A Source Book for Russian History from Early Times to 1917

A SOURCE BOOK FOR RUSSIAN HISTORY

FROM EARLY TIMES TO 1917

VOLUME 3
Alexander II to the February Revolution

George Vernadsky, SENIOR EDITOR
Ralph T. Fisher, Jr., MANAGING EDITOR
Alan D. Ferguson
Andrew Lossky
Sergei Pushkarev, COMPILER

New Haven and London: Yale University Press

1972

Designed by John O. C. McCrillis
and set in IBM Press Roman type.
Printed in the United States of America by
The Murray Printing Co., Forge Village, Mass.

Published in Great Britain, Europe, and Africa by
Yale University Press, Ltd., London.
Distributed in Canada by McGill-Queen's University
Press, Montreal; in Latin America by Kaiman & Polon,
Inc., New York City; in Australasia and Southeast
Asia by John Wiley & Sons Australasia Pty. Ltd.,
Sydney; in India by UBS Publishers' Distributors Pvt.,
Ltd., Delhi; in Japan by John Weatherhill, Inc., Tokyo.

CONTENTS   VOLUME 3

CONTENTS VOLUMES 1 AND 2

PREFACE

Our purpose in this book is to provide, in English, an illustrative sample of the wealth of primary source material that exists for the study of Russia from early times to 1917.

Source books in American and general European history have existed in abundance. They have proved their value as teaching tools to supplement a comprehensive textbook. The need for source books in Russian history has been felt by a great many teachers, to judge from those who offered suggestions to us. It was thanks in large part to their encouragement that we pushed ahead.

As we worked we have had in mind the teacher and especially the purposeful student—the student who is seeking not merely entertainment or native color but solid information as well; the student who does not want to have interpretations handed to him ready-made, but likes to do some evaluating for himself.

Accordingly, in the introductory notes we have avoided either summarizing the document or repeating the background that a text would provide, but we have tried to identify the source and to give enough data to enable the reader to place the document in its historical setting and to figure out what sorts of questions the selection helps to answer.

In the same spirit, we have retained the use of many Russian terms, especially where there is no direct or specific English equivalent, as in the case of territorial divisions, terms of office, and units of measure and money. We believe the hardship this causes to some will work to the net advantage of all of the book's readers—including even the beginner, especially if he is persistent enough in turning to the *Dictionary of Russian Historical Terms* compiled by Mr. Pushkarev.*

In our choice of selections we have sought to achieve a balanced mixture of various types of sources. Along with spirited first-person accounts, there are official documents and other sober fare which require intensive reading. We have included representative samples of the sources that are important enough to be alluded to in the standard textbooks. Often our excerpts are shorter than we would have preferred if expense were no problem, but they are, we think, not too short to convey significant points to the thoughtful reader who is alert to the uses of various kinds of historical evidence.

In response to the wishes of our colleagues, we have emphasized sources not previously published in English translation. About 81 percent of our selections were in that category in 1956 when we began. That proportion is now down to around 75 percent, owing to the new translations that have appeared in recent years. We have cited these new translations in our reference notes for the pertinent items (about 6 percent of our total), so that the reader may locate them easily for further study. About 8 percent of our selections came from publications in English which

---

* A companion volume to this set, the *Dictionary of Russian Historical Terms from the Eleventh Century to 1917* was published by Yale University Press in 1970.

we simply reproduced. Most of these are English in origin, from Richard Chancellor in the sixteenth century to Sir James Buchanan in the twentieth. The remaining selections, about 12 percent, are from sources that had been translated into English but for which we used both the original language and the published translation to produce the version included in this book. In some cases we revised the previous translation only slightly—in other cases, considerably. Our reference notes explain how much.

Scope and coverage. Although our excerpts represent about seven hundred distinct sources (the number could be raised or lowered depending on how one decided to count certain kinds of documents of various dates grouped under one heading), these are of course only a minute fraction of the published sources available. Our original prospectus had to be sharply cut. And although we incorporated about two hundred items from among the additions to our prospectus that were suggested by the letters of our teacher-colleagues, their suggestions totaled around three times that many. It is obvious, then, that much that is worthwhile could not be included here and that many of our choices had to be made on the basis of convenience and availability. At the same time our selections were guided by certain general principles, and these we should explain.

We have felt it necessary to exclude the vast realm of belles lettres, despite its vital importance for the historian. We did not see any way of doing justice to it within the scope of this work. Fortunately that category of source material is widely available in anthologies as well as in translations of individual works.

We have given relatively little space to documents in foreign relations. While we have included some documents bearing on Russia's territorial expansion or on Russian views of certain questions beyond the frontiers, we have generally shunned diplomatic documents which, falling within the scope of general European or world history, are available already in English or are so well summarized in most texts that the marginal gain from an excerpt would be slight.

We have tried to provide sources for political and social history in the broad sense, and have therefore included numerous selections from such fields as intellectual history, church history, economic history, and legal history. We have followed the practice of most textbooks in focusing primarily on the dominant Great Russians, even though by the late nineteenth century they constituted not much over half of the population. We have allotted space to other peoples and areas especially during those periods when they were being brought into the empire. We have not systematically followed the fate of each national element or geographical region thereafter, but have provided occasional illustrations and reminders of the multinational nature of the empire and the problems resulting therefrom.

We have held to a fairly narrow definition of "primary," resisting the temptation to include historical writings that, although "primary" as expressions of the attitudes of their own time, would not generally be classified as such. Our introductions give enough data to enable the student to discern varying degrees of primariness.

In our chronological divisions we have followed the prevailing practice of increasing the coverage as we move closer to the present, but we have given more than the usual emphasis to the 1500s and 1600s, believing, along with many of our colleagues, that we should help to broaden the time span of Russian history beyond that usually taught. On the contemporary end, some of our fellow teachers wanted us to go beyond March 1917. We agree that this would make the book more widely usable in survey courses, but so many sources for Russian history since 1917 had already been translated that we believed such an extension would not be justifiable.

Beyond the problem of achieving a suitable mixture of kinds of sources and a suitable topical and chronological distribution is the at least equally vexing problem of which excerpts to select when, as in most cases, a source is far too long to be included in its entirety. Here, as elsewhere, we have tried not to be unduly influenced by our own preconceptions and have sought to include a wide spectrum of viewpoints from among the voices of the past.

Arrangement, form, style. Our goal in arranging the material has been to make it easy to use this source book along with any textbook in Russian history. Our chapter units thus follow traditional lines. Within them we have arranged the items in a combination of chronological and topical groupings, much as a text might treat them. Particularly where one document touches several topics, our placement has had to be arbitrary. Occasionally—as in the case of the early chronicles—we have broken one source down into separate excerpts by date and topic, but we did not want to overdo this, lest we deemphasize the distinct nature of each source. This means that while it is possible to read the book straight through like a narrative, we have expected, rather, that most users would be reading it by sections or groups of documents, in conjunction with a text or after becoming generally familiar with the period in question. In order to assist both teacher and student in adapting these source readings to any lesson plan, we have provided a Guide to Major Topics.

Our reference notes acknowledge the works we have used as the basis for each item; they are by no means a catalog of all available sources for the same selection. All dates are in the old style or Julian calendar unless labeled N.S. Spaced ellipsis dots indicate that passages in original documents have been omitted in this book; closed-up ellipsis dots represent ellipses contained in the original; double-length dashes represent lacunae—mutilated or otherwise illegible passages—in the original. Unless a selection is identified in our introductory note as a full text, it is an excerpt.

All translators of nonmodern materials understand the compromises required between modern English usage and older expressions which have their counterparts in the Russian of various periods of the past. We felt it unreasonable, in working with so many different kinds of documents, to strive for complete uniformity of style. But even in seeking accuracy we were forced into decisions that will not fully satisfy everyone. Take the example of *tsarskii,* the adjective formed from "tsar." The common rendering, "tsarist," may properly be condemned as now having in English a pejorative connotation that is inappropriate to our uses. But after considering such possibilities as "tsarly" (on the model of "kingly"), "tsarial" (after "imperial"), or "tsarish" (used as "czarish" a few generations back), we returned to "tsarist"—not without dissent in our own ranks. The similar problem of rendering adjectives especially when used as proper names is one familiar to every translator. (Should it be "Resurrection Chronicle" or "Voskresensk Chronicle"? And what about the full adjectival ending and the gender?) We have tried in such cases to follow what seems to be common usage in college textbooks, even though this has led to inconsistencies that may annoy the specialist.

Some of the most frequently used Russian terms have been Anglicized: soft signs have been dropped and plurals have been formed with "s" (for example, "dumas"). In the majority, however, the soft sign and Russian nominative plurals have been retained (*pomest'ia, strel'tsy*). Sometimes this produced results irritating to the Russian speaker, especially when numbers are followed by a nominative case. But the use of genitive forms would have complicated matters unduly for the student who has had no Russian. Where, as an aid to those who have studied Russian, we have added transliterations of Russian words in brackets after the English, we have made some changes toward the modern orthography. But where no confusion would occur we have simply transliterated a term as it stood, thereby preserving changes in spelling, sometimes even within the same document. Our transliterations follow the Library of Congress system with minor modifications.

Family names and patronymics have been simply transliterated. First names have been transliterated except when the English equivalent is very widely used for the person in question (e.g. Tsar Paul). Place names have been transliterated, except where English substitutions are current (Moscow, Archangel). One politically touchy problem is that of rendering place names in the non-Great-Russian parts of the empire. We have in general chosen the solution, favored by English-language texts, of using the Russian form, but we have often added the other names in parentheses.

ACKNOWLEDGMENTS

This book, intended as a service to the teaching profession rather than as a commercial enterprise, owes its existence to many persons and institutions beyond the small group of editors.

Yale University sponsored the project from its very inception. Financial support, working space, materials, and other assistance were provided through the Provost's Office, the Graduate School, and by the Yale Concilium on International and Area Studies and several of its branches: its Council on Russian and East European Studies, its Committee on Faculty Research Grants, and the Henry L. Stimson Fund for Research in World Affairs. We wish to thank the Yale University Press for its continuing interest and support. We depended heavily on Yale's Sterling Memorial Library, and in particular, its reference librarians and its Photographic Division.

The University of Illinois, through its Graduate Research Board, the Russian and East European Center, the James Buchanan Duke Memorial Fund, the Department of History, and the University Library, provided working space and liberal amounts of research assistance, photoduplication, typing, and other clerical support.

A generous grant from the Ford Foundation covered much of the cost of translations, photoduplication, and typing.

The Humanities Fund, thanks to the support of the late Michael Karpovich, contributed toward publication costs. The Rockefeller Foundation, through a half-time fellowship it awarded in 1956-58 to Mr. Fisher for the study of Old Russian and Church Slavic, directly aided his work on documents of the pre-Petrine period for this book.

Assistance came also from many professional colleagues. After we had drawn up a list of the documents we tentatively proposed to include in the sourcebook, we circulated this list to historians and other persons of our acquaintance then active in the Russian field, asking for critical comments. In response, we received helpful suggestions and recommendations of additional documents from over 150 fellow teachers. A mere listing of their names would not indicate the extent of our indebtedness to each of them, and a detailed accounting would be far too lengthy for these pages. As outstanding illustrations we may cite the contributions of Alexander Baltzly, Christopher Becker, Horace William Dewey, Samuel Kucherov, and Dimitri von Mohrenschildt. Mr. Dewey offered us some unpublished translations he had made of early Russian legal documents. Mr. Becker volunteered several translations pertaining to Stolypin. Mr. Mohrenschildt, explaining that he had planned, some years earlier, a handbook of Russian social and political thought, sent us a list of the materials he had assembled, plus microfilms and photostats of untranslated selections, as well as copies of several original and unpublished translations. Messrs Baltzly and Kucherov, who, it turned out, had been working for several years on a project something like ours, placed at our disposal many translations they had completed. The reference notes identify further the materials contributed by the above-mentioned scholars, but we wish to express our appreciation here. They, and the many others who responded with thoughtful suggestions, exhibited a spirit of scholarly generosity that was an inspiration to us.

For initial encouragement and administrative support we are grateful especially to Marian Neal Ash, Radley H. Daly, Norman V. Donaldson, Frederick G. Ludwig, David C. Munford, John H. Ottemiller, and Arthur F. Wright. For assistance with the translations we must first single out for thanks Benjamin P. Uroff. Among the many others who gave translating, editorial, and bibliographic assistance we want to mention especially Norma J. Bruce, Henry L. Eaton, Ida Estrin, J. Gerrit Gantvoort, William G. Gard, Mirra Ginsburg, Judith A. Hill, Peter Hodgson, Stanley Humenuk, Alexandra Kalmykow, Nadezhda S. Kovediaeff, Tamara Kulikauskas, Princess Marie Mestchersky, Vladimir V. Nikouline, Paul L. Roley, and Allen A. Sinel. Our typists included Pauline M. Apperson, Marjorie J. Beauregard, Grey Felstiner, Sandra Swiatowiec Gastineau, Amy Henschen, and Agnes W. Wilson. For the final preparation for printing we are much indebted to our copyeditor, Elizabeth W. Kodama, and to Ellen Graham.

A list of acknowledgments to copyright holders for permission to use selections reprinted in this volume follows the Bibliography.

GUIDE TO MAIN TOPICS, VOLUMES 1-3

This guide is a supplement to both the Contents and the detailed List of Items by Chapters. The reader who wishes to survey the documentary selections for any specific period can locate them through the Contents. The reader who seeks specific documents can locate them through the List of Items by Chapters. The present guide is for the reader who is approaching Russian history topically rather than chronologically, as he might if he were focusing on Russian economic history or on Russian foreign relations. Many of the documents are of course relevant to more than one topic, and the topical categories themselves are so broad that they will serve for general orientation only. Roman numerals indicate chapter numbers; arabic numerals indicate item numbers within each chapter.

POLITICAL, LEGAL, AND ADMINISTRATIVE HISTORY
Including central and local government, armed forces, revolutionary movements

From early times to the late seventeenth century, see:

I: 2, 4, 6, 14, 16	VI: 1-11, 16-21
II: 1, 4-9, 11, 12, 14-21	VII: 1-35, 38-40, 42, 44-47
III: 1-20	VIII: 1-43, 54-59, 61, 62, 65, 67, 71, 77,
IV: 1-28	81, 83-85
V: 1-26	IX: 1-5, 12-18, 20-25

From Peter the Great to Nicholas I, see:

X: 1-29, 33, 35, 40-44, 46-49, 53, 54	XIII: 1, 4, 7, 10-13, 15, 16, 19-48
XI: 1-11, 19	XIV: 1-15, 17, 18, 20, 21, 26-31, 33-35,
XII: 1-28, 31, 34-36, 39-47, 50, 52-55, 57	38, 39, 42

From Alexander II to the February Revolution, see:

XV: 1-22, 24-31, 33, 36-43, 46-63	XVII: 1-25, 27, 28, 30-40, 42, 44-46, 49
XVI: 1-49, 53-66, 78	XVIII: 1-33, 35-47

ECONOMIC HISTORY

From early times to the late seventeenth century, see:

I: 1, 2, 4-6, 14	VII: 2, 5, 7-13, 16, 18, 19, 24, 28, 34,
II: 1-3, 5, 6, 18-21	35, 37-39, 43, 47, 48
III: 3-6, 8-10, 12-14, 17, 19, 20	VIII: 4, 7, 11, 13, 23, 24, 27, 29, 32, 33,
IV: 4-10, 12, 13, 15-19, 22, 27, 28	44-51, 54, 55, 65-71, 77, 83
V: 8, 13, 14, 24-26	IX: 11, 12, 23, 24
VI: 6-8, 10-17	

From Peter the Great to Nicholas I, see:

X: 6-8, 14, 17, 29, 30, 35-44	XIII: 2-6, 8, 14, 18, 24, 25, 34, 38-40
XI: 10-14, 18	XIV: 7, 13, 14, 16-26, 30, 32
XII: 8, 10, 11, 15-19, 21-23, 25-33, 35-38, 40, 46	

SOCIAL, CULTURAL, AND INTELLECTUAL HISTORY
Including literature, science, education,
religion, and the press

HISTORY OF
LITHUANIAN-RUSSIAN STATE, UKRAINE, BELORUSSIA, SIBERIA, COSSACKS
RUSSIAN EXPANSION
NON-RUSSIAN NATIONALITIES

DIPLOMATIC HISTORY
HISTORY OF RUSSIAN FOREIGN RELATIONS

C. Intellectual Trends and Revolutionary Movements

LIST OF ABBREVIATIONS

AAE   *Akty sobrannye v bibliotekakh i arkhivakh Rossiiskoi Imperii arkheograficheskoiu ekspeditsieiu Imperatorskoi Akademii Nauk.* 4 vols. St. Petersburg, 1836.

AN BSSR   Akademiia Nauk Belorusskoi Sovetskoi Sotsialisticheskoi Respubliki.

AN SSSR   Akademiia Nauk Soiuza Sovetskikh Sotsialisticheskikh Respublik.

AOIZR   Arkheograficheskaia Komissiia, ed. *Akty otnosiashchiesia k istorii zapadnoi Rossii,* 5 vols. St. Petersburg, 1846-51.

CIOIDRMU   Obshchestvo Istorii i Drevnostei Rossiiskikh. *Chteniia v Imperatorskom Obshchestve Istorii i Drevnostei Rossiiskikh pri Moskovskom Universitete.* 264 vols. Moscow, 1846-1918.

DAI   Arkheograficheskaia Komissiia, ed. *Dopolneniia k aktam istoricheskim.* 12 vols. St. Petersburg, 1846-72.

Gosiurizdat   Gosudarstvennoe Izdatel'stvo Iuridicheskoi Literatury.

Gosizdat   Gosudarstvennoe Izdatel'stvo.

Goslitizdat   Gosudarstvennoe Izdatel'stvo Khudozhestvennoi Literatury.

Gospolitizdat   Gosudarstvennoe Izdatel'stvo Politicheskoi Literatury.

OGIZ   Ob"edinenie Gosudarstvennykh Izdatel'stv.

PBIPV   *Pis'ma i bumagi Imperatora Petra Velikogo.* 11 vols. Vols. 1-7, St. Petersburg: Gosudarstvennaia Tipografiia, 1887-1918. Vols. 8-11, Moscow: AN SSSR, 1948-64.

PRP   *Pamiatniki russkogo prava.* 8 vols. Moscow: Gosiurizdat, 1952-61.

PSRL   Arkheograficheskaia Komissiia, ed. *Polnoe Sobranie Russkikh Letopisei.* 31 vols. St. Petersburg, 1841-1968.

PSZRI   *Polnoe Sobranie Zakonov Rossiiskoi Imperii . . . 1649-1913.* 134 vols. St. Petersburg, 1830-1916 (1st ser., 46 vols., containing laws of 1649-1825; 2d ser., 55 vols., covering 1825-81; 3d ser., 33 vols., covering 1881-1913).

PVL   V. P. Adrianova-Peretts and D. S. Likhachev, eds. *Povest' vremennykh let.* Moscow: AN SSSR, 1950.

RIB   Arkheograficheskaia Komissiia, ed. *Russkaia istoricheskaia biblioteka.* 39 vols. St. Petersburg, 1872-1927.

RPC   Samuel H. Cross and Olgerd P. Sherbowitz-Wetzor, eds. and trans.
               The Russian Primary Chronicle, Laurentian Text. Cambridge, Mass.:
               Mediaeval Academy of America, 1953.

SIRIO   *Sbornik Imperatorskogo Russkogo Istoricheskogo Obshchestva.*
               148 vols. St. Petersburg: Imperatorskoe Russkoe Istoricheskoe
               Obshchestvo, 1867-1916.

Tsentrarkhiv   Tsentral'nyi Gosudarstvennyi Istoricheskii Arkhiv v Moskve.

VOLUME 3

Alexander II to the February Revolution

CHAPTER XV

Alexander II,
1855-1881

A. THE EMANCIPATION OF THE SERFS

XV:1. ALEXANDER'S ADDRESS TO THE MOSCOW NOBLES, MARCH 30, 1856

On March 30, 1856, Alexander II received the representatives of the nobility of the Moscow guberniia and addressed them in these famous words. (The text, like several others in this chapter, comes from the work of Sergei Spiridonovich Tatishchev [1846-1906], a historian who had access to many official documents of the reign of Alexander II.)

Reference: S. S. Tatishchev, *Imperator Aleksandr II*, 2 vols. (St. Petersburg: A. S. Suvorin, 1911), 1:278.

I have learned, gentlemen, that rumors have spread among you of my intention to abolish serfdom. To refute any groundless gossip on so important a subject I consider it necessary to inform you that I have no intention of doing so immediately. But, of course, and you yourselves realize it, the existing system of serf owning cannot remain unchanged. It is better to begin abolishing serfdom from above than to wait for it to begin to abolish itself from below. I ask you, gentlemen, to think of ways of doing this. Pass on my words to the nobles for consideration.

XV:2. LEVSHIN ON PREPARATIONS FOR EMANCIPATION, 1857-1858

These observations on the background of the peasant reform were written in 1860 by Aleksei Iraklievich Levshin (1799-1879), who, as assistant minister of internal affairs from January 1856 to April 1859, took part in the work of preparing the legislation on the serfs.

Reference: A. I. Levshin, "Dostopamiatnye minuty v moei zhizni, zapiska A. I. Levshina," *Russkii arkhiv*, 1885, no. 8, pp. 498-99, 537.

The start of the work of the Main Committee on the Peasant Question coincided with the beginning of the year 1857; but the first half of the year passed without important results. Some of the members, the chairman [Prince Orlov, who was the president of the State Council] among them, were not at all in sympathy with the matter but had in mind somehow to delay or complicate it without admitting this to the sovereign; others brought to the committee ardent convictions on the necessity of putting an end to serfdom but did not know how to go about it; still others sincerely admitted their ignorance of the subject and asked to be dismissed. In this group were Rostovtsev and Korf. The latter was dismissed after some time; but the first [Rostovtsev] was fated, against his will, to become the chief figure in this matter and to lay down his life for it. . . . In general the composition of the committee was extremely unfortunate, and thus it was not surprising that for the first half year it only gazed at the beast that was shown it and walked around it, not knowing from which side to approach it.

. . .

The example of the Nizhnii-Novgorod nobility was so significant that after it the sovereign began to await with impatience an appeal from the Moscow nobility, and as this did not come for a long time, it was unofficially hinted to the governor general, Count Zakrevskii, that such a delay on the part of the second capital was unseemly. Willy-nilly the Muscovites reacted in the first half of January 1858, and therefore such a rescript was sent to Count Zakrevskii on January 16.

Of the other appeals that came then from the nobility and the rescripts in response to them we will not speak. These were by now normal actions, more or less belated, and stemming not from enthusiasm but from the impossibility for any guberniia to lag behind the others, and from the reminders that came from the ministry to the governors. A genuine appeal to free the serfs, an appeal based on real conviction, did not come from any guberniia at all.

XV:3. NOTES OF SENATOR IA. A. SOLOV'EV ON THE PREPARATIONS FOR THE EMANCIPATION
OF THE SERFS, 1857-1860

One of the men who helped most in preparing the Reform of 1861 was Senator Iakov Aleksandrovich Solov'ev (1820-76), who from 1857 to 1859 was the head of the "Land Department" of the
Ministry of Internal Affairs and then in 1859 and 1860 was a member of the Editorial Commissions. These "notes" were written in the years 1873-75.

   Reference: Ia. A. Solov'ev, "Zapiski Senatora Ia. A. Solov'eva," *Russkaia starina*, 27 (February
1880): 320, 324; 30 (February 1881): 231-32; 30 (April 1881): 754, 756.

The great initiative in the sacred matter of
freeing the serfs belongs entirely to the sovereign emperor Aleksandr Nikolaevich himself.
From the moment that the sovereign announced to the Moscow nobility his intention
to free the serfs, there began a struggle between
the liberal and the conservative elements. The
regulator of the preponderance of one or the
other of these parties was the will of the sovereign emperor. Only this autocratic power,
moved by a deep love for Russia and a pas-
sionate desire for her good, could support the
numerically small and socially weak progressive party, which otherwise could have been
destroyed by the strong and influential representatives of the estate-owners' interests.

· · ·

   Immediately after the publication of the
first rescript, a reactionary movement started
in the committee itself [the so-called Secret
Committee on the Serf Question]. Such a
movement was supported and nourished by
the obvious sympathy of a majority of the
society of the time, in Petersburg as well as
out in the guberniias; the opposition that
came to light in Petersburg fostered and ap-
plauded the opposition movements in the
guberniias. Although not quite consciously,
the representatives of the conservative estate-
owners' party began to strive to carry out a
plan seemingly prepared beforehand. The
aims of this group were either to block the
reform completely or, if that proved impossible, to free the serfs without land and to
receive compensation for having granted them
personal freedom. As a means of attaining
one of these aims they launched a scare
campaign threatening peasant unrest and
democratic revolution and also a general
economic upheaval in the state.

· · ·

   The serfs wanted freedom so badly and
placed so much hope in the government that
every time there was an extraordinary event
they expected it to be the occasion of their
liberation. Thus, on the occasion of the Senate's
decree on naval mobilization in 1854, and later
the manifesto on general mobilization on January 29, 1855, three weeks before the death of
Nikolai Pavlovich [Emperor Nicholas I], a
rumor circulated among the people that serfs
who voluntarily joined the militia would, with
their families, be given freedom and would
forever be rid of working for and being subject to the estate owners.

   The first movements of the peasants took
place in the guberniia of Riazan' and later in
some parts of the guberniias of Tambov,
Vladimir, Simbirsk, Saratov, Voronezh, Nizhnii-
Novgorod, and Penza. In many uezdy of the
Kiev guberniia the manifesto about general
mobilization was interpreted as a general call
to join the Cossacks and be freed from the
estate-owners' authority. In some places the
government was obliged to call in military aid.

· · ·

   A significant majority of estate owners
either did not sympathize at all with the
enterprise that had begun or at least objected
to giving the serfs land along with their freedom. The provincial opposition movement
fed the Petersburg movement, which in turn
supported the provincial movement. In Petersburg drawing rooms, at court functions, at
parades and inspections of the troops, behind the walls of the State Council and the
Senate, and in the offices of the ministers and
members of the State Council were heard
more or less energetic protests against the intentions of the government. These protests
expressed in vigorous terms more or less the
same idea—that the emancipation of the serfs
was premature; the result of the change, said
the numerous enemies of the proposed reform,
would be that the estate owners would remain without working hands, the peasants
because of their natural indolence would not
work even for themselves, the productivity of
the state would decrease, causing general in-
flation, famine, disease, and nationwide misery.

At the same time would come insubordination on the part of the peasants, local disorders followed by widespread rioting—in a word, they predicted another Pugachev rebellion with all its horrors and with the addition of a "deeply plotted" democratic revolution.

.   .   .

There is not the slightest doubt that the information received at the time by the Third Section of His Majesty's Own Chancellery was just as one-sided and was reported to the sovereign in the same vein. The chief of the gendarmes at that time was Prince V. A. Dolgorukov. . . . He was one of the fanatical enemies of the serf reform. The campaign to frighten the sovereign was worked out especially beginning in 1866 [misprint for 1856] and was then put into operation. They tried to scare the sovereign with peasant uprisings and with strong opposition on the part of the nobility.

XV:4. ALEXANDER'S ADDRESSES TO THE NOBLES OF NIZHNII-NOVGOROD AND MOSCOW, AUGUST 19 AND 31, 1858

Here are two samples from the tsar's continuing campaign of appeals to the Russian nobility concerning serfdom.
Reference: Tatishchev, *Imperator Aleksandr II*, 1:310-11.

[From a speech by Alexander II to the nobles in Nizhnii-Novgorod, August 19, 1858:]
I am relying on you; I believe in you and you will not deceive me. . . . The path has been shown. Do not deviate from the principles laid down in my rescript and the program issued to you. Your work will be considered by the Main Committee; but I have allowed you to submit it through two members chosen by you, to whom you will entrust the task of representing your interests to the extent that this is in keeping with the common good. Gentlemen, do what is good for yourselves and what is not bad for others; think of yourselves and think of others. I believe in you and hope you will justify my confidence in you. By carrying out and completing this work conscientiously you will prove to me once again your love and devotion and that unselfish striving for the common good that has always distinguished the nobility of Nizhnii-Novgorod.

[From a speech by Alexander II to the Moscow nobility, August 31, 1858:]

I find it pleasant, gentlemen, when I can thank the nobility, but I cannot say what I do not believe. I always speak the truth, and, unfortunately, I cannot thank you now. You will remember that when I spoke to you here in this very room two years ago I told you that sooner or later it would be necessary to change serfdom and that it was better for this change to begin at the top than at the bottom. My words were misinterpreted. After that I thought about it for a long time and, having prayed to God, decided to set about the task. When as a result of the appeal of the Saint Petersburg and Lithuanian guberniias my rescripts were issued, I must confess I expected the Moscow nobility to be the first to respond; but Nizhnii-Novgorod responded and the guberniia of Moscow was not the first, not the second, nor even the third. This made me sad, for I am proud that I was born in Moscow; I always loved the city when I was heir, and I love it still as my native city. I laid down certain principles for you and I will not deviate from them in any way.

XV:5. DECREES OF THE MAIN COMMITTEE ON PEASANT AFFAIRS, OCTOBER 26 AND DECEMBER 4, 1858

In the fall of 1858 the former Secret Committee was supplanted by the Main Committee on Peasant Affairs [Glavnyi Komitet po Krest'ianskomu Delu]. In the decrees excerpted here, the tsar set forth the general principles he wished the committee to follow.
Reference: *PSZRI*, 2d ser., vol. 36, pt. 3, pp. 38-39 [decree of Oct. 26, 1858], 43-44 [Dec. 4].

[The imperially approved decree of the Main Committee on Peasant Affairs, October 26, 1858:]
The Main Committee on Peasant Affairs

met on October 18, 1858, in the presence of His Imperial Majesty.

.   .   .

After hearing opinions on the matter, His

Imperial Majesty ordered that the following rules be adopted for guidance:

1. In the discussion and subsequent publication of all legislation concerning the present matter, three conditions shall be unfailingly observed:
   a. The peasant must immediately feel that his life has improved.
   b. The estate owner [pomeshchik] must immediately be reassured that his interests are protected.
   c. The government must never waver for a moment at any point in ensuring against any disturbance of law and order.
2. In accordance with these rules the minister of internal affairs by a special circular shall immediately entrust all guberniia committees (except that of Nizhnii-Novgorod, whose work the minister [of internal affairs] considers to be already completed) when submitting their proposals to explain in full detail in what way the condition of the estate owners' peasants will improve in the future, making it clear to the committees that His Majesty the emperor is relying entirely upon their honor as noblemen to assure the justness of their depositions.

[The imperially approved decree of the Main Committee on Peasant Affairs, December 4, 1858:]

The Main Committee on Peasant Affairs met on November 19, 24, and 29, 1858, in the presence of His Majesty the emperor.

... After preliminary consideration of these questions [basic to the work of the committee] ... His Majesty the emperor ordered that during the examination of the guberniia proposals, both on a preliminary basis in the commission attached to the Main Committee and finally in the Main Committee, the following principles should be used as guidance:

1. Upon the promulgation of the new decree on peasants, these peasants shall be granted the rights of the free rural classes in respect to personal rights, property rights, and the right to present complaints.
2. These peasants shall become part of the free rural class within the state.
3. The peasants shall be divided into rural communities which must have their own mir administration.
4. The authority over the individual peasant in regard to the fulfillment or violation of his duties as a member of the rural community lies with the mir and those it elects.
5. The estate owner must deal with the mir alone and not with individuals.
6. The members of the mir bear mutual responsibility for each other in the fulfillment of duties to both the government and the estate owners.
7. The peasants must be induced gradually to acquire ownership of land.

XV:6. THE DECREE ON AND PROGRAM OF THE EDITORIAL COMMISSIONS, MARCH 1859

Another important step was the Senate decree of March 30 establishing the Editorial Commissions [Redaktsionnye Kommissii] and describing their composition and functions. The intended program of the commissions had been set forth earlier that month in a statement submitted by the man Alexander appointed to head them, General Iakov Ivanovich Rostovtsev (1803-60).

Reference: *PSZRI*, 2d ser., vol. 34, pt. 1, p. 249; Nikolai P. Semenov, *Osvobozhdenie krest'ian v tsarstvovanie Imperatora Aleksandra II: Khronika deiatel'nosti komissii po krest'ianskomu delu*, 3 vols. (St. Petersburg, 1889-92), 1:86-87.

[From the Senate decree of March 30, 1859:]

His majesty the emperor has ordered the following:

1. Two Editorial Commissions shall be formed for the purpose of compiling systematically all the proposals submitted by the guberniia noblemen's committees and preparing drafts of the general law concerning the peasants who are about to be emancipated, and other related legislation.

2. Adjutant General Rostovtsev, member of the Main Committee on Peasant Affairs, shall be appointed chairman and immediate superior of both Editorial Commissions.

3. The Editorial Commissions shall consist of (a) members elected with His Imperial Majesty's consent from among experienced estate owners, and (b) members appointed from the Ministries of Internal Affairs, Justice, and State Domains and from the Second De-

partment of His Imperial Majesty's Own Chancery. The following shall be permanent members of both commissions: Actual State Councillor Zhukovskii, executive secretary of the commission attached to the Main Committee on Peasant Affairs, and Collegiate Councillor Solov'ev, a member of the same commission.

4. As the Editorial Commissions complete their drafts, these drafts shall be submitted to the commission attached to the Main Committee on Peasant Affairs, which will pass the drafts, together with its own conclusions, on to the Main Committee.

[From General Rostovtsev's program of March 5, 1859:]

1. The problem before us of eliminating serfdom and improving the welfare of the peasants must be solved with strict fairness and impartiality for both parties, and in such a way as to prevent any grounds at all for hostility between the two classes; in other words, in such a way that Russia may find in the peaceful solution of this problem a true, long-term guarantee against upheaval in the state.

2. Along with individual freedom the peasants must receive full opportunity to acquire enough land of their own to provide for their everyday needs [byt i osedlost'], for without this the life of the peasants would improve merely in word and not in deed. . . .

7. The land to be redeemed by the peasant should consist of a farmstead and a sufficient allotment of land in a plot that is separate from the remaining land possessed by the estate owner.

8. For the land they cede, estate owners must be remunerated justly and as far as possible without loss and impoverishment.

9. The peasants' yearly payment of both interest and redemption dues must not exceed the average amount of their present obligations, or else there will be no improvement in their living conditions.

10. The sooner the redemption of land takes place, or at least commences, the more advantageous it will be (a) to the peasant, since the value of land in Russia is increasing all the time, and (b) to the estate owner, since he needs capital for the economic reforms that will inevitably result from the change in conditions on his estate.

11. Therefore, to speed up the redemption of land and to equalize the interests of the estate owners and peasants, which may well clash, the government must take part in the redemption process by serving as a mediator, extending credit, giving guarantees, or undertaking financial transactions.

12. The question whether the redeemed land is to be owned individually or communally by the peasants should be left to history, and measures should not be imposed by the government, especially since the administrative commune and the economic commune are in essence completely different.

XV:7. THE COMPLAINT OF THE GUBERNIIA COMMITTEES, AUGUST 26, 1859

These passages from the message of August 26, 1859, which a conference of deputies of the guberniia committees approved and sent to the tsar, illustrate the viewpoint and also the tactics of a significant segment of the nobility.

Reference: Semenov, *Osvobozhdenie krest'ian,* 1:615-16.

The drafts of the guberniia committees, however, could represent only local needs, and you, Sire, understanding with keen insight the disadvantages of such disjointed work, enabled it to become smooth and fine by decreeing that the committees, at their own discretion, could elect two deputies each *to sit in the Main Committee and give general consideration to the proposals for improving the conditions of the peasants.* [Footnote: "Underlined in the original by His Imperial Majesty's own hand; opposite these words he wrote 'Never.'"]

The need for this measure, its correctness and its logical nature, ordained by the lustrous mind of the tsar, has aroused universal joy; but while the heart of the tsar and the hearts of the people were uniting for the good of the fatherland, the bureaucracy was sowing seeds of dissension.

Having distorted in the guberniia committees the deeds of the tsar and the people, and having distorted for so many years the tsar's best thoughts and trampled on his most noble feelings, could the bureaucracy tolerate a situation in which the tsar would hear the voice of his people other than through its own untruthful lips?!

. . .

The deputies who arrived in Saint Petersburg were completely neglected. The minister of internal affairs did not bother to present them to Your Majesty, nor even to the Main Committee. Then they were suddenly sent an unsigned invitation to visit the Editorial Commission, and there Adjutant General Rostovstev issued written instructions signed by Butkov, head clerk of the Main Committee, in which, without any regard for the normal system of announcing imperial commands, Your Majesty's orders were countermanded and the deputies were obliged to answer questions which the Editorial Commission considered necessary. . . .

Our grief, Sire, cannot be expressed! More than once in the course of the present matter we have seen the bureaucracy either counterpose one imperial command against another or violate them, but their effrontery had never reached this point before.

Throughout the course of this matter the administrative authorities have continually scorned legality and justice; but they did so out in the provinces in the obscurity of office correspondence, whereas now they are doing it in front of the sovereign and Russia, in plain sight of everyone.

The records of the Editorial Commission and all its administrative actions are filled with harmful and ruinous ideas; we can see them but we are powerless to expose them.

XV:8. LANSKOI'S MEMORANDUM TO THE TSAR, AUGUST 1859

As the nobles through their guberniia committees were submitting their drafts for consideration by the Editorial Commissions, the dominant points of view that emerged were analyzed by Sergei Stepanovich Lanskoi (1787-1862), the minister of internal affairs, in a memorandum to the tsar.
Reference: Semenov, *Osvobozhdenie krest'ian*, 1:828-32.

In general, the majority of the drafts submitted by the [guberniia] committees do not show any sign of impartial consideration for the interests of both classes, nor is there any clear understanding even of the interests of the estate owners themselves. Desires are expressed for emancipation of the peasants without providing land for them and at the same time making the transition difficult. Those compiling the drafts complain that the lack of land and capital will render them [the peasants] helpless and at the same time they seek to reduce the allotments [to the peasants].
. . .

Without going into details, the following predominant opinions can be singled out from the general survey of [guberniia] committee proposals:

The first opinion is held by those who have shown little sympathy for the liberation of the serfs and are motivated by the personal and material interests of the estate owner. They should not be condemned unconditionally and severely. The majority of them, brought up on the concept of serfdom, cannot understand the urgent need for reform and expect it to bring irreparable losses. In their fright they imagine approaching ruin and poverty for themselves and their descendants. Although all the guberniia committees have unanimously set forth the abolition of serfdom as article number one of their proposals, an underlying tendency toward preserving their rights is felt in almost all the committees, and in a great many of them this view is held by the majority of members. . . .

The initial act of the opponents of emancipation was to attempt to stop any action in the peasant question by trying to frighten the government with predictions of revolt. Among such attempts was the anonymous letter to Your Majesty bearing the signature *A.*, which sought to prove that behind the emancipation of the peasants there lay a carefully devised plan for a democratic revolution in Russia. Having become convinced of their inability to stop the reform, these antireformists have begun to try to turn the reform to the greatest advantage of the estate owners. At first they sought reimbursement for the person of the peasant, to be paid by the peasants themselves, by the government, or by all the classes of the state. Having failed in this aim, either they are now trying to retain obligatory work [*barshchina*] by the peasants for the estate owner, and in this way to retain their power over the peasants, or else, by agreeing to unconditional liberation of the individual peasant and praising the freedom to work, they wish to reduce the peasants' land allotments in every possible way and to limit the peasants' use of the land to a twelve-year period, or, if possible, not to give the peasants any land allotment at all. . . .

Second Opinion: . . . This is the trend of *class interest.* It has found adherents primarily among the rich and prominent estate owners. Placing in the forefront the class interests of the nobility, they wish to establish a landed aristocracy, like that of England, and, instead of the present system of privileged ownership by the nobility on the basis of serfdom, to introduce a system no less privileged on the basis of feudalism. In exchange for giving the peasants homesteads and the use of arable lands, the estate owners would retain special rights called "patrimonial rights" which are alien to our laws up to this time and which remind one of the medieval feudal privileges in the West. . . .

The advocates of this view have gained sympathy among the rest of the nobility and possibly among certain members of the Main Committee. The question of "patrimonial rights" was originally brought up by the Saint Petersburg committee, and it spread from there to others.

The third opinion is subscribed to by those desiring the complete abolition of serfdom. They comprise a substantial section of the Russian nobility, though by no means the majority. . . . Nor can one forget the peasants' expectation of a decision. The idea of freedom has long been in the minds of the serfs. There have long been rumors among them that the tsar desired emancipation but that the noblemen were preventing it.

Since the beginning of your reign, the people have been saying that now one and now another date has been fixed for the manifesto on the abolition of serfdom.

XV:9. ROSTOVTSEV'S LETTER TO THE TSAR, OCTOBER 23, 1859

The chairman of the Editorial Commissions reported to the tsar as follows.
Reference: Semenov, *Osvobozhdenie krest'ian,* 2:928-32.

Your Imperial Majesty!

At our last meeting you expressed a desire to know how our sacred cause was proceeding.

With some of the deputies [of the guberniia committees] we have not yet reached agreement on details, but we expect to do so more or less. With others of them we have been unable to agree on fundamentals, and there will be no possibility of coming to terms.

The main divergence is that the [Editorial] Commissions and certain deputies proceed from different premises. The commissions proceed from state necessity and state law, while the deputies base themselves on civil law and private interests. They are right from their viewpoint, and we from ours.

From the standpoint of civil law the entire reform we have undertaken is unjust from beginning to end, since it is a violation of the right to private ownership; but, as a state necessity and on the basis of state law, the reform is legitimate, sacred, and essential.

A large number of enemies of the reform who are unable to see its urgency accuse the Editorial Commissions both verbally and in writing of a desire to fleece the nobles, and others even call some of the members of the commissions "Reds" and accuse them of wanting to cause anarchy.

To desire to fleece the nobles would be both a dishonorable and a pointless thought, all the more so since eight-tenths of the members of the commissions are themselves estate owners and some of them are extremely wealthy.

.   .   .

The efforts of the commissions have been and are still:

First, *to save Russia.* If eleven million persons who have been consoled for two years by the hope of freedom and an improvement in their position are disappointed, they will become despondent and lose their faith in and love for the supreme power; they will attribute the failure of their hopes to the estate owners, and Russia will not be saved.

Second, to carry through *rational and not palliative* changes, that is to say, not for a certain period or by halves, but forever and completely, in order to spare both Russia and Your Majesty's heirs from future upheavals.

Third, to ensure that in her historical future Russia *is not tied by* unfamiliar *knots* like those that Europe has for two centuries been untangling or cutting through.

Fourth, to see that the interests of the estate owners are protected as far as possible and that this revered and most enlightened class, which constitutes, as it were, the flower of Russia, *should not suffer unnecessary loss.*

. . .

The commissions have wholeheartedly desired to balance the interests of both the estate owners and the peasants. If they have failed to achieve this balance up to now, and if there really is more weight on the side of the peasants on certain points, then this is because . . . on particularly difficult questions where the scales had to be weighted, the commissions weighted them on the side of the peasants, because *later on* there will be *many people and much force* tending to tilt the scales in favor of the estate owners and against the peasants, to make the life of the peasants *worse rather than better.*

XV:10. THE TSAR'S LETTER TO ROSTOVTSEV, OCTOBER 25, 1859

Before the close of their conferences, some members of the first convocation of the deputies of the guberniia committees presented their opinions to the tsar, individually and in groups. While Shidlovskii and the group of eighteen criticized the work of the Editorial Commissions as going too far and endangering the interests of the nobility, the group of five (headed by A. M. Unkovskii, the chairman of the Tver' guberniia committee) insisted, on the contrary, that drastic reforms were necessary in Russia's judiciary and administrative system. Alexander commented as follows to Adjutant General Rostovtsev.

Reference: Semenov, *Osvobozhdenie krest'ian*, 2:128.

The review of the state of our sacred cause and the various opinions of members of the noblemen's committees are in complete accordance with the information reaching me from various quarters. Meanwhile, besides [the message from] Shidlovskii, I have received two more messages from [a group of] eighteen and from [a group of] five members. The latter in particular is no good at all and is excessively daring. When you are well again I wish to have them all discussed in my presence by the Main Committee. If these gentlemen think that their efforts to frighten me will succeed, they are greatly mistaken.

I am too certain of the rightness of the sacred cause we have undertaken for anyone to be able to stop me from achieving my aim. But the main task is to know how to achieve it.

As always I am relying on God and on the help of those who, like you, desire it as sincerely as I do and see in it the salvation and future good of Russia.

Do not despair, as I do not despair, though we often have to suffer much grief; and let us pray together to God to guide us and give us strength.

I embrace you from the depths of my heart.

                       A.

XV:11. OPPOSITION TO THE EMANCIPATION (AS GIVEN IN THE MEMOIRS OF MARIIA MILIUTINA), AUGUST AND NOVEMBER 1859

In 1859 and 1860, the assistant minister of internal affairs was Nikolai Alekseevich Miliutin (1818-72). His wife, Mariia Aggeevna, includes in her memoirs documents expressing the views of Lanskoi and his co-workers (including Miliutin and Rostovtsev) on the problem and the opposition they faced.

Reference: Mariia A. Miliutina, "Iz zapisok Marii Aggeevny Miliutinoi," *Russkaia starina*, 98 (Apr. 1899): 105-07, 110-11, 113.

[Mrs. Miliutin writes:] The four autumn months of 1859 (August, September, October, and the first half of November) witnessed strong agitation. This period abounded in denunciations, notes, letters, and foreign brochures [i.e. brochures published abroad to circumvent censorship] against the Editorial Commission. The most noteworthy from the standpoint of tone and content were the note of V. Apraksin, Ziberg-Plater, and Bezobrazov, the brochures by the same Bezobrazov, by

Orlov-Davydov, and by Koshelev, two letters submitted (signed by five and by eighteen members), and a copy of a letter not submitted. The opinion of Nikolai Alekseevich [Miliutin] and his friends toward these messages is revealed in the following notes of the minister of internal affairs, S. S. Lanskoi.

1.

Secret opinion of the minister of the interior concerning the notes from V. Apraksin

which were confided to him by the emperor,
August 31, 1859:

[Having read Apraksin's note, Lanskoi
wrote to the tsar as follows:] ". . . Infected
with aristocratic ideas or, better, with a love
of power and display, some of our fine gentlemen are dreaming about the boyar duma, i.e.
an oligarchy. Others praise the English system
and insist on class self-government; they are
joined by some provincial nobles who, although they are far from aristocratic by birth,
education, and social position, also demand
representation for the nobility. This movement is evidently aroused by a handful of
people who could not move the bulk of the
nobility if they did not stir up passions
brought into play by the serf question. . . .

". . . The most unfair accusations, I will
even say calumnies, against the government
are spread by people unsympathetic to the
reform that has been undertaken, not excluding, unfortunately, persons of even the
highest administrative echelon. In this way,
discontent has been artificially supported
and aroused among the nobility, who, if not
for this, would never have considered constitutional government. . . .

"The saddest fact is that the opposition to
Your Majesty's will finds its most ardent
representatives in that circle which is close
to the court and which from its position produces a strong impression on the masses.
Among the persons in this circle, most either
do not want the emancipation of the serfs *at
all* or insist on emancipation *without land.*

"Now they want to avail themselves of
the arrival here of the members summoned
from the guberniia committees, endeavoring
to give them the status of *deputies* of the
nobility. Some of the most ambitious members are trying to organize general meetings
or assemblies of all the so-called deputies.

. . .

"To you, Sire, they dare to say that *all
confidence in the government* is lost and that
it is *not capable* of undertaking this reform;
without proof they dare to attack all government dispositions; they slander the local

authorities, accusing them of using force in
the election of the guberniia committees;
finally they approach senseless audacity,
charging that the government called on the
nobility to take part in the peasant question
solely in order to relieve itself of responsibility for all the consequences.

"By such acts they try to accuse those
now working on the serf question of harbor-
ing some sort of anarchistic intentions. In
general, all the opponents of the emancipation
of the serfs both openly and secretly focus
all their opposition now against the Editorial
Commissions. They say, as has been brought
to your attention, that *everyone generally is
displeased* with the work of the commissions,
'that they pay no attention to the opinions
of the guberniia committees, and that in them
predominates a one-sided viewpoint, hostile
to the nobility.'

"The displeasure of the estate owners is
comprehensible. It has already been stirred up
by rescripts. It is hard for them to give up
plantation-owners' advantages. And now,
ashamed to admit this, they are endeavoring
to make themselves look like a political opposition.

. . .

"The commissions consist almost entirely
of estate owners, most of whom have lived in
the countryside all their lives and are acquainted
with the nobility in the provinces as well as
with peasant life; although they show sympathy
for *improving* the life of the serfs, they see no
possible reason to sacrifice the lawful interests
of their own class."

. . .

[Mrs. Miliutin adds:] On this genuine note,
in the hand of S. S. Lanskoi, is written: "This
note was returned to me by the emperor personally at Tsarskoe Selo on September 4, with
his own notation in pencil:

"'All that is stated here completely agrees
with my own convictions. All my hopes for
carrying through this matter that is so vital
for Russia I place in God and in those who,
like yourself, serve me *in faith and truth* and
in their thoughts do not separate their fatherland from their emperor.'"

XV:12. A LETTER FROM THE GUBERNIIA COMMITTEES TO PANIN, APRIL 13, 1860

After Rostovtsev's premature death, his place as chairman of the Editorial Commissions was taken
by Count Viktor Nikitich Panin. The letter of April 13, 1860, which he received from the second
convocation of the representatives of the guberniia committees, is a comprehensive statement of a
position endorsed by many of the nobles.

Reference: Semenov, *Osvobozhdenie krest'ian,* vol. 3, pt. 1, pp. 480-81, 483-84, 489.

Having given a detailed analysis of the reports of the sections of the Editorial Commissions, it now remains for us to make some general observations on the significance of the whole system.

By introducing permanent allotments [of land] and unchangeable quitrents for land, the conclusions of the reports undoubtedly violate the fundamental principle of the inviolability of property, excessively and arbitrarily reducing the income received by the estate owners from the land and rendering impossible the cultivation of the estate owners' plowland; they would lead to the ruin of property owners; and in their entirety the measures would result in the enforced sale of land at a loss. At the same time the conclusions would restrict the freedom of the peasants, binding them to the land, placing them on an unfavorable footing with regard to the estate owners and entangling them in a net of almost inescapable dependence upon the mir.

Thus the greatest hopes of all those who wish to free the serfs are dashed. A law based upon such tenets will prove complicated, impracticable, not satisfactory to any side, bothersome to all, an obstacle to the free development of industry and an impediment to all activity. . . . Both classes will suffer great injustices at every step. The peasants will be restricted in their personal rights [by their dependence on the mir], while the estate owners will be restricted in their property rights [by their obligation to furnish land allotments to the peasants]. The inevitable outcome of this will be mutual discontent and animosity between two classes whose close association is essential for the success of agriculture and ought to be reinforced by mutual interest. The voluntary alliance between toil and capital will be broken and an ensuing decline of agriculture would not be surprising.

·   ·   ·

Compulsory relationships are outdated. It is impossible to regulate them properly. They must be entirely abolished. The peasants need complete emancipation, full civil rights, the abolition of all involuntary attachments, and freedom of movement. They need individual independence unrestricted by the power of the mir or by conditions of joint possession and mutual responsibility; they need complete freedom in choosing their occupation and way of life.

·   ·   ·

Having renounced their rights over the serfs, the nobles do not feel it possible to make additional sacrifices in land.

With the abolition of serfdom and with the elimination of the former relationship between the peasants and the estate owners, the previous tie between the peasant and the land of the estate owner is terminated. This tie was created only by the serf-landlord relationship, just like the other duties of the estate owner in regard to the peasants. If the government, therefore, considers that the emancipated peasants must be guaranteed land, the necessary sacrifice should be the lot not of the estate owners alone, but of the entire state. We consider the use of the estate owners' land on this mutually coercive basis to be contrary both to the needs of a free peasantry and to the property rights of the landlords.

It would be as unjust to grant the estate owners the right to compulsory work on the part of free persons as to force those who possess land to share it involuntarily and for an indefinite period. Both one and the other would be a vestige of the former serf-landlord relationship among the rural classes. . . . The peasants can be best and most fairly assured the use of the land of the estate owners by voluntary agreements with them.

·   ·   ·

Except for voluntary agreements and redemption of land, we see no other proper ways of dealing with the present difficulties without infringing upon the right of private ownership, without encroaching upon the freedom of the peasants, and without deviating from the path dictated by fairness and legality. One must either buy the land belonging to the estate owner or allow it to remain his property. In the first case the owner must be paid the full value of the alienated land, and in the second case the estate owner's property must not be deprived of the nature of any private property.

XV:13. ALEXANDER'S ADDRESS IN THE STATE COUNCIL, JANUARY 28, 1861

On January 28, 1861, the drafts of the reform were presented for discussion at a meeting of the State Council. Alexander opened the meeting with these words.
Reference: Tatishchev, *Imperator Aleksandr II*, 1:345-48.

The matter of the liberation of the serfs, which has been submitted for the consideration of the State Council, I consider to be a vital question for Russia, upon which will depend the development of her strength and power. I am sure that all of you, gentlemen, are just as convinced as I am of the benefits and necessity of this measure. I have another conviction, which is that this matter cannot be postponed; therefore I demand that the State Council finish with it in the first half of February so that it can be announced before the start of work in the fields; . . . I repeat—and this is my absolute will—that this matter should be finished right away.

For four years now it has dragged on and has been arousing various fears and anticipations among both the estate owners and the peasants. Any further delay could be disastrous to the state. I cannot help being surprised and happy, and I am sure all of you are happy, at the trust and calm shown by our good people in this matter. Although the apprehensions of the nobility are to a certain extent understandable, for the closest and material interests of each are involved, notwithstanding all this, I have not forgotten and shall never forget that the approach to the matter was made on the initiative of the nobility itself, and I am happy to be able to be a witness to this before posterity. In my private conversations with the guberniia marshals of the nobility, and during my travels about Russia, when receiving the nobility, I did not conceal the trend of my thoughts and opinions on the question that occupies us all and said everywhere that this transformation cannot take place without certain sacrifices on their part and that all my efforts consist in making these sacrifices as little weighty and burdensome as possible for the nobility. I hope, gentlemen, that on inspection of the drafts presented to the State Council, you will assure yourselves that all that can be done for the protection of the interests of the nobility has been done; if on the other hand you find it necessary in any way to alter or to add to the presented work,

then I am ready to receive your comments; but I ask you only not to forget that the basis of the whole work must be the improvement of the life of the peasants—an improvement not in words alone or on paper but in actual fact.

Before proceeding to a detailed examination of this draft itself, I would like to trace briefly the historical background of this affair. You are acquainted with the origin of serfdom. Formerly it did not exist among us; this law was established by autocratic power and only autocratic power can abolish it, and that is my sincere will.

My predecessors felt all the evils of serfdom and continually endeavored, if not to destroy it completely, to work toward the gradual limitation of the arbitrary power of the estate owners.

. . . My late father [Nicholas I] was continuously occupied with the thought of freeing the serfs. Sympathizing completely with this thought, already in 1856, before the coronation, while in Moscow I called the attention of the leaders of the nobility of the Moscow guberniia to the necessity for them to occupy themselves with improving the life of the serfs, adding that serfdom could not continue forever and that it would therefore be better if the transformation took place from above rather than from below. . . .

The Editorial Commissions worked for a year and seven months and, notwithstanding all the reproaches, perhaps partly just, to which the commissions were exposed, they finished their work conscientiously and presented it to the Main Committee. The Main Committee, under the chairmanship of my brother [Grand Duke Konstantin Nikolaevich], toiled with indefatigable energy and zeal. I consider it my duty to thank all the members of the committee, especially my brother, for their conscientious labors in this matter.

There may be various views on the draft presented, and I am willing to listen to all the different opinions. But I have the right to demand one thing from you: that you, putting aside all personal interests, act not like estate owners but like imperial statesmen invested with my trust. Approaching this important matter I have not concealed from myself all those difficulties that awaited us and I do not conceal them now; but, firmly believing in the grace of God and being convinced of the sacredness of this matter, I trust that God will not abandon us but will bless us to finish it for the future prosperity of our beloved fatherland.

XV:14. THE STATUTES ON THE EMANCIPATION OF THE SERFS, FEBRUARY 19, 1861

On February 19 (March 3, N.S.), 1861, the general statute (*polozhenie*) on the emancipation of the serfs and supplementary statutes were approved. Following are some of the most noteworthy provisions enacted that day. It should be noted that the transfer of "temporarily obligated" peasants to the status of "peasant proprietors" was not completed in some cases until twenty years later.

Reference: *PSZRI*, 2d ser., vol. 36, pt. 1, pp. 141, 147-49, 152-53, 155-57, 160, 165, 167, 250. Alexander's emancipation manifesto of the same date is translated in Dmytryshyn, *Imperial Russia,* pp. 220-25.

[From the "general statute":]

1. The serfdom of peasants settled on estate owners' landed properties, and of household serfs, is abolished forever. . . .

2. . . . Peasants and household serfs who have emerged from serfdom are accorded both the personal and the property rights accompanying the legal status [*sostoianie*] of free village dwellers [*svobodnye sel'skie obyvateli*]. . . .

3. Estate owners, retaining the right of ownership to all land belonging to them, accord the peasants, in return for the instituted obligations, the permanent utilization of their homesteads [*usadebnaia osedlost'*] and in addition, in order to provide for their livelihood and the performance of their duties to the government and the estate owner, that amount of fields and other landed resources [*ugod'ia*] which is determined according to the principles set forth in the local statutes [*mestnye polozheniia*].

4. In return for the allotment assigned to them on the basis of the preceding article, the peasants are obliged to discharge to the estate owners, in labor or in money, the obligations defined in the local statutes.

. . .

43. Each volost' is to contain a minimum population of approximately three hundred census souls of the male sex, and a maximum population of approximately two thousand. The distance of the most remote settlements of the volost' from its administrative center is not to exceed approximately twelve versts [about eight miles].

Note: In those localities where, because of the sparsity of population, there are fewer than three hundred peasant souls within the area defined in this article, or where, on the contrary, a population of over two thousand souls is concentrated within an inconsiderable area, deviations from the aforementioned rule are allowed, with the permission of the heads [*nachal'niki*] of the guberniias.

. . .

CHAPTER II. Concerning the administration of the village community. [Note: throughout this document the term *obshchestvo* has been translated as "community," and both *mir* and *obshchina* as "commune."]

46. The administration of the village community is composed of:

a. The village assembly [*sel'skii skhod*].

b. The village elder [starosta].

In addition, those communities that deem it necessary may have: special tax-gatherers; overseers of the granaries, schools, and infirmaries; forest and field wardens; village clerks, and so forth.

47. The "village assembly" is composed of the peasant-householders belonging to the village community and, in addition, all elected village officials.

. . .

51. Under the jurisdiction of the village assembly are:

a. The election of village officials and the appointment of delegates to the volost' assembly.

b. Decisions concerning the expulsion of harmful and pernicious [*porochnye*] members from the community; the temporary removal of peasants from participation in the assemblies, for not more than three years.

c. The release of members from the

community and the acceptance of new ones.

d. The appointment of guardians and trustees; the verification of their actions.

e. The settlement of family divisions [of property; *razdely*].

f. Matters relating to communal utilization of land belonging to the commune, that is: the redistribution of land, the imposition and removal of tiaglo, the final distribution of communal land into permanent plots [*uchastki*], and so forth.

g. Where the land is under plot [*uchastkovoe*] or household [*podvornoe*] (hereditary) utilization, the disposition of plots of communal land that for any reason remain idle or are not under household utilization.

h. Consultations and petitions concerning community needs, the organization of public services, care for the poor, and instruction in reading and writing.

i. The transmission to the appropriate office of complaints and requests dealing with community affairs, through special delegates.

j. The fixing of levies for communal expenses.

k. The apportionment of all fiscal taxes [*kazennye podati*], land [*zemskie*] and communal monetary levies, and likewise the land and communal obligations in kind imposed upon peasants; and the systematic keeping of accounts for the aforesaid taxes and levies.

l. The checking of the accounts of officials elected by the village community, and the fixing of a salary or other recompense for their services.

m. Matters dealing with the discharge of recruit obligations, to the extent that they concern the village community.

n. The apportionment of obrok [quitrent] and obligatory labor services [*izdel'naia povinnost'*] by tiaglo [here meaning a household taxpaying unit], by souls, or in any other customary manner, wherever the obligations to the estate owner are discharged through the joint responsibility of the entire community.

o. The taking of measures for the prevention and recovery of arrears.

p. The allocation of loans from the village reserve storehouses and of sundry kinds of assistance.

q. The bestowal of power of attorney for representing the community in legal matters. . . .

54. For deciding the following matters, the consent of not less than two-thirds of all peasants having a vote in the [village] assembly is required:

a. Replacing communal utilization of land by plot or household (hereditary) utilization.

b. Distributing communal land into permanent hereditary plots.

c. Redistributing communal land.

d. Establishing communal voluntary associations [*skladka*] and using communal capital.

e. Expelling pernicious peasants from the community and placing them at the disposal of the government. . . .

[Concerning the volost' administration:]

69. The volost' administration is composed of:

a. The volost' assembly [*volostnoi skhod*].

b. The volost' elder [*volostnoi starshina*], with the volost' executive board [*pravlenie*].

c. The volost' peasant court [*volostnoi krest'ianskii sud*]. . . .

71. The volost' assembly is composed of village and volost' officials who hold office through election . . . and of peasants elected from each settlement [*selenie*] or hamlet [*poselok*] belonging to the volost', one from every ten households [*dvory*]. . . .

78. Under the jurisdiction of the volost' assembly are:

a. The election of volost' officials and judges of the volost' courts.

b. Decisions on all subjects in general that relate to the economic and public affairs of the entire volost'.

c. Measures of public care for the poor; the establishment of volost' schools; arrangements as to volost' reserve storehouses, where such exist.

d. The transmission to the appropriate office of complaints and requests dealing with volost' affairs, through special delegates.

e. The fixing and apportionment of communal levies and obligations relating to the entire volost'.

f. The checking [of the accounts] of officials elected by the volost' and the verification of their actions.

g. The verification of the recruiting lists and the apportionment of recruit obligations.

h. The bestowal of power of attorney

for representing the volost' in legal matters.
. . .

81. The volost' elder is responsible for the maintenance of general order, peace, and tranquillity in the volost'. In this respect the village elders are fully subordinated to him.
. . .

93. For the formation of the volost' court the volost' assembly shall elect each year . . . from four to twelve . . . judges. . . . Sittings of the court must consist of no less than three judges. . . .

95. The volost' court has jurisdiction over . . . disputes and litigations between peasants and also over minor peasant offenses.

96. The volost' court has final decision over: all disputes and litigations between peasants alone of up to one hundred rubles inclusive in value, concerning, not only immovable and movable property within the limits of the peasant allotment, but also loans, purchases, sales, and sundry kinds of transactions and liabilities, and likewise matters dealing with compensation for losses and damages caused to peasant property. . . .

102. The volost' court is empowered, when dealing with such offenses, to sentence the guilty: to public labor—up to six days; or to a monetary fine—up to three rubles; or to arrest—up to seven days; or, finally, with persons not exempted from corporal punishment, to punishment with rods—up to twenty blows. . . .

104. The volost' elder and the village elder must not interfere in trials of the volost' court and shall not be present while cases are being considered.

[Concerning the release of peasants from the village communities:]

130. For the release of peasants from the village communities the following general conditions must be observed:

a. A peasant who wishes to receive his release from the community, after renouncing forever his share in the communal allotment . . . must give up the plot of land he was using. . . .

c. The family of the person released must not be in arrears in the payment of fiscal, land, or communal taxes, and in addition his own taxes must be paid up to January 1 of the following year.

d. There must not be, upon the person released, any uncontested private proceedings or liabilities which have been presented before the volost' administration.

e. The person released must not be under trial or investigation.

f. The parents of the person released must consent to his release.

g. Those in the family of the released peasant who are underage or otherwise incapable of working, and who remain in the community, must be guaranteed a means of support. . . .

h. The person wishing to obtain his release must present a certificate of acceptance [*priemnyi prigovor*] from that community to which he is transferring. . . .

169. The apportionment of fiscal and land obligations, in money and in kind, among the peasants in the village community is done by the commune. . . .

187. Each village community, whether its land is utilized by the communal method or by the plot or household (hereditary) method, is jointly responsible for the strict discharge of fiscal, land, and communal obligations by each of its members.

[From a supplementary statute:]

113. The communal [*mirskaia*] field land (plowland, hayfields, and other landed resources) remains in the "communal" ["*obshchinnoe*"] utilization of the peasants to whom it is allotted.

Note: By "communal" is meant that customary method of utilization in which the land is "redistributed" or "repartitioned" among the peasants in accordance with the decision of the commune—by souls, by tiagla, or by another method—while the obligations imposed upon the land are discharged through joint responsibility.

XV:15. THE SELECTION OF PEACE ARBITRATORS, IN LANSKOI'S CIRCULAR OF MARCH 22, 1861

On March 22, 1861, the minister of internal affairs, Lanskoi, issued this circular letter to the governors of the various parts of the empire. It laid down principles for filling the office of peace arbitrator (an office that was to be abolished in 1874 upon the establishment of uezd boards for peasant affairs). The term translated here and elsewhere as "arbitrator" (*posrednik*) is etymologically similar to the English word "mediator." However, since the decisions of these officials were not merely advisory but were binding upon the parties, the word "arbitrator" is substantively more accurate.

Reference: *PSZRI*, 2d ser., vol. 36, pt. 1, pp. 490-91. An account by one of those who served as a peace arbitrator has recently been translated in part in Stanley W. Page, ed., *Russia in Revolution: Selected Readings in Russian Domestic History Since 1855* (Princeton: D. Van Nostrand, 1965), pp. 15-18. The first part of Page's book also contains other excerpts—some previously translated and some not—that pertain to the period 1855-1917.

Your Excellency [i.e. each governor] is aware that, according to the new legislation, the appointment of arbitrators from the list compiled by the uezd marshal [of the nobility] . . . is turned over to the heads of the guberniias, and their confirmation in office, to the Governing Senate.

At the present time the successful selection of peace arbitrators [*mirovye posredniki*] constitutes one of the primary concerns of the government, and therefore I consider it necessary to direct the particular, personal attention of Your Excellency to the importance and responsibility of this selection with which you have been entrusted. The arbitrators are charged with making the immediate local arrangements for putting the peasant statutes into operation and with looking after their proper execution. Upon the fortunate choice of these persons will greatly depend the success of the *reform undertaken by the government*, which, in accordance with the expression by the sovereign emperor himself of his supreme will, *"must have as its basis a betterment of the living conditions of the peasants, and a betterment not only in word and on paper, but in actual fact."*

⋅ ⋅ ⋅

The moral qualities required by the office of peace arbitrator are revealed by its very title. His chief function is to conciliate and adjudicate the interests of both classes

[*sosloviia*]. . . . In the present great epoch, so important for the whole future of our fatherland, we must strive in every way possible to attract to the newly created offices men who are impartial, educated, and truly devoted to the sacred work undertaken by our most gracious sovereign. The personal merits of the new arbitrators must substantiate that great significance and general confidence which is accorded to them by the supreme legislative authority. For the success of all impending measures, it is particularly important that the arbitrators should possess not only authority over the peasants but also *their complete confidence*, since the peasants will not always be able to make clear for themselves the nature of their rights and duties from the law itself, and therefore, in case of doubt, it would be desirable that they turn confidently and voluntarily to the arbitrators rather than seek outside advisers who may not always be well intentioned. Such cordial relations between the peasants and the arbitrators will be the most important and very likely the most certain guarantee of the peaceful outcome of the matter at hand. With this aim in mind, it is indispensable for Your Excellency to invite to serve as arbitrators only those . . . among . . . the local estate-owning nobles who are known *for their unquestionable sympathy with the reform and for their good treatment of the peasants.*

XV:16. ENFORCING THE EMANCIPATION: THE MEMOIRS OF LIEUTENANT GENERAL DUBEL'T, 1861

Lieutenant General M. L. Dubel't, who was entrusted with carrying out the emancipation decrees and suppressing disorder in the guberniia of Iaroslavl', recorded the events from his viewpoint.

Reference: M. L. Dubel't, "Iz epokhi osvobozhdeniia krest'ian, rasskaz gen.-leit. M. L. Dubel'ta, 1861," *Russkaia starina*, 69 (Feb. 1891): 469-70.

The highest credit must be given to the Russian people for receiving and assimilating the great gift of freedom, and especially emancipation from the yoke of serfdom, with great wisdom and calm. If here and there in Russia there were at that time misunderstandings and on rare occasions even disorders, they were mostly incited by ill-intentioned people who confused those who were poorly educated.

These difficulties could easily have been averted by patience, wisdom, and tact on the part of the persons who introduced the statutes of 1861. But unfortunately it must be admitted that some of these persons, carried away by the very wide power given them, used it badly, that is to say, immediately, without previously employing measures of persuasion and clarification to inform the ignorant people of their new duties and rights, but instead demanding absolute obedience without such preliminary explanation as was possible. In some guberniias the actions of these persons can even be called extremely cruel.

In the various parts of Russia the disorders that broke out had their own individual characteristics, but we in this short account will occupy ourselves with only those that occurred in the guberniia of Iaroslavl', where I was sent by imperial command to carry out the statutes.

With reluctant pride I recall that in the course of four months during which I personally pacified fourteen estates, I absolutely did not inflict bodily punishment upon a single person; moreover, having recourse to the help of troops in cases of extreme resistance, I did not kill or wound people as others did. Everywhere I tried, and was so glad that I was able, to work patiently on the mind and understanding of the peasants.

XV:17. THE POPULAR RESPONSE TO THE EMANCIPATION, FROM THE MEMOIRS OF PRINCE KROPOTKIN, 1861

In 1861 Prince Petr Alekseevich Kropotkin (1842-1921) was a student in the Corps of Pages, a small and very select military school (for about 150 boys) attached to the imperial court in Saint Petersburg and serving especially the sons and grandsons of those who had achieved one of the top three or four ranks in the military, civil, or court service. In his memoirs, Kropotkin recalls how the emancipation was received by those people with whom he came in contact in the capital and on one of his family estates.

Reference: Peter Kropotkin, *Memoirs of a Revolutionist* (Boston: Houghton Mifflin, 1930), pp. 134-36. Reprint, New York: Horizon Press, 1968. Russian version, Moscow: Izd. Mysl', 1966.

[Kropotkin describes the events of Feb. 21, 1861, after the Emancipation Manifesto had been published:]

We went to the parade; and when all the military performances were over, Alexander II, remaining on horseback, loudly called out, "The officers to me!" They gathered round him, and he began, in a loud voice, a speech about the great event of the day.

"The officers . . . the representatives of the nobility in the army"—these scraps of sentences reached our ears—"an end has been put to centuries of injustice . . . I expect sacrifices from the nobility . . . the loyal nobility will gather round the throne" . . . and so on. Enthusiastic hurrahs resounded amongst the officers as he ended.

We ran rather than marched back on our way to the corps,—hurrying to be in time for the Italian opera, of which the last performance in the season was to be given that afternoon; some manifestation was sure to take place then. Our military attire was flung off with great haste, and several of us dashed, lightfooted, to the sixth-story gallery. The house was crowded.

During the first entr'acte the smoking-room of the opera filled with excited young men, who all talked to one another, whether acquainted or not. We planned at once to return to the hall, and to sing, with the whole public in a mass choir, the hymn "God Save the Tsar."

However, sounds of music reached our ears, and we all hurried back to the hall. The band of the opera was already playing the hymn, which was drowned immediately in enthusiastic hurrahs coming from all parts of the hall. I saw Bavéri, the conductor of the band, waving his stick, but not a sound could be heard from the powerful band. Then Bavéri stopped, but the hurrahs continued. I saw the stick waved again in the air; I saw the fiddle-bows moving, and musicians blowing the brass instruments, but again the sound of voices overwhelmed the band. Bavéri began conducting the hymn once more, and it was only by the end of that third repetition that isolated sounds of the brass instruments pierced through the clamor of human voices.

The same enthusiasm was in the streets. Crowds of peasants and educated men stood in front of the palace, shouting hurrahs, and the Tsar could not appear without being followed by demonstrative crowds running after his carriage. Hérzen was right when, two years later, as Alexander was drowning the Polish insurrection in blood, and "Muravióff the Hanger" was strangling it on the scaffold, he wrote, "Alexander Nikoláevich, why did you not die on that day? Your name would have been transmitted in history as that of a hero."

Where were the uprisings which had been predicted by the champions of slavery? Conditions more indefinite than those which had been created by the Polozhénie (the emancipation law) could not have been invented. If anything could have provoked revolts, it was precisely the perplexing vagueness of the conditions created by the new law. And yet, except in two places where there were insurrections, and a very few other spots where small disturbances entirely due to misunderstandings and immediately appeased took place, Russia remained quiet,—more quiet than ever. With their usual good sense, the peasants had understood that serfdom was done away with, that "freedom had come," and they accepted the conditions imposed upon them, although these conditions were very heavy.

I was in Nikólskoye [a Kropotkin estate in the Kaluga guberniia] in August, 1861, and again in the summer of 1862, and I was struck with the quiet, intelligent way in which the peasants had accepted the new conditions.

They knew perfectly well how difficult it would be to pay the redemption tax for the land, which was in reality an indemnity to the nobles in lieu of the obligations of serfdom. But they so much valued the abolition of their personal enslavement that they accepted the ruinous charges—not without murmuring, but as a hard necessity—the moment that personal freedom was obtained. . . .

When I saw our Nikólskoye peasants, fifteen months after the liberation, I could not but admire them. Their inborn good nature and softness remained with them, but all traces of servility had disappeared. They talked to their masters as equals talk to equals, as if they never had stood in different relations. Besides, such men came out from among them as could make a stand for their rights.

XV:18. LANSKOI'S CIRCULAR REFUTING RUMORS OF ANOTHER EMANCIPATION, DECEMBER 2, 1861

Late in 1861 it was found necessary for the minister of internal affairs to issue these instructions in a circular to the heads of the guberniias.

Reference: *PSZRI*, 2d ser., vol. 36, pt. 2, p. 514. There are many collections of documents on the Emancipation, in addition to those cited on the preceding pages. Among them are: *Otmena krepostnogo prava: Doklady ministrov vnutrennikh del o provedenii krest'ianskoi reformy 1861-1862* (Moscow: AN SSSR, 1950); K. A. Sofronenko, comp., *Krest'ianskaia reforma v Rossii 1861 goda'. Sbornik zakonodatel'nykh aktov* (Moscow: Gosiurizdat, 1954); V. A. Fedorov, ed. and comp., *Padenie krepostnogo prava v Rossii: Dokumenty i materialy,* 3 vols. (Moscow: Izd. Moskovskogo Universiteta, 1966-68).

From information reaching the Ministry of Internal Affairs concerning the state of the peasant matter, it is evident that the further success of this matter, and in particular the compilation of inventory charters [*ustavnaia gramota*], is hindered in many localities by widespread erroneous rumors and false hopes implanted among the peasants. They await what they call a new emancipation, upon the proclamation of which they would receive, after two years, some sort of "new privileges" which were not indicated in the statutes of February 19 (36650), and which peasants who have concluded voluntary agreements with estate owners and have signed inventory charters shall be deprived of. To put an end to such false expectations, the sovereign emperor, at the time of his journey to the Crimea, and in various localities where the elders of communities of temporarily obligated peasants were presented to His Imperial Majesty, was pleased to explain to them personally the nature of the matter and to remind them of the duties resting upon them. The sovereign emperor, on such occasions, deigned to say to the peasants that *there will be no emancipation other than that which has been granted, and that the peasants must therefore perform what is required of them by the general laws and the statutes of February 19.*

In accordance with the supreme command, it was proposed that the heads of the guberniias should inform all the peace arbitrators to make these supreme declarations known to the volost' executive boards, and, whenever the occasion arises in talking with the peasants, to refer in a positive way to the words that the peasants of certain guberniias were fortunate enough to hear directly from the sovereign emperor.

B. OTHER POLITICAL, SOCIAL, AND ECONOMIC DEVELOPMENTS

Note: Developments connected especially with the revolutionary movement are grouped in Section C, below.

XV:19. THE PEACE TREATY OF PARIS, MARCH 18 (30, N.S.), 1856

Russia's defeat in the Crimean War by the allies (Great Britain, France, Sardinia, and Turkey) obliged Alexander II to sign a peace treaty that contained such restrictive provisions as those excerpted here. Article XIII, one of the articles most resented by Russia, was abrogated by Alexander in 1870.

Reference: Edward Hertslet, ed., *The Map of Europe by Treaty since the General Peace of 1814,* 4 vols. (London, 1875-91), 2:1253-62. Russian text in *PSZRI,* 2d ser., vol. 31, pt. 1, pp. 226-30. For this and other diplomatic documents see also E. A. Adamov, ed., *Sbornik dogovorov Rossii s drugimi gosudarstvami 1856-1917* (Moscow: Gospolitizdat, 1952).

ART. III. His Majesty the Emperor of All the Russias engages to restore to His Majesty the Sultan the Town and Citadel of Kars, as well as the other parts of the Ottoman Territory of which the Russian troops are in possession.

ART. IV. Their Majesties the Queen of the United Kingdom of Great Britain and Ireland, the Emperor of the French, the King of Sardinia, and the Sultan, engage to restore to His Majesty the Emperor of All the Russias, the Towns and Ports of Sebastopol, Balaklava, Kamiesch, Eupatoria, Kertch, Jenikale, Kinburn, as well as all other Territories occupied by the Allied Troops. . . .

ART. VII. . . . [The signatories] declare the Sublime Porte admitted to participate in the advantages of the Public Law and System (*Concert*) of Europe. Their Majesties engage, each on his part, to respect the Independence and the Territorial Integrity of the Ottoman Empire; Guarantee in common the strict observance of that engagement. . . .

ART. IX. His Imperial Majesty the Sultan having, in his constant solicitude for the welfare of his subjects, issued a Firman, which, while ameliorating their condition without distinction of Religion or of Race, records his generous intentions towards the Christian population of his Empire, and wishing to give a further proof of his sentiments in that respect, has resolved to communicate to the Contracting Parties the said Firman, emanating spontaneously from his Sovereign will.

The Contracting Powers recognise the high value of this communication. It is clearly understood that it cannot, in any case, give to the said Powers the right to interfere, either collectively or separately, in the relations of His Majesty the Sultan with his subjects, nor in the Internal Administration of his Empire.

ART. X. The Convention of 13th of July, 1841, which maintains the ancient rule of the Ottoman Empire relative to the Closing of the Straits of the Bosphorus and of Dardanelles, has been revised by common consent. . . .

ART. XI. The Black Sea is Neutralised; its Waters and its Ports, thrown open to the Mercantile Marine of every Nation, are formally and in perpetuity interdicted to the Flag of War, either of the Powers possessing its Coasts, or of any other Power. . . .

ART. XII. Free from any impediment, the Commerce in the Ports and Waters of the Black Sea shall be subject only to Regulations of Health, Customs, and Police. . . .

ART. XIII. The Black Sea being Neutralised according to the terms of Article XI, the maintenance or establishment upon its Coast of Military-Maritime Arsenals becomes alike unnecessary and purposeless; in consequence, His Majesty the Emperor of All the Russias, and His Imperial Majesty the Sultan, engage not to establish or to maintain upon that Coast any Military-Maritime Arsenal. . . .

ART. XX. . . . His Majesty the Emperor of All the Russias consents to the rectification of his Frontier in Bessarabia. . . .

ART. XXII. The Principalities of Wallachia and Moldavia shall continue to enjoy under the Suzerainty of the Porte, and under the Guarantee of the Contracting Powers, the Privileges and Immunities of which they are in possession. No exclusive Protection shall be exercised over them by any of the guaranteeing Powers.

There shall be no separate right of interference in their Internal Affairs.

ART. XXIII. The Sublime Porte engages to preserve to the said Principalities an Independent and National Administration, as well as full liberty of Worship, of Legislation, of Commerce, and of Navigation. . . .

ART. XXVIII. The Principality of Servia shall continue to hold of [i.e. to be under] the Sublime Porte, in conformity with the Imperial Hats [decrees] which fix and determine its Rights and Immunities, placed henceforward under the Collective Guarantee of the Contracting Powers.

In consequence, the said Principality shall preserve its Independent and National Administration, as well as full liberty of Worship, of Legislation, of Commerce, and of Navigation.

ART. XXIX. The right of garrison of the Sublime Porte, as stipulated by anterior regulations, is maintained. No Armed Intervention can take place in Servia without previous agreement between the High Contracting Powers.

XV:20. THE DECREE ON RAILWAYS, JANUARY 26, 1857

When Alexander II came to the throne, Russia's only significant railroad was that between Saint Petersburg and Moscow (see the decree of February 1, 1842, Item XIV:22). The following decree, while no doubt providing big profits for some entrepreneurs, paved the way for the construction during Alexander's reign of over twelve thousand miles of railways.

Reference: *PSZRI,* 2d ser., vol. 32, pt. 1, p. 73.

Railways, the need for which has been doubted by many over the last ten years, have now been recognized by all strata as a necessity for the empire and have become a national need and a common and insistent desire.

In this profound conviction we gave orders immediately after the first cessation of hostilities for funds to be arranged so that this urgent need might be satisfied in the best way. Thorough discussion showed that it was best for the sake of convenience and speed to turn, following the example of all other countries, to private enterprise, both domestic and foreign, so as in the latter case to profit from the experience gained in the building of many thousands of miles of railway lines in western Europe.

On this basis various offers were invited, presented, and examined, and after the matter had received due consideration by the Committee of Ministers and been discussed in our presence, the terms offered by the Society of Russian and Foreign Capitalists, at the head of which is our banker, Baron Stieglitz, were unanimously considered the best and were approved by us.

Under these terms the society undertakes: to build at its own expense within ten years and to maintain for eighty-five years the indicated network of about four thousand versts of railway, with the government guaranteeing to pay 5 percent interest on the amount calculated for the construction, and with the entire network becoming the property of the treasury when the time limit expires.

· · ·

The network will extend from Saint Petersburg to Warsaw and the Prussian frontier; from Moscow to Nizhnii-Novgorod; from Moscow through Kursk and the lower reaches of the Dnieper to Feodosiia [in the Crimea]; and from Kursk, or Orel, through Dinaburg [Duenaburg, Dvinsk] to Libava [Liepaja, Libau]—and thereby through twenty-six guberniias it will, by an uninterrupted stretch of railway, link together three capitals, our main navigable rivers, our richest grain regions, and two ports on the Black Sea and Baltic that are open almost all year round. Thus it will facilitate our exports abroad and will ensure the transportation and supply of food at home.

XV:21. PRINCE BARIATINSKII ON RUSSIA AND THE CAUCASUS, 1859 AND 1862

Russia's drive to expand her southern frontiers continued during the mid-nineteenth century. From 1856 to 1862 the tsar's vicegerent in the Caucasus, and commander of the Russian army there, was Field Marshal Prince Aleksandr Ivanovich Bariatinskii (1814-79). Here are excerpts from two documents in which he sets forth his ideas on the people of the area and on the task of subjugation and administration.

Reference: Arnold L. Zisserman, *Fel'dmarshal Kniaz A. I. Bariatinskii, 1815-1877,* 3 vols. (Moscow, 1888-91), vol. 2, app., pp. 277-79 [memorandum of July 10, 1859]; 2:414-18 [letter of December 1862]. A recent publication of sources pertaining to the relationship between the tsar and Bariatinskii is *The Politics of Autocracy: Letters of Alexander II to Prince A. I. Bariatinskii, 1857-64,* ed. Alfred J. Rieber (Paris: Mouton, 1966).

[From Prince Bariatinskii's memorandum of July 10, 1859, concerning internal conditions in the Caucasus:]

With the fall of the aristocracy, the population, which had until then been broken up into separate communities as a result of the continual dissensions among their rulers, thus presenting us with a most convenient situation for the establishment of our rule, coalesced into a single spiritual nationality, making it possible for one man [Shamil] to become the secular and spiritual leader of the entire territory. Agitation for a war against the infidels flared up in the Caucasus and created a religious community which took the form of Muridism. Thus, the religious state of mind, inflamed against our rule, swept the Caucasus mountain range, and all submitted to the Shariat [i.e. the sacred law of the Moslems, including both the teaching of the Koran and the sayings of Mohammed].

. . .

Muridism is not only a religious institution but also a social code, which, leveling all classes and conditions, determines both the judicial law and the system of taxation. It denies the legitimacy of all secular rule and does not recognize any government that is not headed by the legitimate heir of the prophet. The sultan of Turkey, alone, is accepted by Muridism as the lawful sovereign of all Mohammedans. The Shariat—this cornerstone of Muridism—is both a spiritual and a secular court, which assigns equal rights to all Moslems. And this is the reason for the extraordinary influence of Moslem religious leaders in the Caucasus.

. . .

We must endeavor above all to restore the upper class wherever its traces are still preserved. . . . As the nobility is thus restored, the government will have in it the best weapon for the weakening of Islamism, since its revival will spontaneously bring in its wake a strengthening of the Adat [the law based on national customs] as a counterforce to the Shariat. The authority of the Shariat court will then of itself be restricted to purely religious matters. At the same time, we shall invest the people's oral tribunals [*narodnye slovesnye sudilishcha*] established

by us with as much civil jurisdiction as possible. And as we thus separate the principles of civil and religious jurisdiction, it will become easier to draw the former closer to our system of court procedures and, imperceptibly, to lead the people toward all the other forms of our civil organization.

. . .

But the resultant decline of the [Moslem] clergy and the elimination of its civil authority among the people must inevitably lead also to a weakening of the moral postulates so essential for human nature. We should, therefore, take immediate steps to the end that, as they lose their religious faith, the Moslems may have before them another ready-made creed, purer and more reassuring to the dictates of reason and conscience, so that, in any voluntary comparison of this creed with the one that is being abandoned, the former would at the very first glance impress the mind with its unquestionable superiority.

With this in mind I propose that we initiate a restoration of Christian Orthodoxy in the Caucasus. It was my aim to create means for the adequate restoration and erection of churches and the education and maintenance of good preachers of our holy faith. . . .

I therefore venture once more to advance my most earnest plea for the establishment, in the nearest possible future, of a Society for the Restoration of Christianity in the Caucasus.

[From a letter from Prince Bariatinskii to the new vicegerent of the Caucasus, Grand Duke Mikhail Nikolaevich, December 1862:]

It seems to me that the principal fault that is sometimes encountered even among persons in the government lies in an unconscious hostility toward an alien people and an involuntary tendency to force it into submission to our own habits and customs. The effects of this attitude are so strong that, penetrating to the lower strata of officials, they are frequently reflected even in trivial details of ordinary relations, in daily life, offending equally the sensibilities of all classes, from the highest to the lowest, from the most wealthy to the poorest. It may well be asked whether such moral oppression can breed devotion and love for the government among the people.

On the basis of these observations, I have formed convictions and rules by which I have guided myself throughout the period of my office. I believe it is important to win the greatest possible devotion of the territory to the government, and to administer each nationality with affection and complete respect for its cherished customs and traditions. The administrator, in my view, may only prepare the ground and point the way to improvements, but he must permit each nationality to contribute its share to general national progress consistent with its own particular conditions. In this respect the education of native women is, of course, of prime importance. Because of her influence upon the family as a repository of the national manners and customs, a woman has an equal effect on the habits of the child, the adult, and the aged, and therefore she alone can change for the better the domestic customs that are the primary basis for general improvement.

This is why, in a territory where a need is felt for a transformation of customs, attention should be given first of all to increasing the number of schools for women.

· · ·

The problem of such a transformation is more difficult among Moslem peoples, since their civil organization rests on the foundations of Mohammedanism, and all their rules are therefore at odds with the civil principles of Christian government.

Eradication of the [Moslem] clergy's influence must therefore precede all other measures. Yet direct action on our part can only strengthen the people's fanaticism. Hence, it is necessary in this area to find also some means, derived and formed within their midst, which, gradually undermining the importance of the Mullahs, would in time destroy the authority of the Koran.

It was to this end that I restored the power of the khans as a force inimical to the theocratic principle. Although the khans recognize the Shariat, they seek to give precedence to the Adat, a law based on custom and consequently admitting of change. The Adat, based on the rights of the different estates, is extremely onerous, and if—with the decline of the Shariat—the people will no longer be protected against the oppression of the khans,

they will, naturally, prefer to see the introduction of our civil laws.

· · ·

To conclude my survey, permit me, for the sake of greater clarity, to submit to Your Imperial Highness a brief recapitulation of the topics on which I expressed my views and which I regard as the cornerstones of the welfare and happiness of the peoples entrusted to your care:

1. Education of women
2. Eradication of the Shariat
3. Restoration of Christianity
4. Means of communication
5. Irrigation
6. Colonization

· · ·

We have conquered Shamil and, with him, all of the eastern Caucasus. The subjugation of the western Caucasus will be different because here we are not fighting with an established society and an administrative hierarchy. The Circassian tribes do not submit to any social laws; the only things they hold sacred are personal independence, honor, and courage. To deal with them is to deal separately with each individual. This is why cutting them off from the sea and dislodging them from the heart of the western mountain range are the sine qua non for the conquest of the territory, which should subsequently be consolidated by intensive colonization of the trans-Kuban' lands.

There is no doubt that the enemy we are trying to dislodge will defend himself with stubborn fury. But, in my opinion, the desirable outcome can be facilitated by reaching an agreement with the Porte concerning the installation of Shamil on Turkish lands which he should be allowed to colonize with voluntary exiles from the Caucasus. In this manner, we shall soon be rid of malcontents, fanatics, and the entire theocratic party, and we shall pacify simultaneously both European philanthropists and our own conscience, while providing the Circassians with a way out of the present desperate situation. We shall avoid bloodshed, Turkey will acquire an excellent addition to her population, and Shamil, along with gratitude to the emperor, will find fulfillment of his cherished aspirations. [Note: During the 1860s there was indeed a mass resettlement, when several hundred thousand Moslems emigrated from the conquered Caucasus to Turkey.]

XV:22. GORCHAKOV'S JUSTIFICATION OF THE RUSSIAN ADVANCE INTO CENTRAL ASIA, 1864

In 1864, when Russian troops were occupying parts of what is now the Uzbek Republic, Vice-Chancellor Prince Aleksandr Mikhailovich Gorchakov notified the foreign powers of these movements in a detailed circular letter which ran in part as follows.

Reference: Tatishchev, *Imperator Aleksandr II*, 2:107-08.

The situation of Russia in central Asia is similar to that of all civilized states that come into contact with half-savage nomadic tribes without a firm social organization. In such cases, the interests of border security and trade relations always require that the more civilized state have a certain authority over its neighbors, whose wild and unruly customs render them very troublesome. It begins first by curbing raids and pillaging. To put an end to these, it is often compelled to reduce the neighboring tribes to some degree of close subordination. Once this result has been achieved, the latter take on more peaceful habits, but in their turn they are exposed to the attack of tribes living farther off. . . . The state therefore must make a choice: either to give up this continuous effort and doom its borders to constant unrest, which would make prosperity, safety, and cultural progress impossible here, or else to advance farther and farther into the heart of the savage lands, where the vast distances, with every step forward, increase the difficulties and hardships it incurs. Such has been the fate of all states placed in a similar situation. The United States of America, France in Africa, Holland in its colonies, England in the East Indies—they all were inevitably driven to choose the path of onward movement, not so much from ambition as from dire necessity, where the greatest difficulty lies in being able to stop.

XV:23. THE UNIVERSITY REGULATIONS OF JUNE 18, 1863

See also the decrees of 1755, 1803, 1835, and 1851, Items XI:15, XIII:17, XIV:34, and XIV:39, respectively, in preceding chapters.

Reference: *PSZRI*, 2d ser., vol. 38, pt. 1, pp. 622, 624, 625, 626-28, 632-34, 636.

[From the General Charter of the Imperial Russian Universities:]

2. The faculties contained within the universities are the historical-philological, the physico-mathematical, the law, and the medical.

Note: In the University of Saint Petersburg, a faculty of Oriental languages is stipulated, but there is no faculty of medicine.

3. Each university, under the central authority of the minister of education [*narodnogo prosveshcheniia*], is committed to the charge of the superintendent of the educational district [*popechitel' uchebnogo okruga*].

4. The immediate administration of a university devolves upon the rector [*rektor*].

5. Besides the faculties, the component parts of the administration of a university are: (1) the university council; (2) the university executive board [*pravlenie*]; (3) the university court; (4) the prorector or inspector. . . .

6. Each faculty consists of a dean, professors and associate professors [*professory*

ordinarnye i ekstraordinarnye], docents, and lecturers, as provided by the table of organization [*po shtatu*]. In addition to this the universities are permitted to have an unlimited number of privatdocents. . . .

8. The dean is elected at a meeting of his faculty for a term of three years; he is chosen from the ranks of full professors unless there are fewer than three of them within the faculty, in which case he may be chosen from the ranks of associate professors also; and he is confirmed in office by the minister of education. . . .

19. Special lecturers are authorized for modern foreign languages—(1) German, (2) French, (3) English, and (4) Italian—in all universities, and, in addition, for practical instruction in Oriental languages in the University of Saint Petersburg. . . .

24. The rector is elected by the council for a term of four years from among the full professors of the university and is confirmed in this office by imperial [*vysochaishii*] order. . . .

37. The university council is composed of all professors and associate professors of the

university, under the chairmanship of the rector. The rector may invite docents and other instructors to meetings of the council; but they have a consultative voice only in those cases when the council finds it necessary to request their explanation or opinion on some particular question. . . .

42. The subjects the council deals with are: (A) those presented to the council for confirmation, i.e. (1) the assignment of subjects and their method of instruction in all faculties; (2) the awarding of medals and the assignment of scholarships to students; (3) the awarding of prizes for scholarly works on problems offered to scholars for solution in the name of the university; (4) the confirmation of academic degrees [candidate, master, and doctor] . . . (6) the retention of scholarship students in the university to prepare them for professorial rank; (7) arrangements for the publication of scholarly writings in the name of the university; (8) dispositions concerning the program for competitions to fill vacant professorial chairs; (9) the examination of the financial estimate of the university, and likewise the examination and confirmation of the yearly estimate of receipts and expenditures of the special resources it owns . . . (B) those presented to the superintendent for confirmation, i.e. . . . (2) the election of docents, lecturers, laboratory assistants, custodians of offices and museums, and assistants to the prosectors [anatomists] and to the prorector or inspector; (3) the granting of permission for privatdocents to give lectures; (4) the election of honorary members, a librarian and

his assistants, an accountant of the executive board, a treasurer, an architect, a business officer [ekzekutor], an archivist, and secretaries of the council, of the executive board, and of student affairs . . . (C) those presented through the superintendent to the minister for confirmation, i.e. (1) the election of a rector, deans, a prorector or inspector, and professors. . . .

50. The executive board, under the chairmanship of the rector, is composed of: the dean of each faculty and the prorector. . . .

90. Besides students, outsiders are also permitted to attend lectures. . . .

91. The complete course of university instruction embraces five academic years in the faculty of medicine and four years in the other faculties. . . .

105. The tuition for each student attending lectures is fifty rubles a year in the universities of the capital cities [Saint Petersburg and Moscow], and forty rubles in the others. . . .

107. For the relief of needy students, the universities are allowed to grant deferments of payment, or to reduce it by as much as one-half, or even to waive it entirely. . . .

114. Academic degrees may be obtained both by Russian subjects and by foreigners. . . .

129. Universities are accorded the right to import, at liberty and duty free, scholarly texts of any kind from abroad. . . .

130. Books, manuscripts, and periodical publications that the universities receive from foreign countries are not subject to examination by the censorship.

XV:24. THE POLISH NATIONAL COMMITTEE'S PROCLAMATION OF JANUARY 22, 1863

When the Russian government ordered conscription in the hope of removing the rebellious youth from the Polish cities, the National Committee of the Polish revolutionaries, proclaiming itself the temporary government of Poland, issued this proclamation.

Reference: Tytus Filipowicz, ed., *Confidential Correspondence of the British Government respecting the Insurrection in Poland: 1863* (Paris: Soudier, 1914), pp. 12-13, slightly revised on the basis of the curiously not quite complete Polish version in Marjan Dubiecki, comp., *Powstanie styczniowe w swietle zrodel,* Teksty zrodlowe do nauki historji w szkole sredniej, fascicle 54 (Krakow: Nakladem Krakowskiej Spolki Wydawniczej, 1924), p. 7.

The contemptible government of the invaders, rendered furious by the resistance of the victim that it tortures, has determined to strike a decisive blow by carrying away many thousands of its bravest and most strenuous defenders, dressing them in the hated Muscovite

uniform, and driving them thousands of miles to suffer eternal misery and destruction.

Poland will not, cannot, submit to this violence and degradation without an attempt at resistance. It would be a shame before posterity were she to submit to it without an energetic effort. Legions of young men, brave and devoted to the cause of their country, have sworn to cast away the abhorred yoke or to die, and they place their reliance in the just assistance of the Almighty. Follow these, O Polish nation!

The Central National Committee, the only legal government of your country, bids you all appear on the last battlefield, the field of glory and victory, where it pledges itself to give you success before God and Heaven; for the committee knows that as you have been heretofore penitents or avengers, so you are ready to become tomorrow heroes and giants of strength. It knows you are ready to achieve your liberty and independence by deeds of courage, and to make such sacrifices as no people have as yet inscribed in the annals of their history. It knows well that you are ready to give all your blood, your lives, and your freedom without regret, hesitation, or weakness, as an offering to your rising country.

In return the Central National Committee promises to wield the scepter of authority with an unflinching hand, so that your strength will not be wasted. Your sacrifices will not be in vain. It will know how to overcome all difficulties, to break through all impediments; it will pursue and punish every disinclination, nay even every case of lack of sufficient zeal in our holy cause, with the utmost severity required from a tribunal which metes out justice in the name of an offended country.

This being the first day of open resistance, the commencement of the sacred combat, the committee proclaims all the sons of Poland free and equal, without distinction of creed and condition. It proclaims further that the land held heretofore by the agricultural population in fee, for corvée labor or for rent, becomes henceforth their freehold property without any restriction whatsoever. The proprietors will receive compensation from the public treasury. All cottagers and laborers who shall serve the families of those who may die in the service of their country will receive allotments from the national property in land regained from the enemy.

To arms, therefore, you Poles, you Lithuanians, and you [West] Russians [*Rusi*]! The hour of our common deliverance has struck; the ancient sword is drawn from the scabbard; the sacred flag of our common country is unfurled.

And now we appeal to you, Muscovite nation—miserable and tormented, sad and afflicted with ourselves. Your sons have also been dangling on gibbets, or have found a frosty death like our own people in the snows of Siberia; therefore we forgive you the murder of our country, the blood of Praga and Oszmiana, the violence in the streets of Warsaw, the tortures in the dungeons of the citadel: but woe to you if in this solemn hour you give assistance to the tyrant who crushes you while he murders us; if, instead of regret for the past and holy desires for the future, you do this, you shall be accursed and condemned to a shameful and perpetual slavery, and then we must fight you to extermination, the last fight of European civilization with Asiatic barbarity.

XV:25. THE PEASANT REFORM IN POLAND AS DECREED ON FEBRUARY 19, 1864

Early in 1864 the tsarist government decreed land reform for the Polish guberniias of the empire. The language of the decree reflects the government's assessment of the rising of 1863 and its decision on how to deal with the Poles.

Reference: *PSZRI*, 2d ser., vol. 39, pt. 1, pp. 121-22.

The turmoil and disturbances which arose recently and have not yet entirely ceased served as a means for men of evil intent, not only to delay the execution of the definitive arrangement of the mode of life of the peasantry which our parent promised and which we have undertaken, but also to subject to temptation their fidelity to the law and to the throne, and to sow disturbance and unrest in their minds.

The good sense of the peasantry has triumphed, however, over flattering enticements, while their unshakable fidelity, standing fast under all manner of threats and violence, has even been sealed with the blood of many innocent victims.

. . .

ARTICLE 1. Land that is under peasant utilization . . . passes into the full possession of the peasants owning that land. . . .

ART. 2. As of April 3 (15, N.S.), 1864, the peasants are forever freed from all their obligations, without exception, to owners of estates. ... In the future, peasants are obliged to pay to the treasury, in return for the land they have acquired as private property, the land tax instituted by this decree. ...

ART. 3. Owners of estates, whether private, institutional, or conferred inalienably, are to receive compensation from the treasury for the now abolished peasant obligations.

XV:26. THE ZEMSTVO STATUTES OF JANUARY 1, 1864

One logical sequel to the emancipation of the serfs was the establishment of the new zemstvo institutions for local government outside of the large towns. A statute of January 1, 1864, defined the rights and functions of the various zemstvo bodies. Within five years such bodies had been set up in thirty-four guberniias of European Russia, with the notable exception of the western areas where the government doubted the "reliability" of the Polish estate owners. Only in 1911-13 were zemstvos introduced in the western guberniias.

Reference: *PSZRI,* 2d ser., vol. 39, pt. 1, pp. 2-3, 6-8.

1. For the management of affairs relating to the local economic welfare and needs of each guberniia and each uezd, guberniia and uezd zemstvo institutions are to be formed. ...

2. The matters that are subject to the jurisdiction of zemstvo institutions in guberniias and uezdy, as they relate to each, are:

i. The management of the property, capital, and monetary levies of the zemstvo.

ii. The organization and maintenance of buildings belonging to the zemstvo, other equipment, and roads maintained at the expense of the zemstvo.

iii. Measures for assuring foodstuffs for the public.

iv. The management of zemstvo charitable institutions and other measures of care for the poor; methods of eliminating poverty; looking after the building of churches.

v. The administration of matters pertaining to the zemstvo mutual property insurance.

vi. Looking after the development of local trade and industry.

vii. Participation, primarily in an economic capacity and within the limits defined by the law, in looking after public education, public health, and prisons.

viii. Cooperation in preventing cattle plague, and likewise in guarding crops of grain and other plants from destruction by locusts, gophers, and other harmful animals and insects.

ix. The execution of the demands that the military and civil administrations place upon the zemstvo, and participation in matters concerning postal obligations. ...

xi. The fixing, allocation, collection, and expenditure, on the basis of the statutes [ustav] concerning zemstvo obligations, of local levies for satisfying the zemstvo needs of the guberniia or uezd.

xii. The presentation through the guberniia authorities to the central government of information and conclusions on subjects relating to the local economic welfare and needs of the guberniia or uezd, and the bringing of petitions regarding these subjects, likewise through the guberniia authorities; the furnishing of information relating to the economy of the zemstvo upon the demand of the central organs of government and the guberniia heads.

xiii. The holding of elections for membership and for other positions in zemstvo institutions, and the allocation of money for the maintenance of these institutions. ...

6. Zemstvo institutions function independently within the sphere of activity entrusted to them. ...

9. The guberniia head [i.e. the governor] has the right to suspend the execution of any disposition of the zemstvo institutions that is contrary to the laws, or to the general welfare of the state. ...

11. Zemstvo institutions are allowed to present complaints to the Governing Senate against measures of the head of the guberniia and the central administrative authorities that pertain to them. ...

13. The uezd zemstvo institutions are: the uezd zemstvo assembly [*uezdnoe zemskoe sobranie*] and the uezd zemstvo executive board [*uezdnaia zemskaia uprava*].

14. The uezd zemstvo assembly is composed of zemstvo members [*glasnye*], elected:

(a) by the landed proprietors of the uezd;
(b) by the urban communities; and (c) by the
village communities. . . .

37. The verification of the number of
members and the legality and validity of their
election is placed upon the zemstvo assembly
itself.

38. Members are elected for a period of
three years. . . .

39. No prerogatives of service are conferred upon members, nor are they stipulated
any emolument. . . .

43. The uezd zemstvo assembly is under
the chairmanship of the uezd marshal of the
nobility. . . .

46. The uezd zemstvo executive board is
composed of a chairman and two members,
elected for a period of three years by the
uezd zemstvo assembly from among its own
participants. The assemblies may, if they
find it necessary, increase the number of
elected members of the executive board to
six. . . .

48. The chairman of the uezd executive
board, as elected by the zemstvo assembly

(article 46), is confirmed in this office by the
head of the guberniia. . . .

50. The guberniia zemstvo institutions are:
the guberniia zemstvo assembly [*gubernskoe
zemskoe sobranie*] and the guberniia zemstvo
executive board [*gubernskaia zemskaia uprava*].

51. The guberniia zemstvo assembly is composed of members elected by the uezd zemstvo
assemblies for a period of three years. . . .

53. The guberniia zemstvo assembly . . . is
under the chairmanship of the guberniia marshal of the nobility. . . .

56. The guberniia zemstvo executive board
is composed of a chairman and six members,
elected for a period of three years by the
guberniia zemstvo assembly from its own
ranks. . . . The chairman of the guberniia executive board, as elected by the zemstvo assembly, is confirmed in office by the minister
of internal affairs. [The functions enumerated
in article 2, above, fell within the jurisdiction
of the guberniia zemstvo if two or more uezdy
were involved (article 61); the guberniia
zemstvo also had special responsibility for
roads and for fire insurance (article 62).]

XV:27. THE JUDICIAL REFORM OF NOVEMBER 20, 1864

An especially radical innovation of the 1860s—and probably the most successful of all—was the
judicial reform introduced by a series of statutes of November 20, 1864, which were designed to
eliminate the injustice, inefficiency, and cruelty associated with the previous court system.

Reference: *PSZRI*, 2d ser., vol. 39, pt. 2, pp. 180 [no. 41,473], 180-82, 186, 196-97, 199
[no. 41,476], 230, 290.

[From Statute No. 41,473, November 20,
1864:]

Having examined these projects, we find
that they fully correspond to our desire to
establish in Russia courts of justice that are
swift, equitable, merciful, and equal for all
our subjects, to elevate the authority of the
judiciary, to give it the independence that
befits it, and in general to strengthen among
our people that respect for the law without
which the public welfare is made impossible
and which must constantly guide the actions
of one and all, from the most exalted to the
lowliest.

[From Statute No. 41,475, same date:]
The Establishment of Judicial Institutions
[*sudebnye ustanovleniia*]
1. Judicial authority belongs to:
Justices of the peace [*mirovoi sud'ia*]

Sessions [*s"ezd*] of justices of the peace
Circuit courts [*okruzhnoi sud*]
Judicial tribunals [*sudebnaia palata*]
The Governing Senate, in the capacity of
a supreme court of appeal

2. The judicial authority of the institutions
designated in article 1, above, extends to persons of all classes and to all cases, both civil
and criminal.

Note: The judicial authority of ecclesiastical,
military, commercial, peasant, and native tribe
[*inorodtsy*] courts is defined by special regulations concerning them.

3. The justice of the peace is an individual
[*edinolichnyi*] authority; sessions of justices
of the peace, circuit courts, judicial tribunals,
and the Senate are collective [*kollegial'nyi*]
institutions. . . .

6. Examining magistrates [*sudebnyi sledo-
vatel'*] are attached [to the courts] for conduct-

ing investigations in cases involving crimes [*prestuplenie*] and offenses [*prostupok*].

7. For determining the guilt or innocence of the accused in criminal cases, jurors [*prisiazhnye zasedateli*] are added to the composition of the court, in instances designated in the statute [ustav] on criminal procedure.

8. Chief prosecutors [*ober-prokurory*], prosecutors, and their assistants [*prokurory i ikh tovarishchi*] are attached to the courts for supervising prosecutions. . . .

11. Included within the judiciary system are: (a) chanceries [*kantseliariia*]; (b) court bailiffs [*sudebnyi pristav*]; (c) advocates [*prisiazhnyi poverennyi*]; (d) candidates for positions in the judiciary [*po sudebnomu vedomstvu*]; and (e) notaries [*notarius*]. . . .

17. Assemblies [sobranie] of both honorary [*pochetnyi*] and district [*uchastkovyi*] justices of the peace of each judicial circuit [mirovoi okrug] constitute the court of higher instance, which is called the session of justices of the peace. These sessions are under the chairmanship of one of the justices of the peace, elected by their own number. . . .

19. To the post of justice of the peace may be elected those local residents who: first, are at least twenty-five years of age; second, have received a higher or secondary education, or have passed an examination equivalent to it, or have served for not fewer than three years in a post the duties of which could enable them to acquire a practical knowledge of judicial procedure; and third, if in addition they themselves, or their parents or wives, own . . . real estate [in the countryside] with a value of not less than fifteen thousand rubles, or real estate in cities evaluated for purposes of taxation at not less than six thousand rubles in the capital cities, or not less than three thousand rubles in other cities. . . .

23. Both honorary and district justices of the peace are elected for a period of three years.

24. Elections of justices of the peace are held at uezd zemstvo assemblies. . . .

40. In Saint Petersburg and Moscow justices of the peace are elected by the municipal dumas [councils]. . . .

81. Jurors are elected from among all classes [*soslovie*] of local inhabitants. . . .

202. The posts of chairmen, assistant chairmen, and of [other] members of the judiciary, including the examining magistrates, and likewise of prosecuting officials, chief secretaries, secretaries, and their assistants may be filled . . . only by persons who have a certificate from a university or other institution of higher education, testifying to the completion of a course in jurisprudence, or who have passed an examination in this science, or who have demonstrated their knowledge of judicial procedure in some official capacity. . . .

212. Chairmen, assistant chairmen, and [other] members of circuit courts, including the examining magistrate, and likewise senior chairmen, chairmen of departments, and [other] members of judicial tribunals, are appointed by supreme authority, upon the recommendation of the minister of justice.

213. In the event that a post in a circuit court or judicial tribunal, including that of examining magistrate, becomes vacant, a general meeting of the court or tribunal is immediately held, with the participation of the prosecutor, for consultation concerning candidates for this post. . . .

216. Senators of the Senate Departments of Appeal [Kassatsionnyi] and the presidents [pervoprisutstvuiushchii] both of those departments and of their general session [sobranie] are appointed by supreme sovereign decree, at the immediate discretion of His Imperial Majesty. . . .

243. Chairmen, assistant chairmen, and [other] members of the judiciary may neither be discharged except on their request . . . nor transferred from one locality to another without their consent. It is permissible to relieve them temporarily of their duties only in the event that they are brought to trial, and they are subject to final dismissal or suspension from duty only by decision of a criminal court.

[From Statute No. 41,476, concerning criminal proceedings:]

204. Cases involving crimes against the state are tried by the judicial tribunals or by the Supreme Criminal Court. . . . [Note: According to a law promulgated on June 7, 1872, cases involving "crimes against the state" were to be dealt with by the judicial tribunals or "by a special session of the Governing Senate, with the participation of representatives from

the (various) classes," and, in exceptional cases only, by the Supreme Criminal Court (*PSZRI*, 2d ser., vol. 47, pt. 1).] . . .

1051. For trying cases involving crimes against the state, to the members of the criminal department of the judicial tribunals are added: (1) the guberniia marshal of the nobility from that guberniia in which the tribunal is constituted, (2) one of the uezd marshals of the nobility from the circuit of the local circuit court, (3) one of the city mayors [*gorodskoi golova*] from that same circuit, and (4) one of the volost' heads or elders from the local uezd.

XV:28. A PROPOSAL OF THE MOSCOW NOBLES, JANUARY 11, 1865

Soon after zemstvo institutions were established, the nobles of Moscow presented an address to the tsar in which they made this request.

Reference: Boris B. Glinskii, *Revoliutsionnyi period russkoi istorii (1861-1881)* (St. Petersburg: A. S. Suvorin, 1913), pt. 1, p. 259.

The zemstvo which Your Majesty has recalled to life, once fully developed, is destined to consolidate the foundations and strength of Russia for all time. May Your Majesty now complete the state structure you have erected by calling together a general assembly of elected representatives from the Russian land, in order to discuss the common needs of the entire state. Command your loyal nobility to choose for this purpose the best men from among its midst. The nobility has always been the firm mainstay of the Russian throne. Not being officials of the government and not enjoying the rewards that such service brings, doing their duty without remuneration for the benefit of the fatherland and the public order, these men, by virtue of their very position within the state, will have the mission of preserving those moral and political principles that are so valuable for the people and so necessary for their true well-being, and upon which rests the structure of the state. In this way, Your Majesty, you will come to understand the needs of our fatherland in their true light; you will restore confidence in the executive authorities; you will ensure the strict observance of the laws by one and all, and their applicability to the needs of the country.

Truth will reach your throne without hindrance, and your enemies, internal and external, will be reduced to silence when the nation, in the person of its representatives, surrounding the throne with affection, will keep constant watch that treason may not insinuate itself anywhere.

XV:29. THE LAWS CONCERNING THE PRESS, APRIL 6, 1865

The principal press reforms of Alexander II were contained in two laws of April 6, 1865—one a decree and the other an "opinion" of the State Council which was approved by the emperor.

Reference: *PSZRI*, 2d ser., vol. 40, pt. 1, pp. 396, 398–400.

[From the decree:]

Concerning the granting of certain facilities and conveniences to the press of the fatherland.

I. Freed from preliminary censorship are:

   A. In both capitals:

      1. All currently issued periodical publications, if their publishers shall themselves state this desire.

      2. All original writings not less than 160 printed pages [10 *pechatnykh listov*] in length.

   B. Everywhere:

      1. All governmental publications.

      2. All publications of academies, universities, and learned societies and institutions.

      3. All publications in the ancient classical languages and translations from those languages.

      4. Sketches, diagrams, and maps.

II. Periodical and other publications, writings, and translations freed from preliminary censorship are subject to judicial prosecution in the event that they contain a violation of the laws; in addition, periodical publications are also liable to administrative penalties, in accordance with rules specially established for this, in the event that a harmful tendency is noted in them.

III. The management of censorship matters and of the press in general is centered in a newly created Chief Administration [Glavnoe Upravlenie] for these matters within the Ministry of Internal Affairs, under the over-all supervision of the minister.

[From the "opinion" confirmed by the emperor:]

4. Everyone who wishes to issue a new periodical publication in the form of a news-paper, magazine, or anthology is obliged, now as before, to obtain the permission of the minister of internal affairs. . . .

15. Publishers of periodical publications exempt from preliminary censorship are obliged to deposit a guarantee with the Chief Administration.

16. Guarantees are deposited in the follow-ing amounts:

1. For a newspaper issued daily or not fewer than six times a week, 5,000 rubles.

2. For all other periodical publications, 2,500 rubles. . . .

19. The guarantee is used to pay monetary penalties imposed on a periodical publication. . . .

29. The minister of internal affairs is ac-corded the right to issue warnings to periodical publications, indicating the articles giving cause for this. A third warning suspends publication for a period of time designated by the minister of internal affairs upon issue of the warning but not exceeding six months. . . .

30. If after a third warning the minister of internal affairs deems it necessary . . . to pro-hibit this publication altogether, then he is to make representation concerning this to the First Department of the Governing Senate.

XV:30. THE POLICY ON JEWISH ARTISANS (LAW AND MEMORANDUM), JUNE 28, 1865

This law took the form of a declaration by the State Council (supported by a statement from the minister of internal affairs) which the tsar then approved.

Reference: *PSZRI,* 2d ser., vol. 40, pt. 1, pp. 692-93, 699-700.

1. Jewish mechanics, distillers, brewers, and masters [master craftsmen] and artisans in general are permitted to reside, in con-formity with their passports and permits, any-where outside the pale designated for the permanent settlement of Jews. . . .

3. The persons indicated in the first article are permitted, when moving outside the pale designated for the permanent settlement of Jews, to bring with them members of their families, i.e. wives, children, and brothers and sisters who are minors. . . .

4. Jewish youths, not over eighteen years of age, even if they do not belong to the class of artisans, are permitted to move into locali-ties lying outside the pale designated for the permanent settlement of Jews, for the purpose of learning a trade, but their length of resi-dence there is limited to the term of the agree-ment (but in no case over five years) they have concluded with the masters who have accepted them for instruction. . . .

[Then follows the note of the minister of internal affairs recommending to the tsar that he enact the foregoing principles into law:]

The guberniia most heavily populated by Jews is Mogilev, where they constitute 13 per-cent of the total population; then follow the guberniias of: Volynia, 12.16 percent; Kiev,

11.57 percent; Podol'sk, 10.98 percent; Grodno, 10.82 percent; Kovno, 10.25 percent; Vil'no, 9.13 percent; Bessarabia oblast', 8.86 percent; Minsk, 8.72 percent; Vitebsk, 8.68 percent; Kherson, 7.83 percent; Kurland, 4.76 percent; Chernigov, 2.34 percent; Eka-terinoslav, 2.22 percent; Livonia [Lifliand-skaia], 1.65 percent; Poltava, 1.64 percent; and Taurida [Tavricheskaia], 1.41 percent. [Note: These seventeen guberniias (along with the ten guberniias of the "Kingdom of Poland") composed the so-called pale of Jewish settle-ment.]

Comparing the aforesaid number of Jewish inhabitants in the localities indicated with the total population of Russia (excepting the Kingdom of Poland and the Grand Duchy of Finland), which amounts to over 67,235,000, it appears that the Jewish population, in rela-tion to the number of inhabitants of other creeds, constitutes 2.10 percent of the figure cited.

.   .   .

The reason for the decline of the handi-craft industry among the Jews must be sought in the general limitations upon the civil rights of this people which are contained in our legislation, and most of all in the prohibition upon Jewish residence outside the regions designated for their settlement.

From information in the possession of the Ministry of Internal Affairs it is clear that those who suffer most from this limitation upon the right of Jews to live outside the pale designated for their permanent settlement are the class of artisans, Christian as well as Jewish.

. . .

At the same time, the class of Jewish artisans constitutes the most useful, although the poorest, estate amongst their co-religionists; and therefore if the government has already acknowledged it possible to lighten, in relation to merchants, the severity of the regulations existing for Jews in respect to their choice of residence, then the artisans of this nation [*natsiia*] deserve attention all the more. In keeping with these convictions the Ministry of Internal Affairs considers that Jewish artisans should immediately be accorded the opportunity to reside outside their pale of settlement.

There is no doubt that such permission would be advantageous in every respect.

XV:31. LOUBAT ON FOX'S MISSION TO RUSSIA, JULY-AUGUST 1866

Gustavus Vasa Fox, assistant secretary of the navy, was sent to Russia in 1866 to convey a copy of the resolution adopted by the United States Congress bearing congratulations on Alexander II's escape from Karakozov's attempt to assassinate him. On July 25 by the Russian calendar (August 6 by the calendar the Americans were using) the two vessels bringing Fox's mission arrived at Kronstadt, and on July 27 the Americans were received by the emperor at Peterhof. J. F. Loubat, a member of the mission, tells the story of that occasion and what happened to the Americans during the rest of their visit.

Reference: J. F. Loubat, *Narrative of the Mission to Russia, in 1866, of the Hon. Gustavus Vasa Fox, Assistant-Secretary of the Navy, from the Journal and Notes of J. F. Loubat* (New York, 1874), pp. 88-90, 113, 163, 213-14, 234, 243, 282, 307-08, 328, 343-44, 415-16.

Mr. Fox read the following address in the English language:

Sire: The Resolution which I have the honor of presenting to your Imperial Majesty is the voice of a people whose millions of lips speak from a single heart.

The many ties which have long bound together the great Empire of the East, and the great Republic of the West, have been multiplied and strengthened by the unwavering fidelity of the Imperial Government to our own, throughout its recent period of convulsion.

The words of sympathy and friendship then addressed to the Government at Washington, by command of your Imperial Majesty, are fixed in the eternal remembrance of a grateful country. . . .

It is, therefore, with profound emotion that I offer to your Imperial Majesty, to the emancipated subjects, and to all the people of this vast realm, our heart-felt congratulations upon the providential escape from danger.

. . .

His Majesty said that he rejoiced at the friendly relations existing between Russia and the United States, and he was pleased to see that those relations were so well appreciated in America. He was convinced that the national fraternity would be perpetual, and he, for his part, should contribute all his efforts to sustain it, and to strengthen the bonds. He was deeply sensible of the proofs of the personal sympathy and affection of the American people, conveyed in the resolution of Congress, and he was grateful for them. He desired to thank those who had come so great a distance to bear these proofs to him, and he assured them of a warm welcome to the soil of Russia.

His Majesty closed by remarking that the cordial reception which had been given to his squadron in the United States would never be effaced from his memory.

[On July 28, when the Americans were honored by a naval banquet at Kronstadt:]

After the toasts were ended, many of the older officers retired, when the room was cleared. The scene then became very lively. All the American guests were treated to a peculiarly Russian custom—a tossing in the air at the hands of their hosts. The sensation is anything but an agreeable one, but, as it is considered a mark of honor of the highest character, it was submitted to with a good grace by all who were subjected to it.

[On August 3, at a banquet of the merchants' club in Petersburg:]

While the dinner was going on within, a great popular demonstration was taking place in the streets. The space in front of the Club-House and all the avenues of approach to it were densely crowded with people of all classes, who had gathered to do honor to the Americans. Travel was stopped and vehicles were compelled to turn into the adjacent streets. Loud calls were made for Mr. Fox and for others, and he and our officers were obliged to show themselves from time to time on the balcony, each appearance being greeted with extraordinary applause. It was a splendid popular reception, and proved how deeply the masses of the Russian people were moved by the unprecedented act of our Government in sending its sympathy and congratulations by a special envoy.

[On August 12:]

At Tver, where the railway crosses the Volga, another deputation was in waiting to welcome the Americans, notwithstanding the early hour, five A.M., at which the train arrived. The usual greetings and compliments were exchanged here and bread and salt again presented.

At half-past ten o'clock in the morning the train entered the Moscow Station. A great crowd of people and a military band received the visitors with cheers and "Hail Columbia." Prince Stcherbatoff, the mayor of the city, the members of the city council, and numerous representatives of the different corporations, all with red, white, and blue ribbons in their button-holes, welcomed the mission in the most cordial and flattering terms, and informed Mr. Fox that he had been made an honorary citizen of Moscow.

. . .

During the progress of the dinner a military band was heard playing in front of the house, and loud and frequent cheers proclaimed the presence of a great crowd of the citizens of Moscow. Prince Dolgorouky conducted Mr. Fox to the balcony, in answer to the popular appeal. As far as could be seen, the open space in front of the palace was packed with human beings. As soon as the American envoy was descried, the air rang with loud and prolonged hurrahs. It seemed as if the shouts

would never end. It was a grand, spontaneous, popular ovation, and proved that the people of Russia's ancient capital were as profoundly touched by the proffered sympathy of the United States as were those of St. Petersburg. The occasion was a most gratifying one to both host and guests.

[On August 13, at the banquet of the municipality of Moscow:]

Prince Stcherbatoff, the Mayor of Moscow, gave the first toast. He said: . . .

"Distant lands and the ocean divide us, but the spirit of man cares not for space, and our two peoples have long since united in thought and in feeling.

"With a loving interest do we follow each other's successes, with mutual sympathy do we sustain each other in the hour of danger, and we unite to praise the glorious names of the great men whom Providence in mercy sends in the times of great nations' trials. The name of Lincoln is one of those illustrious names."

[Under the date of August 17:]

The journey from Moscow to Nijny-Novgorod, two hundred and seventy-three miles by rail, was a pleasant one, though the country is not very attractive to the eye. . . . The railway-stations are large, commodious buildings of brick and stone, laid in alternate courses, and every thing is provided within them for the comfort of travellers. Crowds of people from the neighboring villages were collected at almost all of them along the route, who greeted the Americans with cheers, music, and the display of flags.

[On August 21, in Kostroma:]

The news of the arrival spread like wildfire, and in a few minutes all the avenues leading to the river were filled with people hurrying to the pier.

. . .

The landing was now black with people. Some barges near by were crowded also, and many row-boats, filled with men and women, covered the river around the steamer. Whenever an American was seen enthusiastic cheers went up, which were echoed and reechoed by the thousands behind them.

[Under the date of August 24:]

Wherever our mission went, it was received by the peasant-class with the utmost enthusiasm; and heart-felt expressions of love and gratitude to the United States were heard in every little village.

[On August 27, at a banquet at the English club in Saint Petersburg, Prince Gorchakov spoke (in French) as follows:]

"There is no need to dwell on the manifestations of sympathy between the two countries. They shine in the broad light of day. It is a fact the most interesting of our epoch, a fact which creates between two nations—I will say rather between two continents—germs of reciprocal good-will and friendship which will bear fruit, which create traditions, and which tend to consolidate between them relations founded upon the true spirit of Christian civilization. This understanding does not rest on geographical proximity—the gulf of oceans separates us. Nor does it rest on parchment—I have not found any trace of it in the archives of the ministry confided to me. It is instinctive; nay, more, I dare to call it providential. I rejoice in its existence; I have faith in its duration. In my political position, all my care shall tend to its consolidation. I say care and not efforts, because efforts are unnecessary when the attraction is spontaneous and reciprocal. ("Bravo!")

"Another motive which induces me to proclaim emphatically my appreciation of this good understanding is, that it is neither a menace nor a peril to any one. It derives its inspiration neither from covetousness nor from any sinister design. God has given to the two countries such conditions of existence that their grand internal life suffices for them. . . ."

[Washington, D.C., February 25, N.S., 1867, from Mr. Fox's report to Mr. W. H. Seward, secretary of state:]

"I have endeavored . . . to comply with the wish often repeated to me by his Majesty, to make known to the Government and my countrymen the feelings of friendship which existed in Russia toward America. But all that I have written myself and all that was written for the press, by persons far more capable than I feel myself to be to describe the manifestations of these feelings, fail to convey any adequate idea of the enthusiasm which pervades the people of Russia toward the United States, and their sincere wishes for the continued prosperity and power of our country.

· · ·

"The crowds that gathered around us at every social meeting, singing the plaintive national songs, the flowers presented by the hands of beauty and innocence, the numerous presents offered upon all suitable occasions, the imperial honor granted at Kostroma of casting down their garments for us to walk upon, the deep feeling which the great mass of the people evinced whenever the name of our country was mentioned, and the many touching incidents which such sympathies evoked, were not produced by curiosity or instigated by officials. The Russians have been familiar with royal embassies from powerful and magnificent courts for many centuries. It was a heart-impulse of the people in favor of our country which occasioned these extraordinary demonstrations toward the messenger of good-will."

XV:32. THE ARRANGEMENTS FOR STATE PEASANTS, AS DECREED ON NOVEMBER 24, 1866

By this decree the state peasants—who comprised roughly half of the peasant population of Russia—received terms that preserved their favorable situation in comparison with the former serfs.

Reference: *PSZRI*, 2d ser., vol. 41, pt. 2, pp. 280-81, 283.

November 24. Concerning the agrarian organization of state peasants in thirty-six guberniias.

· · ·

1. The village communities of state peasants retain all the land and landed resources [*ugod'ia*] reserved to them as allotments and which they are utilizing. In those communities where the land in peasant utilization is not demarcated from the land remaining at the immediate disposal of the treasury, the area of the peasant allotment is determined in proportion to existing utilization, but not more than: 8 desiatinas per soul in uezdy where land is scarce [*malozemel'nye*], and

15 desiatinas in uezdy where land is plentiful [*mnogozemel'nye*]. . . .

3. State peasants who own, on the basis of this decree, the land reserved to them in accordance with the aforesaid deeds [*zapisi,* referred to in article 2] are obliged to make the treasury a yearly payment as determined by law, which is called the "state obrok tax" [*gosudarstvennaia obrochnaia podat'*; this tax was not to exceed by more than 15 percent the amount the state peasants had been assessed by the government before this time]. . . .

4. State peasants are accorded the right of utilizing and disposing of the land given into their ownership in accordance with the deeds, at their own discretion, with the observance of the following rules:

a. With the consent of two-thirds of the members of the community having the right to vote in the assembly, the community may divide the land belonging to it into household plots, in which case the sum total of obrok tax borne by the entire community is divided among the householders, in accordance with the size and quality of the household plots.

b. The allotment of plots to individual householders from land under communal ownership is likewise permitted, with the consent of two-thirds of the members of the commune having the right to vote in the assembly; in which case the amount of obrok on the detached plots is also determined, being proportionately calculated. . . .

12. The amount of obrok tax . . . is to remain unchanged until twenty years have expired from the date of publication of the present decree.

XV:33. THE MUNICIPAL STATUTE OF JUNE 16, 1870

Following are some of the principal provisions of the statute that reformed the government of the towns.

Reference: *PSZRI,* 2d ser., vol. 45, pt. 1, pp. 823-26, 828, 831, 839.

Municipal Statute [Gorodovoe Polozhenie]

1. The responsibility of looking after and directing the municipal economy and the organization of public services is in the hands of the municipal public administration, while the responsibility of supervising the lawful execution of these matters belongs to the governor. . . .

2. The jurisdiction of the municipal public administration includes:

a. Matters relating to the organization of this administration and to the municipal economy. . . .

b. Matters relating to the organization of outdoor public services in the city, namely . . . the building and maintaining of streets, squares, roads, sidewalks, municipal gardens . . . water supply. . . .

c. Matters pertaining to the welfare of the city inhabitants: measures to provide for the public food supply, the organization of markets and bazaars; looking after . . . the maintenance of public health, the adoption of preventive measures against fires and other calamities, and protection against losses incurred through them; looking after the safeguarding and development of local trade and industry, the organization of port facilities, stock exchanges, and credit institutions. . . .

d. The organization, at the expense of the city, of charitable institutions and hospitals, and their management; . . . participation . . . in looking after public education . . . and likewise the organization of theaters, libraries, museums, and other institutions of a similar nature.

e. The presentation to the government of information and conclusions on subjects relating to the local needs and well-being of the city, and the handling of petitions on these subjects. . . .

11. For supervision over the activity of the municipal public administration a "guberniia bureau [prisutstvie] for municipal affairs" is established in each guberniia, composed, under the chairmanship of the governor, of the higher officials of the guberniia administration, the chairman of the guberniia zemstvo executive board, and the mayor of the capital city of the guberniia. . . .

16. The municipal electoral assemblies [*izbiratel'nye sobraniia*] are constituted solely for the election of members [glasnye] of the municipal duma, every four years. . . .

17. Every resident of the city, whatever his legal status [*sostoianie*], has the right to vote in the election of [duma] members, under the following conditions: (1) if he is a Russian

subject; (2) if he is at least twenty-five years of age; (3) if, these conditions being met, he owns within the city limits . . . real estate that is liable to taxation by the city, or maintains a commercial or industrial establishment under a merchant's license, or, having lived for two years in the city . . . pays the tax levied by the city on licenses: as a merchant, or a retail tradesman, or a shop assistant of the first category [prikashchik pervogo razriada]. . . .

24. For holding elections of [duma] members, three electoral assemblies are formed in each city from those inhabitants who have the right to vote in elections; . . . each of these elects one-third of the total number of [duma] members. . . . For this purpose the residents are entered in the lists of electors in the sequence determined by the amounts they have been assessed by the city for taxes which confer the right to vote; then the persons entered in the aforesaid list are divided into three categories or assemblies, to wit: in the first category are entered those electors at the head of the list who, paying the highest tax, together pay one-third of the total amount of taxes paid by all the electors; in

the second category are numbered the electors next on the list, likewise paying together a third of the taxes; in the third category are all remaining electors. . . .

48. The municipal duma is composed of members elected for a period of four years, under the chairmanship of the mayor of the city [gorodskoi golova]. . . .

70. The municipal executive board [gorodskaia uprava] is under the chairmanship of the mayor of the city. . . .

82. The posts of mayor of the city, members of the municipal executive board, and municipal secretary (secretary of the duma) are filled through election by the municipal duma. . . .

92. Persons elected to the post of mayor of the city . . . are confirmed in capital cities of guberniias by the minister of internal affairs and in other cities, by the governor. . . .

150. . . . Complaints against unlawful decisions of the municipal council are brought before the governor, who transmits them to the "guberniia bureau for municipal affairs" for decision. Complaints against decisions of this bureau are brought before the Senate.

XV:34. "CLASSICISM" IN THE SECONDARY SCHOOLS, JUNE 1871

In 1871 the minister of education, Count D. A. Tolstoi, sought to reform the "gymnasiums" or secondary schools in such a way as to discourage radical tendencies. The nature of his approach—referred to as "classicism"—is revealed in a long and authoritative article published in June 1871 in the official journal of Tolstoi's ministry. It included this table and the accompanying explanations. Under regulations endorsed by Alexander a few weeks later (July 30, 1871), only those who had completed a gymnasium or demonstrated mastery of its curriculum were eligible to enter a university. (Other institutions were to be provided for engineering and technical students. On the secondary level these included the real'nye uchilishcha [cf. German Realschule], where the stress was on mathematics and the natural sciences. Graduates of these schools were expected to go on into special higher technical institutions rather than into universities.)

Reference: Zhurnal Ministerstva Narodnogo Prosveshcheniia 155 (June 1871): 142 [table], 165, 194-95.

1. For entrance into the first grade of gymnasiums or progymnasiums a greater and better degree of preparation must be demanded than at present, for which purpose a preparatory grade should be established within each of these institutions.

2. In the interests, not only of greater thoroughness, but in particular of relieving the burden on the pupils, the course of study in the gymnasiums should extend for eight years rather than seven. . . .

3. In the interests of concentrating as much as possible the mental faculties of the pupils

and of bringing them to the requisite maturity, so necessary for the successful and fruitful pursuit of a university course, the total hours of instruction in the chief subjects of the gymnasium course of study, and particularly in the ancient languages, must be considerably increased, and in the less essential subjects conversely decreased.

. . .

The aim of the gymnasium consists primarily in enabling those who wish to devote themselves to learning and in general to the higher spheres of activity (that is, to follow the path

1. Table of Total Weekly Hours of Instruction in the Gymnasiums
(with both ancient languages)

Subjects	Preparatory Grade	I	II	III	IV	V	VI	VII (two years)	Total A*	Total B†
1. Religion	4	2	2	2	2	2	1	1	12	13
2. Russian and church Slavonic	6	4	4	4	3	3	2	2	22	24
3. Survey of the fundamentals of logic	—	—	—	—	—	—	—	(1)	(1)	(1)
4. Latin	—	8	7	5	5	6	6	6	43	49
5. Greek	—	—	—	5	6	6	6	6(7)	29(30)	35(36)
6. Mathematics (with physics, mathematical geography, and a survey of natural science)	6	5	4	3	3	4	6	6	31	37
7. Geography	—	2	2	2	2	—	—	1	9	10
8. History	—	—	—	2	2	2	2	2	10	12
9. French or German	—	—	3	3	3	3	3	2	17	19
10. Penmanship	6	3	2	—	—	—	—	—	5	5
Total:										
For those studying one modern language	22	24	24	26	26	26	26	27	179	206
For those studying two modern languages	22	24	27	29	29	29	29	29	196	225

*Total hours of instruction given by teachers, excluding the preparatory grade [and the eighth year].

† Total hours of instruction compulsory for students in the eight years of the gymnasium course [i.e. including the repetition of the seventh-grade courses in the eighth year].

of a gymnasium and university education) to study in their youthful years as precisely as possible, and directly from the great works of classical antiquity, that historical foundation of all European civilization, that world in which all the arts and sciences originated. . . . But in addition, as we know, Christian doctrine was itself first revealed, interpreted, and preached to the world in the Greek and Latin tongues, without the knowledge of which its original sources remain inaccessible. Along with this, the thorough study of ancient languages and literature is justly esteemed to be the best means of formally developing mental abilities, of aesthetic education, and finally, of forming character itself. In respect to the latter, one of the most noted of German pedagogues, Gustav Muehlmann, has said most justly: "Character is formed and strengthened only when youth exercises all its abilities primarily upon some single academic discipline: upon a single discipline it develops an inclination for hard work, upon a single discipline it attains a consciousness of its activity, upon a single subject it matures for higher scholarly pursuits. The study of classical antiquity is precisely such an academic discipline. . . ." The same author justly sees in the study of classical antiquity, that is, of its best works in the original, "an antidote, in the highest degree beneficial, to the constantly increasing materialism of our time."

In view of the great significance the study of ancient classical languages and their literature has in the development of all aspects of the character of the young, this subject is everywhere assigned almost half the total school hours, as, for example: in the gymnasiums of Prussia (with a nine-year course) 128 hours out of 268 a week (or 47.76 percent of the total hours of instruction) are assigned to ancient languages; in the gymnasiums of Saxony, 134 out of 282 (or 47.52 percent). The schedule currently established for those of our gymnasiums that offer the full classical course allots to this subject only 84 hours out of 206 compulsory hours of instruction, that is, 40.77 percent.

XV:35. AN OFFICIAL JUSTIFICATION OF TOLSTOI'S SCHOOL REFORM, NOVEMBER 1872

This unsigned commentary on the recent reforms in the secondary schools appeared in the official journal of D. A. Tolstoi's ministry of education (*Zhurnal Ministerstva Narodnogo Prosveshcheniia*).

Reference: *Zhurnal Ministerstva Narodnogo Prosveshcheniia* 164 (November 1872): 1-2.

Our educational reform, which marked the years 1871 and 1872 and aroused so much discussion *pro* and *contra* in our press, could not but attract attention in western Europe also. Western Europe cannot be indifferent as to whether the colossal state to its east will assume definitively and permanently a European character or will, after much vacillation, become a half-European, half-Asiatic state. Now it was precisely a question of such universal historical importance that was being decided at the time the educational reform of 1871 and 1872 was under discussion, and, thanks to the wise decision of the sovereign emperor, guided by a divine Providence clearly beneficent to Russia, this question was definitively resolved in principle, that is, by means of legislation, in favor of a European education and a European character for Russia.

In actual fact, what is it that indicates that a country belongs—undoubtedly, truly, and internally—to Europe? First of all, whether Christianity predominates in it, and in this respect the European character of Russia is not subject to the least doubt; but there then arises the question of whether that country is rooted in the common historical soil of Europe, that is, whether it has come to possess the rich common heritage of Europe, bequeathed to humanity by the founders and first promoters of the common culture of Europe—the ancient Greeks and Romans—and in this respect Russia up to the present time was in a state of indecision and vacillation. Now an end has been put to these vacillations, and the fulfillment of a great historical act has been begun; in the person of those younger generations which strive toward the light of knowledge, a nation of one hundred million is being brought into the possession of the age-old heritage of all civilized humanity.

XV:36. COUNT DMITRII MILIUTIN ON THE YEAR 1873

An especially rich source of impressions of the reign of Alexander II is the diary of Field Marshal and Count Dmitrii Alekseevich Miliutin (1816-1912). An outstanding military historian and administrator, Miliutin was minister of war from 1861 to 1881 and a close adviser to Alexander II. In this excerpt he looks back on the year 1873.

Reference: Dmitrii A. Miliutin, *Dnevnik D. A. Miliutina, 1873-1882*, ed. Petr A. Zaionchkovskii, 4 vols. (Moscow [Bibl. Lenina], 1947-50), 1:119-20.

December 31, 1873. On the last day of the year my thoughts involuntarily turn back and quickly run through a whole series of impressions preserved in my memory. For me the year 1873 passed by as a dark shadow; it leaves behind none but melancholy impressions. Not in a single preceding year have I endured so much unpleasantness, sorrow, and failure. The intrigue against me, begun long since, has fully matured and has broken out in all its vileness. My enemies have not succeeded in fully attaining their aims; they cannot consider themselves victorious but have nonetheless managed to injure me in the eyes of the sovereign and to make my position within the government almost impossible. Seeing at every step disaffection and mistrust on the part of the person whose will decides all matters finally and without appeal, I am paralyzed in my activity. . . . By now it is impossible for me to direct the organization of military affairs with the independence and energy with which I have been directing them for over twelve years. As for general affairs of state which lie outside the sphere of the military department, in this respect I have been entirely set aside. Everything is done under the sole influence of Count Shuvalov [i.e. Petr Andreevich Shuvalov, who from 1866 to 1874 was chief of the Corps of Gendarmes and head of the Third Section of His Imperial Majesty's Personal Chancery, that is, in charge of the political police], who has alarmed the sovereign by his daily reports on the fearful dangers to which both the state and the sovereign personally are said to be exposed. All

Shuvalov's power rests upon this bugbear. On the pretext of protecting the person of the sovereign and the monarchy, Count Shuvalov interferes in matters of every kind, and questions of every kind are decided on the basis of his tale bearing. He has surrounded the sovereign with his own supporters; all new appointments are made in accordance with his directions. In this way, by now the majority of members in the Committee of Ministers always acts in unison with Count Shuvalov, the way an orchestra follows the baton of its conductor. Timashev, Count Tolstoi, Count Palen, Valuev—all are the obedient tools of Count Shuvalov. . . .

This is the milieu in which I am fated to operate. Is it possible for one man to struggle against a whole powerful gang? What an amazing and lamentable comparison with the situation as it was when I entered the top echelons of the government thirteen years ago! Then everything surged forward; now everything drags back. Then the sovereign was sympathetic to progress, he moved things forward himself; now he has lost confidence in everything he himself created, in everything that surrounds him, even himself. With such a state of affairs is it possible for me alone to keep my footing amidst the debris of the shipwreck, and would it not be excusable for me to decide to lay down my arms? One soldier doesn't make an army [*Odin v pole ne voin*].

XV:37. THE MANIFESTO AND STATUTE ON UNIVERSAL MILITARY SERVICE, JANUARY 1, 1874

These excerpts give some of the main points of the manifesto and the statute of January 1, 1874, which introduced universal military service. While the law eliminated one of the cherished freedoms of the upper classes, it did reserve considerable privileges to young men on the basis of their family circumstances and education. The drawing of lots, described below, stemmed from the fact that the number of eligible youths was much larger than the number of recruits needed.

Reference: *PSZRI*, 2d ser., vol. 49, pt. 1, pp. 1, 4-5.

[From the manifesto concerning the introduction of universal military service, January 1, 1874:]

Recent events have proved that the power of a state lies not merely in the size of its armed forces but primarily in their moral and mental qualities, which attain their fullest development only when the task of defending the fatherland becomes the common task of the people, when all, irrespective of social status [*zvanie*] or class [*sostoianie*], are united in this sacred task.

[From the statute concerning military service, January 1, 1874:]

1. The defense of the throne and the fatherland is the sacred duty of every Russian subject. All male inhabitants, irrespective of class, are subject to military service. . . .

5. The armed forces of the state consist of a standing army and a militia [*opolchenie*]. The latter is called to duty only in the extreme circumstances of wartime. . . .

10. Conscription into the service is determined by lot, which is drawn once and remains permanent. Those who draw a number exempting them from conscription into the standing army are enrolled in the militia.

11. Each year only one age group of the population is called upon to draw lots: namely, young men who have reached the age of twenty by January 1 of the year in which the levy is held.

12. Those who have satisfied certain educational requirements are entitled to discharge their military service without drawing lots; in the capacity of volunteers [*vol'nooprede-liaiushchiesia*]. [Note: The term of service in the standing army for volunteers was fixed at from three months to two years, according to article 173.] . . .

17. The total term of service in the army [land forces] for those conscripted by lot is fixed at fifteen years, of which six years are on active duty and nine years in the reserve.
. . .

18. The total term of service in the navy is fixed at ten years, of which seven years are on active duty and three years in the reserve. . . .

36. The state militia is composed of all male inhabitants between conscription age and the age of forty who are not enrolled in the standing army but are capable of bearing arms.

XV:38. WALLACE ON RUSSIA, CA. 1870-1875

An exceptionally penetrating foreign observer of Russia during the time of Alexander II was Sir Donald Mackenzie Wallace, who lived and studied there from early in 1870 to late in 1875. Here are excerpts from his work dealing with some of the topics he treated most effectively: the peasants, the provincial towns, the nobility, the zemstvos, and the justices of the peace.

Reference: Donald M. Wallace, *Russia*, rev. and enlarged ed. (London: Cassell, 1912), pp. 101, 128-29, 131, 133-34, 139, 140, 511-12, 513 [all on the peasantry], 182 [on the provincial towns], 318-20 [the nobility], 559-61, 569 [the zemstvos], 593 (justices of the peace). See also the paperback version, ed. C. E. Black (New York: Vintage, 1961), especially chs. 2, 6, and 15.

[From chapter 7, "The Peasantry of the North":]

[In the village of Ivanovka, in the Novgorod guberniia:] Nearly the whole of the female population, and about one-half of the male inhabitants, are habitually engaged in cultivating the Communal land, which comprises about two thousand acres of a light sandy soil. The arable part of this land is divided into three large fields, each of which is cut up into long narrow strips. The first field is reserved for the winter grain—that is to say, rye, which forms, in the shape of black bread, the principal food of the rural population. In the second are raised oats for the horses, and buckwheat, which is largely used for food. The third lies fallow, and is used in the summer as pasturage for the cattle.

All the villagers in this part of the country divide the arable land in this way, in order to suit the triennial rotation of crops. This triennial system is extremely simple. The field which is used this year for raising winter grain will be used next year for raising summer grain, and in the following year will lie fallow. Before being sown with winter grain it ought to receive a certain amount of manure. Every family possesses in each of the two fields under cultivation one or more of the long narrow strips or belts into which they are divided.

[From chapter 8, "The Mir, or Village Community":]

The system of allotment adopted depends entirely on the will of the particular Commune. In this respect the Communes enjoy the most complete autonomy, and no peasant ever dreams of appealing against a Communal decree. The higher authorities not only abstain from all interference in the allotment of the Communal lands, but remain in profound ignorance as to which system the Communes habitually adopt. . . . In spite of the systematic and persistent efforts of the centralised bureaucracy to regulate minutely all departments of the national life, the rural Communes, which contain about five-sixths of the population, remain in many respects entirely beyond its influence, and even beyond its sphere of vision! But let not the reader be astonished overmuch. He will learn in time that Russia is the land of paradoxes; and meanwhile he is about to receive a still more startling bit of information. In "the great stronghold of Caesarian despotism and centralized bureaucracy," these Village Communes, containing about five-sixths of the population, are capital specimens of representative Constitutional government of the extreme democratic type!

· · ·

No class of men in the world are more good-natured and pacific than the Russian peasantry. When sober they never fight.

· · ·

The Assembly discusses all matters affecting the Communal welfare, and, as these matters have never been legally defined, its recognised competence is very wide. It fixes the time for making the hay, and the day for commencing the ploughing of the fallow field; it decrees what measures shall be employed against those who do not punctually pay their taxes; it decides whether a new member shall be admitted into the Commune, and whether an old member shall be allowed to change his domicile; it gives or withholds permission to erect new buildings on the Communal land; it prepares and signs all contracts which the Commune makes with one of its own members or with a stranger; it interferes whenever it thinks necessary in the domestic affairs of its members; it elects the Elder—as well as the Communal tax-collector and watchman, where such offices exist—and the Communal herd-boy; above all, it divides and allots the Communal land among the members as it thinks fit.

... The elections produce little excitement, for the simple reason that, as a rule, no one desires to be elected.

. . .

The peasants are accustomed to work together ... to make concessions for the Communal welfare, and to bow unreservedly to the will of the *Mir*. I know of many instances where the peasants have set at defiance the authority of the police, of the provincial governor, and of the central Government itself, but I have never heard of any instance where the will of the *Mir* was openly opposed by one of its members.

... A share does not mean simply a plot or parcel of land; on the contrary, it always contains at least four, and may contain a large number of distinct plots.

. . .

Communal land in Russia is of three kinds: the land on which the village is built, the arable land, and the meadow or hay-field, if the village is fortunate enough to possess one. On the first of these each family possesses a house and garden, which are the hereditary property of the family, and are never affected by the periodical redistributions. The other two kinds are both subject to redistribution, but on somewhat different principles.

The whole of the Communal arable land is first of all divided into three fields, to suit the triennial rotation of crops already described, and each field is divided into a number of long, narrow strips—corresponding to the number of male members in the Commune—as nearly as possible equal to each other in area and quality. Sometimes it is necessary to divide the field into several portions, according to the quality of the soil, and then subdivide each of these portions into the requisite number of strips. Thus in all cases every household possesses at least one strip in each field; and in those cases where subdivision is necessary, every household possesses a strip in each of the portions into which the field is subdivided. It often happens, therefore, that the strips are very narrow, and the portions belonging to each family very numerous. Strips six feet wide are by no means rare. ... Of these narrow strips a household may possess as many as thirty in a single field! The complicated process of division and subdivision is accomplished by the peasants themselves, with the aid of simple measuring-rods, and the accuracy of the result is truly marvellous.

The meadow, which is reserved for the production of hay, is divided into the same number of shares as the arable land. There, however, the division and distribution take place, not at irregular intervals, but annually.

[From chapter 29, "The Emancipation of the Serfs":]

The work of conciliating and regulating became consequently more difficult, but the great majority of the Arbiters [of the Peace] showed themselves equal to the task, and displayed an impartiality, tact, and patience beyond all praise. To them Russia is in great part indebted for the peaceful character of the Emancipation. ... They played the part of mediators, as their name signified, rather than that of administrators in the bureaucratic sense of the term, and they were animated with a just and humane rather than a merely legal spirit. Instead of simply laying down the law, and ordering their decisions to be immediately executed, they were ever ready to spend hours in trying to conquer, by patient and laborious reasoning, the unjust claims of proprietors or the false conceptions and ignorant obstinacy of the peasants. It was a new spectacle for Russia to see a public function fulfilled by conscientious men who had their heart in their work, who sought neither promotion nor decorations, and who paid less attention to punctilious observance of prescribed formalities than to the real objects in view.

. . .

The serfs were ... not only liberated, but also made Communal proprietors, and the old Communal institutions were preserved and developed. In answer to the question, Who effected this gigantic reform? we may say that the chief merit undoubtedly belongs to Alexander II. Had he not possessed a very great amount of courage he would neither have raised the question nor allowed it to be raised by others, and had he not shown a great deal more decision and energy than was expected, the solution would have been indefinitely postponed.

[On the provincial towns:]

He who wishes to preserve the delusion that Russian provincial towns are picturesque should never enter them, but content himself with viewing them from a distance.

However imposing they may look when seen from the outside, they will be found on closer inspection, with very few exceptions, to be little more than villages in disguise. If they have not a positively rustic, they have at least a suburban, appearance. The streets are straight and wide, and are either miserably paved or not paved at all. *Trottoirs* [sidewalks] are not considered indispensable. The houses are built of wood or brick, generally one-storied, and separated from each other by spacious yards. Many of them do not condescend to turn their facades to the street. The general impression produced is that the majority of the burghers have come from the country, and have brought their country houses with them.

[On the nobility:]

The Russian Noblesse . . . was formed out of more heterogeneous materials, and these materials did not spontaneously combine to form an organic whole but were crushed into a conglomerate mass by the weight of the autocratic power. It never became a semi-independent factor in the State. What rights and privileges it possesses it received from the Monarchy, and consequently it has no deep-rooted jealousy or hatred of the Imperial prerogative. . . . The Russian Noblesse has little or nothing of what we call aristocratic feeling—little or nothing of that haughty, domineering, exclusive spirit which we are accustomed to associate with the word Aristocracy. We find plenty of Russians who are proud of their wealth, of their culture, or of their official position, but we rarely find a Russian who is proud of his birth or imagines that the fact of his having a long pedigree gives him any right to political privileges or social consideration. Hence there is a certain amount of truth in the oft-repeated saying that there is in reality no aristocracy in Russia.

·   ·   ·

New men force their way into it by official distinction, whilst many of the old families are compelled by poverty to retire from its ranks. The son of a small proprietor, or even of a parish priest, may rise to the highest offices of State, whilst the descendants of the half-mythical Rurik may descend to the position of peasants.

[One notices] the readiness of most Russians to afford every possible facility to a foreigner who wishes seriously to study their country. They believe that they have long been misunderstood and systematically calumniated by foreigners, and they are extremely desirous that the prevalent misconceptions regarding their country should be removed. It must be said to their honour that they have little or none of that false patriotism which seeks to conceal national defects; and in judging themselves and their institutions they are inclined to be over-severe rather than unduly lenient. In the time of Nicholas I, those who desired to stand well with the Government proclaimed loudly that they lived in the happiest and best-governed country of the world, but this shallow official optimism has long since gone out of fashion. During all the years which I spent in Russia I found everywhere the utmost readiness to assist me in my investigations, and very rarely noticed that habit of "throwing dust in the eyes of foreigners" of which writers have spoken so much.

[On the zemstvos:]

What surprised me most in this [zemstvo] assembly was that it was composed partly of nobles and partly of peasants—the latter being decidedly in the majority—and that no trace of antagonism seemed to exist between the two classes. Landed proprietors and their *ci-devant* serfs, emancipated only ten years before, evidently met for the moment on a footing of equality. The discussions were carried on chiefly by the nobles, but on more than one occasion peasant members rose to speak, and their remarks, always clear, practical, and to the point, were invariably listened to with respectful attention.

·   ·   ·

The Zemstvo . . . fulfills tolerably well, without scandalous peculation and jobbery, its commonplace, every-day duties. . . . It has done a very great deal to provide medical aid and primary education for the common people, and it has improved wonderfully the condition of the hospitals, lunatic asylums, and other benevolent institutions committed to its charge. In its efforts to aid the peasantry it has helped to improve the native breeds of horses and cattle, and it has created a system of obligatory fire insurance, together with means for preventing and extinguishing fires in the villages—a most important matter in a country where the peasants live in wooden houses and big fires are fearfully frequent.

[On the justices of the peace:]

In the Justice of Peace Courts . . . the justice, always scrupulously polite without distinction of persons, listened patiently to the complaint, tried to arrange the affair amicably, and when his efforts failed, gave his decision at once according to law and common sense. No attention was paid to rank or social position. A general who would not conform to the police regulations was fined like an ordinary workman, and in a dispute between a great dignitary and a man of the people the two were treated in precisely the same way. No wonder such courts became popular among the masses; and their popularity was increased when it became known that the affairs were disposed of expeditiously, without unnecessary formalities and without any bribes or blackmail.

XV:39. P. A. VIAZEMSKII ON THE BALKAN CRISIS, CA. 1876

When Serbia and Montenegro went to war against Turkey in 1876, Russia was swept by a wave of sympathy for the Balkan Slavs, and many volunteers rushed off to help liberate their "brethren" from the Turks. Among the conservative and unheeded minority was the elderly Prince Petr Andreevich Viazemskii (1792-1878), a poet and critic who had earlier been a friend of Pushkin and who in mid-century held several government posts connected with diplomacy, finance, and education. In a letter to a close relative, Prince Viazemskii unburdened himself as follows.

Reference: Tatishchev, *Imperator Aleksandr II*, 2:293-95.

Everything that is being done about the Eastern Question is truly a bewildering nightmare. The government is neither seen nor heard. . . . All the dams are broken, and the torrent is raging and overflowing on all sides; many are the things it will deluge. . . . War at this time may bring us not only harm but ruin. It may drive us into national bankruptcy. Unlike the French, we do not carry billions in our vest pocket—not to mention the other evil consequences of a war. . . . The government tacitly condones this political confusion, and it may have to pay dearly for it. . . . Do we really need to sacrifice our bodies, our blood, possibly our future welfare, that the Serbs may prosper? Let the Serbs tend to their own affairs, and us Russians to ours. This is indeed our chief error, our chief misunderstanding: that we consider ourselves more Slav than Russian. We set Russian blood in the background, while Slavophilism comes first. . . . And why have they raised all this alarm, all this fuss? Why have they let loose the press and those gangs of adventurers? Any time now Europe will catch fire, and a general war will spread. Do they really think that Russia will be strengthened by the resurgence of the Slavic nations? Nothing of the sort; rather the contrary. We shall only ensure and confirm the ill will and ingratitude of a neighbor whom we have revived and put on his feet. . . . It is better for us to have as a neighbor a feeble Turkey, old and decrepit, than a young, strong, democratic Slavic land that will be wary of us but will never love us. And when have the Slavs been of any use to us? Russia to them is only a milch cow and nothing more. And we let them milk us till we bleed. Yet all their sympathies are for the West. . . . Save my letter. . . . I want posterity to have proof that in an intoxicated Russia a few sober voices were raised.

XV:40. ALEXANDER'S MANIFESTO OF WAR AGAINST TURKEY, APRIL 12, 1877

Reference: *PSZRI*, 2d ser., vol. 52, pt. 1, p. 371; translation based on Hertslet, *Map of Europe by Treaty*, 4:2598-99, somewhat revised.

All our faithful and beloved subjects know the lively interest we have always devoted to the destinies of the oppressed Christian population of Turkey. Our desire to ameliorate and guarantee their condition has been shared by the whole of the Russian nation, which shows itself ready today to make fresh sacrifices to relieve the condition of the Christians in the Balkan Peninsula.

The life and property of our faithful subjects have always been dear to us. Our whole reign testifies to our constant anxiety to preserve to Russia the blessings of peace. This anxiety did not cease to animate us at the time of the sad events that came to pass in Herzegovina, Bosnia, and Bulgaria. We originally made it our object to attain the amelioration of the condition of Christians in the East by means of peaceful negotiations and agreements with the great European powers, our allies and friends. For two years we have made incessant efforts to induce the Porte to adopt such reforms as would protect the Christians of Bosnia, Herzegovina, and Bulgaria from the arbitrary rule of the local authorities. The execution of these reforms followed entirely from previous obligations solemnly contracted by the Porte in the sight of all Europe. Our efforts, although supported by the joint diplomatic representations of other governments, have not attained the desired end. The Porte has remained immovable in its categorical refusal of every effectual guarantee for the security of its Christian subjects and has rejected the demands of the Conference of Constantinople. . . .

Having exhausted our peaceful efforts, we are obliged by the haughty obstinacy of the Porte to proceed to more determined action. The feeling of justice and of our own dignity likewise demand this. Turkey, by its refusal, places us under the necessity of having recourse to arms. . . . Now, calling for God's blessing on our valiant troops, we have ordered them to cross the borders of Turkey.

XV:41. THE TREATY OF BERLIN, JULY 1 (13, N.S.), 1878

Russia's gains in the Treaty of San Stefano provoked opposition (especially in England and Austria) that led to the Treaty of Berlin, signed July 1 (13, N.S.), 1878, by Great Britain, Austria-Hungary, France, Germany, Italy, Russia, and Turkey. Here are some of its provisions.

Reference: *PSZRI,* 2d ser., vol. 53, pt. 2, pp. 43-51, 53; translation based on Hertslet, *Map of Europe by Treaty,* 4:2766-98, with minor changes, mostly to conform more closely to the Russian text (which, however, was not any more official than the English text). Hertslet gives the Treaty of San Stefano on pp. 2675-91 of the same volume. The Russian version is in *PSZRI,* vol. 53, pt. 1, pp. 157-64.

ARTICLE I. Bulgaria is constituted an autonomous and tributary principality under the suzerainty of His Imperial Majesty the sultan; it will have a Christian government and a national militia. . . .

ART. III. The Prince of Bulgaria shall be freely elected by the population and confirmed by the Sublime Porte, with the assent of the powers. No member of the reigning dynasties of the great European powers may be elected prince of Bulgaria. . . .

ART. IV. An assembly of notables of Bulgaria, convoked at Tirnovo, shall, before the election of the prince, draw up the organic law of the principality. . . .

ART. VI. The provisional administration of Bulgaria shall be under the direction of an imperial Russian commissioner until the completion of the organic law. An imperial Ottoman commissioner, as well as the consuls delegated ad hoc by the other powers who have signed the present treaty, shall be called to assist him so as to control the working of this provisional administration. . . .

ART. VII. The provisional administration shall not be prolonged beyond a period of nine months from the exchange of the ratifications of the present treaty.

When the organic law is completed the election of the prince of Bulgaria shall proceed immediately. As soon as the prince has been installed, the new organization shall be put into force, and the principality shall enter into the full enjoyment of its autonomy. . . .

ART. IX. The amount of the annual tribute which the principality of Bulgaria shall pay to the suzerain court . . . shall be fixed by an agreement between the powers who have signed the present treaty. . . .

ART. XI. The Ottoman army shall no longer remain in Bulgaria; all the old fortresses shall be razed at the expense of the principality. . . .

ART. XIII. A province will be formed south of the Balkans which will take the name of "Eastern Rumelia" and will remain under the direct political and military authority of His Imperial Majesty the sultan, under conditions of administrative autonomy. It shall have a Christian governor general. . . .

ART. XV. His Majesty the sultan shall have the right of providing for the defense of the land and sea frontiers of the province by erecting fortifications on those frontiers, and maintaining troops there.

Internal order is to be maintained in

Eastern Rumelia by a native gendarmerie assisted by a local militia. . . .

ART. XVII. The governor general of Eastern Rumelia shall be appointed by the Sublime Porte, with the assent of the powers, for a term of five years.

ART. XVIII. Immediately after the exchange of the ratifications of the present treaty, a European commission shall be formed to arrange, in concert with the Ottoman Porte, the organization of Eastern Rumelia. . . .

[ART. XXII.] The period of the occupation of Eastern Rumelia and Bulgaria by imperial Russian troops is fixed at nine months from the date of the exchange of the ratifications of the present treaty. . . .

ART. XXV. The provinces of Bosnia and Herzegovina shall be occupied and administered by Austria-Hungary. The government of Austria-Hungary, not desiring to undertake the administration of the Sanjak of Novi Bazar, which extends between Serbia and Montenegro in a southeasterly direction beyond Mitrovica, the Ottoman Administration will continue to exercise its functions there. Nevertheless, in order to assure the maintenance of the new political state of affairs, as well as freedom and security of communications, Austria-Hungary reserves the right of keeping garrisons and having military and commercial roads in the whole of this part of the former Vilayet of Bosnia. . . .

ART. XXVI. The independence of Montenegro is recognized by the Sublime Porte and by all the High Contracting Parties. . . .

ART. XXXIV. The High Contracting Parties recognize the independence of the Principality of Serbia. . . .

ART. XLIII. The High Contracting Parties recognize the independence of Rumania. . . .

ART. XLV. The Principality of Rumania restores to His Majesty the emperor of Russia that portion of the Bessarabian territory detached from Russia by the Treaty of Paris of 1856, bounded on the west by the mid-channel of the Pruth, and on the south by the channel of the Kiliia arm [of the Danubian delta] and the Staryi-Stambul mouth.

ART. XLVI. The islands forming the delta of the Danube, as well as the Isle of Serpents, the Sanjak of Tulcea, comprising the districts (cazas) of Kiliia, Sulina, Mahmudia, Isaccea, Tulcea, Macin, Babadag, Harsova,

Constanta, Medgidia, are added to Rumania. The principality receives in addition the territory situated to the south of the Dobruja as far as a line starting east of Silistria and terminating on the Black Sea, south of Mangalia.
. . .

ART. LVIII. The Sublime Porte cedes to the Russian Empire in Asia the territories of Ardahan, Kars, and Batum. . . .

ART. LIX. His Majesty the emperor of Russia declares that it is his intention to constitute Batum a free port, essentially commercial.

ART. LX. The valley of Alaschkerd and the town of Bayazit, ceded to Russia by article XIX of the Treaty of San Stefano, are restored to Turkey. . . .

ART. LXI. The Sublime Porte undertakes to carry out, without further delay, the improvements and reforms demanded by local requirements in the provinces inhabited by the Armenians, and to guarantee their security against the Circassians and Kurds. . . .

[ART. LXII.] In no part of the Ottoman Empire shall difference of religion be alleged against any person as a ground for exclusion or incapacity as regards the enjoyment of civil and political rights, admission to public posts, functions, and honors, or the exercise of the various free professions and industries. . . .

The freedom and outward exercise of all forms of worship are assured to all, and no hindrance shall be offered either to the hierarchical organization of the various religious communions or to their relations with their spiritual chiefs.

Ecclesiastics, pilgrims, and monks of all nationalities traveling in European or Asiatic Turkey shall enjoy the same rights, advantages, and privileges.

The right of official protection by the diplomatic and consular agents of the powers in Turkey is recognized both as regards the above-mentioned persons and their religious, charitable, and other establishments in the holy places and elsewhere.

The rights possessed by France are expressly reserved for it, and it is well understood that the *status quo* in the holy places cannot be subject to any violation.

The monks of Mount Athos, of whatever country they may be natives, shall retain their possessions, and shall enjoy, without any exception, complete equality of rights and prerogatives.

XV:42. D. A. MILIUTIN ON THE TSAR AND THE GOVERNMENT, 1876-1880

Minister of War Miliutin, in his famous diary, made these comments on the current scene during the last years of the reign of Alexander II.

Reference: Miliutin, *Dnevnik D. A. Miliutina,* 2:46, 157, 163; 3:72-73, 82, 139-40, 205, 243.

April 15, 1876. . . . The sovereign often displays a fine trait of character: he magnanimously makes concessions, sacrificing his own pride, when he recognizes that this is necessary for the welfare of the state. There is a great deal of gentleness and flexibility in his character and behavior.

· · ·

April 12, 1877 [at the review of troops in Kishinev just after the declaration of war against Turkey]. . . . The troops passed by the sovereign, amongst them both Bulgarian detachments [druzhiny], which presented a highly impressive appearance. When the sovereign, after riding through the mass of assembled troops, uttered several affectionate, cordial words to the officers who surrounded him, the whole throng of both officers and soldiers became animated with enthusiasm such as I had never yet chanced to see among our troops. They shouted and hurled their caps in the air, and many, very many, of them wept sobbingly. Afterward, throngs of people ran after the sovereign with shouts of "Hurrah." It is evident that the present war with Turkey is entirely popular.

· · ·

April 26, 1877. . . . On April 22, at ten o'clock in the evening, we arrived in Moscow. . . . Moscow greeted the sovereign, as was to be expected, with indescribable enthusiasm. Despite the drizzling rain, every street right up to the Kremlin Palace was jammed with masses of people. But the scene on the following morning in the halls of the palace and in the square between the cathedrals is hard to describe. When in the Aleksandrovskii Hall the sovereign, after listening to the welcoming speeches of the marshal of the nobility and the mayor of the city, replied to them briefly, but in words full of meaning and emotion, the entire throng which filled the hall went into a kind of rapture; everyone rushed toward the sovereign, so that only with great difficulty was it possible to shield him, the empress, the heir, and the tsesarevna [wife of the heir]; a large part of the suite was pushed aside. When the sovereign came out on the Red Portico [Krasnoe Kryl'tso; see Item

VIII:43], the entire square resounded with loud shouts of unfeigned enthusiasm. In the customary manner, the sovereign went to the Cathedral of the Dormition, from there to Chudov Monastery, and returned home through the Nikolaevskii Palace. His equipage could hardly move through the dense throng.

At one o'clock in the afternoon a review of the troops of the Moscow garrison was called in Teatral'naia Square; the sovereign with his entire suite rode on horseback from the Kremlin Palace to the scene of the review. Again, countless throngs of people greeted and accompanied him with loud shouts. The sovereign was very pleased with the troops.

· · ·

June 17, 1878. . . . Count Shuvalov . . . [at the Congress of Berlin] tries with all his might to make the best bargain possible. Unfortunately he has desperate and malicious adversaries against him; not only is he forced to struggle daily with the insolent and impudent representatives of England and Austria, but he also encounters resistance on the part of all the other members; even Prince Bismarck, with whom Count Shuvalov was formerly on the best of terms, does not furnish him the support we had a right to expect. The German chancellor is extremely irritable and impatient; at the slightest objection he threatens, in the event of long disputes, to break off the congress and leave for Kissingen. Andrássy and Beaconsfield openly and cynically declare that they do not care at all what happens to this or that Christian people, as long as their own national interests are maintained.

The telegrams received yesterday evening and this morning . . . are not the least consoling. All of Europe shows itself to be against us, even in questions in which we counted confidently on the support of others, as, for example, in Austrian claims to the annexation of Bosnia, Herzegovina, and part of Old Serbia as far as Mitrovica. The insolent demands of Austria stir the depths of my soul with indignation. To my amazement the sovereign accepted these scandalous demands calmly and indulgently; contrary to all expectations, Giers has been ordered without further discussion to telegraph

Count Shuvalov to express his assent to the latest proposal of Count Andrássy. Of course, a refusal in this case would inevitably lead to the closing of the congress and to war; it is already fully apparent that we have not only England against us but all of Europe, and that we cannot expect support from anyone. With matters in such a state, there is no choice: we are compelled to agree to everything, to yield in everything.

      . . .

July 22, 1878. . . . Public opinion in Russia is in an extremely hostile frame of mind toward the government, particularly in Moscow. The Treaty of Berlin arouses almost general displeasure. Its cause may be attributed to disappointment. They expected something colossal, and when the hopes of the idealists were not realized, when the practical reality appeared, everyone raised a cry against our diplomacy and against the whole government. In Moscow Ivan Sergeevich Aksakov constantly leads this chorus; he is seconded by several of his extreme partisans. The extravagant speech of Aksakov before the Slavic Society [Slavianskoe Obshchevstvo] led first to Aksakov's being ordered to resign the post of chairman of the society, and then to the closing of the society itself. A lamentable fact. It will inevitably make a disadvantageous impression for us in the Slavic lands, where they regarded the Moscow Slavic Society as an organ through which the Russian government itself displayed its sympathy and patronage of Slavdom. It is a pity that our not very numerous men of public affairs rarely possess political tact; by getting carried away in their enthusiasm they almost always injure the cause they serve.

      . . .

April 20, 1879. . . . It must be acknowledged that our entire governmental structure demands basic reform from top to bottom. The structure of rural self-government, of the zemstvo, of local administration in uezdy and guberniias, as well as of institutions on the central and national level—all of them have outlived their time; they should all take on new forms in accordance with the great reforms carried out in the sixties. Most regrettably, such a colossal task is beyond the powers of our present statesmen, who are incapable of rising above the viewpoint of a chief of police or even of a city constable.

The higher echelons of the government are intimidated by the impudent displays of socialist propaganda of the past few years and think only of protective police measures, instead of acting against the root of the evil. The disease appears and the government imposes a quarantine, without undertaking anything aimed at healing the disease itself.

Expressing these melancholy thoughts, I involuntarily ask myself the question: Are you acting honestly in keeping these convictions to yourself while actually a member of the higher echelons of the government? This question oppresses me often, almost constantly; but what is there to do? It's no use beating your head against a stone wall; I would be a Don Quixote if I took to the notion of acting upon views that are entirely contrary to those held in the sphere in which I move; these views would make my official position an impossible one and would not bring the least benefit to the cause; I am convinced that the present men are powerless, not only to solve the imminent problem, but even to understand it.

      . . .

January 22, 1880. . . . A few days ago, during a nocturnal search of a house in Saint Petersburg, a printing press was accidentally discovered while it was in operation; leaflets of the revolutionary publication *Narodnaia Volia* [The People's Will] were being printed. There were five people in the apartment, including two women; all of them tried to defend themselves with revolvers but were nevertheless seized, except for one who succeeded in shooting himself. For several days now this event has been a subject of general discussion in the city. . . . So far, however, nightly searches and continual arrests have not led to any positive results but only increase the general displeasure and grumbling. Never before has so much unlimited arbitrary power been granted to the administration and the police. But it is hardly possible to put an end to the revolutionary underground activity, which has already assumed such considerable proportions, by these police measures, terror, and violence alone. It is hard to root out the evil when not in a single layer of society does the government encounter either sympathy or true support. It is saddening to observe what measures are considered indispensable for guarding the person of the sovereign, who only travels surrounded by a convoy. The chief of gendarmes, the governor general, the governor of the city [*gradonachal'nik*], and even the minister of internal affairs likewise travel through the city with Cossacks.

     · · ·

April 23, 1880. . . . Count Loris-Melikov came to visit me and sat with my family for a long time. He is celebrating his triumph over Count Tolstoi, whose dismissal from the posts of minister of education and chief procurator

of the [Holy] Synod produced universal joy. This news instantly spread everywhere; everyone rejoices. . . . Not without great difficulty did Count Loris-Melikov attain his goal; the sovereign stubbornly supported Tolstoi, but finally he had to bring himself to remove a minister who had succeeded in meriting universal hatred. This measure will undoubtedly make a good impression throughout Russia, and Loris-Melikov will receive everyone's sincere thanks.

XV:43. A DECLARATION OF THE TVER' ZEMSTVO, 1879

In 1879 the zemstvo of the guberniia of Tver' presented an address to the tsar embodying this pointed request.
     Reference: Glinskii, *Revoliutsionnyi period*, pt. 2, p. 147. Translation based on Paul Miliukov, *Russia and Its Crisis* (London: T. F. Unwin, 1905), p. 304, slightly revised.

In his concern for the welfare of the Bulgarian people after their liberation from the Turkish yoke, the sovereign emperor has deemed it necessary to grant this people true self-government, the inviolability of the rights of the individual, an independent judiciary, and freedom of the press. The zemstvo of the Tver' guberniia dares to hope that the Russian

people, who bore the entire burden of the war with such complete readiness and with such self-sacrificing love for their tsar-emancipator, will be allowed to enjoy the same blessings, which alone can lead them, in the words of the sovereign, along the path of gradual, peaceful, and legal development.

C. INTELLECTUAL TRENDS AND REVOLUTIONARY MOVEMENTS

XV:44. HERZEN ON RUSSIA AND EUROPE, 1857-1861

These excerpts from some of Alexander Herzen's many writings in the period 1857-61 illustrate facets of his thought in addition to those treated in the preceding chapter. Herzen's influence in Russia remained powerful until 1863, when he became unpopular for siding with the Poles in their uprising.
     Reference: A. I. Gertsen, *Polnoe sobranie sochinenii i pisem*, ed. M. K. Lemke, 22 vols. (Petrograd, Leningrad, Moscow, 1917-25), 8:486-87, 488, 490, 491, 492, 493, 494, 496-97 [letter of 1857], translation based in part on that of Constance Garnett in volume 6 of *My Past and Thoughts: The Memoirs of Alexander Herzen*, 6 vols. (London: Chatto and Windus, 1927), but much revised; Gertsen, *Sochineniia A. I. Gertsena*, 7 vols. (St. Petersburg: F. Pavlenkov, 1905), 6:260-61, 275, 277, 284-85 [1859 piece]; Gertsen, *Polnoe sobranie sochinenii i pisem*, 11:260 [1861 piece]. Recently there has appeared a 4-volume edition of the Garnett translation, as revised by Humphrey Higgens (London: Chatto and Windus, 1968).

[From a letter to the novelist I. S. Turgenev, February 3, 1857:]
     You love European ideas—I love them too. . . . Without them we would sink into Asiatic quietism or African vacuity. *With them, and with them alone,* Russia can be brought into possession of that great part of the heritage which comes to her share.

     · · ·

     The question of the future of Europe I do not regard as finally settled; but, in good

conscience, in obedience to the truth, and with a prejudice rather in favor of the West than against it, after studying it for ten years not in theories and books but in clubs and in public squares, in the center of all its political and social life, I am bound to say that I see neither a speedy nor a happy outcome.

     · · ·

     But outside Europe there are only two progressive regions, America and Russia, with possibly Australia just emerging. All the rest lie in deep slumber or struggle in convulsions which we do not understand and which are as alien to us as a Chinese rebellion with all its piles of corpses and revolting butchery.

. . .

Reading the chronicle of the Bagrov family [*Semeinaia khronika* by S. T. Aksakov] I was struck by the resemblance between the old man who migrated into the Ufa provintsiia and the settlers who migrate from New York somewhere to Wisconsin or Illinois. It is a completely new clearing of uninhabited places and their conversion to agriculture and civic life. . . . In Viatka, in my time, it was still hard to keep the peasants from migrating into the forests and there starting new settlements; in their eyes the land was still common property, the *res nullius* to which every man has a right.

. . .

Russia . . . is a quite special world, with *her own* natural way of life, with her own physiological character—not European, not Asiatic, but Slavic. She participates in the destinies of Europe without having its historical traditions and free from its obligations to the past. . . . Nowhere do we have those hard-and-fast prejudices which like a paralysis deprive Western man of the use of half his limbs. At the basis of our national life lies the village commune, with its repartition of fields, with its communistic possession of land, with an elective administration, with equal rights for each worker (or labor unit [tiaglo]). All this is at present in a depressed, distorted state, but it is all living and has lived through its worst period.

. . .

The stumbling blocks over which Europe has tripped scarcely exist for us. In the natural simplicity of our village life, in our uncertain and unsettled economic and judicial conceptions, in our vague sense of property rights, in our lack of a strong middle class, and in our extraordinary capacity for assimilating foreign ideas, we have an advantage over nations that have been completely formed and are exhausted.

. . .

Communal possession of land, communal government and elections constitute the soil in which a new social order may easily arise, a soil that, like our black earth, scarcely exists in Europe.

. . .

In Russia I see the possibility at hand. I can sense it and feel its presence. There is no such possibility in the West, at least not at this moment. If I were not a Russian, I would long ago have gone away to America.

I feel in my heart and in my mind that history is knocking at our door; if we have not the strength to open it, and if those who have it are unwilling or incapable, the further development of what has gone before will find more competent agencies in America or in Australia, where civic life is being formed on a quite different basis. Perhaps even Europe herself will be remade, will rise up, will take up her bed and walk on her holy land, under which so many martyrs are buried, and on which so much sweat and blood has fallen. Perhaps!

. . .

Eagerly accepting the new civic religion that has arisen on the blood-soaked fields of the Reformation and the [French] Revolution, rereading with throbbing heart the great legends of those days, I turn away from contemporary Europe and have little in common with the pitiful heirs of mighty fathers.

[From the essay "Russian Germans and German Russians," 1859:]

There can be no doubt that European forms of civic life were incomparably superior, not only to those of ancient Russia, but also to our present ones. And the question is not whether we have overtaken the West, but whether we should attempt to overtake it over the same long road when we can take a shortcut instead. It seems to us that after being equipped by Western training we can now stand on our own two feet; and instead of parroting the words of others and trying to fit into worn boots, we ought to consider whether there might not be something in the life of our own people, in our national character, in our thought, and in our art, that might make claim to a social organization incomparably superior to that of the West. Good pupils often skip classes.

. . .

Now the West has been shaken, while we have emerged from our torpor; we struggle to advance, while it tries to hold its place. The point we have reached means that we are finished with pupil-like imitation, that we should be leaving Peter's school, that we should stand on our own two feet and stop parroting the words of others. In our ideas, among our thinking minority, in literature, and in prisons we have lived through Western history, and it would hardly seem necessary for us to repeat it in toto.

Europe has passed from wretched country roads to good highways, and from there to railroads. We still have wretched means of communication—but should we build highways first, and railroads only afterward?

. . .

We are living in the *city of cities*—London. Do you really think that such an absurdity has any sort of future?

Wave after wave of population has descended upon these docks of the universe and has settled here, like locusts on falling grain. And so a throng of three million people has coagulated here, poisoning the air, poisoning the water, crowding together, getting in each other's way, their most morbid parts grown together as if into thick clots. . . . Glance at the dark, dank alleys, at the people burrowed deep into the earth, depriving each other of light and land, of a piece of bread and a filthy hovel. Look at this river running with pus and contagion, this blanket of smoke and stench that covers not only the city but even its environs—and do you think that this will remain, that these are the necessary conditions for civilization?

. . .

The *right to land* and its *communal possession* presuppose a strong *communal organization* as the prime basis of the entire edifice of the state which must evolve on these foundations. Communal organization has survived both foreign domination and the rule of the landowners. . . .

And so, the elements contributed by the Russian peasant commune—elements that

have long existed but are now becoming conscious and encountering the Western aspiration for radical economic change—consist of three principles:

    1. *The right of every man to land*
    2. *Its communal possession*
    3. *Communal government*

It is upon these, and *only these,* principles that the Russia of the future can develop.

[From the essay "The Colossus Awakens!" (1861):]

In Russia the universities have been closed [i.e. closed temporarily because of student disorders]. In Poland the churches, defiled by the police, have shut their own doors. Neither the light of reason, nor the light of religion! Where do they want to lead us in the dark?

. . .

Where then are you to go, young men to whom learning has been barred? Shall I tell you where?

Listen carefully, for darkness does not keep one from hearing: from all parts of our vast homeland, from the Don and the Ural, from the Volga and the Dnieper, there spreads a groan, there arises a murmur; it is the first roar of the ocean wave which is beginning to seethe, rife with storms, after a fearfully wearying calm. *To the people! Toward the people!* This is your place, exiles from learning! Show these Bistroms [Baron Rodrig Grigor'evich Bistrom, commander of the Second Guards Infantry Division in Saint Petersburg, who in 1861 delivered a demagogical speech to his troops denouncing the university students as future "scriveners" who would cheat the common people] that you are fit material not for *scriveners* but for warriors—and not mercenaries without kith or kin, but warriors for the Russian people!

XV:45. CHERNYSHEVSKII IN 1857-1860

Nikolai Gavrilovich Chernyshevskii (1828-89), son of an Orthodox priest, acquired his reputation as a founder of Russian "revolutionary populism" largely through his articles in the journal *Sovremennik* [The Contemporary], in the years preceding the Emancipation. (Most of his life thereafter was spent in Siberian exile.) One does well to keep in mind, while reading these excerpts from his articles, that Chernyshevskii, like others who published legally in Russia, had to observe the limits set by the government censor.

Reference: N. G. Chernyshevskii, *Polnoe sobranie sochinenii N. G. Chernyshevskogo,* 10 vols. (St. Petersburg: I. Kraig, 1905-06), 3:461, 472, 473, 475, 478 [1857 article]; 4:329, 330, 331 [1858 article]; 6:28, 33, 40 [first article of 1860], 229-30, 231, 234, 236 [second article of 1860]. The translation of the last excerpt is based on N. G. Chernyshevsky, *Selected Philosophical Essays* (Moscow: Foreign Languages Publishing House, 1953), pp. 121-22, 124, 128, 130, 132-34.

[From "On the Ownership of Landed Property," 1857:]

There is an immense difference between communal possession without communal production and communal possession with communal production. The former merely averts proletarianization; the second in addition promotes an increase in production.

.   .   .

Private ownership of landed property . . . invariably distributes the territory of the nation so that the majority of the agricultural population either is excluded altogether from sharing in the possession of land or receives as its share paltry, minute scraps, whose cultivation does not provide their holders with a living. Therefore communal possession, which ensures that each farmer will hold land, promotes national prosperity far better than does private ownership of property.

.   .   .

The best form of ownership of landed property for successful agriculture is one that makes owner, manager, and worker one and the same person. Of all forms of property ownership, state ownership of property together with communal possession comes closest to this ideal.

.   .   .

We defend the situation that prevails in our country—state ownership of property along with communal possession—for the very reason that it comes closer than any other form of property ownership to the ideal of landed property ownership.

All the benefits from improvements and labor must belong to those who do the work and make the improvements.

He who cultivates land must also possess it.

.   .   .

Self-interest is the motive force for improvements.

Only communal possession distributes the land in such a manner that profit from land, interest on circulating capital, and labor are united in a single person who therefore has everything to gain from working the best he can, from expending as much capital as possible for raising the productivity of labor through improvements, and from increasing his profit from land as much as he can.

[From "A Critique of the Philosophical Prejudices against Communal Possession," 1858:]

The question we are dealing with is this: Must a given social phenomenon pass through all its logical stages in the actual life of every society, or can it, under favorable circumstances, pass from the first or second level of development directly to the fifth or sixth, omitting the intermediate levels, as happens with phenomena of individual life and in the processes of physical nature?

The unity of laws in all spheres of existence . . . compels us to answer this question affirmatively.

.   .   .

With . . . an accelerated course of development, the intermediate levels bypassed in the life of a formerly backward people, which has utilized the experience and knowledge of an advanced people, attain only theoretical existence, as logical stages that are not actualized by the facts of reality.

.   .   .

The conclusions are rather simple and clear. . . .

1. The highest level of development coincides in form with the earliest.

2. Under the influence of the high level of development that a given phenomenon of social life has attained among advanced peoples, this phenomenon can develop very rapidly among other peoples and can rise from the lowest level directly to the highest, bypassing the intermediate logical stages.

[From "Capital and Labor," 1860:]

The theory of the capitalists had to begin with an analysis of the concepts of production and capital. The result of this analysis was the conclusion that all value is created by labor, and that capital itself is the product of labor. . . . If all value and all capital are produced by labor, then it is evident that labor alone is responsible for all production, and all talk about the participation of movable or immovable capital in production only serves to alter the idea of labor as the sole producing agent. If this is so, then labor must be the sole owner of the values produced. Backward economists are naturally unwilling to accept the conclusion we have presented, but it necessarily follows from the basic concepts of value, capital, and labor discovered by Adam Smith.

.   .   .

The theory of the toilers (as we shall call the theory that corresponds to contemporary needs, in contrast to the backward but dominant theory, which we will call the theory of the capitalists) directs its attention chiefly to the problem of the distribution of values. The principle of the most advantageous distribution is set forth by the words of Adam Smith: that all value is produced only by labor; and by the rules of common sense: that a product must belong to him who produced it. The problem is simply one of discovering the methods of economic organization under which this common-sense demand can be fulfilled.

· · ·

Having no reason for malevolence toward one another, the toilers have no motive for holding themselves apart from each other. On the contrary, they have a direct economic necessity for seeking mutual union. Almost every type of production, to be successful, must be organized on a scale that exceeds the labor power of a single household. The capitalist has no need for union with others, since he has at his disposal the [labor] power of many people. The toiler, who has at his disposal only the [labor] power of his family, must enter into associations with other toilers. This is easy for him to do, since he has no reason to be hostile toward them. Thus the form of production established by the theory of the toilers is the association.

[From "The Anthropological Principle in Philosophy," 1860:]

It is only necessary to examine more closely an action or an emotion that seems to be altruistic to see that all are based on the self-same thought of personal self-interest, personal gratification, personal benefit; they are based on the feeling that is called egoism. . . . Not much . . . difficulty is presented by those cases in which a man makes sacrifices for the object of his love. Even though he sacrifice his very life for it, the basis of the sacrifice is still personal interest, or a paroxysm of egoism.

· · ·

A careful examination of the motives that prompt men's actions shows that all deeds, good and bad, noble and base, heroic and craven, proceed in every case from a single source: a man acts in the way that gives him the most pleasure; he is guided by a calculation that commands him to abstain from a smaller gain, or a lesser pleasure, in order to obtain a larger gain or a greater pleasure. . . .

. . . Usefulness is the criterion of good.

· · ·

If by useful we mean that which serves as a source of numerous pleasures, and by good, simply that which is very useful, not a bit of doubt whatever remains concerning the goal to be ascribed to man—not by any extraneous motives or promptings, not by any problematical presuppositions, or by mysterious relationships with something or other still quite doubtful, but simply by reason, by common sense, by the need for pleasure. That goal is the good. Only good actions are prudent; only he who is good is rational, and he is rational only to the degree that he is good. When a man is not good he is merely an imprudent wastrel who pays thousands of rubles for things that are worth kopecks and spends as much material and moral strength in obtaining a small amount of pleasure as could have enabled him to obtain ever so much more pleasure.

XV:46. REVOLUTIONARY PROCLAMATIONS OF 1861 AND 1862

Although Russia's Emancipation of 1861 went further than that of the same period in the United States, some of the radicals were disappointed. They voiced their anger in revolutionary proclamations like the two excerpted here. The novelist M. I. Mikhailov, who helped write the first, was arrested in September 1861 for distributing subversive literature and was sentenced to hard labor in Siberia. The second proclamation, widely distributed in Saint Petersburg in May 1862, caused a great stir and is considered to be historically significant in the development of the Russian revolutionary movement. P. G. Zaichnevskii, who wrote it with a group of fellow prisoners and sent it to the underground printer via a sentry, said later that as of 1862 neither he nor his co-authors had yet read the Communist Manifesto.

Reference: Mikhail K. Lemke, *Politicheskie protsessy v Rossii 1860-kh gg.*, 2d ed. (Moscow: Gosizdat, 1923), pp. 63-64, 69, 70, 74-75 [1861 item], 508-10, 514-18 [1862 item]. The Lemke volume has recently been reprinted: The Hague: Mouton, 1969.

[From the proclamation *To the Younger Generation* (*K molodomu pokoleniiu*), written by M. I. Mikhailov and N. V. Shelgunov in September 1861, and published that same month in Saint Petersburg without having gone through the censor:]

The sovereign has betrayed the hopes of the people; the freedom he has given them is not real and is not what the people dreamed of and need.

. . .

We do not need a tsar, or an emperor, or the Lord's anointed, or a robe of ermine covering up hereditary incompetence; we want to have as our head an ordinary mortal, a man of the soil, who understands life and the people who have elected him. We do not need an emperor anointed with oil in the Cathedral of the Dormition, but rather an elected elder [starshina] who receives a salary for his services.

. . .

Are the economic conditions and the land situation in Europe the same as they are here? Does the agricultural commune exist there, and is it a possibility? Can every peasant and every citizen there own landed property? No, but here he can. We have enough land to last us tens of thousands of years.

We are a backward people and in this lies our salvation. We should thank our good fortune that we have not lived the life of Europe. Her misfortunes and desperate straits are a lesson to us. We do not want her proletariat, her aristocracy, her state principle, or her imperial power.

. . .

We are advancing to meet the revolution boldly; we even desire it. We believe in our youthful strength; we believe that we are called upon to introduce a new principle into history, to have our own say, and not to parrot the words of Europe. There is no salvation without faith, and our faith in our strength is very great.

If we have to slaughter a hundred thousand landowners in order to realize our aspirations—the distribution of the land among the common people—we would not be afraid of that either. Nor would this really be such a terrible thing.

. . .

We want the authority that governs us to be an intelligent authority which understands the needs of the country and acts in the interests of the people. And in order to be such, it must come from our own midst; it must be elective and limited.

We want freedom of speech, i.e. the abolition of all censorship.

We want the development of the principle of self-government, which already exists to a certain extent among our people. If the peasants have this right, if they can elect elders and heads from their own midst, if communes have the right of administering justice in civil cases and of police enforcement, why should the rest of Russia not enjoy these same rights of election and self-government? . . . Our rural commune is the basic cell, and these cells together make up Russia. There should be a single principle throughout. That is what we need.

We want all citizens of Russia to enjoy equal rights; we do not want privileged classes to exist; we want ability and education, rather than birth, to confer the right to high position; we want appointments to public office to follow the elective principle. We do not want a nobility and titles. We want everyone to be equal in the eyes of the law and equal in [the assessment of] exactions, taxes, and obligations by the state.

. . .

We want the land to belong to the nation and not to individuals; we want each commune to have its allotment, without the existence of private landowners; we do not want land to be sold like potatoes and cabbage; we want to give every citizen, whoever he may be, the opportunity of becoming a member of an agricultural commune, i.e. either by joining an existing commune or by forming a new commune with several other citizens. We want to preserve communal possession of the land, with periodic redistribution at long intervals.

. . .

Naturally, we would like to avoid a violent upheaval. But if there is no other way, we not only shall not renounce it but will willingly call for a revolution to help the people.

[From the proclamation *Young Russia* (*Molodaia Rossiia*), written by P. G. Zaichnevskii and others and published in Saint Petersburg, in or just before May of 1862, without having gone through the censor:]

Russia is entering the revolutionary period of its existence. Examine the life of all its classes and you will see that society is at present divided into two groups, which are hostile to one another because their interests are diametrically opposed.

. . .

The party that is oppressed by all and humiliated by all is the party of the *common people*.

Over it stands a small group of contented and happy men. They are the landowners . . . the merchants . . . the government officials— in short, all those who possess property, either inherited or acquired. At their head stands the tsar. They cannot exist without him, nor he without them. If either falls the other will be destroyed. . . . This is the *imperial* party.

. . .

There is only one way out of this oppressive and terrible situation which is destroying contemporary man, and that is revolution— bloody and merciless revolution—a revolution that must radically change all the foundations of contemporary society without exception and destroy the supporters of the present regime.

We do not fear it, although we know that rivers of blood will flow and innocent victims too will perish; we foresee all this, but we still welcome its approach; we are ready to sacrifice our own lives to hasten the coming of what we have long desired.

. . .

We demand that the present despotic government be converted into a federated republican regional union, with all power transferred to a national assembly and to regional assemblies. We do not know the number of regions into which the Russian land should be divided, nor which guberniias will be included in a given region; the population itself should decide this question.

Each region should consist of agricultural communes, all members of which shall have equal rights.

Every individual must without fail join one of the communes. The commune shall allot him a certain amount of land, which, to be sure, he can refuse or rent out. He shall also have complete freedom to live outside the commune and to practice any trade he wishes, but he shall be obliged to pay in taxes that amount which the commune prescribes.

The land allotted to each member of the commune shall be given to him, not in life tenure, but only for a certain number of years, at the end of which the mir shall carry out a redistribution of the land. All other property of the members of the commune shall remain inviolable during their lifetime, but on their death it shall become the property of the commune.

We demand that all the judicial authorities be elected by the people themselves, that to the communes be reserved the right to try their members in all matters concerning them alone.

We demand that, in addition to a national assembly composed of delegates from the entire Russian land, which shall meet in the [national] capital, there should also be regional assemblies in the capital city of each region, composed solely of representatives from the latter. The national assembly shall decide all matters of foreign policy, examine disputes between regions, pass legislation, supervise the execution of previously enacted laws, appoint administrators for the regions, and determine the overall amount of taxation. The regional assemblies shall decide matters pertaining exclusively to the region in the capital city of which they meet.

. . .

We demand the establishment of community factories which must be managed by persons elected by the community and obligated to render periodic accounts to it; we demand the establishment of community shops in which goods shall be sold at a price that corresponds to their real cost, and not at whatever price the tradesman thinks suitable to enrich himself as rapidly as possible.

We demand that children be brought up by the community, and that they be maintained at public expense until they complete their schooling. . . .

We demand the complete emancipation of women and the granting to them of all those political and civil rights that men will enjoy; we demand the abolition of marriage, as a phenomenon to the highest degree immoral and unthinkable if the sexes are to be completely equal; consequently [we also demand] the abolition of the family, which hampers man's development and makes the abolition of inheritance inconceivable.

· · ·

We demand that all regions be granted the opportunity to decide by majority vote whether or not they wish to join the federated Russian republic.

We fully realize that the clause in our program concerning regional federation cannot be carried into effect immediately. We are even firmly convinced that the revolutionary party that takes over the government—if the movement is successful—must retain the present system of political (although naturally not administrative) centralization, so that by this means the other basic elements of economic and social life can be introduced in the shortest possible time. The party must seize dictatorial power and stop at nothing. The elections to the national assembly must take place under the influence of the government, which will then see to it that its membership does not include any supporters of the present regime (if there are any such left alive).

· · ·

Soon, soon will come the day when we shall unfurl the great banner of the future, the red banner; and with a loud shout—"Long live the social and democratic Russian republic!"—we shall march on the Winter Palace

and destroy those who live there. It may happen that the whole affair will end simply with the extermination of the tsar's family, that is, a hundred or so people; but it may happen—and this is more likely—that the entire imperial party will stand behind the tsar as one man, because this will be a question of its very existence.

In the latter case, with complete faith in ourselves, in our strength, in the sympathy of the people toward us, and in the glorious future of a Russia whose destiny it is to be the first to accomplish the great work of socialism, we need only shout: "Take up your axes!" and then—then kill the men of the imperial party without pity, as they do not pity us now, kill them on the square if that foul scum dares to come out, kill them in their houses, kill them in the narrow alleys of the towns, kill them in the wide streets of the capital cities, kill them in the villages and hamlets!

Remember that when this time comes, he who is not with us will be against us, and he who is against us is our enemy; and enemies must be destroyed by all possible means.

But do not forget to repeat upon every new victory in every battle: "Long live the socialist and democratic Russian republic!"

XV:47. PISAREV'S VIEWS, 1861-1865

Dmitrii Ivanovich Pisarev (1840-68) while still in his early twenties attracted the admiration of the radical younger generation through his articles in the journal *Russkoe slovo* (1861-66), in which he expounded his doctrine of nihilism or, as he called it, "realism." In 1862 Pisarev was arrested for writing an article for an illegal publication, and he spent the next four years in prison in the Petropavlovsk fortress in Saint Petersburg. There, characteristically enough, he was permitted to continue his career as a publicist, so that most of his contributions to *Russkoe slovo*, including some of those excerpted here, were in a sense subsidized by the tsarist government.

Reference: D. I. Pisarev, *Sochineniia*, 4 vols. (Moscow: Gosudarstvennoe Izd. Khudozhestvennoi Literatury, 1955-56), 1:118-19, 120, 133-35 [1861 article]; 2:11 [1862 article], 363-65 [article on "Flowers"]; D. I. Pisarev, *Izbrannye sochineniia*, 2 vols. (Moscow: Gosudarstvennoe Izd. Khudozhestvennoi Literatury, 1935), 2:88, 101-02, 105, 108 [1864 article]. The 1861 article "Nineteenth Century Scholasticism" is translated in full (by J. Katzer) in Dmitry Pisarev, *Selected Philosophical, Social, and Political Essays* (Moscow: Foreign Languages Publishing House, 1958), pp. 72-114. Portions of that article and of "The Realists" are given in Edie, Scanlan, and Zeldin, eds., *Russian Philosophy*, 2:71-78 and 79-96.

[From his article "Nineteenth-Century Scholasticism," published in 1861:]

Common sense and a considerable dose of humor and skepticism form, in my opinion, the most salient feature of the purely Russian mind. . . . On this account it seems to me that no philosophy in the world will be assimilated by the Russian mind as thoroughly and easily

as the healthy and vigorous materialism of our time. . . . If all men would be egoists by conviction in the strictest sense, i.e. if everyone would be concerned only about himself and would obey only his emotional urges, without creating for himself any artificial concepts of ideals and duties, and without interfering in other people's affairs, then truly this world would be a more comfortable place to live in than it is today.

. . .

Man is by nature a very kind creature, and if his temper is not soured by contradictions and inhibitive training, if he is not expected to perform unnatural moral juggling acts, he will spontaneously develop the most amicable feelings toward the people around him and will help them in adversity, for his own satisfaction and not out of a sense of duty, i.e. of his own free will and not under moral constraint.

. . .

Only that which is rotten, only that which, like an Egyptian mummy, crumbles into dust from a current of air, fears the touch of criticism. A living idea, like a fresh flower after the rain, gains strength and grows all the more after meeting the test of skepticism. . . . Every generation destroys the outlook on the world of the preceding generation; what seemed irrefutable yesterday no longer stands up today; absolute eternal verities exist only for nonhistoric peoples like the Eskimos, the Papuans, and the Chinese. . . .

. . . Men who have not yet attained the ultimate limit of their development, i.e. who have not yet stagnated, should be allowed to talk, write, and publish; they should be allowed, by using their native skepticism, to shake up the shopworn goods, the stale rubbish, which you call the "accepted authorities." . . . If the authority is a sham, doubt will smash it to pieces, and a good thing too; if it is necessary and useful, doubt will take it in its hands, turn it this way and that, examine it from all sides, and put it back where it belongs. In a word, here is our ultimatum: what can be smashed, should be smashed; what holds up under the blow is serviceable; what breaks into smithereens is trash. At any rate, strike out right and left; it will and can do no harm.

[From his article "Bazarov" (after the hero of Turgenev's *Fathers and Sons*), 1862:]

Thus, Bazarov in all situations and in all matters acts just as he pleases, or as he finds advantageous and convenient. He is governed solely by personal desires or personal considerations. Neither above himself nor outside himself nor within himself does he recognize any regulating authority, any

moral law, any principle. There is no lofty goal before him; there is no lofty purpose in his mind; but he has enormous strength notwithstanding. "But this is an immoral man! A villain, a monster!" I hear indignant readers exclaim from all sides. . . . If Bazarovism is a disease, it is the disease of our time. . . . You may look upon Bazarovism as you please—that is your affair; but you cannot stop it any more than the cholera.

[From his article "Flowers of Innocent Humor," 1864:]

The acclimatization of natural science in our society is immeasurably more useful to our common people than the publication of books designed especially for them, or all kinds of virtuous talk about the need to draw closer to the common people and to love them.

If natural science enriches our society with thinking men, if our agronomists, industrialists, and capitalists of various types learn how to think, then at the same time these people will learn to understand both their own true interests and the needs of the world that surrounds them. They will then realize that these true interests and these needs merge together completely; they will realize that it is more profitable and more pleasant to increase the general wealth of the country than to squeeze or swindle the last penny out of the meager pockets of the producers and consumers. . . . This assumption may appear idyllic, but to assert that it is unrealizable means to assume that the capitalist is not a human being and cannot be expected ever to become a human being. . . .

. . . To multiply the number of thinking men is the alpha and omega of any rational social development. Consequently, the study of natural science today constitutes the most crying need in our society.

[From his article "The Realists," 1864:]

Now as before, I have always been deeply convinced that thought, and thought alone, can reform and regenerate the whole pattern of human life. Whatever forces us to use our minds and helps us to think is unconditionally useful. Yet the ultimate goal of all our thinking and of all the activities of every honest man must be to solve once and for all the inescapable problem of the hungry and the naked. Outside this problem there is absolutely nothing worth worrying, pondering, or troubling ourselves over.

. . .

The machine age imperatively requires voluntary associations among workers; yet such rational associations are possible only if the workers have reached a rather high level of mental development. For if the workers who come into contact with machines continue to act in a disorganized way, then poverty, stupidity, and demoralization will immediately set in among the working population with amazing ease and rapidity. . . .

. . . The tragic misunderstanding between science and life will recur as long as the pernicious rift between mental labor and muscular labor continues. Until science ceases to be an upper-class luxury, until it becomes the daily bread of every healthy human being, until it penetrates the mind of the artisan, the factory worker, and the simple peasant, the poverty and immorality of the toiling masses will continue to increase, despite all the preaching of moralists, the

almsgiving of philanthropists, the calculations of economists, and the theories of socialists. There is only one evil for mankind: ignorance; and for this evil there is only one remedy: science.

. . .

The capitalist has brains and wealth. These two advantages secure his domination over labor. But this domination, depending on the circumstances, can be either harmful or useful to the people. If the capitalist is given some kind of vague half-education, he will become a leech. But let him receive a thorough, solid, truly human education, and that same capitalist will become not a benevolent philanthropist but an intelligent and judicious director of the people's labor, that is, a person a hundred times more useful than any philanthropist.

. . .

It can be said without the slightest exaggeration that the popularization of science constitutes the most important universal task of our age.

XV:48. BAKUNIN'S ANARCHISM, 1867-1873

Mikhail Aleksandrovich Bakunin (1814-76), the "apostle of anarchy," paid for his participation in the central European revolutions of 1848-49 by being arrested in Austria, turned over to Russia, and removed from circulation for more than a decade. Escaping from Siberian exile in 1861, he spent the last fifteen years of his life back at his old vocation in western Europe. The following excerpts are from works of that mature period of his turbulent career. They illustrate various facets of his ideology, and show, among other things, why and how he clashed with the Marxists.

Reference: M. A. Bakunin, *Izbrannye sochineniia*, 5 vols. (Petrograd: Golos truda, 1920-22), 3:128, 147, 190-91 [selection of 1867], 96-97 [program of 1868]; 5:197-98, 200-01, 202 [Italian letter]; 1:67-68, 95, 140, 233-34, 235, 237, 254. The translations are based in part on G. P. Maximoff, comp. and ed., *The Political Philosophy of Bakunin: Scientific Anarchism* (Glencoe, Ill.: The Free Press, 1953), especially pp. 138-39, 141, 210-11, 274-75, 286-89, 296-97, 374, 378-79, 410, 412-13 (not in the same sequence).

[From "Federalism, Socialism, and Antitheologism," a proposal submitted to the Central Committee of the League of Peace and Liberty, in Geneva, December 1867:]

We recognize the absolute right of every nation, small or large, of every people, weak or strong, and of every province and every commune to complete autonomy, provided the internal organization of any such unit does not constitute a menace and danger to the autonomy and freedom of neighboring lands.

. . .

Freedom without socialism is privilege and injustice; . . . socialism without freedom becomes slavery.

. . .

The state is the most flagrant, the most cynical, and the most complete negation of humanity. It rends apart the universal solidarity of all men upon the earth, and it unites some of them only in order to destroy, conquer, and enslave all the rest. It takes under its protection only its own citizens, and it recognizes human rights, humanity, and civilization only within the confines of its own boundaries. And since it does not recognize any rights outside its own confines, it quite logically arrogates to itself the right to treat with the most ferocious inhumanity all the foreign populations it is able at its own discretion to pillage, exterminate, or enslave.

. . .

This flagrant negation of humanity, which constitutes the very essence of the state, is from the point of view of the latter the supreme duty and the greatest virtue: it is called *patriotism* and it constitutes the *transcendent morality* of the state. . . . From the point of view of ordinary human morality, abuse, oppression, and robbery are considered crimes. On the other hand, in public life and from the point of view of patriotism, when this is done for the greater glory of the state in order to preserve or enlarge its power, all this becomes a duty and a virtue. . . .

. . . The history of ancient and modern states is nothing more than a series of revolting crimes; kings and ministers of past and present, of all times and of all countries, statesmen, diplomats, bureaucrats, and military men, if judged from the point of view of simple morality and human justice, deserve the gallows or penal servitude a hundred times over, a thousand times over; for there is no horror, cruelty, sacrilege, perjury, imposture, infamous transaction, cynical theft, brazen robbery, or foul treason that has not been committed and is not still being committed daily by representatives of the state, with no other excuse than these elastic words, so convenient and at the same time so terrible: *the interest of the state.*

Terrible words indeed! For they have corrupted and dishonored more people in official circles and in the governing classes of society than Christianity itself. As soon as these words are uttered everything falls silent and disappears: honesty, honor, justice, right, compassion itself, and logic and common sense disappear with them; black becomes white and white becomes black, the horrible becomes humane, and the most dastardly treacheries and most atrocious crimes become meritorious acts.

[From "Our Program," composed by Bakunin together with Nikolai Ivanovich Zhukovskii (d. 1895) and published in the émigré newspaper *Narodnoe delo* in 1868:]

We desire the complete intellectual, socioeconomic, and political emancipation of the people.

I. *Intellectual freedom,* because without it political and social freedom cannot be complete or lasting. Belief in God, belief in the immortality of the soul, and all kinds of idealism in general . . . on the one hand serve as an indispensable mainstay and justification for despotism, for all kinds of privilege, and for the exploitation of the people and on the other hand demoralize the people themselves, dividing them into two groups with mutually opposed aspirations and thereby depriving them of the energy required to win their natural rights and to build a fully free and happy life.

From this it clearly follows that we are advocates of atheism and materialism.

II. *The socioeconomic freedom* of the people, without which any freedom would be a detestable and meaningless lie. The economic life of a people has always provided the cornerstone and true explanation of its political existence. All previous or currently existing political and civil organizations in the world have been maintained upon the following basic foundations: conquest, the right of property inheritance, the family rights of father and husband, and the sanctification of all these principles by religion; and all this taken together constitutes the essence of the state. The inevitable result of the entire state system has been and had to be the slavish subordination of the unskilled and ignorant majority to the so-called educated, exploiting minority. A state without political and legal privileges based upon economic privileges is unthinkable.

Desiring the true and complete liberation of the people, we seek (1) the abolition of the right of property inheritance, and (2) the equalization of women's rights, both political and socioeconomic, with those of men; we consequently desire the abolition of family rights and of marriage, both ecclesiastical and civil, which is inseparably connected with the right of inheritance.

. . .

We make two fundamental principles the basis of economic justice:

Land belongs only to those who cultivate it with their own hands—to agricultural communes. Capital and all the implements of labor belong to the workers—to workers' associations.

III. The political organization of the future must be nothing other than a free federation of free workers, both in agriculture and in industrial artels (associations) in the factory.

Therefore, in the name of political freedom,

we want first and foremost the complete destruction of the state; we want the eradication of the state system with all its ecclesiastical, political, bureaucratic (both military and civil), legal, academic, and financial and economic institutions.

We want complete freedom for all peoples now oppressed by the [Russian] Empire, with the right of complete self-determination on the basis of their own instincts, needs, and desires; so that by federating from the bottom up, those among them who *wish* to be members of the Russian nation could jointly create a truly free and happy society in a friendly and federal union with *similar* societies in Europe and throughout the world.

[From "An Epistle to My Italian Friends," published in *La Roma del popolo,* October 1, 1871, in anticipation of the workers' congress called for November 1, 1871, in Rome:]

Our program [is as follows]. . . .

Peace, freedom, and happiness for all the oppressed!

War upon all the oppressors and plunderers!

The full restoration to the workers, organized in associations, of capital, all tools of labor, and raw materials; land to those who cultivate it with their own hands.

Freedom, justice, and brotherhood for all human beings born upon the earth.

Equality for all.

For everyone without distinction, all facilities for his development, upbringing, and education, and an equal opportunity to work for a living.

The organization of society through a free federation, formed from the bottom up, of workers' associations—industrial, agricultural, and scientific, as well as associations of artists and literary men—first into communes, then the federation of communes into regions, of regions into nations, and of nations into a fraternal international union.

. . .

All other classes [except the urban and rural proletariat] must vanish from the face of the earth, not as individuals, but as classes. Socialism is not cruel; it is a thousand times more humane than Jacobinism, by which I mean political revolution. It is not directed against individuals, not even against the most nefarious among them, since it realizes

perfectly well that all men, good or bad, are the inevitable product of the social position created for them by society and history. True, in the first days of the revolution the socialists will naturally not be able to prevent the people from giving vent to their fury by doing away with a few hundred of the most odious, most rabid, and most dangerous individuals. But once that whirlwind passes, they will oppose with all their might hypocritical political and juridical butchery organized in cold blood.

Socialism will wage a ruthless war against "social positions," but not against men. . . .

Consequently, the social revolution will not only spare [the other classes] but, having struck them down and deprived them of their weapons, will raise them up and say to them: "And now, dear comrades, that you have become our equals, get down to work alongside of us. In work, as in everything else, it is the first step that is difficult, and we will help you in a brotherly way to take the first step."

. . .

An uprising of the urban proletariat would not be enough; with that we would have only a political revolution which would necessarily produce a natural and legitimate reaction on the part of the peasantry, and that reaction, or merely the indifference of the peasants, would strangle the urban revolution, as happened recently in France. Only an all-embracing revolution would be sufficiently strong to overthrow the organized power of the state, supported as it is by all the resources of the wealthy classes. But an all-embracing revolution is a social revolution, that is, a simultaneous revolution in cities and villages. This is what must be organized.

[From *The State and Anarchy,* Bakunin's major Russian book, 1873:]

In our present troubled times, a strong state can have only one firm foundation: military and bureaucratic centralization. There is this essential distinction between a monarchy and the most democratic republic: in a monarchy the bureaucratic world oppresses and plunders the people for the greater benefit of the privileged, propertied classes and of their own purses, in the name of the monarch; in a republic it will oppress and plunder the people in exactly the same way, and for the sake of the same classes and

purses, but in the name of the will of the
people. In a republic the self-styled people,
the people in a legal sense, who are allegedly
represented by the state, stifle and will continue to stifle the real and living people. But
it will hardly be any easier on the people if
the stick used to beat them is called the
people's stick. . . .

   . . . No state, however democratic its
forms may be—and not even the reddest
political republic, which is "popular" in the
same sense as that lie that goes by the name
of "popular" representation—is capable of
giving the people what they need, that is,
the free organization of their own interests
from the bottom up, with no interference,
tutelage, or coercion from above, because
every state, even the most republican and
the most democratic state—even the would-
be popular state conceived by Mr. Marx—is
in its essence only a system for governing the
masses from above, through an intelligent and
therefore a privileged minority which allegedly understands the genuine interests of the
people better than the people themselves.

· · ·

But the social revolution cannot be the
solitary revolution of a single people: it is an
international revolution in its very essence.
This means that the Slavs, in seeking their
freedom and for the sake of their freedom,
must join their aspirations and the organization of their national forces with the aspirations and the organization of the national
forces of all other countries: the Slavic
proletariat must enter en masse into the International Association of Workers.

· · ·

The time will come when there will be no
more states (and all the efforts of the social-
revolutionary party in Europe are directed
toward destroying them); the time will come
when upon the ruins of political states there
will be founded, completely freely and
organized from the bottom upward, a voluntary, fraternal union of voluntary producers'
associations, communes, and regional federations, embracing in freedom, and therefore
without distinction, men of all languages and
nationalities; and then the way to the sea will
be equally open to all. . . .

   Air travel will be very important. The
earth's atmosphere is an ocean that penetrates
everywhere; its shores extend everywhere, so

that in relation to it all men without exception
are coastal dwellers, even those living in the
remotest places. But until air travel replaces
sea travel, the coastal dwellers will continue
to be in the forefront in every way and will
comprise a kind of aristocracy among men.

· · ·

We have already expressed several times
our profound abhorrence for the theories of
Lassalle and Marx, which counsel the workers—
if not as an ultimate ideal, at least as a chief
immediate aim—*to form a people's state,*
which, as they explain it, will be nothing less
than "the proletariat raised to the position of
a ruling class."

   One may ask then: if the proletariat is to
be the ruling class, over whom will it rule?
The answer is that there will remain another
proletariat which will be subjected to this
new domination, this new state. It may be,
for example, the peasant "rabble," which, as
we know, does not stand in great favor with
the Marxists, and which, being on a lower
level of culture, probably will be ruled by the
city and factory proletariat; or if we consider
this question from the national point of view,
let us say that the Slavs, for instance, will be
placed, for precisely the same reason, in the
same position of slavish subjection to the
victorious German proletariat as the latter
now occupies with respect to its own bourgeoisie.

   If there is a state, there must necessarily
be domination, and consequently slavery; a
state without slavery, overt or disguised, is
unthinkable—and that is why we are enemies
of the state.

   What does it mean: "the proletariat raised
to the position of a ruling class?" Is it possible
that the proletariat as a whole will be at the
head of the government? There are about forty
million Germans. Will all the forty million
really be members of the government? The
whole people will govern and there will be no
one to be governed. Then there will be no
government, no state; but if there is a state
in existence there will be people who are
governed, and there will be slaves.

   This dilemma is solved very simply in
Marxist theory. By a people's government
they mean that people will be governed by
means of a small number of representatives
elected by the people. General and universal
suffrage—the right of the whole people to

elect its so-called popular representatives and rulers of the state—this is the last word of the Marxists as well as of the democratic school. And this is a lie behind which lurks the despotism of a governing minority, a lie that is all the more dangerous in that it appears as the ostensible expression of the people's will.

Thus, from whatever point of view we approach the problem, we arrive at the same sorry result: the rule of great masses of people by a privileged minority. But, the Marxists say, this minority will consist of workers. Well, if you like, of *former* workers, but ones who, having become rulers or representatives of the people, will cease to be workers and will begin to look down upon the world of the common laborers from their governing heights. They will no longer represent the people but only themselves and their own claims to govern the people.

· · ·

[The Marxists] say that this dictatorial yoke of the state is a necessary transitional measure in order to attain the complete emancipation of the people: anarchism or freedom is the goal, the state or dictatorship is the means. Thus to free the working masses it is first necessary to enslave them.

. . . They maintain that only a dictatorship—their own dictatorship, of course—can create the will of the people; to which we answer: No dictatorship can have any other aim but that of self-perpetuation, and it can only beget and instill slavery in a people that endures it; freedom can be created only by freedom, that is, by a rebellion in which all the people take part and by the voluntary organization of the toiling masses from the bottom up.

· · ·

The proletariat must bring about a revolution in order to capture the state—a heroic expedient. In our opinion, once the proletariat seizes possession of the state, it must immediately proceed to destroy it as an everlasting prison for the toiling masses. Yet according to the theory of Mr. Marx, the people not only should not destroy the state but should strengthen and reinforce it and should transfer it in this form into the hands of their benefactors, guardians, and teachers, the leaders of the Communist Party—in a word, to Mr. Marx and his friends, who will begin to emancipate them in their own fashion. They will concentrate the reins of government in strong hands, because an ignorant people requires a great deal of tutelage. They will create a single state bank, concentrating in its hands all commercial, industrial, agricultural, and even scientific production; and they will divide the mass of people into two armies, industrial and agricultural, under the direct command of state engineers who will constitute a new privileged scientific-political class.

· · ·

On the pan-German banner there is inscribed: "The preservation and strengthening of the state at any cost." But on our social-revolutionary banner there is inscribed in fiery letters of blood: "The destruction of all states, the annihilation of bourgeois civilization, voluntary organization from the bottom up by means of voluntary unions, the organization of the unbound toiling masses and of all liberated mankind—the creation of a new world for all mankind in common."

XV:49. NECHAEV'S PROGRAM, 1869

Sergei Gennadievich Nechaev (1847-82), one of the most fanatic Russian revolutionaries of any generation, rose to notoriety in the late sixties and at that time founded a revolutionary organization called "The People's Retribution" (Narodnaia Rasprava), of which seventy-nine members were brought to trial in 1871. Nechaev himself, turned over by Switzerland to Russia and convicted of the murder of his follower Ivanov, spent the last decade of his life in confinement. While abroad he published in Geneva a small revolutionary journal (also called *Narodnaia rasprava,* 1869-71). The leading article of its first number, in 1869, contained Nechaev's program, reading in part as follows.

Reference: Glinskii, *Revoliutsionnyi period*, pt. 1, p. 411; Vladimir L. Burtsev, comp. and ed., *Za sto let, 1800-1896: Sbornik po istorii politicheskikh i obshchestvennykh dvizhenii v Rossii* (London, 1897), pp. 91, 92, 94. (The Burtsev volume contains most of the article but omits some of the early paragraphs; Glinskii gives them but not the rest.) See also B. P. Koz'min, ed., *Nechaev i nechaevtsy, sbornik materialov* (Moscow: Gos. Sots.-ekonom. Izd., 1931).

The nationwide revolt of the martyred Russian people is inevitable and imminent! . . . We, that is, that part of our nation's youth which has managed in one way or another to obtain an education, must clear a path for it; that is, we must remove all the obstacles in its way and prepare all the favorable conditions.

In view of this inevitability and imminence, we consider it essential to unite all the separate revolutionary forces in Russia into a single and indissoluble whole; in consequence, we have decided to publish, in the name of the Revolutionary Committee, leaflets from which all those who think as we do, scattered in various parts of Russia, all those who work for the sacred cause of regeneration, even if we do not know them, will always be able to see what we want and where we are going.

These leaflets obviously have neither a literary nor a scholarly purpose. Let those who have plenty of leisure time continue to console themselves and mislead others by idle talk of literature and science, of education and upbringing, of progress and civilization!

We have no time!

. . .

A thought has value for us only to the extent that it can serve the great cause of radical and universal destruction. But none of the books available today contains such thoughts. Those who learn the science of revolution from books will always be worthless as revolutionaries. A thought capable of serving a people's revolution can only develop out of the revolutionary actions of the people and must be the result of a series of practical experiments and manifestations which are directed in every way and always unswervingly toward the same goal of merciless destruction. Anything that does not follow this path is for us alien and hostile.

. . .

Bakunin is right in urging us to leave our academies, universities, and schools and go to the people. This idea is correct but far from new. The question is *how to go to the people and what to do among the people.*

. . .

We have but a single negative, unalterable plan—merciless destruction.

We refuse outright to work out a plan for future conditions of life, for such planning is incompatible with the present state of things.

We therefore consider any purely theoretical thinking to be fruitless.

We consider the work of destruction to be such an enormous and difficult task that we are devoting all our efforts to it, and we do not intend to delude ourselves by thinking that we will have sufficient strength and ability left for creation.

For that reason we are undertaking solely the destruction of the existing social system; the task of creating is not for us but for those who follow us.

. . .

Keeping in mind our aim of exterminating the tsar and all his family, servants, and retainers . . . we will nevertheless leave Aleksandr Nikolaevich [Alexander II] alone for the time being, and here is why:

A storm of popular indignation and hatred is already beginning to gather over the head of this weak-minded and colorless despot, who is dependent upon the minds and will of his mistresses and loathsome favorites. The defrauded, despoiled, and hungry people are beginning to open their eyes; they will soon see clearly the cause of their intolerable sufferings. . . . After nine years of their new form of slavery [the peasant emancipation], in 1870, on the anniversary of [the rebellions of] Razin and Pugachev, this well-founded hatred will break like the wrath of God upon the high and mighty, who wallow in debauchery and turpitude. But let him live, this executioner, despoiler, and tormentor of the people, who dares to call himself a liberator; let him live until that time, until that moment, when the wrath of the people bursts forth, when the lowly masses he now tortures awaken from their long, agonizing sleep and solemnly pass sentence on him; when the free peasant, having broken the chains of bondage, personally smashes his skull and with it the odious crown, on the day of the *people's retribution.*

Yes, we will let the tsar live until the day when the peasants pass judgment upon him.

. . .

. . . We will preserve him for a solemn and agonizing execution before the liberated common people on the ruins of the state.

For the present we will set about without delay to exterminate his Arakcheevs—those monsters, considered to be the pillars of the state, who are dressed in resplendent uniforms bespattered with the people's blood.

XV:50. NECHAEV'S "CATECHISM OF A REVOLUTIONIST," 1869

The famous "Catechism of a Revolutionist," written in code, was taken by Nechaev to Russia when he returned from Switzerland in 1869 and is commonly attributed to him. It expresses ideas that he advocated, and it was found by the police when they arrested some of his followers. But it also seems quite possible that the aging Bakunin, temporarily attracted by the twenty-two-year-old zealot, had a hand in its composition. From the excerpts below one can perceive the importance of this document for the subsequent development of certain strains of revolutionary thought in Russia—and one can also understand why the government itself, having deciphered the document, took the initiative in publishing it.

Reference: Vasilii Iakovlevich Iakovlev [known under the pseudonyms B. Bazilevskii and V. Bogucharskii], ed., *Gosudarstvennye prestupleniia v Rossii v XIX veke, sbornik. . . .*3 vols. (St. Petersburg: Russkaia Skoropechatnia, 1906), 1:183-85; translation based on Max Nomad, *Apostles of Revolution* (Boston: Little, Brown, 1939), pp. 228-33. Recently another translation has appeared in Dmytryshyn, *Imperial Russia*, pp. 241-47.

The Revolutionist's Attitude toward Himself

1. The revolutionist is a doomed man. He has no personal interests, no pursuits, sentiments, attachments, property, not even a name. Everything in him is absorbed by a single exclusive interest, a single thought, a single passion—the revolution.

2. In the very depth of his being, not merely in word but in deed, he has broken every connection with the social order and with the entire educated world, with all the laws, proprieties, generally accepted conventions, and morality of that world. He is its ruthless foe, and should he continue to live in it, it would be solely for the purpose of destroying it the more surely.

3. The revolutionist despises every sort of doctrinairism and has renounced all human knowledge, leaving it to future generations. He knows only one science, the science of destruction. For this purpose and for this purpose alone he now makes a study of mechanics, physics, chemistry, and possibly medicine. For this purpose he studies day and night the living science of human beings, their characters, situations, and all the conditions of the present social system in all its various strata. There is but a single goal—the quickest possible destruction of that vile system.

4. He despises public opinion. He despises and hates present-day social morality in all its impulses and manifestations. For him whatever side aids the triumph of the revolution is moral; whatever hinders him is immoral and criminal. . . .

6. Severe toward himself, he must also be severe toward others. All tender, softening sentiments of kinship, friendship, love,

gratitude, and even honor itself must be suppressed in him by a single cold passion for the revolutionary cause. For him there exists only one comfort, one consolation, one reward, and one satisfaction—the success of the revolution. Day and night he must have one thought, one goal—ruthless destruction. Striving coolly and tirelessly toward this goal, he must be ready to perish himself and to destroy with his own hands everything that hinders the realization of his goal. . . .

The Relations of the Revolutionist toward His Revolutionary Comrades

· · ·

10. Each comrade must have at hand several revolutionists of the second and third degree, i.e. such as are not entirely dedicated. He must regard them as part of the total revolutionary capital placed at his disposal. He must spend his portion of the capital economically, always striving to extract the greatest possible use from it. . . .

The Revolutionist's Relations with Society

· · ·

13. The revolutionist enters the world of the state, of classes, and of so-called educated men and lives in it believing only in its fullest and quickest destruction. He is not a revolutionist if he is attached to anything in this world. If he can, he will undertake the destruction of any existing condition, relationship, or person belonging to this world; everybody and everything must be equally hateful to him. . . .

14. With the aim of ruthless destruction, the revolutionist may and frequently must live in society, pretending to be something entirely different from what he is. The revolutionist must penetrate everywhere, into all of the lower and middle classes, into the

merchant's store, into the church, into the nobleman's home, into the bureaucratic and military world, into literature, into the Third Department [the secret police], and even into the Winter Palace. . . .

The Attitude of the Association toward the People

22. The [revolutionary] association has no aim other than the complete liberation and happiness of the people, i.e. of the people who live by manual labor. But, convinced that this liberation and the attainment of this happiness are possible only through an all-destroying popular revolution, the association will exert all its efforts and all its resources to further the development and extension of those misfortunes and those evils that must at length exhaust the patience of the people and drive them to a general uprising.

23. By popular revolution the association does not have in mind a regulated movement after the classical Western model, a movement that, always bowing to property rights and to the traditions of the social systems of so-called civilization and morality, has heretofore limited itself everywhere to overthrowing one political form in order to replace it by another and has striven to create a so-called revolutionary state. The only revolution that will bring salvation to the people is one that completely eradicates any sort of state structure and annihilates all of Russia's state traditions, institutions, and classes.

24. Therefore the association does not intend to foist on the people any sort of organization from above. The future organization will no doubt evolve out of the popular movement and out of life itself. But this is the task of future generations. Our task is terrible, complete, universal, and merciless destruction.

25. Therefore, in getting closer to the people, we must first of all join with those elements of national life which, since the foundation of the Muscovite state power, have never ceased to protest, not in word but in deed, against everything that is directly or indirectly connected with the state: against the nobility, the bureaucracy, the clergy, the merchants' world, and the blood-sucking kulak. Let us join hands with the savage world of the bandits—the only genuine revolutionists in Russia.

26. To unite this world into one invincible, all-destroying force—this is the purpose of our organization, our conspiracy, our cause.

XV:51. LAVROV'S VIEWS CA. 1870-1873

Petr Lavrovich Lavrov (1823-1900), artillery colonel, mathematics professor, and influential ideologist of Russian populism, published his "Historical Letters" in the Petersburg journal *Nedelia* at the end of the sixties, and in 1870 they appeared in book form. Some of the ideas the censor permitted "Mirtov" (his pen name) to express are presented in the first group of excerpts below. The second group of excerpts is from his article "Our Program," printed in an irregular journal called *Vpered* (Forward), which Lavrov published from 1873 to 1877, first in Zurich and then in London.

Reference: P. L. Mirtov (P. L. Lavrov), *Istoricheskie pis'ma* (St. Petersburg, 1870), pp. 30, 43, 63, 108-10, 116, 158-59, 206, 207; Burtsev, *Za sto let,* pp. 106-12 ["Our Program"]. A scholarly translation of the letters has recently appeared: Peter Lavrov, *Historical Letters,* trans. with an introduction and notes by James P. Scanlan (Berkeley and Los Angeles: University of California Press, 1967).

[From "Historical Letters," ca. 1870:]

The physical, mental, and moral development of the individual, the incorporation of truth and justice in social relationships—this is the brief formula that encompasses, I believe, everything that can be regarded as progress.

. . .

Just as in our own day the overwhelming majority of mankind is doomed to ceaseless physical labor, dulling the mind and blunting the moral sense, and to probable death from starvation and disease, so in all times has the majority been in a similar situation. The ever-toiling human machine, often hungry and always anxious for the morrow, is hardly better off today than it was in any other period. For it there has been no progress.

. . .

I will absolve myself of the responsibility for the cost in blood of my own cultural development only by using this very cultural

development to lessen the amount of evil,
present and future. If I am a truly cultured
person, it is *my duty* to do this; nor does
this duty weigh heavily, since it coincides
exactly with what brings me the greatest enjoyment: in seeking out and spreading the
truth, in determining for myself the most
equitable form of society, and in striving to
make it a reality, I increase my own enjoyment, and at the same time I do all I can for
the suffering majority, present and future.

· · ·

What is needed are energetic, fanatical
people ready to take any risk and ready to
make any sacrifice. We need martyrs, whose
legend would outgrow by far their true worth,
their actual merit. . . . Their legend would
inspire thousands with the energy that is
needed for the struggle. . . .

. . . Individuals who can think critically
and strive energetically must fight, not for
the sake of fighting alone, but to win victory.
. . . They must join forces, assume the leadership of a party, and give guidance to others.
Thus an organized force will emerge.

· · ·

The organization of a party is essential to
attain victory.

· · ·

Critical thought organizes the struggle of
labor associations against monopoly capital
and sets up a new economic ideal. It acknowl-
edges the need for economic security, but it
demands a social order within which individuality would be guaranteed. . . . This is an
idealization of labor. . . . It means labor that
provides the worker with security and ob-
tains for him full personal development and
political importance; it is labor that enjoys
all the amenities and even luxuries of life.

· · ·

The ideal of a state is . . . a union in which
the contract is binding only on those who have
had the means and the opportunity to discuss
it, who have weighed and accepted the contract freely, and who can as freely withdraw
from it and renounce everything that follows
from it.

· · ·

However broad the franchise, however
great the difference between the political
system of the United States of America and
the rule of an Asiatic khan, nevertheless both
these systems, just like all intermediate forms,

have one feature in common: the subjection
of a considerable number of people to a
contract they have not deliberately chosen,
or with which they have declared themselves
in disagreement. The state remains everywhere a compulsory obligation for a more or
less considerable part of the population of a
given territory.

[From "Our Program," ca. 1873:]

For us at the present time there are two
overall aims, two struggles in which every
thinking person must take part by siding with
either progress or reaction. . . . First, there is
the struggle of the realistic world outlook
against the theological world outlook, of
clearly recognized human needs against all
idols, theological and metaphysical, theoretical and moral; in short, the struggle of science
against religion. Second, there is the struggle
of toil against the idle enjoyment of the good
things of life, the struggle of complete equality
of the rights of the individual against monopoly
in all its forms and manifestations, the struggle
of free association against a compulsory state
system; in short, the struggle to attain a completely equitable social order.

· · ·

The *social* question is of primary importance
to us. We see in it the most important problem
of the present time, and the only possibility
for a better future. For us the only visible
means of realizing this future is through the
union of a majority of workers into a free association, through the organization of the
union for joint and powerful action, through
the victory of this organization, and through
the establishment of a new social system on
the ruins of the industrial-legal states and
classes of the present time.

· · ·

The *political* question is for us subordinate
to the social and, particularly, the economic
questions. States *in the form in which they
exist* are hostile to the working class movement, and they must all break up once and
for all in order to give way to a new social
order in which the greatest freedom of the
individual will not stand in the way of solidarity among persons with equal rights nor of
broad cooperation for the common goal. But
this is in the distant future and is a social
ideal that should continually be borne in
mind without the self-deception of hoping

that it can be realized either today or to-morrow.

. . .

The *national* question, to our mind, should completely disappear in the face of the important tasks of the social struggle. . . . Any encouragement of rivalry between races or nations is a direct denial of the international character of the social question and the unity of the struggle of the oppressed classes of society against their oppressors. . . .

. . . For the Russians, the communal ownership of land by the peasantry provides the special basis on which the future of the majority of the Russian population can develop in the way indicated by the common tasks of our time. To develop our commune in the direction of communal cultivation of the land and communal utilization of its products, to make the communal assembly the basic political element of the Russian social system, to make private property communal, and to give the peasantry the education and understanding of their social needs without which they will never be able to make use of their legal rights, no matter how extensive they may be, and will never rid themselves of exploitation by a minority, even in the event of the most successful revolution—these are the specific Russian aims that every Russian seeking progress for his native land must promote.

. . .

In our opinion, the contemporary Russian public leader must give up the antiquated notion that revolutionary ideas elaborated by a small section of the more developed minority can be foisted upon the people, or that revolutionary socialists, having overthrown the central government by a single successful blow, can step into its shoes and establish by legislation a new system, conferring benefits upon the unprepared masses. We do not want another regime ruling by force. . . .

. . . Those who desire the welfare of the people should aim, not at taking power through a successful revolution and then leading the people toward a goal that is clear only to the leaders, but at creating among the people a conscious conception of their goals and a conscious aspiration toward those goals, while making themselves no more than the executors of those social aspirations when the time comes for the social revolution.

. . .

Only by strict and intensive personal training can one develop in oneself the *capability* of useful activity among the people.

Only by gaining the confidence of the people in oneself as an individual can one create the *conditions* necessary for such activity.

Only by explaining to the people what their needs are, and by preparing them for independent and conscious activity aimed at attaining clearly understood goals, can one consider oneself a truly useful participant in the present preparation for a better future for Russia.

Only when the course of historical events itself shows that the time for the revolution has come and that the Russian people are prepared for it can one consider that one *has the right* to call upon the people to bring about this revolution. . . .

. . . Revolutions cannot be brought about artificially, for they are the product, not of the individual will, nor of the activity of a small group, but of a whole series of complex historical processes.

XV:52. MIKHAILOVSKII IN 1872-1882

The collected works of Nikolai Konstantinovich Mikhailovskii (1842-1904), literary critic and publicist, run to eight volumes. Here are some samples of his writings extending from his late twenties to his late thirties, covering such topics as the goals of the individual and of society.

Reference: N. K. Mikhailovskii, *Sochineniia N. K. Mikhailovskogo*, vols. 1-3 (of 6), 4th ed. (St. Petersburg: Russkoe Bogatstvo, 1906), vol. 1, cols. 719-21 [1872]; vol. 3, col. 515 [1875-77]; edition published by Russkoe Bogatstvo in 1897, vol. 4, cols. 451-52, 460 [1877]; vol. 5, col. 537 [1881-82].

[From his literary and journalistic notes of 1872:]

And so, where do we go? Shall we follow in the footsteps of Western civilization? But

Cleopatra had many lovers. The [London] *Times* with its apologia for profiteering represents civilization. The radicals who demand that all land be turned into state property

represent civilization. The liberals who advocate the free transfer of land, the liberals who
demand a curb on the freedom to bequeath
property and a change in the inheritance laws,
the liberals who contemplate the communal
landownership of the Middle Ages, and,
finally, the conservatives who stage a fraudulent "new social movement"—all these represent civilization. Well, which path shall we
choose? Obviously, merely to say, "Let us
follow in the footsteps of European civilization," means nothing. One has to take a stand
on some general principles that would shed
light both on the road traveled by Europe
and on our own future course.

The labor problem in Europe bears a revolutionary character, since there it requires the
transfer of the means of production into the
hands of the workers, the expropriation of the
present owners. In Russia the labor problem
is a conservative one, inasmuch as what is
needed here is merely the *retention* of the
means of production in the hands of the
workers, a guarantee of the property rights
of the present owners. In our country, even
right next to Saint Petersburg—that is, in one
of the most "Anglicized" areas, teeming with
factories, plants, parks, country houses—
there exist villages whose inhabitants live on
their own land, burn *their own* wood, eat
their own bread, wear *homemade* coats and
sheepskins from the wool and skins of *their
own* sheep. Give them a firm guarantee that
this will remain theirs, and the Russian labor
problem will be solved. And no price is too
high to achieve this end, if the significance of
a firm guarantee is properly understood. It
will be said: one cannot retain forever the
simple plow [*sokha*], the three-field system
of agriculture, and antediluvian methods of
fabricating coats and sheepskins. That is so.
But there are two ways to overcome this difficulty. One of them, commendable from the
practical point of view, is very simple and
convenient: just raise the tariff and dissolve
the village commune; that would, indeed, be
enough. Industry then would grow like a
mushroom, as in England. But this industry
would devour the worker; it would deprive
him of his property. There is another way,
much more difficult, of course; but an easy
solution is not necessarily the right one. The
other way consists in the development of
those relationships of labor and ownership

that are already in existence, albeit in a very
crude and primitive form. Naturally, this goal
cannot be achieved without large-scale intervention by the state, whose first action should
be the permanent stabilization of the agrarian
commune by means of legislation.

[From "Notes of a Layman," 1875-77:]

A system under which the majority of the
population lives on wages and a system under
which the majority consists of men who are
their own masters belong not to different
levels but to different *types* of development.
It is therefore the types of development that
must be compared here. A certain type of
development may be superior to another and
yet may be on a lower level. If one considers,
for instance, the *level of economic development* in England and in Russia, preference
must be given to the former, but this will not
prevent me from regarding the English economic system as the lower *type*. This distinction between levels and types of development
is very important; if it were always kept in
mind, it might save us from a great many misunderstandings and much futile bickering.

[From "Letters about Truth and Untruth,"
1877:]

All intellectual and psychological processes take place within the individual and
only there; he alone feels, thinks, suffers,
rejoices. This is an elementary truth, yet one
must keep it firmly in mind and hold on to
it without despising its banality, for a great
deal of political sophistry has been built upon
the distortion of this truth. All social groupings, however high sounding and intrinsically
attractive their names, have only relative
value. One should cherish them only insofar
as they contribute to the development of the
individual, preserve him from suffering, and
expand the sphere of his enjoyment. . . . The
individual should never be sacrificed; he is
sacred and inviolable, and all one's mental
efforts should be directed toward watching
as carefully as possible over his fate in every
particular situation and toward taking the
side that will enable him to triumph.

. . .

The interests of the individual are the
criterion by which the value of any association should be judged, be it a party, a group,
the family, the nation, or anything else. . . .

This means that in all political problems one must focus one's thinking not on the interests of the nation, the state, the commune, the province, or the federation but on those of the individual. He will be the center whence the rays of truth will shine forth in every direction, enabling one to understand clearly the significance of a particular social grouping.

[From "Notes of a Contemporary," 1881-82:]

The first French revolution thunderously and crashingly proclaimed the triumph of the principle of the individual, in whose name the old forms of political and economic life were destroyed. The result of this colossal experiment is today evident to all: in practice the individual did not at all become the cornerstone of the new social edifice, and the whole operation merely had the effect of replacing privileges based on birth by privileges based on wealth. But this is not an argument against the idea of the individual as a guiding principle, for although the individual to some extent really did escape from the tight grip of feudalism and the guild system, he immediately fell into the clutches of bourgeois capitalism. In practice, the revolution worked to the advantage not of the individual but of that third estate which Siéyès . . . had said should be "all." Made wiser by grievous historical experience, we must of course begin by giving up this arrogant illusion. And then, if we find it too difficult in our complex social relationships to operate directly, using the principle of the individual, if we find that it is, after all, too abstract to serve as a guiding principle, we shall have to find some social element, serving which may bring us closest to our intended goal. Such a social element exists. It is the people. The people not in the sense of the nation but as the sum total of the working population. Work—the only unifying characteristic of this group of people—carries with it no privileges, and thus in serving it we do not risk favoring some onesided principle; in work the individual expresses himself most vividly and fully.

XV:53. PALEN'S DESCRIPTION OF THE MOVEMENT "TO THE PEOPLE," 1875

In a memorandum of 1875, the minister of justice, Count Konstantin Ivanovich Palen (or Pahlen, 1833-1912), gave this revealing description of the character of the movement "to the people." (For samples of editorials supporting the government's position with respect to revolutionary movements, see the Katkov selections in Item XVI:2, which illustrate views he propounded in the wake of the events of the 1870s.)
Reference: Burtsev, *Za sto let,* pp. 113-23.

The investigation has established that many young people, in some cases abandoning their studies, donned peasant garb, provided themselves with false identification papers, and went under the guise of common laborers "to the people," as they put it, with the purpose of implanting revolutionary ideas in them by means of printed pamphlets and word of mouth propaganda.

· · ·

Early in 1872 there began to circulate among students, in rather considerable quantities, books and publications printed abroad, of an openly revolutionary character, aimed at subverting the existing political system in Russia. These publications, mainly the work of Russian émigrés closely connected in their turn with the International Society [Marx's and Bakunin's First International], either were smuggled into Russia or else were brought in personally by Russian travelers returning from abroad who had absorbed there the theories of Bakunin and other extreme democrats and socialists, and who thereafter spread the poison of these criminal doctrines and democratic aspirations to all parts and classes of Russia.

· · ·

It was natural for the Russian revolutionary party, steadily growing, supported and guided in all its aspirations by its continuing relations with the outside world, to turn its attention to the Russian students and, after insinuating itself among them under the guise of "friends of the people," to assume their leadership as "the heralds of truth and good." The first party formed to this end was the so-called party of the Chaikovtsy [followers of N. V. Chaikovskii], which began its activities in Saint Petersburg but later carried them farther afield.

· · ·

... From 1873 on, the "self-education" groups began to lose their original theoretical character and gradually became assemblages with a clearly defined social and democratic trend. This tendency was intensified under the influence of the journal *Vpered*, published abroad by Lavrov (Mirtov), the first issues of which appeared around this time. Early last year, in 1874, these groups, both in Moscow and Saint Petersburg, became convinced that the time had come "to go to the people," and to begin to act.

   . . .

At the beginning of 1874 the carriers of revolutionary propaganda began their criminal activities simultaneously in various areas and spheres of our society. . . . By the end of 1874 they had succeeded in covering the greater part of Russia with a network, as it were, of revolutionary groups and individual agents. The investigation has uncovered propaganda in thirty-seven guberniias.

   . . .

The total number of defendants brought up for investigation in those guberniias adds up to 770, of whom 612 are men and 158 are women. Two hundred sixty-five are under arrest; 452 are at liberty and subject to other measures; the whereabouts of 53 are unknown. The inquests have established that many persons no longer young, fathers and mothers of families, who enjoy material security and a more or less honored social position, not only failed to oppose the young people but, on the contrary, often gave them open encouragement, help, and support, as if failing to realize, in their blind fanaticism, that the ultimate result of such actions would be society's ruin and their own. . . . Daughters of actual privy councilors— Natalia Armfel'd, Varvara Batiushkova, and Sophia Perovskaia—the daughter of a major general—Sophia Leshern-von-Gertsfel'd— and many others went to live among the people, working as day laborers in the fields, sleeping together with the peasants, their fellow workers. And this behavior apparently encountered sympathy and approval instead of condemnation on the part of some of their relatives and friends. There are many such examples. They must unquestionably serve to confirm the view that the success of the propagandists was due less to their own efforts and activities than to the ease with which their teachings penetrated into various strata of society and the sympathy they evoked there. . . .

To prepare agents, helpers, and future propagandists for themselves from the ranks of the working class, the leaders of the movement spread their views and ideas by word of mouth propaganda, and also by means of enormous quantities of books and pamphlets written in the form of easily comprehensible folk tales.

   . . .

To complete this brief survey of the facts uncovered by the investigation, a few general conclusions must be formulated: (1) There exist in Russia illegal secret associations aiming at the overthrow of the state and the entire existing order and at the establishment of complete anarchy. (2) These associations consist of a multitude of small groups and even individuals, acting independently yet linked together by the absolute solidarity of their goals and methods as well as by constant intercourse. (3) Communication between the groups and the organization of new units are carried out by specially authorized agents. (4) Propaganda is conducted both by word of mouth and by the direct circulation of books, pamphlets, and all kinds of printed and handwritten material. (5) Since their goal is clear and definite—the overthrow of the existing order—the revolutionary agents follow a precise and consistently executed plan. (6) This plan, whose main features are set forth in the program of Prince Kropotkin, presents the danger, among other things, that however energetic may be the investigation and prosecution of the guilty, nonetheless some individual groups would certainly remain undetected and would tirelessly carry on their criminal activities. (7) The swift success of the propaganda may be ascribed, on the one hand, to the fact that the activities of the agitators do not meet with sufficiently vigorous and vocal censure from the public, which does not clearly realize the significance and purpose of these criminal aspirations and up to now has regarded them with apathy, indifference, and sometimes even sympathy; and, on the other hand, especially to the fact that the young people, who form the main contingent of the propagandists, do not encounter any resistance to their pernicious and destructive teachings in the environment where they grow up and develop, since those basic moral principles that can be imparted only by the family appear to be completely undeveloped in many of these young people

who, at the time they enter school, lack any firm principles of respect for religion, for the family, and for personal and property rights.

XV:54. TKACHEV'S VIEWS IN NABAT, CA. 1875

Petr Nikitich Tkachev (1844-85), a former member of Nechaev's circle, published in Geneva from 1875 to 1877 the newspaper *Nabat* (Tocsin). His views are depicted here in some excerpts from that publication as collected by Glinskii and Burtsev.

Reference: Glinskii, *Revoliutsionnyi period*, pt. 1, pp. 507-08; Burtsev, *Za sto let*, pp. 133-35.

[From Glinskii:]

To prepare the revolution is not the task of the revolutionist at all. It is being prepared by the exploiters, the capitalists, the landlords, the priests, the police, the officials, the conservatives, the liberals, the progressives, and so on. . . .

The revolutionist does not prepare the revolution—he "makes the revolution!" . . .

To ring the tocsin, to call to revolution, is to show the need for revolution and its possibility at this very time, to clarify the practical means for bringing it about, and to define its immediate aims.

Such shall be the chief task of our organ.

. . .

Anarchy as the direct, immediate aim of the revolution, propaganda as the practical means for bringing it about, and finally, organization without discipline, hierarchy, and subordination—are these not utopian fantasies, childish dreams?

. . .

A true revolution . . . can be brought about only on one condition: the seizure of governmental power by the revolutionists; in other words, the direct, immediate aim of the revolution must consist in this, and this alone: to take possession of governmental power and to transform the present conservative state into a revolutionary state.

[From Burtsev's collection:]

The immediate aims of the revolution must be the seizure of political power and the creation of a revolutionary state. However, the seizure of power, while a requisite condition of the revolution, is not yet the revolution itself. It is only a prelude to it. The revolution is brought about by a revolutionary state which, on the one hand, fights and destroys the conservative and reactionary elements in society and abolishes all the institutions that obstruct the establishment of

equality and fraternity and, on the other, brings into being the institutions that favor them.

. . .

We recognize . . . that without propaganda the social revolution cannot be achieved, cannot come into being. We affirm, however . . . that propaganda will be really effective and expedient, will produce the expected results, only when material force and political power are in the hands of the revolutionary party.

Consequently, it is not propaganda that must precede the forcible seizure of power but the forcible seizure of power that must precede propaganda.

After consolidating its power the revolutionary state, drawing support from a national assembly [*narodnaia duma*] and making extensive use of propaganda, will bring about the social revolution through a series of reforms in the sphere of economic, political, and legal relationships within the social body. . . .

If the immediate, practically attainable task of the revolutionists consists in forcible assaults upon the existing political power in order to take it into their own hands, then it necessarily follows that all the efforts of a truly revolutionary party must be directed toward achieving this task. . . .

Now more than ever, all sincere and dedicated revolutionists must unite in a closely knit organization . . . disciplined, hierarchical, subordinating individual initiative to guidance by the group, imparting efficacy and unity to the activities of all its members. Only with such an organization can our goal be attained successfully and with the least possible expenditure of effort. . . . *Organization as an instrument for the disorganization and destruction of the existing governmental power, as our most immediate day-to-day task*—this should be at the present time the exclusive program of action of all revolutionists.

XV:55. KROPOTKIN'S VISION OF THE FUTURE, CA. 1876

After being imprisoned as a revolutionary in the mid-1870s and making a daring escape from a prison hospital, Kropotkin (see Item XV:17, above) went abroad, where he became famous as an anarchist theoretician. In this passage from his memoirs he describes his dream of the future as he envisioned it while in Switzerland in about 1876.

Reference: Kropotkin, *Memoirs*, pp. 398-99.

We saw that a new form of society is germinating in the civilized nations, and must take the place of the old one: a society of equals, who will not be compelled to sell their hands and brains to those who choose to employ them in a haphazard way, but who will be able to apply their knowledge and capacities to production, in an organism so constructed as to combine all the efforts for procuring the greatest sum possible of well-being for all, while full, free scope will be left for every individual initiative. This society will be composed of a multitude of associations, federated for all the purposes which require federation: trade federations for production of all sorts,—agricultural, industrial, intellectual, artistic; communes for consumption, making provisions for dwellings, gas works, supplies of food, sanitary arrangements, etc.; federations of communes among themselves, and federations of communes with trade organizations; and finally, wider groups covering all the country, or several countries, composed of men who collaborate for the satisfaction of such economic, intellectual, artistic, and moral needs as are not limited to a given territory. All these will combine directly, by means of free agreements between them.

. . . There will be full freedom for the development of new forms of production, invention, and organization; individual initiative will be encouraged, and the tendency toward uniformity and centralization will be discouraged. Moreover, this society will not be crystallized into certain unchangeable forms, but will continually modify its aspect, because it will be a living, evolving organism; no need of government will be felt; because free agreement and federation take its place in all those functions which governments consider as theirs at the present time, and because, the causes of conflict being reduced in number, those conflicts which may still arise can be submitted to arbitration.

XV:56. WRITINGS OF IVAN S. AKSAKOV, 1863-1883

The views of a prominent Slavophile and pan-Slav are illustrated in these selections from the writings of the publicist Ivan Sergeevich Aksakov (1823-86), between 1863 and 1883. Among the topics touched upon are the nature of the Russo-Slavic world, Russia's relations with "Latin-Germanic Europe," the Russian national spirit, Russian internal political life, and the Orthodox faith. (For some of the opinions of Katkov, who often saw things the same way as Aksakov during this period, see the next chapter, Item XVI:2.)

Reference: I. S. Aksakov, *Polnoe sobranie sochinenii I. S. Aksakova,* 7 vols. (Moscow, 1886-87) [the volumes are arranged in certain overlapping topical categories; hence the shuffling here], 7:447 [July 22, 1863], 32 [July 25, 1864]; 2:260 [Jan. 16, 1865], 367 [Aug. 12, 1867]; 1:173 [Nov. 10, 1867], 175-76 [Nov. 18, 1867], 273 [Sept. 26, 1877]; 5:28 [Mar. 21, 1881], 57 [May 9, 1881]; 2:596 [June 5, 1882]; 1:554, 568-69 [Nov. 15, 1883].

[From *Den'*, a weekly newspaper (1861-65), July 22, 1863:]

Religion is the highest *social* and the highest *cultural* principle; it penetrates into all the recesses of national life; it determines the nation's spiritual development, its moral personality, and its historical course. The Russian nation possesses such a social and cultural principle in its Orthodox faith.

[From *Den'*, July 25, 1864:]

The antipathy of Latin-Germanic Europe to Russia lies deeper than its visible political motivations; it is the antagonism of two different principles of civilization, Latinism and Orthodoxy, of two different historical destinies and missions. Russia must remember that she cannot rely on the friendship of any European nation; that the Latin-Germanic countries, while feuding among themselves, are ready at any time to form a coalition and to stand against Russia as a single unit, under a single banner; that more than once in the future Europe will be forced to divide into two camps: on one side, Russia with the Slavic-Orthodox peoples (including Greece), and on the other, all of Protestant, Catholic, and even Moslem and Jewish Europe together. It follows that Russia must concern herself solely with the strengthening of her own Orthodox-Slavic camp.

[From *Den'*, January 16, 1865:]

Let us give thanks to God that we have our common people, that there exists a seed we have not yet succeeded in crushing under the hammer of the borrowed civilization of the gentry. This seed preserves within itself the entire substance of our national spirit, our national self, our national personality, everything that makes Russia Russia. In it, in this seed, lies our strength and our salvation; in it, in its organic growth, lies our future.

[From *Moskva*, a daily newspaper (1867-68), August 12, 1867:]

"Humane" Europe . . . remains indifferent to the sufferings of millions of Orthodox Christians exposed today, on Crete and in Bulgaria, to the most outrageous tortures by the Turks. Civilized Europe haughtily looks down on the Russian barbarians, while fraternizing with the Asiatics. Christian Europe delivers Orthodox Christians into bondage to the Moslems and prefers the triumph of Islam to the triumph of the Greek "schism"; and the Roman pope gives his blessing to a holy war of Moslems and European Christians against Russia and its co-religionists. Humanity, civilization, Christianity—all this is abandoned in the relationship of western Europe to the Eastern Orthodox world.

[From *Moskva*, November 10, 1867:]

The time is past when the minds of the Slavic peoples could be influenced by Polish and German lies about the alleged plans of Russia—her desire for conquests and for the subjection of the Slavs to her imperial power. Today the Slavs know and believe that the very thought of swallowing up the independence of the Slavic peoples is abhorrent to Russia and that she regards it as her mission to restore them all to life, independence, and freedom.

[From *Moskva*, November 18, 1867:]

Latinism and Orthodoxy . . . are the historical and spiritual principles under whose influence the nationalities of western and eastern Europe have moved in different historical courses and have organized and developed themselves differently. To be a Latin means . . . to be in spiritual communion with the entire Latin Western world. . . . To be an Orthodox means to be in spiritual union with the Eastern church and the Greco-Slavic world. By virtue of this profound spiritual difference the European world is divided into two halves, into two worlds—East and West; these are qualitative rather than geographical terms, signifying a difference in cultural principles which have become powerful forces in the history of mankind. The Eastern world is an Orthodox Slavic world, whose representative is Russia and to which are irresistibly attracted even all those Slavic peoples of a different faith in whom the Latin tradition has not had time to strike deep roots—an indigenous world indubitably destined for a great historical future, a world loathed by western Europe.

[Excerpts from a speech at a meeting of the Moscow Slavic Benevolent Society, September 26, 1877:]

Our people, our simple people, with the humility of wisdom, driven neither by love of power nor by lust for the glory of battle, have accepted the [Russo-Turkish] war as a natural and involuntary moral duty, as an inescapable sacred task imposed upon it by Providence. Why? Because this is a war waged *for the faith,* for Orthodox Christians who moreover belong to its own racial stock, who are oppressed and tormented by the wicked enemies of Christ, the Asiatic Moslems who have enslaved lands that have been Christian from time immemorial.

[From *Rus'*, a twice-monthly newspaper (1880-86), March 21, 1881:]

In our country, by the grace of God, and thanks to the very efforts of the brutally assassinated, martyred tsar [Alexander II], our so-called fourth estate, the peasantry, that is, nearly 80 percent of the entire population of the state, represents the foundation and the real political strength of the entire Russian realm; it is endowed with land, with an organization, and with a vast measure of self-government; to this day it is the repository of the historical instinct, the faith, and all the vital elements in our political organism; the peasantry alone, and not our intelligentsia (most of whose representatives are driven hither and thither by the winds of foreign doctrines), is the mainstay of our fatherland.

[From *Rus'*, May 9, 1881:]

A locally self-governing land headed by an autocratic tsar—this is the Russian political ideal.

[From *Rus'*, June 5, 1882:]

The *peculiar nature* of the Russian national spirit consists in its many-sidedness, its breadth, its all-embracing humanity. It harbors no racial enmity either against the individual German or against *Germans in general.* . . . It harbors no enmity, racial or religious, against Turk or Tatar, or indeed against anyone of alien origin or alien faith, *insofar as* they appear before the Russian people in their *common human* aspect.

[From *Rus'*, November 15, 1883:]

What is pan-Slavism, or, literally translated, all-Slavism? Does it exist? Both yes and no. It does not exist as a political party, nor as a political program, nor even as a definite political ideal. The unification of all the Slavs of East and West in a single political body has so far never been envisaged by anyone in any clear form, not even as a dream. Yet pan-Slavism indubitably exists in our time as the awareness, shared by all the manifold branches of the Slavic race, of their common Slavic character and common ethnic origin.

. . .

There is no power in the world more peace-loving than Russia; there is no race that is naturally more peaceful and good-natured than the Slavs.

. . .

But to renounce *this kind* of pan-Slavism, one that can bring existence, life, and freedom to the Slavic peoples and to the entire Orthodox-Slavic world, would mean for Russia to renounce her very self, her very essence, and her mission among mankind.

. . . Our neighbors the Germans are apt to regard any *Russian national* trend in Russian literature or politics as necessarily *pan-Slavist*, and therefore odious. We repeat: there exists neither a *political* pan-Slavist program nor a *political* pan-Slavist ideal. But as the spiritual solidarity and the gravitation of various branches of the same race toward each other, as the awareness of Slavic brotherhood, as an Orthodox-Slavic *world* headed by Russia and asserting its claim to exist, live, and develop side by side with the Roman and Germanic worlds, pan-Slavism exists both as an idea and as a fact.

XV:57. DOSTOEVSKII'S VIEWS IN 1876-1877 AND 1880

Fedor Mikhailovich Dostoevskii (1821-81) expressed his political and philosophical views in some detail in his *Diary of a Writer* (*Dnevnik pisatelia*). Here are passages from 1876, 1877, and 1880 on such topics as the Russian character, Russia and the Slavs, and Russia and Europe.

Reference: F. M. Dostoevskii, *Polnoe sobranie sochinenii F. M. Dostoevskogo*, 12 vols. (St. Petersburg: A. F. Marks, 1894-95), 10:201 [May 1876], 204, 226 [June 1876], 245, 295-96 [July-August 1876]; 11:26 [January 1877], 117 [April 1877], 384 [November 1877], 469 [June 8, 1880]. The translation is based in part on *The Diary of a Writer: F. M. Dostoevsky*, trans. Boris Brasol, 2 vols. (New York: Charles Scribner's Sons, 1949), 1:340, 342-43, 362, 376-77, 423, 424; 2:581-82, 667-68, 906, 979, considerably revised. The last item (the speech on Pushkin) has recently been translated in Raeff, *Russian Intellectual History*, pp. 289-300.

[May 1876:]

The honesty, disinterestedness, straightforwardness, and open democracy of the greater part of Russian society can no longer be doubted. In this respect, perhaps, we represent or are beginning to represent a phenomenon that has not thus far been manifested in Europe, where democracy even to our own day has usually revealed itself from below. There the struggle is still going on, while the supposedly vanquished upper classes are still offering fierce resistance. Our upper classes were not vanquished; they became democratic, or rather national, of their own accord. Who can deny this? And if this is so, you will agree, our demos can expect a happy future. If at present there is much that is unseemly, it is at least permissible to entertain great hopes that the temporary misfortunes of the demos will unfailingly be alleviated in the future under the unceasing and uninterrupted influence of such enormous *basic foundations* (for they cannot be called anything else) as the *universal democratic mood and general agreement* in this regard of all Russians, starting from the very top.

[June 1876:]

We Russians have two motherlands—our Russia and Europe. . . . All-embracing humanity is the principal personal characteristic and mission of a Russian. . . . The [European] poets are as kindred to us, at least to the majority of our educated men, as to men there in the West. I assert and repeat that every European poet, thinker, and philanthropist is always better understood and more warmly received in Russia than in any other country in the world, with the exception of his native land.

. . .

After Peter [the Great], the first move of our new policy was clearly indicated: it had to involve the unification of all of Slavdom, so to speak, under Russia's wing. And this union is to be effected not for the sake of conquest, not for the sake of oppression, not for the purpose of annihilating Slavic individualities in the face of the Russian colossus, but with the object of regenerating them and placing them in a fitting relation to Europe and to mankind, and of giving them at length an opportunity to be tranquil and to rest after their countless agelong sufferings, to muster their courage, and, once they have felt their new strength, to contribute their own mite to the treasury of the human spirit and to add their share to civilization. . . . But isn't it true that all Russians desire the resurrection of the Slavs precisely on this basis, precisely for the sake of their full individual liberty and the resurrection of their spirit, rather than for Russia's political gain and consequent increase in political power—which is, however, what Europe suspects us of?

[July-August 1876, at the time of the Balkan crisis and the "Bulgarian massacres":]

All of Europe, at least her leading representatives—those same men and nations who vociferated against bondage, who abolished the slave trade, who overthrew despotism at home, who proclaimed the rights of men, who created science and astounded the world with its power, who animated and captivated the human soul with art and its sacred ideals, who kindled enthusiasm and faith in the hearts of men by promising them justice and truth in the very near future—all (nearly all) these same peoples and nations are suddenly turning their backs on millions of unfortunate beings—Christians, men, their own brethren, who are perishing, who have been dishonored— and are waiting, waiting hopefully and impatiently for them all to be crushed like reptiles, like bugs, waiting for their desperate clamors and appeals for salvation to be finally silenced— clamors that annoy and disturb Europe. Yes, just like reptiles and bugs; worse still: tens and hundreds of thousands of Christians are being annihilated as one would an unhealthy scab, are being completely obliterated from the face of the earth, without a trace. . . . Here we are face to face with a system, a method of war, practiced by a huge empire. Bandits are acting upon orders, upon the instructions of ministers and rulers of the state, of the sultan himself. And Europe, Christian Europe, a great civilization, looks on with impatience: "When will these bugs be crushed?" Moreover, in Europe they dispute the facts; they deny them in national parliaments; they do not believe, they pretend not to believe.

. . .

A national idea arose, and national feelings came to the fore: feelings of disinterested love for their [the Russians'] unfortunate and oppressed brethren [in the Balkans], and the idea of an "Orthodox cause." . . . The Slavic idea, in its loftiest sense, ceased to be merely a Slavophile idea; suddenly, under the pressure of circumstances, it thrust itself into the very heart of Russian society; it found precise expression in the common consciousness, while as an *active* feeling it became part of a popular movement. But what is this "Slavic idea in its loftiest sense?" It has become clear to everyone what it is: above all, i.e. prior to any historical, political, or other interpretations, it is a sacrifice, a longing to sacrifice even oneself in behalf of one's brethren, and a feeling of voluntary obligation on the part of the strongest among the Slavic tribes to intercede in defense of the weaker, in order to make one equal to the other in liberty and political independence, and thereby to establish a future great all-Slavic union in the name of Christ's truth, i.e. for the benefit, love, and service of mankind as a whole, for the defense of all the weak and oppressed throughout the world.

[January 1877:]

Under no circumstances can we renounce Europe. Europe is our second fatherland, and I would be the first to profess this ardently; I have always professed this. Europe is *almost* as dear to us *in every way* as Russia; in Europe dwells the entire tribe of Japheth, and our idea is to unify all the nations of that tribe, and even more, much more—to include even Shem and Ham. Now, what are we to do?

First of all and above all we must become Russians. If all-embracing humanity is a Russian national idea, then every one of us must first become a Russian, i.e. himself. Then everything will change, from the very first step. To become a Russian means no longer to despise one's own people. And just as soon as the European perceives that we have begun to respect our people and our nationality, he will at once begin to respect us. . . . Once we become our true selves, we shall at last take on a human rather than an apelike countenance. We shall take on the appearance of free beings and not of slaves or lackeys. . . . We shall even talk with them [the Europeans] more intelligently than at present because we shall find in our people and in their spirit new messages which will unfailingly become more intelligible to Europeans. And we ourselves shall then understand that much of what we used to despise in our people is not darkness but rather light, not stupidity but reason. And having grasped this we shall unfailingly utter in Europe such messages as they have never heard before. We shall then become convinced that genuine social truth resides in none other than our own people; that in their idea and in their spirit lies a living urge for the universal communion of men, a fellowship with full respect for national individuality and for its preservation, for the maintenance of complete human liberty, and with an indication of what such liberty consists of: loving communion, *guaranteed* by practice, by living example, by the practical need for true

brotherhood, and not by the guillotine, not by chopping off millions of heads.

[April 1877:]

We shall be the first to announce to the world that we do not seek to achieve our own welfare through the suppression of national individualities alien to us, but, on the contrary, that we perceive our welfare in the freest and most independent development of all other nations and in a brotherly communion with them, complementing one another, grafting upon ourselves their organic peculiarities and giving them our own twigs for grafting, maintaining spiritual intercourse with them, teaching them, and learning from them, until the time comes when mankind, having attained universal unity through the complementary communion of all the peoples of the earth, shall spread its shade upon the happy earth like a great and beautiful tree. . . . Ask the people; ask the soldier: Why are they arising? Why are they going to war and what do they expect from it? They will all tell you, as one man, that they are going to serve Christ and to liberate the oppressed brethren, and not one of them is thinking about conquest. Yes, right here during this present war we shall prove our whole idea of Russia's future mission in Europe; we shall prove it by the fact that after liberating the Slavic countries we shall acquire for ourselves not even a scrap of their land (as Austria is dreaming to do for itself), and that on the contrary, we shall watch over their mutual harmony and protect their liberty and independence, be it even against all Europe.

[November 1877:]

The Eastern Question is essentially the determination of the destiny of Orthodoxy. The destiny of Orthodoxy is merged with Russia's mission. Now, what is the destiny of Orthodoxy? Roman Catholicism, which long ago betrayed Christ for earthly rule, which has compelled mankind to turn away from itself, and which was thus the prime cause of Europe's materialism and atheism, this Catholicism has naturally generated socialism in Europe. For socialism has as its aim the determination of the destiny of mankind not in accord with Christ but outside of God and outside of Christ. It was inevitably generated of its own accord in Europe to replace the decayed Christian foundations, in keeping with their perversion and loss by the Catholic church itself. The lost image of Christ has been preserved in Orthodoxy in all the light of its purity. And it is from the East that the new message will be uttered to the world to meet the advance of socialism; and this message may again save European mankind. Such is the mission of the East and this is what the Eastern Question means to Russia.

[Diary entry for August 1880, recording a speech on Pushkin, delivered on June 8, 1880, at a meeting of the Society of Lovers of Russian Literature:]

Not with enmity (as one might think) but with friendship and wholehearted affection did we admit into our soul the genius of foreign nations, all together, without any racial discrimination, instinctively managing, almost from the very first step, to recognize and

eliminate contradictions, to excuse and reconcile differences, thereby manifesting our readiness and proclivity—which we ourselves had just realized and felt—to enter into an all-embracing, universal communion with all the nationalities of the great Aryan race. Yes, Russia's destiny is incontestably all-European and universal. To become a true Russian, to become completely Russian simply means, perhaps (and I would like to emphasize this), to become a brother to all men, *a universal man* [*vsechelovek*], if you will. Oh, all this Slavophilism and Westernism of ours is but a great, although historically inevitable, misunderstanding. To a true Russian, Europe and the destiny of the great Aryan race are as dear as Russia herself, as the fate of his native land, because our destiny is universality, attained not by the sword but by the force of brotherhood and our brotherly aspiration for the fellowship of man.

XV:58. THE PROGRAM OF THE "LAND AND FREEDOM" GROUP, OCTOBER 25, 1878

In 1876-77 a group of populists in Saint Petersburg established a secret party which in 1878 took the name "Land and Freedom" (Zemlia i Volia). These passages are from the program article of the first number of the first year of the journal *Zemlia i volia!*, October 25, 1878.

Reference: *Zemlia i volia! Sotsial'no-revoliutsionnoe obozrenie*, vol. 1, no. 1 (Oct. 25, 1878), as given in B. Bazilevskii (V. Ia. Iakovlev), ed., *Revoliutsionnaia zhurnalistika semidesiatykh godov*... (Paris[?], 1906), pp. 71-75. For other documents on the populism of the 1870s, in addition to those contained in the collections cited in this section, see also *Revoliutsionnoe narodnichestvo 70-kh godov XIX veka: Sbornik dokumentov i materialov*, 2 vols. Vol. 1 (1870-75), ed. B. S. Itenberg; vol. 2 (1876-82), ed. S. S. Volk (Moscow: Nauka, 1964-65).

Land and Freedom! These are two magical words that have often called forth powerful elemental movements from the depths of Russia. Twice they came close to overthrowing the Russian state system, and to this day they deeply stir the soul of the simple peasantry from one end of Russia to the other.

Land and Freedom! This is the slogan our forerunners, the socialist-populists of the sixties, faithful to the spirit and history of their people, inscribed on their banner.

We are inscribing the same words on our own banner.

We are convinced that only those cultural forms that are rooted in the minds and aspirations of the masses of the people have a historical future; we do not believe it possible, by means of preliminary work, to inculcate in the people ideals that are at variance with those developed in it by its entire previous history....

The revolution is the work of the masses of the people....

Any historical-revolutionary program must therefore be based upon the ideals of the people, such as have been created by history at a given time and in a given place.

At all times, whenever and in whatever numbers the Russian people have risen up, they have demanded land and freedom.

Land—as the common property of those who toil on it; and freedom—as the common right of all human beings to regulate their own affairs.

The seizure of the lands owned by landlords and boyars; the expulsion and sometimes the general extermination of all superiors, all representatives of the state; the establishment of "Cossack circles," i.e. free autonomous communes with elective, responsible, and always removable executors of the popular will—such invariably was the "program" of the revolutionary socialists from the people: Pugachev, Razin, and their followers.

And there can be no doubt that it has remained the same for the overwhelming majority of the Russian people to this day.

And for that reason we, the revolutionary populists, have made it our own.

Our program places the agrarian problem in the forefront. As for the industrial problem, we leave it in the background, not because we fail to recognize the necessity to expropriate the factories, but because history, which in western Europe has brought the industrial problem into the forefront, in our country has not posed it at all, replacing it with the agrarian issue. Moreover, once the revolutionary movement arises in the cause of land, it cannot help but recognize immediately the need for expropriating the factories and completely abolishing all capitalist production, because in preserving this it would dig its own grave.

. . .

In the sixties, the Russian party movement for the first time inscribed "The People's Revolution" on its banner.

In the seventies, the movement is developing from one of small coteries into a general, sweeping, mass movement which despite bloody persecution advances steadily, becoming broader and more redoubtable with every passing year.

. . .

Socialism is the highest form of universal happiness for all humanity ever conceived by the mind of man. For socialism there are no differences of sex, or age, or religion, or nationality, or class, or rank! It calls one and all to the wonderful feast of life, and to all it offers peace, freedom, and happiness, as much as anyone can have!

In this, and in this alone, lies the irresistible, fascinating force that draws into the ranks of the socialists all that is free, pure, unselfish. Only faith in their service to all that is human can arouse that fervent, truly religious fanaticism that inspires the socialists and makes them invincible and unconquerable, inasmuch as persecution itself becomes for them a source of supreme earthly bliss, the bliss of martyrdom and self-sacrifice.

. . .

[In connection with political terrorism and the political struggle in general:] We must remember that this is not the way we shall achieve the liberation of the toiling masses. Terrorism has nothing to do with the struggle against the foundations of the existing order. Only class can arise against class; only the people itself can destroy the system. It follows that the main contingent of our forces must work in the midst of the people. The terrorists are no more than a protective detachment whose task is to guard those workers against the treacherous blows of their enemies. To dedicate all our strength to the struggle against the power of the government would mean abandoning our direct and permanent goal to pursue a temporary, fortuitous objective.

To direct our activities in this way would be a great mistake. . . . Autocracy, attacked from all sides, will collapse, making way for a more modern constitutional system which, like every other constitution, will bring into the forefront the privileged classes: landlords, merchants, industrialists, all the owners of movable and immovable capital—in short, the bourgeoisie in the economic sense of the word. At present they are disunited and therefore impotent. Constitutional freedom, however modest, will give them, if no one else, the opportunity to organize into a strong party whose first act will be to proclaim a crusade against us, the socialists, as their most dangerous enemies.

If we direct all our strength to the struggle against the government, we shall of course greatly accelerate its downfall. But then, lacking any roots in the people, we shall be unable to take advantage of our victory. It will be a Pyrrhic victory. . . . At the cost of a bloody struggle and inevitable heavy sacrifices, we shall gain nothing for our cause. . . .

Only a close bond with the people will enable us to take advantage of the confusion that always attends a change of system and to create at one stroke the mighty force that will prevent our new enemies from consolidating their power after having sucked the people dry—as they did in Western Europe.

XV:59. THE PROGRAM OF THE "PEOPLE'S WILL" GROUP, JANUARY 1, 1880

Here are the main points in the program issued by the Executive Committee of the group called People's Will (Narodnaia Volia), which, on March 1, 1881, thought it was furthering its "immediate task" by the assassination of Alexander.

Reference: *Narodnaia Volia; Sotsial'no-revoliutsionnoe obozrenie*, vol. 2, no. 3 (Jan. 1, 1880), as given in B. Bazilevskii [V. Ia. Iakovlev], ed., *Literatura partii Narodnoi Voli* (Paris: Société nouvelle de librairie et d'édition, 1905), pp. 162-64. A translation of this document is included in Dmytryshyn, *Imperial Russia*, pp. 248-51 (taken from George Kennan's *Siberia and the Exile System*, 2:495-503).

By our basic convictions we are socialists and populists [*narodniki*]. We are convinced that only socialist principles will enable mankind to embody liberty, equality, and fraternity in its life, will ensure general material prosperity as well as the full harmonious development of the individual, and thus will achieve progress. We are convinced that social forms must be sanctioned only by the *people's will*, that national development is sound only when it advances freely and independently and when every idea that is to be embodied in life *has first passed through the people's will and consciousness.* The welfare of the people and the will of the people—these are our two most sacred principles, indissolubly linked together.

. . . The people is in a state of complete economic and political slavery. . . .

Pressing down upon the enchained people we see a class of exploiters, created and protected by the state. . . .

In the people itself we see its ancient traditional principles still living though constantly repressed: the right of the people to the land, to communal and local self-government, to the rudiments of a federative system, to freedom of conscience and of speech. . . .

We therefore hold that it should be our most immediate task, as socialists and populists, to free the people from the crushing oppression of the present government and to bring about a political upheaval that would transfer power to the people. . . .

It is our opinion that the people's will would be adequately expressed and executed by a constituent assembly [*uchreditel'noe sobranie*], freely elected by universal suffrage and provided with instructions from the voters. . . .

Accordingly this is our goal: to seize power from the existing government and transfer it to the constituent assembly, estab-lished in the way described above, whose duty it will be to reexamine all our political and social institutions and to remodel them in accordance with the instructions from the voters.

While submitting fully to the people's will, we nonetheless deem it our duty as a party to appear before the people with our program. We shall propagate it prior to the revolution, we shall advocate it throughout the election campaign, and we shall defend it in the constituent assembly. This program is as follows:

1. A permanent national representative body, established as described above and having full authority in all matters concerning the entire state.

2. Broad regional self-government, guaranteed by the elective character of all officers, the self-determination of the village commune, and the economic independence of the people.

3. The self-determination of the village commune as an economic and administrative unit.

4. The ownership of the land by the people.

5. A series of measures for transferring all industrial plants and factories to the workers.

6. Complete freedom of conscience, of speech, of the press, of assembly, of association, and of electioneering.

7. Universal suffrage, without any class or property limitations.

8. The replacement of the standing army by a territorial militia.

. . .

The purpose of terroristic activities . . . is to break the spell of governmental power, to give constant proof of the possibility of fighting against the government, to strengthen in this way the revolutionary spirit of the people and its faith in the success of its cause, and, finally, to create cadres suited and accustomed to combat.

XV:60. THE DECREE ON TEMPORARY GOVERNORS GENERAL, APRIL 5, 1879

This was one response to the attempt made against the tsar's life on April 2, 1879.
Reference: *PSZRI*, 2d ser., vol. 54, pt. 1, pp. 298-99.

Recent events have clearly demonstrated the existence in Russia of a gang of evildoers which, if not very numerous, nonetheless persists in its criminal delusions and strives to undermine all the foundations of the structure of state and society. Not confining themselves to propagating, by means of secretly printed and circulated proclamations, the most revolting doctrines aimed at subverting religious dogma, family ties, and property rights, these scoundrels have made repeated attempts on the lives of the highest dignitaries of the empire and of other persons invested with power by the government. The series of outrages has finally culminated in a criminal attempt to assassinate the tsar.

These evil deeds, as well as the absence of any signs of repentance in those machinators who have thus far been apprehended, have called our attention to the necessity of resorting to temporary extraordinary measures which would ensure the exemplary punishment of the culprits and, in the interests of maintaining public order, would accord special powers to persons invested with authority by the government.

To this end we have deemed it proper:

1. To appoint temporary governors general in Saint Petersburg, Khar'kov, and Odessa, with the special extraordinary powers listed in the articles below. The same powers are temporarily accorded to the governors general of Moscow, Kiev, and Warsaw.

2. To subordinate to these governors general . . . certain areas in the adjoining guberniias. . . .

3. In all the designated areas, to place all organs of the local civil administration . . . and the educational institutions of every jurisdiction under the authority of the governors general in matters relating to the maintenance of order and public tranquillity.

4. To authorize the governors general, in the areas under their jurisdiction, to bring persons of civilian status to trial by military courts, applying the penalties established for time of war. . . .

6. To authorize the governors general: (a) to deport from the areas under their jurisdiction, by administrative procedures, all persons whose continued presence in those localities they consider harmful; (b) to arrest, at their personal discretion, any individual, regardless of rank or station, whenever they consider it necessary; (c) to suspend or to forbid altogether the publication of journals and newspapers whose tendency they consider harmful; (d) in general, to adopt any measures they deem necessary, in consideration of local circumstances, for preserving order in the regions entrusted to them.

XV:61. LORIS-MELIKOV'S APPEAL TO THE PEOPLE OF SAINT PETERSBURG, FEBRUARY 14, 1880

Upon assuming the office of chairman of the Supreme Administrative Commission, Count Mikhail Tarielovich Loris-Melikov (1825-88) published this appeal "to the residents of the capital."
Reference: *Pravitel'stvennyi vestnik*, Feb. 14, 1880, as quoted in Tatishchev, *Imperator Aleksandr II*, 2:578.

I am fully aware of the complexity of the task that awaits me, and I do not shut my eyes to the responsibility that rests upon me. This is no time for exaggerated and hasty expectations, and I can promise only one thing— to strive with all my effort and ability, on the one hand, to avoid the slightest weakness and not to recoil from the most severe measures to punish those who are guilty of the criminal acts that are disgracing our society; and, on the other hand, to reassure and safeguard the legitimate interests of the sound elements of society. I am convinced that I shall have the support of all honest men who are loyal to the sovereign and sincerely devoted to their motherland, now undergoing such undeserved tribulations. I regard the support of the public as the principal force capable of assisting the authorities in restoring the normal course of political life, whose disruption most painfully affects the interests of the public itself.

XV:62. LORIS-MELIKOV'S REPORT TO THE TSAR, EARLY APRIL 1880

In April Loris-Melikov proposed these measures. The text of this report is from the work of S. S. Tatishchev (see the first item in this chapter).

Reference: Tatishchev, *Imperator Aleksandr II*, 2:593-94.

1. To act firmly and resolutely with regard to the prosecution of those who conspire against the state structure and the public tranquillity, while distinguishing between them and those persons who do not belong to any criminal social party and are guilty only of offenses having no direct relation to social-revolutionary activities.

2. To strive in every way to achieve complete unity of action by all organs of governmental authority called upon to combat the criminal false doctrines. . . .

3. With the gradual attainment of the above objectives, to strive for a return to normal legal procedures in place of the extraordinary measures.

4. To urge government institutions and officials to show greater solicitude for the manifest daily needs of the common people and of society, and for their representatives. It is imperative that benevolent consideration be given to the needs of the clergy, the pronouncements of the nobility, the activities of the zemstvos, the requirements of the municipalities. . . . It would be useful to draw the nobility, the zemstvos, and the municipalities to participate in matters closely related to their local needs.

5. To restore to the Department of Education the confidence it has lost among all classes and layers of society, without touching the basic foundations of the educational system. The changes this would require in the administrative personnel of the Department of Education will meet with the greatest approval throughout Russia. Without such changes, the success of any measures taken will be gradually paralyzed by new accretions of obnoxious elements, with alarming implications for the present and ominous warnings for the future.

XV:63. LORIS-MELIKOV'S PROPOSAL TO THE TSAR, JANUARY 1881

The further development of Loris-Melikov's plans during the era of the "dictatorship of the heart" is seen in Tatishchev's account of his report to the tsar late in January 1881.

Reference: Tatishchev, *Imperator Aleksandr II*, 2:602-03. Loris-Melikov's memorandum of January 28, 1881 (which Tatishchev is summarizing) has recently been published in English in Raeff, *Plans for Political Reform*, pp. 133-40.

[The count said:] "It seems to me that the best course would be to establish temporary preparatory commissions, similar to the drafting commissions organized in 1859 [to draw up plans for emancipating the serfs], with the provision that the work of these commissions be subject to examination with the participation of representatives of the zemstvos and some of the more important cities."

These commissions, the count proposed, were to be headed by men appointed by the emperor from among the highest dignitaries of the state, and they would include representatives of the various organs of the central government, among them senators charged with inspection [*revizuiushchie senatory,* who from time to time were sent into various guberniias to investigate and report on local affairs and thus were conversant with local conditions and needs], as well as other knowledgeable and reliable persons within and outside the civil service, invited with the sovereign's consent and known for their special contributions to scholarship or their experience in a particular field of public administration or national life. As a beginning, two such commissions were to be created: one administrative-economic, and the other financial. The sphere of action of the former was to include the following subjects: (1) reform of the local guberniia administration . . . (2) supplementation, as proved necessary, of the statute [on emancipation] of February 19, 1861, and of subsequent enactments dealing with the peasant question . . . (4) revision of the statutes on the zemstvos and the municipalities. . . . Within the cognizance of the financial commission would fall problems connected with taxation, passports, and so forth, as directed by the supreme authority.

All legislative bills dealing with the issues listed above, after being drawn up by either of the two preparatory commissions, would be submitted for discussion to a general commission that would also include, besides the chairmen and members of the preparatory commissions, representatives of the zemstvos and municipalities elected by the zemstvo assemblies and the municipal dumas. After being examined and approved or amended by the general commission, the bills, together with the recommendations of the appropriate ministers, would go to the State Council, whose membership Loris-Melikov proposed to enlarge through the inclusion, with voting rights, of ten to fifteen representatives of public institutions [i.e. the zemstvos and municipal governments] who had displayed special knowledge, experience, and outstanding ability.

CHAPTER XVI

Alexander III
and Nicholas II
1881-1906

A. POLITICAL DEVELOPMENTS

Note: Materials on revolutionary movements are in Section B, below.

XVI:1. POBEDONOSTSEV'S LETTERS TO ALEXANDER III, 1877-1882

Konstantin Petrovich Pobedonostsev (1827-1907), who taught law and other subjects to the future Alexander III and continued in a position of influence as over-procurator or executive director of the Holy Synod under his former pupil, maintained in his letters to the heir and tsar a stream of advice. The following excerpts illustrate some of the topics covered and the tone of Pobedonostsev's counsel. (For more of his views, see Item XVI:53, below.)

Reference: K. P. Pobedonostsev, *Pis'ma Pobedonostseva k Aleksandru III*, 2 vols. (Moscow: Novaia Moskva, 1925-26), 1:69-71 [letter of Sept. 17, 1877], 207 [May 17, 1879], 248-49 [Dec. 14, 1879], 315-18 [Mar. 6, 1881], 331-32 [Apr. 26, 1881], 337-39 [May 4, 1881], 346 [July 10, 1881], 367 [Jan. 16, 1882], 381 [May 4, 1882], 382 [May 6, 1882].

[September 17, 1877, after the Russian defeats at Plevna:]

Those who return from the front cannot find words to express their bitterness and indignation at the senseless way in which plans and dispositions are drawn up. One might think that experience should have taught [the generals] a lesson, that they would be more prudent. No, again they launch a mad assault, they sent thousands to a useless death. . . . Nowadays everyone talks and reads [about such things], and I assure you, everyone's heart overflows with bitterness and indignation... Perhaps no news of this reaches you; this is why I have resolved to write you about it.

This is terribly important; this is terribly frightening. This threatens Russia with a great misfortune in the future, if everything in the army remains in its present state. Do they tell the sovereign these things, or don't they dare? Or do they fear to alarm him? But for the sake of saving the whole country, for the sake of keeping intact that hitherto indivisible union between the tsar, his dynasty, and Russia, *something must be done* to allay this anger, to quell this indignation.

I shall tell your Highness frankly against whom this [indignation] is now primarily directed. It is directed against *the grand dukes*, who unfortunately have been placed at the head of many departments of decisive importance in this war. This is what must be changed first of all.

. . .

And the things they say about the com-mander in chief, about Grand Duke Nikolai Nikolaevich! In letters from the front, in the conversation of those who have returned, all ascribe to him the chief blame for all the reverses; they say that he is impossibly stubborn, that he refuses to listen to sensible advice, refuses to recognize his mistakes, and out of stubbornness sends regiments of heroes to die in vain. They even report that resentment seems to be spreading among the troops. "Men are sent to die in vain, and at the crucial moment are refused reinforcements." They now fear lest this resentment should develop into a definite collapse of morale. They complain bitterly of the ignorance, self-esteem, and stubbornness of the chief commanders and staff officers. . . . Everyone says that the most important thing is a new commander in chief.

[May 17, 1879:]

Ah! to my misfortune, I see about me and hear all those men who at present hold the fortunes of the state in their hands. I cannot express the pity and bitter sadness they arouse; I can see no one who knows what he wants, who desires anything with an ardent spirit, who could resolve to act with a firm will, who sees the truth, who speaks the truth firmly. They all are like *eunuchs*, rather than men; the best of them vacillate, shrink from danger, are of two minds on everything, and as a result merely talk but do not act; they are divided among themselves, and there is not a single resolute will which would unite and direct them.

[December 14, 1879:]

Your Imperial Highness.

In the present time of troubles all good Russian men are full of apprehension and sick at heart. Particularly after the events of November 19 [the attempt to assassinate the emperor], this apprehension has increased enormously.

I see a great many people of various rank and station. All the officials and learned men here sicken my heart, as if I were in the company of half-wits or perverted baboons. I hear from all sides that trite, deceitful, and accursed word: constitution. I fear that this word has already made its way into high circles and is taking root.

But I also meet and talk with sane Russian men who are full of apprehension. Their hearts are seized with fear; above all else they fear that basic evil, a constitution. Among the common people everywhere the thought is spreading: better a Russian revolution and ugly turmoil than a constitution. The former could soon be suppressed, with order restored throughout the land; the latter is poison to the entire organism, corroding it by constant deceit which the Russian soul cannot accept.

Your Highness, I must tell you this. Everyone has lost faith in the present government to such an extent that *they expect nothing from it.* They await the future in extreme apprehension, while the common people are deeply convinced that the government is composed of *traitors,* who hold a weak tsar in their power.

All hopes for the future are placed *upon you,* and in everyone's heart stirs one fearful question: What if even the heir might someday begin to think of a constitution? This is what they fear; this is what they talk and think about.

The important thing is that this thought has taken deep hold among the *common people:* in the villages and in the provincial towns the simple folk, who discuss current happenings with simple good sense and fervent hearts, talk about this—there they know what a constitution is and fear it more than anything else on earth.

[March 6, 1881, five days after the assassination of Alexander II:]

Your Imperial Majesty.

I am tortured with anxiety. . . .

I have resolved to write again, for this is a fearful hour and time presses. If Russia and yourself are to be saved, it is either now or never.

If they sing you those old sirens' songs—that you should remain calm, that you must continue on a liberal path, that it is necessary to make concessions to so-called public opinion—oh, for God's sake, do not believe them, Your Majesty, do not listen to them. This will mean ruin, Russia's ruin and yours; this is as clear as day to me. This will not bring you safety but only lessen it still more. The mad villains who killed your father will not be satisfied by any concession and will only burst into a frenzy. They can be repressed, the evil seed can be uprooted, only by a battle to the death with them, by blood and iron. Perish in battle, but conquer. It is not hard to conquer; heretofore everyone wanted to avoid a battle and deceived the late sovereign, you, themselves, and everyone and everything on earth, because those were not men of wisdom, strength, and courage, but flabby eunuchs and tricksters.

No, Your Majesty, there is only one true, direct path: to arise and begin, without a moment's relaxation, the most sacred battle in Russia's history. The entire nation awaits this peremptory decision from you, and as soon as they perceive your sovereign will, everything will rise up, everything will come to life, and there will be a new freshness in the air.

The people are aroused and resentful; and if the uncertainty should long continue, we may expect rebellions and a bloody retribution.

. . . In this [the failure of the authorities to forestall the assassination] the common people see only *treason*—there is no other word. And they will be utterly unable to understand how the present men could be allowed to remain in their posts.

And they cannot be left there, Your Majesty. Forgive me for speaking the truth. Do not let Count Loris-Melikov remain. I do not trust him. He is a trickster and is still capable of playing a double game. If you place yourself in his hands, he will lead you and Russia to destruction. He was good only at putting through liberal projects and he played a game of secret intrigue. But as a statesman he doesn't know himself what he wants, as I myself have told him more than once. And he is not a Russian patriot. [Loris-Melikov was of Armenian descent.] For God's sake, Your Majesty, take care lest he seize hold of your will, and do not let the moment slip by.

And if not he, then who! Your Majesty, I see them all, and know how little they are worth. Of them all I might venture to name Count Nikolai Pavlovich Ignat'ev. He still has sound instincts and a Russian soul, and his name is held in high esteem by the healthy segment of the Russian people—by the simple folk. Take him, to begin with, for someone *loyal* must be taken immediately.

Saint Petersburg should have been placed under martial law from the very first day. . . .

This is an accursed place. Your Majesty ought to *leave here* for a clean place immediately after the burial—even Moscow would be better—and quit this place for a time, until it has been thoroughly cleansed. Your new government, which should also be cleansed from top to bottom, can remain here. . . .

A new policy must be proclaimed immediately and resolutely. This is just the time to put an end, once and for all, to all talk about freedom of the press, freedom of assembly, and a representative assembly. All this is the deceit of vacuous and flabby men, and it must be spurned for the sake of the integrity and welfare of the people.

Saburov cannot be tolerated any longer in his post [as minister of education]; he is completely stupid, and his stupidity has caused much misfortune and continues to cause more every day. It should not be very difficult to find his successor. Of the candidates named the most competent is Baron Nikolai. . . .

Your Majesty. Forgive me for speaking frankly. But I cannot keep silent—it is my duty to speak to you; unless I am mistaken, it was never inconvenient for you to listen to me. You of course have felt that, with all my failings, I never sought anything for myself from you, and that my words were always sincere. God has put me in a position where I was able to speak to you intimately, but, believe me, I would have been happy never to leave Moscow and my small house in a narrow side street.

[April 26, 1881:]

Your Imperial Majesty.

Again I appear and most humbly beg of you not to be angry at my persistence and constant importunity. Not of my own volition or by my own summons did I become known to Your Majesty and come to perceive your confidence and goodwill toward me. And thus, in the present hour, when my heart unceasingly aches and trembles for you and for Russia, how can I keep silent or remain idle and calm?

I hasten to present to Your Majesty the draft of the manifesto I have drawn up, in which I have weighed every word. I am convinced that this draft corresponds entirely to the needs of the present moment. All of Russia awaits such a manifesto and will receive it with enthusiasm, except of course for those madmen who expect a constitution. . . .

. . . In it is expressed the firm and deliberate resolution to preserve the autocratic power; this is the essential point, following which the rumors that a constitution will appear any day should be stilled.

· · ·

And so, if truly Your Majesty has firmly resolved—which I do not doubt—not to tolerate institutions that are senseless and ruinous for Russia, I implore you not to hesitate in expressing your will to the entire nation; as you will vouchsafe to observe, there is nothing harsh in this draft.

· · ·

I venture to say further that there is no need to consult with others about the manifesto and this draft. The matter is as clear as could be of itself; I fear that, if advisers were called in, many of them would say: "What for? Wouldn't it be better to leave the intentions of the sovereign uncertain, so that *anything* could be expected from the new government?"

But in this uncertainty lies the greatest evil of the present moment and the source of great apprehension for all Russian people. [Note: For excerpts from the manifesto, issued April 29, 1881, see Item XVI:5, below.]

[May 4, 1881:]

Your Imperial Majesty.

Permit me once again to disturb you concerning the same matter.

The appearance of the imperial manifesto [of April 29, on the inviolability of the autocracy] has given rise to a bewilderment that still continues. On the following day I learned that Your Majesty accepted Loris-Melikov's request to resign [as minister of internal affairs] and replied in the same vein to Abaza's request [as minister of finance]. Thank God. . . .

Today, to my surprise, I saw Abaza in the State Council and later learned that Your Majesty was pleased to consent to Bunge's request that Abaza continue to perform his duties until the closing of the session of the State Council.

Forgive me, Your Majesty, if I say that this news made me extremely apprehensive. . . . It is my strongest conviction that it was *absolutely necessary* to dismiss Abaza immediately.

Your Majesty, do not choose to be deceived. As of April 29 these men are *your enemies.* They want to prove at any cost that they were right and you were wrong, and the means to do this should never have been left at Abaza's disposal for two more weeks. . . .

As for [Minister of War] Miliutin, his face will not, of course, show any sign of irritation. But he is extremely irritated and resentful; I thought he would be, and everything that I hear about him from Count Ignat'ev confirms my supposition. Believe me, Your Majesty, these men can only be dangerous to you at the present moment.

Among the local officials the manifesto has been greeted with despondency and a kind of irritation; even I could not expect such insane blindness. On the other hand, all sane and simple folk rejoice immeasurably.

. . .

These are difficult times. I shall not rest easily so long as Count Loris-Melikov, Abaza, and Grand Duke Konstantin Nikolaevich remain here. May God grant that they all leave and go their separate ways as soon as possible. The rumors now current will subside as soon as resolute action is undertaken which does not allow of any retreat. But today the rumor has already spread through the city that everything has been changed once again, that Loris-Melikov and Abaza will remain in their posts. No time must be lost in putting an end to this confusion.

. . .

Forgive me, Your Majesty, for all my epistles. They are prompted only by anxiety for you, which gives me no rest.

[July 10, 1881:]

Since 1862 I have seen how [officialdom] has gradually become corrupted, how all

principles and traditions of duty and honor have been destroyed, how firm and indispensable men have been replaced by the weak, indifferent, and insignificant, how they have turned into eunuchs. . . . What has our legislation accomplished? It has separated the courts from the government; it has placed young, weak, and inexperienced judges in a false position of independence from the government, thus corrupting them with the false illusion of an impossible freedom; it has arranged for the election of local judges who know nothing and are answerable for nothing; it has developed a thick network of institutions and forms that are burdensome for the people and unendurable for the treasury; it has created a regiment of new officials—and it has elevated all these things into some sort of sacrosanct ideal of justice and freedom.

[January 16, 1882:]

In the present difficult times the government needs most to pacify minds, to calm public opinion which has been bewildered and perturbed beyond all limits, and to put an end to the unimaginable chatter that everyone engages in, so that there would be less useless talk and something would get accomplished. This is why I have always held that it was impossible to undertake anything lasting and substantial for the establishment of order as long as newspapers and magazines retained complete and unbridled freedom to spread gossip, chatter, and sedition. Unfortunately, no one has yet undertaken this indispensable task with a firm hand, and not only is nothing done to curb the press, but new publications are constantly being authorized.

[May 4, 1882 (in connection with the proposal of the minister of internal affairs, Count Ignat'ev, to summon a zemskii sobor—in this case referring to an assembly of representatives of the zemstvos and other elements of the population:]

Even if I believed in the zemskii sobor of ancient Russia, I would still stop in bewilderment before such a thought. Ancient Russia was all one piece in its simplicity of concepts, customs, and state requirements; it did not get entangled in forms and institutions borrowed from strange and foreign ways of life, it had no newspapers or magazines, and it had no complex problems and requirements. And now it is proposed that we call together a motley, ill-assorted assemblage from contemporary Russia, which is a universe comprising two parts of the earth. Here are the Caucasus, and Siberia, and Central Asia, and the Baltic Germans, and Poland, and Finland! And to this babel of tongues we are supposed to present the question of what to do at the present moment. To my mind, this is the height of absurdity for the state. May God deliver us from such a calamity!

. . . If the *power of decision* and *execution* should pass from the government to any kind of national assembly, this will mean *revolution, the downfall of the government,* and *the downfall of Russia.*

[May 6, 1882, continuing about Count Ignat'ev:]

The activity of a minister with such a sin or such a mistake on his soul cannot be beneficial; nor can his future actions be straightforward. Anyone who could conceive of such an arrangement and adopt such a plan is capable of other plans no less insane. [Note: Within a month, on May 30, Count Ignat'ev was dismissed from his post as minister of internal affairs and replaced by Count D. A. Tolstoi, whose appointment, asserted Pobedonostsev in a letter of June 5, 1882, "will be approved by all sensible men."]

XVI:2. KATKOV'S EDITORIALS, 1881-1887

A youthful liberal who became a highly influential conservative was Mikhail Nikiforovich Katkov (1818-87), who served from 1863 to 1887 as editor of *Moskovskie vedomosti* (Moscow news). In these excerpts from Katkov's editorials over the years from 1881 to 1887 may be seen some of his views on revolutionary movements, on the nature and significance of the Russian monarchy, and on Russian foreign policy.

Reference: M. N. Katkov, *Sobranie peredovykh statei "Moskovskikh Vedomostei," 1881* (Moscow, 1898), pp. 205, 223-24, 526; *Sobranie . . . 1882* (Moscow, 1898), pp. 258-59, 471; *Sobranie . . . 1883* (Moscow, 1898), pp. 228, 482; *Sobranie . . . 1884* (Moscow, 1898), pp. 257, 511-12; *Sobranie . . . 1885* (Moscow, 1898), p. 437; *Sobranie . . . 1887* (Moscow, 1898), p. 117.

[April 25, 1881, on the beginning of Alexander III's reign:]

Many plans are proposed. . . . But there is only one tsarist path.

This is not the path of liberalism or conservatism, novelty or antiquity, progress or retrogression. Nor is this the path of the golden mean between two extremes. From the lofty height of the tsar's throne lies revealed a realm of one hundred million people. The welfare of this hundred million is that ideal and at the same time that compass by which the true tsarist path is determined and directed.

In former ages the interests of separate estates were made preeminent. But this is not the tsarist path. The throne has been elevated in order that distinctions of estate, guild, rank, and class might be equalized before it. Barons and common folk, rich and poor, though there be distinctions between them, are equal before the tsar. A single authority with no other authority in the country, and a nation of one hundred million obedient to it alone—this is what makes a true tsardom.

In the person of the monarch it possesses the strongest central authority for suppressing any sedition and removing all obstacles to the national welfare. In doing away with all other authorities, it still leaves room for the broadest degree of self-government that may be required for the welfare of the people themselves—of the people, and not of parties.

Only through a misunderstanding do people think that monarchy and autocracy preclude "popular freedom"; in actual fact they ensure this better than any sort of trite constitutionalism. Only an autocratic tsar could have freed twenty million slaves without a revolution, by his manifesto alone; and not only freed them personally, but also allotted land to them. It is not words and letters that count but the spirit that animates everything.

May the Lord God of Hosts inspire our sovereign to follow this truly tsarist path, to have in mind neither progress nor retrogression, neither liberal nor reactionary aims, but solely the welfare of his *one hundred million people.*

[May 6, 1881:]

May God aid us in freeing ourselves from the specter of parties, conservative and liberal. Let us be Russians first and foremost, faithful to the spirit and history of our fatherland,

and let us renounce any chimerical experiments in governmental affairs. Let us examine
our affairs through our own eyes, and, lest
we go astray, let us always bear in mind the
indissoluble unity of the interests of the state
and the welfare of the people. There is room
on our firm native soil for all legitimate
interests, all honest aspirations. On this soil
neither conflicting opinions nor clashing
interests present any danger. We shall be
liberal in our conservatism and conservative
in our liberalism.

[November 2, 1881:]
It is essential to organize local administration
so as to make it an extension of the state;
from its center to the smallest local communities, municipal and rural, the state must comprise a single organism in which there must
not be even the shadow of conflicting authority or of antagonism between the state and the
land [zemlia], as we say, so that they would
not form two camps, so that in principle no
rivalry or dispute over rights and interests
could arise between them. It is essential that
even the lowest level of local administration
be a living part of the state, the champion of
its idea, the executor of its tasks.

[May 24, 1882:]
    [Immediately after the peasant emancipa-
tion] . . . plans were prepared for the dis-
memberment of Russia. How many new
states were to be born from the ruins of a
fallen Russia! . . . With the suppression of the
Polish rebellion, this cherished movement
came to a halt. People thought it over, Russian national feeling arose, Russian patriotism
came to the fore; it came to the fore in all
strata of society and in the government. The
intrigue was uncovered, the fraud was de-
tected in all its forms. Common sense, corrob-
orated by events, came into its own; the
unity of Russia became a general watchword;
the traitorous policy of *multi*-nationalism
went into hiding before the idea of a *single*
state nationality in Russia. Then everyone
came to understand that if Russia is destined
to live there can be only one state nationality
in it, and that Russian nationality is not an
ethnographic but a political term, that the
Russian people is not a race, but a political
body composed historically of many racial
elements.

[September 7, 1882:]
    To the Russian tsar has been granted a
special significance distinguishing him from
the other rulers of the world. He is not only
the sovereign of his country and the leader of
his people, but he is ordained by God as the
guardian and defender of the Orthodox
church, which knows not an earthly vicar of
Christ over it and which has abjured any activity save spiritual, leaving all cares concerning its earthly welfare and organization to the
consecrated leader of the great Orthodox
people. The Russian tsar is more than the
heir of his ancestors; he is the successor of
the caesars of Eastern Rome, of the organizers
of the church and of its councils which established the very creed of the Christian faith.
With the fall of Byzantium, Moscow arose and
the greatness of Russia began. Here is the
secret of that profound uniqueness which
distinguishes Russia from the other nations
of the earth.

[May 10, 1883:]
    Russian autocracy has nothing in common
with the way it is depicted by people who judge
it by foreign concepts. Understood in its true
sense, it is found to be the best and truest
guarantor of every blessing mankind holds
dear. It manifests itself as a single authority,
independent of any parties or individual interests, elevated over all, free of any egoism,
equal to the whole. Its sword is drawn not
against freedom but in its defense. It cannot
and must not tolerate any authority in the
country that is not subordinated to it or does
not proceed from it, any state within the
state.
    The contrast between ourselves and the
West consists in the fact that everything there
is based on contractual relations and everything here on faith; this contrast was originally determined by the position the church
adopted in the West and that which it adopted
in the East. A basic dual authority [*dvoevlastie*]
exists there; a single authority [*edinovlastie*]
here.
    Freedom for the church and with it for all
the people, and full and indivisible authority
for the tsar—this is our system.

[October 20, 1883:]
    All of Russia's interests in the East can . . .
only consist in this: that the peoples whose

liberation cost it such great sacrifices be
protected from any form of exploitation,
that they be free and independent, that they
live their own life adhering to their innate
principles and remaining true to their church,
that Serbia be for the Serbs, Bulgaria for the
Bulgarians, Rumania for the Rumanians,
Greece for the Greeks. This, we repeat, is the
sole interest that brings Russia to the East,
and it cannot possibly be called a selfish one.

[May 10, 1884:]

Our Central Asiatic *prestige* – England's
horror—even though supported by the power
of arms, draws its strength from a different
source. The eastern tribes react magically to
Russian kindness, which does not preclude
political firmness and which is so different
from the haughty brusqueness of John Bull.
The Englishman is inclined to despise the
cultural level of a foreigner when it is inferior to his own. The Russian calls everyone
his brother as his very language accustoms
him to doing.

[October 6, 1884:]

The new university charter is not only
important in the educational field; it is also
important because it signifies the beginning
of a new movement in our legislation. Just
as the charter of 1863 marked the beginning
of a system for abolishing the authority of
the state, so does the charter of 1884 antici-
pate the government's revival, authority's
return to duty.

. . .

And so, gentlemen, arise: the government
is moving forward, the government is returning!

[September 10, 1885:]

Alas, there are two Russias: what one ac-
complishes, the other goes and spoils. Where
Russia acts as a great national force impelled
by the spirit of its history, there everything
goes well. Everything great that Russia has attained has been the work of its national spirit;
but when our so-called intelligentsia, which
lacks roots and a guiding principle, goes into
action, then chaos ensues in both our internal
and international affairs.

[March 4, 1887:]

At the present time everything is calm inside Russia, everything is moving toward the
establishment of order, toward the strengthening of authority, toward the protection of
legitimate rights and freedoms, toward the
guaranteeing of sound and fruitful progress.
There is no danger anywhere in internal affairs; everything is headed quietly, but evenly
and firmly, along the path indicated by common sense and by an increasingly active understanding of the true needs of the people
and the real interests of the country. . . . Our
fraudulent revolutionary elements, which
have no ties either with the people or with
any of its classes, or with any of its interests,
serve a cause that is alien and hostile to it.
They seek only turmoil; they want only destruction; and they will obey any command
that prompts them toward this and adds
fuel to the flames in that direction.

XVI:3. THE DIARY OF PERETTS ON THE SESSION OF THE COUNCIL OF MINISTERS OF MARCH 8, 1881

Barely one week after Alexander II's assassination the Council of Ministers and other high officials met, in a session presided over by Alexander III himself, to decide whether or not to put
into effect the proposal of Count Loris-Melikov—previously approved by Alexander II—to summon elected representatives from the zemstvos and towns and to allow them a consultative voice
in legislative activity. Among those present was Egor Abramovich Peretts (1833-99), chief secretary of the State Council (*gosudarstvennyi sekretar'*). His diary contains a detailed account of
the deliberations. (See also D. A. Miliutin's account, below.)

Reference: "Iz dnevnika E. A. Perettsa," in *Krasnyi arkhiv*, vol. 8 (1925), pp. 132, 138, 141-
43. The portion pertaining to Pobedonostsev's remarks has recently been translated at slightly
greater length in Ivar and Marion Spector, eds., *Readings in Russian History and Culture* (Palo
Alto, Calif.: Pacific Books, 1968), pp. 194-96.

A meeting of the Council of Ministers was
scheduled for March 8, at two o'clock in the
afternoon. . . .

Besides the ministers, the chairmen of the
departments of the State Council, myself,
and the director of the chancery of the council

[*zaveduiushchii delami soveta*], State Secretary [*stats-sekretar'*] N. P. Mansurov, there were present the grand dukes Vladimir Aleksandrovich, Konstantin Nikolaevich, and Mikhail Nikolaevich, and Count S. G. Stroganov [a former tutor of Alexander III].

. . .

[After a majority of the ministers had expressed itself in favor of Loris-Melikov's project for summoning representatives from the zemstvos and the towns for legislative activity, with a consultative voice:]

The sovereign: "Yes, but Emperor Wilhelm, when the rumor reached him that my father wished to grant Russia a constitution, implored him in a personal letter not to do this; and in the event that the matter had already gone too far to permit retreat and to dispense with a national representative body altogether, the German emperor advised him to limit its scope as much as possible, giving the representative body less influence and retaining power in the government."

. . .

Chief Procurator of the Holy Synod K. P. Pobedonostsev (white as a sheet, and obviously agitated): "Your Majesty, the duty of my oath and conscience obliges me to express to you everything that is in my heart. I am not only apprehensive but in despair. As in the days before the downfall of Poland they said: 'Finis Poloniae!' now we too are almost driven to say: 'Finis Russiae!' The contemplation of the project proposed for your confirmation wrings my heart. . . . They want to introduce a constitution in Russia, and if not immediately, then at any rate to take the first step toward it... And what is a constitution? Western Europe provides us with the answer to this question. The constitutions existing there are the tools of every kind of falsehood, the tools of every kind of intrigue.

. . .

"And this is the fraud on a foreign model, unsuitable for us, that they want to introduce here, to our misfortune, to our destruction. Russia was strong thanks to autocracy, thanks to the boundless mutual trust and close ties between the people and their tsar. Such ties between the Russian tsar and the people are an inestimable blessing. Our people are the custodians of all our valor and good qualities; there is much to be learned from them! The so-called representatives of the zemstvo only alienate the tsar from the people. In the meantime the government ought to provide for the people; it should come to know their real needs and should help them contend with their often desperate poverty. This is the destiny toward which we must strive; this is the true task of the new reign.

"But instead they propose to organize a chatter shop [*govoril'nia*] for us, something like the French *états généraux*. We suffer enough as it is from chatter shops, which only inflame popular passions under the influence of worthless, good-for-nothing journals. . . .

"New zemstvo and municipal public institutions were established—chatter shops in which, rather than engaging in the business on hand, everyone expounds at random on the most important affairs of state, which do not at all fall under the jurisdiction of the speakers. And who are these expounders, who are the managers of these chatter shops? Worthless, immoral people, among whom leading positions are held by men who do not live with their families, who indulge in debauchery, who think only of personal gain, who seek popularity, and who bring confusion into everything.

"Then new judicial institutions were established—new chatter shops, chatter shops for lawyers, thanks to whom the most fearful crimes, indisputable murders and other heinous misdeeds, remain unpunished.

"Freedom was finally given to the press, that most fearful chatter shop of all, which to every corner of the boundless Russian land, through thousands and tens of thousands of versts, peddles obloquy and reproach upon the regime, sows the seeds of discord and dissatisfaction among peaceful and honest men, inflames passions, and incites the people to the most flagrant lawlessness.

. . .

"In such a terrible time, Sire, we must not think of instituting a new chatter shop, in which new corrupting speeches will be delivered; we must think of action. We must act."

This speech made a very strong impression on many, particularly on the sovereign. . . . A. A. Abaza [minister of finance] spoke in an agitated voice, but with great resolution:

"Your Majesty, the speech of the chief procurator of the Holy Synod is, in essence, an indictment of the reign of that same sovereign whose untimely death we all mourn. If Konstantin Petrovich is right, if his views are correct, then you, Sire, must dismiss from ministerial posts all of us who participated in the reforms of the previous—I will say it boldly—*great* reign.

"Only one who doubts Russia's future, who is unsure of her vitality, can regard our situation as gloomily as does Konstantin Petrovich. I, on my part, decidedly rebel against such views and believe that our fatherland is yet destined for a great future. If certain inauspicious phenomena did arise in the execution of the reforms through which the late emperor summoned Russia to a new life, these were no more than the exceptions that

are possible at any time and in any place, and almost inevitable in a period of transition from complete stagnation to judicious civic freedom. The misfortune that has overtaken us— the assassination of the tsar—cannot be connected with the happy reforms of the past reign. This crime is a fearful thing. But is it really a unique outgrowth of the Russian soil? Is not socialism at the present time a universal cancer which all of Europe is fighting? Was not the German emperor shot at recently, were there no attempts on the life of the king of Italy and of other sovereigns, was there not an attempt a few days ago in London to blow up the quarters of the lord mayor?"

[The tsar decided to postpone the matter for further study.]

XVI:4. D. A. MILIUTIN ON THE YEARS 1881-1882

The following excerpts from D. A. Miliutin's diary (see Items XV:36 and 42, above) touch upon the discussions mentioned in the diary of Peretts (above) as well as upon subsequent developments.

Reference: Dmitrii A. Miliutin, *Dnevnik D. A. Miliutina*, ed. Petr A. Zaionchkovskii, 4 vols. (Moscow: Bibl. Lenina, 1947-50), 4:33-35, 40-41, 51, 131.

March 8, 1881. . . . [In a meeting presided over by the tsar] I expressed the conviction that new legislative measures are indispensable in order to consummate the great reforms of the deceased emperor, which remained unfinished. . . .

. . . Minister of Finance Abaza delivered a fine speech in which, refuting the insinuations of Makov that an attempt was being made to limit the power of the autocracy, he explained that, on the contrary, the call to action of representatives from the zemstvos will strengthen and support the authority of the government. Abaza cited as an example the imminent and absolute indispensable tax reform, which cannot possibly be accomplished without the cooperation of representatives from all classes of society. Despite the convincing arguments of Abaza, Minister of Communications Posiet, speaking after him, voted against the proposed enactments as being untimely and concluded with banal attacks on so-called progress in general. But everything said by Stroganov, Makov, and Tolstoi was pale and insignificant compared to the long, jesuitical speech delivered by Pobedonostsev; this was no mere refutation of the measures currently proposed but a direct, indiscriminate censure of everything that had

been accomplished in the preceding reign; he dared to call the great reforms of the Emperor Alexander II a criminal mistake! The speech of Pobedonostsev, delivered with rhetorical pathos, seemed an echo of vague Slavophile theories; it was a denial of everything that forms the basis of European civilization. Many of us could not conceal a nervous shudder at certain phrases of this fanatical reactionary.

Abaza was the first to raise his voice against the dangerous insinuations of Pobedonostsev. If everything heretofore done in the interests of improving the system and the welfare of Russia was a flagrant and criminal mistake, then all present ministers must immediately be replaced, and what new program will then be proposed by those who condemn everything accomplished in the glorious reign of Alexander II?

Then Prince Urusov, Nabokov, Andrei Saburov, Sol'skii, and Prince Lieven spoke in turn—all in favor of the proposed measures. Sol'skii expressed the bold opinion that representatives from all classes of the population would form a firmer support for autocracy than an army of officials.

. . .

March 16, 1881. . . . After discussing in

absolute privacy the present state of affairs, Loris-Melikov and I reached the conclusion that for a certain time we must both remain in an attitude of waiting, until it becomes clear which of the two opposite paths the emperor will choose. The statesmen of the new reign ought to be selected to correspond with this choice. Of course, neither I nor Loris-Melikov will remain in our posts if the party of Pobedonostsev & Company gains the upper hand. Many others of our best associates will likewise have to leave the scene. What sort of people will take their place? What will be their program? Reaction under the mask of nationality [*narodnost'*] and Orthodoxy— this is a certain road to ruin for the state.

After our conversation we proceeded to the [meeting of the] State Council. The chairman, the grand duke [Konstantin Niko-laevich] (next to whom I sit), began to talk to me in an undertone on the same subject I had just been discussing with Loris-Melikov. The grand duke frankly declared that, if matters continue to go the way they are now going, he too will have to leave the scene.

· · ·

March 31, 1881. My first report [*doklad*] in Gatchina. . . . [Note: As heir to the throne, Alexander III had lived in the Gatchina palace, about thirty miles southwest of Saint Petersburg. He remained in Gatchina during his first days as emperor, since he could have better police protection there than in Saint Petersburg.]

In Gatchina the visitor is struck by the appearance of the palace and the park, which are encircled by several rows of sentries, with additional police officers brought from Saint Petersburg, mounted patrols, secret agents, and so on. The palace has the appearance of a prison; no one is admitted without a permit with a photograph of the bearer on the reverse side. Even without this, Gatchina bears a gloomy, oppressive appearance; now it makes an appalling impression. Their Majesties live in complete seclusion. It has been announced that only on Wednesdays and Fridays will the sovereign receive those who wish to be presented.

· · ·

April 10, 1882. Last night my son arrived in Simeiz [in the Crimea, where Miliutin went when he retired], having spent about six weeks in Saint Petersburg. . . . My son's account of how things are going in Saint Petersburg, together with interesting letters from my brother Boris [a civil servant] and from A. V. Golovnin, disclose a sorry picture of the incompetence of the present government and the depressed mood of the public. Intrigues, the lack of thought and knowledge of one's responsibilities, a sort of lack of hope for the future—these are the distinguishing characteristics of the present time. Confusion reigns in everyone's mind.

XVI:5. THE MANIFESTO ON THE INVIOLABILITY OF THE AUTOCRACY, APRIL 29, 1881

Almost two months after acceding to the throne, Alexander III took Pobedonostsev's advice and formally announced his determination to uphold the autocracy.
Reference: *PSZRI*, 3d ser., 1:54.

Amidst our great sorrow the voice of God enjoins us to take up firmly the reins of government, with trust in divine Providence, with faith in the strength and verity of autocratic power, which we have been called upon to maintain and defend, for the good of the people, against all encroachments upon it.

· · ·

Consecrating ourselves to our great task of service, we call upon all our faithful subjects to serve us and the state with fidelity and truth, for the eradication of the vile sedition disgracing the Russian land, for the strengthening of faith and morality, for the sound upbringing of children, for the extermination of falsehood and rapacity, and for the establishment of order and integrity in the activity of the institutions granted to Russia by her benefactor, our beloved father.

XVI:6. THE STATUTE PROVIDING SPECIAL MEASURES FOR THE MAINTENANCE OF ORDER, AUGUST 14, 1881

The special administrative measures described in this statute, although declared to be temporary, were widely employed and frequently renewed, and in some regions the statute remained in effect until the end of the monarchy.
Reference: *PSZRI*, 3d ser., 1:261–66.

[Note: According to articles 8 and 9, a "state of reinforced protection" (*polozhenie usilennoi okhrany*) and a "state of extraordinary protection" (*polozhenie chrezvychainoi okhrany*) could be proclaimed for individual localities by imperial decree, upon the request of the minister of internal affairs through the Committee of Ministers.]

12. Upon the expiration of one year from the date of establishment of a state of reinforced protection, and six months from the date of establishment of a state of extraordinary protection, the minister of internal affairs shall make representation to the Committee of Ministers for the continuance of these measures, if this proves necessary. . . .

14. In localities declared to be in a state of reinforced protection, the right and duty of maintaining state security and public order shall be entrusted to the governors general, whether permanently or temporarily appointed to those localities, and, in guberniias not under their jurisdiction, to the governors and city governors [*gradonachal'niki*]. . . .

15. Within the boundaries of those localities, the aforesaid authorities may:

a. Publish obligatory ordinances on matters relating to the prevention of violations of public order and state security. . . .

b. Institute penalties, not exceeding three months' arrest or a monetary fine of 500 rubles, for violations of such obligatory ordinances.

16. The governors general, and governors and city governors in localities where they are not subordinated to the former, are also empowered: . . .

b. To forbid any kind of popular, public, or even private assemblies.

c. To make arrangements for the closing of any kind of commercial and industrial establishments whatsoever. . . .

d. To forbid individuals to enter localities in which a state of reinforced protection has been proclaimed. . . .

17. The governors general and, in guberniias not subordinated to them, the minister of internal affairs are empowered:

a. To transfer individual cases concerning crimes covered by the general criminal laws to a military court for examination and trial under martial law, when they deem this necessary for protecting public order and tranquillity.

b. To demand the examination *in camera* of all court cases, the public examination of which could serve as an occasion for the stimulation of emotions and the violation of order. . . .

Local chiefs of police, and likewise heads of gendarme departments [*nachal'niki zhandarmskikh upravlenii*] and their assistants, are permitted to make arrangements:

a. For preliminary detention, for no longer than two weeks, of all persons who arouse well-grounded suspicion of committing a crime against the state or of implication in such, and likewise of belonging to illegal societies.

b. For carrying out searches at any time in all premises, factories, mills, and so forth, without exception. . . .

26. [During a state of extraordinary protection,] those highest in authority [*glavnonachal'stvuiushchie*, i.e., the governors general or their equivalent] . . . are accorded: . . .

f. The right to suspend from duty, for the duration of a proclaimed state of extraordinary protection, officials of all departments and likewise persons serving in class [*soslovnye*], municipal, and zemstvo institutions through election, making an exception only for persons who occupy posts of the first three grades [in the Table of Ranks].

g. The right to permit special assemblies, and to suspend and close regular assemblies, of corporate, municipal, and zemstvo institutions and in each individual case to determine what questions are subject to removal from the agenda of the aforesaid assemblies.

h. The right to suspend periodical publications for the duration of a proclaimed state of extraordinary protection.

i. The right to close educational institutions for a period not exceeding one month.

[Note: Articles 32–36 further provided that administrative exile "to any specific locality of European or Asiatic Russia" for a period of up to five years could be imposed by action of a "special commission" (*osoboe soveshchanie*) consisting of two members from the Ministry of Internal Affairs and two members from the Ministry of Justice, under the chairmanship of the assistant minister of internal affairs.]

XVI:7. TWO MEASURES ON JEWS, MAY 3 AND JUNE 9, 1882

On May 3, 1882, the Committee of Ministers, with Alexander's approval, issued so-called temporary regulations which had far-reaching consequences for Russian Jewry. The first excerpt gives the principal provisions of these "May Laws." Those laws were followed on June 9 by a circular (evidently also approved May 3) which was sent by the minister of internal affairs, Count D. A. Tolstoi, to all governors. The second excerpt below gives its opening paragraphs, enunciating a policy that, although not always appreciated by students of the problem, brought the Jews at least temporary relief from some kinds of maltreatment.

Reference: Vladislav V. Vashkevich, comp., *Sbornik uzakonenii, kasaiushchikhsia evreev* (St. Petersburg, 1884), pp. 341 ["May Laws"], 349 [decree of June 9]. The translation of the "May Laws" is based in part on that in L. Wolf, ed., *The Legal Sufferings of the Jews in Russia* (London: T. F. Unwin, 1912), p. 84, considerably revised.

[From the "temporary regulations" of May 3, 1882:]

1. As a temporary measure and until a general reexamination is made, in due form, of legislation concerning the Jews, they are forbidden henceforth to settle anew outside of cities and towns [*mestechki*], an exception being made only in the case of existing Jewish agricultural colonies.

2. Until further notice, the registration of deeds of sale and mortgages in the names of Jews is forbidden, as well as the attestation, in the name of Jews, of leases on real estate situated outside of cities and towns, or of letters of attorney for the administration or management of such property.

3. Jews are forbidden to carry on trade on Sundays and on the twelve principal [*dvunadesiatye*] holy days.

[From the decree of June 9, 1882:]

By an imperially confirmed resolution of the Committee of Ministers of May 3 of this year [1882], it is decreed:

To make it universally known that the government has decided to prosecute undeviatingly all acts of violence against the person and property of Jews, since they live under the protection of the general laws for the entire population, on an equal basis with the other subjects of His Imperial Majesty.

To make it known to the appropriate guberniia authorities that they bear the responsibility for taking timely preventive measures to avert the occasions for such disturbances, and for halting disturbances at their very inception, should they arise; and that for any negligence in this respect on the part of administrative and police authorities—in a situation where they could have averted an act of violence but did not do so—those who are guilty shall be subject to dismissal.

The promulgation of this imperial resolution has been prompted by the disturbances, accompanied by acts of violence against the Jewish population, which unfortunately have broken out on more than one occasion in various localities of the empire.

XVI:8. THE UNIVERSITY STATUTE OF AUGUST 23, 1884

The autonomy Alexander II had granted in 1863 to the universities (see Item XV:23) was curtailed by his son's statute of August 23, 1884, which contained restrictions that were not lifted until August 27, 1905. This statute, like others of similar tone in the educational sphere, was associated with the name of the man who served as minister of public education from 1882 to 1897, Count Ivan Davydovich Delianov (1818-97). The following excerpts illustrate the nature of Delianov's "reform."

Reference: *PSZRI*, 3d ser., 4:457-63, 466 (arts. 74, 75), 468-69, 472 (arts. 138-39).

3. Each fully constituted university is to contain four faculties: (a) history and philology; (b) physics and mathematics; (c) law; and (d) medicine.

Note: The University of Saint Petersburg contains a special faculty of oriental languages.

4. Each university, under the central juris-diction of the minister of education, is committed to the charge of the superintendent [*popechitel'*] of the local educational district [*uchebnyi okrug*].

5. The direct administration of a university devolves upon the rector, with the participation, in relevant cases, of: (a) the council

[*sovet*]; (b) the executive board [*pravlenie*]; (c) the assemblies [*sobraniia*] and deans of the faculties; and (d) the inspector of students and his assistants.

6. The superintendent of the educational district looks after the welfare of the university; he watches after the manner of instruction in the university and sees to it that all university regulations and functionaries observe the rules prescribed by law or by government order; he halts all violations of these rules; he institutes proceedings for bringing the guilty to account and makes recommendations for rewarding the meritorious. . . .

8. The superintendent is responsible for the overall direction of all arrangements for maintaining order and discipline in the university. . . .

10. The rector is chosen by the minister of education from among the full [*ordinarnyi*] professors of the university and is appointed by imperial order for a period of four years. . . .

23. Each faculty holds its own assemblies, composed of all the professors of the faculty, under the chairmanship of the dean. . . .

24. The deans are chosen by the superintendent of the educational district from among the professors of the corresponding faculty and are confirmed in their posts for a period of four years by the minister of education. . . .

. . .

The council is composed of all the professors of the university, under the chairmanship of the rector. . . .

Matters wherein the decisions of the council are presented, through the superintendent, to the minister of education for judgment or confirmation are (1) the election of honorary members of the university; (2) the selection of persons presented to fill vacant professorial positions; . . . (11) the consideration and approval of academic curricula drawn up by the faculties, and likewise of proposed changes in these curricula; (12) the discussion of programs of instruction drawn up by the faculties, with the scheduling of lectures and laboratory work by days of the week and by hours. . . .

40. The executive board [of the university] is composed of the deans of all the faculties and the inspector, under the chairmanship of the rector. . . .

46. The inspector of students is appointed to his post by the minister of education, upon the nomination of the superintendent of the educational district. . . .

48. The inspector of students has direct supervision over the observance in university buildings—by students as well as outside auditors—of the rules established for them; he sees to it that these persons maintain order and decorum in the aforesaid buildings; if there are infringements of order and decorum, he takes measures to restore the same, bringing such cases to the attention of the rector and requesting, in the more important cases, his consent to the proposed arrangements [for restoring order]. Apart from this, the inspector watches over the behavior of students outside the university buildings also, to the extent possible, following in this respect the direct instructions of the superintendent. . . .

74. University examinations are conducted: (a) by committees specially appointed within the university for this purpose; and (b) by the faculties.

75. . . . The number of committees for each faculty is fixed by the minister of education, who also appoints each year the chairman and members of each committee. . . .

97. The teaching personnel of the university includes: (a) full professors and associate professors [*professory ordinarnye i ekstraordinarnye*]; (b) docents; (c) lecturers. . . .

98. The promotion of an associate professor to the rank of full professor is effected by the minister of education, upon the nomination of the superintendent of the educational district. . . .

99. No one may be a professor who does not have a doctoral degree in the field of knowledge corresponding to his chair. . . .

100. When a professorial vacancy becomes open, the minister of education either fills it at his own discretion with a person who satisfies the conditions stated in article 99 or allows the university to select a candidate for the vacant position and present him for confirmation. . . .

103. A professor selected by the council must be confirmed in his post by the minister. In the event that the candidate presented is not confirmed, the minister is allowed to appoint a professor from among other candidates proposed by the university, or to fill the post

with an outsider who satisfies the requirements of article 99. . . .

138. Publications appearing in the name of a university or with its approval, and in general all things printed in the name of a university, are not subject to preliminary censorship.

139. Printed works, manuscripts, and educational materials received by the universities from abroad are not subject to examination by the censorship or to payment of duty. Bales and boxes with these articles, addressed to universities, are not to be opened in frontier customhouses but are merely to be sealed and then witnessed in the universities in the presence of a customs or police official.

[Note: The key provisions of the decree of August 27, 1905, which restored and enlarged the universities' autonomy, were as follows: "The university council shall be accorded the right to elect the rector and his assistant; each faculty shall elect its own dean and secretary. . . . Persons elected by the council and the faculties shall be presented in due form for confirmation (by the government). . . . Upon the council shall be placed the obligation and responsibility of supervising the maintenance of the proper conduct of academic life in the university." *PSZRI*, 3d. ser., vol. 25, pt. 1, p. 658.]

XVI:9. KENNAN ON SIBERIAN EXILES IN 1885-1886

George Kennan (1845-1924) was a largely self-schooled telegrapher from Ohio, who, at the age of twenty, was sent by Western Union as a member of an expedition that spent about a year exploring the possibility of laying a telegraph line from Alaska across northeastern Siberia. Through lecturing and writing on his experiences after his return (see his book *Tent Life in Siberia*), Kennan turned to journalism, and he traveled through the Caucasus as a journalist in 1870. From June of 1885 to March of 1886, under the sponsorship of the *Century Magazine,* Kennan, accompanied by the artist and photographer George A. Frost, studied the tsarist penal and exile system. The Russian government facilitated Kennan's eight thousand miles of travel but could take little comfort in the result, for Kennan's subsequent lectures, articles, and book (*Siberia and the Exile System*) provided ammunition for critics of many persuasions. Kennan's account, as these excerpts illustrate, suggests many revealing comparisons with the postrevolutionary era.

Reference: George Kennan, *Siberia and the Exile System*, 2 vols. (New York, 1891), 1:79, 81, 87, 89-90, 307, 308; 2:29-30, 38, 159, 372-73, 545, 546, 551.

The relative proportions of these several classes [of exiles to Siberia] for 1885, the year that I spent in Siberia, may be shown in tabular form as follows:

Penal Class	Males	Females	Total
I. Hard-labor convicts (kátorzhniki), punished by sentence of a court	1,440	111	1,551
II. Penal colonists (poseléntsi), punished by sentence of a court	2,526	133	2,659
III. Exiles—(a) Vagrants	1,646	73	1,719
(b) Exiled by judicial sentence	172	10	182
(c) Exiled by village communes	3,535	216	3,751
(d) Exiled by executive order	300	68	368
IV. Voluntaries (dobrovólni), accompanying relatives	2,068	3,468	5,536
Totals	11,687	4,079	15,766

. . .

The political offenders that are exiled to Siberia do not constitute a separate penal class or grade, but are distributed among all of the classes above enumerated. I was not able to obtain full and trustworthy statistics with regard to them from any source of information open to me. A fragmentary record of

them has been kept recently by the inspectors of exile transportation, but this record covers only a few years, and includes only "administratives," or persons banished by executive order for political "untrustworthiness." . . . From the annual reports of Colonel Vinokúrof, inspector of exile transportation for Western

Siberia, it appears that the number of politics banished by administrative process from 1879 to 1884 is as follows:

1879	145
1880	112
1881	108
1882	88
1883	156
1884	140
[Total for] 6 years	749

This is at an average rate of 125 per annum.

· · ·

[In the Tiumen' forwarding prison:] "You see how it is," said the warden, again addressing me. "This cell contains more than four times the number of prisoners that it was intended to hold, and the same condition of things exists throughout the prison." I looked around the cell. There was practically no ventilation whatever, and the air was so poisoned and foul that I could hardly force myself to breathe it. We visited successively in the yard six *kámeras* or cells essentially like the first, and found in every one of them three or four times the number of prisoners for which it was intended, and five or six times the number for which it had adequate air space. In most of the cells there was not room enough on the sleeping-platforms for all of the convicts, and scores of men slept every night on the foul, muddy floors, under the *nári* [*nary*, i.e. plank beds], and in the gangways between them and the walls.

· · ·

We then went to the prison kitchen, a dark, dirty room in the basement of the main building, where three or four half-naked men were baking black rye-bread in loaves about as large as milk-pans, and boiling soup in huge iron kettles on a sort of brick range. I tasted some of the soup in a greasy wooden bowl which a convict hastily cleaned for me with a wad of dirty flax, and found it nutritious and good. The bread was rather sour and heavy, but not worse than that prepared and eaten by Russian peasants generally. The daily ration of the prisoners consisted of two and a half pounds of this black bread, about six ounces of boiled meat, and two or three ounces of coarsely ground barley or oats, with a bowl of *kvas* morning and evening for drink.

· · ·

Our work in all parts of Siberia was greatly facilitated by the attitude of honest and intelligent officials towards the system that we were investigating. Almost without exception they were either hostile to it altogether, or opposed to it in its present form; and they often seemed glad of an opportunity to point out to a foreign observer the evils of exile as a method of punishment, and the frauds, abuses, and cruelties to which, in practice, it gives rise.

· · ·

In Tomsk the condition of the prisons and the evils of the exile system were so well known to everybody, and had been so often commented upon in the local newspapers, that the higher officials did not think it worth while apparently to try to conceal anything from us.

· · ·

The forcible deportation of "politically untrustworthy" citizens by executive order and without trial first became common in the later years of the reign of Alexander II. Administrative banishment had been resorted to, as I have said, before that time as a means of getting rid of obnoxious persons, but in 1878 and 1879, when the struggle between the police and the terrorists grew hot and fierce, exile by administrative process became a common thing, and people who were known to hold liberal opinions, or who were thought to be in sympathy with the revolutionary movement, were sent to Siberia by the score.

· · ·

He [the political exile] examines the "Rules Relating to Police Surveillance," and learns from Section 33 that "administrative exiles who have no pecuniary means of their own shall receive an allowance from the Government treasury for their support." This "allowance," as he soon ascertains, is six *rubles,* or a little less than three dollars, a month. He makes inquiries in the town or village market-place, and finds, as the result of his investigations, that if he receives the Government allowance, and buys only the things that he regards as absolutely essential to life, his monthly budget will stand as follows: [Kennan's footnote: "This is a real, not an imaginary exile balance-sheet, and the prices are those that prevailed in the town of Surgut, province of Tobolsk, Western Siberia, in the spring of 1888."]

RECEIPTS		EXPENDITURES	
Government allowance	$3.00	Rent of a single room	$1.00
Deficit	1.72	40 lbs. of meat	1.50
		40 lbs. of wheat flour	.58
		40 lbs. of rye flour	.33
		10 eggs	.12
		A brick of tea—cheapest	.79
		1 lb. of sugar	.10
		1 lb. of tobacco, cheapest sort	.25
		1 lb. kerosene	.05
	$4.72		$4.72

· · ·

After we had finished our inspection of the cells in the Middle Kará prison, we made an examination of the kitchen. Hard-labor convicts at Kará receive a daily ration consisting of three pounds of black rye-bread; about four ounces of meat, including the bone; a small quantity of barley, which is generally put into the water in which the meat is boiled for the purpose of making soup, and a little brick tea. Occasionally they have potatoes or a few leaves of cabbage; but such luxuries are bought with money made by extra work, or saved by petty "economies" in other ways. This ration seemed to me ample in quantity, but lacking in variety and very deficient in vegetables.

· · ·

In every branch of the administration one is constantly stumbling upon abuses or defects [such as overcrowding] that have long been recognized, that have been commented upon for years, that are apparently prejudicial to the interests of everybody, and that, nevertheless, continue to exist. If you ask an explanation of an official in Siberia, he refers you to St. Petersburg. If you inquire of the chief of the prison department in St. Petersburg, he tells you that he has drawn up a "project" to cope with the evil, but that this "project" has not yet been approved by the Minister of the Interior. If you go to the Ministry of the Interior, you learn that the "project" requires a preliminary appropriation of money—even although its ultimate effect may be to save money—and that it cannot be carried into execution without the assent and cooperation of the Minister of Finance. If you follow the "project" to the Ministry of Finance, you are told that it has been sent back through the Minister of the Interior to the chief of the prison department for "modification." If

you still persist in your determination to find out why this thing is not done, you may chase the modified "project" through the prison department, the Ministry of the Interior, and the Ministry of Finance to the Council of the Empire. There you discover that, inasmuch as certain cross-and-ribbon-decorated senators and generals, who barely know Siberia by name, have expressed a doubt as to the existence of the evil with which the "project" is intended to deal, a special "commission" [with salaries amounting to twenty thousand *rúbles* a year and mileage] has been appointed to investigate the subject and make a report. If you pursue the commission to Siberia and back, and search diligently in the proceedings of the Council of the Empire for its report, you ascertain that the document has been sent to the Ministry of the Interior to serve as a basis for a new "project."

· · ·

[From Kennan's appendix:] A part of the second report of Governor-general Anúchin to the Tsar upon the state of affairs in Eastern Siberia. Delivered to Alexander III in March, 1882. From a "secret" copy.

· · ·

The *étapes,* forwarding prisons, and prisons of other kinds, with the most insignificant exceptions, are tumble-down buildings, in bad sanitary condition, cold in winter, saturated with miasm, and, to crown all, affording very little security against escapes. The prisons in Nízhni Údinsk, Chitá, Nérchinsk, Blagovéishchensk, and particularly Nikoláivsk, astound one by their bad condition.

· · ·

I must offer, for the most gracious consideration of your Imperial Majesty, a few words concerning the State [political] criminals now living in Eastern Siberia. On the 1st of

January, 1882, they numbered in all 430 persons, as follows:

    (a) Sent to Siberia by decree of a court and now

        1. In penal servitude 123

        2. In forced colonization 49

        3. In assigned residences [*na zhityó*] 41

    (b) Sent to Siberia by administrative process and now

        1. In assigned residences [*na zhítelstvo*]........................ <u>217</u>

                    Total 430

XVI:10. THE LAW INSTITUTING LAND CAPTAINS, JULY 12, 1889

Here are some of the provisions of the statute instituting land captains who would be "a firm governmental authority" close to the peasants.

    Reference: *PSZRI*, 3d ser., 9:512-15, 517-18, 528, 531.

I. Statute on district land captains [*zemskie uchastkovye nachal'niki*]. . . .

[Note: According to articles 6-9, local hereditary nobles possessing certain property, educational, or civil service (*sluzhebnyi*) qualifications were eligible to be appointed to the post of land captain.]

13. For every vacant post of land captain the governor shall select one candidate, upon consultation with the marshals of the nobility from the guberniia and the local uezd. . . . The governor shall make representation to the minister of internal affairs concerning candidates selected on this basis, adding to it the opinion of the marshals of the nobility in those cases in which the person presented by the governor has been selected by him against the recommendation of one or both of the marshals.

14. The minister of internal affairs shall confirm in office those of the candidates selected by the governor or proposed by the marshals to whose appointment to the post of land captain he finds no obstacle. . . .

23. The land captain has supervision over all regulations of the peasant community administration, and likewise over any revision of the aforesaid regulations. . . .

31. If the land captain ascertains that a decision of a volost' or village assembly is incompatible with the law, or tends to the obvious detriment of the village community, or violates the legitimate rights of its individual members or of persons enrolled in the volost', then, after halting the execution of this decision, he shall present it, together with his judgment, to the uezd session [*uezdnyi s"ezd*] for consideration [see below, articles 69-71, 73]. . . .

39. The land captain is charged with looking after the economic welfare and moral advancement of the peasants in the district entrusted to him, in matters falling under the jurisdiction of village and volost' assemblies. . . .

47. The land captains shall perform the duties of justices of the peace. . . .

61. In the event that persons under the jurisdiction of the peasant community should fail to comply with the lawful arrangements or demands of the land captains, he has the right to subject the guilty person, without formal trial, to arrest for a period not exceeding three days, or to a monetary fine not exceeding six rubles.

62. The land captain, after considering complaints brought before him against the actions of officials of the village and volost' administration, and likewise in the event of minor delinquencies by the aforesaid persons in the performance of their duties, which he has directly observed himself, has the right to subject them, without any formal trial, to one of the following penalties: a rebuke, a reprimand, a monetary fine not exceeding five rubles, or arrest for a period not exceeding seven days. For more serious violations, the land captain is permitted to remove temporarily from office all aforesaid persons (including volost' judges) and to make representation to the uezd session for removing them permanently from their posts, or for bringing them to trial. . . .

69. An uezd session shall be constituted in each uezd.

70. The uezd session shall contain two bureaus [*prisutstviia*]: administrative and judicial.

71. The administrative bureau of the session shall be composed . . . of all the land captains of the uezd, the police captain [*ispravnik*], and the chairman of the uezd zemstvo executive board, under the chairmanship of the uezd marshal of the nobility. . . .

73. The judicial bureau of the session shall be composed . . . of the uezd member of the district court [*uezdnyi chlen okruzhnogo suda*], the honorary justices of the peace, the municipal judges [*gorodskie sud'i*], and the land captains, under the chairmanship of the uezd marshal of the nobility. . . .

[Note: According to articles 104 and 105, the appellate body for the uezd session is to be the guberniia bureau (*gubernskoe prisutstvie*), under the chairmanship of the governor.]

III. Temporary rules for the volost' courts.
. . .

1. The volost' court shall consist of four judges; one of them, designated by the uezd session, shall be appointed chairman. The session, if it deems it necessary, may confer the duties of chairman upon the local volost' elder.

2. Each village community shall select one candidate for volost' judge; the total number of candidates, however, should not be fewer than eight. . . . From among the candidates, the district land captain shall confirm four in the office of volost' judge for a term of four years and shall appoint the rest as their deputies [*kandidaty*] for the same term. . . .

[Note: According to articles 30-31, complaints against decisions of the volost' court are to be brought before the land captain, who is to present them to the uezd session.]

33. The volost' court may impose, for offenses under its jurisdiction: (1) a reprimand in the presence of the court; (2) a monetary fine of from twenty-five kopecks to thirty rubles; (3) arrest . . . for up to thirty days; and (4) for persons not exempt from corporal punishment . . . punishment with rods, up to twenty blows.

XVI:11. THE NEW ZEMSTVO STATUTE, JUNE 12, 1890

This statute, covering zemstvo institutions in the guberniia and uezd, differed from that of 1864 primarily in that it increased the government's control over zemstvo activities. Here are some of the more important provisions.

Reference: *PSZRI*, 3rd ser., 10:496, 499, 501, 505-06, 509.

5. The governor shall have supervision over the correctness and legality of the actions of zemstvo institutions. . . .

8. For considering, in relevant cases, the correctness and legality of ordinances and arrangements of the zemstvo institutions . . . a guberniia bureau for zemstvo affairs [*gubernskoe po zemskim delam prisutstvie*] shall be instituted in each guberniia. This bureau, under the chairmanship of the governor, shall be composed of the guberniia marshal of the nobility, the vice-governor, the director of the fiscal chamber [*kazennaia palata*], the prosecutor of the district court, the chairman of the guberniia zemstvo executive board, or their legal deputies, and one representative of the guberniia zemstvo assembly, elected by the latter body from among the members of the guberniia executive board or members of the assembly. . . .

[Note: According to article 16, the right to participate in the election of members of the zemstvo assembly was to be enjoyed by landowners who met certain landed property norms (in most guberniias fixed at 150-200 desiatinas), or by owners of other real property with a value of not less than 15,000 rubles. According to article 24, persons who owned not less than one-tenth the amount of land prescribed as the norm would elect representatives (*upolnomochennye*) from their own midst to participate in the zemstvo electoral college (*izbiratel'noe sobranie*).]

28. For holding elections of members of uezd zemstvo assemblies by persons participating in zemstvo electoral colleges, two electoral colleges shall be constituted in each uezd. In the first college shall participate all hereditary and personal nobles, under the chairmanship of the uezd marshal of the nobility; in the second college, other persons having the right to participate in zemstvo elections, under the chairmanship of the mayor of the guberniia or uezd capital, as appropriate. . . .

51. Representatives of village communities shall be elected by the volost' assemblies. . . . From among the candidates [one from each volost', in most cases] the governor shall

appoint the number of representatives of village communities prescribed by law. . . .

87. The governor shall halt the execution of an ordinance of the zemstvo assembly in cases where he ascertains that it: (a) is incompatible with the law or was enacted in violation of the sphere of jurisdiction, the limits of authority, or the order of procedure of zemstvo institutions; or (b) does not correspond to the general welfare and needs of the state or clearly violates the interest of the local inhabitants. [Article 88 provides that ordinances thus halted shall be turned over by the governor within thirty days to the guberniia bureau for zemstvo affairs, which will decide, except in certain categories of cases, whether the ordinance is or is not to be executed.] . . .

89. The zemstvo assembly may bring complaints before the Governing Senate . . . against decisions of the guberniia bureau for zemstvo affairs that repeal an ordinance of the zemstvo assembly. . . .

[Note: According to article 108, the guberniia zemstvo assembly is permitted to draw up obligatory ordinances for local inhabitants on matters relating to the maintenance of order, public services (*blagoustroistvo*), and sanitation.]

118. Persons elected as chairmen of guberniia executive boards shall be confirmed in office by the minister of internal affairs, and those elected as chairmen of uezd executive boards and as members of both guberniia and uezd executive boards, by the governor. . . .

123. The term of service in elected offices of the zemstvo administration shall be fixed at three years.

XVI:12. THE NEW STATUTE CONCERNING TOWN GOVERNMENT, JUNE 11, 1892

The Municipal Statute of 1892, in comparison with that of 1870, increased the controls over city self-government and reduced the number of those who could participate in municipal elections. Some of the means are shown in these excerpts.
Reference: *PSZRI,* 3d ser., 12:434, 435, 437, 440, 445, 450, 451.

11. The governor shall have supervision over the correctness and legality of the actions of the municipal public administration.
. . .

12. The consideration, in appropriate cases, of the correctness and legality of ordinances and arrangements of the municipal public administration . . . shall devolve . . . upon the guberniia bureau for zemstvo and municipal affairs. When this bureau is considering affairs of the municipal public administration, it shall include, instead of a member elected by the guberniia zemstvo assembly, a member of the municipal duma of the guberniia capital, elected by the latter body from among its members. . . .

23. Electoral colleges shall be convoked every four years to elect the members of the duma [*glasnye dumy*] and their deputies [*kandidaty*]. . . .

24. The right to participate in the election of [duma] members shall be enjoyed by: (1) persons who are Russian subjects, and likewise charitable, scientific, and educational institutions, and governmental institutions, if these institutions and persons have owned for not less than one year, within the city limits . . . real estate . . . assessed for purposes of the [city] tax [as follows]: in both capital cities—at not less than three thousand rubles; in guberniia capitals with over 100,000 inhabitants and in the city of Odessa—at not less than fifteen hundred rubles; in other guberniia and oblast' capitals, and in cities under the jurisdiction of a city governor [*gradonachal'nik*], and likewise in the larger uezd capitals—at not less than one thousand rubles; in other municipalities—at not less than three hundred rubles. . . .

56. The duma shall be composed of members elected for a period of four years, under the chairmanship of the mayor. . . .

83. The governor shall halt the execution of ordinances of the duma in those cases in which he ascertains that they: (1) are incompatible with the law or were enacted in violation of the sphere of jurisdiction, the limits of authority, or the order of procedure of the public administration; or (2) do not correspond to the general welfare and needs of the state, or clearly violate the interests of the local inhabitants.

84. Ordinances of the duma halted by the governor as incompatible with the law or enacted in violation of the sphere of jurisdiction, the limits of authority, or the order of

procedure of the public administration shall be transmitted by him, within a month of his receipt of the ordinance, for consideration by the local bureau for zemstvo and municipal affairs or for municipal affairs. . . .

85. The duma may bring complaints before the Governing Senate . . . against decisions of the bureau for zemstvo and municipal affairs or for municipal affairs that repeal an ordinance of the duma. . . .

[Note: According to article 108, the municipal duma was permitted to draw up obligatory ordinances for local inhabitants on matters relating to the maintenance of order, public services, and sanitation in the city.] . . .

114. In Saint Petersburg and Moscow the city mayors shall be appointed by imperial authority, upon the representation of the minister of internal affairs. The dumas of the

capital cities shall be permitted to elect two candidates for this post from among their members.

115. The post of mayor in other municipalities (article 114), and likewise the posts of associate city mayor [*tovarishch gorodskogo golovy*], member of the executive board, assistant to the mayor [*pomoshchnik golovy*], and city secretary, are filled through election by the duma. . . .

118. Persons elected as associate city mayor in the two capital cities, and likewise to the posts of city mayor, assistant to the mayor, and deputy mayor [*zastupaiushchii mesto*] in guberniia capitals . . . are confirmed in office by the minister of internal affairs, and those elected to the post of city mayor and deputy mayor in other municipalities, by the governor.

XVI:13. LAMSDORF ON RUSSIFICATION IN THE BORDER REGIONS IN 1892

Count Vladimir Nikolaevich Lamsdorf (or Lamzdorf, 1841-1907), who later rose to be minister of foreign affairs, was serving in 1891-92 as assistant minister of foreign affairs under N. K. Girs (or Giers). In his diary Lamsdorf includes these comments, among others, on the policy of Russification in the border regions of the empire.

Reference: V. N. Lamzdorf, *Dnevnik 1891-1892* (Moscow: AN SSSR, 1934), p. 251.

Saturday, January 25, 1892.

. . . My brother-in-law Brok . . . is very disturbed by what is taking place in Poland. In his capacity as head of the gendarmerie in this entire region he has had the opportunity to acquaint himself with documents proving that the Austrian government contemplates, in the event of a war with Russia, the restoration of the Kingdom [of Poland] under the Habsburg scepter. . . . But what made the most painful impression on my brother-in-law was the enthusiasm that reigns of late in Warsaw with respect to the emperor Wilhelm; his portraits hang everywhere, and the Poles never stop praising him, representing him very demonstratively as a monarch of genius, and the like.

. . . The thought of restoring Poland as a buffer state between Russia and Europe could really arise in Germany and Austria. We ought

to hinder its realization, but such a danger can certainly not be overcome by means of the offensive measures of persecution adopted in all our "borderlands." . . .

January 26, 1892.

I saw my minister at eleven o'clock. I told him everything that Brok said to me yesterday about Poland; he also found this rather disturbing. Mr. Girs deplores the offensive harshnesses and likewise the arbitrary and imprudent way in which the policy of Russification is carried out in all the border provinces. It only results in general discontent and endless hatred. It is said that the governor general of Kiev, Count Aleksei Ignat'ev, a careerist by nature, proposes endless illegal measures for persecuting the Jews, which leads to the growth of pernicious unrest in this area also.

XVI:14. DIPLOMATIC DOCUMENTS ON THE FORMATION OF THE FRANCO-RUSSIAN ALLIANCE, 1891-1893

Part of the process by which Russia and France drew together in search of security against Germany is shown in these excerpts from pertinent diplomatic documents. They may serve here also as a minute sample of the thousands of documents that have been published dealing with Russia and the events leading to the First World War. Many of these exist in English (as well as French and German) not only in documentary collections but also in monographs like those cited below. In this sourcebook there is room for little more than some reminders of their existence.

Reference: Baron Boris Nolde, *L'Alliance Franco-Russe* (Paris: Librairie Droz, 1936), pp. 632-33 [letter of Aug. 21, 1891]; *Documents diplomatiques français, 1871-1914,* 1st ser., 16 vols. (Paris: Imprimerie Nationale, Alfred Costes, L'Europe Nouvelle, 1929-56), 8:686-87 [letter of Aug. 27, 1891]; 9:643-44 [letter of Aug. 10, 1892] (translation taken partially from William L. Langer, *The Franco-Russian Alliance 1890-1894* [Cambridge: Harvard University Press, 1929]); 10:711-12 [letter of Dec. 30, 1893, and enclosure of Dec. 15].

[Letter from the Russian minister of foreign affairs, Nikolai Karlovich Giers (in Russian, Girs), to Baron de Mohrenheim, Russian ambassador at Paris, August 21, 1891:]

The situation created in Europe by the renewal of the Triple Alliance [Germany, Austria, Italy] and the more or less probable adherence of Great Britain to the political aims of this alliance have prompted an exchange of ideas, during the recent stay here of M. de Laboulaye [French ambassador in Saint Petersburg, 1886-91], between the former French ambassador and myself, in order to define the attitude that would be best suited, under the present circumstances and in view of certain eventualities, to our respective governments, which, while remaining outside any alliances, are yet sincerely desirous of surrounding the maintenance of peace with the most effective safeguards.

Thus we have been led to formulate the two following points:

1. In order to define and perpetuate the cordial understanding that unites them, and desiring to contribute jointly to the maintenance of peace, which is the object of their most sincere wishes, the two governments declare that they will consult together on all issues apt to jeopardize the general peace.

2. If the peace should actually be endangered, and particularly if either of the two parties should be threatened with aggression, the two parties agree to act in accord regarding the measures the two governments would have to adopt immediately and simultaneously as soon as such an eventuality became a fact.

Having reported to the emperor about this exchange of ideas and having submitted to him the text of the conclusions that resulted from it, I have the honor to inform you herewith that His Majesty has deigned to approve these principles of mutual understanding wholly and would favorably view their adoption by the two governments.

In communicating to you these dispositions of the sovereign, I beg you to bring them to the cognizance of the French government and to inform me of the decisions it may reach on its part.

[M. Ribot, minister of foreign affairs, to M. de Mohrenheim, Russian ambassador in Paris:]

Paris, August 27, 1891.

You were kind enough to communicate to me, by order of your government, the text of the letter of the minister of foreign affairs of the [Russian] Empire, which contains the special instructions given you by the emperor Alexander following the recent exchange of ideas between M. de Giers and the ambassador of the French Republic in Saint Petersburg, as occasioned by the general situation in Europe.

Your Excellency was instructed at the same time to express the hope that the contents of that paper, which had been agreed upon and formulated jointly by the two cabinets, would meet with the full approval of the French government.

I take pleasure in thanking Your Excellency for this communication.

The government of the republic could not but view in the same light as the imperial government the situation created in Europe by the circumstances in which the renewal of the Triple Alliance has taken place and considers with it that the time has come to define the attitude that, under the present circumstances and in view of certain eventualities, would be most expedient for the two governments, equally desirous of preserving the safeguards for the maintenance of peace inherent in the equilibrium of the European powers.

Accordingly, I am pleased to inform Your Excellency that the government of the republic gives its complete assent to the two points set forth in the communication from M. de Giers.

. . .

In asking you to bring the reply of the

French government to the cognizance of His Majesty's government, I wish to express my satisfaction in being able to concur, insofar as I am concerned, in the reaffirmation of an understanding that has constantly been the object of our common efforts.

[M. de Montebello, French ambassador to Saint Petersburg, to M. Ribot, minister of foreign affairs, August 10, 1892:]

General Boisdeffre today has seen General Obruchev, who was delegated by the emperor to discuss the draft of the convention.

After an extended discussion, the following text has been proposed:

"France and Russia, being animated with an equal desire to preserve peace, and having no other purpose but to prepare for the exigency of a defensive war provoked by an attack by the forces of the Triple Alliance against either one of them, have agreed upon the following measures:

"1. If France is attacked by Germany or by Italy supported by Germany, Russia shall employ all her available forces to attack Germany.

"If Russia is attacked by Germany or by Austria supported by Germany, France shall employ all her available forces to combat Germany.

"2. In case the forces of the Triple Alliance, or of one of the powers composing it, should mobilize, France and Russia, at the first news of the event and without the necessity of any prior consultation, shall mobilize immediately and simultaneously all their forces and shall transport them as near to the frontiers as possible.

"3. The available forces to be employed against Germany shall be: on the part of France, 1,300,000 men; on the part of Russia, 700,000 or 800,000.

"These forces shall engage to the full with all speed, so that Germany will have to fight on the east and west at the same time.

"4. The chiefs of staff of the armies of the two countries shall consult with each other at all times to prepare for and to facilitate the execution of the measures foreseen above.

"They shall communicate to each other, in time of peace, all information they know, or which shall come to their knowledge, relating to the armaments of the Triple Alliance.

"The ways and means of consulting in time of war shall be studied and planned beforehand.

"5. France and Russia shall not conclude a separate peace with the Triple Alliance.

"6. The present convention shall have the same duration as the Triple Alliance.

"7. All the clauses enumerated above shall be held in strict secrecy."

[M. de Montebello, French ambassador at Saint Petersburg, to M. Casimir-Périer, minister of foreign affairs, December 30, 1893:]

I have just received a letter from M. de Giers informing me that, having been given the orders of the emperor, he has been instructed to let me know that the draft of a military agreement, which had been approved by the emperor in principle and signed by the two chiefs of staff, has been definitely adopted. . . .

Enclosure

M. de Giers, minister of foreign affairs, to M. de Montebello, French ambassador in Saint Petersburg.

Saint Petersburg, December 15 (27, N.S.), 1893.

After studying, by order of the emperor, the draft of a military convention worked out by the Russian and French general staffs in August, 1892, and after submitting it with my appraisal to the emperor, I wish to inform Your Excellency that the text of this understanding, as approved by His Majesty in principle and signed by Adjutant General Obruchev and by Major General Boisdeffre, may henceforth be regarded as definitively adopted in its present form. The two general staffs will thus be able to consult with each other at all times and to convey to each other all the information that may be useful to them.

XVI:15. LETTERS FROM WILLIAM OF GERMANY TO TSAR NICHOLAS, APRIL 26 AND JULY 10, 1895

The German kaiser had his own reasons for joining those who encouraged the young tsar Nicholas to direct his attention eastward. Here are excerpts from two of the numerous letters from "Willy" to "Nicky" apropos of Russia's increased Far Eastern activity just after the Sino-Japanese War.

Reference: Wilhelm II, *The Kaiser's Letters to the Tsar,* ed. N. F. Grant (London: Hodder and Stoughton, 1920), pp. 11, 13.

[From a letter of April 26, 1895:]

For that is clearly the great task of the future for Russia, to cultivate the Asian Continent and to defend Europe from the inroads of the Great Yellow Race. In this you will always find me on your side, ready to help you as best I can. You have well understood that call of Providence, and have quickly grasped the moment; it is of immense political and historical value and much good will come of it.

[From a letter of July 10, 1895:]

Europe had to be thankful to you that you so quickly had perceived the great future for Russia in the cultivation of Asia and in the Defence of the Cross and the old Christian European culture against the inroads of the Mongols and Buddhism. . . . I would let nobody try to interfere with you and attack from behind in Europe during the time you were fulfilling the great mission which Heaven has shaped for you. That was as sure as Amen in Church.

XVI:16. WITTE ON RUSSIAN POLICY IN THE CAUCASUS AND THE FAR EAST, CA. 1896-1905

Sergei Iul'evich Vitte (1849-1915) is usually called "Witte" in English, although his mother was thoroughly Russian, his father's Dutch ancestors had long since been absorbed into the gentry of the Pskov region, and his father himself had made the transition from Lutheranism to Russian Orthodoxy. Witte's celebrated memoirs contain valuable if not always nonpartisan data on countless aspects of public life. Here are some of the comments Witte confided to his memoirs concerning Russian policy in the Caucasus, especially in the period 1896-1905. Witte was born and spent his childhood in Tiflis (Tbilisi), where his father was a government official.

In understanding the frankness with which Witte expresses himself in these excerpts and others later in this chapter, it is helpful to recall that he wrote his memoirs only while abroad, during the months of his vacations at various European resorts. The manuscripts were initially kept in a Paris bank in his wife's name, then were transferred by her to a safe in a Bayonne bank under still another person's name. In this way they escaped the agents of the tsar both during his lifetime and after his death (February 1915), as when an attaché was sent to search through Witte's villa in Biarritz during his widow's absence.

Reference: S. Iu. Vitte, *Vospominaniia: Tsarstvovanie Nikolaia II,* 2 vols. (Berlin: Slovo, 1922), 2:95, 96, 186, 187, 188 [on the Caucasus]; 1:42, 48-49, 65, 129, 131, 200-02, 264, 373 [on the Far East]. The translation of the last excerpt on the Far East is based mostly on Abraham Yarmolinsky's translation in *The Memoirs of Count Witte* (Garden City, N.Y.: Doubleday, Page and Co., 1921), pp. 139-40. The other translations are based directly on the Russian. Edited versions of some of the passages on the Far East are contained in Yarmolinsky, pp. 85-86, 89-90, 97-98, and 106-07.

[On December 12, 1896, Prince Golitsyn was appointed chief administrator in the Caucasus.]

Prince Golitsyn's administration in the Caucasus was noteworthy only in that he aroused the entire Caucasus against him and, indirectly, against the Russian government. Finally, an attempt was made upon his life; he was wounded and thereupon left the Caucasus. But this happened after several years of his rule, when he had already to a considerable extent disorganized that special spirit with which the Caucasus had been governed.

All his predecessors, beginning with the famous serene prince Vorontsov, the vice-gerent of the Caucasus appointed by Emperor Nicholas I, adhered to the principle that the

natives, especially those of the Christian faith and those who had voluntarily submitted to Russian sovereignty, ought to enjoy complete equality of rights. This is why the Caucasus was conquered by the arms both of Russians— that is, persons who had come from Russia— and of natives of the Caucasus. Throughout the sixty-year war in the Caucasus one saw the local natives distinguishing themselves everywhere—not only in the lower ranks of the militia but also in the highest positions. They contributed to the Russian army a whole galaxy of heroes, heroes who attained the highest ranks and decorations. One could cite dozens of such names, for instance, the princes Orbeliani, the princes Bebutov, Prince Ame-

lakhvari, the princes Chavchavadze, the
princes Argutinskii, and so forth. For that
reason, all the administrators of the Caucasus
always treated these natives with the utmost
goodwill and tried not to violate their rights
in any way.

   . . .

It was only by this policy, followed by all
the administrators of the Caucasus (before
Prince Golitsyn), that we conquered that entire region and welded it firmly to the Russian
Empire.

Prince Golitsyn was the first administrator
who put into practice a narrowly nationalistic
point of view. . . . In the final analysis Prince
Golitsyn was a misfit in the Caucasus, and he
left the Caucasus disliked by all, including
the Russians.

   . . .

Prince Golitsyn took action against all the
nationalities inhabiting the Caucasus because
he wanted to Russify them all; but . . . he
displayed the greatest hostility toward the
Armenians. Moreover, in consequence of the
persecution of Turkish Armenians in Turkey
many thousands of Turkish Armenians, infected with a revolutionary spirit, had recently migrated to the Caucasus. These experienced
revolutionaries naturally began to spread revolutionary ideas among their co-religionists
and fellow Armenians who were Russian subjects.

   . . .

To curb the Armenians, Prince Golitsyn
conceived the idea of confiscating the property
of the Armenian churches. For the Armenians
the church is a living thing, it is the spiritual
core of their life; all the charitable and educational activities of the people are centered
in the church. . . .

I objected to this loathsome undertaking
in the most resolute manner, on both political
and ethical grounds.

   . . .

In place of Prince Golitsyn, Count Vo-
rontsov-Dashkov was appointed vicegerent
[1905], which post he holds to this day. He
has reverted to the traditional policy of the
best administrators of the Caucasus, Prince
Vorontsov, Prince Bariatinskii, and the like,
and has put an end to the oppression of the
natives. On his recommendation the decision
to sequestrate the property of the Armenian
churches was rescinded, although in practice

it is proving difficult today to disentangle the
matter, since the bulk of the property had already been taken away. He is liked and
respected in the Caucasus. But now, so long
as the unrest in Russia continues, it is impossible to put an end to the unrest in the Caucasus. It is a recurrence of the phenomenon
that typically troubles the Russian Empire.
All sensible measures come too late. *On vient
toujours trop tard.*

[Witte on the Far East, 1896-1905:]

[For the coronation of Emperor Nicholas
II in May 1896,] China sent Li Hung-chang.
This was the most outstanding of [China's]
statesmen, occupying at that time the highest
office in China, and so the dispatch of Li
Hung-chang to the coronation was meant to
indicate the particular gratitude of China to
our young emperor for the service he had
rendered China in preserving the integrity of
Chinese territory, and likewise for the assistance we had rendered China in her
financial affairs.

In the meantime our great Trans-Siberian
railway had almost reached Trans-Baikalia,
and it became imperative to decide the
further route the railroad should follow.
Quite naturally, I conceived the idea of continuing the road straight across to Vladivostok, cutting across Mongolia and northern
Manchuria. This would speed up its construction considerably. In this way the Trans-
Siberian would become a real transit line,
an artery of worldwide importance, connecting Japan and the entire Far East with Russia
and Europe.

   . . .

I met with Li Hung-chang, and we reached
an agreement on all points, setting forth the
following principles for a secret pact with
China:

1. The Chinese Empire would grant us
permission to build a railroad across its territory along a straight line between Chita and
Vladivostok; but the management of this
railroad must be entrusted to a private
company. Li Hung-chang absolutely refused
to accept my proposal that the road should
be constructed by the treasury, or that it
should belong to the treasury and the state.
For that reason we were forced to form the
Chinese Eastern Railway Company, which of
course was and still is completely in the hands
of the government. . . .

2. Furthermore, a strip of land for the railroad should be alienated to us, as necessary for railway operations. Within this alienated strip we would be sovereign in this respect: that since the territory belonged to us, we would have complete jurisdiction in it, with our own police force and our own guards, i.e. what later comprised the so-called protective guard of the Chinese Eastern Railroad. . . .

On the other hand, we would bind ourselves to defend Chinese territory from any aggressive action on the part of Japan. Thus we would enter into a defensive alliance with China against Japan.

These were essentially the principles on which I reached an agreement with Li Hungchang.

. . .

A treaty with Japan was also signed in Moscow. Prince Lobanov-Rostovskii conducted all the negotiations for this treaty; I also participated, but in a secondary role. I consider that this was a felicitous treaty. By this treaty Russia and Japan arranged for a division of influence in Korea, with Russia obtaining the preponderant influence.

Japan's representatives willingly agreed to this treaty. By this treaty we could keep military instructors and several hundred of our soldiers in Korea, so that in military and financial matters, as regards the management of state finances, Russia was accorded considerable, one might say dominant, rights; thus, by the treaty, we appointed a financial counselor to the Korean emperor, which was equivalent to the appointment of a minister of finance. But influence in Korea was shared by Japan as well as by Russia; Japan could likewise have its industrial companies and carry on trade there; Russia had no special financial privileges that were not accorded to Japan as well, and so forth. In general, as I have already said, I consider this a felicitous treaty.

Thus it seemed that, in Moscow, Russia and Japan had firmly established a division of influence in Korea—now an independent Korea, since before the Sino-Japanese War Korea was considered an autonomous province of China.

. . .

[In December, 1897, a Russian naval squadron entered the harbor of Port Arthur, and on March 15, 1898, an agreement was signed with China for the twenty-five-year

"lease" of the Kwantung region of the Liaotung Peninsula. Witte comments:] This seizure of the Kwantung region [by Russia] . . . was an act of unexampled perfidy.

Several years before our seizure of the Kwantung region we had forced the Japanese to leave it, and, under the pretext that we could not tolerate a violation of China's integrity, we concluded a secret defensive alliance with China against Japan, through which we obtained very considerable advantages in the Far East. Then, after a very short interval, we ourselves occupied a part of the region we had compelled the Japanese after their victory to abandon, on the ground that we could not tolerate any violation of the integrity of the Chinese Empire.

There is no doubt that Emperor Wilhelm incited this action by his seizure of Tsingtao [Ch'ing-tao].

. . .

Our seizure of the Kwantung region made such an overwhelming impression on Japan that Count Murav'ev, fearing an armed conflict with Japan, yielded to her demands and withdrew our military instructors and our military forces from Korea; subsequently [K. A.] Alekseev, our counselor to the Korean emperor, was also forced to leave.

Military as well as financial and economic influence in Korea passed from our agents to agents of Japan.

As a result, in order to pacify Japan, an agreement with Japan was concluded on April 13, 1898, by which we clearly yielded dominant influence in Korea to Japan. Japan understood this and was pacified for the moment.

If we had adhered scrupulously not only to the letter but to the spirit of this agreement, i.e. if we had unreservedly left Korea under complete Japanese influence, there is no doubt that peaceful relations would have been established between Russia and Japan for a long time to come.

. . .

Around November 15, 1901, the remarkable and even great Japanese statesman, Marquis Ito, arrived in Saint Petersburg.

The purpose of Marquis Ito's visit was to establish, at last, an agreement between Russia and Japan which would avert the unfortunate war that later broke out. The agreement was to be based on the following principles. Russia definitely had to yield to Japan complete influence in Korea. Japan would accept the seizure of the Kwantung region and the construction of the eastern branch of the Chinese Railroad to Port Arthur, but on the condition that we would withdraw our troops from Manchuria, leaving only the railroad guards, and would then apply the open door policy to Manchuria. This was, properly speaking, the substance of his proposals. . . .

Ito met with a very cool reception in Saint Petersburg. . . .

. . . We gave no definite reply to the proposed agreement that Ito presented.

. . .

In the summer of 1902 the sovereign emperor went to Revel' to attend naval maneuvers. In June the German emperor came for the maneuvers. When the maneuvers were over, the following interesting incident took place, revealing the frame of mind of the German emperor. When his yacht was bearing off and the usual farewell signals were being exchanged, the German emperor gave the following signal: the admiral of the Atlantic Ocean salutes the admiral of the Pacific Ocean. The sovereign was greatly embarrassed for an answer to this salute. I do not know how His Majesty replied, but I know for a fact that the German emperor sent to ours a message that, if translated into ordinary language, meant: I aim to seize or acquire a dominant position in the Atlantic Ocean, and I advise you and will give you my support to obtain a dominant position in the Pacific Ocean.

. . . Emperor Wilhelm pushed us into the Far Eastern affair, realizing that if he distracted us in the Far East he would have a free hand in Europe; by this signal he was continuing that same typical game.

I do not know whether it was the influence of Emperor Wilhelm, reflected, among other things, in that signal, or whether it was something else; but from that time onward, and still more in 1903, the dispatches sent to His Majesty's vicegerent in the Far East and other documents repeatedly expressed the sovereign's desire that Russia acquire a dominant influence in the Pacific Ocean.

. . .

[On the Russo-Japanese War:]

On February 8, [1904] Minister of War Kuropatkin was appointed commander of the army [in Manchuria].

This appointment followed the wishes of public opinion; public opinion unanimously demanded the appointment of Kuropatkin, in whom it had great trust. . . .

The appointment itself nonetheless was rather absurd, for it turned out that the Russian army now had two commanders: on the one hand [E. I.] Alekseev, vicegerent of the Far East, as commander in chief; and on the other, the former minister of war, Adjutant General Kuropatkin, commanding the army. Such a combination was obviously incompatible with the most elementary rules of military science, which always requires single leadership, particularly in time of war. Therefore it was natural that this appointment could result in nothing but confusion.

. . .

[While en route to the United States in the summer of 1905, after Russia's humiliating reverses in the Far East, to seek peace with the Japanese at Portsmouth, New Hampshire:]

On board ship I had ample opportunity to remain alone and to reflect. I resolved to base my tactics on the following principles: (1) not to show that we were in the least anxious to make peace, and to convey the impression that, if His Majesty had consented to the negotiations, it was merely because of the universal desire on the part of all countries to see the war terminated; (2) to act as befitted the representative of Russia, that is, the representative of a mighty empire involved temporarily in a slight difficulty; (3) in view of the tremendous influence of the press in America, to show it every attention and to be accessible to all its representatives; (4) to behave with democratic simplicity and without a shadow of snobbishness, so as to win the sympathy of the extremely democratic Americans; (5) in view of the considerable influence of the Jews on the press, especially in New York, not to exhibit any hostility toward them—which conduct was entirely in keeping with my opinion of the Jewish question. I followed this program of action strictly throughout my stay in the United States, where I lived, by virtue of the peculiar circumstances in which I found myself, always in everybody's sight like an actor on the stage.

XVI:17. THE PEACE TREATY WITH JAPAN AT PORTSMOUTH, AUGUST 23, 1905

Here are some of the main provisions of the peace treaty which, through the mediation of President Theodore Roosevelt, was concluded between Russia and Japan at Portsmouth, New Hampshire, August 23 (September 5, N.S.), 1905. Witte headed the Russian delegation.

Refererence: *PSZRI*, 3d ser., vol. 25, pt. 1, pp. 713-15; translation based, with some changes, on *Traités et conventions entre l'Empire du Japon et les puissances etrangères* (Tokyo: Z. P. Maruya, 1908), pp. 585-97. Russian and English versions are also contained in *Sbornik dogovorov i diplomaticheskikh dokumentov po delam Dal'nego Vostoka 1895-1905 gg.* (St. Petersburg: Izd. Ministerstva Inostrannykh Del, 1906), pp. 741-53.

We hereby declare that in pursuance of a mutual agreement between ourselves [the emperor of Russia] and His Majesty the emperor of Japan, our plenipotentiaries have concluded and signed, in Portsmouth, on August 23, 1905, a treaty of peace.

. . .

ARTICLE II. The imperial Russian government, acknowledging that Japan possesses paramount political, military, and economic interests in Korea, engages neither to obstruct nor to interfere with the measures of guidance, protection, and control which the imperial government of Japan may find it necessary to take in Korea. . . .

ART. III. Russia and Japan mutually engage:

1. To evacuate Manchuria completely and simultaneously, except for the territory covered by the lease of the Liaotung Peninsula. . . .

2. To restore entirely and completely to the exclusive administration of China all portions of Manchuria now occupied or controlled by Japanese or Russian troops, with the exception of the territory mentioned above.

The imperial government of Russia declares that it does not have any territorial advantages or preferential or exclusive concessions in Manchuria that could impair Chinese sovereign rights or are inconsistent with the principle of parity of rights. . . .

ART. V. The imperial Russian government cedes to the imperial government of Japan, with the consent of the government of China, the lease of Port Arthur, Talien, and the adjacent territories and territorial waters, and likewise all rights, privileges, and concessions connected with or constituting a part of this lease; it also cedes to the imperial government of Japan all public works and properties in the territory covered by the above-mentioned lease. . . .

ART. VI. The imperial Russian government engages to cede to the imperial government of Japan, without compensation and with the consent of the Chinese government, the railway between Ch'ang-ch'un (K'uanch'eng-tzu) and Port Arthur, with all its branch lines and the rights, privileges, and properties in that locality, as well as all coal mines in the said region belonging to or worked for the benefit of the above-mentioned railway. . . .

ART. IX. The imperial Russian government cedes to the imperial government of Japan, in perpetuity and full sovereignty, the southern portion of the island of Sakhalin and all islands adjacent thereto. . . .

Japan and Russia mutually agree not to construct in their possessions on the island of Sakhalin or the adjacent islands any fortifications or similar military works. They also mutually engage not to take any military measures that may impede the free navigation of the straits of La Perouse and Tartary. . . .

ART. XI. Russia engages to enter into an agreement with Japan for granting to Japanese subjects fishing rights along the coasts of the Russian possessions in the seas of Japan, Okhotsk, and Bering.

XVI:18. A REPORT FROM ZUBATOV, SEPTEMBER 19, 1900

This excerpt from a secret report of September 19, 1900, by Sergei Vasil'evich Zubatov (1864-1917), head of the Moscow section of the Okhrana, helps to explain the experiment in "police socialism" which Zubatov was permitted to conduct in Moscow from 1901 to 1903.

Reference: *Krasnyi arkhiv*, vol. 19 (1926), p. 211.

We must woo the masses. They have a staunch faith in us, but both oppositional and revolutionary propaganda is trying to weaken their faith. It is essential to nurture this faith with proof of our solicitude, and then any opposition will be powerless, no matter how hard it tries.

. . .

In other words, the moral is this: (1) ideologists always exploit the masses politically on the basis of their want and poverty, and we must catch hold of them; and (2) in struggling with them, we must always remember to "strike at the root," disarming the masses by means of timely and constant improvement of their condition by the government, on the basis of their petty wants and demands (by themselves the masses never demand more than this at one time). But the government must definitely do this itself and must do it constantly, without delay. . . . In the present circumstances the motto of our internal policy must be the "maintenance of equilibrium among the classes," which now regard each other with hatred. An autocracy that stands above classes must follow a policy of *divide et impera*. Only let them not come to terms (which is all it takes for a revolution)—a development that could be promoted by the strategems of ideologists and by our own one-sidedness. And this is why we must keep a tight grip on these ideologists and must undertake a reformation in regard to the masses. In order to create a counterpoise (as an antidote) to the bourgeoisie, which feels proud and acts insolently, we must attract the workers, thereby killing two birds with one stone: restraining the bourgeoisie and the ideologists, and making the workers and peasants favorably disposed toward us.

XVI:19. THE DIARY OF A. A. POLOVTSEV CONCERNING THE GOVERNMENT IN 1901 AND 1902

Aleksandr Aleksandrovich Polovtsev (1832-1909) was appointed senator in 1873, chief secretary of the State Council (*gosudarstvennyi sekretar'*) in 1883, and member of the State Council in 1892. His personal diary—published only after the Revolution—affords glimpses of the highest echelon of the government, as shown in these excerpts of 1901 and 1902.

Reference: "Dnevnik A. A. Polovtseva, 1901-1903 gg.," *Krasnyi arkhiv*, 3 (1923): 99, 161.

[From his entry of July 22, 1901:]

Living in the seclusion of Tsarskoe Selo one learns only in bits and snatches what is going on in the circles that guide the destiny of our country. There is no policy based on principle, well reasoned and firmly directed, in any field. Everything is being done piecemeal and fortuitously, on momentary impulse, through the intrigues of one person or another, or through the importunities of various fortune seekers who crawl out of their dark corners. The young tsar is becoming more and more contemptuous of the organs of his own authority and is beginning to believe in the beneficent effect of his autocratic power, which he exercises sporadically, without prior deliberation and without reference to the general course of affairs.

[From his entry of September 22, 1902:]

After four weeks spent first at Tsarskoe Selo and then in Saint Petersburg . . . I am obliged to return to the south to gather my strength for the winter legislative season in the State Council. I take with me the saddest impressions of difficult times for our fatherland. Because of the unrestrained abuse of power by officialdom, senseless bureaucratic whims, regulations bordering on the ridiculous, the absence of any sound policy discussed in advance, capricious interference in affairs and especially in appointments by the empresses, the grand dukes and duchesses, and the crowd of scoundrels surrounding them, the Russian people are sinking deeper and deeper into oppression and misery. Their patience is wearing thin; the ground for anarchy is becoming ever more propitious. The young tsar, who hears from all sides that salvation lies in autocracy, has a wrong conception of this profound truth, and what he gives to Russia is not a tsarist but a bureaucratic autocracy. Great disasters are in store for Russia.

XVI:20. URUSOV ON THE KISHINEV POGROM OF APRIL 1903

One significant source concerning the Kishinev pogrom of April 1903 is Prince Sergei Dmitrievich Urusov, who became governor of Bessarabia in May, shortly after the disorders. Urusov, born in

1862, was from a distinguished noble family. He had served three terms as the elected marshal of the nobility in the Kaluga guberniia and was also president of the guberniia zemstvo institutions. In 1902 Minister of the Interior Pleve had appointed him vice-governor of Tambov, and it was from there that he was promoted to the post in Kishinev. His term there lasted through much of the judicial investigation pursuant to the pogrom. His memoirs are of special interest also for what they reveal of him as an administrator and as an analyst of the political process.

Reference: S. D. Urusov [Urussov], *Memoirs of a Russian Governor, Prince S. D. Urussov,* trans. Herman Rosenthal (New York: Harper and Brothers, 1908), pp. 77, 79-85, 148.

The real cause of the Kishinev massacre still remains obscure. The April riots of 1903 gave rise to an amount of agitation and burning interest in Russia and abroad not weakened by the subsequent massacres of Jews that took place after the October manifesto of 1903 [actually 1905—eds.] in various cities and towns, and afterwards in 1906, at Homel, Byelostok, and Siedlce. . . .

I must, therefore, speak of the impressions made upon me by the factors antecedent to the disorders of Easter, 1903, which deprived the Kishinev Jews of forty-two lives, and inflicted on them a loss of at least a million rubles.

But in spite of every effort to give a clear account of the entire matter, and notwithstanding my wish to detail impartially my impressions, I can but faintly sketch the events that preceded the portents of the massacre.

⋅ ⋅ ⋅

A significant role in preparing for the pogrom was played by the press, this especially by Krushevan's local paper [Krushevan was a local estate owner of Moldavian extraction] and the St. Petersburg publications of similar tendencies, shipped to Kishinev for distribution. Issues of these papers were filled with accusations against the Jews, as well as statements and arguments calculated to stir up the passions. Krushevan's authority, in the eyes of his readers, was to a certain degree supported by the open patronage of the chief bureau of the press censorship. The effect was that the local administration was powerless to temper his anti-Semitic zeal. . . . Moreover, the local resident could not help noting the government's favorable attitude toward those who endeavored to develop the "Russian spirit," in patriotic garb, thus advancing their private interests.

The monstrous manifestations of this spirit, which called into existence later on the notorious leagues of the "True Russians," are universally known. Most people free from bias doubtless noticed that these "patriotic bodies" include many persons of dubious antecedents, of unenviable reputation, and utter lack of scruple. Hatred of the Jews is one of their chief articles of faith. Among those of this notorious class at Kishinev were Pronin [a prominent local citizen] and his companion, and these individuals openly boasted themselves the mainstay of the Russian government and the pioneers of Russian interests in a non-Slavic province. It cannot be doubted that such people did enjoy a certain degree of protection from a government that regarded the autocracy as a "sound foundation," a patriotic bulwark of the autocracy and Russian nativism. It was equally true that in this crowd could be found any number who were ready to beat and plunder the Jews in the name of the Orthodox Church, in defence of the orthodox people, and for the glory of the autocratic Russian Czar.

The connection of these Russians with the police, especially with the secret service, already existed at the time I describe. The Kishinev police, as probably the police in other cities where the Jewish population predominated, noted the central tendency and its manifestations in their vicinity. The police, therefore, thought that a hostile attitude towards the Jews was a sort of government watchword; that Jews might be oppressed not out of "fear," but as a matter of "conscience." In connection with this, the conviction grew among the ignorant masses that hostile acts against the Jews could be undertaken with impunity. Things went so far that a legend appeared among the people that the Czar had ordered a three days' massacre of the Jews. . . .

Thus, in my opinion, the central government cannot shake off its moral responsibility for the slaughter and plunder that went on at Kishinev. I consider our government guilty of encouraging the narrow, nationalistic tendencies. It inaugurated a short-sighted policy, coarse in its methods, with regard to the frontier country and the non-Slavic population—a policy fostering among the several nationalities mutual distrust and hatred. Finally, the authorities connived at the militant jingoism. Thus are indirectly encouraged those barbarous instincts that vanish the moment the government openly announces that a pogrom founded on race hatred is a crime—a crime for which an administration that condones it in any way must be held responsible. This was demonstrated in the eighties by the famous circular of Count Tolstoi [that of June 9, 1882, Item XVI:7, above], the Minister of the Interior. Thus I regard the charge of connivance lodged against the government.

But can one fully exonerate the government of the suspicion that—at least through its secret agents—it did take a direct part in the massacres? And can it be maintained that the immediate cause of the massacres was of a natural, an accidental character, and not the execution of "an order"?

. . .

I do not care to pass my suppositions for facts. I only pointed out the way in which the anti-Semitism of Plehve, Minister of the Interior, possibly voiced by him as a mere matter of conviction, could be interpreted by his colleague Wahl, who was guided, in addition, by other extraministerial influences. These influences might well have suggested to him the desirability of trying the experiment of applying the pogrom policy. Moreover, I showed how this hint, rolling down the hierarchic incline of the gendarmerie corps, reached Lewendal [head of the secret police in Kishinev] in the guise of a *wish* on the part of the higher authorities, reached Pronin and Krushevan as a *call* for a patriotic exploit, and reached the Moldavian rioters as an *order* of the Czar. The pogrom trial lasted a very long time, and I did not continue in office at Kishinev until the end. To the best of my recollection, the number of men acquitted was approximately equal to the number of those convicted. The penalties meted out were, with rare exceptions, very lenient. The suits for damages were mostly left unsatisfied, as it was impossible to prove the extent of the damage done by any one of the defendants.

. . .

The staff of the Prosecuting Attorney of Bessarabia was a most respectable one. At the head of it stood the Prosecuting Attorney, V. N. Goremykin, a graduate of the Lyceum, nephew of I. L. Goremykin, formerly Minister of the Interior and subsequently Prime-Minister during the first Duma. With V. N. Goremykin I became very intimate. We worked together very cordially, and often met to confer on questions in which the Governor and the prosecuting attorney have some points in common.

. . .

He [Goremykin] was not, properly speaking, a judophile, but simply an intelligent and educated man, free from animosity and intolerance towards all non-Russian nationalities. But, as is well known, with us it is just these qualities which give one the name of a judophile. V. N. Goremykin did not escape the unpleasant effects of his impartial and strictly lawful attitude toward the Jews. . . .

The preliminary inquest held in the pogrom case and the indictment drawn up by Goremykin resulted in a number of charges and complaints of the prosecuting attorney's partiality towards the Jews. Not only the notorious, small-calibered, "patriotic" press, but even the *Novoye Vremya*, expressed indignation at the fact that not a single Jew was indicted in the pogrom case. Goremykin had even to furnish to his superiors an explanation of the matter. Yet, indeed, while forty-two Jews were killed during the pogrom, and none but Jewish property was looted, of the Christians only one boy perished, and he by a stray bullet. The Jewish defence, as was established by the inquest, was nothing more than that they were congregating in several places and arming themselves with sticks that injured nobody, and did nothing to hinder the success of the rioters. Not a single complaint of violence committed by Jews reached either the police or the prosecuting attorney. Still, our attorney did not escape the reproach of having conducted the preliminary inquest with partiality and one-sidedness.

. . .

It is self-evident that trades and commerce on anything like a paying basis, leaving a margin above the point of mere subsistence, are unthinkable in the cities and towns where Jewish destitution reigns supreme. The result is that in such communities there is a wholesale exodus of the artisans and small merchants of other nationalities from their occupations, and along with this comes the usual complaint against the invasion of the Jews into all branches of industry and commerce, to the exclusion of everybody else. Anti-Jewish discontent grows in proportion to the increasing number of Jews, preparing in this way the ground on which pogroms have of late so richly bloomed.

XVI:21. NICHOLAS'S DECREE LIMITING FINNISH AUTONOMY, MARCH 20, 1903

In August 1898, the appointment of General N. I. Bobrikov as governor general of the Grand Duchy of Finland inaugurated a period of progressive encroachments on Finnish autonomy. The Russian measures of 1899-1901 aroused Finnish opposition, which in turn led the tsar to issue on March 20 (April 2, N.S.), 1903, a decree containing these measures to preserve "public tranquillity."

Reference: *PSZRI*, 3d ser., 23:170-71.

1. The governor general is authorized:

a. To order the temporary closure of hotels, wholesale and retail bookstores, and any commercial and industrial establishments whatsoever.

b. To forbid any kind of public or private gatherings.

c. To dissolve private associations and their branches.

d. To forbid persons regarded by him as detrimental to political order and public tranquillity from residing in Finland. . . .

5. Municipal magistracies, as well as municipal and rural communal administrations, are subject to the supreme authority of the governor general and to the direct authority of the governors, on the following basis:

a. The names of persons elected as mayors and aldermen, as chairmen and vice-chairmen of municipal councils, and to other offices in the municipal and rural communal administrations shall be submitted to the local governor for confirmation. Should he twice refuse to confirm the person elected, the office shall be filled through appointment by the Economic Department of the Senate in agreement with the governor general.

b. Mayors and municipal aldermen, chairmen and vice-chairmen of municipal councils, and other persons holding office in municipal and rural communal administrations can, by administrative process, be removed from office by the Economic Department of the Senate in agreement with the governor general. . . .

c. The governors are authorized to suspend the execution of decisions adopted by communal authorities subordinate to them, if such decisions do not conform to the general national interests or the needs of the local population, or if they violate the requirements of the law.

XVI:22. PLEVE'S LETTER TO GENERAL KIREEV, AUGUST 31, 1903

When Minister of Internal Affairs D. S. Sipiagin was assassinated in April 1902, the man named to succeed him was Viacheslav Konstantinovich Pleve (or von Plehve, 1846-1904), who had been director of police. In his short term as minister of internal affairs (until his assassination by Sazonov in July 1904) Pleve gained the reputation of being oppressively reactionary. Something of his own viewpoint is expressed in his letter of August 31, 1903 (published only in 1926) to Aleksandr Alekseevich Kireev, a retired general of Slavophile persuasions who was trying to urge Pleve to be more liberal.

Reference: *Krasnyi arkhiv*, vol. 18 (1926), p. 202.

The campaign against bureaucracy is only the slogan for a struggle pursuing broader objectives and dictated by more complex factors than the predominance of officialdom over the public element in our government.

. . . The swiftly unfolding evolution of society has outstripped the efforts of the state to bring order into newly formed relationships. Hence the doubt about the ability of the state apparatus to cope with imminent administrative tasks. Hence also the aspiration of a certain part of educated society for a governmental system based on political liberty, which has come to be considered a panacea for all social evils. . . .

Such are the social currents that feed this longing for a constitution from a pure spring; but there are other, muddier springs: first, the activities of political self-seekers of every description, using every opportunity to organize something in the way of public protests; second, the intrigues of various centrifugal movements of non-Russian origin. We must steer a wise course amidst these different currents. Some must be combatted by putting various obstacles in their way; others must be guided into channels of fruitful political activity under gradually and organically improving norms of civil life. I have already mentioned what, in my opinion, is the best means of pacifying agitated minds: it consists of depriving the opposition of its reason for being, by means of constructive work directed toward the general welfare.

. . . The methods of administration have themselves become obsolete and are in need of considerable improvement.

Only our historic autocracy has the strength necessary to carry out the comprehensive program that has fallen to the lot of the present generation. Autocracy alone can maintain a just balance between all interests and needs. Only under its banner will the official executors of autocracy's will work together in harmony with all worthy men who respond to their duty not only as subjects but also as citizens.

XVI:23. THE MANIFESTO ON THE CREATION OF A STATE DUMA, AUGUST 6, 1905

The tsar's manifesto of August 6, 1905, accompanying the statutes on the "Bulygin Duma" (so called after the then minister of internal affairs), contained these explanatory passages.

Reference: *PSZRI*, 3d ser., vol. 25, pt. 1, pp. 637-38. Recently a translation of this document was published in Raeff, *Plans for Political Reform*, pp. 142-44. For some of the Russian collections of documents on this period, in addition to the collections cited elsewhere in this and the following chapter, see F. I. Kalinychev, comp., *Gosudarstvennaia Duma v Rossii v dokumentakh i materialakh* (Moscow: Gosiurizdat, 1957); and N. I. Lazarevskii, ed., *Zakonodatel'nye akty perekhodnogo vremeni 1904-1908* (Saint Petersburg: Izd. Pravo, 1909).

The Russian state was created and grew strong through the indissoluble union of the tsar with the people and of the people with the tsar. The concord and union of tsar and people constitute the great moral force that has created Russia in the course of centuries, has defended it from all manner of evils and misfortunes, and is to this day the guarantee of its unity, independence, and integrity, its material well-being and spiritual development, both present and future.

. . .

Now the time has come, following the happy undertakings [of former tsars in the field of elective public institutions], to summon elected men from the entire Russian land to permanent and active participation in drafting legislation, by including for this purpose among the highest organs of the state a consultative legislative body, to which shall be entrusted the preliminary drafting and discussing of legislative proposals and the

examining of the budget of state revenues and expenditures.

In these considerations, while preserving the inviolability of the fundamental law of the Russian Empire on the substance of the autocratic power, we have deemed it beneficial to establish a State Duma and have confirmed a statute on elections to this duma.

. . .

We cherish the belief that the men elected by the confidence of the entire nation, now summoned to joint legislative work with the government, will show themselves worthy before all Russia of that monarchical confidence with which they have been summoned to this great task and, acting in complete concord with other organs of government and with the authorities we have ordained, shall render us useful and zealous assistance in our labors for the good of our common mother Russia, for strengthening the unity, security, and grandeur of the state and public order and prosperity.

XVI:24. THE STATUTE CONCERNING THE STATE DUMA, AUGUST 6, 1905

The following provisions are from the statute of August 6, 1905, establishing the "Bulygin Duma." Some of the reasons why this conciliatory step by the tsar evoked an unfavorable reaction may be seen here, especially in the wording of article 1.

Reference: *PSZRI*, 3d ser., vol. 25, pt. 1, pp. 640-45. For a recent translation of some additional portions of this statute, see Raeff, *Plans for Political Reform*, pp. 144-49.

1. A State Duma shall be established for the preliminary drafting and discussion of legislative proposals, which by virtue of the fundamental laws shall then be brought, through the State Council, before the supreme autocratic power.

2. The State Duma shall be composed of members elected by the population of the Russian Empire for a period of five years, on the principles indicated in the statute on elections to the Duma. . . .

9. The chairman of the State Duma and his deputy shall be elected by the Duma from among its deputies for a period of one year and may be reelected upon the expiration of this term. . . .

14. Deputies to the State Duma shall enjoy full freedom of judgment and opinion on matters subject to the jurisdiction of the Duma and shall not be held accountable to those people who elect them. . . .

33. The following shall be subject to the jurisdiction of the Duma:

a. Matters on which it is necessary to issue laws and tables of organization, and likewise to amend, supplement, suspend, and repeal them.

b. The financial estimates of the ministries and main departments, and the state budget of revenues and expenditures, as well as monetary appropriations from the treasury not provided for in the budget—on the basis of special rules for this matter.

c. The report of the State Board of Comptrollers [Gosudarstvennyi Kontrol'] dealing with the administration of the state budget.

d. Matters concerning the transfer of part of the state revenues or property, requiring imperial approval.

e. Matters concerning the construction of railways under the direct management of the treasury and at its expense. . . .

34. The State Duma is accorded the right to initiate proposals for the repeal or amendment of existing laws and for the promulgation of new laws. . . . These proposals must not relate to the principles of the governmental structure as established by the fundamental laws.

35. The State Duma is accorded the right to request ministers and chief directors of separate departments legally subordinated to the Governing Senate to provide information and explanations regarding such actions of ministers or chief directors, and likewise of persons and institutions under their jurisdiction, that in the opinion of the Duma violate existing statutes. . . .

61. If the State Duma, by a majority of two-thirds of its deputies in plenary session, deems the explanation of a minister or chief director of a separate department unsatisfactory, then the matter shall be brought, through the State Council, before the sovereign for consideration.

XVI:25. WITTE'S MEMORANDUM TO THE TSAR, OCTOBER 9, 1905

On October 9, 1905, as revolutionary disorders increased, Witte addressed to Nicholas a memorandum containing these significant observations. The memorandum was published by the Soviet government after the Revolution.

Reference: *Krasnyi arkhiv,* vols. 11-12 (1925), pp. 51, 54-55.

The basic watchword of the present-day movement of public opinion in Russia is freedom.

. . .

We live in a time dominated wholly by extremist ideas. No one stops to consider whether a given idea is realizable. To impetuous minds everything seems attainable and realizable, simply and easily.

Such a mood among the public is the most dangerous sign of an imminent explosion. The ranks of those who fervently advocate the regeneration of all aspects of Russian life, but only through peaceful evolution, are growing thinner each day. Each day it is

becoming more and more difficult for them to restrain the movement.

Their position is especially difficult because they must fight on two fronts: with those who deliberately work for a forcible overthrow, and with a government that does not distinguish them from the anarchists and subjects them to the same persecution, a government that keeps to the same old methods and modes of action.

. . .

The inconsistent and clumsy actions and the indiscriminate methods the administration resorted to in the past, and which continue to this day, have produced fatal results. The public is not only dissatisfied; it has nurtured a hatred for the government which grows from day to day. The government is not respected and not trusted. The most beneficial undertakings inspire protest. At the same time, the public has come to feel confident of its importance and its powers, of its ability to withdraw support from the government and compel it to capitulate. The daily course of events confirms public opinion as to the impotence, ignorance, and bewilderment of the authorities.

· · ·

The government should give real rather than fictitious leadership to the country. . . .

Leadership demands above all else a clearly formulated goal, an ideological, high-principled goal accepted by everyone.

The public has set such a goal, a goal of great and completely invincible significance, for justice and truth are on its side. The government must therefore accept it. The watchword of freedom should become the watchword of all government activity. There is no other way to save the state.

The course of historical progress cannot be stemmed. The idea of civil freedom will triumph, if not by reform then by revolution. But in the latter case it will be regenerated from the ashes of an overthrown millennial past. A Russian rebellion, mindless and merciless, will sweep everything away, will crumble everything into dust.

XVI:26. WITTE'S REPORT TO THE TSAR, OCTOBER 13, 1905

On October 13, 1905, Witte submitted upon the tsar's request this "most respectful report" concerning measures for pacifying the country. On October 17 the tsar approved Witte's report and made it public, together with the imperial manifesto of that same day, as the program of the government in which Witte was to be chairman of the Council of Ministers.

Reference: *Pravo*, no. 41 (Oct. 25, 1905), cols. 3409-11. A rather free translation of this document appears in Yarmolinsky, *Memoirs of Count Witte*, pp. 234-36, some phrases from which have been used here.

The unrest that has seized the various classes of Russian society cannot be looked upon as the consequence of isolated imperfections in the political and social order, or as the result of the organized activity of extremist parties. The roots of this unrest unquestionably lie deeper. They lie in the disturbed equilibrium between the ideological aspirations of the thinking elements of Russian society and the external forms of their life. Russia has outgrown the existing regime and aspires to a rule of law based on civil liberty.

The external forms of Russian life must be raised to the level of the ideas that animate the reasonably inclined majority of the people. As its first task, the government must strive to establish immediately, without waiting for legislative sanction by the State Duma, the basic elements of a rule of law: personal inviolability and freedom of the press, of conscience, of assembly, and of association. The strengthening of these fundamental aspects of the political life of the country must be effected through regular legislative channels, along with the work of granting legal equality to all subjects of Your Imperial Majesty, without distinction of religion or nationality. . . .

The next task of the government is to establish institutions and legislative principles that harmonize with the political ideals of the majority of the Russian people and firmly guarantee the inalienability of the previously granted blessings of civil liberty. This task is a matter of instituting a rule of law. In keeping with the aim of establishing tranquillity and security in the state, the economic policy of the government must strive to benefit the broad masses of the people, while naturally safeguarding those property and civil rights that are recognized in all civilized countries.

· · ·

To bring this about it is imperative for the government to be homogeneous in composition and united in the aims it pursues. . . .

In relation to the future State Duma, the government must take care to uphold its prestige, to have confidence in its work, and to assure this institution of the importance it deserves. The government must not be an element that counteracts the decisions of the Duma. . . .

It is very important to reform the State Council so as to provide for the participation of a considerable group of elected members.

. . .

... On all levels the activity of the government must be guided by the following principles:

1. Frankness and sincerity in consolidating in every sphere the benefits of civil liberty granted to the people, and the establishment of guarantees for these liberties.

2. The desire to eliminate all extraordinary legislative measures.

3. The coordination of the activities of all organs of government.

4. The elimination of repressive measures directed against actions that clearly do not threaten either society or the state.

5. The firm suppression of all activity menacing society and the state, in strict accordance with the law and in spiritual unity with the reasonably inclined majority of the people.

XVI:27. THE MANIFESTO OF OCTOBER 17, 1905

Here is the complete text of the "October Manifesto," signed on the seventeenth of that month by Nicholas.

Reference: *PSZRI,* 3d ser., vol. 25, pt. 1, pp. 754-55; translation based in part on Bernard Pares, *The Fall of the Russian Monarchy: A Study of the Evidence* (New York: Alfred A. Knopf, 1939), pp. 503-04, and Yarmolinsky, *Memoirs of Count Witte,* pp. 232-33. More recently this manifesto has been translated in Dmytryshyn, *Imperial Russia,* pp. 314-15.

The turmoil and unrest in the capitals [Saint Petersburg and Moscow] and in many localities of our empire fill our heart to overflowing with great and heavy sorrow. The welfare of the Russian sovereign is inseparable from the welfare of the people, and the affliction of the people is his affliction. The turmoil that has now arisen may create a profound disturbance among the people and a threat to the integrity and unity of our empire.

The great vow of imperial service commands us to strive with every effort of reason and authority to put the speediest end possible to a turmoil that so endangers the state. Having ordered the proper authorities to take measures for the suppression of direct manifestations of disorder, illegality, and violence, and for the protection of peaceful men who seek to carry out in tranquillity the duties incumbent upon everyone, we have deemed it necessary, in order to carry out more effectively the general measures designed by us for pacifying the life of the state, to unify the actions of the higher organs of government.

We impose upon the government the duty of executing our inflexible will:

1. To grant the population unshakable foundations of civil liberty on the principles of true inviolability of person, freedom of conscience, speech, assembly, and association.

2. Without halting the appointed elections to the State Duma, to admit to participation in the Duma, insofar as this is feasible in the brief period of time left before the Duma convenes, those classes of the population that at present are altogether deprived of the franchise, leaving the further development of the principle of universal suffrage to the newly established legislative system [i.e. the Duma and the Council of State, in extension of the law of August 6, 1905].

3. To establish as an unshakable principle that no law can be put into effect without the consent of the State Duma, and that the elected representatives of the people should be guaranteed the opportunity of real participation in control over the legality of actions of the authorities appointed by us.

We summon all faithful sons of Russia to remember their duty to the motherland, to help in putting an end to the unprecedented turmoil, and together with us to make every effort to restore tranquillity and peace in our native land.

B. IDEOLOGICAL TRENDS AND REVOLUTIONARY MOVEMENTS

Note: Some of the items in Chapter XV, Section C, pertain also to the period 1881-1905. See especially the selections from Mikhailovskii and Ivan Aksakov, Items XV:52 and 56.

XVI:28. PLEKHANOV'S OUR DIFFERENCES, 1884

Georgii Valentinovich Plekhanov (1856-1918) first came to prominence among Russian revolutionists in 1879, when the secret Land and Freedom society split over the use of political murder.

Plekhanov, opposed to a reliance on terror, was a leader of the short-lived group that called itself Chernyi Peredel (Black Partition, meaning "total redistribution of the land"). Emigrating in 1880 to Switzerland, however, Plekhanov soon abandoned populism, embraced Marxism, and became one of Russia's foremost socialist theoreticians. Among his influential works was *Nashi raznoglasiia* (Our differences *or* Our disagreements), written in 1884 and published abroad the next year, though not published in Russia till 1906. Here are some representative passages from that revolutionary classic.

Reference: G. V. Plekhanov, *Nashi raznoglasiia* (St. Petersburg: Novyi Mir, 1906), pp. 33, 190, 203, 241, 250, 278-79, 298, 300-01, 305. In connection with these selections, the editors gratefully acknowledge materials contributed by Professor Dimitri von Mohrenschildt.

In our revolutionary calculations the intelligentsia played the role of the beneficent providence of the Russian people—a providence whose will would determine the direction in which the wheel of history would turn. ... The propagandists were convinced that without much effort they could teach the peasantry the truths of scientific socialism. The rebels demanded the immediate formation of "battle" organizations among the people, without imagining that this might encounter serious obstacles. Finally, the adherents of the Nabat [Tocsin] group believed that our revolutionaries had only to "seize power," and the people would immediately adopt the socialist forms of communal life. The self-confidence of the intelligentsia went hand in hand with a boundless idealization of the people.

· · ·

All the principles of a modern economy, all the mainsprings of contemporary economic life, are irreconcilably hostile to the commune. To expect its further independent "development" is therefore as preposterous as to expect fish thrown out on the shore to go on living and reproducing. ... The very atmosphere of our contemporary monetary economy destroys our archaic form of land ownership; it undermines its very roots.

· · ·

If ... we ask ourselves once again, "Will Russia have to pass through the school of capitalism?" we shall reply unhesitatingly with another question: "Why should she not finish the school she has already entered?"

· · ·

From the point of view of a social democrat, a truly revolutionary movement is possible in our time only among the working class. ... The social democrat wants the worker to *make his own revolution;* the Blanquist demands that the worker *support* a revolution

that others have instigated and directed in his behalf and in his name—as, for example, the officers did in the case of the Decembrist conspiracy.

· · ·

If real popular sovereignty were established in our country, then the sovereign people, in reply to the question of whether they needed land and whether land should be taken from the landlords, would answer: "Yes, land is needed and it should be taken." But to the question of whether they needed "the principle of socialist organization," the people would first reply that they did not understand the question, and then, after having grasped the meaning with difficulty, they would say: "No, we have no need for that." And since the expropriation of the large landowners is not at all equivalent to the "principle of socialist organization," the seizure of power by the revolutionaries would not lead to any kind of socialism.

· · ·

Russian socialism as expressed by the People's Will party will remain estranged from the great tasks of European socialism until it completely abandons its intermediate position between the anarchism of Bakunin and the Blanquism of Tkachev. ...

... [Then] our socialism will cease to be "Russian," and will merge with world socialism, as expressed in the works of Marx, Engels, and, to some extent, Lassalle.

Its adherents will then come to understand that:

1. The *Communist* revolution of the working class cannot possibly grow out of the petty bourgeois and peasant socialism that almost all our revolutionaries are preaching today.

2. Because of the internal characteristics of its organization, the village commune tends to give way to bourgeois rather than communistic forms of society.

3. In the transition to communism the commune will play a *passive* rather than an *active* role; the commune is incapable of *impelling* Russia toward communism; it can be expected only to *offer less resistance* to such a movement than a system of small-scale individual landownership.

4. Only the working class in our industrial centers is able to assume the initiative for a communist movement.

5. This class can achieve its liberation only by its own conscious efforts.

. . .

In furthering the formation of a workers' party, our revolutionaries will be performing the most fruitful and important task that the contemporary Russian "progressive man" could possibly fulfill.

. . .

The speediest possible formation of a workers' party is the only means for solving all the economic and political contradictions in present-day Russia. Success and victory await us along this road; all other roads lead only to defeat and impotence.

. . .

In no way do we deny the important role of the terrorist struggle in the present liberation movement. . . . But, taken in itself, so-called terrorism, while destroying the power of the government, contributes very little to the conscious organization of the forces of its opponents. The terrorist struggle does not enlarge the sphere of our revolutionary movement; on the contrary, it reduces it to the heroic activities of small guerrilla bands. After a few brilliant successes, our revolutionary party has been visibly weakened by the great exertion and cannot recover without the influx of fresh forces from new strata of the population. We recommend that the party turn to the working class as the most revolutionary of all the classes of contemporary society. Does this mean that we recommend temporary abandonment of the active struggle against the government? By no means. On the contrary, we point out a way to extend the struggle, to make it more versatile, hence more successful.

. . .

Our program . . . does not sacrifice the village to the interests of the city, nor does it ignore the peasants for the sake of the industrial workers. *It sets itself the task of organizing the social-revolutionary forces of the city in order to draw the village into the channel of a universal historical movement.*

XVI:29. PLEKHANOV'S PROGRAM FOR THE EMANCIPATION OF LABOR GROUP, 1884

The Emancipation of Labor group (Osvobozhdenie Truda) organized in Geneva in 1883 was the first Russian revolutionary organization dedicated to Marxist principles, and Plekhanov was its chief ideologist. These passages from its program, written by Plekhanov in 1884, indicate its outlook on various questions of the day.

Reference: G. V. Plekhanov, *Sochineniia*, 24 vols. (Moscow: Gosizdat, 1923-27), 2:357, 358, 359, 361-62. From materials contributed by Professor von Mohrenschildt. A translation of the whole document is in Plekhanov, *Selected Philosophical Works*, 2 vols. (Moscow: Foreign Languages Publishing House, 1959), 1:400-05. That translation is included in Dmytryshyn, *Imperial Russia*, pp. 285-89.

The Emancipation of Labor group sets itself the goal of propagating socialist ideas in Russia and preparing the ground for the organization of a Russian *socialist workers' party*.

The essence of its views can be expressed in the following few statements:

I. The economic emancipation of the working class will be achieved only by transferring all the means and the output of production to the collective ownership of the workers and by organizing all the functions of socioeconomic life to comply with social needs.

II. The contemporary technological develop-

ments of civilized societies not only provides the *material prerequisites* for such organization but also renders it *necessary and inevitable,* in order to solve the contradictions that obstruct the peaceful and harmonious development of these societies.

III. This radical economic revolution will entail the most fundamental changes in the whole tenor of social and international relations.

. . .

It is already possible to foresee the international character of the impending economic revolution. The contemporary development of the international exchange of commodities makes it necessary for all civilized societies to participate in this revolution.

Therefore, the socialist parties of all countries recognize the international character of the contemporary labor movement and proclaim the principle of the international solidarity of the producers.

The Emancipation of Labor group further reaffirms the great principles of the International Workers' Association and the identity of interests among the toilers of the entire civilized world.

. . .

The working population of Russia squarely bears the entire burden of the huge machinery of a despotic police state, while at the same time suffering all the miseries peculiar to the era of capitalist *accumulation;* and in certain localities—in our industrial centers—it is already experiencing the oppression of capitalist *production,* which thus far as not been restricted either by energetic government intervention or by an organized resistance of the workers themselves. Present-day Russia, as Marx once said of western Europe, suffers not only from the development of capitalist production but also from the insufficiency of that development.

One of the most harmful consequences of this backwardness of production has been and still is the underdevelopment of our middle class, which in this country is unable to assume the *initiative* in the struggle against absolutism.

For this reason the socialist intelligentsia has had to assume leadership of the present liberation movement, the immediate task of which must be to create free political institu-

tions in our fatherland. The socialists on their part must strive to furnish to the working class an opportunity for active and productive participation in the future political life of Russia.

The principal means to this end must be agitation in favor of a democratic constitution.
. . .

The Emancipation of Labor group sets itself the task of propagating modern socialism in Russia and preparing the working class for conscious participation in the sociopolitical movement; to this goal it dedicates all its strength, calling upon our revolutionary youth for its help and support.

While pursuing this aim with all the means at its disposal, the Emancipation of Labor group recognizes the necessity for a terroristic struggle against absolute rule and differs with the People's Will party only on the issue of the so-called seizure of power by the revolutionary party and on *the objectives of the direct activity of the socialists among the working class.*

The Emancipation of Labor group in no way ignores the peasantry, which forms by far the largest part of Russia's working population. But it believes that the efforts of the intelligentsia, especially under the present conditions of the sociopolitical struggle, must be directed primarily toward a more advanced stratum of this population, as represented by the industrial workers. Once the strong support of this element is secured, the socialist intelligentsia can extend its influence to the peasantry with much greater hope for success, especially if by this time it has succeeded in obtaining freedom for propaganda and agitation.

XVI:30. PLEKHANOV ON PROLETARIAN AND PEASANT IN 1892

The famine of 1891-92, attributable in part to the system of land tenure and cultivation, injected new vigor into the Russian revolutionary movement. Plekhanov's outlook at the time is revealed in his *On the Tasks of the Socialists in the Campaign against Famine in Russia,* a booklet published in 1892 in Geneva.
Reference: Plekhanov, *Sochineniia,* 3:386-87, 388, 389.

The proletarian and the "little peasant" are genuine political antipodes. The historical role of the proletarian is as revolutionary as the role of the little peasant is conservative. Oriental despotism stood firm for entire millennia on the shoulders of the little peasant. The

proletariat within relatively a very short time has shaken loose all the "foundations" of western European society. And in Russia its development and political education are proceeding at a pace much faster than in the West. In Russia the proletariat is growing, maturing, and gaining strength not from day to day but literally from hour to hour, like the giant in the fairy tale. In the space of ten or twelve years its growth has altered it beyond recognition. . . . The Russian proletariat developed and gained in strength especially under the reign of Alexander III, that is, during an era of the fiercest reaction and the dreariest stagnation, an era when the "intelligentsia" succumbed to hopeless depression, losing faith both in itself and in its "ideals." . . . While the disenchanted intelligentsia derides the ideals of its "old-timers," or becomes absorbed in the strange fantasies of a strange count [Lev Tolstoi], the working class studies, reads, acquaints itself with the Western proletarian movement, becomes imbued with an irreconcilable hatred for despotism and an awareness of its own strength, its own interests, and its own dignity, thereby nullifying completely all the efforts of a decade of reaction. The Russia of the nineties is proving to be more ripe for revolution than was the Russia of the seventies, when the revolutionary movement of that period was in full swing.

· · ·

The development of capitalism not only has utterly ruined the peasant economy and exhausted the Russian soil but has undermined the foundations of autocracy and has brought to life those very social classes that are destined to be its gravediggers. The best representatives of the *proletariat*, the most revolutionary of these new social classes in

Russia, are already well aware of their political tasks. Another class—a backward one, the bourgeoisie—will have to become aware of *its* own tasks or else face ruin. This is already an enormous step forward; this is a reliable guarantee of a better future; this is a complete negation of the Asiatic stagnation that once was Russia's distinctive feature. Our Slavophiles and conservatives of every sort used to be terribly fond of contrasting calm, conservative Russia with the restless, revolutionary West. Such an antithesis was valid only so long as the internal conditions of Russia were not yet comparable to those of western Europe. Today it is becoming meaningless, because the old economic order of Russia is collapsing like a house of cards, like a piece of rotten wood decaying and turning to dust. And now all of us, enemies of the existing order, at last feel firm ground under our feet. *Our time has come.*

· · ·

Our populists are shedding bitter tears over the transformation of the Russian peasant into a proletarian. Their imagination sees no further than the poverty that threatens the proletarian. But did the peasant suffer little misery? . . . The time has come to dispel the Slavophile fog; it has long been time to realize that the rise of the proletariat does not promise to increase the people's sufferings—the Russian people can go no further in this direction—but promises *an opportunity for a successful struggle against such suffering.*

XVI:31. A PROCLAMATION OF THE LEAGUE OF THE STRUGGLE FOR THE EMANCIPATION OF THE WORKING CLASS, APRIL 19, 1896

In 1895 the secret League of the Struggle for the Emancipation of the Working Class was formed in Saint Petersburg under the leadership of Lenin and others. The league propagandized the factory workers in language like that contained in this proclamation.

Reference: Vladimir L. Burtsev, comp. and ed., *Za sto let, 1800-1896: Sbornik po istorii politicheskikh i obshchestvennykh dvizhenii v Rossii* (London, 1897), pp. 262-63.

We, the workers of Saint Petersburg, members of the league, invite all our other comrades to join our league and to aid the great cause of uniting all workers in the struggle for their interests. The time has come for us, the Russian workers, to break the chains with which

the capitalists and the government have bound us in order to keep us in submission; the time has come for us to join the struggle of our brothers, the workers of other countries, and to stand with them under a common banner on which is written:

"Workers of the world, unite!"

XVI:32. THE MANIFESTO OF THE FIRST CONGRESS OF THE RSDWP, MARCH 1898

The meeting that became known as the First Congress of the Russian Social-Democratic Workers' Party took place in Minsk, March 1-3, 1898. Its manifesto read in part as follows.

Reference: *Manifest Rossiiskoi Sotsial'-demokraticheskoi Rabochei Partii, 1898 g.* (Geneva: T. A. Kuklin, 1903), pp. 2-3. From materials contributed by Dimitri von Mohrenschildt.

The farther east one goes in Europe, the greater become the political weakness, cowardice, and vileness of the bourgeoisie, and the greater become the cultural and political tasks that fall to the lot of the proletariat. The Russian working class must bear and shall bear upon its own strong shoulders the cause of achieving political freedom. This is indispensable, but it is only the first step toward accomplishing the great historical mission of the proletariat to create a social order in which there shall be no place for man's exploitation of man.

The Russian proletariat shall throw off the yoke of autocracy, so as to carry on with still greater energy the struggle with capitalism and the bourgeoisie to the final victory of socialism.

The first steps of the Russian workers' movement and of Russian social democracy necessarily lacked cohesion, were in a certain sense fortuitous, and lacked unity and planning. Now the time has come to unite local forces, groups, and organizations of Russian social democracy into a single Russian Social-Democratic Workers' Party. Recognizing this, representatives of the Unions Fighting for the Liberation of the Working Class [Soiuzy Bor'by za Osvobozhdenie Rabochego Klassa], of the group that publishes *Rabochaia Gazeta* [The Workers' Paper], and of the All-Jewish Workers' Union in Russia and Poland [Obshcheevreiskii Rabochii Soiuz v Rossii i Pol'she] have organized a congress. . . .

The local groups, by uniting into a party . . . definitively mark the transition of the Russian revolutionary movement to a new era of conscious class struggle. As a socialist movement and current, the Russian Social-Democratic Workers' Party carries on the cause and traditions of the entire past revolutionary movement in Russia; in making the attainment of political freedom the chief immediate task of the party as a whole, social democracy moves toward the goal clearly marked out by the glorious members of the old People's Will [Narodnaia Volia]. But the methods and path that social democracy chooses are different. This choice is determined by the fact that it consciously wishes to be and to remain a class movement of the organized working masses. It is firmly convinced that "the liberation of the working class can come about only through its own efforts."

XVI:33. LENIN'S WHAT IS TO BE DONE? *1902*

One of Lenin's most influential early works was his booklet *What Is to Be Done? Burning Questions of Our Movement (Chto delat'? Nabolevshie voprosy nashego dvizheniia).* It was printed in Stuttgart in 1902, after Lenin had returned from Siberia, gone to western Europe, and taken up his work as an editor of the revolutionary paper *Iskra* (The spark). Some of its points, like those quoted here, presage the coming split between Bolshevism and Menshevism, although Lenin's main target of the moment was the heresy of economism, which stressed improving the conditions of the working class.

Reference: V. I. Lenin, *Sochineniia,* 2d ed., 30 vols. (Moscow: Gosizdat, 1926-30), 4:384-85, 447, 458, 460-61, 462, 464-65, 469; translation based largely on *The Essential of Lenin in Two Volumes* (London: Lawrence and Wishart, 1947), 1:169-70, 225, 236-38, 239-40, 242, 246. In addition to many English translations of this work published in the Soviet Union, there is a recent American one by Sergei V. and Patricia Utechin (New York: Oxford University Press, 1963).

The strikes of the nineties, in spite of the enormous progress they represented as compared with the [earlier factory] "riots," remained a purely spontaneous movement.

. . . *There could not yet be* any social-democratic consciousness among the workers. This consciousness could only be brought to them from without. The history of all countries shows that the working class, exclusively by its own efforts, is able to develop only trade union consciousness, i.e. it may itself realize the necessity for combining in unions, for fighting against the employers, and for striving to compel the government to pass necessary labor legislation, and so forth. The theory of socialism, however, grew out of the philosophical, historical, and economic theories that were elaborated by educated representatives of the propertied classes, the intelligentsia. According to their social status, the founders of modern scientific socialism, Marx and Engels, themselves belonged to the bourgeois intelligentsia. Similarly in Russia, the theoretical doctrine of social democracy arose quite independently of the spontaneous growth of the labor movement; it arose as a natural and inevitable outcome of the development of ideas among the revolutionary socialist intelligentsia.

. . .

On questions of organization and politics the Economists are forever lapsing from social democracy into trade unionism. The political struggle carried on by the social democrats is far more extensive and complex than the economic struggle the workers carry on against the employers and the government. Similarly (and indeed for that reason), the organization of a revolutionary social-democratic party must inevitably *differ* from the organizations of workers designed for the latter struggle. A workers' organization must in the first place be a trade organization; second, it must be as extensive as possible; and third, it must be as public as conditions will allow (here and further on, of course, I have only autocratic Russia in mind). On the other hand, the organizations of revolutionaries must consist first and foremost of people whose profession is that of a revolutionary. . . . Such organizations must of necessity be not too extensive and as conspiratorial as possible.

. . .

Give us an organization of revolutionaries, and we shall overturn the whole of Russia!

. . .

Lack of specialization is one of our most serious technical defects. . . . On the other hand, in order to unite all these tiny fractions into a single whole, in order to avoid breaking up the movement while breaking up functions, and in order to imbue those who carry out these minute functions with the conviction that their work is necessary and important—for without this they will never do the work—it is necessary to have a strong organization of tried revolutionaries. . . . In a word, specialization necessarily presupposes centralization, and in its turn unquestionably demands it.

. . . Our very first and most imperative duty is to help to train working-class revolutionaries. . . . Therefore, attention must be devoted *primarily* to the task of *raising* the workers to the level of revolutionaries, and not to lowering ourselves to the level of the "laboring masses" as the Economists wish to do.

. . .

The working-class revolutionary must also become a professional revolutionary.

. . .

Only a gross failure to understand Marxism (or an "understanding" of it in the spirit of Struve-ism) could prompt the opinion that the rise of a mass, spontaneous labor movement *relieves* us of the duty of creating as good an organization of revolutionaries as Land and Freedom had in its time, and even an incomparably better one. On the contrary, this movement *imposes* this duty upon us, because the spontaneous struggle of the proletariat will not become a genuine "class struggle" until it is led by a strong organization of revolutionaries.

. . .

The only serious organizational principle the active workers of our movement can accept is strict secrecy, strict selection of members, and the training of professional revolutionaries.

XVI:34. THE PROGRAM ADOPTED BY THE SECOND CONGRESS OF THE RSDWP, AUGUST 1903

The Second Congress of the Russian Social-Democratic Workers' Party met from July 17 (30, N.S.) into August 1903, in Brussels and London. Although this congress was sufficiently disharmonious to produce the Bolshevik-Menshevik split, it agreed on the program whose principal provisions are given here and which, with little change (see the program of 1906, Item XVII:27), remained the official party program until 1918.

Reference: *Izveshchenie o vtorom ocherednom s"ezde Rossiiskoi Sotsial'-demokraticheskoi Rabochei Partii* (Geneva: Izd. Ts.K. RSDRP, 1903), pp. 7, 9-12, 14-15. A translation of this document is included in the recently published Dmytryshyn, *Imperial Russia*, pp. 325-31.

The development of trade has established such a close bond between all peoples of the civilized world that the great liberation movement of the proletariat had to become and has long since become international.

Considering itself one of the detachments

of the universal army of the proletariat, Russian social democracy pursues the same final goal toward which social democrats of all other countries strive.

. . .

As . . . the contradictions inherent in bourgeois society increase and develop, there is also an increase in the discontent of the toiling and exploited masses with the existing order of things, an increase in the number and solidarity of proletarians, and an intensification of their struggle with their exploiters. At the same time technical improvements, which concentrate the means of production and distribution and collectivize the labor process in capitalist enterprises, create with increasing rapidity the material possibility of replacing capitalist relations of production with socialist ones, i.e. that social revolution which is the ultimate goal of all the activity of international social democracy, as the conscious spokesman of the class movement of the proletariat.

. . .

The indispensable condition for this social revolution is the dictatorship of the proletariat, i.e. the proletariat's attainment of such political power as to enable it to suppress any resistance on the part of the exploiters.

Setting itself the task of making the proletariat capable of carrying out its great historical mission, international social democracy is now organizing it into an independent political party, in opposition to all bourgeois parties; it directs all manifestations of [the proletariat's] class struggle, unmasks before it the irreconcilable opposition between the interests of the exploiters and the interests of the exploited, and makes clear to it the historical significance and essential conditions of the forthcoming social revolution.

. . .

In Russia, where capitalism has already become the dominant mode of production, there still remain very numerous remnants of our old precapitalist order, which was based on the enslavement of the toiling masses to the landowners, the state, or the head of the state. . . .

The most important of all these survivals and the most powerful bulwark of all this barbarism is the tsarist autocracy. By its very nature it is hostile to any social movement and must necessarily be the most vicious opponent of all the aspirations of the proletariat for liberation.

Therefore, the Russian Social-Democratic Workers' Party sets as its most immediate political task the overthrow of tsarist autocracy and its replacement by a democratic republic, whose constitution would guarantee:

1. Popular sovereignty, i.e. the concentration of all supreme state power in the hands of a legislative assembly composed of representatives of the people and constituted as a single chamber.

2. Universal, equal, and direct suffrage in elections both to the legislative assembly and to all local organs of self-government, for all citizens of both sexes who have reached the age of twenty; secret balloting in elections; the right of every voter to be elected to all representative bodies; biennial parliaments; a salary for the representatives of the people.

3. Broad local self-government. . . .

4. Inviolability of persons and domiciles.

5. Unlimited freedom of conscience, speech, the press, assembly, strikes, and unions.

6. Freedom of movement and occupation.

7. The abolition of classes [*sosloviia*, i.e. legal class categories or estates] and the complete legal equality of all citizens irrespective of sex, religion, race, and nationality.

8. The right of all inhabitants to obtain an education in their native tongue. . . .

9. The right of self-determination for all nations entering into the composition of the state. . . .

11. The popular election of judges.

12. The replacement of the standing army by a national militia.

13. The separation of church and state, and of school and church.

14. Free and compulsory general and professional education for all children of both sexes up to the age of sixteen; the furnishing of food, clothing, and textbooks to needy children at state expense.

As the basic condition of the democratization of our state economy, the Russian Social-Democratic Workers' Party demands: *the abolition of all indirect taxes and the establishment of a progressive income and inheritance tax.*

[The program goes on to enumerate a series of sixteen demands dealing with the protection of the working class, including an eight-hour working day (point 1) and state insurance of workers (point 8).]

. . .

With the aim of eliminating the remnants of serfdom, which are a heavy burden lying directly upon the peasants, and in the interests of the free development of the class struggle in the villages, the party demands, first of all:

1. The abolition of redemption and obrok [quitrent] payments, as well as all duties falling at the present time upon the peasantry as a specially obligated class [*podatnoe soslovie*].

2. The repeal of all laws hindering the peasant in disposing of his land.

3. The return to the peasants of the monies taken from them as redemption and obrok payments; the confiscation, for this purpose, of monastery and church property, and also of appanage land [the revenue from which went to the members of the imperial family]

and cabinet land [the revenue from which went to the emperor], and of other land belonging to members of the imperial family; likewise the imposition of a special tax on land belonging to noble landowners who received redemption payments [at the time of the emancipation] and the conversion of money thus obtained into a special national fund for the cultural and charitable needs of village communities.

4. The establishment of peasants' committees: (a) for the return to village communities (by means of expropriation or—in the event that land has changed hands—redemption by the state at the expense of large-scale noble landownership) of those lands that were cut off [*otrezany*] from the peasants [at the time of the emancipation], and which serve the estate owners as a means of enslaving them.

XVI:35. LENIN AND PLEKHANOV ON THE DIFFERENCES BETWEEN BOLSHEVIKS AND MENSHEVIKS, 1904

The division between Bolsheviks and Mensheviks produced a vast literature dealing with revolutionary strategy and tactics. Anything approaching a comprehensive treatment would require more space than is available here. The following excerpts from writings of Lenin and Plekhanov in 1904 do, however, at least suggest the flavor of some of the initial exchanges.

Reference: Lenin, *Sochineniia*, 6:160, 272 (translation based on *Essential of Lenin*, 1:276, 318); Plekhanov, *Sochineniia*, 13:92, 114.

[From Lenin's *One Step Forward, Two Steps Back (The Crisis in Our Party) (Shag vpered, dva shaga nazad [Krizis v nashei partii])*, a book first published in Geneva in 1904:]

The "majority" is the revolutionary, and the "minority" the opportunist wing of our party; the dissensions that divide the two wings at the present moment for the most part concern only questions of organization, and not questions of program or tactics. . . .

. . . As a matter of fact, comrade Aksel'rod and comrade Martov are now only deepening, developing, and extending their initial error with regard to paragraph one [of the party statute of 1903]. As a matter of fact, the entire position of the opportunists on questions of organization had already begun to be revealed in the controversy over paragraph one: their advocacy of a diffuse, not strongly welded, party organization; their hostility to the idea (the "bureaucratic" idea) of building the party from the top downward, starting with the party congress and the bodies set up by it; their tendency to proceed from the bottom upward, which would allow every

professor, every gymnasium student, and "every striker" to declare himself a member of the party; their hostility toward the "formalism" which demands that a party member belong to an organization recognized by the party; their inclination toward the mentality of the bourgeois intellectual, who is only prepared "platonically to recognize organizational relations"; . . . their partiality for autonomy as against centralism—in a word, all that is now blossoming so luxuriantly in the new *Iskra*.

. . .

It is an unquestionable and incontrovertible fact that *the minority was composed of those members of our party who were most inclined to gravitate toward opportunism*. The minority was composed of the elements in our party *who were the least stable* in theory *and the least consistent in matters of principle*. It was from the *right wing* of the party that the minority was formed. The division into a majority and a minority is a direct and inevitable continuation of that division of the Social Democrats into a revolutionary wing and an opportunist wing, into a Mountain and a Gironde, which did not appear only yesterday, not in the Russian Workers' Party alone, and which no doubt will not disappear tomorrow.

[From Plekhanov's "Centralism or Bonapartism?" an article in *Iskra,* May 1, 1904:]

If our party actually conferred such an organizational structure upon itself, then very soon there would be no room left in its ranks either for men of intelligence or for hardened warriors; it would be left only with little frogs who had at last received their desired king, and a king heron which would be free to swallow these little frogs one after the other.

[From Plekhanov's "An Answer to Comrade Liadov," *Iskra,* June 1, 1904:]

I do not find it necessary to argue with comrade Liadov about the alleged opportunism of the minority. I have already demonstrated time and again that talking about the opportunism of such comrades as P. Aksel'-rod, Martov, Starover, and so on, indicates one's ignorance of what the word means, and if he still drags it out, then he is clearly hopeless.

A strange business! We have started calling those people opportunists who *do not want to accommodate their viewpoints to Lenin's outlook and "morals,"* i.e. those who are devoid of the opportunism this little parody of a Solon desires. At the same time, those *who excel in this opportunism* are for some reason called *firm.* And the more opportunistic they are, the firmer they appear to themselves and to others.

XVI:36. RESOLUTIONS OF THE THIRD CONGRESS OF THE RSDWP, APRIL 1905

The Mensheviks did not attend the Third Congress of the RSDWP, which met in London in April 1905. Here are passages from three of the resolutions adopted by the assembled Bolsheviks.
      Reference: *Izveshchenie o III s''ezde Rossiiskoi Sotsial'-demokraticheskoi Rabochei Partii* (Geneva: Izd. RSDRP, 1905), pp. 12-13, 14, 15.

[From the "Resolution on the Attitude toward the Peasant Movement":]

The Third Congress of the RSDWP directs all party organizations:

      a. To spread propaganda among the broad ranks of the people, saying that social democracy sets as its task the most energetic support of all revolutionary actions of the peasantry that can improve its status, including the confiscation of estates belonging to landowners, the state, the church, monasteries, and members of the imperial family.

      b. As a practical slogan for agitation among the peasantry and as a means of bringing the greatest possible degree of consciousness into the peasant movement, to urge the necessity of immediately organizing revolutionary peasant committees with the aim of carrying out all revolutionary democratic reforms for the purpose of delivering the peasantry from the oppression of policemen, officials, and landowners.

      c. With the aim of disorganizing the autocracy and supporting the revolutionary onslaught upon it, to summon the peasantry and the rural proletariat to all possible political demonstrations and to a collective refusal to pay taxes, perform military service, and obey

the decrees and orders of the government and its agents.

      d. To strive to organize the village proletariat independently, to amalgamate it with the urban proletariat under the banner of the Social-Democratic Party, and to draw its representatives into the peasant committees.

[From the "Resolution on Practical Agreements with the Socialist Revolutionaries":]

The Third Congress of the RSDWP directs the Central Committee and local committees to enter, when necessary, into temporary battle agreements with organizations of Socialist Revolutionaries, local agreements being permitted only under the control of the Central Committee.

[From the "Resolution on Relations with the Liberals":]

The Third Congress of the RSDWP urgently recommends to its comrades:

      1. That they explain to workers the antirevolutionary and antiproletarian character of the bourgeois-democratic movement in all its shadings, beginning with the moderate liberal, represented by large groups of landowners and manufacturers, and ending with

the more radical, represented by the Union of Liberation and numerous groups of professional men.

2. That they struggle energetically, in view of what has been said above, against all attempts of bourgeois democracy to gain control of the workers' movement and to speak in the name of the proletariat or its individual groups.

Note: The present resolution repeals Comrade Starover's resolution concerning relations with liberals, adopted at the Second Congress. [Note: This resolution held that "temporary agreements with liberal movements" were permissible for Social Democrats.]

XVI:37. LENIN ON THE PEASANTRY, MARCH AND SEPTEMBER 1905

One of the important questions of revolutionary strategy was treated this way by Lenin in 1905.

Reference: Lenin, *Sochineniia,* 7:158, 160; 8:186; translation of the second article taken, with minor changes, from *Essential of Lenin,* 1:452.

[From "The Proletariat and the Peasantry," an article in the journal *Vpered,* March 10 (23, N.S.), 1905:]

Peasant uprisings are breaking out. . . . The problem of the attitude of the conscious vanguard of the proletariat, the Social-Democratic Party, toward the peasant movement is acquiring immediate practical significance and must have priority on the agenda of all our party organizations and in all the speeches of our agitators and propagandists.

The Social-Democratic Party has repeatedly pointed out that the peasant movement poses a double problem for us. Insofar as it is a revolutionary democratic movement, we must support it unconditionally and drive it forward. At the same time we must hold firmly to our proletarian class viewpoint and organize the rural proletariat on the same basis as the urban workers and together with them into an independent class party, making clear to the rural proletariat the antagonism between its interests and those of the bourgeois peasantry, and calling it to fight for the socialist revolution. We must point out to it that liberation from oppression and poverty lies, not in transforming a few layers of the peasantry into petty bourgeois, but in replacing the entire bourgeois system with a socialist one.

. . .

There can be only one solution to this problem: to support the peasant bourgeoisie against any kind of feudalism and against the feudal landlords; to support the urban proletariat against the peasant bourgeoisie and any other bourgeoisie. That is the "line" of the rural proletariat and its ideologist, the social democrat.

[From "The Attitude of Social Democracy toward the Peasant Movement," an article in *Proletarii,* no. 16, September 1 (14, N.S.), 1905:]

There will always be reactionary admixtures in the peasant movement, and we declare war on them in advance. Class antagonism between the rural proletariat and the peasant bourgeoisie is unavoidable, and we reveal it in advance, explain it, and *prepare for a struggle on this ground.* One of the occasions of such a struggle may very likely be the question: to whom shall the confiscated land be given, and how? . . . There we shall certainly be with the rural proletariat, with the entire working class, *against* the peasant bourgeoisie. In practice, this may mean the transfer of land to the class of petty peasant proprietors wherever big estates based on bondage and feudal servitude still prevail, where there are as yet no material prerequisites for large-scale socialist production; it may mean nationalization, provided the democratic revolution is completely victorious; or the big capitalist estates may be transferred to *workers' associations;* for from the democratic revolution we shall at once, and exactly in accordance with the measure of our strength, the strength of the class-conscious and organized proletariat, begin to proceed to the socialist revolution. We stand for continuous revolution. We shall not stop halfway. The reason we do not now immediately promise all sorts of "socialization" is simply because we know what is actually required for that task and do not gloss over but reveal the new class struggle that is ripening within the ranks of the peasantry.

At first we shall support the peasantry in general against the landlords, support it to the limit and by every means, including confiscation, and then (or rather not "then," but at the same time) we shall support the proletariat against the peasantry in general.

XVI:38. MENSHEVIKS MARTYNOV AND AKSEL'ROD ON DIFFERENCES WITH THE BOLSHEVIKS, APRIL 1906

In these excerpts from speeches at the Fourth Congress of the RSDWP, held in Stockholm in April 1906, A. S. Martynov and P. B. Aksel'rod explain further the Menshevik position.

Reference: *Protokoly ob"edinitel'nogo s"ezda Rossiiskoi Sotsial'-demokraticheskoi Rabochei Partii, sostoiavshegosia v Stokgol'me v 1906 g.* (Moscow: Izd. RSDRP, 1907), pp. 159, 165 [Martynov], 206, 208, 210 [Aksel'rod]. Aksel'rod's speech was subsequently published as a separate pamphlet under the title *Dve taktiki* (St. Petersburg: Novyi Mir, 1907).

[From the thirteenth session. A discussion of the second point on the agenda: "On the present situation and class tasks of the proletariat":]

MARTYNOV: Comrades! We, the so-called Mensheviks and Bolsheviks, differ not only in our present tactical directives, but in the very criteria, in our very conception of the course of any revolution. For just this reason we evaluate the present situation in different ways; for just this reason we come to different tactical conclusions. The Bolsheviks say: either the erection of a constitutional structure or an armed uprising. . . . Such a conception of the course of revolution is completely utopian; in all major revolutions elemental outbursts and violent clashes are accompanied by the breakup of political institutions, that is, by the erection of a constitutional structure; and these two processes not only do not exclude, but on the contrary are mutually conditioned to each other. . . .

The conception of the course of revolution held by the comrades of the majority is a return to the utopian outlook of our populist rebels. . . . Tkachev and Bakunin wrote the same thing about uprisings that Comrade Lenin has told us here.

· · ·

Our disagreements with the Bolsheviks are very profound; we differ even in our conceptions of what the psychological type of a good revolutionary ought to be. The comrades of the majority eagerly imitate Blanqui; unfortunately, they know little about this major historical personage. Blanqui used to say that a good revolutionary ought to have *"du feu sous la glace"*—his heart should be aflame, but his head should be cold as ice. Among our comrades of the majority has taken shape another type of revolutionary, one whose imagination is on fire instead of his heart, whose brain is inflamed, who babbles revolutionary phrases. Just now I witnessed an extremely characteristic scene. While I was talking with Comrade Lenin, Voinov ran out to us from the meeting hall and breathlessly shouted to Lenin: "They don't want to insert the word 'revolutionary.'" Lenin and Voinov instantly ran into the hall and raised their hands, voting for the word "revolutionary," although Lenin didn't even know where this word was supposed to be inserted. Comrades! If our proletariat is going to fight under the direction of such leaders and such parties, it will not triumph but will only repeat the unsuccessful experiment of the February revolution [of 1848 in France], which Marx called a revolution of revolutionary phrases and pretty gestures.

· · ·

[AKSEL'ROD:] . . . The tactical disagreements that underlie the majority and minority resolutions proposed by the committee on the question of our tactics regarding the State Duma are matters of principle having paramount significance. These disagreements come as the logical conclusion, reflection, or expression of the basic antagonism between two fundamental tendencies struggling within our party, tendencies irreconcilably hostile to each other and mutually exclusive.

· · ·

The tactical point of view of the opponents of our resolution may be characterized in a word as rebel-conspiratorial, as a mixture of anarchist and Blanquist tendencies, screened behind Marxist or social-democratic phraseology.

· · ·

We cannot entirely avoid by any devices, verbal or tactical, the objective historical demand of "political cooperation" between the proletariat and the bourgeoisie in absolutist Russia. On the contrary, in the organic, systematic conjunction of our essentially proletarian task with this general democratic demand, conditioned by the social content of our revolution, lies the core of all the political problems of Russian social democracy.

XVI:39. CHERNOV ON SOCIALISM AND REVOLUTION, 1900

Viktor Mikhailovich Chernov (1873-1952), ideologist and leader of the Socialist Revolutionary Party, wrote about socialism and the revolutionary process in these words when his party was just getting organized. These passages are from *The Immediate Task of the Revolutionary Cause*, a booklet published anonymously in London (in Russian) in 1900.

Reference: *Ocherednoi vopros revoliutsionnogo dela* (London: Agrarian-Socialist League, 1900), pp. 8, 23, 26.

There is no historical law that says that the socialist organization of any branch of production may be possible only as a product of preceding capitalist development. There is no historical law that requires that in all branches of production the direct producers first have to pass through a kind of purgatory—the proletarian state—before entering the socialist paradise. For a certain part of the direct producers, for certain branches of production, a more direct transition is possible through the evolution of various types of communal ownership, including the village commune, to the nationalization of the land, and through cooperative associations to socialism.

. . .

We are deeply convinced that in Russia the future can belong only to the party that manages to find a fulcrum for its struggle not only in the city but also in the village, a party that can construct a harmonious program which would enable it to represent and defend simultaneously the interests of the industrial working class and those of the toiling peasantry. Without some support among the peasantry—and still less *against its will*—no revolutionary party in Russia will be able to strike a serious, decisive blow to the bourgeois-capitalist regime, which in our country knows how to live in peaceful harmony with the relics of an age of serf-owning gentry under the wing of Russian absolutism.

. . .

. . . Only an alliance between the intelligentsia and the people can transform the spontaneous popular movements of our time into conscious action and direct them along sensible paths. And only an alliance between urban and rural workers will represent a vital force strong enough to break the power of the existing order and prepare the triumph of the ideals of socialism and revolution.

XVI:40. CHERNOV ON HIS AND THE SOCIALIST REVOLUTIONARIES' POLICIES TOWARD THE PEASANTRY AS PURSUED CA. 1900-1917

A comprehensive, though unfortunately not a contemporary, statement of Chernov's policies toward the rural segment of society is seen in his book *Konstruktivnyi sotsializm* (Constructive socialism). It was published in Prague in 1925, well before the drive for collectivization in the Soviet Union, and at a time when the policies Chernov had advocated as prerevolutionary leader of the Socialist Revolutionaries were still very close to his heart.

Reference: Viktor M. Chernov, *Konstruktivnyi sotsializm* (Prague: Volia Rossii, 1925), pp. 119-21, 280-81.

The Socialist Revolutionaries believed . . . that the working peasantry was not simply a "remnant" of the past but rather an indispensable "vital element" of the present and future. From the first they refused to follow the dogma which declares that the agricultural economy develops, albeit belatedly, along the same pattern as urban industry. They met with skepticism all these dogmatic "last rites" for the peasant and the small-scale labor economy, all these categorical forecasts of the imminent advent of large-scale capitalist "grain factories" and their triumphal march through the arena of the rural economy. Of course, they expected that unification and socialization of labor and property would come even in the field of agriculture, but from below, not from above; not under the rod of a tutelary capitalism but through the independent economic action of the tillers of the soil themselves. In other words, they envisaged the future of agriculture not as a capitalistic but as a cooperative evolution.

. . .

In analyzing the nature of the agrarian commune as a peculiar form of cooperative labor, the Socialist Revolutionaries discovered in it a progressive series of forms which balanced, reconciled, and synthesized two essentially different rights: the *right to work* (a right guaranteed in the commune by means of allotting a plot of land to each of its members in an amount equivalent to the expenditure of labor), and the *right to the product of work* (the right to the product of work which, once invested in the land and made inseparable from it, becomes part of the land in the form of *soil improvement*). . . . The Socialist Revolutionaries attempted to cleanse these two basic work principles of peasant land cooperatives from alien accretions and local limitations and to extend them to the entire agrarian territory of the country. All of agricultural Russia would be transformed, as it were, into a single huge "agrarian commune," and the separate local associations of neighboring agrarian units would become its branches and organs. In this way the land would not be regarded by the peasant as "alien"; it would not become the "property" of a remote, many-headed, yet impersonal, half-mythical creature—the state. The land would not be taken away from the peasant to become state property, nor would the peasant himself thus become a "proletarian," making use of the land by the gracious "permission" of the state. He would remain in possession of his individual "right to the land" under its double aspect: the right, equally shared with every other tiller of the soil, to the allotment of a plot of land; and the right, equally shared with every other tiller of the soil, to extract a value from the land equivalent to his invested work. Within the limits of this right he would be unassailable, he would have firm footing on a position inaccessible to interference from any side. But this right would not be a "monopoly," a basis for exploiting the labor of others; rather it would be essentially a right to work the land and use it on equal terms with others.

This scheme undoubtedly contains a certain indigenous element, a vivid reflection of purely Russian national conditions. However, this element should not be exaggerated. What is "indigenous" and purely "national" here is merely the method of *linking* the concepts of land ownership held by the socialists with customary law, with the natural philosophy of labor held by the Russian agriculturalists. This is what to a large extent accounts for the extraordinary success of the Socialist Revolutionaries in the village, in preaching the socialization of the land. They worked a "miracle" by knowing how to represent the socialization of the land as a logical outgrowth of the laboring peasantry's traditional and current views of land ownership, simply deepening and interpreting these views. The elemental agrarian movement of the land-poor peasants, having swept along with it the bulk of the Russian peasantry, advanced solidly under the agrarian slogans of the Socialist Revolutionary Party; and in the first really free popular elections to the Constituent Assembly it gave this party an absolute majority. It was an event without precedent in history. At the very first application of the right of universal suffrage in the country, a socialist party, which had publicly declared its intention of abolishing private ownership of land, attained the position of a ruling party *by means of the peasant vote!*

. . .

The basic feature of the agrarian program of the Socialist Revolutionaries—the "communization [*obmirshchenie*] of the land"— can thus be described as an extension of the great principle of self-government into a new field, that of agrarian relations. Into the area encompassed by self-government it introduced an immense social good—land as the object of labor. The land reform of the Socialist Revolutionaries was to create a great economic peasant democracy on a national scale. As a true democracy, it expected not simply a despotic autocracy of the majority but the abolition of all absolutism, by guaranteeing the rights, not only of the minority, but of every separate individual. The absolutism of the property owner, based on Roman law, was not replaced in the Socialist Revolutionary program either by the absolutism of regional authorities or by the absolutism of the state. The goal was a profoundly democratic, complex agricultural community with authority delegated from the bottom up, or, to put it differently, a cooperative distribution of the land for exploitation by the labor of groups and individuals.

The further development of this cooperative organization would consist of a gradual collectivization of individual labor rights. The basic "cooperative distribution of the land" would gradually be supplemented by various other kinds of cooperative organizations until at length the logical end point of development was reached, that is, until the "great all-Russian cooperative *distribution* of the land" was transformed into a similar cooperative *utilization of the land by labor*—that is, until the basic problem of socialism in this area was solved.

XVI:41. AN EARLY MANIFESTO OF THE SOCIALIST REVOLUTIONARY PARTY, JUNE 25, 1902

These phrases from an early manifesto of the Socialist Revolutionary Party underscore the party's special interest in the peasantry. This manifesto was published in Paris in the journal *Revoliutsionnaia Rossiia*, and was addressed "to all workers for revolutionary socialism in Russia."

Reference: "Nashi zadachi v derevne" [Our tasks in the village], in *Po voprosam programmy i taktiki: Sbornik statei iz "Revoliutsionnoi Rossii"* ([Paris:] Tip. Partii Sotsialistov-Revoliutsionerov, 1903), pp. 27, 28.

What can the intelligentsia and proletariat do *without the peasantry*, much less *in defiance of the peasantry?* . . . Is it enough to ignite a revolutionary blaze among hundreds of thousands or even *millions* of proletarians, if the *tens of millions* of peasants will move upon it like a cold, glacial mass and extinguish it in its very inception?

. . .

What can the intelligentsia and proletariat do *together with the peasantry?* Everything.

The peasantry gives autocracy an enormous portion of its material strength: money and soldiers; tsarist power rests upon peasant ignorance as a heretofore unshakable foundation. Therefore, it is not even absolutely necessary for the entire peasantry to attack autocracy with armed force in order to destroy it. At the critical moment, for example, merely a mass refusal to pay taxes and furnish recruits may prove sufficient for the chief props of autocracy to totter, and for it to crash down with the first strong push.

XVI:42. THE BULLETIN AND PROGRAM OF THE FIRST CONGRESS OF THE SOCIALIST REVOLUTIONARY PARTY, JANUARY 1906

The First Congress of the Socialist Revolutionary Party met in December 1905 and January 1906 in the Grand Duchy of Finland. The congress issued an announcement and a program, excerpts from which are presented here. Both were published in 1906 by the Central Committee of the party.

Reference: *Programma i organizatsionnyi ustav Partii Sotsialistov-Revoliutsionerov* (Paris: Izd. TsK PS-R, 1906), pp. 15-16, 17 [party bulletin], pp. 18, 22, 24-27, 28 [party program]. A translation of the program is included in the recently published Dmytryshyn, *Imperial Russia*, pp. 331-37.

[From the "Bulletin of the Party Congress":]

While preparing for . . . a general uprising, the party, in the meantime, not only does not withdraw from the direct struggle but, on the contrary, recognizes that training for battle is unthinkable without the process of battle; it recognizes that battle not only wins rights but also develops that strength which wins rights. And therefore, in all major spontaneous uprisings of the people the task of party men is clear: they must be in the front ranks of the people; they must seal with blood their bond with the working masses. . . . That same battle training and development is also acquired by means of terroristic struggle, central and local, individual and mass. The specific methods for carrying on this struggle, which corresponds to the particular features of the moment, are not to be made public, but the basic principle remains the same. Not of its own will, nor out of preference for bloody methods of struggle, did the party take up this weapon, but in fulfillment of its stern duty to the cause of revolution, to the cause of the working people. This was a profoundly serious and responsible decision. History has justified it. And the new debauch of arbitrary rule finds the party once again at its battle station. It will cease terroristic tactics as a system of political struggle only when it secures political institutions that make the will of the people the source of power and legislation.

In the name of this principle of real popular sovereignty, the party energetically rises in revolution against the pitiful attempt of the government to conceal its crimes against the country by the manipulated elections to the State Duma—that deformed and ludicrous parody of a national representative body. As was to be expected, the congress unanimously decided upon a boycott of the elections to the [First] Duma and of the Duma itself. . . . [Note: This policy was changed before the elections to the Second State Duma.]

. . .

The party . . . boldly advances to meet the political storms and crises that await it.

Long live international revolutionary socialism!

Long live the Socialist Revolutionary Party, a detachment of the worldwide socialist army of labor!

Long live the social revolution!

[From the "Program of the Socialist Revolutionary Party":]

Contemporary Russia, in its historical development, is entering into increasingly closer relations with the advanced countries of the civilized world, while at the same time preserving certain distinctive features conditioned by the nature of its previous history, its local conditions, and its international position.

. . .

The Socialist Revolutionary Party in Russia regards itself as one of the detachments of the army of international socialism and carries on its activity in the spirit of the common interests of this struggle, in the forms that correspond to the concrete conditions of Russian reality.

. . .

The complete attainment of the party program, i.e. the expropriation of capitalist property and the reorganization of production and the entire social structure along socialistic principles, presupposes the complete triumph of the working class, organized into a social-revolutionary party, and, if need be, its establishment of a temporary revolutionary dictatorship.

. . .

During the [present] period the Socialist Revolutionary Party will defend, support, or endeavor to extort by its revolutionary struggle the following measures:

A. In the political and legal sphere: the acknowledgment of the following rights of men and citizens as inalienable: full freedom of conscience, speech, press, assembly, and association; freedom of movement, choice of occupation, and collective refusal to work (freedom to strike); the inviolability of persons and domiciles; universal and equal suffrage for every citizen over the age of twenty without distinction of sex, religion, or nationality, with direct elections and a secret ballot; a democratic republic established upon these principles, with broad autonomy on the regional level and for municipal and rural communes; the widest possible application of the federative principle to the relations between the different nationalities, with the acknowledgment of their unconditional right to self-determination; proportional representation; direct legislation by the people (referendum and initiative); the right to elect, remove at any time, and bring to justice all officials, including deputies and judges; the free administration of justice; the use of the native language in all local, public, and governmental institutions; the establishment of compulsory, equal, universal, and secular education at the expense of the state; . . . the complete separation of church and state and the recognition of religion as a strictly private matter of conscience; the abolition of the standing army, to be replaced by a national militia.

B. In the sphere of the national economy:

1. In matters concerning the economy and the financial policy of the state, the party will agitate for the establishment of a progressive income and inheritance tax, with complete tax exemption for small incomes below a certain norm, and for the abolition of indirect taxes (excluding luxury taxes), protective duties, and all taxes whatsoever imposed on labor.

2. In matters of labor legislation the SR Party establishes as its goal the safeguarding of the moral and physical forces of the urban and rural working class, and the increase of its powers in the further struggle for socialism. . . . The party will strive for: the greatest possible reduction in the length of the working day, in accordance with the norms prescribed by scientific hygiene (in the

immediate future, for an eight-hour working day in most branches of industry, and a correspondingly shorter day in those more dangerous or injurious to health); the establishment of minimum wages by agreement between the organs of self-government and the workers' trade unions; governmental insurance in all its forms (against accidents, unemployment, old age, illness, and so forth), supported by the state and the employers on the basis of management by the insured; legislative protection of labor in all branches of industry and commerce. . . .

3. In matters involving the reorganization of agrarian relations the SR Party wishes, in the interests of socialism and the struggle against the principles of bourgeois property, to base itself upon the communal and labor-oriented attitudes, traditions, and way of life of the Russian peasantry, and particularly upon the widespread conviction within it that the land does not belong to anyone, that the right to utilize it can be obtained only by labor. In agreement with its general views on the tasks of the revolution in the village, the party will stand for the socialization of land, i.e. for withdrawing it from circulation as a commodity and transferring it from the private ownership of single individuals or groups into the possession of the entire nation on the following principles: all land shall come under the management of central and local organs of popular self-government, starting with democratically organized classless rural and municipal communes and culminating with regional and central institutions (for

settlement and migration, management of the land fund, and so forth); the utilization of land must be based upon the principles of equality and labor, i.e. the consumer needs [of each family] must be provided for, but solely by the application of personal labor, whether singly or in associations; rents, collected through a special assessment, must be used for public needs; the use of land that is of more than strictly local importance (extensive forests, fisheries, and the like) shall be regulated by correspondingly more extensive organs of self-government; the mineral wealth of the earth shall remain in the hands of the state; the land shall become the common property of all the people, without redemption; those who have suffered from these property changes may claim no more than the right to public support for the period of time necessary to adjust themselves to new conditions of personal existence.

· · ·

The SR Party, while waging a direct revolutionary struggle with autocracy, carries on agitation for the convocation of a constituent assembly on the democratic principles indicated above, for the liquidation of the autocratic regime and the reorganization of the entire present system with the aim of establishing a free government of the people and the necessary personal freedoms, and of defending the interests of labor. It will defend its program for reorganization in the constituent assembly, and likewise strive directly to carry it through during the revolutionary period.

XVI:43. STRUVE'S OSVOBOZHDENIE, 1902-1905

Osvobozhdenie (Liberation), a fortnightly review edited by the former Marxist Petr Berngardovich Struve (1870-1944), was published first in Stuttgart beginning in 1902, and then, from October 1904 to October 1905, in Paris. Copies were smuggled into Russia. Struve's journal, excerpts from which are given here, expressed the views of the zemstvo constitutionalists and the Union of Liberation (Soiuz Osvobozhdeniia)—the progenitors of the Kadet or Constitutional Democratic Party.

Reference: *Osvobozhdenie*, no. 1 (June 18 [July 1, N.S.], 1902), pp. 2, 5, 9, 10; no. 7 (Sept. 18 [Oct. 1, N.S.], 1902), p. 105; no. 20 (Mar. 19 [Apr. 1, N.S.], 1904), p. 346; no. 64 (Jan. 12 [25, N.S.], 1905), p. 233. For translations of Struve's writings, the editors wish to express their appreciation to Professor Dimitri von Mohrenschildt.

[From *Osvobozhdenie*, no. 1, June 18 (July 1, N.S.), 1902, an introductory statement from the editor:]

Our journal is not going to be "revolutionary," but its entire content will call for a great *change* in the life of Russia: replacing the arbitrary rule of an autocratic bureaucracy

with a regime of civil rights, individual and public. We expect that some will find this statement too moderate and others too radical. We do not fear the reproaches of either side. Our point of view is simple and clear. Basing ourselves on this point of view, which in its guiding principles is shared by all honest

Russians of awakened social consciousness, we shall calmly face accusations both of opportunism and of radicalism. We shall preach not adaptation to the existing political regime, which saps the best forces of our nation, but, on the contrary, a fight against it; we shall not pass over in diplomatic silence all the implications deriving from a demand for political freedom. But neither shall we invent, create, or foster any artificial strife between the various trends of public and individual endeavor, between the different minds and personalities all aiming more or less consciously at the one great goal. Our task will be to unite, not to split. The cultural and political liberation of Russia cannot be exclusively or preeminently the task of one class, one party, one school of thought. It must become a national task which embraces all the people.

· · ·

The great liberation movement . . . is in its very essence liberal and democratic. Liberal because it aims at winning freedom, democratic because it defends the most vital material and spiritual interests of the masses. Even the extreme Russian parties do not go, in their practical demands, beyond far-reaching political and economic reforms in a democratic spirit. These are the tasks that actually unite all Russians with the exception of self-seeking partisans of the existing bureaucratic disorder. But while the extremist movements of our country are organized, the liberal-moderate core of Russian society remains in an almost amorphous state. Yet the historical period in which we live calls for the utmost exertion of all social forces in fighting for the reforms the government has been so long and so stubbornly denying the country. This strenuous struggle against arbitrary bureaucracy must be carried on at every point, using all morally permissible means; and such a struggle requires the elaboration of a clear program and a stable organization. It is our belief that one of the chief tasks of our journal is to further this important undertaking, on which unquestionably depends the further success of national liberation. To become clearly aware of the liberal-democratic movement in the country and to give it form means nothing other than the organization of a politically clear and unified public opinion that would be strong because of its very awareness and solidarity. We dedicate our publication

to this task in full consciousness of its importance.

[From the same issue, in an article entitled "From the Russian Constitutionalists":]

The first clauses of our program must be.
. . .

1. *Personal liberty* guaranteed by an *independent* judiciary. . . .

2. *Legal equality for all.* . . .

These indispensable provisions of personal liberty and equality of civil and political rights must be followed by the no less indispensable recognition of the elementary prerequisites of free political thought and criticism:

1. Freedom of the press; the right to publish periodicals without preliminary permission and without furnishing security [against fines that might be imposed on the editor or publisher]; abolition of censorship and responsibility of the press before the courts.

2. Freedom of assembly and association.

3. The right of petition.

· · ·

Popular representation without class distinctions, in the form of a permanent, annually convoked supreme institution with the right to exercise control over the executive, to issue laws, and to ratify the budget.

[From *Osvobozhdenie,* no. 7, September 18 (October 1, N.S.), 1902, in an article by P. B. Struve, entitled "Liberalism and the So-called Revolutionary Elements":]

An end must be put to the mutual lack of understanding between the various elements of the Russian opposition; and we are firmly convinced that this can be done, provided a way is found to establish complete sincerity and broad tolerance. Sincere and consistent liberals must, and will, understand more and more clearly that, however great in many respects may be the distance between them and the socialists and revolutionaries, revolutionary socialism can never mean to them what it means to the reactionary government, that is, "sedition." The publicist of the bureaucratic autocracy, Katkov, was right from his point of view in branding the entire Russian opposition as "seditious." But if the entire opposition is "seditious," this means that *there is no sedition in Russia; there is only an opposition.* This is the political truth that Russian liberalism should have learned from the hard school of the two decades from 1881 to 1901, and which it should candidly and honestly declare for all to hear. Even twenty years ago it was strange that men should be mistaken about the nature of the Russian revolutionary movement, which is primarily a wholesome protest against the arbitrary policies of the government and its criminal neglect of the people's most urgent needs. The revolutionary movement can create neither "chaos" nor "anarchy." To expect chaos from it is to misunderstand its very essence, on the one hand, and infinitely to exaggerate its strength, on the other.

Two conclusions must be drawn from the aforesaid. First, a sincere and consistent liberalism must realize and acknowledge its solidarity with the so-called revolutionary elements in their political objectives, insofar as these aim at establishing a rule of law in Russia. Second, the "revolutionaries" must renounce their intolerance, which is an outgrowth of their doctrine and their political immaturity, and accept liberalism as their ally in the struggle for political freedom, that is, in the task that is the real and vital substance of the Russian revolution.

[From *Osvobozhdenie*, no. 20, March 19 (April 1, N.S.), 1904, in an editorial entitled "The Policy of the Liberal Party":]

Our party, defined in its negative aspect as a party of revolution striving to abolish autocracy, finds its positive basis in affirming freedom to be an essential requirement of life. We regard this principle, not only as the key to solving all pressing social problems, not only as the soundest practical instrument of our present policy, but also as a fundamental social blessing that we value highly for itself, independently of practical results. We consider freedom of the individual the alpha and omega of our political credo; in our program it is both the point of departure upon which everything is based and the ultimate end to which everything is directed. We deem it especially important to insist upon this principle in Russian society, where not only the reactionaries but also the progressive parties have often neglected this essential requirement of social life.

No less than the other opposition parties, we contemplate economic and social reforms. In our day a liberal program is unthinkable

and impossible without a broad plan of social improvements in which and by which freedom will find its concrete realization. Land reform, factory and labor legislation, and the sum total of all the tasks of social and economic policy must find a place in our program; but all this must be based upon and linked with our fundamental principle—individual freedom.

In this connection we further accept as necessary the democratic consequences of liberalism. Freedom, as a sincere and universal principle of politics, certainly means freedom for all, not just for a few. The democratic principle is a logical and ethical consequence of a liberal program.

[From *Osvobozhdenie*, no. 64, January 12 (25, N.S.), 1905, the full text of an editorial by Struve under the heading "The Revolution in Russia—The People's Executioner":]

The people came to him, the people waited for him. The tsar met his people. Whips, sabers, and bullets were his answer to words of sorrow and trust. Blood has been shed in the streets of Saint Petersburg, and the bond between the people and this tsar has been broken forever. It matters little what he is, whether an arrogant despot unwilling to descend to the people, or a contemptible coward afraid to face the very element from which he draws his power; after the events of January 9/22, 1905, Nicholas has openly become the enemy and executioner of the people. More than this we shall not say of him; after this we shall no longer speak to him. He has destroyed himself in our eyes, and there is no return to the past. Not one among us can forgive this blood. It chokes us with spasms; it possesses us; it leads us on; and it will take us where we must go and where we shall arrive.

Yesterday there were still disputes and factions. Today the Russian liberation movement must have a single body and a single will, a single twofold thought: revenge and freedom, whatever the cost. This thought inflames our soul like a sacred oath, and its constant call pierces our mind.

All who possess a simple human conscience must arise against the terrible crimes committed in the streets of Saint Petersburg at the tsar's command. There can be no argument that the crime must be punished, and that its root must be destroyed. It is impossible to live on like this. The annals of autocratic violence, outrage, and crime must be closed.

We cannot think or write about anything but revenge and freedom.

Through vengeance we shall become free, through freedom we shall take revenge.

P. S.

XVI:44. THE PROGRAM OF THE UNION OF LIBERATION, NOVEMBER 1904

The Union of Liberation (Soiuz Osvobozhdeniia) was founded secretly in 1903-04 by zemstvo elements along with other professional people and intellectuals. In November 1904, representatives of the various subgroups of the union agreed on the following statement of general principles.

Reference: *Osvobozhdenie*, no. 17 (Nov. 19 [Dec. 2, N.S.], 1904), p. 2. The translation is from George Fischer, *Russian Liberalism* (Cambridge: Harvard University Press, 1958), p. 147.

The first and main aim of the Union of Liberation is the political liberation of Russia. Considering political liberty in even its most minimal form completely incompatible with the absolute character of the Russian monarchy, the union will seek before all else the abolition of autocracy and the establishment in Russia of a constitutional regime. In determining the concrete forms in which a constitutional regime can be realized in Russia, the Union of Liberation will make all efforts to have the political problem resolved in the spirit of extensive democracy. Above all, it recognizes as fundamentally essential that the principles of universal, equal, secret, and direct elections be made the basis of the political reform.

Putting the political demands in the forefront, the Union of Liberation recognizes as essential the definition of its attitude in principle to the socioeconomic problems created by life itself. In the realm of socioeconomic policy, the Union of Liberation will follow the same basic principle of democracy, making the direct goal of its activity the defense of the interests of the laboring masses.

In the sphere of national questions, the union recognizes the right of self-determination of different nationalities entering into the composition of the Russian state. In relation to Finland the union supports the demand for the restoration of the political and legal status which existed in that country until its illegal abrogation during the present reign.

XVI:45. THE PROGRAM OF THE KADET PARTY, OCTOBER 1905

The Constitutional Democratic Party (called "Kadet" from the initials "KD") was established when representatives of two earlier groups came together in an organizing convention in Saint Petersburg from October 12 to October 18, 1905. The program drawn up by that convention expressed the views of a significant segment of Russia's professional and educated people at this time—views that achieved added importance because of the leading role played by the Kadets in the first two Dumas.

(Concerning paragraph 13, it should be noted that the Kadets' second convention, in January 1906, voted that Russia should be a "constitutional and parliamentary monarchy.")

Reference: *Pravo*, no. 41 (Oct. 25, 1905), cols. 3424-32. A translation of most of this program is included in the recently published Dmytryshyn, *Imperial Russia*, pp. 338-43.

I. Fundamental rights of citizens.

1. All Russian citizens are equal before the law, regardless of sex, creed, and nationality. All legal distinctions among classes and all restrictions upon the personal and property rights of Poles, Jews, and all other population groups, without exception, must be abolished.

2. Every citizen is guaranteed freedom of conscience and religion. . . .

3. Everyone is free to express his ideas orally and in writing, as well as to publish and disseminate them through the press or in any other manner. Censorship, both general and special, whatever it may be called, is abolished and cannot be reestablished. . . .

4. All Russian citizens have the right to hold public meetings, both in buildings and under the open sky, to discuss any type of question.

5. All Russian citizens have the right to form leagues and societies, without requesting permission.

6. The right of petition belongs both to individual citizens and to all types of groups, leagues, assemblies, and so forth.

7. Everyone's person and home must be inviolable. . . .

8. No one can be persecuted or punished except on the basis of the law—by judicial authorities and legally established courts. There must be no extraordinary courts. . . .

11. The fundamental law of the Russian Empire should guarantee all the nationalities inhabiting the empire the right of free cultural self-determination, in addition to full civil and political equality for all citizens. . . .

II. State organization.

13. The constitutional structure of the Russian state is determined by the fundamental law.

14. The people's representatives are elected by universal, equal, direct, and secret ballot, without distinction as to religion, nationality, or sex. [Footnote in this text of the program: "As to the question of the immediate extension of the vote to women, the minority retained its own opinion, for practical considerations. The convention therefore declared the party's decision on this matter not obligatory for the minority."]

The party admits of difference of opinion in its midst on the question of organizing popular representation in the form of one or two chambers, of which the second should consist of representatives of local self-government organs, reorganized on the basis of the universal ballot and extended throughout Russia. . . .

16. No enactment, decree, edict, order, or similar measure can have legal force, whatever its name or source, unless it is based on the decision of a popular representative body. . . .

19. The ministers are responsible before the assembly of the people's representatives, whose members shall have the right of inquiry and interpellation.

III. Local self-government and autonomy. . . .

24. After the establishment of civil rights [prav grazhdanskoi svobody] and proper representation, with constitutional rights for the entire Russian state, a legal way must be opened, by means of nationwide legislation, for the establishment of local autonomy and of regional representative assemblies possessing the right to participate in the legislative process in regard to certain matters, in accordance with the needs of the people.

25. Immediately upon the establishment of empire-wide democratic representation with constitutional rights, autonomous organizations shall be instituted in the Kingdom of Poland, with a sejm [diet] to be elected on the same basis as the general national representative bodies [of the empire], under conditions providing for the preservation of state unity and of Poland's participation in the central representative body on the same basis as the other parts of the empire. . . .

VI. Agrarian legislation.

36. There shall be an increase in the area of land under cultivation by people who work the land by their own personal labor, such as landless and land-poor peasants, as well as other categories of small-owner farmers, [this increase to be accomplished] by the addition of state lands, appanage lands, lands belonging to the emperor's central office [kabinetskie zemli], and monastery lands, as well as privately owned lands purchased by the state for this purpose in the amounts needed, the present owners being paid according to a just appraisal of value rather than the market price. . . .

VII. Labor legislation.

41. Freedom of labor unions and assemblies.

42. The right to strike. . . .

44. Establishment by law of the eight-hour workday. . . .

47. Obligatory insurance, through the intermediary of the state, against illness (for specified periods), accidents, and occupational diseases, the expenses to be paid by the employers.

48. State insurance against old age and disability for all persons living by their own labor. . . .

VIII. Education.

53. Complete autonomy and freedom of instruction at universities and other higher educational institutions. . . .

55. Establishment of universal, free, and compulsory primary education. Transfer of primary education to the jurisdiction of local organs of self-government.

XVI:46. MILIUKOV'S ADDRESS AT THE FOUNDING CONGRESS OF THE KADET PARTY, OCTOBER 14, 1905

Pavel Nikolaevich Miliukov (1859-1943), historian and leader of the Constitutional Democratic Party, stated these views in his opening address at the founding congress of the party in Moscow.

Reference: P. N. Miliukov, *God bor'by, 1905-1906* (St. Petersburg: Obshchestvennaia Pol'za, 1907), pp. 97-98, 100.

The purpose of the present congress is to create and to proclaim formally a large political party, the first open political party in Russia, to which the public has already given the name *Constitutional Democratic.* This purpose is so natural, so uncontrived, indeed, so necessary and inevitable in view of the present political situation, that life has already anticipated our formal resolutions, and the Constitutional Democratic Party is regarded as an entity that has been in existence for a long time, which even possesses its own traditions and its own definite political physiognomy. . . .

. . . The party as it now exists has been formed chiefly from two groups, already linked with one another both in membership and in the character of their social views and activity. The first of these groups is the well-known Union of Liberation [Soiuz Osvobozhdeniia]; the other is the Union of Zemstvo Constitutionalists [Soiuz Zemskikh Konstitutsionalistov]. Each of the two groups has its own background and a more or less lengthy history. . . . In its present phase, the activity of both groups dates back to 1903. I shall not describe this activity but shall merely say that its political scope has been very broad. It may be said that in recent years the entire Russian liberation movement—insofar as it was not the result of the activity of the socialist parties—has in one way or another been connected with the activities of the above-mentioned organizations.

. . .

On the Right . . . our opponents raise against us the principles of Russian *unity* and the inviolability of private property, as if we were rejecting unity and private property. The Kadet Party naturally does not repudiate either of these, but it is irreconcilably opposed to bureaucratic centralization and to the [present] administration. The true boundary line, therefore, is by no means where our opponents on the Right would like to draw it, to their own advantage. This boundary lies where they speak in the name of the narrow class interests of Russian agrarians and industrialists. Our party will never stand guard over these interests, to the detriment of the interests of the working class.

Between us and what we would like to call, not our opponents, but our allies, on the Left, there is also a certain dividing line, but it is of a different nature from the one we draw on the Right. We do not join them in demanding a democratic republic and the socialization of the means of production. Some of us do not subscribe to these slogans because they find them generally unacceptable; others, because they regard these demands as lying outside the realm of practical politics.

XVI:47. THE PROGRAM OF THE OCTOBRISTS, 1905

The moderate-liberal party called the Union [or League] of October 17, organized after the issuance of the October Manifesto, attracted the support of many merchants and industrialists as well as a considerable segment of the noble landowning class. The leader of the party was the Moscow industrialist Aleksandr Ivanovich Guchkov (1862-1936). The Octobrists occupied the central position in the Third and Fourth Dumas.

Reference: *Polnyi sbornik platform vsekh russkikh politicheskikh partii,* 4th ed. (St. Petersburg, 1907), pp. 111-23.

Program of the Union of October 17 . . . The Manifesto of October 17 signals a great change in the destinies of our fatherland: henceforth our people becomes a politically free people, and our state a legal state; and a new principle is introduced into our state structure—the principle of constitutional monarchy.

The new order, calling all Russian people, without distinction as to class, nationality, or religion, to free political life, opens before them a wide opportunity to influence the

destiny of their fatherland by legal means
and make it possible for them to defend their
interests on the basis of the law and to seek
a victory for their ideas and convictions through
peaceful and open struggle. At the same time
the new order imposes upon all those who
sincerely desire the peaceful revival of the
country and the triumph of law and order,
those who reject both stagnation and revolutionary upheavals, the sacred duty at this
moment in the life of our fatherland, a moment that is solemn but fraught with great
danger, to rally harmoniously around the
principles proclaimed in the Manifesto of
October 17; to insist on the speediest possible,
full, and broad realization of these principles
by the government, with firm guarantees of
their inviolability; and to cooperate with the
government, which is following the path of
salutary reforms aimed at the complete and
all-around renewal of the political and social
structure of Russia.

. . . The great danger resulting from centuries of stagnation in the development of
our political forms, threatening not only the
well-being but the very existence of our
fatherland, calls everyone to unity, to active
work toward the creation of a strong and
authoritative government which will find
support in the confidence and cooperation of
the people and which alone is capable, by
way of peaceful reforms, of bringing the
country out of the present social chaos and
assuring it internal peace and external security.

     . . .

1. Preservation of the unity and indivisibility
    of the Russian state.

. . . The vital condition for the strengthening of the external might of Russia and for
her internal prosperity is the safeguarding of
the unity of her political body . . . while
recognizing the broadest rights of the individual nationalities to the satisfaction and protection of their cultural needs within limits
set by the interests of the whole country and
the interests of other nationalities. . . .

2. Development and consolidation of the
    principles of constitutional monarchy,
    with popular representation based on uni-
    versal suffrage.

. . . Although the will of the constitutional
monarch is limited by the rights of popular
representation, nevertheless, in his very unity
with the people and union with the land under

the new governmental system, he gains new
power and the new exalted task of serving as
the supreme leader of a free people. . . .

3. Assurance of civil rights.

    . . .

This includes, first of all: freedom of
religion, freedom of expression, spoken and
printed, and freedom of assembly and association. It also includes protection of freedom of movement and of choice of place of
residence and occupation, assurance of freedom of labor, industry, and trade, and freedom in acquiring and disposing of property.
Civil freedom also presupposes the inviolability of person, home, correspondence, and
property. . . .

The urgent need for convocation of the State
Duma.

    . . .

. . . As it begins its fundamental, constructive labors, the State Duma should, in the
opinion of the Union [of October 17], set
itself the following problems of prime state
importance for consideration and gradual
solution.

a. The peasant question.

First among all the vital reforms should be
steps for the decisive and irreversible extension of full civil rights to the peasants, in complete equality with the rest of the citizens.
This includes: revocation of special laws that
place in juridically inferior position those
classes that pay the *podat'* [a direct tax];
abolition of administrative tutelage; and
recognition of communal land ownership [i.e.
ownership by the mir] as an institution under
civil law. In addition to constant state concern with raising agricultural productivity,
other measures needed for the improvement
of peasant life are: the regulation of petty
land rents; the reorganization of the work of
the Peasant Land Bank [see Item XVI:67,
below]; assistance in settlement and resettlement; a proclamation that state and appanage
lands constitute a fund which may be drawn
upon in order to meet the land needs of
former peasants and other categories of small
landholders; the redistribution of lands where
the strips belonging to peasants and estate
owners are intermingled, with obligatory
transfer of title in the case of parcels of land
that interfere with the economic unity of
holdings; and, finally, should these measures
prove insufficient, the transfer [to the peasants]

of part of the privately owned lands—permissible in cases important for the state—with fair compensation as established by legislative authority.

b. The labor question.

. . . This also includes measures for assuring workers and their families against illness, disability, and death; measures toward the gradual achievement of insurance for workers in all types of labor; and measures for limiting working hours for women and children, and in industries particularly hazardous to health.

While giving full recognition to trade unions and the freedom to strike as instruments by which workers may protect their interests, it is nevertheless important for us to recognize the need for legislative regulation of the conditions of this economic struggle. . . .

c. The development and consolidation of the principles of local self-government. . . .

d. Concern for popular education. . . .

e. Judicial and administrative reforms. . . .

f. Economic and financial measures.

. . . It is possible, already within the very near future, to achieve a more rational and just tax system and to shift the tax burden from weaker to stronger shoulders.

XVI:48. THE PROGRAM OF THE UNION OF THE RUSSIAN PEOPLE, 1905

Founded in the autumn of 1905, the political party that called itself the Union of the Russian People strove, under the leadership of such men as A. I. Dubrovin, N. E. Markov, and V. M. Purishkevich, and with the sympathy of the tsar himself, to reverse the current of events.

Reference: *Polnyi sbornik platform vsekh russkikh politicheskikh partii*, pp. 46-48.

I. The purpose of the union.

1. The Union of the Russian People sets itself the undeviating goal of developing national Russian consciousness and achieving the firm unification of Russian people of all classes and conditions for common work to the benefit of our dear fatherland—united and indivisible Russia.

II. Program.

2. The welfare of the homeland lies in the inviolate preservation of Orthodoxy, Russian unlimited autocracy, and nationality [or "nationhood"—*narodnost'*].

3. The Russian people is an Orthodox people, and therefore the Orthodox Christian church . . . should be given a prime and dominant position in the state.

4. Russian autocracy was created by the wisdom of the people, blessed by the church, and vindicated by history; our autocracy is in the unity of the tsar with the people.

Note. . . . The modern bureaucratic structure, intervening between the glorious person of the Russian tsar and the people and usurping a portion of the immemorial rights of Russian autocratic power, has brought our fatherland to grave misfortunes, and should therefore be radically altered; . . . the change of the existing system should by no means express itself in the establishment of restrictive principles in the form of any constitutional or constituent assemblies, but only by the institution of the State Duma as the organ representing a direct link between the sovereign will of the tsar and the people's sense of justice.

5. To the Russian nationality, the gatherer of the Russian land, which has created our great and powerful state, belongs the leading place in the life of the state and in the building up of the state.

· · ·

6. The State Duma, not having any idea of restricting the supreme sovereign power, should be nationally Russian. By truthfully informing the lawgiver [the tsar] about the actual needs of the people and the state, it should help him to carry out the needed changes.

7. The immediate activity of the reigning authorities should be steadfastly directed toward the establishment of strict law and order upon the firm foundations of freedom of speech, of the press, and of assembly and association, and of the inviolability of the person, but with the establishment of rules defining the limits of such freedom, in order to prevent violation of the state's legal order and the rights of individual citizens, and in order to protect the freedom itself from arbitrariness.

XVI:49. KROPOTKIN'S ANARCHISM, CA. 1901

Prince Peter Kropotkin (see Items XV:17 and XV:55)—general's son, Guards officer, explorer, geographer, geologist—ran afoul of the government in 1874 for spreading revolutionary propaganda. Escaping from prison and from Russia in 1876, he became part of the émigré revolutionary colony in Switzerland and later, from 1886 to 1917, in England. It was in England that most of his works were published, including the two cited here. These excerpts convey various aspects of Kropotkin's "scientific anarchism" as he was expounding it around the turn of the century. Kropotkin returned to Russia in 1917 but soon turned against the Soviet regime.

Reference: Peter Kropotkin, *Modern Science and Anarchism,* 2d ed. (London: Freedom Press, 1923), pp. 45, 92; Kropotkin, *Mutual Aid: a Factor of Evolution* (New York: MacLure Phillips, 1902), pp. 5, 54, 114, 272-74, 300.

[From his book *Modern Science and Anarchism,* first published in London in 1901:]

The Anarchists conceive a society in which all the mutual relations of its members are regulated, not by laws, not by authorities, whether self-imposed or elected, but by mutual agreements between the members of that society, and by a sum of social customs and habits—not petrified by law, routine, or superstition, but continually developing and continually readjusted, in accordance with the ever-growing requirements of a free life, stimulated by the progress of science, invention, and the steady growth of higher ideals.

No ruling authorities, then. No government of man by man; no crystallisation and immobility, but a continual evolution—such as we see in Nature. Free play for the individual, for the full development of his individual gifts—*for his individualisation.* In other words, no actions are *imposed* upon the individual by a fear of punishment; none is required from him by society, but those which receive his free acceptance. *In a society of equals* this would be quite sufficient for preventing those unsociable actions that might be harmful to other individuals and to society itself, and for favouring the steady moral growth of that society.

This is the conception developed and advocated by the Anarchists.

. . .

On the basis of historical data accumulated by modern science, Anarchism has demonstrated that State authority, which steadily grows in our days, is in reality but a noxious and a useless superstructure which, for us Europeans, only dates from the fifteenth and sixteenth centuries: a superstructure built to the advantage of Landlordism, Capitalism, and Officialism, and which in ancient times has caused already the downfall of Rome and Greece and many other centres of civilisation once flourishing in the East and in Egypt.

In political economy, Anarchism has come to the conclusion that the evils of the present day are not caused by the capitalist appropriating for himself the "surplus value," or "net price," but by the fact itself that "net profit" or "surplus value" is possible. Such an appropriation of the produce of human labour by the owners of capital exists only because millions of men have literally nothing to live upon, unless they sell their labour force and their intelligence at a price that will make the net profit of the capitalist and "surplus value" possible.

. . . In the coming revolution, the Anarchists see a first step toward *free Communism,* untrammelled by the State.

[From his book *Mutual Aid: A Factor of Evolution,* first published in London and New York in 1902:]

As soon as we study animals—not in laboratories and museums only, but in the forest and the prairie, in the steppe and the mountains—we at once perceive that though there is an immense amount of warfare and extermination going on amidst various species, and especially amidst various classes of animals, there is, at the same time, as much, or perhaps even more, of mutual support, mutual aid, and mutual defence amidst animals belonging to the same species or, at least, to the same society. Sociability is as much a law of nature as mutual struggle.

. . .

Sociability—that is, the need of the animal

of associating with its like—the love of society for society's sake, combined with the "joy of life," only now begins to receive due attention from the zoologists.

. . .

Wars and invasions created military authority, as also castes of warriors, whose associations or clubs acquired great powers. However, at no period of man's life were wars the *normal* state of existence. While warriors exterminated each other, and the priests celebrated their massacres, the masses continued to live their daily life, they prosecuted their daily toil. And it is one of the most interesting studies to follow that life of the masses; to study the means by which they maintained their own social organization, which was based upon their own conceptions of equity, mutual aid, and mutual support—of common law, in a word, even when they were submitted to the most ferocious theocracy or autocracy in the State.

. . .

The annalists of old never failed to chronicle the petty wars and calamities which harassed their contemporaries; but they paid no attention whatever to the life of the masses, although the masses chiefly used to toil peacefully while the few indulged in fighting. The epic poems, the inscriptions on monuments, the treaties of peace—nearly all historical documents bear the same character; they deal with breaches of peace, not with peace itself. So that the best-intentioned historian unconsciously draws a distorted picture of the times he endeavours to depict.

. . .

In Russia . . . the *artel* makes the very substance of Russian peasant life. The history of "the making of Russia," and of the colonization of Siberia, is a history of the hunting and trading *artels* or guilds, followed by village communities, and at the present time we find the *artel* everywhere: among each group of ten to fifty peasants who come from the same village to work at a factory, in all the building trades, among fishermen and hunters, among convicts on their way to and in Siberia, among railway porters, Exchange merchants, Customs House labourers, everywhere in the village industries, which give occupation to 7,000,000 men—from top to bottom of the working world, permanent and temporary, for production and consumption under all possible aspects. Until now, many of the

fishing-grounds on the tributaries of the Caspian Sea are held by immense *artels,* the Ural river belonging to the whole of the Ural Cossacks, who allot and re-allot the fishing-grounds—perhaps the richest in the world—among the villages, without any interference of the authorities. Fishing is always made by *artels* in the Ural, the Volga, and all the lakes of Northern Russia. Besides these permanent organizations, there are the simply countless temporary *artels,* constituted for each special purpose. When ten or twenty peasants come from some locality to a big town, to work as weavers, carpenters, masons, boat-builders, and so on, they always constitute an *artel.* They hire rooms, hire a cook (very often the wife of one of them acts in this capacity), elect an elder, and take their meals in common, each one paying his share for food and lodging to the *artel.* A party of convicts on its way to Siberia always does the same, and its elected elder is the officially recognized intermediary between the convicts and military chief of the party. In the hard-labour prisons they have the same organization. The railway porters, the messengers at the Exchange, the workers at the Custom House, the town messengers in the capitals, who are collectively responsible for each member, enjoy such a reputation that any amount of money or bank-notes is trusted to the *artel*-member by the merchants. In the building trades, *artels* of from 10 to 200 members are formed; and the serious builders and railway contractors always prefer to deal with an *artel* than with separately hired workers. The last attempts of the Ministry of War to deal directly with productive *artels,* formed *ad hoc* in the domestic trades, and to give them orders for boots and all sorts of brass and iron goods, are described as most satisfactory; while the renting of a Crown iron work (*Votkinsk*) to an *artel* of workers, which took place seven or eight years ago, has been a decided success.

. . .

In the practice of mutual aid, which we can retrace to the earliest beginnings of evolution, we thus find the positive and undoubted origin of our ethical conceptions; and we can affirm that in the ethical progress of man, mutual support—not mutual struggle—has had the leading part. In its wide extension, even at the present time, we also see the best guarantee of a still loftier evolution of our race.

XVI:50. VLADIMIR SOLOV'EV ON NATIONS AND NATIONALISM, 1888-1889

One of Russia's outstanding philosophers of the last quarter of the nineteenth century was Vladimir Sergeevich Solov'ev (1853-1900). His views on many questions of religion, ethics, and morality were widely read if not always clearly understood. The excerpts selected here, concerning nations and nationalism, were published in one volume in 1901, immediately after his premature death, but they had appeared originally in various publications of the period 1888-89, as indicated.

Reference: V. S. Solov'ev, *Sobranie sochinenii Vladimira Sergeevicha Solov'eva*, 9 vols. (St. Petersburg: Obshchestvennaia Pol'za, 1901-07), 5:78-79, 206-07, 209, 248-49.

[From the article "Russia and Europe," originally published in 1888:]

Every nationality has the right to live and freely to develop its forces, without violating the same rights of other nationalities. This demand of *equal rights* for *all* nations brings into politics a certain higher moral idea, to which national egoism must be subordinated. In this higher idea all nations have a bond of solidarity with each other, and to the extent that this solidarity exists, humanity is not an empty word. But, on the other hand, this stimulation of national self-consciousness in every nation, particularly in the larger and stronger nations, is conducive to the development of national egoism or nationalism, which has nothing in common with justice and is expressed by a quite different formula: "Our nation is the best of all nations, and therefore it is destined in one way or another to subject all other nations to itself, or in any case to take the first and highest place among them." Such a formula is used to sanctify every kind of violence, oppression, endless wars—everything evil and dark in the history of the world.

[From the article "Slavophilism and Its Degeneration," originally published in 1889:]

Our chief infirmity here lies in the weak development of individuality, and, through this, in the weak development of social life too, since these two elements are correlative to each other: if the individual principle is suppressed, men constitute a herd rather than a society. Then there can be no thought of legality, of justice, of human dignity, of public morality—all this is replaced by arbitrariness and servility. And so the cult of strong authority *with nothing else behind it,* extending to the apotheosis of Ivan the Terrible, elevates the fundamental calamity of our life into a principle and finds in it our chief superiority over Western civilization, which is allegedly perishing from doctrinaire

ideas of legality and justice. Our latter-day patriots share this hatred for the juridical element in national life with the old Slavophiles, with the difference, to be sure, that as a higher principle the latter counterpose to law and justice, brotherly love, while the former counterpose the fist and the stick. . . .

Idolizing our nation as the preeminent bearer of universal truth; then idolizing it as an elemental force independent of universal truth; finally, idolizing those national peculiarities and historical anomalies that isolate the nation from civilized humanity, i.e. idolizing the nation with the blunt denial of the very idea of universal truth—these are the three gradual phases of our nationalism, successively represented by the Slavophiles, Katkov, and the latter-day obscurantists. The first were pure visionaries in their teaching; the second was a realist with a vision; the last, finally, are realists without any visions, but likewise without any shame.

. . .

The greatest representatives of Russian literature were entirely free from national exclusiveness; they were deeply inspired by what was good in others, and mercilessly condemned what was bad in ourselves—all those aspects of Russian life that are particularly dear to our obscurantists.

[From the article "On Sins and Ailments," originally published in 1889:]

I consider it worthwhile to remind [the reader], in several brief theses, of my thoughts on nationality generally and in Russia specifically.

1. Nationality is a positive force, and every nation has the right to an existence independent (from other nations) and to the free development of its national capacities.

2. Nationality is the most important factor of innate human life, and the development of national self-consciousness is a great achievement in human history.

3. The national idea, understood as it relates to political justice, in whose name weak and oppressed nationalities are defended and liberated, has a lofty moral significance and deserves full respect and sympathy.

4. Nationalism or national egoism, i.e. the aspiration of an individual nation to assert itself at the expense of other nationalities, to dominate them, is a complete perversion of the national idea; it changes nationality from a healthy, positive force into a morbid, negative *effort,* which is dangerous to the higher interests of mankind and leads the nation itself toward decline and ruin.

5. The Russian nation possesses great elemental forces and rich potentialities for spiritual development.

6. The national self-existence of Russia—

as manifested, among other things, in our belles lettres—is beyond doubt.

7. The true spirit of Russian nationality, as defined by the highest moral principles, has been expressed in the circumstances attending the origin of the Russian state (the calling of the Varangians and also the Christianization of Russia), then in the reforms of Peter the Great, and finally, in the receptive, responsive, and universal character of Russian poetry.

8. At the present time, because of the artificial stimulation of grossly egoistic instincts and aspirations in Russian society, and also in consequence of certain particular historical conditions, the spiritual development of Russia is retarded and deeply perverted; national life is in a depressed and sickly state and requires radical healing.

XVI:51. *VLADIMIR SOLOV'EV'S* THE JUSTIFICATION OF THE GOOD, *1897*

The Justification of the Good: The Moral Philosophy of Vladimir Solov'ev was published in 1897. These selections are from two chapters of that influential book.

Reference: V. S. Solov'ev, *Opravdanie dobra: Nravstvennaia filosofiia Vladimira Solov'eva,* 2d ed. (Moscow, 1899), pp. 344, 350, 351, 358, 360, 369, 371, 372-73; translation based on V. Solovyof, *The Justification of the Good,* trans. Nathalie A. Duddington (London: Constable, 1918), pp. 273, 278-79, 284, 286, 295, 296-97, slightly revised.

[From chapter 13, "The Moral Norm of Social Life":]

Christianity, being the embodiment of an absolute moral ideal, is as universal as the moral principle itself, and originally it had this character. But the historical institutions that in the course of history came to be connected with it did not remain universal and therefore lost their pure and all-embracing moral character. . . . Universality expresses itself, not only by the absence of external, national, denominational, and other limitations, but still more by freedom from inner limitations. To be truly universal, religion must not separate itself from intellectual enlightenment, from science, from social and political progress. A religion that fears all these things obviously has no faith in its own power and is inwardly permeated with unbelief. While claiming to be the sole moral norm of society, it fails to fulfill the most elementary moral condition—sincerity.

[From chapter 14, "The National Question from the Moral Point of View":]

Patriotism may be *irrational,* do harm instead of the intended good, and lead nations to disaster; patriotism may be *shallow* and express no more than unfounded pretensions; and finally, patriotism may simply be *false* and serve merely as a cloak for low and selfish motives.

· · ·

Everyone would grant that it is impermissible to use criminal means to enrich oneself or a friend, or one's own family or his, or even one's town or province. But this moral truth, which is as clear as day, suddenly becomes dim and altogether obscure as soon as it becomes a matter of *one's own nation.* Everything becomes permissible in the service of its supposed interests, the end justifies the means, black becomes white, falsehood is preferred to truth, and violence is extolled as a virtue. Nationality here becomes the final and unquestioned end, the highest good and the standard of good for human activity. Such undue glorification is, however, purely illusory and is in practice degrading to the nation.

· · ·

Pan-humanism (or that church which the apostles preached) is not an abstract idea but is a *harmonious union of all the positive characteristics* of a new or regenerated creation. It therefore includes *national as well as personal* characteristics. The body of Christ is a *perfect* organism and cannot consist of simple cells alone; it must contain larger and more complex organs, which in this connection are naturally represented by the different nations.

· · ·

Before they could realize in themselves the ideal of pan-humanism, nations first had to be formed as distinct independent bodies.

· · ·

Peter the Great and Pushkin—these two names are sufficient to prove that the dignity of our national spirit finds its realization only in open communion with the rest of humanity, and not apart from it.

· · ·

National hostility and opposition no doubt exist, just as cannibalism once existed everywhere; they exist as a zoological fact, condemned by the best human consciousness of the peoples themselves. Elevated into an abstract principle this zoological fact hangs heavy over the life of nations, obscuring its significance and destroying its inspiration— for *the significance and the inspiration of the particular are to be found only in its connection and harmony with the universal.*

· · ·

If we love a man we must love his nationality, which he loves and from which he does not separate himself. The highest moral ideal demands that we should love all men as we love ourselves. But since men do not exist outside of their nationality (just as nationalities do not exist apart from individual men), and since this connection has already become moral and inward as well as physical, the direct logical deduction is that *we must love all nationalities as we love our own.*

XVI:52. LEO TOLSTOI'S VIEWS ON RELIGION, SOCIETY, AND THE STATE, CA. 1882-1905

While most of the millions who worshiped the novels of Leo Tolstoi either ridiculed or ignored the philosophical outpourings of his later years, he retained a not inconsiderable following, and his ideas—of which these are some samples—are of more than purely biographical importance.

Reference: Essay of 1882: Lev N. Tolstoi, *Polnoe sobranie sochinenii,* 90 vols. (Moscow: Gosudarstvennoe Izd. Khudozhestvennoi Literatury, 1957), 23:479; translation based on *The Works of Leo Tolstoy: Tolstoy Centenary Edition,* 21 vols. (London: Oxford University Press, 1928-37), vol. 12, *On Life and Essays on Religion,* pp. 338-39, somewhat revised. Essay of 1893: *Polnoe sob. soch.,* 28:167-68, 192, 211-12, 218-19, 258, 292; translation based on *Tolstoy Cent. Ed.,* vol. 20, *The Kingdom of God and Peace Essays,* pp. 252, 291, 320-21, 331-32, 392, 442, slightly revised. Essay of 1894: *Polnoe sob. soch.,* 39:61, 63, 65, 74; translation based on *Tolstoy Cent. Ed.,* 20:511, 514, 517, 530, slightly revised. Essay of 1900: *Sochineniia grafa L. N. Tolstogo,* 12th ed., 20 vols. (Moscow: T. and I. N. Kushnerev, 1911), pp. 169, 177, 179, 181, 186, 187, 188; translation based on *Tolstoy Cent. Ed.,* 20:547, 557-58, 560-61, 562-64, 569, 570, 571, considerably revised. Essay of 1905: *Polnoe sob. soch.,* 36:214; translation based on *Tolstoy Cent. Ed.,* vol. 21, *Recollections and Essays,* p. 283, slightly revised.

[From the essay "Church and State," written ca. 1882, published 1904:]

The sanctification of political power by Christianity is blasphemy; it is the negation of Christianity. After fifteen hundred years of this blasphemous alliance of pseudo-Christianity with the state, a strong effort is needed to free oneself from all the complex sophistries by which (to please the authorities) the sanctity and righteousness of state power, and the possibility of its being Christian, have always and everywhere been defended. In reality the words "Christian state" are like the words "hot ice." Either there is no state, or there is no Christianity.

In order to understand this clearly we must forget all those fantastic notions with which we have been carefully brought up and must ask plainly: What is the purpose of such historical and juridical science as has been taught us? Such science has no sound basis; its purpose is merely to supply a justification for the use of violence.

[From the essay "The Kingdom of God Is Within You," 1893:]

A Christian is bound only by the inner and divine law and can neither obey the requirements of external laws when they are incompatible with the divine law of love of which he is conscious (as is the case with exactions of the state) nor acknowledge an obligation to submit to any individual or institution or to the duty of what is called allegiance. For a Christian the oath of allegiance to any government whatever—the act that is considered the very basis of political life—is the direct negation of Christianity. For the man who promises in advance unconditional obedience to all the laws that have been and will be enacted by certain men, by that very promise, completely renounces Christianity, which consists of exclusive and unconditional obedience to the divine law of love of which man is conscious within himself.

. . .

All the revolutions in history are merely the seizure of power by evil men and their domination over the good.

. . .

The rich men and those who now stand at the head of governments no longer constitute the flower of society as in olden times but, on the contrary, are below the average.

In Russia and Turkey, as in France and America, in spite of the constant change of government officials, the majority of these are self-seeking and venal men of such a low moral standard that they do not even satisfy the low demand of simple integrity expected of them. . . .

The majority of rich people today no longer constitute the most refined and educated portion of society as before, but are either coarse money grubbers concerned only with enriching themselves (frequently by shady methods) or else the degenerate heirs of such money grubbers, who, far from playing any prominent part in society, are for the most part held in general contempt.

. . .

The condition of Christian mankind, with its fortresses, cannon, dynamite, rifles, torpedoes, prisons, gallows, churches, factories, customhouses, and palaces, is truly terrible. But neither the fortresses nor the cannon nor the rifles will attack anyone of themselves, the prisons will not of themselves lock anyone up, the gallows will not of themselves hang anyone, the churches will not

delude anyone nor will the customhouses detain anyone, and the palaces and factories do not build themselves or maintain themselves. All this is done by men. And if they once understand that there is no need for all these things, these things will disappear.

And men are already beginning to understand.

. . .

The ruling classes, having no longer any reasonable justification for the advantageous position they hold, are obliged, in order to maintain this position, to repress their higher rational capacities and love for their fellow men and to hypnotize themselves into the belief that their exceptional position is necessary. And the lower classes, crushed by toil and deliberately stupefied, live in a continual state of hypnosis, intentionally and ceaselessly induced by men of the upper classes.

Only in this way can one explain the amazing contradictions that fill our life.

. . .

There is one and only one thing in life in which it is granted man to be free and over which he has full control—all else being beyond his power. That one thing is to perceive the truth and to profess it.

[From the essay "Christianity and Patriotism," 1894:]

Patriotism may have been a virtue in the ancient world when it demanded of a man devotion to the highest ideal then attainable—that of his fatherland. But how can it be a virtue in our time, when it demands what is contrary to the ideals of both our religion and our morality, and recognizes not the equality and brotherhood of men but the predominance of one state and one people over all others?

. . .

Patriotism was necessary in forming and consolidating strong states composed of heterogeneous populations and needing defense against barbarians. But when Christian enlightenment had transformed those states from within, giving to them all the same basic principles, patriotism became the sole obstacle to that union among nations for which Christian consciousness had prepared them.

Patriotism in our day is a cruel tradition surviving an outlived past. It is maintained only by inertia and because governments and ruling classes, feeling that their power and even their existence is tied to it, persistently arouse and maintain it among the people by cunning and by violence.

· · ·

Patriotism in its simplest, clearest, and most indubitable sense is nothing but an instrument for the attainment of the ambitious and mercenary aims of the government; it means a renunciation of human dignity, common sense, and conscience by the governed, and their slavish submission to those who hold power. That is what is really preached wherever patriotism is championed.

Patriotism is slavery.

· · ·

No feats of heroism are needed to bring about the greatest and most important changes in the life of mankind; neither the arming of millions of men, nor the construction of new railways and machines, nor the organization of exhibitions or trade unions, nor revolutions, nor barricades, nor dynamite outrages, nor the perfection of aerial navigation, and so forth. All that is needed is a change in public opinion.

[From the essay "Patriotism and Government," 1900:]

Patriotism as an emotion is bad and harmful, and as a doctrine it is stupid. For it is clear that if each nation and each state considers itself the best of nations and states, they must all live under a gross and harmful delusion.

· · ·

After the Hague Conference it became obvious that as long as governments with armies continue to exist, the termination of armaments and of wars is impossible. For an agreement to become possible it is necessary that the parties to it should trust each other. And in order that the powers should trust each other they must lay down their arms, as is done by those who bear a flag of truce when they meet for a conference.

So long as governments continue to distrust one another, and instead of disbanding or reducing their armies continually increase them to keep pace with their neighbors, and use spies to watch every troop movement, knowing that each of the powers will attack its neighbor as soon as the opportunity presents itself, no agreement is possible, and every conference is either foolishness, or a

game, or a fraud, or an impertinence, or all of these together.

· · ·

A government is therefore the most terrible and dangerous institution in the world, especially when it is entrusted with military power.

A government in the broadest sense, including both the capitalists and the press, is nothing but an organization that places the majority of men in the power of a minority which dominates it.

· · ·

To deliver men from the terrible and ever increasing evils of armaments and wars, we need neither congresses nor conferences nor treaties nor courts of arbitration, but the destruction of those instruments of violence that are called governments and from which humanity's greatest evils flow.

To destroy them it is only necessary for people to understand that the feeling of patriotism which alone supports that instrument of violence is a crass, harmful, shameful, and base emotion, and above all immoral. . . .

It is only necessary for people to understand this, and then the terrible shackles we call government will fall apart of themselves without a struggle, and with this the terrible and useless evils they inflict upon mankind will cease.

· · ·

"But," it is usually asked, "what will happen if there is no government?"

Nothing will happen. All that will happen is that something long useless and therefore superfluous and bad will be abolished.

· · ·

The abolition of the organization of government, formed to do violence to men, in no way entails the abolition of what is reasonable and good, and therefore not based on violence, in laws, or in courts of justice, or in property, or in police regulations, or in financial arrangements, or in popular education. On the contrary, the absence of the brutal power of government, which is needed only to maintain itself, will facilitate a more just and reasonable social organization which does not need violence. Courts of justice and public affairs and popular education will all continue to exist to the extent that they are needed by the people, but in a form that will not contain the evils associated with the present form of government. Only that will be destroyed which was bad and hindered the free expression of the people's will.

· · ·

So that even if the absence of government really meant anarchy in the negative disorderly sense of that word (which is far from being the case), even then no anarchical disorder could be worse than the condition to which governments have already brought their peoples, and to which they are now bringing them.

And therefore emancipation from patriotism, and the destruction of the despotism of government that rests upon it, cannot but be beneficial to mankind.

[From the essay "A Great Iniquity," 1905:]

We once had cannibalism, we once had human sacrifices, we once had religious prostitution and the killing of sickly children and girls, we once had blood vengeance and the slaughter of entire populations, judicial tortures, quarterings, burnings at the stake, the lash, and—what has disappeared only within our own memory—the gauntlet and slavery. But if we have outlived those dreadful customs and institutions, this does not prove that there do not exist among us institutions and customs that have become as abhorrent to enlightened reason and conscience as those which in their day were abolished and which exist for us now only as a dreadful memory. The path of mankind toward perfection is endless, and at every moment of history there are superstitions, deceptions, and pernicious and evil institutions that men have already outlived and that belong to the past, others that present themselves to us as in the mists of a distant future, and some that we have with us now, whose suppression constitutes the problem of our own day. Such in our time are capital punishment and punishment in general, such also are prostitution, the eating of meat, militarism and war, and—most immediate and urgent of all—private property in land.

XVI:53. POBEDONOSTSEV'S REFLECTIONS, 1896

Konstantin P. Pobedonostsev (see Item XVI:1, above)—close adviser to Alexander III and, as director of the Holy Synod from 1880 to 1905, a major figure also in the first decade of Nicholas's reign—published in 1896 a comprehensive exposition of his views in a volume called *Moskovskii sbornik* (Moscow collection). It has become widely known in its unfortunately rather loose English translation of 1898, aptly entitled *Reflexions of a Russian Statesman*.

Reference: K. P. Pobedonostsev, *Moskovskii sbornik* (Moscow, 1896), pp. 1, 9, 10, 18 [Church and State], 26-28 [The New Democracy], 33-36, 38-43 [The Great Falsehood of Our Time], 57, 60, 62, 65 [The Press], 183 [The Spiritual Life], 213 [The Church], 249-50, 258 [Power and Authority]. The translation is based in part on K. P. Pobyedonostseff, *Reflexions of a Russian Statesman,* trans. Robert C. Long, preface by Olga Novikoff (London, 1898), pp. 1, 9-11, 19, 27-28, 34-45, 62, 65, 67, 70, 184, 211, 255-56, 266, but much revised and in many cases completely retranslated.

[In the chapter called "Church and State":]

No matter how immense the power of the state may be, it maintains itself solely upon an identity of spiritual consciousness between the people and the government, upon the religious faith of the people; authority is undermined the moment that this consciousness, founded on religion, begins to lose its unity.

· · ·

There are those who advocate the separation of church and state. . . .

. . . Wise and learned men define it thus: the state should not concern itself with the church, nor the church with the state. Thus mankind must move in two great spheres, so that in one sphere will dwell mankind's body, and in the other its spirit; and there will be as great a distance between these spheres as between heaven and earth. But how is this possible? The body cannot be separated from the spirit; both spirit and body live a single life.

· · ·

The moral principle is indivisible. It cannot be separated so as to provide one moral doctrine for the individual and another for society, one secular, the other spiritual. There is a single moral principle that embraces all relations—personal, domestic, and political; and no church that retains the consciousness of its own worthiness will ever renounce its legitimate

influence over matters relating to the family
or to civil society.

. . .

The irreligious state is no more than an
unrealizable utopia, for irreligion is the direct
negation of the state. Religion and, above all,
Christianity is the spiritual foundation of
every right in political and civil life, and of
all true culture.

["The New Democracy":]

Under a democratic form of government,
those people, with their adherents, come to
rule who are skilled at gathering votes; mechanics who adroitly operate the hidden
springs that move the puppets in the arena
of democratic elections. . . .

In our time the game of vote gathering
under the banner of democracy constitutes
a common phenomenon in almost all European states, and it would seem to have revealed itself to everyone as a lie; yet no one
dares openly to rise up against this lie. . . .
Votes, insignificant units in themselves, acquire value in the hands of dexterous agents.
Their value is realized by various means—
mainly, by the most varied forms of bribery,
ranging from trifling gifts of money and
articles to the distribution of profitable posts
in the excise offices, the financial departments,
and the administration.

["The Great Falsehood of Our Time":]

Parliament is *an institution serving to
satisfy the personal ambition, vanity, and self-
interest of its members. . . .*

. . . In the parliamentary fiction, the representative, as such, surrenders his personality
and must serve as the embodiment of the will
and opinions of his constituents; in reality,
the constituents in the very act of election
surrender all their rights in favor of their
elected representative. . . . To him his constituents are a herd, an aggregation of votes,
and he, as the master of these herds, resembles
those rich nomads whose herds constitute
their capital, the foundation of their power
and eminence in society. Thus is developed
to perfection the art of playing on the instincts and passions of the masses, in order to
attain the personal ends of ambition and
power. Then these masses lose all importance
for their elected representative, until it becomes necessary to act upon them again;

then flattering and lying phrases are lavished
as before, to please some and to frighten
others: that long endless chain of uniform
maneuvers that constitutes the mechanics of
parliamentarism. Yet this electoral farce continues to deceive humanity, and to be regarded
as the institution that crowns the edifice of
state. Poor humanity! In truth may it be said:
Mundus vult decipi, decipiatur [The world
wishes to be deceived; let it be deceived].

. . . By his position, and by the role he has
chosen, [the democratic politician] is *forced*
to be a hypocrite and liar in front of people
whom he detests; he must associate, fraternize,
and be obliging with them in order to win
their goodwill; he must lavish promises, knowing that he cannot fulfill them; he must pander
to the basest tendencies and prejudices of the
masses to obtain a majority for himself. What
honorable person would accept such a role?

. . .

Almost no one knows the man [nominated
by the party], or is aware of his character,
ability, and convictions; they vote for him
because they have heard his name so often.

. . .

In theory, the elected candidate must be
the favorite of the majority; but in reality he
is the favorite of a minority, which sometimes
is very small but represents an organized force;
while the majority, like sand, has no cohesive-
ness, and is therefore powerless before a clique
or a party. . . .

. . . The leader of a party requires above
all a resolute will. This is an organic attribute,
like physical strength, and therefore does not
necessarily presuppose moral qualities. A
man whose mental abilities are extremely
limited, in whom egoism and even hatred are
infinitely developed, whose motives are base
and dishonest, but who possesses a strong
will, may become the leader of his party, and
then he becomes the guiding and dominant
figure in a clique or party which may include
men far surpassing him in moral and intellectual qualities. . . . To this is joined still another decisive force—eloquence. This also is
a natural faculty, presupposing neither moral
character nor lofty spiritual development. A
man may be a deep thinker, a poet, a skillful
military commander, a subtle jurist, or an
experienced legislator, and at the same time
be unable to speak effectively; while, on the
contrary, a man with the most ordinary

intellectual abilities and knowledge may possess a special gift of eloquence. . . . Experience unquestionably shows that in great assemblies the decisive voice is carried, not by reasonable, but by glib and glittering words; that the masses react most readily, not to clear and logical arguments which penetrate deeply into the heart of the matter, but to resounding words and phrases, artfully selected, constantly reiterated, and calculated on the instinct of banality always dormant in the people. The masses are easily carried away by outbursts of empty declamation, and under the influences of an impulse often make sudden decisions, which they come to regret upon calm consideration of the matter.

. . .

All important actions in a parliamentary system are performed by the leaders of the party: they make the decisions, lead the battle, and celebrate the victory. The public sessions are no more than a spectacle for the public.

. . .

It is sad and painful to think that even in the Russian land there were and are men who aspire to the establishment of this falsehood among us; that our professors preach to their young audience about representative government as the ideal of political science; that our newspapers and journals stress this in their articles and stories, under the name of justice and order, without troubling to examine more closely, without prejudice, the workings of the parliamentary machine.

. . .

Democracy is the most complex and the most intricate form of government known to human history. . . . The duty of the state is to act and to ordain; its actions are manifestations of a single will; without this government is inconceivable. But how can a multitude of men, or a popular assembly, act with a single will?

["The Press":]
From the time of the fall of man, falsehood has established itself in the world, in human speech, in the practical business of life, in all relationships and institutions. But it would seem that never did the Father of Lies invent such a web of falsehood of every kind as in these troubled times when from all sides we hear so many *falsehoods* about *truth*.

. . .

. . . We are bidden to believe that the voice of newspapers and journals, or of the so-called *press*, is the expression of public opinion. Alas! This is a great falsehood, and the press is one of the most lying institutions of our time.

. . .

Any vagabond babbler or unrecognized genius, anyone who is trying to make a fast ruble, by using his own money or obtaining it from others for profit and speculation, can found a newspaper, even a large newspaper, gather around him at the first call a throng of scribblers and columnists ready to make pronouncements on any subject, and reporters to keep him supplied with rumors and scandals--and his staff is ready; the next day he can assume a position of authority to judge each and every one, influence ministers and rulers, literature and art, finance and industry.

. . .

The journalist, whose power in practice extends over everything, requires no sanction. No one elects him or confirms him. His newspaper becomes a power in the state, and for this power alone no endorsement is required. Anyone who wishes, any man in the street may become the organ of this power, the representative of this power, and moreover be completely *irresponsible* as no other power in the world can be.

. . .

A newspaper, which addresses itself daily . . . to all men, as long as they can make out a page of print, offers to each a ready-made judgment upon everything; and thus, little by little, by force of habit, it breaks the reader of any desire or effort to have his own opinions.

["The Spiritual Life":]
Old institutions, old traditions, old customs, are no small matter. The people treasures them as the ark of the covenant of its forefathers.

["The Church":]
The spirit is the essential thing in all human institutions; this is what must be most zealously protected from distortion and adulteration.

From time immemorial our church has been and still continues to be a church for all the people, retaining the spirit of love, and with equality of communion for all. It is through faith that our people has maintained itself to this day amidst privation and calamity, and if anything can sustain, strengthen, and regenerate it in future history, it is faith, and the faith of the church alone.

["Power and Authority":]

The task of power is the task of ceaseless service and thus is, in essence, a labor of *self-sacrifice*. . . . The first condition of power is faith in itself, that is, in its calling. Happy is

power when this faith is combined with a recognition of duty and of moral responsibility. . . .

Power, as the bearer of truth, above all needs men of truth, men of clear intellects, of strong understanding, and of sincere speech.   · · ·

Great and sacred is the vocation of power. A power worthy of its mission inspires men and lends wings to their activity; it serves everyone as a mirror of truth, dignity, and energy.

XVI:54. A STUDENT'S ACCOUNT OF THE PROTEST AT SAINT PETERSBURG UNIVERSITY, FEBRUARY 1899

February 1899 marked the beginning of a new period of student disorders in Russian universities, after some years of relative tranquillity. The opening incident occurred at Saint Petersburg University. There, on February 8, at the annual ceremony (*akt*) commemorating the founding of the university, students who took offense at the rector's warning against drunkenness and rowdiness on that day interrupted the rector's speech by whistling and shouting, left the hall, and marched along the Neva quay. There a squadron of mounted police used whips to disperse them. In this excerpt one of the participating students tells of their response. It led within a few days to a student strike which closed most higher educational institutions until that fall.

Reference: Vladimir G. Chertkov, ed., *Studencheskoe dvizhenie 1899 goda* (Purleigh, Eng.: Svobodnoe slovo, 1900), p. 7.

News of the beatings spread with lightning speed. Indignation was absolutely universal; everyone was talking about a meeting the following day at the university. . . . By ten o'clock the next day great numbers of people had already begun to gather at the university. The meeting opened at eleven o'clock, but, since there was only room for a small portion [of the people] in the vestibule, a request that the assembly hall [*aktovyi zal*] be opened was addressed to the inspectorate. The frightened inspectorate fulfilled this request. And for the next three days this hall witnessed events unparalleled in the chronicles of the university. The meeting, with over 2,000 people in attendance, after a prolonged discussion concerning, however, only the form the protest should take, and acting with remarkable restraint, calmness, and solidarity,

voted unanimously (or almost unanimously) by show of hands that the university be closed until the government guaranteed that in the future the elementary rights of the individual would no longer be violated so shamelessly and insolently. All other means or forms of protest, i.e. petitions, joint withdrawals from the university, were rejected by an overwhelming majority. It was decided to press for the closing of the university with all one's might, using obstructionist tactics and agreements with professors, many of whom on the day of the notable battle [the dispersal of students by the police on February 8] in the Rumiantsevskii Public Gardens expressed their desire to join the movement actively in whatever form it took. It must be said that the meeting in the assembly hall was held with surprising tact, calmness, and solidarity.

XVI:55. DOCUMENTS ON THE STUDENT MOVEMENT IN 1901-1902

The combination of specific student grievances, repressive actions by the government, and growing discontent in other elements of Russian society led the Russian student movement to assume an increasingly revolutionary character in 1901-02. Various aspects of the movement are seen in these excerpts from student proclamations, a police report, and a student resolution.

Reference: *Krasnyi arkhiv*, vol. 75 (vol. 2 in 2d series; 1936), pp. 101-02 [Moscow proclamation], 102-03 [St. Petersburg proclamation]; vols. 89-90 (4-5 in 2d series; 1938), p. 265 [Khar'kov police report], p. 279 [Moscow bulletin].

[Excerpt from a proclamation of the executive committee of the union of *zemliachestva* (associations of students from the same city or province) and other organizations of the Moscow students, February 26, 1901:]

Not only the student body but all of Russian society is living through significant days. In all the years of the university's existence, society has never before dared to express so openly and actively its solidarity with the "rebellious" students and its sympathy with their situation. Yesterday's demonstration reached an unprecedented size. The entire Tverskoi Boulevard with its side streets, as well as Mokhovaia Street, were overflowing with demonstrators whose number must have reached the thousands. The overwhelming majority were workers and factory hands, who displayed their sympathy with the students.

We students should be especially appreciative of their presence and their sympathy toward us; after all, they have their own tasks, incomparably broader and more pressing. Nevertheless, they attended the demonstration at the risk of harming themselves. More than once the police attempted to disperse the demonstrators, knocking down women and children with their galloping horses. In the late afternoon they made use of whips and fists, and again mostly women and children were beaten. Yet the workers and factory hands were equal to the situation, loyally defending the men and women students [*studenty i kursistki*] and protecting the weak.

[Complete text of a proclamation of the students of Saint Petersburg on the occasion of the demonstration in front of Kazan' Cathedral in Saint Petersburg, on March 4, 1901:]

We, the students of Saint Petersburg, appear before Russian society in defense of the violated rights of the individual.

On February 8, 1899, we were subjected to brutal treatment: we were beaten with whips.

We came forward with a demand for personal inviolability and demanded that all actions of the police be subject to the jurisdiction of the general courts.

Young people rose up everywhere. Society sympathized. The government yielded. A high commission was appointed.

Former Minister of War Vannovskii has acknowledged the guilt of the police. [Yet] society received a reprimand, and the students were given "temporary rules" providing for conscription into the army for the slightest "group" disobedience to the authorities. And the police force goes unpunished.

At this moment over two hundred and fifty students of the universities of Kiev, Khar'kov, and Saint Petersburg are soldiers because they attended meetings in the university. A stroke of the pen, and the "sacred duty of defending the fatherland" becomes a punishment; certain citizens have been placed outside the "general statute on military service." The law has been trampled underfoot.

In response to this provocation demonstrations are taking place in Khar'kov. People are maimed, injured, killed, and arrested, but nothing can stop the protest. The workers rise, the public takes part; the students do not stand alone. In Moscow thousands crowd the streets; clashes with the police take place. The city is changed. For the first time the voice of the people is raised in defense of a violated law, in defense of humiliated and insulted human beings. The movement is spreading to other university cities. The government is attempting to suppress these protests against the illegal "temporary rules" by employing equally illegal temporary rules—the "statute on reinforced protection" which for the last twenty years has devastatingly [paralyzed] [brackets in Russian edition—eds.] the civil laws protecting, however slightly, the inviolability of the individual.

Nor can we, the students of Saint Petersburg, remain impassive spectators. We emphatically declare our protest against the arbitrariness of the police which bears equally as hard upon you as upon us, and we call you to join us in demanding:

1. The cancellation of the temporary rules of July 29, 1899.

2. The guarantee of personal inviolability, by according the right to seek redress from administrative action through trial by jury.

Long live that law which protects the rights of man!

[Excerpt from a report of the gendarme administration of the Khar'kov guberniia to the Department of Police, December 3, 1901:]

On the evening [of December 2] . . .

students began assembling in groups on Sumskaia Street, and at 6:30 P.M., quickly banding together, they formed a crowd of some 150 or 200 people; whistling and singing the "Dubinushka" [a revolutionary song] they proceeded down Sumskaia to Moskovskaia Street. At the corner of Moskovskaia Street a red flag was raised from the crowd; shouts were heard: "Down with the government!" "Down with autocracy!" "Long live freedom!" An order of the police to disperse was met, as during the demonstration of November 29, with abusive language directed against the police and the government. A crowd of about 3,000 people, composed of persons of all classes, including factory workers and artisans, accompanied the demonstrators. At the corner of Moskovskaia Street and Petrovskii Lane, the demonstrators were overtaken by Cossacks and dispersed with whips.

Half an hour later, the scattered student demonstrators reassembled near University Hill and were joined there by some artisans. When the crowd was about 200 strong, a red flag was raised; they started singing the "Dubinushka" and marched along Ekaterinoslavskaia Street where the Cossacks again overtook them and dispersed them with whips. After this, small groups of demonstrators formed here and there but were driven away by the police. While the demonstration was in progress, stones were thrown by the crowd at the police and the Cossacks.

[Complete text of bulletin no. 50 of the executive committee of the union of student organizations of Moscow University, February 9, 1902:]

On February 9, 1902, in the assembly hall of Moscow University, a meeting took place of students in institutions of higher learning, attended by 518 persons. The following resolution was adopted:

We, the students of institutions of higher learning in Moscow, gathered in a general assembly numbering 518 persons, after thorough deliberation, have unanimously resolved:

Inasmuch as we regard the abnormality of the existing academic situation as a manifestation of the general Russian lack of legal rights, we abandon forever the illusion of campaigning on an academic level and now raise the banner of general political demands. We are deeply convinced that the normal course of public life requires the reconstruction of the entire political and social system on the basis of the recognition of the civil rights of the individual. We are convinced that without this Russian life will never move ahead, that the best elements will be periodically torn away from the social body, and that the shameful stagnation will never be overcome. We demand: (1) inviolability of persons, (2) freedom of the press, (3) freedom of conscience, (4) freedom of assembly and association, (5) direct responsibility of members of the administration, (6) education accessible to all, (7) admission of women to the universities, (8) equal rights for all nationalities. We join with the workers in demanding (1) an eight-hour working day, and (2) the right to strike.

Inasmuch as we do not consider the existing government capable of reconstructing the social system on these principles, we address ourselves to all Russians of independent mind and political maturity, to call their attention to the timeliness of convoking a constituent assembly. This general political program compels us to carry our protest into the streets, where we are ready, together with the cadres of labor, to support our demands by force.

XVI:56. THE RESOLUTION OF THE ZEMSTVO CONGRESS OF NOVEMBER 6-9, 1904

Cooperation among various zemstvo groups was stimulated from 1894 on by the head of the Moscow zemstvo, Dmitrii N. Shipov, and from 1903 on by the Union of Liberation (Soiuz Osvobozhdeniia). This led in 1904 to an unofficial conference of zemstvo delegates. The conference, held November 6-9 in Saint Petersburg under Shipov's chairmanship, adopted the resolution excerpted here. The resolution was endorsed during succeeding weeks by many groups of professional men as well as by town councils and representatives of the nobility.

Reference: *Zemskii s''ezd 6-go i sl. noiabria 1904 g.* (Paris: Izd. Red. "Osvobozhdenie," 1905), pp. 16-17. Translation taken almost entirely from Fischer, *Russian Liberalism*, pp. 182-88.

1. The abnormality of the state's existing administrative system has manifested itself especially since the beginning of the 1880s.

This abnormality consists in the complete separation of the government from the public and the absence of that mutual confidence that is essential for national life.

2. The relationship of the government to the public has been based on the fear of developing political independence and the constant effort to prevent the people from participating in the administration of the state. Proceeding from these premises, the government has sought to institute administrative centralization in all branches of local government, and to control all aspects of public life. Relations with the public have been maintained by the government exclusively in terms of bringing the activities of public institutions into line with the views of the government.

3. The bureaucratic system, separating the supreme authority from the population, creates the basis for numerous occasions of arbitrary and personal abuse. Under such a system, the public lacks the ever essential assurance of strict protection of each individual's lawful rights, and its confidence in the government is undermined.

4. The regular flow and development of state and public life is possible only under the condition of an active and close contact, of unification of the state authority with society.

5. To prevent possible occurrences of administrative license, it is essential to establish and carry out consistently the principles of the inviolability of the individual and of private domicile. Without a ruling by an independent court authority no one should be subjected to search or limited in his rights. For the purpose indicated above it is essential, furthermore, that procedures be established for civil and criminal prosecution of officials violating the law to ensure the practical realization of the principles of lawfulness in administration.

6. For the full development of the spiritual forces of the people, for a universal clarification of popular needs and the unobstructed expression of public opinion, it is essential to provide freedom of conscience and religion, freedom of speech and press, and also freedom of assembly and association.

7. The individual, civil, and political rights of all citizens of the Russian Empire must be equal.

8. The independence of the public is the main condition for a proper and successful development of the country's political and economic life. Since a considerable majority of Russia's population belongs to the peasant estate, it is therefore necessary to begin by putting the latter in a position in which it can develop initiative and energy. This can be achieved only through a fundamental change of the present wrong and degraded condition of peasants. For this purpose it is essential: (a) to make the peasants equal in individual rights with persons of other estates; (b) to free the village population from administrative tutelage in all aspects of its personal and public life; and (c) to protect it through a proper system of courts.

9. Zemstvo and municipal institutions, in which local public life is mainly concentrated, must be put in a position where they can successfully fulfill the responsibilities appropriate for properly and broadly organized organs of self-government. For this the following is essential:

a. That zemstvo representation not be based on class lines, [but] that to the extent possible all available elements of the local population be drawn into participation in zemstvo and municipal self-government.

b. That zemstvo institutions be brought closer to the population through the creation of small zemstvo units along lines guaranteeing their actual independence.

c. That the sphere of jurisdiction of zemstvo and municipal institutions be extended to all areas of local welfare and needs.

d. That the aforesaid institutions be granted the required stability and independence. Only if these exist is the correct development of their activities, as well as the creation of the proper relations between governmental and public institutions, possible.

e. [That] local self-government should be extended to all parts of Russia. . . .

10. But in order to create and preserve an always active and close contact and unity of the state with society, on the basis of the above principles guaranteeing the proper development of state and public life, the following is absolutely essential:

Opinion of the Majority

The regular participation of popular representatives, in a distinct elected institution, in
carrying out legislative functions, in establishing a state budget of income and expenditures, and in supervising the legality of the
administration's actions.

11. In view of the importance and difficulty of external and internal conditions being experienced by Russia, the private conference expresses the hope that the supreme
authority will call together freely elected

Opinion of the Minority

The regular participation in legislation of
popular representatives in a distinct elected
institution.

representatives of the people, in order to lead
our fatherland with their collaboration on a
new path of state development, of establishing principles of law and interaction between
state and people.

XVI:57. AN OFFICIAL REPORT ON BLOODY SUNDAY, JANUARY 9, 1905

On January 18, 1905, nine days after Bloody Sunday, the journal *Pravo* (Justice) carried this official government report, dated January 10-11, of the events of the preceding days. Concerning
the last sentence in this excerpt, there is some evidence that the number of dead was 126 and
that the number of wounded was much higher than the figure in the official report.

Reference: *Pravo*, no. 2 (Jan. 18, 1905), cols. 98-100. A convenient collection of documents
on the Revolution of 1905 is L. M. Ivanov et al., eds., *Revoliutsiia 1905-1907 gg. v Rossii. Dokumenty i materialy,* 2 vols. (Moscow: AN SSSR, 1955).

At the beginning of 1904, upon the petition
of several workers in the factories and mills
of Saint Petersburg, a charter was confirmed,
in due legal form, for the Saint Petersburg
Society of Factory and Mill Workers, which
had the aim of satisfying their spiritual and
intellectual needs and diverting the workers
from the influence of criminal propaganda.
As it spread to all the factory areas of Saint
Petersburg, this society, which chose as its
chairman the chaplain of the Saint Petersburg
Exile Prison [*peresyl'naia tiur'ma,* for the
temporary detention of persons sentenced to
exile], Georgii Gapon, began to engage in the
discussion of worker-employee relations existing in individual factories and plants. . . .
Incited by the priest Gapon and by members
of the aforesaid society, the workers of the
Putilov factory stopped work on January 2.
. . . Under the influence of these same persons
the workers of several other large factories
of Saint Petersburg joined this strike one by
one; then the strike began to spread rapidly,
embracing almost all the industrial enterprises
of the capital. Along with this, as the strike
spread the demands of the workers increased
correspondingly. Written statements of these
demands, prepared in most cases by the priest
Gapon, were distributed among the workers.
At first they dealt only with local issues con-

cerning individual factories and plants, but
then they went on to general issues: an eight-
hour working day, the participation of workers'
organizations in settling disputes between
workers and employers, and so forth. . . . In
view of the fact that the strike was not accompanied by any violation of order, no
repressive measures were taken by the authorities, and from the time of its outbreak
not a single arrest or search was made among
the workers. However, incitement by underground revolutionary groups was soon added
to the agitation conducted by the Society of
Factory and Mill Workers. On the morning of
January 8 the above-mentioned society, with
the priest Gapon at its head, itself passed over
to clearly revolutionary propaganda. On this
day the priest Gapon prepared and distributed
a petition from the workers addressed to the
sovereign, in which rude demands of a political
nature were expressed along with wishes for
changes in working conditions. Rumors were
spread among the workers and written statements were distributed to the effect that they
must assemble in Palace Square at two o'clock
on January 9 and present a petition to the
sovereign emperor, through the priest Gapon,
concerning the needs of the working class. In
these rumors and statements no mention was
made of demands of a political character, and

the majority of workers were led astray concerning the purpose of the summons to Palace Square.

The fanatical preaching of the priest Gapon, forgetful of the sanctity of his calling, and the criminal agitation of persons of evil intent excited the workers to such an extent that on January 9 they began heading in great throngs toward the center of the city. In some places

bloody clashes took place between them and the troops, in consequence of the stubborn refusal of the crowd to obey the command to disperse, and sometimes even in consequence of attacks upon the troops.

. . .

The number of victims on [January] 9 proved to be, by accurate count: 96 dead and 333 wounded.

XVI:58. THE DEMANDS OF THE RAILWAY WORKERS' UNION, OCTOBER 7, 1905

The principal demands made by the striking railway workers on October 7, 1905, are reported here as they were printed in the journal *Pravo* a few weeks later.
Reference: *Pravo*, no. 43 (Nov. 8, 1905), app., cols. 1-2, initialed "R. V."

The Moscow Junction Committee of the Railroad Workers' Union has raised the following general demands, as the goal of the general strike of railroad workers:

1. An increase in the wages of workers and employees to the level necessary to satisfy the material and spiritual needs of the worker and his family.

2. The establishment of working hours, for all railroad workers without exception, not to exceed eight hours a day or forty-eight hours per week. . . .

6. The opening, at the expense of the railroads, of an adequate number of educational institutions, libraries, and reading rooms for workers and employees and their families.

7. Freedom of assembly, meeting, unions, organizations, speech, the press, and strikes; and the inviolability of persons and domiciles.

8. The convocation of an all-Russian congress of delegates of the employees and workers of all railroads to draft a new statute on railroad employees and workers.

9. Since, as has been shown by recent experience, the above demands cannot be satisfied under the existing police and bureaucratic regime, it is essential to convene representatives of the people, invested with legislative powers and elected by the entire population of the country by universal, direct, secret, and equal ballot, without distinction of nationality, sex, or religion, to draft new fundamental laws for the country in the interests of the laboring classes.

10. The inviolability of all the participants in the strike, and the reinstatement of all who have been penalized for participation in strikes and unions.

11. Full amnesty for all those penalized for so-called political and religious offenses.

XVI:59. THE RESOLUTION OF THE MOSCOW STRIKE COMMITTEE, OCTOBER 18, 1905

At 2:00 P.M. on October 18, 1905, the day after the proclamation of the October Manifesto, the Moscow Strike Committee issued this declaration, which is reproduced here in its entirety on the basis of the text published in *Pravo* shortly thereafter.
Reference: *Pravo*, no. 43 (Nov. 8, 1905), col. 114.

The Moscow Strike Committee declares that the united proletariat of all Russia has won recognition of certain demands, albeit thus far in words only. Advising our brother proletarians to discontinue temporarily the general strike, the committee asks them to declare that the proletariat, and those who have joined it in the strike, are returning to work in order to organize themselves as perfectly as possible, to gather the necessary means, to organize the general armament of the proletariat, and to continue the further struggle

under the banner of socialism until the following demands are attained in the near future:

1. The actual realization of the inviolability of persons and domiciles, and freedom of speech, the press, assembly, unions, and strikes.

2. The convocation of a constituent assembly on the basis of universal, direct, and equal suffrage, regardless of sex or nationality.

3. Amnesty for all who have suffered for their political or religious beliefs, as well as for strikes and peasant movements.

4. The satisfaction, by legislative means, of

the fundamental, urgent, and economic needs of the workers and employees.

The Moscow Strike Committee also urges all workers and employees to empower their delegates, the strike committees, and the committees of the Social-Democratic and Socialist Revolutionary parties jointly to discuss and set the date for a new general political strike whenever that proves necessary.

XVI:60. DECLARATIONS IN IZVESTIIA, OCTOBER 17-20, 1905

On October 17, 1905, there began the publication of *Izvestiia Soveta Rabochikh Deputatov* (News of the Soviet of Workers' Deputies), the official organ of the new Saint Petersburg Soviet. The following excerpts are from proclamations and reports published in the first few issues of that paper.

Reference: Vladimir I. Nevskii, comp., *1905: Sovetskaia pechat' i literatura o sovetakh, 1905: Materialy i dokumenty*, vol. 3 (Moscow: Gosizdat, 1925), pp. 3, 8, 12, 21, 22, 23-24.

From the Soviet of Deputies.

Comrades! Elect deputies to the soviet in those plants and factories where elections have not yet taken place.

Comrades, organize meetings at factories and plants that are operating, and persuade your comrades to join the general strike at once.

Comrades, remove from the job those workers who refuse to stop work, despite all our efforts at persuasion and despite the decrees of the Soviet of Deputies. Those who are not with us are against us, and the Soviet of Deputies has decreed the use of extreme means—force—in dealing with them.

The Soviet of Deputies has unanimously resolved to issue the following appeal:

To All Men and Women Workers: Comrades!

The all-Russian strike has begun. The working class, which has firmly endorsed the demands for a constituent assembly and universal suffrage, and has not received any rights, has resorted to the ultimate mighty instrument of the world labor movement— the general strike. And the blind power of the autocracy has trembled before the conscious power of proletarian solidarity.

[From *Izvestiia Soveta Rabochikh Deputatov*, no. 2 (Saint Petersburg, October 18, 1905:]

The political strike of the workers for freedom and happiness continues. The revolutionary struggle of the proletariat against the tsarist government and for a democratic republic is following its course.

· · ·

Our path is one of implacable revolutionary struggle to the death.

The people do not want imperial edicts; they want arms. When the people of Saint Petersburg take guns into their hands, they will write their great edict with the point of a bayonet upon the blood-red walls of the Winter Palace. This edict will be the death warrant of the tsarist government and the proclamation of a free republican life for the people.

The revolutionary strike goes on. There is no retreat for the people. Ahead lies a bitter struggle. The struggle requires weapons.

· · ·

The workers' deputation will demand, in the name of the Saint Petersburg proletariat, that the [municipal] duma fulfill its duty: the duma must recognize that a people's militia is indispensable for saving our life and honor and for winning freedom. The duma must recognize that every citizen has a right to bear arms. The duma must come to the aid of the proletariat and assign the necessary sums from the people's own money for the creation of a people's militia.

[Another item in the same issue:]
News of the Day
A manifesto has been issued!

The whole night through, to the morning of October 18, demonstrators with red flags marched through the streets of Saint Petersburg. Speeches were made pointing out that the proclaimed "constitution" is a rump constitution, that it cannot for a moment satisfy the Social Democrats even as a preliminary step toward a democratic republic and the ultimate goal of the proletarian party— the triumph of socialism.

[From *Izvestiia Soveta Rabochikh Deputatov*, no. 3 (Saint Petersburg, October 20, 1905):]

The slogans of the struggle are the same: a constituent assembly, withdrawal of the troops, formation of a militia, amnesty, and an eight-hour working day.

Neither the villainous order "not to spare cartridges" nor the treacherous manifesto of October 17 can change the tactics of the proletariat.

What the strike does not win shall be achieved by an armed uprising.

[Another item in the same issue:]
The Tsar's Manifesto on Freedom and Our
Demands
· · ·

On the strength of the rights we have won, we should at once begin openly to assemble, speak, and write about our affairs. We should organize into unions, and these unions should openly join the Russian Social-Democratic Workers' Party.

This party alone is the true spokesman for the interests of the proletariat, not only in Russia, but throughout the world. It alone boldly and truthfully shows the proletariat the way to escape modern slavery, the way to socialism. United into a mighty organiza-tion under the banners of the Russian Social-Democratic Workers' Party, the Russian proletariat shall win that full political freedom which will enable it, by joining the great army of international social democracy, to achieve socialism, that is, the transfer of all land and all means of production into the hands of the workers.

[From the same issue:]
To Our Brothers—the Soldiers!
Soldiers! The hour approaches of the people's judgment upon all the bloodsuckers, headed by Tsar Nicholas the Bloody. It is at hand... And the tsar and all his henchmen feel this and tremble. They tremble for their right to drink the people's blood unpunished, as of old; they tremble for their riches, soaked through and through with the people's sweat and blood; they tremble for their criminal, vile, predatory life.
· · ·

Soldiers! In the name of the people fighting for their liberation, we call upon you: do not spare cartridges in exterminating the people's oppressors, with the last of the tsars at their head!

XVI:61. THE "FINANCIAL MANIFESTO" OF DECEMBER 2, 1905

Here are the key portions of the "financial manifesto" of December 2, 1905, published in an un-dated *Izvestiia* issue which evidently appeared December 5 in Saint Petersburg.

Reference: Nevskii, *1905: Materialy i dokumenty,* 3:87-88.

There is only one way out: to overthrow the government and remove its last supports. We must cut off its last source of existence: financial revenues. . . .

We therefore resolve: to refuse to make redemption payments or any other payments to the treasury; to demand that all business transactions and the payment of wages and salaries shall be made in gold or, if the amount is less than five rubles, in standard specie; and to withdraw all deposits from savings banks and the State Bank, demanding payment of the entire sum in gold. The autocracy has never enjoyed the confidence of the people and has never received any mandate from it.

At the present time, the government rules within the boundaries of its own state as if it were a conquered country. Therefore we resolve to permit no payment of debts on any of the loans contracted by the tsarist government while manifestly and openly waging war against the entire people.

The Soviet of Workers' Deputies
The Chief Committee of the All-
Russian Peasant Union
The Central Committee and the
Organizational Committee of the
Russian Social-Democratic
Workers' Party
The Central Committee of the
Socialist Revolutionary Party
The Central Committee of the
Polish Socialist Party

XVI:62. STRIKE APPEALS OF DECEMBER 7 AND 8, 1905

In Moscow on December 7 and in Saint Petersburg on December 8, 1905, the respective soviets issued the following calls to strike.

Reference: Nevskii, *1905: Sovetskaia pechat'*, 109, 89-90.

[From *Izvestiia Moskovskogo Soveta Rabo-chikh Deputatov*, no. 1, December 7, 1905:]

The Moscow Soviet of Workers' Deputies, the committee and group of the Russian Social Democratic Workers' Party, and the committee of the Socialist Revolutionary Party have resolved: to proclaim a general political strike in Moscow on Wednesday, December 7, at twelve o'clock noon, and to seek to transform it into an armed uprising.

To all workers, soldiers, and citizens! Comrade workers, soldiers, and citizens!

· · ·

The revolutionary proletariat can no longer tolerate the mockery and crimes of the tsarist government and thus declares decisive and merciless war against it!

Comrade workers! We, your elected deputies, the Moscow committee and group of the RSDWP, and the committee of the Socialist Revolutionary Party, proclaim a general political strike and call upon you to leave and stop work on Wednesday, December 7, at twelve o'clock noon, in all factories and plants, in all municipal and governmental establishments.

Long live the merciless struggle against the criminal tsarist government!

Comrade soldiers! We are your blood brothers, the children of the same mother, long-suffering Russia. You have already recognized and confirmed this by participating in the common struggle. Now, when the proletariat is declaring decisive war against the hated enemy of the people, the tsarist government, we call you also to bold and decisive action.

Refuse to obey your bloodthirsty commanders, drive them out and arrest them. Elect trusty leaders from your own midst and join the revolutionary people with arms in hand!

[From *Izvestiia Soveta Rabochikh Deputatov*, no. 9, Saint Petersburg, December 11, 1905:]

To the Entire People

· · ·

The government is arresting the representatives of the people, to whom the people entrusted the defense of its interests. It arrested the bureau of the Peasant Congress, arrested the bureau of the Union of Postal and Tele-graph Employees, seized the chairman of the Soviet of Workers' Deputies, Khrustalev [-Nosar'], and, finally, arrested on December 3 the entire assembly of the Soviet of Deputies of the Saint Petersburg workers—two hundred and fifty persons, elected by more than two hundred thousand workers. Brother workers, shall we not come to the defense of our elected representatives? . . .

Workers, peasants, and all who hold freedom dear! Will you permit your political rights to be taken from you? You must defend your fundamental political rights. You must defend your hard-won freedom. . . . *The Soviet of Deputies of the Saint Petersburg Workers has therefore resolved upon and hereby proclaims a general political strike throughout Saint Petersburg and its environs.*

On Thursday, December 8, at twelve o'clock noon, work must cease in all plants, factories, workshops, commercial enterprises, offices, banks, stores, warehouses, and all transportation facilities both in Saint Petersburg proper and connecting Saint Petersburg with the rest of Russia.

The struggle is launched. It will exact great sacrifices and may cost many lives. But whatever happens, we shall not put down our arms until the following is assured:

A constituent assembly, on the basis of universal, direct, equal, and secret suffrage.

· · ·

Transfer of land to the people.

Recognition of the eight-hour working day as a fundamental political right of the people, along with freedom of speech, conscience, and other fundamental political rights.

. . . Join with us—and we will stop production, we will stop trade, we will stop transportation throughout the country, and we will destroy the remnants of the autocracy by our common efforts. Better to die fighting than to live in slavery.

Soldiers and sailors! You are a part of the people, but you are led against the people. All your demands are ours also, but you are led against us. And you will drown your own freedom in the people's blood. Disobey orders, obey the voice of the people. Join us. Rise up together with us.

XVI:63. STATEMENTS OF KHRUSTALEV-NOSAR' AND TROTSKII WHEN ON TRIAL, OCTOBER 1 AND 3, 1906

In December of 1905, the approximately 300 members of the Saint Petersburg Soviet of Workers' Deputies were arrested for their antigovernment declarations. Of these only 29 (of whom 12 were acquitted) were actually brought to trial. The charge was conspiracy to overthrow the government. The most serious punishment meted out by this civil court was sentence to penal exile. Here are statements made during the trial, on October 1 and 3, 1906, by two of those who received that sentence. It may be noted that Trotskii had little trouble in escaping, and by the following spring had already reached a safe haven abroad.

Reference: *Pravo*, no. 39 (Oct. 1, 1906), col. 3019; no. 42 (Oct. 22, 1906), cols. 3256-57.

[From the record of the pleas of the defendants:]

DEFENDANT [KHRUSTALEV-]NOSAR': I plead not guilty to the charges presented against me, since the entire activity of the Soviet of Workers' Deputies was not an expression of individual malice but a historical and political necessity. In the subsequent stages of the trial I shall deal with this aspect of the question in detail. For the present, I wish to state that I was elected to the Soviet of Printing Trades Workers; I was chairman of the Soviet [of Workers' Deputies]; I was chairman of its Executive Committee; and I was chairman of the Unemployment Commission. In my political views, which determined my activity in the soviet, I belong to the Russian Social-Democratic Workers' Party.

DEFENDANT BRONSHTEIN-TROTSKII: I was chosen a delegate to the Soviet of Workers' Deputies by the Russian Social-Democratic Workers' Party, to which I belonged and belong today. After the arrest of Comrade Khrustalev, I was elected by the soviet to membership in the Presidium. In my activities, I have guided myself by the principles of social democracy, which expresses the interests of the proletariat. Do I plead guilty? No!

[From Trotskii's speech at the session of October 3, 1906:]

The prosecution is constantly trying to prove that the Soviet of Workers' Deputies armed the laboring masses specifically against the state authority. I am ready to assume this guilt. I am prepared to reply to this in the affirmative.

We Social Democrats have always sought to prove that in this country there is no state authority as a definite form of government; there is only an automaton for mass murder.

XVI:64. WITTE ON THE REVOLUTION OF 1905

These excerpts from the aforementioned memoirs of Witte reveal something of his thoughts concerning the momentous revolutionary upheaval of 1905-06, when he was at the apogee of his career.

Reference: Vitte, *Vospominaniia*, 1:275, 329, 441, 476, 493-94.

Both my family traditions and the inclinations of my own heart and soul prompt me to favor absolute monarchy. But after all that we have experienced, after all that I have seen and still see on this high level, my mind leads me to conclude that there is no other solution than reasonable limitation, than the erection of walls along the broad highway to limit the movements of the autocracy. This, evidently, is the inevitable historical law under the present condition of the creatures who inhabit our planet.

         . . .

In my opinion, the greatest danger confronting Russia is the degeneration of the official Orthodox church and the extinction of the living religious spirit of the people. If respectable Slavophilism has performed any real service to the country, it is by emphasizing this truth as far back as fifty years ago.

The present revolution has demonstrated it with even more clarity. No state can exist without higher spiritual ideals. These ideals can only sway the masses if they are simple, lofty, and accessible to everyone, in a word, if they bear the imprint of the Divine. Without a living church, religion becomes philosophy and loses its power to enter into the life of men and to regulate it. Without religion the masses turn into herds of beasts, but beasts of a particularly evil type, for these beasts possess a greater intelligence than animals.

Our church has unfortunately long since become a dead, bureaucratic institution; our priests serve not the high God but earthly gods; Orthodoxy has become orthodox paganism. Gradually we are becoming less Christian than the members of any other Christian church. We have less faith than any other nation. Japan has defeated us because she believes in her god incomparably more than we do in ours.

. . .

The present life of all peoples is based wholly on individualism. All their fundamental premises and psychology are based on individualism. And the state itself was formed in accordance with it. The "I" organizes and moves everything. . . .

One of the causes, perhaps the principal one, of our revolution is the lag in the development of the principle of individuality and consequently of the sense of property and civic needs, including civil liberty.

. . .

I regard and have always regarded Russia as the most democratic among all the states of western Europe, but democratic in a special sense of this word. It would perhaps be more accurate to say: as a "peasant" state, since the entire essence, the entire future of the Russian land, the entire history of Russia, present and future, is bound, if not solely then mainly, with the interests, life, and culture of the peasantry. And if, despite the terrible times we are now experiencing, I am still convinced that Russia has a tremendous future, that, out of all the misfortunes that have befallen her and that, unfortunately, are probably still to come, Russia will emerge transformed and great, I am convinced of this precisely because I believe in the Russian peasantry, in its world significance for the destinies of our planet.

. . .

When I returned from America on September 16, 1907 [actually 1905—eds.], I found Russia in total unrest, with the revolution everywhere beginning to break to the surface from underground. The government had lost its capacity for action. People either did nothing or acted at odds with one another, while the authority of the existing regime and of its supreme head was utterly disregarded. Sedition was spreading, not by the day, but by the hour, and the revolution was ever more menacingly bursting out into the street, drawing with it all the classes of our population. The entire upper class was dissatisfied and embittered. The youth, not only in the universities but also in the upper grades of secondary schools, recognized no authorities except those who preached the most extreme revolutionary and antistate theories. The vast majority of the professors took up a position against the government and the existing regime and proclaimed with great authority, both for the youth and for most of the adults: "Enough! We must change everything." Zemstvo and municipal leaders had long declared that "the only salvation is a constitution." The commercial and industrial classes, the wealthy elements, had taken the side of the zemstvo and urban leaders and the professors, and some of them (Morozov, Chetverikov, and the widow Tereshchenko) gave large monetary contributions, not only for the support of the liberation movement, but directly for the revolution (like Savva Morozov, who subsequently shot himself abroad). The workers were falling entirely under the leadership of the revolutionaries and were most active where physical action was needed. All the various *inorodtsy* [ethnic groups with a special legal status]—and these constitute 35 percent of the population of the Russian Empire—seeing the empire thus weakened, raised their heads and decided that the moment had come to realize their cherished dreams and aspirations. This meant "autonomy" for the Poles, "equal rights," and so on, for the Jews, and for all the others abolition of all the restrictions that surrounded their lives—and in many cases these restrictions were outrageous, anti-Christian, rude and, what is especially unforgivable, often stupid. The peasants raised with renewed energy the question of landlessness and, generally, their oppressed state. The officials and clerks who saw at close range the situation in the offices and the system of patronage that developed to gigantic proportions during the reign of Nicholas II set themselves against the regime they served. The army was upset about all the disgraceful defeats in the war and quite properly blamed everything on the government. Besides, the conclusion of peace brought about a special condition which created much disaffection among the troops, especially those who remained in Russia. According to the law, all the soldiers mobilized in wartime were to be discharged when peace was reached. But since the armed forces remaining in Russia were very small, the soldiers were not demobilized, and they became greatly agitated. Because of this the revolutionaries found easy access to the troops, and outbursts of disobedience began to spread among them.

. . .

It may be said without exaggeration that all of Russia rebelled, and that a general slogan was contained in the heart's cry: "This cannot go on!"—in other words, that an end must be put to the existing regime. . . . Everyone was united in hatred of the regime. . . . October 17 destroyed the unanimous hatred of the existing situation and broke up the struggle aimed solely at the "existing regime" into partisan struggles and hatreds.

XVI:65. OFFICIALLY PUBLISHED STATISTICS ON ARRESTS AND DEPORTATIONS, 1905-1906

The journal *Pravo* for May 21, 1906, published this government communiqué (complete text).
    Reference: *Pravo,* no. 20 (May 21, 1906), col. 1819.

According to available information, during the period from the end of October of last year [1905] to the end of April last, 6,825 persons were deported through administrative action by decree of the Special Commission [Osoboe Soveshchanie, consisting of two officials each from the Ministries of Justice and Internal Affairs, under the chairmanship of the assistant minister of internal affairs], formed on the basis of article 34 of the statute on security [of 1881], and by order of governors general on the basis of articles 17 and 19 of the military regulations. Of this number,

5,446 persons were deported by decree of the Special Commission proper.
    . . . As of May 1, 2,627 persons were held in custody on the basis of . . . the statute on security. In addition, on the same date 3,351 persons were under arrest, held under charges for investigations conducted on the basis of article 1035 of the criminal code, their cases being subject in due course either to presentation for court trial, or to discontinuance because of insufficient evidence or on other legal grounds.

XVI:66. CONFIDENTIAL GOVERNMENT STATISTICS ON TERRORISM IN THE YEARS 1905-1909

The following statistics on the victims of terrorism and on the punishment of terrorists in the period from 1905 to May 1909 were reportedly contained in two coded telegrams of June 29 and August 10, 1909, sent by the minister of foreign affairs, Sazonov, to the Russian ambassador in London, Count Benkendorf, at the latter's request. After the Revolution the Soviet government came upon the telegrams and published this table based on them.
    Reference: *Krasnyi arkhiv,* vol. 8 (1925), p. 242.

Years	Victims of Terrorist Acts			Sentenced to Death and Executed	
	Killed	Wounded	Total	Sentenced	Executed
1905	233	358	591	72	10
1906	768	820	1,588	450	144
1907	1,231	1,312	2,543	1,056	456
Additional number sentenced by court martial August 19, 1906-April 20, 1907	—	—	—	683	683
1908	394	615	1,009	1,741	825
1909 up to May 1	65	117	182	628	272
Total	2,691	3,222	5,913	4,630	2,390

C. OTHER SOCIAL AND ECONOMIC DEVELOPMENTS

XVI:67. THE STATUTE ESTABLISHING THE PEASANT LAND BANK, MAY 18, 1882

Here are a few short excerpts from the statute establishing the Peasant Land Bank. The bank's role was enhanced when, in 1885, it was permitted to buy land in its own name for future sale to peasants. By the end of 1913 this bank had aided peasants in the purchase of more than seventeen million desiatinas (about forty-six million acres).

Reference: *PSZRI*, 3d ser., 2:219, 221.

1. The Peasant Land Bank is established for assisting peasants of all categories in purchasing land that its owners desire to sell and the peasants wish to acquire.

2. The Peasant Land Bank is a governmental institution under the jurisdiction of the Ministry of Finance. . . .

25. Loans from the Peasant Land Bank are granted for twenty-four and one-half or for thirty-four and one-half years, according to the wishes of the borrower.

26. Village communities, peasant associations [*tovarishchestva iz krest'ian*], and individual peasants who receive a loan from the bank are required to pay, at the expiration of every half-year, on a date fixed by the minister of finance: (1) as interest, 2.75 percent; (2) for the liquidation of principal: on loans granted for twenty-four and one-half years, 1 percent, and on loans for thirty-four and one-half years, .5 percent; and (3) for the administrative expenses of the bank and for the accumulation of reserve capital, .5 percent.

XVI:68. PROVISIONS FOR THE ESTABLISHMENT OF A NOBLES' LAND BANK, APRIL 21 AND JUNE 3, 1885

On the centennial of Catherine II's Charter to the Nobility, Alexander III issued his imperial rescript of April 21, 1885. It was followed on June 3 by his statute formally establishing the Nobles' Land Bank.

Reference: *PSZRI*, 3d ser., 5:169, 264, 267–68.

[From the rescript of April 21, 1885:]

The nobility of Russia, following the precept of its ancestors . . . has steadfastedly served the tsars of the Russian land as their chief mainstay in the administration of the state and in its defense against external foes; in difficult times of trial it has responded with unexampled ardor to the summons of the fatherland. It pleases our heart to acknowledge this and testify to it by our sovereign word.

And in recent times, when at the summons of the monarch—our never-to-be-forgotten father—it was necessary to undertake the abolition of serfdom, the nobility readily responded to this summons and, while enduring no small sacrifice of their fortune, presented an example of magnanimity rare in the history of any country or people.

On this present noteworthy day, pausing in grateful thought on the history of the noble class [*soslovie*, estate] which is inseparable from the history of the Russian state and people, we set firm hopes that the sons of valiant fathers who served the state will show themselves worthy members of this class in serving the fatherland. Along with this our solicitude is addressed toward assisting them to fulfill with honor so lofty a calling in the days ahead. Mindful of the needs of noble estate-ownership, in many places disarranged by the impoverishment of economic resources and the difficulty of obtaining credit, we have ordered the minister of finance to proceed, along principles indicated by us, to the establishment of a special Nobles' Land Bank, so that the nobles might be more attracted to reside permanently on their estates, where it is primarily their task to apply their energies to the activity that the duty of their station demands of them. Confident that the continuation of this activity will also be in keeping with splendid successes in other fields of endeavor, as prescribed for the nobility from olden times by history and the monarchical will, we, for the welfare of the state, deem it right for the nobles to retain, now as heretofore, a preeminent place in military leadership, in the affairs of local administration and justice, in unselfish solicitude for the needs of the people, and in the propagation by their example of the precepts of faith and loyalty and sound principles of popular education.

[From the statute of June 3, 1885:]

1. The State Nobles' Land Bank is established for granting long-term loans to landowning hereditary nobles, on mortgage of landed property belonging to them. . . .

47. On loans granted by the bank, bor-

rowers are obliged to pay every six months, for the entire term of the loan: (1) as interest, 2½ percent; (2) for the liquidation of principal: on loans granted for 48 years, ¼ percent, on loans for 36 years, ½ percent; and (3) for administrative expenses of the bank and for the accumulation of reserve capital $^1/_8$ percent. In addition to this, borrowers are to pay ¼ percent of the obtained loan at the time the mortgage is taken out. . . . [Note: A manifesto of November 14, 1894, ordered that the interest rate on loans from the State Nobles' Land Bank be lowered to 4 percent per year.]

XVI:69. THE DECISION OF THE STATE COUNCIL ON THE EMPLOYMENT OF MINORS, JUNE 1, 1882

Among the early attempts of Alexander III, and especially his minister of finance, Bunge, to cope with the problems of industrialization was the State Council's decision of June 1, 1882, confirmed by the emperor, concerning the industrial employment of minors. These were among the key provisions.

Reference: *PSZRI,* 3d ser., 2:265-66.

I. . . . 1. Children under the age of twelve are not permitted to work.

2. Minors between the ages of twelve and fifteen cannot be employed at work for more than eight hours a day. . . .

3. Minors under the age of fifteen cannot be employed at work between nine o'clock in the evening and five o'clock in the morning, or on Sundays and high [*vysokotorzhestvennye*] holidays.

4. Minors referred to in article 3 are forbidden to be employed in industries, or at particular jobs in such industries, which by their nature are harmful to the health of

minors or must be regarded as exhausting for them. . . .

5. Owners of mills, plants, and factories are obliged to afford those minors working in their establishments, who do not have a certificate of course completion from at least a one-grade primary school [*odnoklassnoe narodnoe uchilishche*] or another equivalent school, the opportunity to attend the aforesaid educational institutions for no less than three hours daily, or eighteen hours a week.

II. For supervising the observance of the ordinances on labor and education for underage workers, a special inspectorate is instituted.

XVI:70. THE FACTORY REGULATIONS OF JUNE 3, 1886

Another significant piece of legislation to alleviate industrial strife was the regulations of June 3, 1886, including these points.

Reference: *PSZRI,* 3d ser., 6:262-66, 268, 270.

A. Decision of the State Council, confirmed by the emperor.

[I.] 11. It is forbidden to lower the wages of workers before the expiration of a term contract negotiated with them, or without giving two-weeks' notice to workers hired for an indefinite term. . . . Workers likewise have no right, before the expiration of their contract, to demand any changes in its conditions. . . .

13. A worker who has failed to receive the wages due him on time has the right to demand the legal dissolution of the contract negotiated with him. . . .

14. It is forbidden to pay workers in coupons, promissory notes, bread, merchandise, or other articles in place of money. . . .

17. It is forbidden to charge workers for . . . medical assistance. . . .

20. A hiring contract may be canceled by the manager of a mill or factory:

a. In consequence of the absence from work of a worker for more than three consecutive days without a satisfactory reason. . . .

c. In consequence of insolence or bad behavior on the part of a worker, if it threatens the property interest of the factory or the personal safety of any member of the factory administration. . . .

21. Besides the circumstances indicated in article 13, a worker is also permitted to demand the cancellation of a contract:

a. In consequence of beatings, severe insults, and mistreatment in general on the part of the owner, his family, or persons entrusted with supervision of workers.

b. In consequence of the violation of conditions relating to the furnishing of food and living quarters to the workers.

c. In consequence of work detrimental to his health. . . .

[III.] 2. For stopping work in a mill or factory through a strike among workers, with the aim of forcing mill or factory owners to raise wages or change other conditions of the hiring contract before the expiration date of the latter, those guilty are subject to: imprisonment for a term of four to eight months, for instigating the beginning or continuation of a strike; imprisonment for a term of two to four months, for otherwise participating.

Those participants in a strike who discontinue the same and commence work upon the first demand of the police authorities, are freed from imprisonment. . . .

[IV.] 1. For an arbitrary refusal to work before the expiration date of the hiring contract, guilty mill or factory workers are subject to arrest for not more than one month.
. . .

B. Rules for supervision over industrial factory establishments and for mutual relations between factory owners and workers.

1. Supervision over the observance of proper organization and order in mills and factories is entrusted to the local guberniia authorities and is carried out by them with the assistance of guberniia bureaus for factory affairs [*gubernskie po fabrichnym delam prisutstviia*], officials of the factory inspectorate, and the police.

2. Guberniia bureaus for factory affairs, under the chairmanship of the governor, are composed of the vice-governor, the prosecutor of the district [*prokuror okruzhnogo suda*] or his assistant, the head of the guberniia department of gendarmes, the district factory inspector or his assistant, the chairman or a member of the guberniia zemstvo executive board (who shall be elected by this executive board), and the mayor of the capital city of the guberniia or a member of the local municipal executive board (who shall be elected by the latter body). . . .

Note b. In the two capitals and in cities where a consultative institution dealing with trade and industry exists, the bureau members representing the zemstvo and municipal executive boards are replaced by two members: in Saint Petersburg, from the council on trade and industry; in Moscow, from a department of the same; and in other localities, from the committees on trade and industry. . . .

21. Every worker . . . must be issued a pay book. . . .

42. The manager of a mill or factory is subject to a monetary fine of from fifty to three hundred rubles:

a. For charging workers for articles the use of which should be accorded them free of charge. . . .

c. For paying workers in promissory notes, bread, goods, or other articles including coupons, instead of in money.

XVI:71. THE STATE COUNCIL'S EXPLANATION OF FACTORY LEGISLATION, 1886

The official account of the legislative activity of the State Council in 1886 contains this partial explanation, clothed in good bureaucratic phraseology, of what lay behind the factory laws of the 1880s.

Reference: *Otchet po Gosudarstvennomu Sovetu za 1886 god* (St. Petersburg, 1888), pp. 426-29.

Our legislative enactments concerning the mutual relations between manufacturers and workers (articles 50-60 of the factory ordinance), issued more than fifty years ago (in 1835) and now considerably antiquated, were marked by deficiencies and did not correspond to the contemporary needs of factory life.

These inadequacies in legislation relating to such an important subject, which provoked the frequent occurrence of abuses on the part of factory owners and workers both, have long since attracted the attention of the government and have given occasion to the adoption of various measures over the past forty years directed toward the regularization of factory employment. But these measures, in consequence of their fragmentary and one-sided nature, were found to be inadequate and did not achieve their goal. . . .

Meanwhile, in consequence of the rapid growth of industry, which has of late created entire branches of production that previously did not exist, the mutual relations between manufacturers and workers have begun to grow increasingly complicated. The disturbances that arose among the factory workers of the Moscow and Vladimir guberniias at the end of 1884 and the beginning of 1885, and the disorders that took place in certain factories, palpably revealed many extremely unattractive aspects of factory life. The investigation that was conducted proved that the causes behind these disorders were by no means of an accidental nature, but were conditioned by incorrect relations between manufacturers and workers. The owners of certain factories, taking advantage of their position, did not hesitate to violate the contracts concluded with the people they hired and resorted to various means of extracting excessive profits. Reductions of workers' wages, in violation of the agreements concluded, took place either openly or by reductions in the number of working hours and days per week. Furthermore, deductions and fines from the workers, which the manufacturers were turning to their own benefit, in some cases attained huge proportions, comprising a total of up to 40 percent of the wages paid. Finally, forcing the workers to purchase articles they needed from factory stores and at high prices

was found to be a common practice. Such a state of affairs naturally entailed very harmful consequences for the development of industry and directly affected factory owners who managed their business conscientiously. . . . The position of the workers proved to be still more deplorable. Burdened to excess by their helpless indebtedness to the owner, they were often placed in a position where it was impossible for them, not only to discharge their obligations and to support their families, but even to earn enough money for their own subsistence. The irritation against the manufacturers that would arise therefrom, in view of the difficulty for ignorant folk of finding lawful means of protecting their rights, constantly bolstered the workers' tendency to seek the restoration of these rights by means of strikes and disorders, accompanied by rude displays of insubordination and violence.

In view of this, being anxious to discover means for the possible elimination of factory strikes and disorders in the future, the Ministry of Internal Affairs has become convinced that it is essential to begin without delay a reappraisal of those enactments of the ordinance on factory and mill industry that are currently in force, to regulate the mutual relations between manufacturers and workers, with the aim of introducing into these enactments those rules that, by supplementing the existing law with instructions defining the rights of owners and workers, would guarantee the strict execution by both parties of their obligations and would show them more effective methods for restoring infringed interests.

With this aim, a special commission was established, with imperial sanction, within the aforesaid ministry, consisting of representatives of the departments concerned, under the chairmanship of Senator Privy Councillor Pleve, which has drafted a set of rules for supervision over industrial plant establishments and for the relations between their owners and the people working for them.

XVI:72. KRAVCHINSKII (STEPNIAK) ON THE RUSSIAN PEASANTRY, 1888

Sergei Mikhailovich Kravchinskii (1851-95), whose literary pseudonym was "Stepniak," was trained as a military man but in his early twenties abandoned that career and embraced the movement "to the people." In 1878, as a member of the Land and Freedom organization, he assassinated General Mezentsev, the chief of police. Soon escaping abroad, he made his home from 1884 onward in England, where his life was cut short by a train accident in 1895. The following excerpts are from his book *The Russian Peasantry: Their Agrarian Condition, Social Life, and*

Religion, first published in New York in 1888. (In the following year, through the land captains, the rights of the mir were significantly curtailed, to be restored only by a law of October 5, 1906.)

Reference: S. M. Kravchinskii [Stepniak], *The Russian Peasantry: Their Agrarian Condition, Social Life, and Religion* (New York: Harper and Brothers, 1905), pp. 117, 126-27, 132, 134-35, 137-39, 147, 156, 635-37.

Far from being degraded and brutalised by slavery, the peasants, united in their semi-patriarchal, semi-republican village communes, exhibited a great share of self-respect, and even capacity to stand boldly by their rights, where the whole of the commune was concerned. Diffident in their dealings with strangers, they showed a remarkable truthfulness and frankness in their dealings among themselves, and a sense of duty and loyalty and unselfish devotion to their little communes.

· · ·

A Russian village has never been a mere aggregation of individuals, but a very intimate association, having much work and life in common. These associations are called *mirs* among the Great and White Russians, *hromadas* among the Ruthenians.

Up to the present time the law has allowed them a considerable amount of self-government. They are free to manage all their economical concerns in common: the land, if they hold it as common property—which is the case everywhere save in the Ruthenian provinces—the forests, the fisheries, the renting of public-houses standing on their territory, etc. They distribute among themselves as they choose, the taxes falling to the share of the commune according to the Government schedules. They elect the rural executive administration—*Starost[as]* and *Starshinas*—who are (nominally at least) under their permanent control.

Another very important privilege which they possess is that they, the village communes composing the *Volost,* in general meeting assembled, elect the ten judges of the *Volost.* All these must be peasants, members of some village commune. The jurisdiction of the peasants' tribunal is very extensive; all the civil, and a good many criminal offences (save the capital ones), in which one of the parties, at least, is a peasant of the district, are amenable to it. The peasants sitting as judges are not bound to abide in their verdicts by the official code of law. They administer justice according to the customary laws and traditions of the local peasantry.

· · ·

The peasants have applied their collective intelligence not to material questions alone, nor within the domain apportioned to them by law; the *mir* recognises no restraint on its autonomy. In the opinion of the peasants themselves, the *mir's* authority embraces, indeed, all domains and branches of peasant life. Unless the police and the local officers are at hand to prevent what is considered an abuse of power, the peasants' *mir* is always likely to exceed its authority.

· · ·

In the olden times, as late as the sixteenth century, it was the *mir* who elected the parson (as the dissenting villages are doing nowadays), the bishops only imposing hands on [i.e. endorsing] the *mir's* nominees.

· · ·

The *mir* forms indeed a *microcosm,* a small world of its own. The people living in it have to exercise their judgment on everything, on the moral side of man's life as on the material, shaping it so as to afford to their small communities as much peace and happiness as is possible under their very arduous circumstances.

· · ·

"Each for himself," they say—"but God and the *mir* for all." The *mir* is no egotist; it pities everybody alike, and should it have to settle any difference it does not look to the numerical strength or respective influence of the contending parties, but to the absolute justice of the cause.

· · ·

The Russian *moujik* is proverbially benevolent towards strangers of his own race. He is accustomed to feel something like family attachment to most, or to very many, of the members of his *mir.* . . .

There is no people on the face of the earth who treat aliens so kindly as do the Russian *moujiks.* They live peacefully side by side with hundreds of tribes, differing in race and religion—Tartars, Circassians, Bouriats, and German colonists. . . .

The *mir* in the management of its affairs recognizes no permanent laws restricting or guiding its decisions. It is the personification of the living law, speaking through the collective voice of the commune. Every case brought before the *mir* is judged on its own merits, according to the endless variety of its peculiar circumstances.

· · ·

A passion for Equality and Fraternity is and will ever be the strongest, we may say the only strong social feeling in Russia.

· · ·

Every Russian village commune elects its elder or mayor, who is by virtue of his office its spokesman and delegate before the authorities. In the village itself the elder is neither the chief nor even the *primus inter pares,* but simply the trusted servant and executor of the orders of the *mir.* The *mir* discusses and regulates everything that falls within its narrow and simple sphere of action, leaving hardly anything to the discrimination and judgment of its agent. So simple and subordinate are the elder's duties, that any peasant, provided he be neither a drunkard nor a thief, is eligible for the post. In many villages, in order to avoid discussion, the office of elder is filled in turn by all the members of the *mir.*

· · ·

There exist no people on the face of the earth, or, to keep within the boundaries of the better known, on the face of Europe, who, as a body, are so well trained for collective labour as our *moujiks* are. Whenever a group or a crowd of them have some common economical interest to look after, or some common work to perform, they invariably form themselves into an *artel,* or kind of trades union, which is a free, purely economical *mir,* purged of the compulsory, despotic elements of political authority. It is a free union of people, who combine for the mutual advantages of cooperation in labour, or consumption, or of both. Its membership is voluntary, not imposed, and each member is free to withdraw at the close of the season, or upon the conclusion of the particular work for which the *artel* was formed, and to enter into a new *artel.* . . . The *artel* has no legal authority over its members. Expulsion from the *artel* is the only punishment, or rather the only protection, these associations possess against those who break their rules. Yet the *artels* do very well, and in permanent work often prove to be lifelong partnerships. The fishermen of the north; the carpenters who go to work in the towns; the bricklayers and builders; the diggers and the freight-carriers,—all the hundreds of thousands of peasants who move from the villages in search of work, either start by forming *artels,* or join some *artel* when they reach their destination. Every *artel* accepts work, makes engagements, etc., as a body, distributing or dividing the work they have to do amongst themselves. The principle followed is, that every man's pay shall be strictly proportioned to the amount of his individual labour, or, that this ideal shall be approached as nearly as the nature of the particular industry will admit of.

There is endless variety in the economical characters and the size of these *artels,* some being regular owners of industrial establishments or trading companies (a machine manufactory in Ural), whilst others are only temporary and limited associations of vast numbers of men, blown together by the four winds of heaven, such as those of bargemen or railway servants, etc., though in substance they all reproduce the leading features of the village *mir.*

The principle of co-operation is applied as frequently and as naturally to agricultural as to non-agricultural work.

XVI:73. THE LAW RESTRICTING THE ALIENATION OF ALLOTMENT LAND, DECEMBER 14, 1893

The law that is reproduced in part here repealed article 165 of the redemption statute of February 19, 1861, which had obligated the community to allow a householder to obtain separate tenure on his plot if he paid the entire share of the redemption dues on that plot and demanded its withdrawal from communal tenure.
Reference: *PSZRI,* 3d ser., 13:653-54.

[I.] 1. The sale of allotment land by the entire village community is permitted only on the basis of a special decision to that effect by the community, laid down with the consent of not less than two-thirds of all peasants with a vote in the assembly, and confirmed by the guberniia bureau. . . . If the value of the alienated plot [*uchastok*] exceeds five hundred rubles, then its sale requires, in addition, the permission of the minister of internal affairs, by agreement with the minister of finance. . . .

3. Peasant communities and individual peasants are forbidden to mortgage allotment land to private parties and private institutions, even if the redemption loan on this land has been liquidated. . . .

II. . . . As long as the redemption loan has not been repaid [by the entire community],

individual householders shall not be permitted separation of tenure [*vydel*, by which a peasant converted his allotment into a hereditary holding and withdrew from the commune] and advance redemption of individual plots of communal land, except with the consent of the community and on the conditions stated in the decision of the corresponding village assembly.

XVI:74. THE FACTORY LAW OF JUNE 2, 1897

Here are some of the key provisions of the factory law of June 2, 1897, as recommended by the State Council and approved by the tsar.

Reference: *PSZRI*, 3d ser., vol. 17, pt. 1, p. 355.

4. For workers employed exclusively in the daytime the working day (article 2) shall not exceed eleven and a half hours, and on Saturdays and the eves of the . . . holidays designated in article 6, ten hours. On Christmas Eve work must be terminated no later than noon. . . .

[Note: Article 6 lists fourteen obligatory

holidays, not counting Sundays.]

8. . . . Overtime work is permitted only by special agreement between the manager of the industrial establishment and the worker. The hiring contract may include provisions regarding such overtime work only as required by the technical needs of production.

XVI:75. WITTE'S SECRET MEMORANDUM ON THE INDUSTRIALIZATION OF RUSSIA, MARCH 22, 1899

These passages from a secret report he made to Tsar Nicholas II on March 22, 1899, explain some of Witte's policies.

Reference: Theodore H. von Laue, "A Secret Memorandum of Sergei Witte on the Industrialization of Imperial Russia," *Journal of Modern History,* 26 (March 1954): 64-73. The translation is Professor von Laue's.

The entire economic structure of the empire has been transformed in the course of the second half of the current century, so that now the market and its price structure represent the collective interest of all private enterprises which constitute our national economy.

· · ·

I realized, of course, that there were very weighty arguments against the protectionist system and against high tariffs. But I supposed that even the proponents of free trade must be aware that it would be extremely harmful from the government viewpoint to repudiate the protective system before those industries had been securely established for whose creation whole generations had paid by a high tariff. . . . I did not waver in my fundamental aim to complete in detail what was so boldly begun in the reign of Alexander III and of Your Imperial Majesty. The results of state policy in economic matters are the work of decades, and the most harmful of all

commercial and industrial systems is that which is inconstant and wavering.

· · ·

The economic relations of Russia with western Europe are fully comparable to the relations of colonial countries with their metropolises. The latter consider their colonies as advantageous markets in which they can freely sell the products of their labor and of their industry and from which they can draw with a powerful hand the raw materials necessary for them. . . . Russia was, and to a considerable extent still is, such a hospitable colony for all industrially developed states, generously providing them with the cheap products of her soil and buying dearly the products of their labor. But there is a radical difference between Russia and a colony: Russia is an independent and strong power. She has the right and the strength not to want to be the eternal handmaiden of states which are more developed economically.

. . .

It must be stated first of all that the system, because it is coherently carried out, is already beginning to show results. Industry numbers now more than 30,000 factories and mills, with an annual production surpassing 2,000,000,000 rubles. That by itself is a big figure. A widespread and tight net of economic interests is linked to the welfare of that industry.

. . .

We need capital, knowledge, and the spirit of enterprise. Only these three factors can speed up the creation of a fully independent national industry.

. . .

Industry gives birth to capital; capital gives rise to enterprise and love of learning; and knowledge, enterprise, and capital combined create new industries. Such is the eternal cycle of economic life, and by the succession of such turns our national economy moves ahead in the process of its natural growth. In Russia this growth is yet too slow, because there is yet too little industry, capital, and spirit of enterprise. But we cannot be content with the continuation of such slow growth.

. . .

The influx of foreign capital is, in the considered opinion of the minister of finance, the sole means by which our industry can speedily furnish our country with abundant and cheap goods. . . . Hence the natural riches of the Russian land and the productive energies of its population will be utilized to a considerably greater extent; our economy will begin to work with greater intensity.

. . .

The extent of the influx of foreign capital into Russia is usually much exaggerated. . . . It would seem, then, that of the total amount of capital invested every year in the further development of our industries, foreign capital scarcely constitutes more than one-fifth or one-sixth.

. . . [It has been] 376,000,000 rubles all together since 1887—do these statistics prove that there is a danger for our vast Russian economy?

. . .

Either way we have to pay the foreigner, but obviously in the case of imported capital that payment will be considerably less than in the case of imported goods.

. . . If in our present situation we cannot satisfy all our demands from our own resources and have to resort to purchasing abroad, it will be more advantageous for us to buy not finished goods but capital, which is one of the most necessary productive forces, particularly in industry. . . . Foreign capital . . . works its way into our industry only because it is satisfied wherever it goes with smaller profits than its Russian predecessors. A new hundred million, flowing into the country from abroad during a given year, lowers by the laws of competition the rate of interest of all capital previously invested in Russian industry, which amounts to billions. If the country pays for these new hundred million rubles ten million in dividends, it gains still a considerably larger sum from the lower interest rates for the capital already invested in its economy. As the billions of national capital become cheaper, the prices of all industrial products will also fall considerably. We have at our disposal cheap labor, tremendous natural riches, and only the high price of capital now stands in the way of getting cheap goods. So why not let foreign capital help us to obtain still more cheaply that productive force of which alone we are destitute?

. . .

The imported cultural forces thus become an inseparable part of the country itself. Only a disintegrating nation has to fear foreign enslavement. Russia, however, is not China!

I have now analyzed the chief bases of the economic system which has been followed in Russia since the reign of Alexander III.

Its starting point is the protective tariff of 1891, somewhat lowered by the subsequent trade treaties with France, Germany, Austria-Hungary, and other governments.

That protective system has for its aim the creation of a Russian national industry, which would contribute to the growth of our economic, and consequently also our political, independence and would make possible more favorable terms for both international and domestic trade.

That task, demanding great sacrifices from the population, has in some respects already been fulfilled. Russia has now an industry of tremendous size. The interests of our entire economy are closely tied to its future.

This industry, however, has not yet reached such an extent and such technical perfection as to furnish the country with an abundance of cheap goods. Its services cost the country too dearly, and these excessive costs have a destructive influence over the welfare of the population, particularly in agriculture. They cannot be sustained much longer.

We cannot possibly count on an adequate growth of our industry out of our own national resources, because our store of capital, knowledge, and the spirit of enterprise is altogether insufficient to provide us with cheap industrial goods.

To obtain cheaper goods, of which the population stands in such urgent need, by a substantial tariff reduction would be too expensive. It would forever deprive the country of the positive results of the protective system, for which a whole generation has made sacrifices; it would upset the industries which we have created with so much effort just when they were ready to repay the nation for its sacrifices.

It would be very dangerous to rely on the competition of foreign goods for the lowering of our prices. But we can attain the same results with the help of the competition of foreign capital, which, by coming into Russia, will help Russian enterprise to promote native industry and speed up the accumulation of native capital.

XVI:76. V. I. GURKO ON WITTE AS MINISTER OF FINANCE, 1892-1903

Vladimir Iosifovich Gurko (1862-1927), son of a field marshal and brother of a general (Vasilii), graduated from Moscow University in 1885. In 1902, having served in several bureaucratic posts and having published two books on agrarian problems, he was appointed to a high post in the Ministry of Internal Affairs, and in 1906 he served briefly as assistant minister. Subsequently turning to zemstvo activity, he was elected in 1912 to the State Council, where he served until the Revolution. In this passage from his posthumously published memoirs, Gurko gives his appraisal of Witte as minister of finance.

Reference: Vladimir I. Gurko, *Features and Figures of the Past: Government and Opinion in the Reign of Nicholas II* (Palo Alto: Stanford University Press, 1939), pp. 56-57, 66-67.

Witte's economic policy was but a program to meet the current need and showed that simplicity of conception which was his distinctive trait. This policy was, in brief, the accumulation of funds in the state treasury and the accumulation of private capital in the country. Realizing that the best method of increasing state resources was to develop the country's economic life, he encouraged such development; but he considered that the only means to attain this end was to develop industry, heavy industry especially, since it was the source of all great private fortunes.

. . . Witte held that agriculture is but a limited field for the application of human labor, while industry, unconfined by material limitations, may develop indefinitely and thereby use an indefinite amount of labor. Agriculture to him was a necessary but purely subordinate branch of public economy; agriculture was necessary to feed the population, but could not serve as the sole source of its well-being. This explains his negative attitude toward all measures designed to improve the agricultural situation.

· · ·

As to selection of method, Witte was . . . an opportunist; he was facile also in shifting his opinion when he considered such shifts advisable. But his aim of promoting the economic development of Russia as a basis for political strength was steady and unswerving.

In summary, Witte's accomplishments as Minister of Finance reveal his great merit as an organizer of our state economy. He brought order into the state budget, avoided deficits, and achieved even a pronounced increase of revenues; he strengthened Russian finances as much by the introduction of the gold standard as by his successful conversion of state loans to a lower rate of interest, to four instead of six per cent. He extended the network of our railways; he introduced and developed university and secondary technical education; he assembled a fine group of assistants and other officers in the Ministry of Finance; he organized the department of tax supervision; he most successfully introduced and organized the large-scale liquor monopoly. All these were the fruits of Witte's strenous labor. Thanks to him our industry began to develop at an almost incredible speed and attracted a part of the population away from agricultural pursuits which could not absorb all the peasant labor as the population increased.

XVI:77. THE REGULATIONS ON TRANS-URAL SETTLEMENT, JUNE 29, 1899

In the migration of more than three million settlers beyond the Urals in the years 1893-1913, it was to be expected that often those who most wanted to go were those who lacked the means to do so. Hence the government was led to furnish assistance of the types illustrated in these passages from regulations of June 29, 1899 (which followed "provisional regulations" of 1893 and 1896). The full title of this document is "Regulations concerning Government Grants-in-Aid to Settlers Migrating with Required Authorization to Siberia and the Steppe Governorship General." It was prepared by the Committee of the Siberian Railway.

Reference: *PSZRI*, 3d ser., 23 (suppl. to vol. 19): 50-53.

Regulations

1. The government may give assistance to settlers migrating with the required authorization to Siberia and the Steppe governorship general and settling in these territories: (a) by granting loans for travel; (b) by granting loans for farming equipment, seed, and housing construction, and (c) by distributing free lumber from state forests for building purposes. . . .

5. No interest or fines shall be charged on the loans issued to settlers. . . .

7. Travel loans of not more than 30 rubles may be issued to individual scouts [*khodoki*] and to families of settlers migrating with the proper documents. . . . For settlers going to the Amur governorship general, the loan may be increased to 100 rubles. . . .

11. Loans for farming equipment and seed may be issued in response to a written or oral application by the settlers within three years of settlement and should not exceed 150 rubles in the Amur governorship general and 100 rubles in the remaining territories of Siberia and the Steppe governorship general.
. . .

19. In those cases where the resettlement lands do not provide a sufficient quantity of timber for construction, the settlers may be issued free lumber from the state forests nearest the land assigned to them, in quantities of not more than 200 trees suitable for house timbers and 50 poles per household, and, in addition, up to 20 trees for bathhouses and up to 60 trees for threshing barns and threshing floors. . . .

24. After five years during which no payment is required, the loans are to be repaid in the course of the following ten years, on fixed dates in equal annual payments.

XVI:78. THE TABLE OF RANKS IN 1901

The Table of Ranks promulgated by Peter I in 1722 (see above, Item X:25) underwent changes with the passage of time. Some of the titles widely encountered by readers of nineteenth-century Russian history and literature were not included in the original table. We therefore present here a table published in 1901. It has been abridged even more than the earlier document, and the courtiers' and Guards' ranks have been omitted altogether. (See also the law of June 11, 1845, Item XIV:28, above.)

Reference: *Entsiklopedicheskii Slovar'*, 41 vols. (St. Petersburg: Brokgauz and Efron, 1890-1904), 32:440-41.

CLASS	CIVIL RANKS	CORRESPONDING RANKS	
		ARMY	NAVY
1.	Chancellor [Kantsler]	Field Marshal General	Admiral General
2.	Actual (or Right) Privy Councillor [Deistvitel'nyi Tainyi Sovetnik]	General of Cavalry; General of Infantry; General of Artillery	Admiral
3.	Privy Councillor [Tainyi Sovetnik]	Lieutenant General	Vice-Admiral
4.	Actual (or Right) State Councillor [Deistvitel'nyi Statskii Sovetnik]; High Procurator [Ober-Prokuror]; Master Herald [Gerol'dmeister]	Major General	Rear Admiral [Kontr-admiral]
5.	State Councillor [Statskii Sovetnik]	—	—

CLASS	CIVIL RANKS	ARMY	NAVY
6.	Collegiate Councillor [Kollezhskii Sovetnik]	Colonel [Polkovnik]	Captain, 1st Grade
7.	Court Councillor [Nadvornyi Sovetnik]	Lieutenant Colonel [Podpolkovnik]	Captain, 2d Grade
8.	Collegiate Assessor [Kollezhskii Assesor]	Captain [Kapitan and also Rotmistr]	–
9.	Titular Councillor [Tituliarnyi Sovetnik]	Staff Captain [Shtabs-kapitan and Shtabs-rotmistr]	Lieutenant
10.	Collegiate Secretary [Kollezhskii Sekretar']	Lieutenant [Poruchik]	Warrant Officer [Michman]
11.	–	–	–
12.	Guberniia Secretary [Gubernskii Sekretar']	Sub-lieutenant [Podporuchik]	–
13.	–	Ensign [Praporshchik]	–
14.	Collegiate registrar [Kollezhskii Registrator]	–	–

XVI:79. RITTIKH ON THE PEASANT COMMUNE, 1903

The pros and cons of the peasant land commune were hotly debated at the opening of the twentieth century, especially in local committees of the Special Conference on the Needs of Agriculture (Osoboe Soveshchanie o Nuzhdakh Sel'skokhoziaistvennoi Promyshlennosti), established in 1902 in forty-nine guberniias of European Russia. Aleksandr Aleksandrovich Rittikh, an expert on the peasantry, published in 1903 a summary of the views expressed in these local committees. It is interesting to evaluate his comments, as excerpted here, in the light of the subsequent developments in the rural sector. (For other observations on the peasantry at about the same time, see Stolypin's report from Saratov in 1904, Item XVII:28.)

Reference: A. A. Rittikh, ed., *Krest'ianskoe zemlepol'zovanie* (St. Petersburg: V. F. Kirsbaum, 1903), pp. 2, 14-15, 18-19, 22, 33, 35, 36.

Section I. Communal Ownership
Chapter 1. Positive Aspects of the Commune

Recognizing the necessity for basic changes in the legal structure of the peasant economy, the members of the local committees differ in evaluating the various particular aspects of this structure. The conflict is most clearly marked in the question of the commune: a considerable majority admits the extreme harm done by the equalizing form of land utilization, and may even see in it the basic cause of the decline of agricultural production; a minority, however, expresses its conviction that this form of land ownership is advantageous both for the economy as a whole and for private economic relationships.

From the latter point of view it is maintained that this form of utilization is quite profitable for the peasant economy, and at the same time presents no particular obstacles to the development of agriculture.

. . .

Propositions concerning the possible development of the commune into a cooperative union are linked to a considerable degree with considerations of socioeconomic significance. From the latter point of view the stress is laid primarily upon the positive aspects of the equalizing system of land ownership, even when it is admitted that from the point of view of the individual economy this system presents a serious obstacle to the progress of agriculture.

This important defect is compensated for in that the land belongs not to individuals, but to the entire commune, with each person belonging to it and born into it having the right to a land allotment equal to that of every other member. Under these conditions, the supply of land, which is the chief and, in the majority of cases, the sole source of subsistence, is protected against monopolization by a minority of the population, and our entire communal peasantry is guaranteed a share of this basic and immediate source of existence that will be just and commensurate with the needs of each. On the other hand, the right of private property converts the land into a commodity which, under the influence of unequal competition between men who differ in capacities, and especially between the rich and the poor, gradually accumulates in the hands of the former and places in their power the dispossessed, displaced masses, who become farmhands and proletarians. The history of all the countries of western Europe demonstrates that with the abolition of the commune begins the transfer and great diminution of small landed property as a result of its concentration in the hands of the few. From that, as a result of this same process, stems the abnormal development of the proletariat, which is at present the incurable disease of the political organisms of western Europe. The same process would undoubtedly take place in Russia; if the land were divided by households into private plots, one or two bad harvests, i.e. one or two decades, would be enough to bring about the dispossession of the overwhelming majority to the advantage of the numerically insignificant portion of the population that is more enterprising and economically secure. In Russia this would be particularly dangerous, because in countries with a higher cultural level a considerable part of the dispossessed population finds employment and income in manufacturing and commercial activity, which in Russia is underdeveloped, and which in any case is incapable of providing an income for the millions who would undoubtedly be left without land following a transfer from communal to household ownership. Therefore the commune, with its characteristic equalizing procedures, must be protected by all means from destruction; it is the sole guarantee against the development of an economically undesirable and politically dangerous proletariat.

. . .

Chapter 2. Undesirable Aspects of the Commune

. . . The amount of arable land is . . . greatly diminishing as a result of the ruining of the soil, which the opponents of the equalizing system of land utilization trace directly to the instability of possession, as this hinders an increase in soil productivity through in-tensive cultivation and leads people to "plow as much as possible, no matter how." Hence the hayfields, the pastures, the slopes of gullies are put to the plow, the forests are cut down and turned into meadowland or pastures, which in a short time will also come under the plow. Under such conditions the sandy subsoil is laid bare, and the plowed-under slopes of gullies cause the emergence of a series of ravines that eat up the soil, depriving it of moisture and facilitating the removal of the topsoil by spring floods.

The deterioration of the arable land and its careless cultivation have an extremely harmful effect on peasant cattle raising both qualitatively and quantitatively, as a result of which the area under cultivation is fertilized less and worked less beneficially. Agriculture becomes unprofitable on the exhausted land. This is particularly noticeable in relation to fields distant from settlements, where the scant harvest barely repays the time and work spent in their cultivation. The peasants neglect them, and the periphery of the allotment, formerly plowland, now becomes wasteland. In this way, after the rapid growth of the cultivated area comes its gradual diminution, but in place of lands formerly arable and useful for fodder there now appear wastelands, completely exhausted and agriculturally worthless. Under these conditions the allotment becomes more and more inadequate for feeding the growing population, and the peasants, in the search for unexhausted land, are forced to buy it and in large measure resort to renting it outside the allotment. The constantly increasing demand for land raises its price out of all proportion to its potential income, in consequence of which the peasant barely gets back the price of his labor from the rented plot, gaining no net profit. Everywhere there are complaints of too little land, while at the same time the percentage of agriculturally worthless areas, such as marshes, sands, ravines, and wastelands, steadily increases, replacing former fields and plowlands. . . .

Ascribing this desire of the peasantry for a quantitative rather than a qualitative economy to the impermanence of communal land use, the opponents of the equalizing system see this as the chief cause of the constant complaints of too little land. Holding such [land scarcity] to be merely conditional, they claim that, with proper cultivation of allotments, which is possible only where the user has permanent property rights, the problem of too little land would cease to exist for the majority of peasants now complaining of it.

. . .

Reports from the Kursk guberniia made clear what an indescribable amount of work it takes for even the most energetic communal peasants to introduce intensive cultivation on land they hold only temporarily: "The peasant lacks not only the possibility but also the right to improve and develop his agricultural enterprise. He cannot, on a plot allotted to him for twelve years by a general reapportionment, put up a fence and plant a garden, for his fence will be broken down and his garden trampled under by cattle; he cannot plant on it whatever he wants—grasses, grains, or garden vegetables, for these too will be pulled up and trampled down. At the will of the mir, he is obliged in a designated place to sow winter crops, in another place to sow spring crops, and in a third place—for all his desire to make some use of it—to do nothing at all. Part of his meadows he cannot improve because he does not know where it is. Part of his woods he must cut down when the communal meeting so orders. Only in his little yard does the peasant have rights equal to those of a private landowner."

. . .

The basic cause of all the undesirable aspects of the peasant economy as detailed above is held to be the absence, under an equalizing system of land tenure, of the main incentive to work—of the knowledge and conviction that the results of labor will be enjoyed by the laborer himself, or by persons near to him by kinship and attachment. . . . Under such conditions, the economic prudence, the enterprising spirit, and the energy of the individual are pointless and, in the majority of cases, inapplicable. These mainsprings of any material progress find an insuperable obstacle in the conditions of the communal system. Hence an apathetic and negligent attitude toward one's work, laziness, and a tendency to shiftlessness and drunkenness develop among the peasantry. Along with this, the impermanence of those rights of land tenure most vital to the peasants, and their dependence on the whim of a majority vote formed by chance, teach them not to respect the rights of others,

and give rise to mutual distrust, sometimes even to open enmity, among commune members.

. . .

The communal system is not a voluntary association on artel principles, but has a sharply formulated compulsory character. In contradiction of the general principle of civil rights, that no one may be constrained to remain in a corporate holding, the legislation regulating the communal system deprives individual peasants of the right to withdraw their share of land out of the communal allotment without the consent of the mir, or even to receive compensation for it. The right to transfer to private holding [*vydel*] existed, however, up to the year 1893, and until that time every communal peasant who had paid his redemption debt had the possibility of transferring his land to homestead tenure, even without the consent of the commune. As is well known, the law of December 14, 1893 [see Item XVI:73, above], which abrogated this right, was intended to prevent the dispossession of the peasantry. . . . At present it is generally impossible to withdraw one's share out of the communal allotment, due to the difficulty of getting the consent of the mir; consequently, every member of a land commune is forced either to stay in it or to renounce his share of the land.

. . .

On the other hand, each commune member has the right to an allotment of land, with the result that persons permanently residing elsewhere and firmly established in nonagricultural occupations appear in the village at the time of reapportionment and demand allotments, which they then rent to fellow villagers, most often to kulaks.

The compulsory tie with the land, coupled with the contrary principle of the right of all to receive an allotment, has the consequence that the communal landholding is split up so as to correspond exactly with the growth of the population bound to it, while at the same time the decrease in the size of individual household allotments is not compensated for by a corresponding increase in yield per acre.

. . .

The result of such a splitting up is that in the majority of cases the allotments of the individual commune members are sufficient neither for subsistence nor for the full employment of the available working force.

XVI:80. STATISTICS ON LANDED PROPERTY IN RUSSIA IN 1905

In the last century and especially the last half-century of the tsarist era, the machinery for collecting statistics developed in Russia as in other modern states, and a mountain of information is available on the empire's economic growth and condition. Little of this material lends itself to inclusion in this sourcebook, and yet some of it constitutes exceedingly valuable data for the student of Russian history. An example is the *Ezhegodnik Rossii 1906 g.,* the statistical annual for 1906 prepared by the Central Statistical Committee of the Ministry of Internal Affairs. Here are excerpts from the section covering landholding in the fifty guberniias of European Russia (i.e. excluding Finland, Poland, and the Caucasus) in 1905.

Reference: Tsentral'nyi Statisticheskii Komitet, *Ezhegodnik Rossii 1906 g.* (St. Petersburg: Ministerstvo Vnutrennikh Del, 1907), pp. 26, 31, 36-38, 50-51.

[Landholding in fifty guberniias of European Russia in 1905 (sum totals from the table):]

Type of Landholding	Land Area (in thousand desiatinas)	Percent of Total Area	Number of Households with Allotment Land (in thousands)	Average Amount of Allotment Land per Household (in desiatinas)
Private property	101,735	25.8	–	–
Allotment land	138,768	35.1	12,298	11.1
State, church, and [other] institutions	154,689	39.1	–	–
Total	395,192		12,298	11.1

[Note: Of the 154,689,000 desiatinas in the third category, 138,086,000 were treasury lands situated predominantly in the nontillable forests and tundras of the north.]

· · ·

Group I (private holdings). . . .
Personal property [of individuals] . . .

Landholder	Landholding (in desiatinas)	Landholding as Percent of Total Area	Landholding as Percent of Personal Property
Nobles	53,169,008	13.5	61.9
Clergy	337,206	0.1	0.4
Merchants and honorary citizens [*potomstvennye pochetnye grazhdane*]	12,906,795	3.3	15.0
Meshchane	3,763,822	0.9	4.4
Peasants	13,214,025	3.3	15.4
Other classes	2,213,372	0.6	2.5
Foreign subjects	352,438	0.1	0.4
Total belonging to individual property owners	85,956,666	21.8	100.0

· · ·

Collective private property. The second form of private property consists of holdings of societies and associations, to which belong 15,778,667 desiatinas, or 4.0 percent of the total area, or 15.5 percent of all private property.

· · ·

Group II (allotment lands). The second category of holdings includes the allotment lands of peasants and of the Don, Orenburg, and Astrakhan' Cossack hosts. The total area of allotment land . . . is calculated at 138,767,587 desiatinas, which comprises 35.1 percent of the total area of fifty guberniias of European Russia; or, if the northern region, with its exceptional size and composition, is excluded, 130,873,445 desiatinas or 47.2 percent of the total area.

. . .

The number of households among which the aforesaid allotment area [Note in text: "With the exclusion of 1,837,121 desiatinas not distributed by households"] is distributed, is calculated at 12,297,905, which consequently comes to an average of 11.1 desiatinas per household. In the separate parts of Russia this percentage varies . . . by guberniias from 3.8 desiatinas (in the Podolia guberniia) to 65.1 (in the Olonets guberniia).

If the guberniias are arranged in the order of the greatest average size of peasant allotment land per household, it is as follows:

Desiatinas per Household

Over 10		7 to 10		7 or Fewer	
Olonets	65.1	Saint Petersburg	9.7	Orel	7.0
Orenburg	29.8	Voronezh	9.6	Tambov	7.0
Astrakhan'	28.4	Saratov	9.5	Simbirsk	6.8
Samara	19.8	Ekaterinoslav	9.3	Riazan'	6.6
Ufa	18.8	Pskov	9.2	Bessarabia	6.5
Grodno	16.5	Minsk	9.1	Chernigov	6.3
Viatka	16.0	Smolensk	9.0	Tula	6.3
Perm'	15.8	Vladimir	8.9	Archangel	6.1
Vologda	15.5	Kostroma	8.9	Kiev	5.5
Tavrida	14.7	Tver'	8.6	Poltava	4.9
Kovno	14.6	Kazan'	8.6	Don	4.4
Vilna	13.5	Mogilev	8.2	Podolia	3.8
Novgorod	13.5	Kaluga	8.1		
Vitebsk	11.5	Volynia	7.8		
		Kherson	7.8		
		Moscow	7.5		
		Penza	7.5		
		Nizhnii-Novgorod	7.4		
		Khar'kov	7.3		
		Kursk	7.3		
		Iaroslavl'	7.1		

[Note: There were no allotment lands in the Baltic guberniias of Estonia, Courland, and Livonia.]

. . .

If the allotment land is divided according to its manner of utilization—communal or household—into two parts . . . the following figures are obtained:

Land held as personal property	85,956,666 desiatinas
[Allotment] land held under household tenure	22,981,193 desiatinas
[Allotment] land held under communal utilization	115,786,390 desiatinas
Land held as property of societies and associations	15,778,677 desiatinas

. . .

If we turn to an investigation of the composition of private landholding by *classes* [*soslovia*], and add to the allotment land of peasants the land that is held as their personal property and as the property of societies and associations (the latter including both exclusively peasant and mixed peasant-meshchane associations); if we add to the personal property of me- shchane, land belonging to meschane associations; and if we add to the personal holdings of merchants, land belonging to commercial-industrial associations: it will be found that out of the total amount of 240,502,930 desiatinas of nonpublic [*chastnyi*, in the sense of excluding lands of the state and the church] land there belongs to:

Peasants	148,735,808 desiatinas or 61.84 percent of total area
Nobles	53,169,008 desiatinas or 22.11 percent of total area
Merchants	16,669,049 desiatinas or 6.93 percent of total area
Cossacks	14,689,498 desiatinas or 6.11 percent of total area
Meshchane	3,828,537 desiatinas or 1.59 percent of total area
Clergy	337,206 desiatinas or 0.14 percent of total area
Others	2,721,386 desiatinas or 1.13 percent of total area
Foreigners	352,438 desiatinas or 0.15 percent of total area

And if the land belonging to Cossacks and meshchane is added to peasant land, we see that about 70 percent of all nonpublic landholdings belongs to this entire group.

. . .

The area of *noble* landholding comprises only [about] one-fifth (22.11 percent) of the [total] area and . . . is concentrated primarily in the western borderlands—in the Baltic, north-western, and Trans-Dnieper regions. . . .

. . . The *peasant* group of landholdings is distributed as follows:

	Desiatinas	Percent of Total
Allotment land	124,078,089	83.4
Personal property	13,214,025	8.9
Land belonging to associations	7,654,006	5.2
Land belonging to societies	3,729,352	2.5

XVI:81. A DECREE ON RELIGIOUS TOLERANCE, APRIL 17, 1905

Here are some of the main provisions of an imperial decree that was intended to alleviate the position of religious dissenters.

Reference: *PSZRI*, 3d ser., vol. 25, pt. 1, pp. 257-58. To supplement the works in English already cited in this volume, students especially interested in Russian religious, ethical, and epistemological writings may consult Louis J. Shein, ed. and trans., *Readings in Russian Philosophical Thought* (The Hague: Mouton, 1968). Its chronological focus is the late nineteenth and early twentieth century.

1. Withdrawal from the Orthodox faith into another Christian confession or religious teaching shall not be subject to persecution and must not involve any unfavorable consequences in relation to personal or civil rights.
. . .

3. . . . Persons registered as Orthodox, but in actuality practicing that non-Christian faith to which they themselves or their ancestors belonged before joining the Orthodox church, may be stricken from the Orthodox registers if they so desire. . . .

6. The legal enactments that confer the right to hold public religious services and de-fine the civil status of schismatics shall extend to the followers of both the Old Ritualist [or Old Believer—*staroobriadcheskii*] congregations and the sectarian doctrines. . . .

8. The erection of Old Ritualist and sectarian houses of prayer, permission to repair them, and their closing must conform with the regulations that exist or shall be enacted for temples of non-Orthodox confessions. . . .

10. These same ecclesiastics [Old Ritualist and sectarian] shall be permitted to perform religious ceremonies freely both in private homes and in houses of prayer, and in other necessary cases.

CHAPTER XVII

The Duma Monarchy
1906-1914

Note: Although the Introduction as well as the content of previous chapters have made it clear that we do not pretend to provide more than a minimal sample of sources in the sphere of foreign relations, a special comment seems warranted for the period 1906-14. On the one hand, Russia's foreign involvements in those years, especially in the Balkans, cannot be disregarded by the student of Russian domestic development, for they brought Russia into a war that proved fatal to the tsarist system. On the other hand, the story of those involvements is an integral part of one of the most voluminously documented segments of world history—the history of the events, interrelationships, human errors, and institutional machinery that led to the war of 1914—and a great many of the most important sources have already appeared in English, either in collections of treaties and other documents or in monographic studies. Any group of excerpts on Russia's foreign relations in 1906-14 that was brief enough to fit within the scope of this chapter would therefore add little to what is already available in English and could add little, if anything, to the student's understanding of the same topic as treated by a comprehensive textbook (see, for example, chapter 42 in Michael T. Florinsky's *Russia: A History and an Interpretation,* 2 vols. New York: Macmillan, 1953). Accordingly, while pursuing in this chapter our policy of emphasizing the largely untranslated sources of Russia's domestic history, we wish to reiterate our earlier warnings that for the student the sources presented here are no substitute for a standard textbook.

A. POLITICAL DEVELOPMENTS

XVII:1. THE MANIFESTO AND DECREE ON THE REFORM OF THE STATE COUNCIL, FEBRUARY 20, 1906

On February 20, 1906, a manifesto concerning changes in the establishing acts of both the State Council and the State Duma, a decree spelling out the changes to be made in the State Council, and a new establishing act for the Duma were issued. Here are excerpts from the first and second of these documents.

Reference: *PSZRI,* 3d ser., vol. 26, pt. 1, pp. 148-49, 154-55. For some of the Russian collections of documents on this period, in addition to those cited in this chapter, see the reference notes to items XVI:23 and 57.

[From the manifesto of February 20, 1906, concerning the amendment of the establishing act for the State Council and the revision of the establishing act for the State Duma:]

Elected representatives of the nobility, the zemstvos, and the clergy of the Orthodox church, which is dominant in Russia, as well as representatives of science, commerce, and industry, are invited to participate in the legislative activity of the State Council, in equal numbers with the members appointed by us. The State Council thus reorganized shall have equal rights with the State Duma in legislative affairs.

Preserving inviolate the basic principle of the Fundamental State Laws, according to which no law can become effective without our ratification, we decree henceforth as a general rule that, from the time of the convocation of the State Council and State Duma,

no law can become effective without the confirmation of the Council and the Duma.

. . .

The State Council and the State Duma may, in the manner defined in their statutes, initiate bills for the repeal or amendment of existing laws and the promulgation of new ones, with the exception of the Fundamental State Laws, whose revision we reserve for ourselves the right to initiate.

Legislative bills shall be considered by the State Duma and, upon approval, shall be sent to the State Council. Legislative bills drafted on the initiative of the State Council shall be considered in the Council and, upon approval, shall be sent to the Duma.

Legislative bills approved by the State Council and the State Duma shall be presented to us for consideration. Legislative bills not accepted by the State Council or the State Duma shall be considered rejected.

The State Council and the State Duma may, in the manner defined by their statutes, interpellate ministers and chief administrators of separate departments legally subordinated to the Governing Senate concerning actions taken by them, or by persons or agencies under their jurisdiction, that are held to be illegal.

[From the decree of February 20, 1906, concerning the revision of the establishing act for the State Council:]

1. The State Council shall be composed of members appointed by His Imperial Majesty and members elected: (a) by the clergy of the Russian Orthodox church; (b) by the guberniia zemstvo assemblies; (c) by the corporations of the nobility [*dvorianskie obshchestva*]; (d) by the Imperial Academy of Sciences and the imperial Russian universities; and (e) by the Council of Trade and Manufactures, its Moscow branch, local trade and manufacturing committees, stock exchange committees, and merchants' boards.

2. The total number of members of the State Council summoned by His Imperial Majesty from among the imperially appointed Council members must not exceed the total number of elected Council members. . . .

3. The chairman and vice-chairman of the State Council shall be appointed annually by His Imperial Majesty from among the imperially appointed members of the Council. . . .

4. The clergy of the Russian Orthodox Church shall be represented on the State Council by six members . . . chosen by the Holy Synod: three from the monastic Orthodox clergy, and three from the secular Orthodox clergy.

5. Each guberniia zemstvo assembly shall elect one member of the State Council.

6. Corporations of the nobility in those guberniias and oblasti where the nobility holds elections shall each elect two electors from their midst. A congress of these electors shall meet in Saint Petersburg and elect from its midst eighteen members of the State Council.

7. The Imperial Academy of Sciences and every imperial Russian university shall elect three electors each. The academy, in full academic assembly, shall elect these from among the full members of the academy, and the council of each university, from among its full professors. A congress of these electors shall meet in Saint Petersburg and elect, from its midst, six members of the State Council.

8. . . . A congress . . . of electors [representing commercial and industrial organizations] shall meet in Saint Petersburg and elect, from its midst, twelve members of the State Council, including six from industry and six from commerce.

9. Elected members of the State Council shall serve for terms of nine years, with one third of each category of members completing its term every three years.

[Note: In addition to the thirty-four guberniias that had zemstvo assemblies, there were twenty-six in European Russia that did not. Most of these were in the western areas. In the ten Polish guberniias, the property owners were to elect a total of six members. In the other sixteen guberniias, the property owners were to elect one member per guberniia. Hence the total of elected members was ninety-eight.]

XVII:2. NICHOLAS'S DELIBERATIONS CONCERNING THE FUNDAMENTAL STATE LAWS, APRIL 9, 1906

From April 7 to 12, 1906, at Tsarskoe Selo, Nicholas II himself presided over discussions of the draft of the Fundamental State Laws that had been prepared by the Council of Ministers. (At this time Nicholas had recently received Witte's resignation as chairman of the Council, and had selected I. L. Goremykin to succeed him.) On April 9, as these excerpts from the official record indicate, the emperor took up the question—decided three days later—whether his power should or should not still be referred to as unlimited. The point at issue was in article 4 of the new version and in article 1 of the old; hence the use of both numbers. The old article 1 declared: "The emperor of all the Russias is an autocratic and unlimited monarch [*Monarkh Samoderzhavnyi i neogranichennyi*]. That his authority be obeyed not only out of fear, but also out of conscience, God himself commands." In the draft prepared by the Council of Ministers, article 4 read: "The emperor of all the Russias possesses supreme autocratic power [*Verkhovnaia*

Samoderzhavnaia vlast']. That his authority be obeyed, not only out of fear, but also out of conscience, God himself commands."

Reference: *Protokoly zasedanii soveshchaniia . . . po peresmotru osnovnykh gosudarstvennykh zakonov* (St. Petersburg: Gosudarstvennaia Tip., 1906), pp. 28-29, 32-35, 94.

HIS IMPERIAL MAJESTY: Let us now take up article 4. It contains the most important point in this entire matter. I have not ceased thinking about this question since I first beheld the draft of the revision of the Fundamental Laws. I kept the draft for a whole month and have thought about this question constantly also since the chairman of the Council of Ministers submitted the altered draft to me. All this time I have been troubled by the doubt whether I have the right, in the face of my ancestors, to alter the limits of the power I have received from them. This conflict within me continues. I have not yet reached a final decision. One month ago it seemed easier to decide this question than it does now, after long reflection, when the moment for decision is drawing near. During all this time I have daily received scores of telegrams, letters, and petitions from all ends and corners of the Russian Land, from people of all classes. They express their touching feelings of loyalty to me, pleading with me not to limit my power and thanking me for the rights granted by the Manifesto of October 17. As I ponder the idea of these people, I feel that they wish the Manifesto of October 17, and the rights granted by it to my subjects, to be preserved, but that not one step further be taken and that I remain the autocrat of all the Russias.

I tell you most sincerely, believe me, that if I were convinced that Russia wanted me to abdicate my autocratic powers, I should gladly do it for the sake of its welfare. I issued the Manifesto of October 17 with all deliberateness, and I am firmly resolved to bring it to completion. But I am not convinced that it is necessary at the same time to abdicate my autocratic powers and to alter the definition of supreme authority [or "sovereign power"—Verkhovnaia vlast'] as contained in article 1 of the Fundamental Laws for the past 109 years. It is my conviction that, for many reasons, it is highly dangerous to change this article. . . . I know, moreover, that leaving article 1 without changes will provoke agitation and attacks. But we should consider the source whence the reproach will come. It will come, of course, from the entire so-called educated element, the proletarians, the third estate. But I am confident that 80 percent of the Russian people will be with me, will support me, and will be grateful to me for such a decision. . . .

Article 4 is the most important in the entire draft. But the question of my prerogatives is a matter for my conscience, and I shall decide whether the article should be left as it is or altered.

I. L. GOREMYKIN: Eighty percent of the population will be disturbed, and many of them will be displeased, by a limitation of the boundaries of sovereign power. . . .

· · ·

COUNT K. I. PALEN [PAHLEN]: The entire question is whether the word "unlimited" [*neogranichennyi*] is to be left in article 1 [i.e. in the old version]. I entertain no sympathies for the Manifesto of October 17, but it exists. Until that time, you possessed the unlimited right to issue laws; but since October 17, Your Majesty can no longer issue laws by yourself, without the legislative institutions. . . . The word "unlimited" cannot remain in the Fundamental Laws.

M. G. AKIMOV: There is no need to be confused by what is easily resolved. I too am not a supporter of the freedoms granted to the people. But on October 17, Your Majesty voluntarily limited yourself in the field of legislation. . . . Where legislative power does not belong fully to the emperor, the monarch is limited. To use the word "unlimited" at this time means throwing down the gauntlet and creating irreconcilable enmity in the Duma. . . . The word "unlimited" must be excluded.

· · ·

COUNT D. M. SOL'SKII: Since you have decided, Sire, to carry out the Manifesto of October 17, article 1 must be changed. . . . If you cannot bring yourself to do so, it would be best not to publish the Fundamental Laws at all.

· · ·

HIS IMPERIAL HIGHNESS, THE GRAND DUKE NIKOLAI NIKOLAEVICH: By the

Manifesto of October 17, Your Imperial Majesty has already stricken out the word "unlimited."

HIS IMPERIAL HIGHNESS, THE GRAND DUKE VLADIMIR ALEKSANDROVICH: I agree with my cousin.

P. N. DURNOVO: Half-educated and educated persons can stir up even a well-intentioned people. The entire unrest comes, not from the people, but from educated society, which must be reckoned with: the state is governed by educated society. It is important to have as many well-disposed persons as possible among the educated elements. After the manifestos of October 17 and February 20, the unlimited sovereignty of the monarch ceased to exist. . . . The word "unlimited" cannot be left to stand, since this will not correspond to the manifestos of October 17 and February 20. It will produce sedition in the minds of educated persons, and that will lead to nationwide sedition.

· · ·

HIS IMPERIAL MAJESTY: We shall now recess for fifteen minutes.

· · ·

HIS IMPERIAL MAJESTY: I shall announce my decision later. Let us now take up further questions.

· · ·

[Meeting of April 12:]

COUNT D. M. SOL'SKII: Your Imperial Majesty was pleased to postpone decision on article 4. What is your command: shall the word "unlimited" be preserved, or excluded?

HIS IMPERIAL MAJESTY: I have resolved to accept the wording of the Council of Ministers.

COUNT D. M. SOL'SKII: Consequently, the word "unlimited" is to be excluded?

HIS IMPERIAL MAJESTY: Yes, it is to be excluded.

XVII:3. THE FUNDAMENTAL STATE LAWS OF APRIL 23, 1906

On April 23, 1906, were published the Fundamental State Laws (Osnovnye Gosudarstvennye Zakony), setting forth the structure of the state in the new constitutional era (the opening of the Duma was only four days off). Here are some of the most significant articles.

Reference: *Svod Zakonov Rossiiskoi Imperii*, 3d ed., 16 vols. (St. Petersburg: Gosudarstvennaia Tip., 1857-1916), vol. 1, pt. 1, pp. 5, 6, 14-15, 17, 18-19, 20, 22, 23, 24, 26. A translation of this document is included in the recently published book of Dmytryshyn, *Imperial Russia*, pp. 317-24.

CHAPTER 1. On the nature of supreme autocratic power (articles 4-24).

[ARTICLE] 4. Supreme autocratic power belongs to the emperor of all Russia. . . .

7. The sovereign emperor exercises legislative authority jointly with the State Council and the State Duma.

8. The sovereign emperor possesses the initiative in all legislative matters. The Fundamental State Laws may be subject to revision in the State Council and the State Duma only at his initiative.

9. The sovereign emperor ratifies the laws, and no law can become valid without his ratification. . . .

13. The sovereign emperor declares war and concludes peace, as well as treaties with foreign states. . . .

CHAP. 2. On the order of succession to the throne (articles 25-39). . . .

CHAP. 3. On the majority of the sovereign emperor and the government by regency (articles 40-52). . . .

CHAP. 4. On the accession to the throne and the oath of allegiance (articles 53-56).

. . .

CHAP. 5. On the holy coronation and anointment (articles 57-58). . . .

CHAP. 6. On the title of His Imperial Majesty and the state coat of arms (articles 59-61).

59. The full title of His Imperial Majesty is as follows:

"With the help of God's grace, we, NN, emperor and autocrat of all Russia, of Moscow, Kiev, Vladimir, and Novgorod; tsar of Kazan', tsar of Astrakhan', tsar of Poland, tsar of Siberia, tsar of the Chersonesus Taurica, tsar of Georgia; sovereign of Pskov and grand prince of Smolensk, Lithuania, Volynia, Podolia, and Finland; prince of Estonia, Livonia, Courland and Semigallia, Samogitia, Bialystok, Karelia, Tver', Ugria, Perm', Viatka, Bulgaria, and others; sovereign and grand prince of the lower land of [Nizhnii] Novgorod [i.e. the Middle Volga] and Chernigov; ruler of Riazan', Polotsk, Rostov, Iaroslavl', Beloozero, Udoria, Obdoria, Kondinia, Vitebsk, Mstislavl', and all the northern lands; and sovereign of the lands of Iberia, Kartalinia, and Kabarda, and the land of Armenia; hereditary sovereign and master of the Circassian and [Caucasian] Mountain princes and others; sovereign of Turkestan; heir of Norway, duke of Schleswig-Holstein, Stormarn, Ditmarsen, and Oldenburg, etcetera, etcetera, etcetera. . . ."

CHAP. 7. On religion (articles 62-68). . . .

63. The emperor who holds the throne of all Russia cannot profess any religion save the Orthodox.

64. The emperor, as a Christian monarch, is the supreme defender and protector of the dogmas of the dominant religion and the guardian of true faith and decorum within the holy church.

65. In the administration of the church, the autocratic power acts through the intermediary of the Holy Governing Synod which it has instituted.

66. All subjects of the Russian state who do not belong to the dominant church . . . as well as foreigners . . . residing in Russia, shall everywhere be free to profess their religion, and to worship in accordance with its ritual.

67. Freedom of religion is accorded, not only to Christians of foreign denominations, but also to Jews, Mohammedans, and heathens. . . .

CHAP. 8. On the rights and duties of Russian subjects (articles 69-83). . . .

72. No one can be prosecuted for criminal offenses except in the manner prescribed by law.

73. No one can be held under arrest except in cases prescribed by law.

74. No one can be tried and punished except for criminal acts that are so defined by the criminal laws in effect at the time when such acts were committed. . . .

75. All dwellings are inviolable. No search or seizure may take place in a dwelling without the consent of the head of the household, except in cases and in a manner prescribed by law.

76. Every Russian subject has the right freely to choose his place of residence and occupation, to acquire and dispose of property, and to travel beyond the frontiers of the state without hindrance. Limitations of these rights are regulated by special laws.

77. Property is inviolable. Compulsory alienation of real property, when such is necessary for the welfare of the state or the public, is permissible only on the basis of just and adequate compensation.

78. Russian subjects have the right to organize meetings for purposes that are not in contravention to the laws, peacefully, and without weapons. . . .

79. Everyone may, within the limits prescribed by law, express his ideas orally and in writing and may also disseminate them by means of the press or by other methods.

80. Russian subjects have the right to form societies and associations for purposes that are not in contravention to the laws. . . .

CHAP. 9. On laws (articles 84-97).

84. The Russian Empire is governed on the firm foundation of laws promulgated in the prescribed manner. . . .

86. No new law may appear without the approval of the State Council and the State Duma or become effective without ratification by the sovereign emperor.

87. While the Duma is not in session, if extraordinary circumstances demand a measure requiring legislative sanction, the Council of Ministers shall submit the matter directly to the emperor. Such a measure, however, may not introduce any changes into the Fundamental State Laws, the establishing acts of the State Council or the State Duma, or the laws governing elections to the Council or the Duma. Such a measure becomes inoperative if the appropriate minister or chief administrator of a separate department does not introduce in the State Duma a legislative bill corresponding to the adopted measure within the first two months of the next Duma session, or if it is rejected by the State Duma or the State Council. . . .

CHAP. 10. On the State Council and the State Duma, and their manner of operation (articles 98-119). . . .

100. The State Council is composed of members by imperial appointment and members by election. The total number of . . . imperially appointed members should not exceed the total number of elected Council members. . . .

106. The State Council and the State Duma possess equal legislative powers.

107. The State Council and the State Duma may, in the manner prescribed in their statutes, initiate bills for the repeal or amendment of existing laws and the promulgation of new ones, with the exception of the Fundamental State Laws, the revision of which may be initiated only by the sovereign emperor.

108. The State Council and the State Duma may, in the manner prescribed in their statutes, interpellate ministers or chief administrators of separate departments legally subordinated to the Governing Senate concerning such actions taken by them, or by persons or agencies under their jurisdiction, that are held to be illegal. . . .

111. Legislative bills that are not adopted by the State Council or the State Duma shall be considered rejected. . . .

CHAP. 11. On the Council of Ministers and chief administrators of separate departments (articles 120-24). . . .

123. The chairman of the Council of Ministers, the ministers, and the chief administrators of separate departments are responsible before the sovereign emperor for the general operation of the state administration. Each of them is individually responsible for his own actions and orders.

XVII:4. KOKOVTSOV ON THE OPENING OF THE FIRST DUMA, APRIL 27, 1906

The tsar's initial meeting with the representatives of the people at the opening of the First Duma on April 27, 1906, is here described vividly by Count Vladimir Nikolaevich Kokovtsov. Born in 1853 (d. 1942), Kokovtsov had a long career of distinguished government service, culminating in almost ten years as minister of finance (beginning in 1904) and almost three as chairman of the Council of Ministers following Stolypin's assassination in 1911. This excerpt and others below are from his memoirs, which constitute an especially valuable source on the upper echelons of the government in the decade before 1914. The English version of his memoirs, while briefer than the Russian, was approved by him and may be regarded as equally authoritative.

Reference: V. N. Kokovtsov, *Iz moego proshlogo, vospominaniia, 1903-1919,* 2 vols. (Paris: Illiustrirovannaia Rossiia, 1933), 1:173; translation based on Harold H. Fisher, ed., *The Memoirs of Count Kokovtsov: Out of My Past,* trans. Laura Matveev (Palo Alto: Stanford University Press, 1935), pp. 129-30, somewhat revised. Reprint, The Hague: Mouton, 1970.

Saint George's Room, the throne room, presented a queer spectacle at this moment, and I believe its walls had never before witnessed such a sight as the crowd then gathered there. The entire right side of the room was filled with uniformed people, members of the State Council, and, farther on, the Senate and the tsar's retinue. The left side, in the literal sense of the word, was crowded with the members of the State Duma, a small number of whom had appeared in tails and frock coats, while the overwhelming majority, demonstratively occupying the first places near the throne, were dressed as if intentionally in workers' blouses and cotton shirts, and behind them was a crowd of peasants in the most varied costumes, some in national dress, and a multitude of Duma representatives from the clergy. The first place among these representatives of the people was occupied by a man of tall stature, dressed in a worker's blouse and high, oiled boots, who examined the throne and those about it with a derisive and insolent air. It was the famous Onipko, who later won great renown by his bold statements in the First Duma and who also played a prominent role in the Kronstadt insurrection. While the tsar read his speech addressed to the newly elected members of the State Duma, I could not take my eyes off Onipko, so much contempt and hate did his insolent face show. I was not the only one who was thus impressed. Near me stood P. A. Stolypin, the new minister of internal affairs, who turned to me and said: "We both seem to be engrossed in the same spectacle. I even have the feeling that this man might be carrying a bomb."

XVII:5. V. I. GURKO ON THE OPENING OF THE FIRST DUMA, APRIL 27, 1906

Here Gurko (see Item XVI:76, above), who by 1906 had attained a high position within the Ministry of Internal Affairs, describes the same scene.

Reference: Vladimir I. Gurko, *Features and Figures of the Past: Government and Opinion in the Reign of Nicholas II* (Palo Alto: Stanford University Press, 1939), p. 470.

The hostility of the majority of the First Duma toward the throne was clearly shown on the first day of its sessions. All the Duma members attended the Imperial reception in the throne room of the Winter Palace dressed in a deliberately careless fashion. Be it said, however, that there was a certain lack of tact on both sides. The court had decided that this reception was to be particularly solemn and brilliant. The Imperial regalia had been brought from Moscow, and these were to be borne by the highest officials, ranged on both sides of the throne. The throne was draped in the Imperial ermine mantle; it was said that the Tsarina herself had draped the mantle so that it would hang in artistic folds. Velvet ropes down the center of the room formed a sort of corridor through which the Imperial suite was to pass. On one side of this corridor were members of the State Duma and on the other members of the State

Council, senators, and the other higher civil and military officials. The contrast was striking. The court and the government, flourishing gold-laced uniforms and numerous decorations, was set opposite the gray, almost rustic group representing the people of Russia. Naïvely believing that the people's representatives, many of whom were peasants, would be awed by the splendor of the Imperial court, the ladies of the Imperial family had worn nearly all their jewels; they were literally covered with pearls and diamonds. But the effect was altogether different. This Oriental method of impressing upon spectators a reverence for the bearers of supreme power was quite unsuited to the occasion. What it did achieve was to set in juxtaposition the boundless Imperial luxury and the poverty of the people. The demagogues did not fail to comment upon this ominous contrast. Nor did the Tsar's address of welcome improve matters.

XVII:6. POLOVTSEV ON THE OPENING OF THE FIRST DUMA, APRIL 27, 1906

This eyewitness report of the ceremony that opened the First Duma comes from the private diary of A. A. Polovtsev, a longtime member of the State Council (see Item XVI:19, above).
Reference: "Dnevnik A. A. Polovtseva, 1905-1908 gg.," *Krasnyi arkhiv*, 4 (1923): 105-06.

[From his entry of April 27, 1906, concerning the ceremony that opened the First Duma:]

I arrive at the Winter Palace . . . and proceed to the Hermitage Pavilion where the members of the reorganized State Council are assembling. From here we are soon led through the Romanov portrait gallery to the Saint George throne room. To the right of the throne the State Council takes its position; to the left, the members of the Duma. Most of them are dressed in black frock coats; the workingmen and peasants wear jackboots and here and there grey peasant coats; a considerable minority is attired in white tie and tails. Next to the Duma members, closer to the throne, stand the senators in their scarlet uniforms. Next to the State Council stand the honorary guardians [*pochetnye opekuny*, of the Office of the Empress Maria, which maintained educational and charitable institutions], the state secretaries, and the sovereign's suite; behind it, far in the rear of the room, on a specially built platform, the diplomatic corps is seated. At 1:45 the emperor enters, preceded by the highest ranking court officials and followed by the two empresses and numerous grand dukes. As for

the grand duchesses, they pass through the inner rooms, enter by a side door at the right of the throne, and ascend the platform set up for them, where they are joined by the two empresses at the end of the Te Deum celebrated in the center of the room. The sovereign advances with slow steps and takes his seat on the throne. The imperial robe is thrown over one of the armrests of the throne; on one side stands General Roop holding the imperial sword; on the other, Count Ignat'ev holding the imperial standard. On four stools are disposed the crown, the scepter, the orb, and the seal of state. . . . As silence falls, the tsar reads the speech handed to him by the minister of the imperial court; he reads very distinctly. Immediately after the speech a military band breaks into the national anthem, "God Save the Tsar," and the right-thinking part of the assembly begins to shout "hurrah!" thus preventing Messrs. Petrunkevich, Rodichev, et al., from carrying out the intention ascribed to them of replying to the sovereign's speech. The procession slowly returns to the inner chambers. The entire ceremony was conducted and concluded with extraordinary decorum and success. To be sure, this success was assisted by the fine weather, warm and sunny, and by the great number of troops stationed in the squares and the streets surrounding the palace.

XVII:7. THE FIRST DUMA'S ADDRESS TO THE TSAR, MAY 5, 1906

At its fifth meeting, on May 5, 1906, the Duma approved (with no dissents and only eleven abstentions) a statement in reply to the tsar's address from the throne a few days earlier. The Duma's address, here given from the stenographic report of its reading before the vote, made several far-reaching demands.

Reference: Gosudarstvennaia Duma, *Stenograficheskie otchety, 1906 god, Sessiia 1*, vol. 1 (St. Petersburg, 1906), pp. 239-41.

Your Imperial Majesty!

Your Majesty was pleased, in your speech to the representatives of the people, to declare your determination to protect the unshakable institutions through which the people has been summoned to exercise legislative authority together with its monarch. The State Duma regards this solemn pledge given by the monarch to the people as a firm guarantee of the consolidation and further development of a legislative system in accord with strictly constitutional principles. The State Duma, on its part, will endeavor to perfect the principles of popular representation and will submit for Your Majesty's approval a law concerning popular representation, based, in accordance with the unanimously expressed will of the people, upon the principles of universal suffrage.

. . . The State Duma, composed of representatives of all classes and nationalities inhabiting Russia, is united in the common fervent desire to reinvigorate Russia and to create in it a government order based on the peaceful coexistence of all classes and nationalities and on the firm foundations of civil freedom.

. . .

No pacification of the country is possible until . . . all the ministers are made responsible before the people's representatives, and until the administrative apparatus on all levels of the civil service is reorganized accordingly.

. . . First of all is it necessary to free Russia from the influence of those extraordinary laws—reinforced [protection] and extraordinary protection and state of war—under cover of which there has developed a great deal of arbitrary rule by irresponsible officials.

. . . The entire people will fulfill the creative task of renewing our life with true energy and enthusiasm . . . only when it is not divided from the throne by the State Council, composed of appointed dignitaries and those elected by the upper classes; when the assessment and levying of taxes is placed under the jurisdiction of the people's representatives; and when there are no special laws to restrict the legislative competence of the people's representatives. . . .

In the field of future legislative activity, the State Duma, faithful to the duty clearly imposed upon it by the people, considers it immediately essential to provide the country with exact laws assuring inviolability of the individual, freedom of conscience, freedom of speech and of the press, freedom of association, of meetings and strikes. . . . The State Duma proceeds further from its unshakable conviction that neither freedom nor order based on law can be firmly consolidated without the establishment of the general principle of the equality of all citizens, without exception, before the law. . . . Striving toward the liberation of the country from the shackles of administrative tutelage, and placing the right to impose any restriction on the freedom of citizens solely in the hands of an independent judiciary, the State Duma, however, considers the death penalty inadmissible, even under court sentence. Capital punishment may not be imposed at any time or under any circumstances. . . .

Determination of the needs of the rural population and adoption of appropriate legislative measures will constitute the immediate task of the State Duma. The most numerous part of the country's population— the toiling peasantry—awaits impatiently the satisfaction of its acute land needs, and the first Russian State Duma would be remiss in its duty if it did not prepare a law for the satisfaction of this urgent need by drawing for this purpose upon state lands, appanage lands, cabinet lands [*kabinetskie zemli,* lands belonging to the tsar and managed by his central office or *Kabinet Ego Imperatorskogo Velichestva*], monastery lands, and church lands, as well as by the compulsory transfer of privately owned lands.

The State Duma also deems it essential to draft laws proclaiming the equality of the peasants and freeing them from the yoke of arbitrary rule and tutelage. The State Duma considers it equally urgent to satisfy the needs of the working class by means of legislative measures protecting hired labor. . . .

The State Duma will also consider it a duty to do its utmost to improve popular education and, above all, to draft and enact a law concerning universal free education.

Along with these measures, the Duma will give special attention to the equitable distribution of the tax burden, hitherto imposed unjustly upon the poorer classes of the population, and to the proper use of state funds. An equally important legislative effort will be the radical transformation of local government and self-government, drawing the whole population into equal participation in the latter, on the basis of the universal ballot.

. . .

Finally, the State Duma considers it essential also to include among its urgent tasks the problem of satisfying the long-pressing demands of individual nationalities. Russia is a state inhabited by a multitude of different tribes and nationalities. The spiritual unification of all these tribes and nationalities is possible only if the needs of each of them to preserve and develop its own unique character in various aspects of its life are met and satisfied. The State Duma will concern itself with the broad fulfillment of these just needs.

. . . The first word spoken within the walls of the State Duma, and greeted with cries of approval on the part of the entire Duma, was the word "amnesty." The country longs for an amnesty applied to all actions, as defined in the criminal law, that were prompted by religious or political causes, as well as to all agrarian offenses. There are demands of the popular conscience that cannot be denied and that must be fulfilled without delay. Sire, the Duma awaits from you a full political amnesty, as the first token of mutual understanding and mutual harmony between the tsar and the people.

XVII:8. THE GOVERNMENT'S ANSWER TO THE DUMA, MAY 13, 1906

The Duma's demands of May 5, 1906, brought the chairman of the Council of Ministers, Ivan Logginovich Goremykin (1839-1917), to the Duma meeting of May 13, 1906, with this sober reply.

Reference: Gosudarstvennaia Duma, *Stenograficheskie otchety, 1906 god, Sessiia 1,* 1:321-23.

The Council of Ministers approaches with particular attention the questions raised by the State Duma concerning the immediate satisfaction of the urgent needs of the rural population and the promulgation of a law proclaiming the peasants equal to persons of other classes, the satisfaction of the needs of the working class, the drafting of a law concerning universal elementary education, the study of possible methods by which the wealthier strata of the population may be made to carry more of the tax burdens, and the reorganization of local government and self-government, with consideration for the special characteristics of outlying regions.

Equally important, in the opinion of the Council of Ministers, is the question, mentioned by the State Duma, of promulgating a new law guaranteeing the inviolability of

the individual and freedom of conscience, speech, and the press, assembly and association, in place of the temporary provisions that are currently in effect. . . . The Council of Ministers deems it necessary, however, to specify that in carrying out this legislative work it is important to arm the administrative authorities with effective methods so that, even under the laws designed for the peaceful course of civil life, the government may be able to prevent abuses of the freedoms thus granted and to counteract encroachments that endanger society and the state.

As for the proposal of the State Duma that the peasant land question be solved by drawing upon appanage lands, cabinet lands, monastery lands, and church lands and by compulsorily transferring private lands— among which are the lands of peasant owners, acquired by purchase—the Council of Ministers deems it necessary to state that the solution of this question on the basis proposed by the State Duma is absolutely inadmissible. The government cannot recognize the right of some people to ownership of land and at the same time deprive others of this right. Nor can it deny generally the right of private property in land, without simultaneously denying the right to ownership of every other type of property. The principle of inalienability and inviolability of property is, throughout the world and at every level of civic development, the cornerstone of the people's welfare and of social development, the fundamental bulwark of civic life, without which the very existence of the state is unthinkable. Nor is the proposed measure called for by the essential facts. With the wide and far-from-exhausted means at the command of the state, and with the broad employment of all available legal methods, the land question can without doubt be successfully solved without disintegrating the very foundations of our statehood and undermining the vital forces of our fatherland.

The rest of the legislative proposals con-

tained in the address of the State Duma are: the establishment of the responsibility of ministers having the confidence of the Duma majority to the people's representatives; the abolition of the State Council; and the elimination of the restrictions that certain special laws impose upon the legislative activity of the State Duma. The Council of Ministers does not feel that it has the right to dwell on these proposals; they involve a radical alteration of fundamental state laws, which are not subject to revision at the initiative of the State Duma.

. . .

Pardon of those condemned by a court, whatever the nature of the crimes committed, is the prerogative of the supreme authority, which alone can decide whether imperial mercy for those who have fallen into criminal ways is in accord with the general welfare. The Council of Ministers, for its part, feels that such welfare would not be served, during the present troubled times, by pardoning criminals who participated in murders, robberies, and violence.

XVII:9. THE DUMA'S REPLY, MAY 13, 1906

Having heard Goremykin's declaration of May 13, 1906, the Duma on that same day endorsed—with only eleven negative votes—the following resolution.

Reference: Gosudarstvennaia Duma, *Stenograficheskie otchety, 1906 god, Sessiia 1,* 1:353.

Finding in the statement of the chairman of the Council of Ministers a decisive indication that the government has no wish whatsoever to meet the people's demands and expectations in regard to land, rights, and freedom, which were outlined by the State Duma in its answering address to the speech from the throne, and without the satisfaction of which tranquillity in the land and fruitful work by the people's representatives are impossible;

Finding that, by its refusal to satisfy the people's demands, the government reveals manifest contempt for the true interests of the people and obvious unwillingness to forestall new upheavals in our country, ex-

hausted by poverty, lawlessness, and the continued irresponsible reign of arbitrary officials;

Expressing before the face of the country complete lack of confidence in the ministry, which is not responsible to the people's representatives;

And regarding the immediate resignation of the present ministry and its replacement by a ministry that will enjoy the confidence of the State Duma as the most essential condition for the pacification of the state and for fruitful work by the people's representatives;

The State Duma now undertakes consideration of current business.

XVII:10. THE MANIFESTO ON THE DISSOLUTION OF THE DUMA, JULY 9, 1906

As the conflict between the First Duma and the ministry of Goremykin over the land question grew sharper, the peasants became increasingly rebellious. The government sought to dampen radical hopes by rejecting publicly on June 20 the principle of the compulsory transfer of private lands. The Duma in its turn, addressing the populace directly, urged that that principle be insisted upon. The government thereupon dissolved the First Duma on July 8 and issued next day a manifesto that contained this explanation of the government's position.

Reference: *PSZRI*, 3d ser., vol. 26, pt. 1, pp. 738-39.

Instead of legislative work, the people's elected representatives have digressed into an area outside their competence, undertaking to investigate the actions of the local authorities appointed by us, to point out to us faults in the Fundamental Laws, which may be changed only at the instance of our sovereign will, and engaging in such clearly illegal actions as an appeal to the people in the name of the Duma.

Stirred up by such improper actions and expecting no legal improvement in its condition, the peasantry has turned, in a number of guberniias, to open looting, appropriation of other people's property, and disobedience of the law and of legal authorities.

But let our subjects remember that lasting improvement in the life of the people is possible only under conditions of complete order and tranquillity. Let it be known that we shall not tolerate any insubordination or lawlessness and shall employ every power of the state to bring those who disobey the law to submission to our imperial will. We call upon all men of good will in Russia to unite for the support of the legal government and the restoration of peace in our beloved fatherland.

May tranquillity return to the Russian land, and may the Almighty help us to accomplish the most important of our imperial labors— the improvement of the welfare of the peasantry. Our will to this end is unshakable, and the tiller of the Russian soil shall be given a legal and honest means of enlarging his landholdings, without detriment to other people's property, wherever there is a shortage of land.

. . .

Loyal sons of Russia!

Your tsar calls to you, as a father to his children, to rally with him in the cause of renewing and reviving our holy homeland.

We believe that valiant men of thought and action will come forth and by their selfless labors will bring shining glory to the Russian land.

XVII:11. THE VYBORG MANIFESTO, JULY 10, 1906

The First Duma having been dissolved by the government, about 180 Duma members on July 9 went by train a few miles north of Saint Petersburg to Vyborg, in the autonomous Duchy of Finland. There they adopted on July 10 this manifesto—for which most of them later (1908) had to pay by spending three months in jail and thereby becoming ineligible for membership in future dumas.

Reference: *Pravo*, no. 51 (Dec. 23, 1907), col. 3316. On the Vyborg Conference, see *Krasnyi arkhiv*, 57 (1933): 85-99.

To the people, from the people's representatives.

Citizens throughout Russia! The decree of July 8 dissolved the State Duma. When you elected us your representatives, you entrusted us with the task of securing land and freedom. Fulfilling your charge and our duty, we drafted laws to assure the people's freedom and demanded the removal of irresponsible ministers who suppressed freedom with impunity, in violation of the laws. But above all we wished to promulgate a law concerning the allotment of land to the working peasantry by drawing for this purpose on state lands, appanage lands, cabinet lands, monastery lands, and church lands, and by the compulsory alienation of privately owned lands. The government declared such a law inadmissible and replied to the Duma's insistent reaffirmation of its resolution concerning compulsory alienation by dismissing the people's representatives. . . .

Citizens, stand firmly for the trampled rights of the people's representatives, stand firmly for the State Duma. Russia must not remain a single day without popular representatives. We have the means of achieving this: The government has no right either to collect taxes from the people or to mobilize men for military duty without the consent of the people's representatives. Now, therefore, when the government has dismissed the State Duma, you have the right not to give it either soldiers or money. And if, in order to obtain funds, the government begins to resort to borrowing, then such loans, made without the consent of the people's representatives, are henceforth invalid, and the Russian people will never recognize them or repay them. And so, until the convocation of the people's representatives, do not give a single copeck to the treasury or a single soldier to the army. Be firm in your refusal. Defend your rights like a single man. No force can

prevail before the united and unbending will
of the people. Citizens, in this forced and

unavoidable struggle your elected representatives will be with you.

XVII:12. MILIUKOV ON THE DUMA, MAY 10, 1906

Miliukov (see Item XVI:46, above) expressed these views in an article entitled "The Duma's
Principal Task and the Extremist Parties," in *Rech'*, May 10, 1906.

Reference: P. N. Miliukov, *God bor'by, 1905-1906* (St. Petersburg: Obshchestvennaia Pol'za,
1907), pp. 348-49, quoting *Rech'*, no. 69, May 10, 1906, in the article "Glavnoe delo Dumy i
krainie partii."

An attempt is being made in advance from
two directions to undermine the cause of
popular representation. To the advocates of a
revolution from above, popular representation
appears to be as much of a hindrance as it
does to the advocates of a revolution from
below. We are once more told again and
again that when the "black" and the "red"
are engaged in a life-and-death struggle there
is no room for intermediate shades between
them. . . . Our extreme leftists are repeating
all the tactical mistakes that have just been
condemned by the more reasonable and
enlightened of their own comrades. . . .

The viewpoint of our extreme leftists is
based on the rejection, as a matter of principle,
of parliamentary methods of struggle. In re-
fusing to adapt their tactics to the new opportunities and possibilities that are created
by new forms of public life, they are, in essence, trying to keep the revolutionary movement in its earlier, "conspiratorial" stage.
And, in protesting against "parliamentary
illusions," they are reestablishing archaic
revolutionary illusions. The essence of these
"revolutionary illusions" has always consisted
in the belief that a victorious revolution can
be organized by conspiratorial means. It is
superfluous to point out that, as a matter of
principle, such "Blanquist" tactics have long
been condemned by the theoreticians of the

extremist parties themselves. As for their
practical application, they can at best bring
about the paroxysms of an "elemental" mass
movement, which cannot be predicted or controlled by the leaders of the "conspirators."

. . .

Single combat between the revolutionaries
and the government is hopeless and utopian if
it sets itself the goal of immediate victory for
the revolution. But it is inevitable and socially
useful if there are no other ways and means
of struggle. The difficulty in the position of
parliamentary parties in a time like ours lies
in the fact that, while we urge the extremist
parties to adopt parliamentary forms of struggle, we ourselves cannot feel that these forms
have yet been fully mastered by Russian life.
To the extent that the parliamentary forms of
struggle prove to be inadequate or precarious,
a return to the old forms is inevitable. The
Party of National Freedom [Partiia Narodnoi
Svobody, another name for the Kadets] has
been and is reproached for having an ambigu-
ous position toward the revolution and revolutionaries. There is no ambiguity here: the party
has always made its stand on this question entirely clear. But, undoubtedly, there is a certain lack of clarity in the situation itself, re-
flecting as it does all the confusions and contradictions of a transitional period.

XVII:13. V. A. MAKLAKOV ON THE FIRST DUMA, 1906

Vasilii (not to be confused with Nikolai) Alekseevich Maklakov, born in 1870, was a Moscow
lawyer and political figure—a member of the Central Committee of the Constitutional Democratic Party and a member of the Second, Third, and Fourth Dumas. Under the Provisional
Government he served as commissar of the Ministry of Justice and as Russian ambassador to
France. In emigration (where he lived until 1957) he wrote several significant volumes of reminiscences fortified by extensive study and reflection. These passages are from his volume on the
First Duma.

Reference: Vasilii A. Maklakov, *Pervaia Gosudarstvennaia Duma: Vospominaniia sovremennika* (Paris: Dom Knigi, 1939), pp. 13-14, 138, 145, 148, 239. Since this translation was
prepared there has appeared a translation of Maklakov's whole book by Mary Belkin (Bloomington: Indiana University Press, 1964).

[After October 17, 1905] the liberals needed but to recognize that, with the proclamation of a constitution, their former *irreconcilable* attitude toward the government had lost its raison d'etre, that an understanding had become possible and necessary, and that it [the understanding] should have been given an honest trial on the basis of the constitution that had been granted.

But liberalism, as represented by the Kadets, set itself a different task. It did not want an understanding with the government. It sought immediate and full victory over it, demanded its capitulation, and accomplished only this: that the government accepted the challenge, took the offensive, and conquered Kadet liberalism.

· · ·

The [First] Duma did not avoid work. But the Duma was even more fond of striking effects and grandiloquent phrases, even if they were detrimental to the results of its work. The ideal of the Duma leaders was not a working parliament, laboring over positive legislation, but the *Assemblée Nationale* of 1789, casting "principles" into the world. But this Assemblée Nationale had the historical mission of carrying out a revolution, not of peacefully reorganizing a state.

· · ·

On the eve of the convocation of the Duma, political leaders said openly that, in order for the inevitable conflict between the Duma and the monarch to have a successful outcome, it was necessary to provoke a conflict over the *land* question, which *alone* agitated the peasants. Thus the Kadet agrarian bill was inspired not by concern for the welfare of the peasants but by "politics," by the struggle, first for a constitution, and then only for this particular Duma. In *this respect* it played into the hands of *revolution*, rather than *pacification*. As always, the Kadets were straddling the fence: they both stirred up revolutionary sentiments and offered measures for their pacification.

There was another, no less harmful side to such "politics." By their agrarian reform bill, the Kadets opened a gulf between themselves and the nonrevolutionary liberal parties. Indeed, the agrarian bill would have resulted in the abolition of the landowner class. Even without that, this class was dwindling rapidly. The land was naturally passing from the land-owners to the peasants. This trend was inevitable and therefore on the whole healthy. It would have been sufficient to *assist* this process, instead of fighting it. Encouraging the transfer of land into the hands of peasants, accelerating this by the pressures of progressive taxation on land, putting an end to illegal privileges for landowners' mortgaged lands, and so forth—all this would have been sufficient to accelerate the transfer of landowners' holdings to those who could use the land, who would not have allowed it to lie idle. This would have been a natural and therefore beneficial process.

· · ·

It was absurd . . . in Russia . . . to speak of acute land shortage. Russia still possessed vast, untapped reserves of land. Resettlement and internal colonization of these lands should have been encouraged. The much simpler alternative of seizing the neighboring landowners' holdings and destroying advanced agricultural enterprises would have been a turning aside from *this* policy.

· · ·

The consolidation of the victory of 1905 demanded the joint efforts of idealists and practical men, of sensible proponents of the *new* and the best representatives of the *old* order.

But the "real political figures" did not want to yield their primary role. Compromises and gradual steps seemed to them a "lowering of the flag." They wanted *everything* and *immediately*. Of course, the ideal of liberalism in 1906, i.e. a "constitutional monarchy," was entirely attainable; however, it could not be realized in full at once. It was impossible without a transitional period to confer on Russia a "four-tailed" [*4-khvostka,* a formula to indicate universal, equal, direct, and secret suffrage] single chamber and a ministry that was responsible to it, regardless of the extent to which the country was ready for them.

The intolerance of the doctrinaires expressed itself most sharply in questions bearing on "theoretical statements" and "principles." These were the main baggage of the theoreticians. A concession in *this* area [i.e. in theoretical principles] was regarded as treason. From this resulted the unreal and harmful attitude of the Kadet "politicians" toward the position of the monarchy in Russia.

According to the ideology of the "theoreticians," the basis of state authority was "the sovereignty of the people" [*narodovlastie*]. But this was understood, as is customary in infancy, in a *simplified* scheme as sovereignty in popular *representation*. The monarchy was regarded as a no longer necessary vestige of retarded political customs. Therefore, only the *Constituent Assembly* had the right to frame a constitution. Witte as early as 1905 was told this in the name of the Bureau of Zemstvo Congresses.

XVII:14. A CONTEMPORARY ACCOUNT OF THE ATTEMPT TO MURDER STOLYPIN, AUGUST 12, 1906

The journal *Pravo* published on August 20, 1906, this account of the terrorists' attempt to assassinate P. A. Stolypin a few days earlier.
     Reference: *Pravo*, no. 33 (Aug. 20, 1906), cols. 2659-60.

An attempt has been made in Saint Petersburg on the life of Prime Minister P. A. Stolypin. The details are as follows. On August 12, at 3:15 P.M., while the chairman of the Council of Ministers was receiving visitors, a landau drove up to his country house near the Botanical Gardens. In the landau were three men, two of them in officers' uniforms. . . . They tried to force their way from the entrance hall into the reception room, where there were numerous visitors awaiting their audience and also the entire official staff of the chairman of the Council of Ministers. During the ensuing scuffle with the servants, one of the plotters, wearing an officer's uniform most nearly resembling that of the gendarmerie, dropped a bomb which exploded immediately with terrible force. The blast wrecked the entrance hall where the bomb was dropped, the adjoining orderly room, and part of the reception room beyond it; it also demolished the porch, brought down the second-story balcony, and caused the collapse of the wooden walls of the first and second stories facing the garden. The tremendous force of the explosion shook the entire building. The minister, who was receiving visitors in his office, was unharmed. His son and daughter, who were on the second-story balcony, were injured. . . . According to preliminary estimates, twenty-five persons were killed. . . . Twenty-five persons were injured.

XVII:15. V. I. GURKO ON STOLYPIN IN 1906

Another excerpt from the postrevolutionary memoirs of V. I. Gurko (see Item XVI:76, above) is presented here.
     Reference: Gurko, *Features and Figures of the Past*, pp. 494, 498.

Although the Emperor dreamed only of reducing as far as possible all liberties granted the people, Stolypin was of an entirely different opinion. He had set himself the task of reconciling public and government. He believed steadfastly that even the most malevolent representatives of the public were opposed to the government because of its continuation of certain out-of-date practices of the past. He was thoroughly convinced that as soon as the government proved its sincere desire to heed the voice of the people by effecting certain liberal reforms and by repealing certain regulations which caused the most exasperation, the opposition would be disarmed and public sympathy would be his. In particular, he believed that the government would have to make certain important concessions to the Duma's demands concerning the land question.

. . .

[After the explosion in Stolypin's house on Aptekarskii Island, on August 12, 1906:] Stolypin's courage was equal to the occasion. He himself carried his son from under the debris. In spite of the shock of the whole affair he maintained his composure. . . . A falling inkpot had smeared Stolypin's neck and the back of his head.

     Kokovtsov arrived soon after I did. How vividly I recall the scene that followed. In a tiny washroom that faced the garden Stolypin was trying to remove the ink from his neck. Kokovtsov was standing on one side of him, I on the other. Wet and with water streaming from him, Stolypin exclaimed with animation: "This shall not alter our program. We shall continue to carry out our reforms. They are Russia's salvation." Nor was this by any means a pose, for Stolypin was at that period of his ministry in the first flush of creative effort and sincerely devoted to the idea of reform.

XVII:16. THE DECREE ON FIELD COURTS-MARTIAL, AUGUST 19, 1906

After the First Duma was dissolved the sharp increase in revolutionary disturbances, including the attempted assassination of Stolypin, prompted the government to respond on August 19 with this decree. During the eight-month period until these courts were discontinued (April 20, 1907), their sentences led to the execution of 683 persons. Revolutionary violence during the year 1906 is estimated to have killed 768 and wounded 820. (See Item XVI:66, above.)

Reference: *PSZRI*, 3d ser., vol. 26, pt. 1, p. 814.

I. In accordance with article 87 of the Fundamental State Laws, edition of 1906, it is decreed that: in areas placed under martial law or under a state of extraordinary protection [*polozhenie chrezvychainoi okhrany*], the governors general, chief administrators [*glavnonachal'stvuiushchie*], or persons invested with their authority, may, in cases when a crime committed by a civilian is so clear as to require no investigation, turn over the accused to a field court-martial [*voenno-polevoi sud*], subject to punishment according to wartime laws, for trial under the following rules:

1. A field court-martial is instituted, at the demand of the governor general . . . and at a place he designates, by the commanders of garrisons or detachments and the chief commanders and commanders of ports, according to jurisdiction, to consist of a chairman and four members, from among officers of the army or navy. . . .

3. The court proceeds immediately to examine the case, and completes this work within no longer than two days.

4. The case is tried behind closed doors. . . .

5. The sentence pronounced by the court takes immediate legal effect and shall be executed, at the order of the military authorities, without delay, and in any event not later than within twenty-four hours.

XVII:17. STOLYPIN'S STATEMENTS OF POLICY, JULY-AUGUST 1906

The slogan "First pacification, then reforms," quite erroneously attributed to Stolypin, expresses rather the view of those rightist and court circles whose influence Stolypin energetically combatted. The following two documents—Stolypin's telegram of July 11, 1906, to the governors, and his government's communiqué of August 24, 1906—show his strategy in the multifront campaign ahead.

Reference: *Pravo*, no. 28 (July 16, 1906), col. 2373; no. 34 (Aug. 27, 1906), cols. 2697-2701. The translation was contributed by Christopher Becker.

[Telegram of July 11, 1906, from Stolypin, then chairman of the Council of Ministers and minister of internal affairs, to the governors general, governors, and other territorial officials throughout the empire:]

In accordance with instructions received from His Majesty the emperor, I hereby inform you, with a view to coordinating completely the actions of the local authorities, that you are requested to furnish the most decisive and unwavering leadership to the organs of government subordinate to you in swiftly, firmly, and unflinchingly effecting the restoration of order. Overt disorders must be assiduously repressed. Revolutionary plots must be forestalled by every legitimate means. At the same time, the measures undertaken must be marked by the most careful planning. We are struggling not against society but against the enemies of society. For this reason sweeping repressions cannot be approved. Irregular and incautious actions which create animosity instead of restoring calm will not be tolerated. His Majesty's intentions are immutable. The administration, therefore, is imbued with the firm intention of carrying out, in legitimate fashion, the abolition and replacement of those laws which are outdated and no longer achieve their ends. The old system will be renovated. Order, however, must be fully maintained. To achieve this you must manifest your own initiative, and the responsibility for this rests upon you. A strong and firm authority acting in the manner indicated above will undoubtedly find support in the better part of society.

[Government communiqué of August 24, 1906:]

In the last two years the revolutionary movement has manifested itself with extreme intensity. Since this spring it has increased extraordinarily. Hardly a day goes by without some new crime. Mutinies at Sevastopol', at Sveaborg, in Revel' harbor and in Kronstadt, murders of government and police officials, attacks and robberies follow one after the other. In the course of this summer alone, the following high government officials were killed: the commander of the Black Sea Fleet, Chukhnin; the governor of Samara, Blok; the acting governor general of Warsaw, General of Cavalry Vonliarliarskii; the police assistant of the governor general of Warsaw, General Markgrafskii; and the commander of the Semenovskii Guards regiment, Major General Min. Independently of this, a number of outrageous attempts, accompanied by numerous deaths, have been made upon the lives of high officials, such as the attempt in Sevastopol' on the fortress commander, Nepliuev, and that on the chairman of the Council of Ministers [Stolypin], on Aptekarskii Island. Lastly, the police force suffers an enormous loss in dead and wounded every day.

· · ·

After the dissolution of the State Duma, the speedy suppression of the Kronstadt and Sveaborg mutinies, the failure of the projected general strike, and the initiation of decisive measures against the agrarian disorders, the revolutionary extremists, hoping to counteract the impression made by the failure of their plots and to impede the constructive labors of the government, decided to make an impression on the country and to create panic in government circles by means of the extermination of high state officials.

· · ·

But it would be a great mistake to believe the protection of the state from criminal attacks to be the sole task of the state authority, forgetting the profound causes that have given birth to such monstrous manifestations.

The government cannot, as some groups in society demand of it, call a halt to all reforms, call a halt to the entire life of the country, and direct the entire power of the state toward the struggle with sedition, concentrating on the symptoms of the evil without penetrating to its essence. Nor would the circumstances and the interests of Russia be served by the other solution proposed by the opponents of the first opinion: to concentrate exclusively on the realization of liberating reforms, in the belief that in this case sedition will cease of itself, having lost its whole meaning. This latter opinion is inacceptable if for no other reason than that the revolution is fighting, not for reforms, which the government also considers it its duty to enact, but rather to achieve the destruction of the political order itself, the destruction of the monarchy and the introduction of a socialistic system. Hence it is clear what the path of the government must be: to preserve order and, by decisive measures, to protect the population from revolutionary disturbances, while, at the same time, it employs all its political power to follow a constructive path, so as to reestablish an abiding order of things founded on legitimacy and a genuine, intelligently conceived liberty.

· · ·

At present the government is at work on a whole series of problems of the greatest political importance. The most important of these are the following:

1. Freedom of conscience.

2. The inviolability of the individual and civil equality, in the sense of the removal of the limitations and checks placed on separate groups of the population.

3. The improvement of peasant land tenure.

4. The improvement of the way of life of the workers and, in particular, their state insurance.

5. The reform of local administration, which it is proposed to organize in such a fashion that the guberniia and uezd administrative institutions should be placed in immediate contact with reformed organs of self-government, the latter to include also the small zemstvo unit.

6. The introduction of zemstvo self-government into the Baltic region and also into

the northern and southwestern regions.

7. The introduction of zemstvo and town self-government into the guberniias of the Kingdom of Poland.

8. The reform of the local courts.

9. The reform of secondary and higher education.

10. An income tax.

11. A reform of the police, directed, in part, toward a merger of the general police force with the gendarmerie.

12. Means for the special protection of the political order and of the public tranquillity, with the uniting of the various kinds of special protection now used into a single law.

Finally, along with this the preparatory labors are continuing for the approaching summons, by imperial command, to an all-Russian church council.

XVII:18. STOLYPIN IN THE SECOND DUMA, MARCH 6, 1907

In the Second Duma's historic session in the afternoon of March 6, 1907, Stolypin set forth his ministry's program of reform—a program that was sharply attacked by leftist deputies. Here are excerpts from Stolypin's statement, Tsereteli's criticism, and Stolypin's reply. The assembly, in which leftists were numerous, turned to the next item on the agenda without taking any formal position on Stolypin's program. (For more on Stolypin's program, see Items XVII:28-33.)

Reference: Gosudarstvennaia Duma, vtoroi sozyv, *Stenograficheskie otchety, 1907 god,* vol. 1 (St. Petersburg, 1907), cols. 108-19 [Stolypin], 122-29 [Tsereteli], 168-69 [Stolypin]. Translation contributed by Christopher Becker.

THE CHAIRMAN OF THE COUNCIL OF MINISTERS [Stolypin]: I must bring up the matter of those laws which, in view of their exceptional importance and urgency, were promulgated by the procedure provided in article 87 of the Fundamental Laws, and which are likewise subject to consideration by the State Duma and [State] Council.

. . .

With the aim of giving peasants the opportunity to withdraw from the commune, a law has been issued that simplifies the transfer to [hereditary] homestead and consolidated plot tenure. In this matter all coercion has been avoided; only the forcible attachment of the peasant to the commune is removed; the subjection of the individual, incompatible with the idea of the freedom of man and of human labor, is abolished.

. . .

With the aim of putting into effect the imperial decrees confirming the principles of religious tolerance and freedom of conscience, the ministry is placing before the State Duma and Council a group of legislative bills regulating changes of confession, freedom of worship, the erection of houses of prayer, the organization of church congregations, the removal of restrictions based solely on religion, and so forth.

Turning now to the inviolability of persons, the State Duma will find in the bills proposed by the ministry those guarantees that are customary in all states governed by a rule of law. Personal arrest, search, and the opening of correspondence are to be permitted only upon warrant by the proper judicial authority, which shall also be responsible for examining, within a twenty-four-hour period, the legal grounds for arrests made by order of the police.

. . .

The ministry has had to undertake a reform of zemstvo and municipal self-government, a reform of the guberniia, uezd, and district [*uchastkovoe*] administrations, and a police reform.

. . .

A close connection exists between local administrative reform and court reform. When the office of land captain and the volost' courts are abolished, it will be necessary to create a local court that is accessible, inexpensive, speedy, and close to the population. In accordance with these considerations, the Ministry of Justice is placing before the State Duma a bill for the reform of the local courts, concentrating judicial authority in local matters in the hands of justices of the peace elected by the population from its midst.

. . .

The Chief Administration [of Land Organization and Cultivation] has set itself the goal of increasing the acreage of peasant landholding, and of improving the organization of landholding through agronomy.

. . .

The Chief Administration proposes, as a means of eliminating the severe land shortage, the preferential sale of land to farmers at a price commensurate with the value of the land and with the buying power of the purchaser. To this end the government, by the terms of the decrees of August 12 and 27, 1906, has at its disposal nine million desiatinas, as well as over two million desiatinas bought by the Peasant [Land] Bank since November 3, 1905. But in order for the project of increasing peasant landholdings to succeed, it must be coordinated with the improvement of techniques of cultivation; for this purpose various incentives and, most important of all, measures of credit must be offered. The Chief Administration intends to pursue this goal by developing and organizing a large-scale system of credit for land purchases, agricultural improvements, and peasant resettlement.

. . .

The reform of labor legislation must be undertaken with two goals in mind: to render the worker positive aid, and to limit administrative interference in the relations between industrialists and workers, while allowing each the necessary freedom of action through the mediation of trade unions and by letting economic strikes go unpunished.

The main task involved in rendering positive aid to the worker is that of state provision for incapacitated workers, which can be accomplished by insuring them against sickness, mutilation, disablement, and old age. Connected with this is a bill for the organization of medical aid for workers.

With the aim of protecting the life and health of the younger generation of workers, the present rules governing the labor of children and adolescents should be reexamined, and night and underground labor should be forbidden for both them and women. In connection with this we propose to shorten the maximum working day for adult workers, as established by the law of June 2, 1897.

. . .

An educational reform on all levels of schooling is being planned by the Ministry of Education, on the principle of an uninterrupted chain of primary, secondary, and higher schools, with provision made for a self-contained curriculum on each educational level. The Ministry of Education shall make a special effort to prepare instructors for all school levels, and to improve their financial position.

Further, the Ministry of Education regards its most immediate task to be the establishment, by the combined efforts of the government and society, of a system of primary education that shall be first accessible and in time compulsory for the entire population of the empire.

. . .

The Ministry of Finance has been guided to the extent possible by the aims of establishing proportional taxation and of exempting the great masses of the unpropertied populace from any additional tax burdens. The bill proposed by the Ministry of Finance, by introducing an income tax, will correct to a certain extent the inequity of our tax system.

. . .

TSERETELI (Kutais guberniia) [Social Democrat]: . . . All . . . the efforts of the government between the [First and Second] Dumas are but the last desperate attempts of the bureaucracy, with its serf-owning mentality, to halt a historical development which has irrevocably condemned a regime founded on the oppression and enslavement of all of Russia. Tossing us a few scraps of reforms, long ago outdated by life and incapable of satisfying anyone, the government is attempting by means of unheard-of repressions to smother every sign of life in the country.

. . .

The people, in electing this Duma, have already made their decision. Hatred of the government broke through the thousand obstacles erected to block the will of the people at the elections. Now everyone can perceive this sovereign will; but we, the representatives of the people, cannot carry it out without the aid of the people themselves. And so now when the people, having been able to express their political will, are gathering strength to put it into practice, the servants of the people must direct all their energies, all their intellectual efforts toward the end of uniting the people. (*Voices from the Right:* "That's enough, that's enough. . . .") For only with the direct support of the people will it be possible to check the savage debauch of the tyrants who ravage the country. You will remember, representatives of the people, how ten months ago the deputy Nabokov, from the height of the Duma tribunal, basing himself on indisputable law, addressed the government with the words: "Let the executive power be subordinated to the legislative power." Two months later the executive power, supported by bayonets, disbanded the legislative power. As long as the organized force of the government is not opposed by the organized force of the people, the executive power will not yield, will not retreat, will not submit to the legislative power.

. . .

The Social-Democratic faction of the State Duma declares that it expects nothing from the government of an autocratic bureaucracy; it remembers that the last Duma could not carry its struggle with the government to victory because it did not have time to create a close bond with the people; it knows that the present Duma is equally incapable of breaking the resistance of the bureaucracy by mere votes of nonconfidence, that the Duma has yet to become a force capable of serving as the powerful weapon of national liberation; it places all its hopes on the awakening of the people themselves, for the people alone can put an end to the reign of arbitrary despotism.

. . .

THE CHAIRMAN OF THE COUNCIL OF MINISTERS, STOLYPIN: . . . It must be remembered that at the time when, a few miles away from the capital and from the imperial residence, Kronstadt stood in mutiny, when treason burst forth in Sveaborg, when the Baltic region was ablaze, when the wave of revolution flowed through Poland and the Caucasus, when all activity had ceased in the southern industrial region, when peasant disorders were spreading, when fear and terror had begun to reign, the government was then forced either to abdicate and make way for revolution, to forget that its authority is the guardian of the statehood and the integrity of the Russian nation, or to act and defend its trust. . . . I find myself forced to declare—and I wish that my declaration could be heard far beyond the walls of this assembly—that here, by the monarchical will, there are neither judges nor accused, and that this is the government bench and not a prisoner's dock. . . . These attacks are calculated to create a paralysis of will and thought in the government, among those in authority. They can all be reduced to two words, addressed to those in authority: "Hands up." To these two words, gentlemen, the government, with complete calm and with assurance that it is in the right, can answer very simply: "You will not frighten us."

XVII:19. THE MANIFESTO CONCERNING THE DISSOLUTION OF THE SECOND DUMA, JUNE 3, 1907

The decree dissolving the Second Duma, June 3, 1907, was accompanied by Nicholas's manifesto of the same date, containing these words of explanation.
Reference: *PSZRI,* 3d ser., 27:319-20.

To our sorrow, a substantial portion of the representatives to the Second Duma has not justified our expectations. Many of the delegates sent by the people approached their work, not with sincerity, not with a desire to strengthen Russia and to improve its organization, but with an obvious desire to increase sedition and to further the disintegration of the state.

The activity of these persons in the State Duma has been an insuperable obstacle to fruitful work. A spirit of hostility has been brought into the Duma itself, preventing a sufficient number of its members, desirous of working for the good of their native land, to unite for such work.

For this reason, the Duma either failed entirely to consider the broad measures drafted by our government, or delayed their discussion, or rejected them, not hesitating even to reject laws punishing the overt praising of crimes and particularly punishing the sowers of discord among the troops. Avoiding the censure of murders and violence, the State Duma did not render moral support to the government in the matter of establishing order, and Russia continues to endure the ignominy of criminally evil times.

The State Duma's sluggish discussion of the state budget rendered difficult the prompt satisfaction of many of the people's urgent needs.

A substantial portion of the Duma turned the right to interrogate the government into a way of struggling with the government, and of fomenting distrust of the government among wide sections of the population.

Finally, there took place an action unprecedented in the annals of history. Judicial authorities discovered a conspiracy by an entire section of the State Duma against the state and the authority of the tsar. When our government demanded a temporary suspension, until the completion of their trial, of the fifty-five Duma members accused of this crime, and the imprisonment of the most culpable, the State Duma did not fulfill immediately the legitimate demand of the authorities, a demand that admitted of no delay.

All this has prompted us to dissolve the Second State Duma by a decree issued to the Governing Senate on June 3, setting November 1, 1907, as the date for the convocation of a new Duma.

However, having faith in our people's love for their native land and in their political sense, we have discovered that the reason for the twice-repeated failure in the activity of the State Duma is that, because of the novelty of this business and the imperfections in the electoral law, this legislative body was filled with members who were not true spokesmen for the needs and aspirations of the people.

Hence, while leaving in force all the rights granted to our subjects by our manifesto of October 17, 1905, and by the Fundamental Laws, we have resolved merely to alter the method of electing the people's representatives to the State Duma, so that each sector of the people may have its own electees in it.

Established to strengthen the Russian state, the State Duma should be Russian in spirit also.

Other nationalities that become members of our empire should have spokesmen for their needs in the State Duma, but these spokesmen should not and will not be present in such numbers as would make it possible for them to have the decisive voice on purely Russian questions.

In those outlying districts of the state where the population has not yet reached a sufficient level of civic development, elections to the State Duma should be temporarily suspended.

All these changes in the system of elections cannot be introduced in the usual legislative way through the State Duma, whose membership we find unsatisfactory as a result of the imperfections in the very method of electing its members. Only the authority that granted the first electoral law, the historic authority of the Russian tsar, has the right to revoke it and replace it by another.

The Lord God has entrusted us with sovereign power over our people. Before his throne we shall answer for the fate of the Russian empire.

XVII:20. THE GOVERNMENT'S PROPOSAL TO THE THIRD DUMA, NOVEMBER 16, 1907

On November 16, 1907, Stolypin presented and defended before the Third Duma the government's program. The following excerpts from the stenographic report of that session give not only the gist of Stolypin's argument but also two illustrative responses, from the Left and the Right. (Guchkov's motion, incidentally, was defeated on November 22 by a vote of 182 to 179.)

Reference: Gosudarstvennaia Duma, tretii sozyv. *Stenograficheskie otchety, 1907-1908 gg., Sessiia 1,* vol. 1 (St. Petersburg: Gosudarsvennaia Tipografiia, 1908), 7th sitting, cols. 307, 309-12, 328, 351. Translation contributed by Christopher Becker.

THE PRESIDENT OF THE COUNCIL OF MINISTERS: . . . It has now become evident to all that the destructive movement created by the parties of the extreme Left has degenerated into open robbery and has brought to the fore all the antisocial and criminal elements, causing the ruin of the honest workingmen and corrupting the younger generation.

. . .

This development can be opposed only by force. . . .

Heretofore the government has taken the path of rooting out criminal actions, and it will take this path in the future as well.

· · ·

By placing the rural population of many millions on its feet and giving it the possibility of attaining economic independence, the legislative body will lay the foundation on which will be built the reconstructed edifice of the Russian state.

Therefore, the basic thought of the present

government, its guiding idea, has always been the matter of agrarian reform.

Not a disorganized giveaway of land, nor the quieting of a riot with handouts—riots will be put down with force—but the recognition of the inviolability of private property and, as a necessary result, the creation of small private landed property (*applause from the Center and Right*), the genuine right of exit from the commune, and the resolution of the problems of improved land use: these are the tasks whose realization the government has held and still holds to be the vital questions of the Russian state.

. . .

The government is proposing to you to carry out the reforms necessary for the country—by the extension and rebuilding of local self-government, by the reform of local administration, by the broadening of education, and by the introduction of a whole series of improvements in the structure of local life, among which government aid to incapacitated workers, workers' insurance, and the provision of medical care for workers are at present occupying the especial attention of the government. Appropriate plans have been prepared.

. . .

In the sphere of local reforms, the most important is the plan presented by the Ministry of Justice to the Duma, concerning the reform of the local courts, because the passage of this bill is necessary for the realization of another, which concerns the inviolability of the person and a number of reforms in local administration.

. . .

GUCHKOV (City of Moscow): In the name of the Union of October 17 faction, and in the name of the moderate rightist faction, I have the honor to propose to the State Duma that it accept the following motion to take up the next items on the agenda: "The State Duma, having heard the message of the president of the Council of Ministers, and having firmly decided to proceed without delay in the legislative labors necessary for the implementation of the imminent reforms necessary to the state, and to carry out unflinchingly, within the limits prescribed by law, its right of inspecting the legitimacy of the activity of the government, moves to take up the next items on the agenda."

. . .

POKROVSKII (Kuban' and Terek provinces, and the Black Sea guberniia): . . . The Social-Democratic faction . . . draws its strength from its awareness of being a part of a mighty whole, of being borne by the wave of the movement which cannot for long be held back by mere police barricades. (*Applause from the Left.*) It is aware that history has entrusted it with a glorious responsibility—to be the direct successor of that faction of the Second State Duma which the counterrevolution placed in the dock of the accused. Observing with contempt the slanders and attacks of its foes, it will march toward the single goal it has set itself—toward socialism by way of a democratic system, as the Russian detachment of the great international army of the socialist proletariat.

. . .

THE PRESIDENT OF THE COUNCIL OF MINISTERS: . . . The government has been given the task, along with that of putting down revolution, of helping the population as much as possible to enjoy in actuality the benefits it has been given. As long as the peasant is poor, as long as he owns no private landed property, as long as he is forcibly kept in the bonds of the commune, he will remain a slave, and no written law can give him the blessing of civil freedom. (*Applause from the Center and Right.*) In order to make use of these benefits, one must obviously have a certain amount of wealth, even if to a very small degree. . . . That is why, before all, and above all, the government is helping the peasants to reorganize and improve their economic life and wishes to create a source of private property from a combination of their allotment lands and the lands obtained by the government. The small private landowner is indisputably the nucleus of the small zemstvo unit of the future; hard-working, possessing a sense of his own worth, he will bring culture, enlightenment, and abundance to the village.

And then, only then, will freedom on paper be transformed, be converted, into freedom in fact, which is surely made up of civil liberties and of a feeling of statehood and patriotism. (*Applause from the Center and Right. Exclamations of "bravo!"*)

XVII:21. WALLACE ON STOLYPIN AND THE DUMA, 1906-1911

After his initial years of intensive study of Russia in the 1870s, Wallace (see above, Item XV:38) kept in touch with developments there and made other, shorter visits. In the 1912 edition of his work he made these comments in a chapter on the Duma.

Reference: Donald Mackenzie Wallace, *Russia,* rev. ed. (London: Cassell, 1912), pp. 728, 740, 740-41, 742. See also the paperback version ed. by C. E. Black (New York: Vintage, 1961), ch. 3.

In theory the Cadets were a moderate constitutional party, and if they had possessed a little more prudence and patience they might have led the country gradually into the paths of genuine constitutional government; but, like everyone in Russia at the time, they were in a hurry, and they greatly overestimated their own strength. Their impatience was curiously illustrated during a friendly conversation which I had one evening with a leader of the party. With all due deference, I ventured to suggest that, instead of maintaining an attitude of systematic and uncompromising hostility to the Ministry, the party might cooperate with the Government and thereby gradually create something like the English parliamentary system, for which they professed such admiration; possibly in eight or ten years this desirable result might be obtained. On hearing these last words my friend suddenly interrupted me and exclaimed:

"Eight or ten years? We cannot wait so long as that!"

"Well," I replied, "you must know your own affairs best; but in England, which constitutionalists of other countries often take as their model, we had to wait for several centuries."

. . .

M. Stolypin . . . formed two resolves, and he clung to them with marvellous tenacity: To suppress disorders relentlessly by every means at his disposal, and to preserve the Duma as long as hopes could be entertained of its doing useful work, while keeping it strictly within the functions assigned to it by the Emperor. Until the assembling of the

third Duma he found no cordial support in any of the parties or groups; all were leagued against him. For the Conservative and Reactionary Right, he was too Liberal; for the Revolutionary Left, he was a pillar of Autocracy, an advocate of police repression and drum-head courts martial.

. . .

In order to appreciate fully the difficulties of M. Stolypin's task, we must remember that he had to struggle not only with political opposition in the Duma and among the Court officials, but also with the revolutionary agitation, conspiracies, terrorism, and all manner of disorders throughout the country. During the first five weeks of his premiership he had to deal with five local mutinies in the army and navy, and with a long series of murderous attacks with bombs and revolvers on provincial governors, vice-governors, generals, minor officials, and policemen of all grades. He himself had a very narrow escape. His villa in St. Petersburg was blown up with bombs while he was sitting in it at work; he remained unhurt, but a number of his officials and servants were killed or wounded, and one of his daughters, when extricated from the wreckage, was found to be dangerously injured.

. . .

Of the many distinguished Russians whom I have known, he [Stolypin] was certainly one of the most sympathetic, and even his enemies, while denying to him the qualities of a great statesman, were constrained to admit that he was an honest, courageous, truthful, and in all respects honourable man.

XVII:22. IZVOL'SKII ON STOLYPIN, CA. 1906-1911

The memoirs of Aleksandr Petrovich Izvol'skii (1856-1919), minister of foreign affairs from 1906 to 1910 and ambassador to France from 1910 to 1917, contain valuable observations not only on Russian foreign policy but also on the situation at home. Here are excerpts showing his evaluation of Stolypin's character and works.

Reference: A. P. Izvol'skii, *The Memoirs of Alexander Iswolsky,* ed. and trans. C. L. Seeger (London: Hutchinson, 1920), pp. 97-98, 100-01, 219, 230, 237-38.

Totally out of his element in the bureaucratic world of the capital, this country gentleman of a rather provincial aspect appeared at first to play an insignificant part at the meeting of the Council of Ministers, but very soon his robust and original personality imposed itself strongly upon the routine functionaries who composed the majority of the Cabinet. As for me, I fell a victim to his charm at once, and was happy to find among my chance companions a man to whom I felt drawn by a communion of ideas and political convictions, for at that time M. Stolypine appeared to me to be an especially sincere partisan of the new order of things, resolved to collaborate with the Douma in every way possible.

· · ·

But that which constituted the incontestable and undisputed superiority of M. Stolypine and established from the outset his ascendancy over his colleagues was a rare *ensemble* of qualities, both of heart and of character. . . . When meeting him for the first time, one was impressed and attracted by a simplicity and a sweetness which gave to his personality an irresistible charm, and, upon further acquaintance, one discovered in him a high-mindedness and a nobility of soul that the exercise of a power, which, at certain times, became even dictatorial, never in the least affected. His exalted and chivalrous conception of duty made of him a servant, devoted to the point of martyrdom, of his Sovereign and his country, but, at the same time, he was so proud of his name and jealous of his liberty that he ever maintained, toward a Court and a bureaucracy which regarded him in the light of an intruder and were more or less hostile to him from the beginning, an attitude of reserve and independence to which one was little accustomed in that sphere, and which, I am sorry to say, was never appreciated at its worth by the Czar and his intimates.

The portrait which I have essayed to draw of this distinguished man would be incomplete were I to omit to mention his marvellous gift of oratory; in his first address to the Douma he revealed himself as a public speaker of extraordinary power.

· · ·

On Saturday, the 25th of August [N.S.; August 12, O.S., 1906], about three o'clock in the afternoon, a formidable explosion

destroyed a part of the villa occupied by M. Stolypine on the Islands [in the northern section of Saint Petersburg]. The Prime Minister was not injured, but some thirty people were killed and as many more wounded, several of them seriously, among these two of M. Stolypine's children.

· · ·

The Council of Ministers, held in the evening of August 25th, after the explosion, at the town residence of the Prime Minister, was of great moment. M. Stolypine opened it with an address, in which he began by declaring in the most energetic manner that the attack upon him, which had barely missed depriving him of his children, could not influence in the slightest degree his political course; his programme remained unchanged: pitiless repression of all disorders and all revolutionary or terrorist acts; carrying into effect, with the help of the next Douma, a far-reaching plan of reforms in the direction of liberalism; immediate solution of the most urgent problems by executive decrees and, first of all, a settlement of the agrarian question. M. Stolypine added that we must expect the reactionary party to profit by the occasion and make it a pretext for inciting the Emperor to proclaim a military dictatorship, and even to annul the charter of 1905 and return to the old regime of absolute power. He announced that he would oppose with all his strength any such reaction and, rather than abandon his constitutional course, he would resign his office.

· · ·

The agrarian reforms were adopted by the lower House [the Duma] with scarcely any modification and by a heavy majority, but in the Council of the Empire they met with a lively opposition and were passed by a majority of one vote, counting those of the Ministers who were members of that assembly. . . .

Curiously enough, this reform was opposed simultaneously by the two extremes, both Right and Left. The Socialists rejected it because of their communistic theories, and as for the reactionaries, they regarded it as an attack upon the sacrosanct traditions of the past and a step in the direction of the equalization of the classes—a strange aberration on the part of a party calling itself Conservative, but at the same time joining hands with the revolutionaries to defeat a law which had for its object the strengthening of the principle of ownership of property.

It was the reactionary party that had organized the opposition to agrarian reform in the Council of the Empire. When the law came up for discussion that party was particularly strong because the Emperor had limited his appointments to persons who were well known for their reactionary tendencies. . . .

M. Stolypine's agrarian reforms met with extraordinary success, surpassing the most optimistic expectations. The Russian peasant, prone as he is to listen to revolutionary propaganda when it appeals to his dominant passion for more land, is nevertheless possessed of a keen intelligence. He was not slow in going ahead of the measures decreed for facilitating the ownership of the land which he

farmed and finding means of acquiring additional land by proper and legal methods. Under the able and firm direction of M. Krivocheine [Krivoshein], who succeeded Prince Wassiltchikoff [Vasil'chikov] as Minister of Agriculture, the new legislation, reinforced by a considerable extension of the activity and power of the "Peasants' Bank," produced wide-spread results in a surprisingly short time. These results were so satisfactory that, on the eve of the revolution of 1917, it is safe to say that the entire agrarian problem was in a way to be definitely solved, and that only a comparatively short period would have sufficed to put the agrarian regime in Russia on a solid foundation. The social and economic upheaval caused by the revolution destroyed, alas, those magnificent results.

XVII:23. KOKOVTSOV ON THE ADMINISTRATION OF STOLYPIN, 1906-1911

The following excerpts are a small sample of the extensive observations on the administration of Stolypin contained in the memoirs of Kokovtsov (see Item XVII:4, above).
Reference: Kokovtsov, *Memoirs of Count Kokovtsov*, pp. 164-65, 167-68, 178.

[After the bomb attempt of August 12, 1906] Stolypin's calm and self-control won the admiration of everyone. In fact, his conduct at the time unquestionably worked a great change in the way he was treated not only by the court and St. Petersburg society but by his colleagues as well. Theretofore he had been criticized for his provincialism and lack of knowledge of the capital's established bureaucratic customs. After August 12, however, he acquired great moral prestige. His nobility, courage, and devotion to the state were indisputable. He gained in stature and was unanimously acclaimed master of the situation.

. . . Stolypin and most of the ministers, with the possible exception of A. P. Izvolsky, clearly recognized that another election according to the provisions of the law of December 11, 1905, would only lead to the same result and paralyze the normal work of the government, which, after all, was appointed by the Tsar and responsible to him and not to the lower chamber [the Duma]. We also recognized that if the government arbitrarily changed the law we should be accused of illegal actions, but at the same time we knew that it would be impossible to persuade the Duma to revise the law. In this dilemma all of us, with the exception of

Izvolsky, agreed that in view of the issues at stake an arbitrary revision of the law was ultimately unavoidable.

I mention all this because I want to relieve Stolypin of the full responsibility for the Council's decision on this subject by saying quite definitely that all the ministers at that time, including myself, were perfectly in accord with the Chairman of the Ministers' Council; we all must bear the same responsibility, just as we all must share the same merit—that of having had enough courage to face the unfortunate situation squarely and of having assured the country of peaceful legislative work until the turbulent period begun by the events of 1914.

· · · ·

[In October 1906, Stolypin and the Council of Ministers compiled a list of those restrictions on the Jews which they all agreed should be abolished and presented it to the tsar for confirmation.] The recommendation of the Ministers' Council remained for a long time in the Tsar's possession. We often asked Stolypin what its fate had been and why it had not been returned, and his replies were always assured and confident. Finally, on December 10, 1906, the recommendation was returned to Stolypin accompanied by a letter from the Tsar, which Stolypin permitted me to copy.

Here it is: "I am returning to you without my confirmation the recommendation of the Council on the Jewish problem. Despite most convincing arguments in favor of adopting a positive decision in this matter, an inner voice keeps on insisting more and more that I do not accept responsibility for it. So far my conscience has not deceived me. Therefore I intend in this case also to follow its dictates. I know that you, too, believe that 'A Tsar's heart is in God's hand.' Let it be so. For all laws established by me I bear a great responsibility before God, and I am ready to answer for this decision at any time." None of the documents in my possession shows so clearly the Tsar's mystical attitude toward the nature of his imperial power as this letter to the Chairman of his Ministers' Council.

· · ·

[Speaking of the period February-June 1907:] Stolypin had had a great struggle with his own conscience before he had undertaken the task of revising the electoral law. In making this change without the consent of the Duma he violated the Tsar's earlier decree, but he did so solely in the name of preserving the principle of public representation.

In this respect the position of the government, and of Stolypin in particular, was truly tragic. Personally, he was a confirmed champion not only of popular representation but of the principle of legality. . . . He openly and honestly desired to attract into the government men who had popular support. Yet he also recognized that the Emperor was unsympathetic to this idea, and, further, that such public men as he had in mind were less than frank in their dealings with him and were far from anxious to exchange the freedom of opposition for responsibility. Deep in his heart Stolypin certainly craved power, loved it, and was loath to let it slip from his hands. But he was unquestionably an honorable and honest man, and he perceived that the problem was either to safeguard public order in the form in which it had recently been established or to take the easy road of making concessions which might lead to the destruction of the entire regime.

XVII:24. DURNOVO'S ADVICE TO THE TSAR IN FEBRUARY 1914

Petr Nikolaevich Durnovo (1845-1915) began his career in the naval and military service, transferred in 1881 to the Police Department of the Ministry of Internal Affairs, and from 1884 to 1893 was that department's director. He went on to high posts in other parts of the same ministry, including a short term as its head (1905-06). His principal position during the last decade of his life was that of member of the State Council. In February 1914 he offered to the tsar the memorandum from which excerpts are given here. Whatever present-day readers of Durnovo may say about his premises, they cannot but be fascinated by his analysis and his prophecies.

Reference: "Zapiska P. N. Durnovo," in *Krasnaia nov'*, no. 10 (November-December 1922), pp. 182-99; translation based largely on Frank A. Golder, ed., *Documents of Russian History 1914-1917*, trans. Emanuel Aronsberg (New York: Century, 1927), pp. 3-23, with slight revisions. The Aronsberg translation is reprinted in Thomas Riha, ed., *Readings in Russian Civilization*, 2 vols. (Chicago: University of Chicago Press, 1964), 2:457-70.

The central factor of the period of world history through which we are now passing is the rivalry between England and Germany. This rivalry must inevitably lead to an armed struggle between them, the outcome of which will, in all probability, prove fatal to the vanquished side. . . . The armed conflict impending as a result of this rivalry cannot in any case be confined to a duel between England and Germany alone. . . . The future Anglo-German war will be transformed into an armed conflict between two groups of powers, one with a German, the other with an English, orientation.

· · ·

The Russo-Japanese War radically changed the relations among the great powers and brought England out of her isolation. As we know, all through the Russo-Japanese War England and America observed benevolent neutrality toward Japan, while we enjoyed a similar benevolent neutrality from France and Germany. Here, it would seem, should have been the inception of the most natural political combination for us. But after the war our diplomacy faced abruptly about and definitely started along the road toward rapprochement with England. France was drawn into the orbit of British policy; there was formed a group of powers of the Triple

Entente, with England playing the dominant part; and a clash became inevitable, sooner or later, with the powers grouping themselves around Germany.

. . .

We find it difficult to perceive any practical advantages gained by us in rapprochement with England. The only benefit—improved relations with Japan—is hardly a result of the Russo-English rapprochement. As a matter of fact, Russia and Japan were created to live in peace since there is no decisive issue to divide them. All Russia's objectives in the Far East, if correctly understood, are entirely compatible with Japan's interests. . . .

. . . Japan . . . does not covet our Far Eastern possessions. The Japanese, by their very nature, are a southern people and the rigorous conditions of our Far Eastern outlying districts could not entice them. . . . Possessing Korea and Formosa, Japan would hardly go further north, and its desires, one must suppose, would sooner lie in the direction of the Philippine Islands, Indochina, Java, Sumatra, and Borneo. . . .

In a word, peaceful neighborly life [*mirnoe sozhitel'stvo*], nay, more, a close rapprochement, between Russia and Japan in the Far East is perfectly natural, regardless of any mediation by England.

. . .

The worst results, however, of the accord with England—and of the consequent radical break with Germany—have been felt in the Near East. . . .

. . . The Russo-British rapprochement evidently seems to Turkey to be tantamount to England's renouncing her traditional policy of closing the Dardanelles to us, while the creation of the Balkan League, under the auspices of Russia, appeared as a direct threat to the continued existence of Turkey as a European power. To sum up, the Anglo-Russian accord has brought us nothing of practical value up to this time. In the future, it inevitably threatens us with an armed clash with Germany.

. . . The fundamental groupings in a future war are self-evident: Russia, France, and England, on the one side; Germany, Austria, and Turkey, on the other.

It is more than likely that other powers, too, will participate in that war, depending upon circumstances as they may exist at the war's outbreak. . . . Italy, if she has any conception of her real interest, will not enter on the side of Germany.

. . . The possibility of Italy's entering the war on the side of the anti-German coalition would appear all the more likely if the scales of war inclined in her favor, i.e. if she were guaranteed the most favorable conditions for participating in the subsequent sharing of the spoils. In this respect Italy's position coincides with the probable position of Rumania, which, one must suppose, will remain neutral until fortune leans to one side or another. Then, guided by a healthy political egoism, it will join the victor to be rewarded at the cost of either Russia or Austria. . . .

. . . Under these conditions the struggle with Germany presents great difficulties for us and will require incalculable sacrifices. The war will not catch our opponent napping and the stage of his preparedness will probably exceed the most exaggerated of our expectations. . . .

The Main Burden of the War Will Fall on Russia

The main burden of the war will undoubtedly fall on us, since England is hardly capable of large-scale participation in a continental war, while France, poor in manpower, will probably confine itself to strictly defensive tactics, in view of the enormous losses by which war will be attended under the present conditions of military technique. The part of a battering-ram, making a breach in the very thick of the German defense, will be ours. . . .

The Far East should be excluded from the list of unfavorable factors [in a future war]. Both America and Japan are hostile to Germany, the former by nature and the latter because of its present-day political orientation; and there is no reason to expect them to enter on Germany's side. . . .

. . . And what is more, one should not exclude the possibility of America or Japan entering [the war] on the side of Germany's opponents. . . . However, an outburst of hostility toward us is certain in Persia, and disturbances among the Moslems are likely in the Caucasus and Turkestan. . . .

Are we prepared for so stubborn a struggle as the future war of the European nations will undoubtedly prove to be? We must answer this question, without evasion, in the negative.

. . .

In this respect we must note, first of all, the insufficiency of our military supplies, which, certainly, cannot be blamed upon the war department, since the procurement plans are still far from being fulfilled, owing to the low productivity of our factories. This insufficiency of munitions is the more significant since, on account of the embryonic condition of our industries, we shall, during the war, have no opportunity to remedy the ascertained shortage by our own efforts, while the blockade of the Baltic as well as the Black Sea will make impossible the importation from abroad of the defense materials we lack.

Another circumstance unfavorable to our defenses is our excessive dependence, generally speaking, upon foreign industry, a fact which, in connection with the above-noted interruption of more or less convenient transport routes abroad, will create a series of obstacles difficult to overcome. . . .

The network of strategic railways is inadequate. The railways possess a rolling stock sufficient, perhaps, for normal traffic, but not commensurate with the colossal demands that will be made upon them in the event of a European war. Finally, it should not be forgotten that the impending war will be fought among the most civilized and technically most advanced nations. Every war up till now has invariably been accompanied by something new in the realm of military technique, but the technical backwardness of our industries will not create favorable conditions for our adopting the new inventions.

The Vital Interests of Germany and Russia Nowhere Conflict

. . .

Is this orientation, however, correct, and does even a favorable outcome of the war promise us such advantages as would compensate us for all the hardships and sacrifices which must attend a war unparalleled in its probable strain?

The vital interests of Russia and Germany do not conflict anywhere, and they provide a solid foundation for peaceful coexistence between these two states. Germany's future lies on the sea, that is, in a realm where Russia, in essence the most continental of all the great powers, has no interests whatever. . . . We have no surplus population which would require territorial expansion, but even from the viewpoint of new conquests, what can we gain from a victory over Germany? Posen, or East Prussia? But why do we need these regions, densely populated as they are by Poles, when we find it difficult enough to manage the Poles in Russia? Why encourage centrifugal tendencies, which have not subsided even to this day in the Vistula territory, by incorporating into the Russian state the restless Posnanian and East Prussian Poles, whose national aspirations even the German government, which is more firm than the Russian, cannot stifle?

Exactly the same thing applies to Galicia. It is obviously disadvantageous to us to annex, in the interests of national sentimentalism, a territory that has lost every vital connection with our fatherland. For, together with a negligible handful of Galicians who are Russian in spirit, how many Poles, Jews, and Ukrainianized Uniates would we receive? The so-called Ukrainian or Mazeppist movement is not a menace to us at present, but we ought not to enable it to expand by increasing the number of turbulent Ukrainian elements, for this movement undoubtedly contains the seed of an extremely dangerous Little Russian separatism which, under favorable conditions, may assume quite unexpected proportions. The obvious aim of our diplomacy in the rapprochement with England has been the opening of the Straits. But the attainment of this object hardly seems to require a war with Germany, for it was England, and not Germany at all, that closed our exit from the Black Sea. . . .

Also, there is good reason to believe that the Germans would agree sooner than the English to let us have the Straits, in the fate of which they are only slightly interested, and at the price of which they would gladly purchase our alliance.

. . .

The Straits would not give us an outlet to the open sea, however, since beyond them lies a sea consisting almost wholly of territorial waters, a sea dotted with numerous islands where the British navy, for instance, would have no trouble in actually closing to us all entrances and exits, irrespective of the Straits. Therefore, Russia might safely welcome an arrangement which, while not turning the Straits over to us directly, would safeguard us against the penetration of the

Black Sea by a hostile fleet. Such an arrangement, attainable under favorable circumstances without any war, has the additional advantage that it would not violate the interests of the Balkan States, which would regard our seizure of the Straits with alarm and quite understandable jealousy.

. . . Those territorial and economic acquisitions which might really prove useful to us are located only in places where our ambitions may meet opposition from England, but by no means from Germany. Persia, the Pamirs, Kuldja, Kashgaria, Dzungaria, Mongolia, the Uriankhai territory [Tuva]— all these are regions where the interests of Russia and Germany do not conflict, whereas the interests of Russia and England have clashed there repeatedly.

. . .

With respect to Germany's economic future, the interests of Russia and England are diametrically opposed.

It is to England's advantage to destroy Germany's industry and maritime trade, turning her into a poor and, as far as possible, agricultural country. It is to our advantage for Germany to develop her maritime trade and the industry which serves it, so as to supply the remotest world markets, and at the same time to open her domestic market to our agricultural products to supply her large working population.

. . .

As the German colonies increase and there is an attendant growth of German industry and maritime commerce, the German colonization movement decreases, and the day is not far off when the *Drang nach Osten* will pass into the realm of historical reminiscences. . . . As regards German dominance of our economic life, this phenomenon hardly justifies the complaints usually voiced against it. Russia is far too poor both in capital and in industrial entrepreneurship to get along without a large influx of foreign capital.

. . .

Even a Victory over Germany Promises Russia an Exceedingly Unfavorable Prospect

In any case, even if we were to admit that it was necessary to eradicate German dominance in our economic life, if only at the cost of total proscription of German capital in Russian industry, appropriate measures could be taken, it would seem, without war against Germany. Such a war will demand such enormous expenditures that they will many times exceed the more than doubtful advantages we would receive as a result of the abolition of German [economic] domination. Moreover, the result of such a war will be an economic situation compared with which the yoke of German capital will seem light.

There can certainly be no doubt that the war will require expenditures exceeding Russia's limited financial resources. We shall have to turn for credit to allied and neutral countries, but this will not be granted gratuitously. There is no point in discussing now what will happen if the war should end disastrously for us. The financial and economic consequences of defeat can be neither calculated nor even foreseen, and will undoubtedly spell the total disintegration of our entire national economy. But even victory promises us extremely unfavorable financial prospects; a totally ruined Germany will not be in a position to compensate us for the cost involved. A peace treaty dictated by English interests will not afford Germany an opportunity for sufficient economic recovery to cover our war expenditures, even long afterward. The little we may perhaps succeed in extorting from her will have to be divided with our allies, and our share will be but negligible crumbs compared with the cost of the war. . . . It is inevitable that even after a victorious conclusion of the war we shall fall into the same sort of financial and economic bondage to our creditors, compared with which our present dependence upon German capital will seem ideal. However, no matter how tragic may be the economic prospects which face us as a result of union with England and consequently of war with Germany, they still fade into the background in the face of the political consequences of this essentially unnatural alliance.

A Struggle between Russia and Germany Is Profoundly Undesirable for Both Sides, as Involving a Weakening Monarchical Principle

It should not be forgotten that Russia and Germany are the representatives of the conservative principle in the civilized world, as opposed to the democratic principle, embodied in England and, to an infinitely lesser degree, in France. Strange as it may seem, England, monarchistic and conservative to the core at home, has in her foreign relations always acted as the protector of the most demagogical tendencies, invariably encouraging all popular movements aimed at the weakening of the monarchical principle.

From this point of view a struggle between Germany and Russia, regardless of its outcome, is profoundly undesirable for both sides, as undoubtedly leading to a weakening of the conservative principle of which the above-named two great powers are the only reliable bulwarks. More than that, one must foresee that under the exceptional conditions that exist, a general European war is mortally dangerous both for Russia and Germany, no matter who wins. It is our firm conviction, based upon a long and careful study of all contemporary subversive tendencies, that there must inevitably break out in the defeated country a social revolution which, by the very nature of things, will spread to the country of the victor.

. . . An especially favorable soil for social upheavals is found, of course, in Russia, where the masses undoubtedly profess the principles of an unconscious sort of socialism. In spite of the spirit of antagonism to the government in Russian society, which spirit is just as unconscious as the socialism of the broad masses of the people, a [purely] political revolution is not possible in Russia, and any revolutionary movement will inevitably degenerate into a socialist movement. The opponents of the government have no support among the common people, who see no difference between a government official and a member of the intelligentsia. The Russian masses, whether workmen or peasants, are not looking for political rights, which they neither need nor comprehend.

The peasant dreams of obtaining free a share of somebody else's land; the workman, of getting hold of the entire capital and profits of the manufacturer. Beyond this, they have no aspirations. If these slogans are scattered far and wide among the populace, and the government permits agitation along these lines, Russia undoubtedly will be flung into anarchy such as she suffered in the ever memorable period of troubles in 1905-1906. War with Germany would create exceptionally favorable conditions for such agitation. As already stated, this war is fraught with enormous difficulties for us, and cannot turn out to be a triumphal march to Berlin. Both military disasters—partial ones, let us hope—and all kinds of shortages in our supply are inevitable. Because of the excessive nervousness of our society these events will be given an exaggerated importance, and because of the spirit of opposition in this society all the blame will be laid on the government.

. . .

If the war ends in victory, the suppression of the socialist movement will not after all present insurmountable obstacles. There will be agrarian disturbances as a result of agitation for compensating the soldiers with additional land allotments; there will be labor troubles during the transition from the probably inflated earnings of wartime to normal wage scales; and this, it is to be hoped, will be all, so long as the wave of the German social revolution has not reached us. But in the event of defeat, the possibility of which in a struggle with a foe like Germany cannot be overlooked, social revolution in its most extreme form is inevitable.

. . . It will start with all disasters being attributed to the government. In the legislative institutions a bitter campaign against the government will begin, which will result in revolutionary agitation throughout the country. There will immediately ensue Socialist slogans—which alone are capable of arousing and rallying the masses—first the complete reapportionment of land [chernyi peredel] and then the reapportionment of all valuables and property. The defeated army, having lost its most dependable men during the war, and carried away for the most part by the tide of the general elemental desire of the peasant for land, will prove to be too demoralized to serve as a bulwark of law and order. The legislative institutions and the opposition intelligentsia parties, lacking real authority in the eyes of the people, will be powerless to stem the rising popular tide, which they themselves had aroused, and Russia will be flung into hopeless anarchy, the outcome of which cannot even be foreseen.

. . .

A summary of all that has been stated above must lead to the conclusion that a rapprochement with England does not promise us any benefits, and that the English orientation of our diplomacy is in essence profoundly wrong. We do not travel the same road as England; she should be left to go her own way, and we must not quarrel on her account with Germany.

The Triple Entente is an artificial combination, not founded on genuine interests. The future belongs not to it but to an incomparably more vital, close rapprochement of Russia, Germany, a France reconciled with Germany, and a Japan allied to Russia by a strictly defensive alliance. A political combination like this, nonaggressive in its relation with other states, would safeguard for many years the *peaceful coexistence of civilized nations,* threatened, not by the bellicose intentions of Germany, as English diplomacy is trying to show, but solely by the perfectly natural

striving of England to retain at all costs her vanishing domination of the seas. In this direction, and not in the fruitless search for a basis of agreement with England, an agreement that is in its very nature contrary to our national views and aims, should all the efforts of our diplomacy be concentrated.

It goes without saying that Germany, on her part, must meet our desire to restore our tested relations of amicable alliance with her, and to elaborate, in closest agreement with us, such terms of our neighborly life as to afford no basis for anti-German agitation on the part of our constitutional-liberal parties, which, by their very nature, are forced to adhere, not to a conservative German, but to a liberal English orientation.

P. N. Durnovo

February 1914

XVII:25. SAZONOV ON HOW THE WAR CAME, SUMMER 1914

Sergei Dmitrievich Sazonov (1861-1927), Russia's minister for foreign affairs in 1910-16, wrote his reminiscences of those years. Here is part of his explanation of how Russia and Germany came to blows in 1914.

Reference: Sergei D. Sazonov, *Fateful Years 1909-1916: The Reminiscences of Serge Sazonov* (London: J. Cape, 1928), pp. 174, 175, 177-78, 197, 208, 210-13. Russian ed.: *Vospominaniia* (Paris: Izd. E. Siial'skoi, 1927).

The Triple Entente had no offensive plans; it only desired to prevent the establishment of a German hegemony in Europe, which would constitute a serious threat to its vital interests.

. . .

In order to achieve these aims, there was no need to "encircle" Germany—a term which, as its strategical origin indicates, suggests some idea of aggression. Such an idea was equally foreign to every member of the Entente.

. . .

Austria-Hungary impatiently awaited the moment when, with the support of Germany, she would be able to fall upon her small neighbour. . . . In order to make sure of her pretext for war, the ultimatum to Serbia was worded in such a way as to exclude all possibility of its being accepted.

. . .

Serbia accepted all the demands of the Austrian ultimatum, except that which stipulated that Austro-Hungarian officials should take part in the inquiry into the alleged complicity of the Serbian authorities in the Sarajevo crime. Even this reservation held good only if the participation of the

Austro-Hungarian officials in the inquiry was not in accordance with the usages of international law. At the same time, M. Pashich expressed his readiness to submit the Serbian case to the decision of the International Court of Justice at the Hague. . . .

. . . The Serbian Crown Prince appealed to the Emperor Nicholas, from whom alone he could hope to obtain active help. This appeal frankly acknowledged the impossibility of self-defense, and begged for prompt cooperation. The Emperor, in a reply which indicated his sincere sympathy with the Serbian people and the Crown Prince, spoke of the strenuous efforts of the Russian Government to overcome the difficulties of the moment, and expressed his belief in Serbia's desire to find, without loss of dignity, some way out of the situation that would avoid the horror of a new war. "As long as there remains the faintest hope of avoiding bloodshed," the Emperor's telegram concludes, "all my efforts will tend in that direction. If we fail to attain this object, in spite of our sincere desire for peace, Your Royal Highness may rest assured that Russia will in no case remain indifferent to the fate of Serbia."

... The Austrian ultimatum, although accepted by Serbia—with the reservations ... which could in no way be construed as a rejection—was but the first step towards her complete subjugation. This was apparent from its text, and even more so from the haste which the Austro-Hungarian Legation displayed in leaving Belgrade as soon as the Serbian reply had been delivered, thus showing its complete indifference to the nature of that reply. The rupture had already been decided upon.

. . .

On July 30 [N.S., July 17 O.S.] I had another interview with the German Ambassador, in the course of which he asked me whether we would be content with Austria's promise to leave Serbian territory intact, and begged me to state on what conditions we should be ready to stop our preparations for war. I immediately wrote down on a piece of paper and handed him the following statement: "If, admitting that the Austro-Serbian conflict has become a European question, Austria is ready to withdraw from her ultimatum the clauses which infringe upon the sovereign rights of Serbia, Russia will undertake to stop her preparations for war."

. . .

General mobilization orders were only issued in Russia on July 31 [N.S.], i.e. on the day that *Kriegsgefahrzustand* was declared in Berlin earlier in the day than they had received the news of our mobilization. This declaration of the "state of war danger" differed from mobilization hardly in anything but name, and was a German trick for beginning the mobilization before the actual word had been pronounced.

. . .

At midnight on July 31 the German Ambassador handed me the ultimatum in which Germany required us to demobilize within twelve hours the reservists called up against Austria and Germany. It would have been impossible, on technical grounds, to comply with this request, which was indeed simply an act of bullying, since Germany and Austria did not promise that if we demobilized they would do likewise. Austria had by that time already completed her mobilization, and Germany began hers on that very day by declaring "an imminent state of war"—or, if we believe Kurt Eisner, the head of the temporary Bavarian Government, who was assassinated later, she had begun it three days previously. . . .

The German requests were, of course, utterly inadmissible both on formal grounds and in themselves. The military preparations of our Western neighbors were of the greatest danger to us, and the only way to dispel the danger would be for them to stop their mobilization at once. There is no need to add that our demobilization at that moment would have introduced a complete and hopeless disorder into our military organization, and our enemies would have immediately taken advantage of this to carry out their designs unhindered.

. . .

The last and irrevocable step was taken by Germany on Saturday, August 1 [July 19 O.S.]. Count Pourtalès came to see me at seven o'clock in the evening, and after the very first words asked me whether the Russian Government was ready to give a favourable answer to the ultimatum presented the day before. I answered in the negative. . . .

... Deeply moved, the Ambassador said to me, speaking with difficulty:

"In that case my Government charges me to give you the following note."

And with a shaking hand Pourtalès handed me the Declaration of War. . . .

After handing the note to me, the Ambassador, who had evidently found it a great strain to carry out his orders, lost all self-control and leaning against the window burst into tears. With a gesture of despair he repeated: "Who could have thought that I should be leaving St. Petersburg under such circumstances!"

In spite of my own emotion, which I managed to overcome, I felt sincerely sorry for him. We embraced each other and with tottering steps he walked out of the room.

B. SOCIAL AND ECONOMIC DEVELOPMENTS

Note: Some of the selections in Section B of Chapter XVI also deal with the period 1906-14.

XVII:26. THE DECLARATION OF THE NOBLES' CONVENTION, JUNE 11, 1906

In June 1906, while the struggle raged between the Duma and the ministry over the question of compulsory transfer of private lands, a nationwide nobles' congress or convention addressed these words to the tsar.

Reference: *Pravo,* no. 23 (June 11, 1906), cols. 2061-63.

Sire!

At the present signal moment, when the Russian state order is being transformed by the will of Your Imperial Majesty, we ask that you hear the voice of the class [*soslovie*] your crowned forebears throughout the centuries have called to counsel and to civic labors at decisive moments in the life of our state.

At this moment, perhaps the gravest in a thousand years of our history, when we stand before a great danger which threatens the integrity and the existence of the state, the deputies of the united nobility address you, our sovereign. . . . Seeking to achieve political and economic dominance, the enemies of Russian statehood [*gosudarstvennost'*] are trying, by using the dream of land, to win the blind confidence of the peasants and, by awakening base instincts, to rouse the peasant masses to unthinking struggle. . . .

. . . Unafraid of the reproach that we are supposedly concerned solely with the protection of our own interests, the nobility declares in all firmness that the passage of a land law based on compulsory alienation of private possession will shake to the very foundations one of the firmest mainstays of state life—the inviolability of property rights—and will have a ruinous effect upon the entire national welfare and the proper development of the country. At the same time, recognition of the full right of the peasants to ownership of the land in their possession, and their confirmation in this right, is the foremost need in our national life. Consolidation of the peasants' property rights is in accord with the fundamental views and desires of the Russian people. It will develop the desire to work and will strengthen the force of attachment for one's own possessions and respect for the possessions of others.

The preaching of the alienation of land conceals behind it, and is the first step toward, a victory of the idea of socialism, which denies all property. An obstacle to the realization of this idea in Russia is private land ownership, which also protects the inviolability of peasant ownership. Therefore, the complete abolition of land ownership is essential to socialism, in view of the subsequent opportunity to abolish easily the land ownership of the peasants as well, and to turn the entire people, impoverished and robbed of its land, into slavery to the all-powerful force of international capital.

The destruction of private land ownership will also undermine at the very root the common interests of the national economy, lowering the productivity of Russia's land which, in turn, will affect all the commercial and monetary affairs of the country. . . .

. . . The nobility considers the enlargement of the peasants' arable land area an urgent and pressing task before the state administration, to be accomplished both by the proper organization of resettlement on the basis of ownership and by the development of state land credits. Besides this, it is most important to encourage improvement in agricultural methods on the allotted land. All obstacles to completely free, independent, and creative agricultural labor should be eliminated; all tutelage should be abolished, especially in the economic realm; transition to the use of land on the basis of full ownership, which constitutes the principal lever for economic effort and progress, should be facilitated; the development of industries everywhere should guarantee the opportunity for work during periods when there is no farm work to be done; and, finally, well-organized popular education should provide a moral upbringing in the spirit of the Christian faith and on the basis of our people's fundamental attitudes, the roots of which are alive despite the false teachings brought in from the outside.

XVII:27. THE AGRARIAN PROGRAM OF THE FOURTH CONGRESS OF THE RSDWP, APRIL 1906

The Fourth Congress of the RSDWP, held in Stockholm in April 1906, brought the Bolshevik and Menshevik factions together for the time being. This congress adopted a change in the party program of 1903 in respect to the vexed question of peasant landholdings, where the Social-Democratic view of the historical process conflicted with the party's desire for immediate peasant support. (Concerning the Bolsheviks and Mensheviks, see also several of the documents in Chapter XVI, Section B.)

Reference: *Programma i ustav Rossiiskoi Sotsial'-demokraticheskoi Rabochei Partii* (Paris: *Sotsial'demokrat,* 1909), pp. 9-10.

With the aim of eliminating the remnants of serfdom, which are a heavy burden lying directly upon the peasants, and in the interests of the unhindered development of the class struggle in the village, the Russian Social-Democratic Workers' Party demands:

1. The abolition of all legal restrictions on the person and property of peasants as a separate class.

2. The abolition of all payments and obligations that discriminate against the peasantry as a class, and the annulment of debtor obligations of an oppressive character.

3. The confiscation of church, monastery, appanage, and cabinet [see Item XVII:7] lands, and their transfer, along with state lands, to large-scale organs of local self-government, combining municipal and rural districts; land required for the resettlement fund, and likewise forests and waters of importance to the state as a whole, are to be transferred into the possession of a democratic state.

4. The confiscation of privately owned land, except for small landholdings, and its placement at the disposal of large-scale organs of local self-government, elected on democratic principles; the minimum size of plots of land subject to confiscation shall be determined by these large-scale organs of local self-government.

While supporting the revolutionary actions of the peasantry, including the confiscation of landowners' estates, the Russian Social-Democratic Workers' Party shall always and unfailingly oppose any attempt to retard the course of economic development. In the event of the triumphal outcome of a revolution, the Russian Social-Democratic Workers' Party, while striving to transfer confiscated lands into the possession of democratic institutions of local self-government, shall, if conditions do not favor this, support the division among the peasants of those estate lands that are actually used for small-scale economic operations, or lands that are necessary for rounding them off. Along with this, the party, in any event and whatever the status of democratic agrarian reforms, sets itself the task of striving undeviatingly toward the independent class organization of the village proletariat, of making clear to it the irreconcilable opposition of its interests to the interests of the peasant bourgeoisie, of cautioning it against seduction by an economic system of small-scale enterprises which, given the existence of commodity production, would never be able to eliminate the poverty of the masses, and, finally, of indicating the necessity of a complete socialist upheaval as the sole means of eliminating all poverty and all exploitation.

XVII:28. STOLYPIN'S REPORT FROM SARATOV, 1904

One stage in the development of Stolypin's attitudes on agrarian problems is seen in these excerpts from the report that, in his capacity as governor of the Saratov guberniia, he submitted to the tsar covering the year 1904.

Reference: *Krasnyi arkhiv,* 17 (1926): 84-85. This translation and those of the next five items were contributed by Christopher Becker.

The Russian peasant has a passion for making everyone equal, for reducing everything to a common denominator, and since the masses cannot be raised to the level of the most capable, the most active, and the most intelligent, the best elements must be brought

down to the level of understanding and ambition prevailing among the inferior, inert majority. This can be seen both in the difficulty of implanting improved agricultural techniques into the communal economy, and in the frequent difficulties encountered in arranging for a whole commune to acquire land with the aid of the Peasant Bank.

. . .

The extent of the peasant's need for land and his love for it is demonstrated by the disproportionately high rental fees he pays to lease land in certain uezdy. In good years the harvest barely justifies these fees; in poor, and even in average, years the peasant works for nothing. This leads not only to poverty but also to the hatred of one class for another and to animosity toward the existing order, which can easily be exploited by propaganda and can give rise to agrarian disorders spreading with unbelievable rapidity, even into prosperous neighboring localities. This has been demonstrated again the past year.

The hunger for land and the agrarian disorders themselves indicate the measures that could rescue the peasant population from its present abnormal situation. The natural counterbalance to the communal principle is individual ownership of property. It serves also as a guarantee of order, since the small property owner is the cornerstone of any durable political structure. At present the stronger peasant usually turns into a kulak, into an exploiter of his fellows in the commune. . . . If another outlet could be found for the energy and initiative of the best forces of the peasantry, and if the industrious farmer could be given the opportunity first to obtain temporarily, as a trial venture, and then to secure possession of a separate plot of land, taken from the state lands or from the lands at the disposal of the Peasant Bank, with provision for a water supply and the other conditions essential to the proper cultivation of land, then alongside the commune, where the commune is a vital force, the independent, prosperous peasant would make his appearance.

XVII:29. THE DECREE ON PEASANT RIGHTS, OCTOBER 5, 1906

On October 5, 1906, the government under Stolypin issued a decree—whose importance is sometimes overlooked—"on the repeal of certain restrictions on the rights of village dwellers." This decree marked the virtual completion of the process of emancipating the peasants. Here are its principal provisions.

Reference: *PSZRI*, 3d ser., vol. 26, pt. 1, pp. 891-93.

The great reform of February 19, 1861, which admitted millions of village dwellers [peasants] to participation in general civic life, laid the foundation for gradually extending to the peasants equal rights with the rest of the population of the empire. Now, following our manifestos of August 6 and October 17 of the past year [1905], which summoned the rural population to participate in legislative work, it remains to consummate the sage plans of the tsar-liberator according to the principles, which we have proclaimed, of civil liberty and the equality before the law of all Russian citizens.

. . . In regard to the peasantry . . . the law still retains certain individual restrictions that are not in agreement with the basic provisions and general spirit of the manifestos of August 6 and October 17, 1905; some of these [restrictions] have indeed already lost their original significance as a result of the abolition of collective responsibility [of the community for arrears, by the decree of March 12, 1903] and redemption payments [by the decree of November 3, 1905].

. . . We hereby issue these commands:

I. To give all Russian subjects regardless of their origin, with the exception of the *inorodtsy* [ethnic groups with a special legal status, including native tribes of Siberia, Central Asia, and Trans-Caspia, the Samoyeds, Kalmyks, and Jews], equal rights with regard to state service, so as to conform with the rights enjoyed by persons of noble estate [or class]. . . .

II. To free village dwellers and persons belonging to other estates formerly under special obligations [*podatnoe sostoianie*] from the requirement of presenting certificates of discharge from their communes upon entering educational institutions or the civil service.
. . .

III. To discontinue the obligatory exclusion from their commune . . . of village dwellers . . . who have obtained the rights of a higher estate, and to permit such persons to remain members of their commune. . . .

IV. To permit village dwellers who are members of a village commune to become members of other village communes without

compulsory exclusion from the first commune.
. . .

V. To give village dwellers and persons belonging to other estates formerly under special obligations the freedom to choose their place of permanent residence, on the same . . . basis as persons of other estates. . . .

VII. To repeal the special regulations on punishments imposed on village residents and other persons under the jurisdiction of volost' courts. [Note: Corporal punishment for "village dwellers" had been abolished by the manifesto of August 11, 1904.] . . .

X. To repeal the regulation that gives governors the right to appoint the zemstvo representatives of the village communes from among the candidates nominated by the volost' assemblies . . . and to allow the nominated candidates themselves to elect from their own number the specified number of representatives. . . .

XI. To repeal the articles . . . of the statute

on the institutions for the management of peasant affairs . . . in virtue of which persons under the jurisdiction of the volost', village, and inorodtsy administrations are [at present] subject, at the discretion of the land and peasant captains [*zemskie i krest'ianskie nachal'niki*, the former being in European Russia, the latter in Siberia], to administrative punishment without formal prosecution in cases of failure to carry out the orders of the aforementioned officials.

XII. To establish that the uezd sessions [*uezdnye s"ezdy;* see the law of 1889 establishing the land captains, Item XVI:10, above] may rescind decisions of the communal peasant assemblies, upon the representation of the land and peasant captains . . . only in those cases where the decision rendered is incompatible with the law, or where a decision violating the legal rights of members of a village commune, or persons registered in the volost', has been appealed by the persons involved.

XVII:30. THE DECREE ON PEASANT ALLOTMENTS, NOVEMBER 9, 1906

Among the many laws enacted by the government during the period August to November 1906 for the benefit of the peasantry, including laws opening new land to purchase by peasants and making it easier for peasants to borrow, the most important of all was the decree of November 9—a decree that found a broad response among the peasantry and brought great changes to the Russian countryside during the ensuing decade. Here are its main provisions.

Reference: *PSZRI*, 3d ser., vol. 26, pt. 1, pp. 970-73.

By our manifesto of November 3, 1905 . . . the collection of redemption payments from peasants for allotment land will cease as of January 1, 1907. From that date onward the aforementioned lands will be freed of the limitations placed upon them because of redemption debts, and the peasants will have the right of free withdrawal from the communes, in which case individual householders who make the transfer to personal ownership will be accorded property rights over plots of land from the communal allotment.

. . .

I. . . . 1. Every householder who holds allotment lands on a communal basis may at any time demand that his due share of the aforementioned lands be accorded to him as private property. . . .

3. . . . If a householder who desires to make the transfer to private ownership holds in constant use more land than would fall to his share on the basis of the quota established by the most recent repartition, taking into

account the number of quota units [consisting of every male, every worker, or every member of the family, depending on local custom] in his family at the time of application [for separation of title], then he shall be accorded as private property [only] that amount of communal land which is his due share according to the aforementioned calculation. . . .

4. Householders who have been accorded the right of private ownership over plots of communal land held [by them] in constant use (articles 1-3) retain the right to use, to the same extent as before, all those hayfields, forests, and other appurtenances that have been repartitioned on a special basis . . . and likewise the right to share in the use . . . of homestead land belonging to the entire commune, commons, pastures, items of revenue, and so forth. . . .

12. Every householder accorded plots of allotment land [as private property] . . . has the right to demand at any time that in ex-

change for these plots the commune shall allocate to him, if possible, a corresponding consolidated plot.

13. In those cases where a demand for the allocation of a consolidated plot does not coincide with a general repartition, and where such an allocation appears inconvenient or impossible, then the commune must provide monetary compensation to the householder desiring consolidation, by mutual agreement or, failing agreement, according to an estimate made by the volost' court. . . .

III. . . . 1. Household plots [*podvornye uchastki*] including both those granted in [hereditary] household tenure [*podvornoe vladenie*] to peasants at the time they were

alloted land, and those subsequently made over from communal land to individual peasants as private property, and likewise house-and-garden plots [*usadebnye uchastki*] in communes with repartitional tenure [*obshchinnoe zemlepol'zovanie*], constitute the private property of the householder. . . .

IV. . . . The transfer of entire [peasant] communities from either communal [repartitional] or from homestead [hereditary] tenure to consolidated plot tenure [*vladenie v otrubnykh uchastkakh*] shall be carried out by the decision of a two-thirds majority of all peasants having the right to vote in the [communal] assembly.

XVII:31. STOLYPIN'S SPEECH TO THE DUMA ON THE AGRARIAN QUESTION, MAY 10, 1907

Stolypin's arguments for his land program and against the proposals of the radicals are set forth in these passages from his speech to the Second Duma on May 10, 1907.

Reference: Gosudarstvennaia Duma, vtoroi sozyv, *Stenograficheskie otchety, 1907 god,* vol. 2 (St. Petersburg, 1907), cols. 434-45.

The equal distribution [among the peasants] of all [nonpeasant] land would hardly satisfy local needs for land; it would be necessary to resort to the same method proposed by the government, i.e. to resettlement. . . . I suspect that land which would be divided among the citizens, expropriated from some and turned over to others by a local Social-Democratic bureau, would soon take on the characteristics of water and air. It would be utilized; but as for improving it, as for putting one's labor into it when the results of this labor would go to someone else, no one would do that. More generally, the stimulus to work, the motive that makes people work, would be removed. Every citizen—and there always have been and always will be slackers among them—will know that he has the right to declare his desire to receive land, to put his labor into the land, and then, when he begins to tire of this occupation, to leave it and go wandering again through the wide world. Everything will be equal, but it is possible to make everyone equal only at the lowest level. A lazy man cannot be made the equal of a hard worker, a dull-witted man cannot be brought to the level of a capable one. As a result the level of agriculture in the country will be lowered. The good farmer, the farmer with initiative, will in the nature of things be deprived of the possibility of applying his

talents to the land. . . . The reapportionment of all the land will not bring the state as a whole a single additional ear of grain. All advanced agricultural enterprises will certainly be destroyed. Temporarily the peasant allotments will be increased in size, but with an increase in population they will soon become microscopically small, and this atomized land will send masses of impoverished proletarians into the cities.

. . .

The government considers that the nationalization of land would be ruinous for the country, while the plan of the Party of National Freedom [Kadets], i.e. semiexpropriation and seminationalization, would, in the last analysis, in our opinion, lead to the same results as the proposals of the parties of the Left.

. . . The aim of the government is quite definite: the government wants to increase peasant landholdings; it wishes to see the peasant rich and prosperous, since where there is prosperity, there are also, of course, enlightenment and true liberty. But to this end it is essential to provide the capable, hard-working Russian peasant, the salt of the Russian earth, with the opportunity to free himself from the hindrances and the conditions of life which he now faces. We must give him the opportunity to keep the fruits of his own labor, and to make them his inalienable property. Let this property be held in common wherever the commune is not yet moribund, let it be held as homestead property [*podvornaia sobstvennost'*] where the commune is no longer a living force, but let it be strong, let it be hereditary. The government has an obligation to help the property-holding farmer with counsel and with credit, that is, with money.... At the present time our state is ailing. Its sickest and weakest part, the part that is growing feeble and sluggish, is the peasantry. It must be helped. There has been proposed a simple, completely automatic, completely mechanical method: to seize and divide all 130,000 estates existing at present. Would this be statesmanlike? Wouldn't this be like the story of Trishka's dressing gown [in a fable of Krylov]—cutting off the flaps to make the sleeves? . . . The idea that all the resources of the state should be employed to help its weakest part may call to mind the principles of socialism; but if this is a principle of socialism, then it is one of state socialism, which has been applied more than once in western Europe and which has produced real and substantial results. This principle could be applied in Russia by the government's assuming the payment of part of the interest the peasants are required to pay for the land placed at their disposal. In general terms the arrangement would be as follows: the government would buy the private lands put up for sale; these, together with the appanage [*udel'nye*] and state [*gosudarstvennye*] lands, would constitute a state land fund. Considering the large amount of land that would be put up for sale, land prices would not rise. From this fund, the peasants with little land who can use more and who are actually putting their labor into the land at present, and also the peasants who need to improve their form of land tenure [i.e. toward the ownership of consolidated plots] at present, could receive land on favorable terms.... At the same time, once withdrawal from the commune is per-

mitted and individual property ownership is firmly established, once resettlement is properly organized, once it becomes easier to receive loans on allotment land, and once large-scale credit for land improvement is granted, although the program of land reforms proposed by the government would not be fully realized, some hopeful features would appear in examining the problem as a whole, and perhaps even the notorious issue of compulsory expropriation would present itself in a clearer light. It is time to place this matter [expropriation] in perspective; it is time, gentlemen, to stop looking upon this as a magic remedy, as a panacea for all ills. This seems like a bold remedy only because in an impoverished Russia it would create still another class of utterly impoverished landowners. Compulsory expropriation, gentlemen, may in fact prove necessary, but only as an exception and not as a general rule, and only if hedged with clear and exact legal guarantees. Compulsory expropriation must be qualitative rather than quantitative in character. It should be employed, for the most part, only where the peasants can be taken care of locally, as a means of improving methods of land utilization; it should be resorted to only when essential agricultural techniques are being improved—to provide for watering places and cattle-drives to pasture, to build roads, and, finally, to eliminate the pernicious system of scattered strip holding. . . .

After spending roughly ten years working for agricultural development, I have become profoundly convinced that this is a task that demands tenacious application and long preparatory labors. We cannot solve this problem; we can only work toward a solution. This has taken the Western governments decades. The path we propose to you is modest but true. The opponents of state authority would like to take the path of radicalism, the path of emancipation from the historical past of Russia, of emancipation from its cultural traditions. They want great upheavals, we want a great Russia!

XVII:32. STOLYPIN'S "WAGER ON THE STRONG" SPEECH IN THE THIRD DUMA, DECEMBER 5, 1908

When the Third Duma took up the agrarian bill—a bill the Duma's Agrarian Commission had prepared in order to amend and expand the terms of the decree of November 9, 1906—much of the debate centered around the question of family as opposed to individual ownership. These excerpts from the stenographic report of the Duma sessions of December 1 and 5, 1908, include, not only Stolypin's own words defending the bill, but also some of the opposing arguments, so that the reader may have some means of judging for himself what Stolypin had in mind when he uttered his famous and often misunderstood words about the "wager on the strong."

Reference: Gosudarstvennaia Duma, tretii sozyv, *Stenograficheskie otchety, 1908 god, Sessiia 2*, vol. 1 (St. Petersburg, 1908), 24th sitting, cols. 2002-05, 2024, 2053, 2280-84.

[December 1:]

OBRAZTSOV (Ekaterinoslav guberniia) [from the Right]: . . . [The plan drawn up by the Agrarian Commission] intends to convert 50,000,000 commune peasants into private landowners with a single stroke of the pen. This is unthinkable, this is impossible. It is unthinkable juridically: the last reapportionment in our commune, in our village, took place twenty-four years ago. I was alloted the ten desiatinas of land which I am using today. Three days ago the State Duma declared that I am no longer a commune member, but a homesteading [podvornyi] plot holder, and today it wants to declare that I am no longer a homesteader, but a private householder, and that the ten desiatinas are my private property. But the question is, what are these ten desiatinas, and why ten rather than two or twenty? Ten because at the reapportionment I was apportioned two desiatinas, and two desiatinas for each of my four sons, and that made ten desiatinas. But how is it that I now prove to be the owner of someone else's land, the private owner of land that does not at all belong to me? . . . I repeat, this is unthinkable in law and impossible in fact. Even if you mobilize the whole Russian army for a civil war with the people, even then you will fail. How can you take land away from 50,000,000 people, land which belongs to them, belongs to them on legal grounds, belongs to them by right of inheritance, belongs to them by economic right, since they paid taxes and duties on it; belongs to them by right of labor, since they have worked it? How can you take this land away from them? . . . The immoderate application of the law of November 9 [1906] . . . has created a most serious danger, not only to the well-being, but also to the very existence of Russia. The danger is extreme. Now the time has come . . . to sound the alarm. . . . The Russian peasant . . . used to sell for drink things that were not worth saving—he drank away a poor horse cart, drank away his clothes, his boots. . . . Now he will drink away his land (*applause from Left and Right*), now he will drink away his

own children, now he will drink away the fate of his grandchildren and the destiny of his fatherland. Now is the time to sound the alarm.

· · ·

SHINGAREV (Voronezh guberniia) [Kadet]: . . . I maintain that to change in this fashion a way of life, to change the forms of landholding, is impossible, that the institution of private property can never be established by shifting over to it in one minute. . . . Woe to that legislation which attempts, contrary to life, in favor of an abstract principle, no matter how perfect, to change immediately the way of life of a people. Woe to the legislation that attempts, without considering the peculiarities of a people's life, its psychology, its beliefs, its habits, to introduce reforms instantly in abstract fashion. This procedure, gentlemen, will never establish the institution of private property. This way is the way of alarm, the way to troubles, the way to mutual misunderstanding and disagreement, and not the way to the extension of law and order, not the way to a renewal of Russian life.

· · ·

MARKOV II (Kursk guberniia) [leader of the rightist segment]: . . . The peasantry, across the wide expanse of Russia . . . makes use of lands in communal ownership, makes use of them as a household, as a family, but not as a separate person, not as a householder. . . . The whole family . . . all of them, work and bring to the family the fruits of their labors. . . . This way of life cannot be shattered with a single stroke of the pen. . . . In this respect the bill of the Agrarian Commission, in my opinion, has failed; it did not wish to take account of life or of conditions.

· · ·

[December 5:]

PRESIDENT OF THE COUNCIL OF MINISTERS STOLYPIN: . . . In those localities of Russia where the individuality of the peasant is already definitely developed, where the commune as a coercive union constitutes an obstacle to his independent activity, there must be given the freedom to apply his labors to the land; there he must be given the liberty to work, to enrich himself, to have charge of his own property; he must be given control over the land, he must be saved from the slavery of the obsolescent communal system. . . . One cannot preach, on the one hand, that people are mature enough to dispose freely, without guardians, of their spiritual forces, to apply their energies freely to the land as they think best, and, on the other hand, admit that these same people are too untrustworthy to be allowed to take proper care of their property without pressure from the other members of their family. . . . The law must place certain limitations, certain restrictions, on the land, but not on its owner. Our laws contain such restrictions and limitations, and we, gentlemen, have retained these limitations in our bill: allotment lands may not be alienated to a person of another class [soslovie]; allotment lands may not be mortgaged except to the Peasant Bank; they may not be sold for private debts; they may not be bequeathed otherwise than according to custom. But what is family ownership? . . . Why is it necessary? First of all, it creates certain limitations, and these limitations relate not to the land but to its owner. These limitations are quite serious: the owner of the land, according to the proposal of the proponents of family ownership, may not, without the agreement of the members of the family, without the agreement of the children of the householder, either sell his plot, or mortgage it, or even, it seems, secure it for himself or shift his allotment into a single location; he is hindered in his every

action. . . . The small family commune . . . will undoubtedly paralyze both the personal liberty and the private initiative of the villager. In the name of what is this all to be done? Do you think that by this you will protect the property of the children of fathers who are drunken or spendthrift, or who have remarried? . . . We cannot create a general law for exceptional, abnormal cases. . . . We must, when we write laws for the whole country, keep in mind the judicious and the strong, and not the drunken and the weak. . . . The government . . . by using the provisions of article 87 in order to enact the law of November 9, 1906 . . . placed its wager not on the poor and the drunken, but on the firm and the strong. . . . In Russia such strong people are in the majority. . . . Isn't it clear enough that the slavery of the commune, the yoke of family ownership, is a bitter and unwanted hardship for ninety million of our population? Have you forgotten that this path has already been tried, that the colossal [experiment] of guardianship over a huge part of our population has already suffered a great defeat? . . . The partisans of family ownership, both on the Right and on the Left, in my opinion, are profoundly wrong. . . . All the efforts both of the legislator and of the government should be directed toward raising the productive forces of the sole source of our well-being—the land. By applying to it individual labor, private property—by attaching to it all, absolutely all the strength of the people—we must lift up our impoverished, our weakened, our exhausted land; for the land is the promise of our future strength; the land is Russia.

XVII:33. THE LAND LAW OF JUNE 14, 1910

Here are some of the most important passages from the very complicated but highly important land law which was worked out by the Agrarian Commission of the Third Duma and, with Stolypin's support and despite much opposition, made its way slowly through the Duma and the State Council, finally to be signed by the emperor on June 14, 1910.

Reference: *PSZRI,* 3d ser., vol. 30, pt. 1, pp. 746-50.

1. Those communities [*obshchestva*] and settlements . . . in which there have been no general repartitions since they were allotted land are regarded as having been transferred to hereditary (plot [*uchastkovoe*] or homestead [*podvornoe*]) ownership. . . .

2. In the communities and settlements mentioned in article 1, plots that, at the time of publication of the present law, are held in

indisputable constant (not rented) use by individual householders are declared to be their private property, or, in the requisite cases (article 48), to be property held in common with the other members of the family. . . .

9. Any householder possessing allotment land by communal right may at any time demand that the portion of the aforemen-

tioned land that is due to be rendered to persons who leave the commune be made his private property, or, in the requisite cases (article 48), be made property held in common with the other members of the family. . . .

17. Householders who have had plots of communal land transferred to them as their private property (articles 11-16) retain the right to use, to the same extent as before, all those haying, forest, and other lands that are shared on special conditions, for instance, according to the products of the soil, and so forth. . . .

19. Rights of sharing in the use of undivided benefits, such as communal gardening plots [*mirskaia usadebnaia zemlia*], thoroughfares, roads leading to pastures, watering places, common pastures, quitrent incomes, and the like, are confirmed without change. . . .

32. Every householder who has had plots of allotment land transferred to him . . . has the right to demand that the commune apportion to him, in place of these plots, a corresponding plot in one place, if possible.

33. If such an apportionment (article 32) is found to be inconvenient or impossible by the proper authorities (articles 37 and 60), then the commune is obliged to indemnify the householder desiring to withdraw by a money payment reached by mutual agreement, or, if no agreement can be reached, in accordance with a valuation made by the uezd land-organizing [*zemleustroitel'naia*] commission. If the householder desiring to withdraw finds the valuation set by the commission unfavorable to himself, then he may refuse the money payment and may continue to hold the plots transferred to his ownership, with their previous boundaries.

34. Such an apportionment in one place, if possible (article 32), is mandatory upon a commune, and the right to indemnify those withdrawing by a money payment is nullified, in the following cases: (1) during general repartitions, if application for this apportion-

ment has been made prior to the passage of the resolution to repartition, and (2) apart from general repartitions, (a) if not less than a fifth of all householders demand such apportionment, or, in communities where the number of householders is greater than 250, no fewer than 50 demand it, and (b) upon application of even a single householder, where the apportionment is declared (articles 33 and 37) to be possible and not to entail special inconveniences. . . .

39. Plots transferred to private ownership . . . are subject, both before and after their consolidation in a single place, to the regulations concerning allotment lands. [See Stolypin's speech of December 5, 1908, above.] . . .

46. The conversion of entire communities [*obshchestva*] and settlements from communal or mixed landholding to consolidated-plot [*otrubnye uchastki*] ownership is accomplished by the passing of a resolution by a majority of two-thirds of all householders having the right to vote in the [communal] assembly. . . .

47. Both those plots given to peasants in homestead ownership at the time when they were allotted land and also those plots that were consequently transferred from communal lands to the ownership of individual peasants . . . constitute the private property of the householders. . . .

48. In those cases where the plots referred to in article 47 are in the common possession of a mother and her children, or of several persons not related to each other in a direct line of descent, the plots constitute their common property. . . .

56. For the time being, until peasant landholding legislation is reviewed, it is forbidden, within the boundaries of a single uezd, to consolidate in a single holding, by purchasing or receiving as a gift, allotment lands . . . equivalent to the standard or above-standard allotments of more than six souls, in guberniias and oblasti where the regional Great Russian and Ukrainian codes apply.

XVII:34. LENIN ON THE PEASANTRY IN HIS REPORT TO THE FIFTH PARTY CONGRESS, MAY 12, 1907

The question of revolutionary policy among the peasantry was treated this way by Lenin on May 12 (25, N.S.), 1907, in his report at the Fifth Congress of the Russian Social-Democratic Workers' Party, meeting in London.

Reference: Vladimir I. Lenin, *Sochineniia*, 2d ed., 30 vols. (Moscow: Gosizdat, 1926-30), 11:246-47, 251, 252.

The bourgeoisie can be neither the prime mover nor the leader of the revolution. The proletariat alone is capable of leading it to the end, that is, to complete victory. But this victory can be achieved only on the condition that the proletariat manages to enlist the majority of the peasants in its support. The victory of the present revolution in Russia is possible only in the form of a revolutionary democratic dictatorship of the proletariat and the peasantry.

. . .

Keep in mind that we are now appraising the significance of peasant ideals not in the framework of the socialist movement but in *this particular* bourgeois democratic revolution. Would it be utopian or reactionary in *this particular* revolution for all the land to be taken away from the landowners and distributed or alloted equally among the peasants? No! Far from being reactionary, this would be the most definite, the most consistent expression of the aspiration to destroy completely the entire old order, all the remnants of serfdom. What is utopian is the belief that "equalization" could endure under a system of commodity production and could even serve as the beginning of a semi-

socialist system. But the peasants' desire to seize the estates of the landlords right away and to distribute them equally is not utopian but revolutionary in the fullest, strictest, most scientific meaning of the word. Such a seizure and such a distribution would create the basis for the swiftest, broadest, and freest development of capitalism.

. . .

The class-conscious proletariat knows that there is and can be no other road to socialism than through a bourgeois democratic revolution.

This means that the less complete and decisive this revolution, the longer will the proletariat be burdened, not with socialist tasks, nor with purely proletarian tasks, but with general democratic tasks. The more complete the victory of the peasantry, the sooner will the proletariat definitely emerge as a separate class, the more clearly will it bring to the fore its own purely socialist tasks and goals.

From this it is clear that the peasants' ideas about [land] equalization are reactionary and utopian from the viewpoint of socialism and revolutionary from the viewpoint of bourgeois democracy.

XVII:35. A CONTEMPORARY ACCOUNT OF THE ASSASSINATION OF A. M. MAKSIMOVSKII, OCTOBER 15, 1907

In its issue of October 21, 1907, the journal *Pravo* printed this account of a not atypical assassination and of the character and behavior of the assassin. (Concerning terrorism in the years 1905-09, see also Item XVI:65, above.)

Reference: *Pravo*, no. 42 (Oct. 21, 1907), cols. 2734-35.

On October 15, 1907, the director of the Chief Prison Administration, Actual State Councillor A. M. Maksimovskii, was assassinated in Saint Petersburg under the following circumstances. A young woman of eighteen or twenty, of the educated class in appearance, came to the headquarters of the Chief Prison Administration. When the official on duty approached her to inquire, she declared that she had come to appeal for alleviating [prison] conditions for her husband's brother and insisted on a personal interview with the director of the Chief Administration. She was informed that the director would receive her after seeing the many petitioners in the waiting room who already had appointments. The young woman sat down to wait on a chair near the door to the office. Shortly before five o'clock the door to the office opened, and Mr. Maksimovskii appeared in

the doorway. He had barely appeared when the young woman quickly arose and, taking several steps toward him, shot at him point-blank with a Browning. The bullet hit him in the upper lip, shattered his jaw, and lodged in the brain. M[aksimovskii] fell across the doorway to his office. The assassin was seized at once. On her breast was found a package tightly bound to her body with cord. Between two thin layers of cotton wadding was found a small pouch made of white elastic fabric, equipped with a detonating cord.

According to experts, the pouch contained about thirteen pounds of nitroglycerin, which would have been quite sufficient not only to kill everyone in the building but also to demolish the building itself. The assassin, Ragozinnikova, is a *meshchanka* [feminine of *meshchanin*, someone of the tradesman-craftsman class] of the town of Krasnoufimsk and a former student at the conservatory.

. . . On the morning of October 16, Ragozinnikova was handed her indictment, and at 3:00 P.M. she was brought to court. The prison inspector and three watchmen from the [Chief Prison] Administration were called as witnesses in the case of the murder of the director . . . A. M. Maksimovskii. The interrogation of the defendant—who replied to the questions of the presiding judge either with laughter or with silence—and of the witnesses was completed by four o'clock. The prosecutor's speech and the presiding judge's summation were short. Following this, the

court retired for deliberation. At four o'clock [sic] the court pronounced the verdict, sentencing the meshchanka Ragozinnikova to death by hanging, under article 279, volume 22 of the military regulations, for membership in a criminal organization and for the murder of the director of the Chief Prison Administration, Actual State Councillor A. M. Maksimovskii. The sentence was forwarded for confirmation to the commander in chief of the armed forces of the Saint Petersburg [military] district. After the sentence was read, Ragozinnikova made a deep bow to the judges and burst into laughter. She gave no testimony.

XVII:36. THE PROCEEDINGS OF THE SOCIALIST REVOLUTIONARY PARTY CONFERENCE OF 1908

These passages from the published record of the First General Party Conference of the Socialist Revolutionary Party, held in August 1908 in London, give some ideas of how the SRs viewed the situation in Russia at that time and what they thought they ought to do about it. "Olenin" was one of the pseudonyms of the SR leader Viktor M. Chernov. (On Chernov, see Item XVI:40, above.)

Reference: *Protokoly pervoi obshchepartiinoi konferentsii P.S-R., 1908 g.* (Paris: Izd. TsK PS-R, 1908), pp. 56-57 [Chernov], 228-29 [resolution].

[From the "Report of Comrade Olenin on the Activities of the C.C. (Central Committee)":]

The period covered by this report was a period of definite crisis for the social-revolutionary parties in Russia, and this crisis was bound to influence strongly the nature of the activity of the C[entral] C[ommittee]. Our party has suffered very severe damage; the Social-Democratic Party, rent as before by disputes between "Bolsheviks" and "Mensheviks," who are only nominally united but in reality separately organized, has probably suffered even more than ours; the P[olish] S[ocialist] P[arty] has broken up into two parts; the Bund has faded away. . . . The general crisis has created immensely difficult conditions for party work, which have greatly hampered the activity of the C.C. There are extremely few local workers left, and as a result of this the intermediate links between the masses and the central organs of the party have become weak.

. . . Almost all [of those presenting reports] note that over the current period we have unfortunately become estranged from the masses—not because the masses have become disillusioned in revolution and have abandoned it, but because the organization has melted

away and evaporated. . . . Among local Russian [party] workers this problem—that many comrades have stopped working [for the party] — has become a terribly sore point. "The grievous need for party workers," which has been spoken of here, is what paralyzes work and saps the strength of the comrades who remain at their posts by swamping them with all kinds of work, by forcing them to do too many things at once and to knock themselves out, by absorbing all their time in organizational hustle and bustle, and by denying them the possibility of putting their work on a more solid basis. . . . For us as an organization, herein lies a real tragedy. At a time when the demands of the masses are growing so, when there is such a need for qualified and extra-qualified propagandists, what have we to offer the workers? Weak little groups of party men, who complain that they are overwhelmed by organizational hustle and bustle! For us this quite often means bankruptcy. The party is not living through a *political* crisis, its program and tactics have not been undermined by stern experience, but there is no doubt that it is experiencing an *organizational* crisis, and a very severe one.

[From the resolution "On the Struggle against the Agrarian Laws":]

The government, having suppressed attempts at open rebellion and seizure of land in the villages, has set itself the goals: (a) of calming the peasant masses by minor concessions in the economic and legal spheres; (b) of sowing dissension among them by encouraging the plunder of communal land; (c) of atomizing the peasantry by an intensified implantation of individual private property and the *khutor* [enclosed individual farmstead] economy. Every success of the government in this direction inflicts serious damage on the cause of the revolution and creates obstacles to the realization of the agrarian program of our party. On the other hand, the landowning class, relying on the victory of the government and the dissension sown among the peasantry, is organizing itself and attempting to regain the positions it has forfeited in the village.

In such circumstances the village becomes the chief sociopolitical battlefield. The outcome of the struggle in the village will determine the history of our country for a long time to come. Therefore the party must pay particular attention to its tasks in the village, and to the immediate questions of peasant policy.

From this point of view the present situation in the village demands first and foremost from the party:

1. Intensification of propaganda as regards: (a) a more concrete elucidation of our agrarian program . . . (b) steadfast criticism of private ownership of land, criticism that will not brook any compromise with individualistic inclinations, and (c) elucidation of the entire scope of the agrarian measures of the government.

2. Special discussion—in peasant organizations and at assemblies of their representatives—of methods of struggle against the corrupting influence of agrarian legislation and against the landowners, working out the decisions that are most expedient in the conditions of a given locality.

3. Development from among the peasants of active workers who will be capable of carrying on independently the sum total of party work in the village.

4. Strengthening of party organizations in the village and the rallying around them of the toiling peasantry on the basis of struggle against the agrarian legislation of the government, and against the landowners and the Peasant [Land] Bank over the renting of land and hiring of labor.

Turning in particular to the struggle against the separation of holdings [*vydel*, by which a peasant acquired clear title to his land and withdrew from the commune], [the following measures] are considered expedient: (a) the improvement of working procedures within the commune . . . (b) the struggle, by means of communal decisions, against demands for the separation of holdings; (c) the boycott of kulaks and those members of a commune who desire the separation of holdings so as to seize a larger amount of land than would fall to their family in the event of a new repartition.

XVII:37. A BOLSHEVIK APPRAISAL OF 1910

This passage from the platform drawn up by the group of Bolsheviks associated with the newspaper *Vpered* (Forward) shows something of their view of the state of the revolutionary movement in 1910, before the upsurge of industrial strikes that was soon to come.

Reference: *Sovremennoe polozhenie i zadachi partii. Platforma, vyrabotannaia gruppoi Bol'shevikov* (Paris: Izd. Gruppy "Vpered," 1910), p. 1.

Our party is in a very serious condition. In the two and one-half years since the time of the London congress [of May 1907], at which from 130,000 to 140,000 organized workers were represented, our organizations have grown much smaller: where there were thousands [of members] before, there are only hundreds now; where there were hundreds, there are only scores; and many local groups have disintegrated altogether. To the same degree, or still more, all local activity has been curtailed. Because of countless arrests and banishments, and also because of the desertion of the intelligentsia, there is an enormous shortage of forces for leadership and propaganda. There are almost no local publications; and where they do spring up it develops that, for absence of writers, it is too difficult to run them. From abroad no propaganda literature is received at all, and only an insignificant amount of literature that gives political guidance, and even this is unsatisfactory to the local [party] workers. The ties between organizations have become extremely weak; all-party and even regional centers hardly function in Russia at all. There are insufficient forces for directing party work in the trade unions, cooperatives, and clubs that still survive; the party has no success in guiding the activity of its Duma faction in any systematic way, or making any serious use of it. Work in the armed forces and among the peasantry has died down altogether. The decline has undoubtedly been severe.

At the same time, however, our proletarian organizations display in practice a very great vitality, a very great capacity for work and development. After thousands of comrades were thrown out of the ranks of the party, and the unstable intelligentsia took flight along with those circles of social-democratic workers less imbued with class consciousness, there remained a firm and steady proletarian nucleus of party organizations. It bears the entire burden of reaction, makes innumerable sacrifices for the party cause, and carries it on, over all the difficulties and obstacles, with hardly any help and support.

XVII:38. VEKHI, 1909

The volume *Vekhi* (Road markers), published in 1909, contained many provocative criticisms of the Russian intelligentsia. Here are excerpts from the articles of S. N. Bulgakov, P. B. Struve, and S. L. Frank.

Reference: *Vekhi: Sbornik statei o russkoi intelligentsii*, 4th ed. (Moscow: T. and I. N. Kushnerev, 1909), pp. 30-31, 39, 41, 60-61 [Bulgakov], 170-71 [Struve], 185, 188-89, 204-05 [Frank]. Reprinted: Frankfurt a. M.: Posev, 1967.

[From Sergei Nikolaevich Bulgakov (1871-1944), "Heroism and Selfless Devotion [*podvizhnichestvo*]":]

It is well known that there is no intelligentsia more atheistic than the Russian. Atheism is the common creed in which all, both those from the educated classes and those from the people, who enter into the bosom of the intellectual humanistic church are christened. And it dates back to the very beginning, to the spiritual father of the Russian intelligentsia, Belinskii. And just as every social milieu evolves its own particular customs, its own particular beliefs, so has the traditional atheism of the Russian intelligentsia become an obvious peculiarity which is not even discussed, as if it were a sign of good taste. A certain degree of education and enlightenment is, in the eyes of our intelligentsia, synonymous with indifference to and denial of religion. There is no debate among the various factions, parties, and "orientations" on this point; in this they are all united. . . . And at the same time it must be admitted that Russian atheism is by no means a conscious denial, the result of a complex, anguished, and prolonged effort of the mind, heart, and will, the summoning up of one's private life. No, it is most frequently taken on faith and preserves the features of a naïve religious faith only turned inside out; and this [view] is in no wise altered because it

[Russian atheism] assumes militant, dogmatic, pseudo-scientific forms.

· · ·

The heroic member of the intelligentsia is not satisfied . . . with the role of modest worker (even when he is perforce limited to such a role). His dream is to be the savior of mankind or, at least, of the Russian people. . . . Maximalism is an integral feature of the heroism of the intelligentsia, revealed with such startling clarity during the Russian revolution [of 1905]. It is not an attribute of any one party, it is the very soul of heroism, for the hero will, in general, not tolerate anything on a small scale. Even if he does not see any opportunity for the immediate realization of the maximum, and never will see it, his mind is occupied solely with it. He makes a historical leap in his imagination and, little interested in the path he has jumped over, he fixes his gaze only upon the bright spot on the very edge of the historical horizon. Such maximalism bears the marks of an ideological obsession, of self-hypnosis; it paralyzes thought and produces a fanaticism that is deaf to the voice of reality. This also provides an answer to the problem faced by the historian, of why the most extreme tendencies triumphed in the revolution, while the tasks of the moment were given an increasingly maximalist definition (going so far as the establishment of a socialist republic or anarchy).

· · ·

Our intelligentsia, which almost to a man aspires to collectivism, to the greatest possible organic togetherness [*sobornost'*] in human existence, is by its very nature anticollective, anticooperative, for it carries within itself the divisive element of heroic self-affirmation. A hero is to a certain extent a superman who strikes with respect to his fellow men the proud and challenging attitude of a savior; and for all its striving for democracy, the intelligentsia represents merely a special variety of class aristocratism, haughtily contrasting itself with the "philistines." Whoever has lived among the intelligentsia is quite familiar with this arrogance and conceit, this sense of infallibility, this scorn for those of a different mind, and this abstract dogmatism in whose mold all its doctrines are cast. Because of its maximalism, the intelligentsia remains deaf to the arguments both of historical realism and of scientific knowledge. Socialism itself is for the intelligentsia not a general concept designating a gradual socioeconomic transformation made up of a series of specific and quite concrete reforms; not a "historical movement," but a suprahistorical "ultimate goal" (according to the terminology of the well-known debate with Bernstein), the attainment of which requires a historical leap accomplished by an act of heroism by the intelligentsia. Hence their insufficient consciousness of historic reality, hence the geometric rectilinearity of their judgments and evaluations, their notorious "principledness."

. . .

Equally well known is the cosmopolitanism of the Russian intelligentsia. Reared on the abstract schemes of the enlightenment, the member of the intelligentsia most naturally assumes the pose of the Marquis de Posa [in Schiller's drama *Don Carlos*]. He thinks of himself as a citizen of the world [*Weltbuerger*] and this empty cosmopolitanism, this absence of a healthy national sense which prevents the development of national self-awareness, is connected with the extranationality [*vnenarodnost'*] of the intelligentsia.

The intelligentsia has not yet reflected on the national problem, which has concerned only the Slavophiles, but has been satisfied with "natural" explanations of the origin of nationality (beginning with Chernyshevskii,

who assiduously blots out the independent significance of the national problem), right up to the contemporary Marxists, who dissolve it entirely in the class struggle.

[From Petr Berngardovich Struve (1870-1944), "The Intelligentsia and the Revolution":]

The grafting of the political radicalism of the intelligentsia's ideas onto the social radicalism of the people's instincts has taken place with astonishing rapidity. . . .

Political flippancy and inefficiency have been added to this fundamental moral error. Although the intelligentsia possessed the form of religiosity without its content, its "positivism," on the contrary, was something completely formless. Its "positive," "scientific" ideas were devoid of any real positiveness, any knowledge of life and people. It was "empiricism" without experience, "rationalism" without wisdom and even without common sense.

The revolution was poorly concocted. Today it is perfectly clear that a cleverly staged provocation played a role in the making of the revolution. This, however, merely illustrates strikingly the amazing inefficiency of the revolutionaries, their helplessness in practical affairs; but this is not the main point. The main point is not how they made the revolution, but that they did on the whole *make* it. They made it at a time when the task was to concentrate all efforts on political education and self-education. . . .

Thus, the irreligious apostasy from the state, which characterizes the political outlook of the Russian intelligentsia, has determined both its moral flippancy and its impracticality in politics.

[From Semen Ludvigovich Frank (1877-1950), "The Ethics of Nihilism":]

Nihilist moralism is the fundamental and most profound feature of the spiritual physiognomy of the Russian member of the intelligentsia. The negation of objective values leads to the deification of the subjective interests of one's fellow man ("the people"); hence the assertion that the supreme and the only task of man is to serve the people; and hence, in turn, an ascetic hatred of all that hinders or even merely does not abet the fulfillment of this task. Life has no objective, intrinsic meaning; its sole blessing is material security, the satisfaction of subjective needs. Therefore, man must devote all his energies to bettering the lot of the majority, and everything that diverts him from this is evil and must be mercilessly destroyed. Such is the strange chain of ideas, poorly grounded in logic but firmly welded by psychology, which guides all judgments and behavior of the Russian member of the intelligentsia.

. . .

The concept of "populism" [*narodnichestvo*] combines all the fundamental features of the spiritual temper we have described: a *nihilist utilitarianism*, which denies all absolute values and discovers in service to the subjective, material interests of the "majority" (or the people) the sole moral goal; a *moralism*, which demands from the individual uncompromising self-sacrifice and complete subordination of personal interests (even the loftiest and the purest) to the cause of public service; and finally, an *anticultural tendency*, which strives to convert all people into "working men" and to curtail and reduce higher needs to a minimum in the name of universal equality and solidarity in the realization of moral demands. . . . As an ethical being the Russian member of the intelligentsia has remained, from roughly the seventies to our day, a stubborn and inveterate *populist*. His God is the people, his only goal the happiness of the majority; his morality consists in a devotion to this goal, combined with an ascetic self-restraint and a hatred of and contempt for intrinsically valuable spiritual interests.

The Russian member of the intelligentsia has preserved this populist soul in its pristine form for decades, despite all the diversity of the political and social theories he has professed.

. . .

We may define the classic Russian member of the intelligentsia as a *militant monk of the nihilist religion of earthly well-being. . . .* But, having retired to his monastery, the member of the intelligentsia is not indifferent to the world. On the contrary, from his monastery he wants to rule the world and propagate his faith. He is a militant monk, a monk-revolutionary. The intelligentsia's entire attitude to politics—its fanaticism and intolerance, its impracticality and ineptness in political activity, its intolerable tendency to factional strife, its lack of comprehension of state interests—all this is the result of its monastic-religious character, of its regarding the purpose of political activity to be, not so much the realization of some reform that is objectively beneficial in a temporal sense, but the extermination of enemies of the faith and the forcible conversion of the world to its creed. And, finally, the *content* of this creed is a deification, based on atheism, of earthly, material welfare. All the enthusiasm of this monastic army is aimed at earthly, material interests and needs, at the creation of an earthly paradise of satiety and security. It regards all that is transcendental, otherworldly and genuinely religious, all belief in absolute values, as a real and hateful enemy.

XVII:39. REACTIONS TO VEKHI, 1910

The spirited response to the *Vekhi* volume of 1909 is illustrated in these passages from the articles of P. N. Miliukov, M. I. Tugan-Baranovskii, and N. D. Avksent'ev, published in two collections of articles, one by liberals and radicals (entitled *The Intelligentsia in Russia*) and one by socialists (*Vekhi as a Sign of the Times*).

Reference: *Intelligentsiia v Rossii: Sbornik statei* (St. Petersburg: Knigoizdat. "Zemlia," 1910), pp. 187, 189 [Miliukov], 236, 239-40 [Tugan-Baranovskii]; *"Vekhi," kak znamenie vremeni: Sbornik statei* (Moscow: "Zveno," 1910), pp. 128-29, 141 [Avksent'ev].

[From P. N. Miliukov, "The Intelligentsia and Historical Tradition":]

A "scientific" spirit in politics and in civic education is the only effective remedy that can be opposed to the panaceas the authors of *Vekhi* proclaim with such pomp and aplomb and paint with such brilliant colors

of literary enthusiasm. The act of "humility" which is urged by one of these authors and to which all the others less emphatically but fatally incline is an act that would lead us not forward but backward, not to civic consciousness [*grazhdanskaia soznatel'nost'*], but to traditional passivity and disorder.

This is why I think that the seeds cast by the authors of *Vekhi* on soil, unfortunately, far too receptive, are poisonous seeds, and the cause in which they labor is—irrespective, of course, of their own intentions—a dangerous and harmful cause.

. . .

What must the intelligentsia do? On this point we radically and irreconcilably disagree with the religious moralists of *Vekhi*. We must do exactly the opposite of what they advise. We must apply all our efforts to the "external [sociopolitical] organization of life," in order to complete, roof and all, our "spacious," but unfinished house. In doing this, we shall be doing essentially what the Russian intelligentsia has always done.

[From M. I. Tugan-Baranovskii (1865-1919), "The Intelligentsia and Socialism":]

The historical development of Russia has followed an altogether different path. Russia has not gone through the stage of the city economy [i.e. when the city had a monopoly of trade and industry] and has not experienced the guild organization of industry. Herein lies its most fundamental and profound difference from the West, a difference from which all the others have resulted as a natural consequence. Russia, being foreign to the city economic system, has not had that distinctive industrial culture which represented the starting point for the subsequent economic history of the West. Also because of this, the bourgeoisie, the social group that in the West was the principal factor in economic progress, was unable to develop to a significant degree in Russia.

. . .

Why, then, did socialism find so fertile a soil precisely among the Russian intelligentsia? The Russian member of the intelligentsia was and remains, as Herzen long ago pointed out, a remarkably free being, culturally. In the West there has existed and still exists a powerful historical national culture, the principal bearer of which in modern times has been the bourgeoisie. The educated classes of the West until quite recently were closely linked with the bourgeoisie in all their interests. The Russian member of the intelligentsia, on the contrary, has stood outside the influence of bourgeois culture, if only because no such culture existed in our country. . . .

Being entirely free culturally, the Russian member of the intelligentsia, in the person of his leading representatives, has naturally cleaved in spirit to that social ideal which promises most for improving conditions of the life of society. The western European did not have to choose for himself an ideology and social ideal. He received them ready-made from the social environment surrounding him. The Russian member of the intelligentsia, on the contrary, alienated from his historical soil, has therefore chosen for himself the social ideal that seemed the most valid from a rationalist viewpoint. Socialism represents such a cosmopolitan, supranational and suprahistorical ideal.

[From N. D. Avksent'ev (1878-1943), "The Creation of Culture":]

The first demand of socialism is . . . the realization of the basic postulate of culture—the integral emancipation of the creator in man, the emancipation of *labor*. Both sides of the ethical problem—the striving for the establishment of social justice, for the creation of a realm of free and equal men, and the autonomy of the freely creative human personality—are potentially included in this demand. . . .

Thus, the struggle for the *emancipation of labor* is defined, in the end, by a positive demand for the organization of free creative activity; the struggle for the emancipation of labor turns into the *poetry of emancipated labor*. Emancipated labor is the basis of the new cultural system which socialism carries with it. . . .

In this sphere, also, the ideal of socialism is, like every ideal, infinite. We, the puny builders of a great future, can in ecstatic anticipation merely foresee all the beauty and nobility of this future. It extends before us infinite and wonderful, ever nobler, ever more perfect. Its ultimate heights disappear in the endless sky of ideal values, for the creativity of free creators is limitless. The ethical ideal, intertwining and combining with the esthetic, gives birth to the most exalted [being], the harmoniously developed creative personality in the midst of a harmonious, intimate community of men. The creation of values, the boundless development along the path to the ideal, the tireless striving forward and upward—this is what the

socialist ideal indicates, this is what it teaches.
   . . . All-encompassing, deep, free, like the
sea, the social milieu gives birth to the most
wonderful [being] in the world, the individual creator of higher values!

                     ·   ·   ·

   The aspiration for freedom and the longing for the freedom of self-determination
have been the basic substance of the spiritual
experience of Russian society, of the Russian
people for the past forty years. To realize
this aspiration is the fundamental task of the
cultural creativity of present-day Russia. And
the great Russian liberation movement is also,
from this philosophical point of view, a great
cultural movement, the common creative
work of the entire people in the realization

of long-recognized and obligatory values.
   The nature of this movement itself is clearly the result of this aspect of creative work.
The old edifice was being destroyed, but in
the very process of destruction new feelings,
new social relations, were born, new forms
of association were crystallized, and a new,
more mature citizen was coming into being.
The din of this very destruction is producing
a symphony of a new, unprecedented, not-
yet-experienced social solidarity. And he
who, like the gentlemen of *Vekhi,* has seen
only strikes and uprisings, who has heard
only the noise of falling buildings, he has
seen nothing, heard nothing, and—alas!—
understood nothing!

XVII:40. LEO TOLSTOI ON THE REVOLUTIONARY MOVEMENT, JANUARY 30, 1909

Near the end of his life the sage of Iasnaia Poliana wrote "A Letter to a Revolutionary," in
which he expounded his views on the various contemporary recipes for remaking the Russian
state.
   Reference: Lev N. Tolstoi, *Polnoe sobranie sochinenii,* 90 vols. (Moscow: Gosudarstvennoe
Izd. Khudozhestvennoi Literatury, 1936), 38:263-67.

People see the injustice and poverty suffered
by the working people, deprived of the opportunity to enjoy the fruits of their labor,
which are taken from them by the minority
of powerful persons and capitalists, and they
ponder on the ways and means by which the
condition of the vast majority of mankind
may be changed and corrected. And, to change
and remedy such a situation, various people
propose various methods of social order.
Some suggest a constitutional monarchy with
socialist organization of the workers, and
there are those who defend absolute monarchy.
Others, such as the Mensheviks, Bolsheviks,
Trudoviks, Maximalists, and Syndicalists,
propose a republic, with various systems of
organization. A third group proposes direct
legislation by the people, and a fourth,
anarchy with a communal system, and so on.
Each party, confident that it knows what is
needed for the good of mankind, says: "Just
give me power, and I shall bring about general
prosperity." But, despite the fact that many
of these parties have been, or are even now,
in power, the promised general prosperity
still has not been achieved and the position
of the workers continues to deteriorate. This
is so because a ruling minority, whatever its
name—whether it be called an absolute

monarchy, a constitutional state, or a democratic republic, as in France, Switzerland, or
America—finding itself in power and being
prompted by the selfishness native to man,
naturally uses this power in order to retain
for itself by force the advantages that are
acquired at the expense of the working
people, and which cannot be acquired in any
other way. So that, in all the revolutions and
changes of government, only the rulers are
changed: one set of rulers is replaced by another, but the position of the working people
remains the same.

                     ·   ·   ·

   It is impossible not to see that all the
mountains of socialist political and economic
works, filled with erudition and wit, are in
essence nothing but empty, entirely unnecessary, and, furthermore, even very harmful writings, diverting human thought from
the natural and sensible path and directing it
into a path that is artificial, false, and
ruinous. . . .
   One thing is needed for the improvement
of the condition of the working people: not
dissertations about a future order, but only
the liberation of one's own self from that
constraint that one places upon himself according to the will of the rulers.

. . .

And so, the deliverance of the working people from oppression and the alteration of their position can be achieved, not by any schemes for the best possible social system, and still less by attempts to introduce this system by force, but only in one way—the very way that is denied by the zealots of the people: by affirming and spreading among the people such religious consciousness as would make it impossible for a man to violate in any way his unity with and respect for his fellow man and would therefore make it morally impossible for him to practice any kind of coercion over another. And it appears that such a religious consciousness which would preclude the possibility of coercion could easily be adopted and acknowledged, not only by the Christian world but by all of mankind today, if it were not for the existence, on the one hand, of pseudo-religious superstition, and, on the other, of the still more harmful pseudo-scientific superstition.

XVII:41. KOVALEVSKII'S SPEECH IN THE DUMA ON PUBLIC EDUCATION, MARCH 11, 1908

On March 11, 1908, the Third Duma took up a bill calling for the allocation of sizable sums for schools, with the aim of making free primary schooling universally compulsory in the not-too-distant future. The bill, proposed by the Ministry of Public Education, was supported in the Duma by the Commission on Public Education. Here is a portion of the speech by Evgraf Petrovich Kovalevskii (1865-1941), an Octobrist and secretary of the commission, introducing the bill in the Duma on that day. The Duma passed the bill on April 3 and it became law on May 3, 1908. Expenditures on education under the zemstvos increased sharply in subsequent years.

Reference: Gosudarstvennaia duma, tretii sozyv, *Stenograficheskie otchety, 1908 god, Sessiia 1*, vol. 2 (St. Petersburg, 1908), cols. 399, 406, 407.

KOVALEVSKII (Voronezh guberniia):

Today the State Duma is to discuss the bill providing for the allocation of [an additional] 6,900,000 rubles for public education, "with the aim of universal schooling."

. . .

[The teachers] work day after day, year after year, under poor conditions, often for the most meager wages, not even resting on holidays, since behind the school stands the village, and they cannot remain indifferent to its needs. They sometimes must organize Sunday schools, discussions, and readings, and must help the illiterate peasants. It requires a great love of people, great idealism, and great faith in one's work to retain for many years one's energy and zeal, far removed from an intellectual environment. In most cases, because of the barbarous conditions surrounding him, the Russian public primary-school teacher is an entirely unique type, quite unlike his German or French colleague. He is often half-saint, rather than public official. His work demands great self-sacrifice. . . . The activity of a public school teacher requires creativeness. His work is an art; his responsibility is great, far greater than we think. This is why our first thought was of the teacher, and our first step, to assure his material welfare. The unanimity with which the Commission on Public Education and the Budget Commission approved the bill and the allocation of funds gives us every reason to count on equally unanimous support of this allocation on the part of the State Duma.

In conclusion, I shall venture to share with you some of the apprehensions I have come to feel after discussions with various persons who are connected with the business of public education. "Why are you hurrying?" said some. "You want to achieve universal education too quickly—in ten or fifteen years! Why so soon? Look at Germany, it has taken a hundred years to introduce universal education." Others anxiously said: "A hundred million [people]! That's no joke!" Without agreeing with either of these views, I wish to quote, in closing, the words of a French educator, Jules Simon, who said: "In the work of public education, we must be generous with funds and economical with time." And I hope, as do all who have dedicated themselves to the cause of public education, that the labors of the representative assembly of the Third Duma will yield results that will permit our Duma in the future to be called the "Duma of public education."

XVII:42. DECREES SETTING QUOTAS FOR JEWS IN EDUCATIONAL INSTITUTIONS,
1908 AND 1909

Some of the government's restrictions on Jews are illustrated in these excerpts from decrees of
September 16, 1908, and August 22, 1909.
Reference: *PSZRI*, 3d ser., vol. 28, pt. 1, p. 720; vol. 29, pt. 1, pp. 723-24.

[The imperially confirmed decree of the
Council of Ministers "concerning the establishment of quotas for the admission of persons
of the Jewish faith to educational institutions,"
September 16, 1908:]

I. As regards the admission of Jews to the
institutions of higher education of all government departments, with the exception of the
conservatories of the Imperial Russian Musical
Society [it is decreed that where not otherwise ordained] . . . the following quotas in
relation to the total number of students shall
be maintained: 3 percent for the educational
institutions in the capitals; 5 percent in the
rest of the territories of the empire outside
the Jewish Pale of Settlement; and 10 percent inside the Pale of Settlement.

[The imperially confirmed decree of the
Council of Ministers "concerning conditions
governing the admission of Jews to institutions of secondary education," August 22,
1909:]

1. The quotas for the admission of Jews
to the state-supported institutions of secondary education of all departments shall be
fixed at 5 percent of the total number of
students in educational institutions in the
capitals, 10 percent in educational institutions elsewhere in the empire outside the
Pale of Jewish Settlement, and 15 percent
within the Pale. . . .

4. No restrictions shall be imposed on the
admission of Jews to institutions of secondary
education that confer no rights upon their
students and do not qualify them for entrance
into higher educational institutions.

5. Nor shall there be any restrictions on
the admission of Jews to secondary-level art
schools, to commercial, industrial art, technical, and trade schools under the jurisdiction
of the Ministry of Trade and Industry, to
dental schools, and to the lower-level technical
schools of the Ministry of Public Education.
. . .

7. The number of Jews admitted to university lectures because they are apothecary's
assistants wishing to prepare for the calling
of pharmacist is restricted, in relation to the
total number of such students in each university, by the following quotas: Moscow
University—6 percent; universities elsewhere
in the empire outside the Pale of Jewish
Settlement—10 percent; universities within
the Pale of Settlement—20 percent.

XVII:43. LAWS ON TRANS-URAL SETTLEMENT, APRIL 19, 1909, AND JULY 5, 1912

Among the measures that greatly expanded the flow of settlers beyond the Urals in the years
1906-13 were the laws whose key passages are given here. (See also Item XVI:77, above.)
Reference: *PSZRI*, 3d ser., vol. 29, pt. 1, pp. 266-67; vol. 32, pt. 1, pp. 1091-92.

[The statute "imperially confirmed and approved by the State Council and the State
Duma, concerning loans for the community
needs of settlers," April 19, 1909:]

1. Loans for community needs [*obshche-
poleznye nadobnosti*] may be issued to agricultural communities of settlers, to settlements, and to associations of peasant householders as follows: (a) for irrigation and
drainage installations (wells, dams, dikes, and
ditches); (b) for road construction (roads,
corduroy roads, bridges, and fords); (c) for
the construction of public buildings (schools,
granaries, volost' and village administration
buildings, Orthodox churches, Christian
prayer houses, and homes for the clergy);
(d) for protecting the village buildings
against fire (fire engines and fire fighting
equipment); (e) for agricultural enterprises
(mills, brickyards, and the like); (f) for fixing boundaries within the land alloted them.

Note 1. Loans for community undertakings may also be issued to individuals if peti-
tioned for and guaranteed by the communities and associations. . . .

5. No interest or fines shall be charged on
the loans. . . .

7. Repayment of loans shall be made with-

in a period of not more than ten years . . . in equal annual payments at fixed dates. . . .

9. In cases meriting special consideration, repayment may be spread over a period of up to twenty years.

[The statute "imperially confirmed and approved by the State Council and the State Duma, concerning the amendment of the regulations governing the issuance of loans to settlers for the establishment of a homestead," July 5, 1912:]

1. Loans for the establishment of a homestead may be granted in response to an oral or written application by the settlers within three years of settlement. . . .

3. Loans for the establishment of a household . . . may not exceed 400 rubles per household in the taiga sections of the Trans-Baikal region, and 250 rubles in the remaining territories of Asiatic Russia.

4. A portion, but no more than half, of a loan for the establishment of a household issued to settlers who have permanently established themselves in areas where settlement is regarded essential, for reasons of state, shall be considered an outright subsidy. . . .

8. Loans for the establishment of a household are issued by peasant captains [krest'-ianskie nachal'niki] or their deputies, who grant top priority to cases of this type.

XVII:44. THE FIELD SERVICE REGULATIONS OF APRIL 27, 1912

The imperially ratified statute of April 27, 1912, prescribing the field service regulations for the Russian army, addressed these commands to Russian soldiers and noncommissioned officers.

Reference: *PSZRI*, 3d ser., vol. 32, pt. 1, p. 83.

1. You are fighting against enemy troops, not against peaceful inhabitants. . . .

2. Spare the life of an unarmed enemy asking for mercy.

3. Respect an alien faith and its temples.

4. Do not harm the peaceful inhabitants of an enemy territory; do not damage or take their property yourself, and restrain your comrades from so doing. Cruelty to civilian residents merely increases the number of our enemies. Remember, a soldier is the warrior of Christ and the emperor and must therefore conduct himself as a Christ-loving warrior.

5. When the battle is over, have pity on the wounded and try to help him as much as you can, regardless of whether or not he is an enemy soldier. The wounded man is no longer your enemy.

6. Treat the prisoner of war humanely; do not mock his faith; do not oppress him.

7. The plundering of prisoners of war, and, even worse, of the dead and wounded, is the most shameful act for an honest soldier. Those who allow themselves to be tempted into such action shall be subject to the most severe penalties, just as for brigandage.

XVII:45. THE JUDICIAL REFORM OF JUNE 15, 1912

The judicial reform of June 15, 1912, comprising the law and the supplementary rules issued on that date, brought back the elected justices of the peace at the expense of the appointed land captains. In 1913 the new legal institutions were introduced in ten guberniias, mostly in the south and southwest.

Reference: *PSZRI*, 3d ser., vol. 32, pt. 1, pp. 662-64; pt. 2, pp. 212-13.

[The law of June 15, 1912, concerning the reform of local courts:]

12. Justices of the peace are established in uezdy and cities. . . .

17. The assembly of honorary, district [uchastkovye], and auxiliary [dobavochnye] justices of the peace of every judicial okrug [mirovoi okrug] constitutes the highest local judicial authority [vysshaia mirovaia instantsiia] and is named the conference of justices of the peace [s"ezd mirovykh sudei].

The chairman of the conference of justices of the peace is appointed by the emperor, on the recommendation of the minister of justice, from among those who can be assigned to a position in the justice department [sudebnoe vedomstvo] with a rank no lower than member of an okrug court [okruzhnoi sud] or from among district justices of the peace who have served in this capacity not less than three years.

In the cities of Saint Petersburg, Moscow,

Khar'kov, Saratov, Kishinev, Odessa, and Kazan', the chairman of the conference of justices of the peace is elected for a term of three years by the justices of the peace from their own ranks. . . . [The number 18 is skipped in the numeration of articles.]

19. Eligible for election to the post of justice of the peace are those local residents:

a. Who are at least twenty-five years of age.

b. Who hold a certificate or diploma from a university or other institution of higher education testifying to their completion of a course of study; or who hold a certificate of completion of a course of study in a secondary school or who have passed the corresponding examinations and have subsequently served not less than three years in positions whose duties would enable them to acquire practical knowledge of the conduct of judicial affairs; or who, lacking the above educational qualifications, have served not less than six years as marshals of the nobility or as secretaries of the conference of justices of the peace or who have occupied, for not less than six years prior to the promulgation of the law concerning the reform of local courts, the posts of district land captain [*zemskii uchastkovyi nachal'nik*] or secretary of the uezd congress [of land captains].

c. If, in addition, they, their parents, or their wives have owned for not less than one year, even if in different guberniias, either: (i) sufficient land assessed for zemstvo taxes to make them eligible to participate directly in the election of delegates to the uezd zemstvo assemblies . . . or (ii) other real estate not located in cities and assessed for zemstvo taxes at a value of not less than fifteen thousand rubles; or (iii) real estate in cities assessed for purposes of taxation as follows: in the capitals, at not less then fifteen thousand rubles; in cities with a population of more than one hundred thousand, at not less than six thousand rubles; and in the rest, at not less than three thousand rubles. . . .

23. Justices of the peace, including honorary as well as district and auxiliary justices of the peace, are elected for three-year terms [by the zemstvo assembly, as explained in article 32]. District and auxiliary justices of the peace who have served their three-year elected terms are reelected for six years if their reelection occurs in the same judicial district and immediately following their term of service.

[The provisional rules concerning volost' courts, June 15, 1912:]

I. Establishment of volost' courts and higher rural courts [*verkhnii sel'skii sud*].

A. Volost' courts. . . .

4. The volost' court shall consist of a chairman, two members, and two candidates for membership. . . .

5. Eligible for election to the posts of volost' judges (the chairmen of the volost' court, its members and candidates) are literate peasant householders of at least thirty years of age. . . .

8. A list of those persons elected to volost' courts shall be presented to the conference of justices of the peace for confirmation. . . .

B. Higher rural courts.

29. A special session known as the higher rural court shall be instituted in each judicial district [*mirovoi uchastok*] to hear complaints against the decisions and resolutions of the volost' courts.

30. The higher rural court, under the chairmanship of the district justice of the peace, shall have as its members the chairmen of the volost' courts of the judicial district.

31. A session of the higher rural court shall consist of a chairman and no fewer than two members.

XVII:46. THE DUMA'S DISCUSSION OF THE LENA GOLDFIELD INCIDENT, APRIL 9-11, 1912

The incident of April 4, 1912, in which about two hundred striking workers at the Lena goldfields were killed, led to heated exchanges in the Duma. Here are brief excerpts from the stenographic record of the Duma sessions at which statements of inquiry addressed to the government were introduced by the Constitutional Democrats, Social Democrats, Octobrists, and Nationalists. The subsequent investigation did not strengthen Makarov's position.

Reference: Gosudarstvennaia Duma, tretii sozyv, *Stenograficheskie otchety, 1912 god, Sessiia 5*, vol. 3 (St. Petersburg, 1912), cols. 1658-59, 1952-53, 1963.

[Session of April 9, 1912:]

THE SECRETARY OF THE STATE DUMA: The statement concerning the inquiry of the Constitutional Democratic faction: "To the chairman of the State Duma. At the end of February of this year, in the Lena goldfield district, the workers in the enterprises of the Lena Gold Mining Association went on strike. This circumstance fully justified the workers' presenting a series of economic demands aimed at the improvement of their material conditions. . . . The strike proceeded quite peacefully for more than a month, and the workers gave no cause for anyone to assume the possibility of any violent action on their part. . . . The arrest, without apparent reason, of the workers' elected representatives had an extremely grave effect on the mass of the workers, who naturally regarded this act as administrative intervention in the economic struggle for the purpose of aiding the employers. On April 4, the day after the arrest of their representatives, the workers moved en masse to the building occupied by the assistant procurator assigned to the area, in order to obtain from him the release of the arrested men. When the workers were about 250 yards from the assistant procurator's house, the okrug engineer, Tul'chinskii, accompanied by two guards, addressed an appeal to the crowd to stop. The men in the front ranks stopped and entered into negotiations with Tul'chinskii, but those in the rear did not understand the reason for the halt, and continued to move forward. At that moment the order to fire was quite unexpectedly given to the soldiers, and a number of volleys killed approximately two hundred workers and wounded an even greater number."

[Session of April 11, 1912:]

MINISTER OF INTERNAL AFFAIRS MAKAROV: . . . Despite the warning and the signals, the crowd advanced upon the troops . . . and Assistant Procurator Preobrazhenskii reports that the situation was so dangerous that in a moment the troops would have been overrun, and the soldiers, only 110 men, and without reserves, were alarmed and, fearful of an onrush, demanded orders to fire. . . . Such were the circumstances under which firearms were resorted to.

. . .

When a crowd that has lost all reason under the influence of malicious agitators attacks the troops, then there is nothing left for the troops to do but shoot. (*Voices on the Right:* "That's right.") So it was, and so it shall be in the future.

. . .

KUZNETSOV (Ekaterinoslav guberniia) [Social Democrat]: Gentlemen, members of the State Duma. In the name of the working class, I wish to express my profound gratitude to the minister of internal affairs for the speech he delivered today from the Duma's rostrum. This speech is a more effective proclamation than any the socialist parties have ever published in their appeals. I recommend that the working class print and distribute today's speech more energetically than any Social-Democratic proclamation, or any Social-Democratic appeal. [Makarov's] speech confirmed everything that I said from the Duma's rostrum at the last meeting—namely, that this is how it was, and this is how it will be in the future. We categorically assert that the working class has been shot down and will continue to be shot down as long as the political regime headed by men like Makarov exists.

XVII:47. THE LAWS PROVIDING SOCIAL INSURANCE FOR WORKERS, JUNE 23, 1912

Here are some of the important passages from the laws that provided sickness and accident insurance to industrial workers.

Reference: *PSZRI,* 3d ser., vol. 32, pt. 1, pp. 857, 863, 865-66 [sickness], 872-73 [accidents].

[The "Statute concerning Insurance for Workers against Sickness":]

8. Medical assistance is provided at the expense of the employers.

9. Financial assistance is given by the sick benefit fund [*bol'nichnaia kassa*] at its expense.

64. The sick benefit funds are financed by: (1) participants' dues and additional payments by employers; (2) income from the properties of the fund; (3) grants and contributions. . . .

65. The amount of dues to be paid by participants in the sick benefit fund is set by a

general meeting of the fund at from 1 to 2 percent of one's earnings. . . .

67. The amount of additional payments to the sick benefit fund by the employer (articles 64 and 1) is fixed at two-thirds the dues paid by the participants. . . .

85. The affairs of the sick benefit fund are managed by: the fund's general meeting and its executive board.

86. The fund's general meeting comprises: (1) delegates from participants in the fund; and (2) representatives of the employer.

87. The fund's participants elect from their midst the number of delegates fixed by the statutes of the fund and not to exceed one hundred persons. . . .

88. . . . The representatives of the employer at the general meeting have two-thirds the number of votes belonging to the [participants'] delegates attending the meeting.
. . .

90. An employer or someone designated by him presides over the meeting. An employer may decline his right to the chair, in which case the meeting elects a chairman from those present. . . .

97. The executive board of the sick benefit fund comprises an uneven number of members as fixed by its statutes. It is composed of elected and appointed members. The former are elected by the general meeting

from among its members; the latter are participants of the fund or outside persons and are appointed by the employers. The elected members of the board are chosen by a secret ballot in which the employer and his representatives do not participate. The number of elected members of the board should exceed by one the number of appointed members.
. . .

99. The board members elect their chairman and deputy chairmen from their midst.

[The "Statute concerning Accident Insurance for Workers":]

8. The insurance is provided at the expense of the employers [who form "insurance associations" for this purpose]. These persons are mutually responsible for the obligations of the association. . . .

21. The pensions granted those suffering permanent disability are as follows: for total disability, two-thirds of one's annual earnings; and for partial disability, a percentage of two-thirds of one's annual earnings corresponding to the degree of disability.

In cases of insanity, total loss of vision, loss of both arms or both legs, or total helplessness requiring outside care, the pension shall equal the full annual earnings of the victim.

XVII:48. OFFICIAL STATISTICS ON STATE FINANCES, 1900-1913

Although statistical records are an important category of primary sources, their form of presentation does not easily lend itself to inclusion in a sourcebook of limited size. As a compromise, in order to illustrate some of the kinds of data that are available for the Russian economy in the early years of the present century, we offer below not a direct quotation but an abbreviated and condensed version of data for the years 1900, 1906, and 1913 from the official statistical publications of 1911 and 1915. From these figures the reader can also gain some impression of the changes in various sectors of the state budget in the years 1906-13 as compared with the previous period.

Reference: Tsentral'nyi Statisticheskii Komitet, *Ezhegodnik Rossii 1910* (St. Petersburg: Izd. Tsentral'nogo Statisticheskogo Komiteta M.V.D., 1911), pp. 625-27, 634; *Statisticheskii Ezhegodnik Rossii 1914* (St. Petersburg: Izd. Tsentral'nogo Statisticheskogo Komiteta M.V.D., 1915), sec. 12, pp. 1-6, 12-19.

State Revenues

Direct taxes	1900 Millions of Rubles	1900 Percent of Total Revenues	1906 Millions of Rubles	1906 Percent of Total Revenues	1913 Millions of Rubles	1913 Percent of Total Revenues
Taxes on land and other real estate	46.0	2.7	60.5	2.7	87.3	2.55
Tax on commerce and industries	69.8	4.1	82.5	3.6	150.1	4.4
Tax on monetary assets	16.1	0.9	20.2	0.9	35.1	1.0
Total	131.9	7.7	163.2	7.2	272.5	8.0

Indirect taxes	1900		1906		1913	
	Millions of Rubles	Percent of Total Revenues	Millions of Rubles	Percent of Total Revenues	Millions of Rubles	Percent of Total Revenues
Excise on alcoholic beverages	164.4	9.7	40.0	1.8	53.7	1.6
Excise on tobacco	41.2	2.4	59.9	2.6	83.7	2.45
Excise on sugar	63.3	3.8	108.8	4.8	149.2	4.4
Excise on petroleum products	25.5	1.5	29.9	1.3	48.6	1.4
Excise on matches	7.4	0.4	15.0	0.7	20.0	0.6
Customs revenue	203.6	12.0	241.3	10.6	352.9	10.3
Total	505.4	29.8	494.2	21.8	708.1	20.7
Duties (of various kinds)	88.7	5.2	113.3	5.0	231.2	6.8
State royalties						
Mining revenue	4.7	0.3	0.04	0.0	0.7	0.02
Mint	4.2	0.2	5.3	0.2	5.1	0.15
Post, telegraph, and telephone revenue	50.0	3.0	74.3	3.2	119.8	3.5
Revenue from the spirits monopoly	270.3	15.9	697.5	30.7	899.3	26.3
Total	329.2	19.4	777.1	34.2	1024.9	30.0
Property and funds belonging to the state						
Forests	55.7	3.3	57.5	2.5	92.4	2.7
State railways	361.7	21.2	490.9	21.6	813.6	23.8
Other state property and funds	56.7	3.2	54.9	2.4	140.6	4.2
Total	474.1	27.8	603.3	26.5	1046.6	30.7
Redemption payments	96.2	5.6	35.0	1.5	1.2	0.04
Incidental revenues	78.6	4.6	85.6	3.8	132.9	3.9
All regular state revenues	1,704.1	100.0	2,271.7	100.0	3,417.4	100.0

Regular State Expenditures
[not including expenditures on war and railroad construction]

	1900		1906		1913	
	Millions of Rubles	Percent of Total Budget	Millions of Rubles	Percent of Total Budget	Millions of Rubles	Percent of Total Budget
Ministry of the Imperial Court	12.9	0.8	16.5	0.8	17.4	0.6
Central organs of government[a]	3.2	0.2	5.7	0.3	9.4	0.3
Department of the Holy Synod	23.7	1.5	29.2	1.4	45.7	1.5
Ministry of Internal Affairs	88.2	5.5	136.3	6.6	185.4	6.0
Ministry of Finance	280.2	17.5	353.2	17.1	482.3	15.6
(of which expenditures on the state spirits monopoly totaled:)	(112.8)	(7.1)	(178.3)	(8.6)	(235.0)	(7.6)

	1900		1906		1913	
	Millions of Rubles	Percent of Total Budget	Millions of Rubles	Percent of Total Budget	Millions of Rubles	Percent of Total Budget
Ministry of Justice	45.9	2.9	53.5	2.6	92.7	3.0
Ministry of Foreign Affairs	5.4	0.4	5.9	0.3	11.5	0.4
Ministry of Public Education	33.6	2.1	44.0	2.1	143.1	4.6
Ministry of Transportation	366.8	22.9	477.2	23.2	640.6	20.7
(of which expenditures for the operation and maintenance of the state railways totaled:)	(326.8)	(20.4)	(448.7)	(21.8)	(586.5)	(18.95)
Ministry of Trade and Industry[b]	—	—	31.85	1.5	64.6	2.1
Chief Administration of Land Organization and Agriculture[c]	40.7	2.5	36.2	1.7	135.8	4.4
Chief Administration of State Stud Farms	1.8	0.1	1.75	0.1	3.3	0.1
Ministry of War	333.5	20.9	392.5	19.0	581.1	18.8
Ministry of the Navy	88.6	5.5	111.6	5.4	244.8	7.9
State Control	7.7	0.5	9.1	0.4	12.1	0.4
Service of state debt	267.0	16.7	356.5	17.3	424.4	13.7
(of which payments on railroad loans totaled:)	(112.3)	(7.0)	(134.9)	(6.5)	(142.1)	(4.6)
All regular state expenditures	1,599.2	100.0	2,061.1	100.0	3,094.2	100.0

a. Including the Senate, State Council, and, after 1906, the State Duma.
b. Established at the end of 1905.
c. Before 1906, the Ministry of Agriculture and State Property.

XVII:49. KOKOVTSOV ON RUSSIAN ECONOMIC DEVELOPMENT, CA. 1904-1914

In these passages from his memoirs, Kokovtsov (see Item XVII:4, above) summarizes Russia's economic development during the period of almost a decade when he served as minister of finance.

Reference: Kokovtsov, *Memoirs of Count Kokovtsov*, pp. 460, 462-66.

I might take time just to mention some of the fields in which progress was made in these years [1904-14]. In 1910 the government took steps to introduce general education throughout the country and made the necessary financial appropriations. It was estimated that this undertaking would be complete by 1920. Vast sums were appropriated also for land reorganization, for the development of agriculture, including improved methods of cultivation, adequate distribution of proper fertilizers and agricultural machinery, and the manufacture in Russia of such machinery. This work received a great stimulus from the series of splendid crops beginning with 1909, the crops of that year and of 1910 being particularly good. Prosperity in agriculture was reflected, too, in other branches of state life. Steps were taken to make credit available for the lower classes of the population; attention was paid to the whole problem of savings; special forms of credit were created for municipalities and zemstvos. In all this progressive work private enterprise worked hand in hand with the departments of the government.

. . .

The sum total of ordinary expenditures during 1913 amounted to 3,070,000,000 rubles, as against a total of 1,883,000,000 in 1904. This represents an increase in expenditures of a little more than 63 per cent.

Of the 1913 total of 3,070,000,000 rubles,

a) 503,000,000 were spent on administration as against 327,400,000 in 1904, an increase of almost 54 percent.

b) 402,800,000 were spent in payment of state debts as against 327,400,000 in 1904, an increase of 39 per cent.

c) 816,500,000 were spent on national defense as against 466,300,000 in 1904, an increase of more than 75 per cent.

d) 519,200,000 were spent on cultural and productive projects as against 213,700,000 in 1904, an increase of 143 per cent.

e) 828,500,000 were spent on state enterprises (liquor monopoly and state railways) as against 586,900,000 in 1904, an increase of more than 41 per cent.

These figures show beyond a doubt that during the decade 1904-1913 "cultural" expenditures showed an absolute increase of 305,400,000 [305,500,000?] rubles, and a greater percentage increase than any other appropriations. True, the absolute increase (350,200,000) of expenditures for national defense from 1904 to 1913 is greater than cultural expenditures, but its percentage increase is only 75. The greater absolute increase can be explained by the necessity of rebuilding our fleet after 1905 and of restoring military materials lost in the war with Japan.

. . .

The increase of capital—as represented by money and securities—in banks of different types, in insurance companies, and in state savings banks may be illustrated by the following few figures.

On January 1, 1904, the total amount of money in Russian financial institutions—currency, interest-bearing securities, and mortgages—was 11,300,000,000 rubles. Five years later, January 1, 1909, it was 14,300,000,000; after five more years, on January 1, 1913 [1914], it was 19,000,000,000 rubles. Of this total, interest-bearing securities amounted to 8,300,000,000 in 1904, and to 13,300,000,000 in 1913—an increase of over 60 per cent.

Still more deserving of attention are the operations of the state savings banks. In the beginning of 1904 the money and securities deposited in them amounted to 1,022,000,000 rubles; in 1913 the amount was 2,100,000,000—it had more than doubled. The number of savings books had increased from 4,854,000 to 8,597,000.

. . .

The development of agriculture and the increase in peasant purchasing-power had always been the basic factors of Russia's economic progress. Now, from 1904 to 1913, under the influence of the agrarian reform aimed at the development and growth of small peasant properties and of the measures designed to improve and intensify agricultural production, to increase the demand for agricultural machinery and chemical fertilizers, to spread agricultural education, to increase the number of agricultural schools and experimental farms, and so on, the Russian peasantry was becoming stronger. Good crops were becoming more regular and the productivity of the cultivated land was increasing. A foundation for the sound and rational development of all the productive forces of the country was thus laid, improved, and widened.

The progress of Russian industry during the decade was a normal development, based upon the economic and political foundations of the state. And on these firm foundations, had it not been for the Bolshevik catastrophe, it would have continued its swift and powerful development in perfect harmony with other manifest developments in the country's economic life and with the parallel growth of public prosperity.

In the manufacture of staple commodities, cotton-fiber production increased from fifteen million puds in 1905 to twenty-three million in 1913, and the manufacture of cotton goods increased from thirteen to twenty million puds. Refined-sugar production amounted to fifty million puds in 1905 and to 180 million puds in 1913. Cigarette manufacture yielded twelve billion cigarettes in 1905 and twenty-six billion in 1913. In the field of heavy industry, the amount of coal mined increased from 1,091,000,000 puds in 1903 to 2,214,000,000 puds in 1913. Cast-iron production increased from 152 million puds in 1903 to 283 million puds in 1913. As for the oil industry, the damage done in 1905 had been so great that the output before the World War had not yet reached the 1904 level and only during the War, with the exploitation of the Grozny oil fields, did the oil output almost reach the 1904 level (656 million puds in 1904 and 602 million puds in 1916).

As for the railways, no other decade saw such advances as did the years 1904-1914. . . .

It is not exaggerating to say that without the results achieved in railway development there would have been no tangible progress in the other branches of Russian economic life at that time. On December 31, 1903, the length of the Russian railways, excluding those in Finland and the Chinese Eastern Railway, totaled 55,314 versts. In January 1914 it had grown to 65,526 versts, two-thirds of which, that is, 43,383 versts, were included in the state railway network; 33,416 versts for European Russia, and 9,969 versts for Asiatic Russia.

XVII:50. P. A. BURYSHKIN ON THE MERCHANTS OF MOSCOW, CA. 1911-1914

These excerpts from the memoirs of a merchant and civic leader of Moscow show something of the role of the merchant class in Russia in the years just before World War I.

Reference: Pavel A. Buryshkin, *Moskva kupecheskaia* (New York: Chekhov, 1954), pp. 9-10, 54-57, 104-05.

On the one hand, Moscow was considered a merchant city, where representatives of trade and industry occupied leading positions, especially in the Moscow public administration; on the other hand, among all the nonmerchant strata of Muscovite society—the nobility, the officialdom, and the intellectual circles, both Right and Left—the attitude toward the "moneybags" was, on the whole, unfriendly, derisive, and somewhat condescending. At any rate, the tradesmen and industrialists did not enjoy that importance or that share of influence which they should have had by virtue of their leading part in Russian economic life and which was enjoyed by their Western European, and particularly by their trans-atlantic colleagues in their respective countries.

· · ·

Moscow was the largest domestic reservoir of industrial and commercial capital. From every corner of Russia, merchants thronged there for goods, and vast quantities of raw material entered the city for resale or process-ing in the numerous factories both in Moscow proper and in the surrounding towns and vil-lages. It would be no exaggeration to say that the main bulk of Russia's entire domestic and foreign trade was concentrated in Moscow. For a long time the stock of predominantly practi-cal, technical knowledge had been accumulat-ing in Moscow among the various strata of its population, and the most enterprising workers, who built industrial establishments not only in Moscow but elsewhere, were to be found here. Moscow, therefore, was in a sense the main

seedbed of trade, not only for all interior Russia, but even for the Caucasus and Central Asia.

· · ·

The final ten years of the last century and the first years of the present were characterized by the extraordinary growth of industry in Russia. A number of fields of production be-gan to develop with remarkable rapidity; new forms of industry appeared, hitherto unknown in Russia. This development took place both in the manufacturing and in the extracting industries. Mining and metallurgical industries, ironworks, sugar production, and textiles, especially cotton, prospered greatly. . . . The growth of . . . [Russian industry] was furth-ered both by Russia's immense natural re-sources and by a series of necessary govern-ment measures promulgated during S. Iu. Witte's administration of Russia's finances, for example, the monetary reform or the protective tariff policy, which had existed in Russia even earlier, from the beginning of the nineteenth century. The general atmo-sphere that developed and prevailed among Russian business and, in part, government circles also stimulated this growth. The slogan of the day was the development of Russia's productive forces, the building of its own industry, the organization of Russia's own production to utilize the country's enormously rich productive capacities.

· · ·

Qualitative improvement of factory equip-ment went along with quantitative growth.

Many of the textile mills in Russia, especially in the Moscow district, were among the best equipped in the world.

· · ·

Broad philanthropic activity and support for every type of cultural effort were characteristic of the Russian commercial and industrial milieu. There were the Tret'iakov Gallery; the Shchukin and Morozov museums of contemporary French painting; the Bakhrushin Theatrical Museum; A. V. Morozov's collection of Russian porcelain; S. P. Riabushinskii's collection of icons; the painting collections of V. O. Girshman, E. I. Loseva, and M. P. Riabushinskii; S. M. Mamontov's private opera; S. I. Zimin's opera, the Art Theater of V. S. Alekseev-Stanislavskii and S. T. Morozov . . . the Soldatenkov Hospital; the Solodovnikov Hospital; the Bakhrushin, Khludov, Mazurin, and Gorbov hostels and asylums; the Arnol'd and Tret'iakov school for deaf-mutes; the Shelaputin and Medvednikov gymnasiums; the Aleksandrov Commercial School; the Practical Academy of Commercial Sciences; and the Commercial Institute of the Moscow Society for the Dissemination of Commercial Education.

CHAPTER XVIII

The War
and the Road to Revolution
1914-1917

XVIII:1. RODZIANKO ON THE DECLARATION OF WAR AGAINST GERMANY, JULY 20, 1914

Among the important sources on the closing years of the empire are the memoirs of Mikhail Vladimirovich Rodzianko (1859-1924). Rodzianko, by 1900, had become chairman of the zemstvo board for the guberniia of Ekaterinoslav (now Dnepropetrovsk). After the revolution of 1905 he was one of the leaders of the Octobrist Party, and was a member and the chairman of the Third and Fourth Dumas. Here is his description of the scene in Petrograd on July 20 (August 2, N.S.), 1914.

Reference: M. V. Rodzianko, "Krushenie Imperii," in *Arkhiv russkoi revoliutsii,* ed. I. V. Gessen, 22 vols. (Berlin: Slovo, 1921-27), 17:79.

On the day of the manifesto of war with Germany a great crowd gathered before the Winter Palace. After a prayer for the granting of victory, the tsar spoke a few words, ending with the solemn promise not to end the war while the enemy still occupied one inch of Russian soil. A loud "hurrah" filled the palace and was taken up by an answering echo from the crowd on the square. After the prayer, the tsar came out on the balcony to his people, the empress behind him. The huge crowd filled the square and the nearby streets, and when the tsar appeared it was as if an electric spark had run through the crowd, and an enormous "hurrah" filled the air. Flags and placards with the inscription "Long live Russia and Slavdom" bowed to the ground, and the entire crowd fell to its knees as one man before the tsar. The tsar wanted to say something; he raised his hand; those in front began to sh-sh-sh; but the noise of the crowd, the unceasing "hurrah," did not allow him to speak. He bowed his head and stood for some time overcome by the solemnity of this moment of the union of the tsar with his people. Then he turned and went to his chambers.

Coming out of the palace onto the square, we mingled with the crowd. Some workers came by. I stopped them and asked how they happened to be there when not long before they had been striking and presenting economic and political demands almost with weapons in hand. The workers answered: "That was our private affair. We found that the reforms were going too slowly through the Duma. But now all of Russia is concerned. We came to the tsar as to our banner, and we will go with him in the name of victory over the Germans."

XVIII:2. PALÉOLOGUE, RODZIANKO, AND MILIUKOV ON THE DUMA SESSION OF JULY 26, 1914

On July 26 (August 8, N.S.), a few days after Germany's declaration of war, a special Duma session was held. Its atmosphere is conveyed, not only in the official stenographic record, but in some respects more vividly in the reports of participants and observers. Here are three samples of such sources: Georges Maurice Paléologue, the French ambassador; Mikhail Vladimirovich Rodzianko, the Octobrist leader and chairman of the Duma; and Pavel Nikolaevich Miliukov, the leader of the Kadets or Constitutional Democrats.

Reference: [Georges] Maurice Paléologue, *An Ambassador's Memoirs,* trans. F. A. Holt, 4th ed., 3 vols. (New York: George H. Doran, 1924-25), 1:68-70; M. V. Rodzianko, "Gosudarstvennaia Duma i fevral'skaia 1917 g. revoliutsiia," *Arkhiv russkoi revoliutsii,* 6:19; P. N. Miliukov, *Vospominaniia 1859-1917,* 2 vols. (New York: Chekhov, 1955), 2:190-91.

[Paléologue:]

August 8 [N.S.], 1914. . . . To-day there was a sitting . . . of the [State] Duma. . . .

I sat with Sir George Buchanan in the front row of the diplomatic gallery.

The session opened with a moving speech by the President, Rodzianko. His eloquent and sonorous oratory roused the assembly to great enthusiasm.

Next the aged Goremykin tottered to the tribune. Forcing out his words with difficulty in a feeble voice, which seemed every now and then to be exhausted and about to expire, he declared that "Russia did not desire the war, that the Imperial Government had done everything possible to save the cause of Peace, clinging even to the slightest chance of damming the deluge of blood which threatens to engulf the world." He concluded by saying that Russia could not shrink from the challenge thrown down to her by the German powers and in any case "if we had yielded our humiliation would not have changed the course of affairs. . . ."

Sazonov followed him on the tribune. He was pale and nervous. From the very outset he cleared his conscience: "When history brings the day of unbiased judgment I am convinced it will justify us." He vigorously reminded his audience that "It was not Russian policy which imperilled the peace of the world," and that if Germany had so desired she could "with one word, one authoritative word," have stopped Austria in her bellicose career. Then in warm tones he exalted "magnanimous France, chivalrous France which has risen at our side in the defence of right and justice." At these words all the deputies rose, turned towards me and gave round after round of cheers for France. All the same I observed that the cheers were not very enthusiastic on the benches occupied by the Left: the liberal parties have never forgiven us for prolonging the life of Tsarism by our financial subsidies.

The cheering broke out afresh when Sazonov said that England also had recognized the moral impossibility of remaining indifferent to the outrage on Serbia. His peroration accurately translated the thought which has inspired all our actions and reflections in the last weeks: "We will not accept the yoke of Germany and her ally in Europe." He descended from the tribune to the accompaniment of further cheers.

After the sitting was suspended all the party leaders furnished proof of their patriotism by declaring their readiness to make any sacrifice to save Russia and the Slav peoples from German hegemony. When the President put the credits asked for by the Government to the vote the Socialist [Social-Democratic] Party announced that it would abstain from voting, being unwilling to accept any responsibility for the policy of Tsarism: but it exhorted the democracy of Russia to defend its native soil against foreign invasion. "Workmen and peasants, summon up all your energies to defend our country; we will free it afterwards!" Except for the abstention of the Socialists [Social Democrats] the military credits have been voted without a single dissentient voice.

When I left the Tauride Palace with Buchanan our cars had some difficulty in making their way through the crowd that swarmed round and warmly cheered us."

[Rodzianko:]

At this historic session [of July 26] there were no parties. This is all the more significant since, before this, quarrels on party grounds often led to excesses and scandals, and the chairman of the State Duma was forced to exercise all his authority to obtain at least an outward calm and order.

At the session of July 26 all the existing party barriers fell without exception. The members of the Duma affirmed the necessity of war until victory, in the name of the honor and dignity of their beloved fatherland, and they drew harmoniously together in this feeling and resolved to support the government in every way possible.

Everyone without distinction of nationality understood that this was a national [*narodnaia*] war, that it must remain so until the end, and that the defeat of intolerable German militarism was an absolute necessity. . . . One need only read the stenographic account of this meeting to see how great this national enthusiasm was and to what extent all the nationalities that make up the Russian state represented at this moment a single family, fired by one goal and one desire.

[Miliukov:]

Realizing the importance of a united statement by the people's representatives, the government called a one-day extraordinary session of the Duma for July 26. Following Rodzianko's speech at this session three ministers—Goremykin, Sazonov, and Bark—addressed the Duma, and statements were made by representatives of various nationalities—Poles, Latvians, Lithuanians, Jews, Moslems, Baltic Germans, and German colonists from the Volga regions. All of them, of course, similarly expressed their readiness to defend the homeland and their loyalty to the state and the people. These were followed by statements by the "responsible opposition," the Progressives and Kadets. Our declaration was written by me and approved by the [Kadet] faction and the Central Committee, particularly by I. I. Petrunkevich. It stressed the objectives of the war. "We are fighting for the liberation of our homeland from foreign invasion, for the liberation of Europe and Slavdom from German hegemony, for the liberation of the entire world from the intolerable burden of ever increasing armaments... In this struggle we stand united. We set no conditions; we make no demands. We simply place on the scales of war our firm will to victory." Such a statement, while stressing our solidarity with our allies, individualized our own role in the war, emphasized its defensive character, assigned to the war the pacifist aim of disarmament, and based our cooperation with the government on one task only, that of winning the war.

The "sacred unity," which was presented to the government voluntarily—and evidently despite its apprehensions—was, however, short-lived. And its breakdown was not the fault of the Duma.

XVIII:3. LENIN'S VIEWS ON THE WAR, SEPTEMBER-OCTOBER 1914

The way Lenin interpreted World War I and the program he advocated for his followers are shown in these passages from his writings. The first document was written by Lenin early in September 1914 and unanimously approved on September 6-7 by a small group of Bolsheviks (including Krupskaia and Zinov'ev) in Berne. These "theses" were then circulated and discussed in party groups in Russia and in western Europe and were incorporated, after some changes, into the manifesto which is the second item below.

Reference: Vladimir I. Lenin, *Sochineniia*, 2d ed., 30 vols. (Moscow: Gosizdat, 1926-30), 18: 46 [statement of September 1914], 61, 62, 65-66 [Central Committee Manifesto], 70, 71 [article of November 1914]. The translation of the second item is taken, with minor changes, from *The Essential of Lenin in Two Volumes* (London: Lawrence and Wishart, 1947), 1:619-20, 623-24.

[From "The Tasks of Revolutionary Social Democracy in the European War" ("Zadachi revoliutsionnoi sotsial-demokratii v evropeiskoi voine"), written by Lenin early in September 1914:]

The slogans of social democracy at this time must be: First, all-embracing propaganda extending to the army and to the theater of war, propagating the socialist revolution, and the necessity of using weapons not against one's own brothers, the hired slaves of other countries, but against the reactionary and bourgeois governments and parties of all nations; the absolute necessity of organizing illegal cells and groups in the armies of all nations for carrying on this propaganda in all languages; a ruthless struggle against the chauvinism and "patriotism" of the petty bourgeoisie and bourgeoisie of all countries without exception; an appeal to the revolutionary consciousness of the toiling masses, who bear the full burden of the war and who in most cases are hostile to opportunism and chauvinism, against the leaders of the present International, who have betrayed socialism. Second, propaganda calling for the immediate establishment of republics in Germany, Poland, Russia, and so forth, and for the organization of the separate European states into a republican United States of Europe. Third, a struggle against the tsarist monarchy and Great Russian pan-Slav chauvinism; agitation for a revolution in Russia and for the liberation and self-determination of all peoples oppressed by Russia, with emphasis on the immediate aims—a democratic republic, confiscation of estate lands, and an eight-hour working day.

[From "The War and Russian Social Democracy" ("Voina i rossiiskaia sotsial'-demokratiia"), a front-page manifesto signed by the "Central Committee of the Russian S.D. Workers' Party," in the newspaper *Sotsial-Demokrat* (Geneva), no. 33, November 1, 1914:]

The German bourgeoisie heads one group of belligerent nations. It is deluding the working class and the laboring masses by asserting that it is waging war in defense of the fatherland, freedom, and civilization, for the liberation of the peoples oppressed by tsardom, for the destruction of reactionary tsardom. . . . In reality, whatever the outcome of the war may be, this bourgeoisie will, together with the Junkers, exert every effort to support the tsarist monarchy against a revolution in Russia.

· · ·

The other group of belligerent nations is headed by the British and French bourgeoisie, which is deluding the working class and the laboring masses by asserting that it is waging war for the defense of their native lands, freedom, and civilization, against the militarism and despotism of Germany. But as a matter of fact, this bourgeoisie has long been using its billions to hire the armies of the Russian tsardom, the most reactionary and barbarous monarchy in Europe, and to prepare them for an attack on Germany.

In reality, the object of the struggle of the British and French bourgeoisie is to seize the German colonies and to ruin a competing nation which has displayed a more rapid rate of economic development. And, in pursuit of this noble aim, the "advanced" democratic nations are helping the savage tsarist regime to strangle Poland, the Ukraine, and so on, and to throttle revolution in Russia more thoroughly.

· · ·

For us, the Russian social democrats, there can be no doubt that from the standpoint of the working class and of the laboring masses of all the nations of Russia, the lesser evil would be the defeat of the tsarist monarchy, the most reactionary and barbarous of governments, which is oppressing the greatest number of nations and the largest mass of the population of Europe and Asia.

The immediate political slogan of the social democrats of Europe must be the formation of a republican United States of Europe. But in contrast with the bourgeoisie, which is ready to "promise" anything in order to draw the proletariat into the general current of chauvinism, the social democrats will reveal that this slogan is utterly false and senseless without the revolutionary overthrow of the German, Austrian, and Russian monarchies.

. . . The war has placed the slogan of socialist revolution on the agenda of all the advanced countries. . . .

The only correct proletarian slogan is the transformation of the present imperialist war into a civil war.

[From "The Condition and Tasks of the Socialist International" ("Polozhenie i zadachi sotsialisticheskogo internatsionala"), an article published in the newspaper *Sotsial-Demokrat* (Geneva), no. 33, November 1, 1914:]

The socialist movement cannot be victorious within the old framework of the fatherland. It creates new and higher forms of social relationships whereby the legitimate needs and progressive aspirations of the toiling masses of *every* nationality will for the first time be satisfied with an international union, upon the destruction of present national barriers. . . .

The bourgeoisie deludes the masses when it disguises its imperialistic pillage with the old ideology of a "national war." The proletariat exposes this deception by proclaiming the slogan of the transformation of the imperialistic war into a civil war.

· · ·

Even in wartime the socialist must propagate the class struggle; the task of transforming the war of nations into a civil war is the sole task of socialists in an era of armed imperialist conflict between the bourgeoisie of all nations. Away with the silly priestly sentimental yearnings for "peace at any price!" Let us raise the banner of civil war! . . .

The Second International is dead, vanquished by opportunism. Away with opportunism, and long live . . . the Third International, cleansed of opportunism.

. . . The Third International faces the task of organizing the forces of the proletariat for a revolutionary assault upon the capitalist governments, for a civil war against the bourgeoisie of all nations, for political power, for the victory of socialism!

XVIII:4. PALÉOLOGUE ON SUKHOMLINOV AND BELIAEV AND THE QUESTION OF MUNITIONS, NOVEMBER 25, 1914, AND JULY 7, 1915

Georges Maurice Paléologue (1859-1944), the French ambassador to Petrograd from just before the war in 1914 until May 1917, published in 1921-23 three volumes of memoirs. Here are two items he recorded under the dates indicated.

Reference: [Georges] Maurice Paléologue, *An Ambassador's Memoirs,* trans. F. A. Holt, 4th ed., 3 vols. (New York: George H. Doran, 1925), 1:217; 2:34.

[November 25 (December 8, N.S.), 1914:]

I am getting reports from many quarters that the Russian army is running short of gun ammunition and rifles. I have been to General Sukhomlinov, the War Minister, to ask him for definite information on this matter.

He gave me a very friendly reception.

. . .

I questioned him very closely. He kept on answering: "Don't worry; I've prepared for everything," and he produced to me the most comforting figures.

[July 7 (20, N.S.), 1915, in an interview with General M. A. Beliaev, chief of the general staff of the army:]

[General Beliaev said to M. Paléologue:] "You know all about the dearth of munitions. We are not producing more than 24,000 shells a day. It's a pittance for so vast a front! But our shortage of rifles alarms me far more. Just think! In several infantry regiments which have taken part in the recent battles at least one third of the men had no rifles. These poor devils had to wait patiently, under a shower of shrapnel, until their comrades fell before their eyes and they could pick up their arms. It's a perfect marvel under the circumstances that there was no panic. It is quite true that our *muzhiks* have an amazing capacity for endurance and resignation, but that doesn't make it any less ghastly. . . . One of our army commanders wrote to me the other day: '*At the beginning of the war, when we had gun ammunition and rifles, we were the victors. When the supply of munitions and arms began to give out we still fought brilliantly. To-day, with its artillery and infantry dumb, our army is drowning in its own blood.*' For how long will our men survive such a fiery trial? After all, these massacres are perfectly ghastly!"

XVIII:5. PARES ON THE RUSSIAN ARMY IN 1914-1915

Before 1914, Sir Bernard Pares, professor of Russian at the University of Liverpool, had spent much time in Russia and had achieved prominence lecturing on Russia to his fellow Britons. An ardent admirer of the Russian people, he spent most of the war years at their side. His experiences in the first year of the war were published at the time in his *Day by Day with the Russian Army, 1914-1915.* These excerpts illustrate how Pares saw the events at the front in those relatively hopeful months.

Reference: Bernard Pares, *Day by Day with the Russian Army, 1914-1915* (London: Constable 1915), pp. ix-x, xi, 34, 47, 176-77, 222-24, 258.

[Preface:]
When Germany declared war on Russia, I volunteered for service, and was arranging to start for Russia when we, too, were involved in the war. I arrived there some two weeks afterwards, and after a stay in Petrograd and Moscow was asked to take up the duty of official correspondent with the Russian army. . . . I had the great satisfaction of sharing in the life of the army, where I was entertained with the kindest hospitality and invited to see and take part in anything that was doing.

· · ·

It was a delight to be with these splendid men. I never saw anything base all the while that I was with the army. There was no drunkenness; every one was at his best, and it was the simplest and noblest atmosphere in which I have ever lived.

· · ·

[October 1914:] But the most impressive thing of all is the extraordinary endurance of the men in the trenches. It is a common experience for a man to be five to eight days in the trenches in pouring rain, almost, or sometimes altogether without food, then perhaps to rush on the enemy, to fall and see half his comrades fall, but the rest still going forward, to lie perhaps through a night, and then to the hospital to lose a limb: and yet, spite of the reaction [of shock from being wounded], such men are not only patient and affectionate to all who do anything for them, but really cheerful and contented, often literally jovial and always in no doubt of the ultimate issue.

· · ·

[November 4, 1914:] The Polish population shows the greatest alacrity in assisting the Russian troops both in the country and in the towns. All Poles now readily speak Russian. Yesterday the Warsaw Press entertained the Russian and foreign correspondents. There was a distinguished gathering, and both Russians and Poles spoke with striking frankness and feeling. One eminent Polish leader, Mr. Dmowski, said that all the blood shed between the two nations was drowned in the heavy sacrifices of the present common struggle. Polish politicians are keenly enthusiastic for France and Great Britain, and are studying the development of closer economic and other relations with Great Britain.

· · ·

[April 1915:] We had in England no adequate army when the war began; we had not reckoned on the shameless violation of Belgian territory or on the obligations of a joint struggle with allies for the independence of Europe. . . . But it is Russia who has given us time for preparing our action on land; and the sacrifices which this has cost her are heavy indeed. The tremendous impact at Rava Ruska was followed by another prolonged and exterminating effort on the San, and this takes no account of the work which was done in holding the furious attacks of the main enemy in Russian Poland. These efforts put a terrible drain on the Russian resources. While we stood firm on the west, whole Russian regiments were almost annihilated in the victorious storming of one Austrian position after another. In my earlier visits to regiments I have often asked how many men of the first call still remain; sometimes only six of a company were still left, sometimes it was hardly more out of a whole regiment. It was an army already replaced at almost every point which had to attempt the conquest of the Carpathians.

· · ·

[May 10, 1915:] . . . The number of wounded officers is not surprising, for . . .

they stand and walk while their men are ordered to crawl; but the sacrifice in officers is particularly impressive.

. . . Seven officers led the last counterattack of this regiment. Of some regiments the news was that they were practically all gone; in one case the answer was "The regiment does not exist. . . ." Of forty officers and four thousand men, in the end two hundred and fifty were left.

The enemy was in overwhelming numbers; but prisoners continued to come in in great batches.

· · ·

[June 1915:] By now I was coming to a conclusion which I had long been considering. I had visited these last corps to complete my information on some points which seemed to me to be of the first importance, not only to the army, but to Russia and to the allies. The data, of which I now had much more than enough, were overwhelming in what they indicated. Clearly the troops had lost not an atom of their fighting spirit; equally clearly they were fighting under the most unfair conditions and would continue to do so until their technical equipment, in arms and munitions, was much more on a level with that of the enemy.

XVIII:6. KNOX ON THE RUSSIAN ARMY, 1914-1917

Major General Sir Alfred Knox published a two-volume work entitled *With the Russian Army 1914-1917: Being Chiefly Extracts from the Diary of a Military Attaché*. Here are a few excerpts from that valuable account of Knox's three and one-half years of service in various parts of the Russian forces.

Reference: Alfred Knox, *With the Russian Army 1914-1917: Being Chiefly Extracts from the Diary of a Military Attaché*, 2 vols. (New York: E. P. Dutton, 1921), 1:39-40, 189-90, 194, 216, 219-20, 270, 282, 322-23, 332, 348-49; 2:389, 412, 422-25, 549-52.

I arrived in Petrograd on the morning of Friday, July 31st [N.S.; July 18, O.S.]. Germany declared war on Russia at 6 p.m. the following day—Saturday, August 1st.

The mobilisation went smoothly and the number of men called up in comparison with the partial mobilisation of 1904 caused general astonishment.

The spirit of the people appeared excellent. All the wine-shops were closed and there was no drunkenness—a striking contrast to the scenes witnessed in 1904. Wives and mothers with children accompanied the reservists from point to point, deferring the hour of parting, and one saw cruel scenes, but the women cried silently and there were no hysterics. The men

generally were quiet and grave, but parties cheered one another as they met in the street.

The war was undoubtedly popular with the middle classes, and even the strikers, who Russians believed had been subsidised with German money, at once on mobilisation returned to work. The Warsaw Press summoned the Poles to rally to the defence of Slavdom. A mass of a quarter of a million people uncovered in the Palace Square before the sacred eikons while the Emperor swore in the words of Alexander I. that he would never make peace as long as an enemy remained on Russian soil. Patriotic crowds cheered nightly in front of the British and French Embassies and the Serbian Legation.

. . .

[November 25, N.S., 1914:] The Grena-
derski Regiment yesterday lost very heavily,
and has now only nine officers and 500 men.
The Moskovski Regiment has only sixteen
officers left. The Semenovski Regiment has
lost ten officers killed and twenty wounded
since the beginning of the war, and 3,000
rank and file. The Preobrajenski Regiment has
lost forty-eight officers killed and wounded out
of seventy.

. . .

[December 2, N.S., 1914:] The losses
among officers have been very great. A General Staff officer of the 18th Division told me
that his Division has now only forty left out
of the 350 with which it commenced the war,
but some of the absent are sick and wounded
who will no doubt return. Battalions are com-
manded by ensigns. At present a single officer
has often a verst of trench to watch, and in
consequence cannot hope to control expenditure of ammunition. One regiment has been
losing as many as seven men per day in deser-
tions to the enemy. The men are tried beyond
their strength by having to remain in the
trenches without relief.

. . .

[January to March 1915:] The chief
deficiencies were in rifles and gun ammunition.

. . .

The secretiveness of many responsible
Russian officials and their suicidal desire to
represent the situation in a falsely favourable
light made it at all times exceedingly difficult
for allied representatives in Russia to keep
their Governments posted with timely and accurate information. The following is an
instance. On September 25th [N.S., 1914]
General Joffre had enquired by telegram
whether the resources of the British and Russian Governments permitted of the indefinite
continuance of the war at the then rate of
expenditure of ammunition, and, if they did
not, up to what date did the supply suffice.
The French Ambassador at Petrograd passed
on the question to the Russian Government
in an official letter. The Minister of War replied
on September 28th that the question of the
supply of ammunition in the Russian army
gave no cause for anxiety, and that the Ministry of War was taking all necessary steps to
provide everything required. At the same
time the French Military Attaché learned
from an unofficial source that the output of
factories in Russia then amounted to only
35,000 shells *a month*. Unfortunately, he had
no means of ascertaining that the rate of expenditure at the front then averaged 45,000
a day, and he believed that the initial stock
on mobilisation was more than twice as large
as it really was.

. . .

[Summer of 1915:] Unfortunately, the
situation on the front since the first realisa-
tion in November [1914] of the shortage of
rifles and shell had not permitted of the accumulation of any reserve. Apart from the
large quantities of material lost in the disaster
to the 10th Army, the normal monthly
wastage exceeded in quantity the supplies
received from the rear. The greatest lack was
still of rifles. Unarmed men had to be sent
into the trenches to wait till their comrades
were killed or wounded and their rifles became available.

. . .

[On the German offensive on the Dunajec
and the Russian retreat from Poland, April-
August 1915:]
The Russian General Staff at Petrograd
issued later a sort of official apology for the
retirement. This document stated that the
Germans concentrated upwards of 1,500
guns, of which many were of medium calibre,
against the right of the 3rd Army. They fired
700,000 shell in the four hours preceding the
attack. It was calculated that they used ten
medium-calibre shell for every pace and a half
of front, and as a natural result all the Russians
in the danger zone who were not killed or
wounded were stunned or contusioned.

The Russians had nothing with which to
reply. It is believed that there were not more
than three medium-calibre batteries in the
whole of the 3rd Army.

. . .

A strikingly pathetic feature of the retreat
was the mass of fugitives that blocked all the
roads as the Russian troops retired. The whole
of the Polish peasantry seemed to migrate from
the districts east of the Vistula. The Russians
said that they did not compel them to move
unless their villages were likely to be the scene
of fighting. The requisition, however, had
been ordered from all who remained of all
cattle, horses, bacon, tea and sugar, and it

was impossible for the people to remain behind when deprived of their means of livelihood. Unfortunately the civil staff was always the first to leave, and it was left to the Corps Intendance to carry out the requisitions. This, having no proper staff for the purpose, carried out its task in a slipshod manner. The authorities in rear were put to it to cope with a movement that had assumed the dimensions of a national migration. Even if trains had been available, they would have been of no use to the peasantry, whose only wealth was of too bulky a nature. They travelled in their long Polish carts drawn generally by two horses, the father driving and the mother sitting on the top of the family belongings in a cluster of her younger children. The elder sons and daughters drove flocks of cows or geese or pigs along the roadside.

Near Byelsk I passed twenty continuous miles of such fugitives. Some of them had come from as far as Plotsk, and had been on the road a month. If asked why they left their homes they would say that if they had stayed they would have starved, for "the Germans took everything," and "Russia will at any rate not allow us to starve." If asked where they were going, they replied that they did not know.

The Polish peasantry is one of the finest in the world—sober, hard-working and religious. The self-control with which these poor people met their trouble made one's heart go out to them. The women were often quietly crying, and there were many faces of absolute despair, but there was no bad temper and never a complaint.

. . .

[From the middle of August to the middle of October 1915:]

Most officers of the army regretted the Grand Duke's dismissal, for they regarded him as an honest man who stood apart from Court intrigue. They would have been content to pay that dismissal as the price of the much-desired removal of Yanushkevich and Danilov, many of them thinking . . . that the "Grand Duke was completely in the hands of those men." Misgiving, however, was almost universal regarding the Emperor's assumption of the Supreme Command.

. . .

This army was formidable on paper. Unfortunately in strength it was only a third of war establishment. From calculations made at the time, I estimated the total strength of the Russian army on the Western Frontier at the commencement of the winter of 1915-1916 at only 650,000 rifles, 2,590 machine-guns, and 4,000 three-inch field guns.

Six hundred and fifty thousand rifles to defend a front that from Reval to Czernowitz was not far short of one thousand miles were little enough. It was impossible for the moment for the Russians to bring their divisions up to establishment, first because the depots had been drained dry, and, secondly, because even if trained men had been available, there were no rifles to arm them. The prospect of the army being able to resume the offensive in the spring with any chance of success depended primarily on the balance-sheet of rifles.

The army was, however, weak in other ways. The number of officers of every kind in the normal division of sixteen battalions and six batteries had fallen to an average of 110. Few infantry units still retained more than 12 to 20 per cent. of their original establishment of professional officers.

. . .

[January-March, 1916:] During a visit to the Northern Front in February I was struck by the enthusiasm with which officers spoke of the spirit of the rank and file. The censors in the 12th Army (on the extreme right) read all letters and classified them according to their general spirit, as (a) "Good", (b) "Discontented or depressed," (c) "Complaining of officers," (d) "Complaining of food," etc. In all units 80 per cent. of the letters were said to show a good spirit, and in some units 100 per cent.

. . .

[April-July 1916:] Unfortunately, General Polivanov, who had succeeded Sukhomlinov as Minister of War in the summer of 1915, had been dismissed from his post on March 20th [N.S., 1916]. He was informed by Imperial letter that the Emperor felt that in serious times like the present he must have as Minister of War a man whom he could trust to work in less close co-operation with non-official organisations that were openly hostile to the Government.

Polivanov was undoubtedly the ablest military organise   'ussia, and his dismissal was a disaster.

   . . .

Generally speaking, the Russian military position had improved by the commencement of the summer of 1916 far beyond the expectations of any foreign observer who had taken part in the retreat of the previous year. The fighting of 1915 had taught the value of defenses, and the autumn of that year and the succeeding winter had seen the construction of several defensive lines. All units at the front by the middle of May possessed their full complement of rifles. The output of small arms ammunition had increased. The number of machine guns had increased to an average of ten to twelve per four-battalion regiment. Most of the infantry divisions had now thirty-six field guns, and there was a reserve of some 8,000,000 of 3″ shell. Most of the corps had a division of eight 4.8″ howitzers. A considerable number of trench mortars and hand grenades had been provided.

The troops at the front had benefited by their long rest, and their spirit was good.

   . . .

The transport, owing to lack of automobiles, was still archaic, and very little had been done to improve the railways.

   . . .

On June 20th [N.S., 1916] I reported:

The greatest danger of all is the danger of discontent in the large towns in the winter owing to the dearness of the necessities of life. The rise in prices is caused partly by speculation and partly by the fewness of the railways and the inefficiency of their working. In Moscow bread has risen 47 per cent. in price, in Odessa 80 per cent. Firewood has risen from 100 to 125 per cent.; sugar, when obtainable, by from 65 to 70 per cent. Meat is unobtainable by the general public, though there are abundant supplies in Siberia. The country folk are contented enough, for they have grown rich through the high price of grain and the closing of the wine-shops, but the more dangerous town population may give trouble in the winter.

The provisioning of the town population requires thought, for there are limits to the patience of even the Russian people.

   . . .

In the autumn of 1915 the allied prospects in the Eastern theatre looked black indeed, but in the spring of 1916 the Russian "grey great-coats" came again grandly, and the Russian Supreme Command held the initiative till the intervention of Rumania increased its liabilities without adding to its strength.

   . . .

"Brusilov's offensive" was the outstanding military event of the year. In the extent of territory regained, in the number of the enemy killed and taken prisoner and in the number of enemy units absorbed, it surpassed other allied offensives. Russia, owing to this advance, and the bait of Rumania, absorbed enormous enemy forces. . . . This contribution to the allied cause was attained with equipment that would have been laughed at in the Western theatre, and Russia paid the price in blood. Brusilov's armies lost 375,000 men in twenty-seven days in June, and their losses up till the end of October exceeded a million.

[Early in 1917:] On the eve of the Revolution the prospects for the 1917 campaign were brighter than they had been in March, 1916, for the campaign of that year.

   . . .

The Russian infantry was tired, but less tired than it had been twelve months earlier. It was evident that the Russian Command must in future squander men less lavishly on the front, but still the depots contained 1,900,000 men, and 600,000 more of excellent material were joining from their homes.

The stocks of arms, ammunition and technical equipment were, almost under every heading, larger than they had been even on mobilisation—much larger than they were in the spring of 1915 or of 1916, and for the first time supplies from overseas were arriving in appreciable quantities. England and France were sending much-needed aeroplanes. . . .

The leading was improving every day. The army was sound at heart. The men in the rest of the winter would have forgotten the trials of the past, and would have attacked again with the élan of 1916. There can be no doubt that if the national fabric in the rear had held together, or, even granted the Revolution, if a man had been forthcoming

who was man enough to protect the troops
from pacifist propaganda, the Russian army
would have gained fresh laurels in the campaign of 1917, and in all human probability

would have exercised a pressure which would
have made possible an allied victory by the
end of the year.

XVIII:7. MILIUKOV AND POLNER ON THE ALL-RUSSIAN UNION OF ZEMSTVOS, 1914-1916

Given the scope and nature of the activities of the All-Russian Union of Zemstvos (Vserossiiskii
Zemskii Soiuz) during the war, a full view can best be obtained through sources that combine
primary with secondary material, like the two quoted here: Miliukov's reminiscences and Tikhon
J. Polner's comprehensive study.

Reference: Miliukov, *Vospominaniia*, 2:201-02; Tikhon J. Polner, *Russian Local Government
during the War and the Union of Zemstvos*, Russian Series, "Economic and Social History of the
World War," vol. 9 (New Haven: Yale University Press, 1930), pp. 56, 57, 70, 269, 302-03.

[Miliukov:]

At the very beginning of the war, the Moscow zemstvo board [*zemskaia uprava*] raised
the question of establishing an All-Russian
Union of Zemstvos for the Relief of Sick and
Wounded Soldiers. In the atmosphere of
"sacred unity," it was impossible to reject
this proposal. [Georgii Evgenevich] L'vov
was received by the tsar, who expressed his
"sympathy" for the undertaking, and on
August 25, 1914, an imperial decree was published concerning the existence and activity
of the union, analogous to the Red Cross.
. . . The work of the Zemstvo Union was
superior in quality to that of the government,
and, most important, it brought aid more
quickly. Personal ties were established between military authorities and sections of the
Zemstvo Union. Everything from surgical
instruments and dressings to evacuation
trains, distribution stations, medical personnel
and hospitals was attended to and opportunely
provided by the zemstvo organization. These
operations required, in addition to the
12,000,000 rubles assigned from zemstvo
funds, huge sums which the government was
obliged to supply. By the end of June 1915,
the government had allocated to the zemstvos
72,000,000 rubles; by January 1, 1916, the
total had risen to 187,000,000. By the end
of 1916 nearly 8,000 zemstvo agencies of
various types, employing hundreds of thousands of persons, were spread throughout
Russia and the front. Naturally, the government was obliged to reckon with an organization of such scope.

And yet, despite the apolitical attitude of
G. E. L'vov, the political antagonism between
the public as represented by the zemstvo and
the government not only was not mitigated

but continued to grow in proportion to the
zemstvo successes. [Nikolai Alekseevich]
Maklakov, as minister of internal affairs,
played the main role in this intensification
of hostility.

[Polner:]

On July 30, 1914 . . . a conference attended by representatives of thirty-five
provincial zemstvos assembled at Moscow.
The other zemstvos sent word that they
were in full sympathy and joined the Union.
. . .

The conference approved the constitution
of the Union. The supreme power in the
Union was vested in the conference of the
deputies of the provincial zemstvos, each
zemstvo having two representatives, one
elected by the provincial assembly and the
other by the provincial board. Moscow was
selected as the meeting place of the conference.
It chose the president of the Union—the High
Commissioner—and a Central Committee
composed of ten members.

· · ·

The local organs of the Zemstvo Union
were the provincial and district committees.
. . .

Prince [G. E.] Lvov was elected President
of the Union.

· · ·

About the middle of 1916, when the
Central Committee undertook the classifica-
tion of the various institutions that had been
established in the war zone, it was able to
register 146 types and varieties grouped in
the following main categories: medical, sanitary, canteens, transport of wounded, freight,
charities, trading, veterinary, workshops,

factories, abattoirs, dairy farms, laboratories, storage depots and warehouses, and institutions for the purchase of raw materials.

Toward the close of 1916 the number of such institutions belonging to the Zemstvo Union was as follows:

Institutions of the Union of Zemstvos in 1916

Medical and sanitary	4,983
Canteens	850
Transport	395
Hospital trains	70
Workshops and factories	498
Stores	146
Depots	481
Others	305
Total	7,728

. . .

In the second half of 1916 the Zemstvo Union had grown to such an extent as to constitute a veritable state within a state. . . . Hundreds of thousands of persons, women as well as men, drawn from all paths of life, were employed directly and indirectly in the service of the Union. Donations were constantly flowing into its treasury. Gifts and parcels for the troops were being received in such quantities that they had to be sent to the front by special trains in charge of special commissioners. While it cannot be said that cash donations played any considerable part in the enormous budget of the Union, it should be noted that these small gifts and contributions in cash came from every part of the country and all classes of the popula-

tion, thus demonstrating the confidence that the Union enjoyed.

. . .

The World War found the zemstvo's work in full swing. It aroused immense patriotic enthusiasm in zemstvo circles and the determination to serve the nation in the calamities which had come upon it. Men of the most diverse political opinions forgot their differences and, joining hands, and combining their efforts, succeeded in creating a powerful central organization, which rested locally upon the provincial and district zemstvos and upon committees of the Zemstvo Union. These local organs succeeded in rallying around them local forces. . . .

This task was accomplished by the Unions of Zemstvos and of Towns. Amongst the educated classes the work of the unions was almost everywhere greeted with understanding, sympathy, and support. At the front the activities of the Zemstvo Union gradually won the recognition of the army, and most military men looked upon the zemstvo workers as messengers from their far-away homes conveying to them in a tangible form the sympathy of the nation and its desire to mitigate the sufferings of the army. The very nature of the work of the Union could not but win the cordial welcome and approval of the army. . . .

Radically different was the attitude toward the zemstvos of the high government functionaries in Petrograd. . . . Distrusting and fearing the Zemstvo Union, the Council of Ministers tried to limit its field of work and to place obstacles in the way of its further development.

XVIII:8. THE REGULATIONS OF THE WAR-INDUSTRY COMMITTEES, SEPTEMBER 9, 1915

The war-industry committees (*voenno-promyshlennye komitety*), under the vigorous leadership of A. I. Guchkov, became an active force in the latter part of the war.

Reference: Frank A. Golder, ed., *Documents of Russian History 1914-1917*, trans. Emanuel Aronsberg (New York: Century, 1927), pp. 125-26, citing the source: *Izvestiia Glavnogo Komiteta po snabzhenii armii*, no. 2-3 (Oct. 14, 1915), pp. 141-42 (not available to the editors).

On September 9 [1915], His Majesty confirmed the following regulations, recommended by the Council of Ministers, relating to the War-Industry Committees:

1. To help government organizations supply the army and navy with all necessary military and food supplies, there are being formed, for the duration of the war, central,

regional, and local war-industry committees.

2. The war-industry committees are public organizations which have no commercial aims. Consequently economic institutions belonging to them furnish military and food supplies at cost. When placing orders with private industries and business houses, the committees, to cover general expenses, may

have a rebate, the amount of which to be determined by the committees with the factories and business houses, but in no case is it to be more than one per cent of the cost of the order.

3. The composition, resources, relations [with other institutions] and activities of the Central War-Industry Committee are determined by the committee itself. The composition, resources, relations and activities of regional and local committees are determined by these committees in accordance with the general principles of organization and activities of war-industry committees, in agreement with the Central War-Industry Committee.

4. The relations between government institutions and war-industry committees in the matter of supplying the army and navy with military and food supplies are determined by

mutual agreement between the committees and the military and civil authorities concerned.

5. The Central War-Industry Committee has the right to take over every kind of movable and unmovable property; to conclude contracts with private individuals, with government and public institutions; to assume all kinds of obligations; in particular to carry out government orders for supplies and work; to organize, in agreement with the Ministries of War and Navy, methods of receiving and delivering war materials, etc.; to sue and be sued. Similar rights are enjoyed by the regional committees, organized and confirmed by the Central War-Industry Committee, as well as the local committees, organized and confirmed by the regional committees.

XVIII:9. THE RUSSIAN CO-OPERATOR *ON THE COOPERATIVE MOVEMENT, 1905-1916*

A noteworthy feature of the Russian economy in the last prerevolutionary decade is described in these excerpts from the first issue of the *Russian Co-operator: a Journal of Co-operative Unity,* launched in Britain in December 1916. The leading article, "Towards Co-operative Unity," indicated that the journal was designed to foster contact between commercial men in western Europe and the organizations of consumers and producers in Russia. Next came a historical sketch by W. Maisky, which read in part as follows.

Reference: *The Russian Co-operator, a Journal of Co-operative Unity* (London), 1 (December 1916):4-6.

Most English people would probably be greatly surprised to learn that the Russian co-operative movement celebrated its fiftieth anniversary last year. Russian co-operation was, in fact, born in 1865.

. . .

Unfortunately, the first successes won by the co-operative movement were of short duration, lasting only for a decade. In the middle of the 'seventies came an unwelcome change. The Government, after wavering for a while, embarked definitely on a policy of reaction. . . .

Even the publication of the "model rules" issued by the Government in 1897, which entitled the new societies adopting these rules to a somewhat shorter procedure in obtaining official recognition, did not infuse fresh life into the movement. . . .

The year 1905 may be regarded as the turning point in the whole history of Russian co-operation. Two causes contributed chiefly

to this effect. The first and most important was the great popular movement of this year, which gave the country the beginnings of a constitutional system of government. . . . The second reason for the enormous successes achieved by Russian co-operation during the next ten years can be found in the promulgation of the Act of 1904, which made it easier to open new credit societies, and in the establishment of a special Government Department for promoting small credit, chiefly for agricultural purposes.

The new successes of the Russian co-operative movement which mark the period 1905-1916, surpassed the most optimistic expectations of its leaders and supporters. To give an idea of the changes brought about by the last decade it is sufficient to quote a few figures. Agricultural credit societies are the backbone of Russian co-operation. Their development is well illustrated by the following figures:

	Number of Societies	Membership	Turnover (million £)
On January 1st, 1905 ...	1,434	564,000	6.4
On January 1st, 1916 ...	15,454	10,084,000	81.6

The number of societies has increased ten-fold, the membership nearly twenty-fold, and the turnover nearly fourteen-fold, this marvellous development being the work of only eleven years. At present the co-operative societies are spread throughout the country, from Archangel to the Caucasus, and from the Baltic Provinces to Eastern Siberia. Their chief centres, however, are to be found in districts of Central, Southern and Northern Russia.

Successes, not so great, but still notable, have been achieved during the last ten years by the consumers' societies. We have already seen that their number, at the beginning of this century, was about a thousand, with a membership of some 250,000. On January 1st, 1914, the total number of consumers' societies amounted to 10,080, with a membership of 1,459,000. The annual turnover of all these organisations reached £30,000,000, their net profit £1,000,000.

It was practically during the last decade that the co-operative organisations for agricultural produce grew up, which now occupy a distinguished place in the Russian co-operative world. In this connection the Siberian Creamery Associations, "the pride of Russian co-operation"—to use the popular expression one frequently hears amongst Russian co-operators—must be especially mentioned. In 1905 the number of creamery associations was very small, and their productive capacity rather limited; in 1915 there were 2,000 co-operative creamery associations with a total membership of 300,000 and an annual turnover of £6,000,000.

Another important branch of productive co-operation is formed by the societies of tar makers, situated chiefly in the Northern part of European Russia (in the provinces of Archangel, Vologda, Nijni Novgorod, etc.). In 1905 they hardly existed, but in 1915 the number of tar makers' societies amounted to 1,000. During recent years there have also been founded many co-operative organisations of flax growers, of tricot makers, and

other producers. The total number of the various productive societies reaches at present about 4,000.

We omit particulars concerning the less important organisations of the Russian co-operative world. It is sufficient, in summing up, to say that Russia has now 40,000 local co-operative societies, numbering more than 12,000,000, their members representing, if we include their families, nearly one-third of the total population of Russia.

Simultaneously with the rapid development of the movement, there was a growing tendency towards centralisation. Here Russian co-operators had to overcome great difficulties of a legal and administrative nature. The Government, suspicious in its attitude towards co-operation, tried as usual to prevent the union of local societies into bigger combinations. The formation of co-operative unions was, of course, not altogether forbidden, but to obtain a Ministerial permission to establish such a union was a long and complicated process. Co-operative congresses and conferences underwent similar difficulties.

Step by step, however, the co-operative movement extended the right of combination. In 1898 the Moscow Union of Consumers' Societies was established as the first co-operative union in Russia, and in 1901 the Berdiansk Union of Credit Societies was opened as the first union of Agricultural Credit Societies. These were followed by others, among them The Union of the Siberian Creamery Associations, which at present embraces about 1,200 co-operative societies of that kind. In 1908 the first Russian Co-operative Congress was allowed to be held in Moscow, in 1913 the second Co-operative Congress took place at Kiev. In 1912 the Moscow Narodny (People's) Bank was established as the central financial institution of the Russian co-operative movement.

Under the pressure of war conditions the Government has abandoned its former policy towards co-operative associations, and allowed the formation of co-operative unions.

The result of this step was really remarkable. During last year alone the number of such unions increased from 12 to 76, and it still continues to increase. One of the most important steps towards the centralisation of the Russian co-operative movement was a Conference of 36 District Unions of Consumers' Societies held in June, 1915, at Moscow, with a view to reorganising the Moscow Union of Consumers' Societies, to which 1,747 societies are now affiliated, on the lines of a co-operative wholesale society, embracing the whole of Russia. The Conference agreed to this plan, and all the necessary measures to put it in effect are now in preparation. Recent reports from Russia show also that during the last two years central associations of flax growers and tar makers have been formed, and that other central unions of a similar kind are on the way to commence business shortly.

XVIII:10. THE REPORT OF DUMA CHAIRMAN RODZIANKO TO THE TSAR, AUGUST 12, 1915

When it became known that the tsar intended to relieve the popular commander in chief, Grand Duke Nikolai Nikolaevich, and assume supreme command of the Russian armies himself, the chairman of the State Duma, Mikhail Rodzianko, addressed this report to the tsar (complete text).

Reference: Vladimir P. Semennikov, *Politika Romanovykh nakanune revoliutsii* (Moscow: Gosizdat, 1926), pp. 84-85; translation based largely, but with some changes, on Golder, *Documents of Russian History,* pp. 208-10.

To His Imperial Majesty,
the most humble report of
the chairman of the State Duma
Your Imperial Majesty:

Supplementing my verbal report, which I had the honor to lay before you on the eleventh of August, I make bold to beg Your Majesty again not to subject your sacred person to the dangers in which you may be placed as a consequence of your decision.

Sire! You are the symbol and the standard around which all the peoples of Russia rally. This standard cannot and must not be crumpled by the stress and storm of the adversities that have rushed upon us. It must shine radiantly as the torch for all national aspirations and must be the invincible bulwark of all the sons of Russia and the hope that will calm their minds, alarmed by these events.

Sire! You have no right to allow anything to happen before the nation that might possibly cast the faintest shadow to fall upon this sacred standard.

At this dreadful hour, unprecedented in the history of Russia, when the possibility arises of a heavy Teutonic yoke over the Russian land, you, Sire, must be outside and above those organs of government whose responsibility is the immediate repulsion of the enemy.

You cannot be the executive: you must be the judge, a benign encourager or implacable punisher.

But if you, Sire, should assume the direct command of our glorious army—you, Sire, the last refuge of your people—who will then pass judgment, in the event of failure or defeat? Is it not obvious, Sire, that you will then voluntarily have surrendered your inviolable person to the judgment of the people? And that is fatal to Russia.

Consider, Sire, what you are laying hands on—on yourself, Sire!

Our native land is going through a serious crisis. General mistrust surrounds the government now in power, which has lost its composure and will power. Any concept of authority has been shattered by its disorderly measures, and yet now, more than ever before, there has grown up in the country a realization of the need for a firm, unshakable faith in oneself and in the popular forces of authority. The minds and emotions of all Russians have reached a state of unprecedented strain, fearing for the fate of Russia.

The nation longs for and impatiently awaits that authority which will be capable of instilling confidence and leading our native land onto the path of victory. Yet at such a time, Your Majesty, you decide to remove the supreme commander in chief, whom the Russian people still trusts absolutely. The people must interpret your move as one inspired by the Germans around you, who are identified in the minds of the people with our enemies and with treason to the Russian cause.

Your Majesty's decision will appear to the people to be a confession of the hopelessness of the situation and of the chaos that has invaded the administration.

Sire! The situation will be even worse if the army, deprived of a leader enjoying its complete confidence, loses courage.

In this event defeat is inevitable, and within the country revolution and anarchy will then inevitably break out, sweeping everything from their path.

Your Majesty! Before it is too late, revoke your decision, no matter how hard it may be for you.

Retain Grand Duke Nikolai Nikolaevich at the head of the army.

Reassure troubled and already alarmed minds by forming a government from among those who enjoy your confidence and are known to the country by their public activities.

Sire, it is not yet too late!

On bended knees I beg you fervently not to delay the decision that will protect from approaching harm the sacred person of the Russian tsar and the reigning dynasty.

Sire, give heed to this truthful, heartfelt word from your loyal servant.

The President of the State Duma
Mikhail Rodzianko

Petrograd, August 12, 1915

XVIII:11. THE COLLECTIVE MESSAGE OF THE MINISTERS TO THE TSAR, AUGUST 21, 1915

In addition to the report of the chairman of the Duma, Nicholas received this "collective address" of August 21, 1915, from his ministers (complete text).

Reference: Semennikov, *Politika Romanovykh nakanune revoliutsii*, pp. 87-88; translation based largely, but with some changes, on Golder, *Documents of Russian History*, pp. 210-11. Recently there has appeared a translation of the discussions within the Council of Ministers at this time: Michael Cherniavsky, ed., *Prologue to Revolution: Notes of A. N. Iakhontov on the Secret Meetings of the Council of Ministers, 1915* (Englewood Cliffs, N.J.: Prentice-Hall, 1967). The message of August 21, 1915 is on pp. 166-67.

Most Gracious Sovereign:

Do not reproach us for our bold and candid address. We are driven to this action by our duty as loyal subjects, by our love for you and our native country, and by our alarmed consciousness of the dire portent of events now taking place.

Yesterday, at the meeting of the Council of Ministers over which you personally presided, we laid before you our unanimous appeal that Grand Duke Nikolai Nikolaevich not be removed from participation in the supreme command of the army. But we fear that Your Imperial Majesty did not deign to yield to our plea, and, in our opinion, the plea of all loyal Russia.

Sire, we make bold once more to tell you that, to the best of our understanding, your adoption of such a decision threatens Russia, yourself, and your dynasty with serious consequences.

At the same meeting the radical difference of opinion between the president of the Council of Ministers [Goremykin] and us in assessing events within the country and in determining the government's course of action became manifest. A situation such as this, intolerable at any time, is fatal in these days.

Under these circumstances, we are losing faith in the possibility of our consciously being of service to you and our country.

Your Imperial Majesty's loyal subjects:
Petr Kharitonov
Aleksandr Krivoshein
Sergei Sazonov
Petr Bark
Prince N. Shcherbatov
Aleksandr Samarin
Count Pavel Ignat'ev
Prince Vsevolod Shakhovskoi

August 21, 1915

XVIII:12. THE PROGRAM OF THE PROGRESSIVE BLOC, AUGUST 25, 1915

Here is the full text of the program agreed to on August 25, 1915, by those elements in the Duma and in the State Council that joined together to form the Progressive Bloc.

Reference: A. N. Iakhontov, "Tiazhelye dni," *Arkhiv russkoi revoliutsii*, 18:109-10; translation based largely on Golder, *Documents of Russian History,* pp. 134-36, and Bernard Pares, *The Fall of the Russian Monarchy: A Study of the Evidence* (New York: Alfred A. Knopf, 1939), pp. 271-73.

The undersigned representatives of parties and groups in the State Council and in the State Duma, out of the conviction that only a strong, firm, and active authority can lead our fatherland to victory, and that such an authority can only be one supported by the confidence of the public and capable of organizing the active cooperation of all citizens, have come to the unanimous conclusion that the most essential and important task of creating such an authority cannot be realized without the fulfillment of the following conditions:

The formation of a united government, consisting of persons who enjoy the confidence of the country and are in agreement with the legislative institutions as to carrying out, at the earliest time, a definite program; a decisive change in the methods of government hitherto employed, which have been founded on distrust of public initiative, in particular: (a) strict observance of the principle of legality in administration; (b) removal of the dual power of military and civil authority in questions that have no immediate relation to the conduct of military operations; (c) renovation of the personnel of local administration; (d) an intelligent and consistent policy directed to the maintenance of internal peace and the removal of discord between nationalities and classes.

For the realization of such a policy, the following measures must be taken in both the administrative and the legislative systems:

1. By amnesty from the Sovereign, the withdrawal of cases initiated on charges of purely political and religious offences which are not complicated by offences of a criminal character; the remission of punishment and restoration of rights, including that of taking part in elections to the State Duma, to zemstvo and town institutions, and so on, for persons condemned for such offences, and some mitigation for others who have been condemned for political and religious offences, with the exception of spies and traitors.

2. The return of those administratively exiled for offences of a political character.

3. Full and decisive cessation of persecution for religion under any pretext whatso-

ever, and repeal of circulars limiting and distorting the meaning of the decree of April 17, 1905 [on religious tolerance].

4. A settlement of the Russo-Polish question, that is: repeal of limitations on the rights of Poles all over Russia, the immediate preparation and introduction into the legislative institutions of a bill on the autonomy of Russian Poland [Tsarstvo Pol'skoe], and the simultaneous revision of the laws on Polish land ownership.

5. A beginning toward abolishing the limitations on the rights of Jews, in particular, further steps for the abolition of the Jewish Pale, facilitation of access to educational institutions, and a repeal of limitations on the choice of a profession; the restoration of the Jewish press.

6. A policy of conciliation in the Finnish question—in particular, a change in the personnel of the administration and the Senate, and the cessation of persecution of officials.

7. Restoration of the Little Russian press; the immediate review of the cases of inhabitants of Galicia kept under arrest or exiled, and the liberation of those of them who, though innocent, were subjected to prosecution.

8. The restoration of the work of trade unions, and cessation of persecution of the workers' representatives in sick benefit funds, on suspicion of belonging to an illegal party; restoration of the labor press.

9. Agreement between the government and the legislative institutions as to the speediest introduction of:

a. All bills that are most closely related to national defense, the supplying of the army, the care of the wounded, the regulation of the lot of refugees, and other problems directly connected with the war.

b. The following program of legislative work, directed toward organizing the country to contribute to victory and toward the maintenance of internal peace: equalization of the rights of peasants with those of other classes; the introduction of volost' zemstvos; the revision of the zemstvo law of 1890; the revision of the municipal law of 1892; the introduction of zemstvo institutions in outlying areas, such as Siberia, the Archangel guberniia, the Don region, the Caucasus, and so on; bills on cooperative societies, on rest days for shop assistants, on improving the lot of postal and telegraph employees, on approving temperance forever, on zemstvo and town congresses and unions, on the statute concerning inspections [*ustav revizii*], and on the introduction of justices of the peace in those guberniias where their introduction has been halted for financial reasons; and the carrying out of such legislative measures as may be found to be necessary for the administrative execution of the above-described program of action.

Signed:
For the Progressive Nationalist Group,
    V. A. Bobrinskii
For the Center Faction,
    V. N. L'vov
For the Zemstvo-Octobrist Faction,
    I. I. Dmitriukov
For the Union of 17 October Group,
    S. I. Shidlovskii
For the Progressivist Faction,
    I. N. Efremov
For the People's Freedom [Kadet] Faction,
    P. N. Miliukov
For the Academic Group of the State Council,
    D. D. Grimm
For the Center Group of the State Council,
    Baron V. Meller-Zakomel'skii

XVIII:13. LETTERS FROM THE TSARITSA TO THE TSAR, 1915- 1916

The private correspondence between emperor and empress—in part a by-product of the tsar's fateful decision of August 1915 to assume the supreme command at the front—is unexcelled as a source of information on the highest echelon of the tsarist government. Alexandra's letters, of which only a few excerpts can be given here, were written in her own variety of English. They were discovered in a black box in Nicholas's last place of imprisonment in Ekaterinburg, after the murder of the tsar's family (July 1918) and the capture of the area by the Whites.

Reference: *Letters of the Tsaritsa to the Tsar*, intro. by Bernard Pares (London: Duckworth, 1923), pp. 100, 106, 110, 114, 145, 152 [Sept. 9, 1915], 171, 174-76 [Sept. 17, 1915], 221, 283, 355, 394, 409, 411, 412, 416, 433-34, 438, 439-40 [Nov. 11, 1916], 444, 453-54, 455-56.

[Tsarskoe Selo, June 17, 1915:]

Now the Duma is to come together in August, & our Friend [Rasputin] begged you several times to do it as late as possible & not now, as they ought all to be working in their own places—& here they will try to mix in & speak about things that do not concern them. Never forget that *you are* & *must* remain authocratic Emperor,—we are not ready for a constitutional government, N's [Grand Duke Nikolai Mikhailovich] fault & Wittes it was the *Duma* exists, & it has caused you more worry than joy.

[Tsarskoe Selo, June 22, 1915:]

Ah my love, when at last will you thump with your hand upon the table & scream at *Dzhunkovsky* [commanding officer of the Palace Guards] & others when they act wrongly—one does not fear you—& one must— they must be frightened of you, otherwise all sit upon us, & its enough Deary—don't let me speak in vain. If *Dzhunkovsky* is with you, call him, tell him you know (*no* names) he has shown that paper [denunciation of Rasputin written by Dzhunkovsky] in town & that you order him to tear it up & *not to dare* to speak of *Gregory* [Rasputin] as he does & that he acts as a traitor & not as a devoted subject, who ought to stand up for the Friends of his Sovereign, as one does in every other country. Oh my Boy, make one tremble before you— to love you is not enough, one must be affraid of hurting, displeasing you. You are always too kind & all profit. It cannot go on like that Deary, beleive me once, its honest truth I speak. All, who really love you, long that you should be more decided & show your displeasure stronger, be more severe—things cant go well so. If your Ministers feared you, all would be better. The old man, *Goremykin,* also finds you ought to be more sure of yourself & energetically speak, & show more strongly when you are displeased.

[Tsarskoe Selo, June 25, 1915:]

Deary, I heard that that horrid *Rodzianko* & others went to *Goremykin* to beg the *Duma* to be at once called together—oh please dont, its not their business, they want to discuss things not concerning them & bring more discontent—they must be kept away—I assure you only harm will arise—they speak too much.

Russia, thank God, is not a constitutional country, tho' those creatures try to play a part & meddle in affairs they dare not. Do not allow them to press upon you—its fright if one gives in & their heads will go up.

[Tsarskoe Selo, August 22, 1915:]

Do not fear for what remains behind—one must be severe & stop all at once. Lovy, I am here, dont laugh at silly old wify, but she has "trousers" on unseen, & I can get the old man [Goremykin] to come & keep him up to be energetic—whenever, I can be of the smallest use, tell me what to do—use me— at such a time God will give me the strength to help you—because our souls are fighting for the right against evil. It is all much deeper than appears to the eye—we, who have been taught to look at all from another side, see what the struggle here really is & means— you showing your mastery, proving yourself the *Autocrat* without wh. Russia cannot exist. Had you given in now in these different questions, they would have dragged out yet more of you. Being firm is the only saving— I *know* what it costs you, & have & do suffer hideously for you, forgive me, I beseech you, my Angel, for having left you no peace & worried you so much—but I too well know yr. marvelously gentle character—& you had to shake it off this time, had to win your fight alone against all. It will be a glorious page in yr. reign & Russian history the story of these weeks & days—& God, who is just & near you—will save your country & throne through your firmness.

[Tsarskoe Selo, September 7, 1915:]

Your poor dear head must be awfully tired with all this work & especially the interior questions? Then, to recapitulate what the old man said: to think of a new minister of the interior, (I told him you had not yet fixed upon Neidhardt [conservative, loyalist, later recommended for the post of minister of transport]; perhaps, when you return you can think once more about *Khvostov*) [Aleksei N. Khvostov, whom Rasputin recommended to become minister of internal affairs]; a successor to *Sazonov* [minister of foreign

affairs 1910-16], whom he finds quite impossible, has lost his head, cries & agitates against *Goremykin*, & then the question, whether you intend keeping the latter or not. But certainly not a minister who answers before the *Duma*, as they want,—we are not ripe for it & it would be Russia's ruin—we are *not* a Constitutional country & *dare not* be it, our people are not educated for it & thank God our Emperor is an *Autocrat* & must stick to this, as you do— only you must show more power & decision. I should have cleared out quickly still *Samarin* [overprocurator of the Holy Synod] & *Krivoshein* [minister of agriculture 1908-15], the latter displeases the old man greatly, right & left & excited beyond words.

Goremykin hopes you won't receive *Rodzianko.* (Could one but get another instead of him, an energetic, good man in his place wld. keep the *Duma* in Order.)—Poor old man came to me, as a "soutien" & because he says I am "l'énergie". To my mind, much better clear out ministers who strike & not change the President who with decent, energetic, well-intentioned cooperates can serve still perfectly well. He only lives & serves you & yr. country & knows his days are counted & fears not death of age, or by knife or shot—but God will protect him & the holy Virgin. Our Friend wanted to wire to him an encouraging telegram.

[Tsarskoe Selo, September 9, 1915:]

Clean out all, give *Goremykin* new ministers to work with & God will bless you & their work.

Please Lovebird, and *quickly.*

. . .

And you my love, try to heed to what I say, its not my wisdom but a certain instinct given by God *beyond myself* so as to be your help.

[Tsarskoe Selo, September 17, 1915:]

Some are afraid I am meddling in state affairs (the ministers) & others look upon me as the one to help as you are not here (*Andronnikov* [social and political adventurer and a friend of Rasputin], *Khvostov* [soon thereafter named minister of internal affairs], *Varnava* [archbishop of Tobol'sk and a friend of Rasputin] & some others) that shows who is devoted to you in the *real* sense of the word— they will seek me out & the others will avoid me—is it not true, Sweetheart?

[Tsarskoe Selo, September 17, 1915:]

... I sent you two wires because of *Khvostov* & hoped you would mention a wee word.

. . .

With pleasure I continue thinking over Khvostov's talk & wish you had been there too—a man, no petticoats—& then one who will *not* let *anything* touch us, & will do all in his power to stop the attacks upon our Friend [Rasputin], as then he stopped them & now they intend beginning again.

. . .

Well dear, there is nothing to be done with those Ministers, and the sooner you change them, the better.

[Tsarskoe Selo, November 15, 1915:]

Now, before I forget, I must give you over a message from our Friend, prompted by what He saw in the night. He begs you to order that one should advance near Riga, says it is necessary, otherwise the Germans will settle down so firmly through all the winter, that it will cost endless bloodshed and trouble to make them move—now it will take them so aback that we shall succeed in making them retrace their steps—he says this is *just now* the most essential thing and begs you *seriously* to order ours to advance, he says *we can* and we must, and I was to write it to you at once.

[Tsarskoe Selo, March 2, 1916:]

Am so wretched that we, through *Gregory* recommended *Khvostov* to you—it leaves me not peace—you were against it and I let myself be imposed upon by them, tho' fr. the very first told Ania [Anna Vyrubova] that I like his great energy but that too selflove and something not pleasing to me; and the devil got hold of him, one cannot call it otherwise. I wld. not write to you about it last time not to bother you—but we passed through trying times, and therefore wld. have been calmer if, now that you go, something could be settled. As long as *Khvostov* is in power and has money and police in hands—I honestly am not quiet for *Gregory* and Ania. [A. N. Khvostov was dismissed March 16, 1916.]

[Tsarskoe Selo, June 16, 1916:]

I forgot to tell you that our Friend begs you should give the order that one should not augment the prices of going in town in trains—instead of *5 kopeeks* now one must pay *10 kopeeks* and thats not fair upon the poor people—let the rich be taxed but the others who daily have often more than once to go by train.—Write it on one of yr. papers to *Sturmer* [Shtiurmer, then chairman of the Council of Ministers] to tell Obolensky [Prince A. N., prefect of police], who I suppose gave this foolish order.

[Tsarskoe Selo, September 7, 1916:]

Gregory begs you *earnestly* to name *Protopopov* [as minister of internal affairs] there. You know him & had such a good impression of him—happens to be of the *Duma* (is *not* left) & so will know how to be with them. Those rotten people came together & want *Rodzianko* to go to you and ask you to change all the ministers & take their candidates—impertinent brutes.

I think you could not do better than name him. . . . About Poland He begs you to wait, *Sturmer* too; only *not* before we cross the frontier—do listen to Him who only wants yr. good & whom God has given more insight, wisdom & enlightenment than all the military put together. His love for you & Russia is so intense & God has sent Him to be yr. help & guide & prays so hard for you.

[Tsarskoe Selo, September 22, 1916:]

I am no longer the slightest bit shy or affraid of the ministers & speak like a waterfall in Russia[n]!!! And they kindly don't laugh at my faults. They see I am energetic & tell all to you I hear & see & that I am yr. wall in the rear wh. is a very firm one & with God's mercy I hope I may be of some wee use to you.

[Tsarskoe Selo, September 23, 1916:]

Our Friend says about the new orders you gave to Brussilov [General Brusilov] etc.: *"Very satisfied with father's orders, all will be well."* He won't mention it to a soul but I had to ask His blessing for yr. decision.

[Tsarskoe Selo, September 24, 1916:]

Lovy, our Friend is much put out that *Brussilov* has not listened to yr. order to stop the advance—says you were inspired from above to give that order & the crossing of the Carpathians before winter & God wld. bless it.—Now he says again useless losses.

[Tsarskoe Selo, September 27, 1916:]

Speak to *Pr.* [Protopopov, the sixth and

last to serve as minister of internal affairs in
1915-16] about:

1. Sukh. [Sukhomlinov, former minister
of war], order to find a way to get him out.

2. Rubinstein [D. L., Jewish banker accused of financial scandals] to send away.

3. *Prefect.*

4. Augment *wages* of the *officials* as *your
kindness* to them, not fr. the ministers.

5. About *food supplies* tell him *strictly,*
severely that all must be done to set it to
rights—you *order* it.

6. Tell him to listen to our Friend's councils, it will bring him blessings & help his work
& Yours—*please* say this, let him see yr. trust
in him—he knows him several years already.

Keep this paper before you.

[Tsarskoe Selo, November 4, 1916:]

Warmest thanks for yr. dear letter just received. I read Nikolai's [Grand Duke Nikolai
Mikhailovich, letter of about November 1,
1916, Item 24 in this chapter] & am utterly
disgusted. Had you stopped him in the middle
of his talk & told him that, if he only once
more touched that subject or me, you will
send him to Siberia—as it becomes next to
high treason. He has always hated & spoken
badly of me since 22 years & in the club too
(this same conversation I had with him this
year).—but during the war & at such a time
to crawl behin yr. Mama & Sisters & not stick
up bravely (agreeing or not) for his Emperor's
Wife—is loathsome & treachery. He feels
people count with me, begin to understand
me & are for my opinion & he cant bear. He
is the incarnation of all that's evil, *all* devoted
people loathe him, even those who do not
much like us are disgusted with him and his
talks.—And Fred. [Count Fredericks, minister
of the imperial court] old & no good & cant
shut him up & wash his head & you my Love,
far too good & kind & soft—such a man needs
to be held in awe of you—He & *Nikolasha*
[Grand Duke Nikolai Nikolaevich] are my
greatest enemies in the family, not counting
the black women [two Montenegrin princesses
married to the grand dukes Nikolai Nikolaevich
and Petr Nikolaevich]—& Sergei [Grand Duke
Sergei Mikhailovich]—He simply cld. not bear
Ania & me—not so much the cold rooms, I
assure you. I don't care personal nastiness,
but as yr. chosen wife—they dare not Sweety
mine, you must back me up, for your and

Baby's sake. Had we not got Him [Rasputin]—
all wld. long have been finished, of that I am
utterly convinced.—I am seeing Him a moment
before *Sturmer.* Poor old man may die fr. the
vile way his spoken to & of at the *Duma—
Miliukov's* speech yesterday when he quotes
Buchanan's [the British ambassador's] words
that *Sturmer* is a traitor & Buch. [Buchanan]
to whom he turned in the box—held his
tongue—vile behavior. We are living through
hardest times, but God will help us through,
I have no fear. *Let* they scream—we must
show we have no fear & are firm. Wify is your
staunch One & stands as a rock behind you.
I'll ask our Friend, whether He thinks it advisable I go in a week's time, or, as you cant
move—whether I shld. remain here to help
the "weak" minister [Sturmer]. They have
again chosen *Rodzianko* & his speeches are
quite bad & what he says to the ministers.

I hope Sweetheart's leg will soon be better.
And *Alexeiev* [Chief of Staff Alekseev] ill—
all worries at one time—but God will not for-
sake you & our beloved Country through the
prayers & help of our Friend.

[Tsarskoe Selo, November 10, 1916:]

I received old *Sturmer* & he told me yr.
decisions—God grant, all is for the good, tho'
it gave me a painful shock you also take him
away fr. the *Council of Ministers.*

I had a big lump in my throat—such a
devoted, honest, sure man. Yr. kindness &
trust touched him so much & the beautiful
nomination. I regret, because he likes our
Friend & was so right in that way—*Trepov*
[who succeeded Shtiurmer as chairman of
the Council of Ministers], I personally do
not like & can never have the same fealing
for him as to old *Goremykin* & *Sturmer*—
they were of the good old sort. The other, I
trust, will be firm (I fear at heart a hard man)—
but far more difficult to talk to—those two
loved me & came for every question that worried them, so as not to disturb you—this one
I, alas, doubt caring for me & if he does not
trust me or our Friend, thinks will be difficult. I told *Sturmer* to tell him how to behave
about *Gregory* & to safeguard him always.
Oh, may it be for the good & you have an
honest man, in him to help you. You, Lovy,
will tell him to come to me too sometimes—
I know him so little & would like to "understand" him.

[Tsarskoe Selo, November 11, 1916:]

Forgive me, deary, believe me—I entreat you *dont* go and change *Protopopov* now, he will be alright, give him the chance to get the *food supply matter* into his hands & I assure you, all will go. . . . *Protopopov* is honestly for us. Oh, Lovy, you can trust me. I may not be clever *enough*—but I have a strong feeling & that helps more than the brain often. *Dont change anybody until* we meet, I entreat you, lets speak it over *quietly together.* Let *Trepov* come a day later or keep the papers & names back, Lovy dear—for Wify's sake. You dont know how hard it is now—so much to live through & such hatred of the "rotten upper sets". The *food supply* must be in *Protopopov's* hands. . . . *Protopopov* venerates our Friend & will be blessed—*Sturmer* got frightened & for months did not see him—so wrong & he lost his footing.

[Tsarskoe Selo, December 5, 1916:]

You have said yr. say & had yr. fight about Protopopov & it shall not be in vain we suffered—stick to him, be firm, don't give in—as then never more any peace, they will begin worrying you in the future yet worse when you don't agree, as they see that by persistent obstinacy they force you to give in—as hard as they, I mean *Trepov* & *Rodzianko* (with the evil) on one side—I shall stand against them, (with God's holy man) don't you stick to them, but to us, who live only for you, Baby [their twelve-year-old son, Alexis], & Russia. To follow our Friend's councils, lovy—I assure is right—He prays *so* hard day & night for you . . . only one must listen trust & ask advice—not think He does not know. God open—everything to Him, that is why people, who do not grasp His soul, so immensely admire His wonderful brain—ready to understand anything; & when He blesses an undertaking—it succeeds & if He advises people—one can be quiet that they are good—if they later on change that is already not His fault—but He will be less mistaken in people than we are—*experience in life* blessed by God.

[Tsarskoe Selo, December 13, 1916:]

Thank God, you at last fixed no date in Jan. & can call them together in Feb. or not at all. They do not work & *Trepov* flirts with *Rodzianko* all know that, 2 a day they meet—that is not decent—why does he make up &

try to work with him (who is false) & not with *Protopopov* (who is true)—that pictures the man. . . . My Angel, we dined yesterday at Ania's [Anna Vyrubova] with our Friend. . . . He *entreats* you to be firm, to be Master & not always to give in to *Trepov*—you know *much* better than that man (still let him lead you)—& why not our Friend who leads through God. Remember why I am disliked—shows it right to be firm & feared & you be the same, you a man,—only believe more in our Friend (instead of *Trepov*). He lives for you & Russia. And we must give a strong country to Baby, & *dare not* be weak for his sake, else he will have a yet harder reign, setting our faults to right & drawing the reins in tightly which you let loose. You have to suffer for faults in the reigns of your predecessors & God knows what hardships are yours. Let our legacy be a lighter one for Alexei. He has a strong will & mind of his own, don't let things slip through yr. fingers & make him have to build up all again. Be firm, I, your wall, am behind you & won't give way—I know He leads us right—& you listen gently to a false man as *Trepov*. Only out of love which you bear for me & Baby—take no big steps without warning me & speaking over all quietly. . . . Only not a *responsible cabinet* which all are mad about. Its *all* getting calmer & better, only one wants to feel Your hand—how long, years, people have told me the same—"Russia loves to feel whip"—its their nature—tender love & then the iron hand to punish & guide.—How I wish I could pour my will into your veins. . . .

. . . *Forgive* this letter, but I could not sleep this night, worrying over you—don't hide things from me—I am strong—but listen to me, wh. means our Friend & trust us through all—& beware of *Trepov*—you *can't* love or venerate him. I suffer over you as over a tender softhearted child—wh. needs giding, but listens to bad advisers whilst a man of God's tells him what to do.

[Tsarskoe Selo, December 14, 1916:]

Trepov behaves now, as a traitor & is false as a cat—do not trust him, he concocts everything with *Rodzianko* together, its only too well known.

. . . Be Peter the Great, John the Terrible, Emperor Paul—crush them all under you—now don't you laugh, noughty one—but I long to see you so with those men who try to govern you—& it must be the contrary. . . . And here the contrast, telegr. fr. "*Union of the Russian People*" asking me to give over things to you.—One is rotten, weak, immoral society—the other, healthy, right thinking, devoted subjects—& to these one must listen, their voice is Russia's & not society or the *Duma's.* One sees the right so clearly & they know the *Duma* ought to be closed & to them *Trepov* won't listen. If one does not listen to these, they will take things into their own hands to save you and more harm unwillingly may be done—than a simple word from you to *close the Duma*—but till February, if earlier—they will all stick here. I cld. hang *Trepov* for his bad counsels. . . . Disperse the *Duma* at once—I should have quietly & with a clear conscience before the *whole* of Russia have sent *Lvov* to Siberia (one did so for far less grave acts) . . . *Miliukov, Gutchkov* [Octobrist leader] & *Polivanov* [minister of war 1915-16] also to Siberia. It is *war* and at such a time *interior* war is high treason, why don't you look at it like that, I really cannot

understand. I am but a woman, but my soul & brain tell me it wld. be the saving of Russia— they sin far worse than anything the Sukhomli- nov's ever did.—Forbid *Brussilov* etc. when they come to touch any political subjects, fool, who wants *responsible cabinet* as *Georgi* [Grand Duke Georgii Mikhailovich] writes.

Remember even Mr. Philippe said one dare not give constitution, as it would be yr. & Russia's ruin, & all true Russians say the same. . . . I know I worry you . . . but my duty as wife & mother & Russia's mother obliges me to say all to you—blessed by our Friend. Sweetheart, Sunshine of my life, if in battle you had to meet the enemy, you wld. never waver & go forth like a lion—be it now in battle against the small *handful* of brutes & republicans—be the Master, & all will bow down to you. . . . we have been placed by God on a throne & we must keep it firm & give it over to our Son untouched—if you keep that in mind you will remember to be the Sover- eign—& how much easier for an *autocratic* sovereign than one who has sworn the Consti- tution.

XVIII:14. LETTERS FROM THE TSAR TO THE TSARITSA, 1915-1917

Here are a few illustrative excerpts from the wartime letters "Nicky" wrote to "Sunny" from the Stavka or general headquarters of the Russian armies at Mogilev. It was on August 20, 1915, that he assumed direct command. The tsar's end of the correspondence, like the tsaritsa's, was carried on in English, but in this case the original has not been made available, and one can work only from the Russian version edited shortly after the Revolution by M. N. Pokrovskii, which was retranslated into an approximation of the tsar's English by A. L. Hynes.

Reference: Tsentrarkhiv, ed., *Perepiska Nikolaia i Aleksandry Romanovykh 1914-1917*, vols. 3-5 (Moscow: Gosizdat, 1923), 3:53 [Nov. 19, 1914], 266-68 [Aug. 25, 1915], 273-74 [Aug. 27, 1915], 329 [Sept. 9, 1915]; 4:149 [Mar. 14, 1916], 152 [Mar. 15, 1916], 290-91 [June 5, 1916], 295 [June 7, 1916], 321 [June 17, 1916]; 5:16-17 [Sept. 9, 1916], 46 [Sept. 20, 1916], 60 [Sept. 23, 1916], 63-64 [Sept. 24, 1916], 134 [Nov. 5, 1916], 146 [Nov. 10, 1916], 213 [Feb. 23, 1917], 217 [Feb. 24, 1917]. The translations are based largely, with occasional changes, on those by A. L. Hynes in C. E. Vulliamy, ed., *The Letters of the Tsar to the Tsaritsa, 1914-1917* (London: J. Lane, 1929), pp. 14, 70-72, 73-74, 85, 157-59, 200, 202-03, 212, 256- 57, 266, 269, 270, 293, 297-98, 313-14, 315.

[Stavka, November 19, 1914:]

The only great and serious difficulty for our troops is that we again do not have suf- ficient munitions. Therefore, during battle our troops have to observe economy and discretion, which means that the brunt of the fighting falls upon the infantry; owing to that, the losses at once become colossal. Some of the army corps have become divisions, the brigades have shrunk into regiments, and so forth.

[Stavka, August 25, 1915:]

My own beloved, darling Sunny,

Thank God it is all over, and here I am with this *new* heavy responsibility on my shoulders! But God's will be fulfilled—I feel so calm—a sort of feeling after the Holy Com- munion!

The whole morning of that memorable day, August 23, while coming here, I prayed much and read your first letter over and over again. The nearer the moment of our meeting, the greater the peace that reigned in my heart.

N. [Grand Duke Nikolai Nikolaevich] came in with a kind, brave smile, and asked simply when I would order him to go. I answered in the same manner that he could remain for two days; then we discussed the questions connected with military operations, some of the generals and so forth, and *that was all*.

. . .

A new clean page begins, and only God Almighty knows what will be written on it!

I have signed my first prikaz [order] and have added a few words with a rather shaky hand!

. . .

Think, my Wifey, will you not come to the assistance of your hubby now that he is absent? What a pity that you have not been fulfilling this duty for a long time or at least during the war!

I know of no more pleasant feeling than to be proud of you, as I have been all these past months, when you urged me on with untiring importunity, exhorting me to be firm and to stick to my own opinions.

We had only just finished playing dominoes when I received through [Chief of Staff] Alekseev a telegram from Ivanov [General N. Iu. Ivanov, commanding the Southwest Front], who reports that today our Eleventh Army (Shcherbatchev's) in Galicia attacked two German divisions (the Third Guard and the Forty-eighth Infantry) with the result that they have captured over 150 officers and 7,000 men, 30 guns and many *pulemety* [machine guns].

And this happened immediately after our troops learned that I have taken upon myself the supreme command. This is truly God's blessing, and such a swift one!

Now I must finish; it is already late, and I must go to bed.

God bless you, my beloved treasure, my ray of sunshine!

Tenderly and again tenderly do I kiss you and the dear children.

Always your old hubby,
Nicky

[Mogilev, August 27, 1915:]

The trains move very irregularly, owing to the tremendous work on the lines. From a military point of view this is one of our greatest difficulties.

Troops, war materials, supplies go in one direction, and the evacuation—and especially these unhappy *bezhentsy* [refugees]—in the opposite!

It is impossible to restrain these poor people from abandoning their homes in the face of the advancing enemy, as nobody wishes to risk being left in the hands of the Germans or Austrians. Those for whom there is no room in the trains walk or ride along the roads, and, as the cold weather is coming, this pilgrimage is beginning to be terribly difficult; the children suffer very acutely, and many of them, unfortunately, die on the way.

All local authorities and the members of various committees work hard and do all in their power—I know that; but they confess frankly that they cannot do everything. It is frightful to think how many *unforeseen* sufferings the war has brought with it.

[Mogilev, September 9, 1915:]
My dear, beloved Sunny,

Thank you, thank you for your nice, long letters, which now come more regularly—about 9:30 in the evening. You write just as you talk. The behavior of some of the ministers continues to amaze me! After all that I told them at that famous evening session, I thought they understood both me and the fact that I was seriously explaining precisely what I thought. What matter—so much the worse for them! They were afraid to close the Duma—it was done! I came here and replaced N. [Grand Duke Nikolai Nikolaevich], in spite of their advice; the people accepted this move as a natural thing and understood it, as we did. As proof—the heaps of telegrams which I receive from all sides, with the most touching expressions. All this clearly shows me one thing: that the ministers, continuously residing *in the city,* know terribly little of what is happening in the country as a whole. Here *I can judge* correctly the real *mood* among the various classes of the people: everything must be done to bring the war to a victorious ending, and no doubts are expressed on that score. I was officially told *this* by all the deputations I received the other day, and so it is all over Russia. Petrograd and Moscow constitute the only exceptions—two minute points on the map of our fatherland!

[Stavka, March 14, 1916:]
Things are moving very slowly at the front;

in several places we have sustained heavy losses, and many generals are making serious blunders. Worst of all, we have so few good generals. It seems to me that during the long winter rest they have forgotten all the experience they acquired last year! . . .

[Stavka, March 15, 1916:]
My Treasure!

I thank you tenderly for your dear letters. I cannot tell you how I sympathize with you when you are oppressed by those terrible pains in the face, and how I long to be near you at those times in order to comfort you! It is quite impossible for me to determine when I shall be able to come home for a few days—perhaps not for some time, and perhaps in about a week!

What I was afraid of has happened. Such a great thaw has set in that the positions occupied by our troops where we have moved forward are flooded with water knee deep, so that it is impossible either to sit or to lie down in the trenches. The roads are rapidly deteriorating; the artillery and transport are scarcely moving. Even the most heroic troops cannot fight under such conditions, when it is impossible even to entrench oneself. In consequence, our offensive was brought to a halt, and another plan has to be worked out.

[Stavka, June 5, 1916:]

Some days ago *Alekseev* and I decided not to attack in the north, but to concentrate all our efforts a little more to the south—*but I beg you not to tell anybody about it,* not even our Friend [Rasputin]. Nobody must know about it.

[Stavka, June 7, 1916:]

I told *Alekseev* how interested you were in military affairs, and of those details which you asked me for in your last letter, no. 511. He smiled and listened silently. Of course, these things have been, and are being, taken into consideration; our pursuit will end at the Suchava River; all the narrow- and broad-gauge railways are being put right, and new ones are being constructed immediately behind our troops. Do not be surprised if a temporary lull now occurs in military operations. Our troops will not move there until new reinforcements arrive and until a diversion has been made near *Pinsk.* I beg you to

keep this *to yourself;* not a single soul must know of it!

[Stavka, June 17, 1916:]

Next Tuesday our second offensive will begin there and higher up, almost all along the whole front. If only we had sufficient ammunition for the *heavy* artillery, I should be quite calm. But now we shall be obliged to call the offensive to a halt in a week or two, in order to replenish our supplies, and this is done too slowly because of the shortage of fuel!

Thus, our military operations are being hindered only by the fact that the army does not receive a sufficient quantity of heavy ammunition.

One could crawl up a wall in sheer desperation!

[Stavka, September 9, 1916:]

Thank you with all my heart for your dear, long letter, in which you pass on our Friend's instructions. It seems to me that this *Protopopov* [whom Rasputin had urged as minister of internal affairs] is a good man, but he has much to do with factories, etc. *Rodzianko* has for a long time suggested him for the post of minister of trade, instead of *Shakhovskoi.* I must consider this question, as it has taken me completely by surprise. Our Friend's opinions of people are sometimes very strange, as you yourself know—therefore one must be careful, especially with appointments to high offices. I do not personally know this Klimovich [General E. S., chief of police, an enemy of Rasputin]. Would it be wise to discharge them at the same time, i.e. I mean to say, the minister of the interior [A. A. Khvostov, uncle of A. N.] and the chief of police? This must be carefully thought out. And whom am I to begin with? All these changes make my head spin. In my opinion, they are too frequent. In any case, they are not good for the internal situation of the country, as each new man brings with him alterations in the administration.

[Stavka, September 20, 1916:]

Together with military matters, the eternal question of *supplies* troubles me most of all. *Alekseev* gave me today a letter he received from the charming Prince Obolenskii, the chairman of the Committee *on Supplies.* He confesses frankly that they *cannot alleviate the situation in any way,* that they are working in vain, that the Ministry of *Agriculture* pays no attention to their regulations, that all prices are soaring and the people beginning to starve. It is obvious where such a state of affairs may lead the country.

Old Sht. [Shtiurmer] cannot overcome all these difficulties. I do not see any other way out, except transferring the matter to the military authorities, but that also has its disadvantages! It is the most damnable problem I have ever come across! I never was a merchant and simply do not understand anything in these questions of supplies and provisioning!

[Stavka, September 23, 1916:]

Yes, truly, you ought to be my eyes and ears there in the capital, while I have to sit here. It rests with you to keep peace and harmony among the ministers—thereby you are being of great benefit to me and to our country. Oh, my precious Sunny, I am so happy to think that you have found at last an occupation suitable for you! Now I shall, of course, be calm, and at least need not worry over internal affairs.

[Stavka, September 24, 1916:]
My precious darling,

. . . You will really help me a great deal by speaking to the ministers and watching them. I have only just received your telegram, in which you inform me that our Friend is very disturbed about my plan not being carried out. When I gave this order I did not know that [General V. I.] *Gurko* had decided to gather almost all the forces at his disposal and prepare a joint attack with the Guards and the neighboring troops. This combination doubles our forces in this place and gives hopes for the possibility of success. That is why, when *Al.* [Alekseev] read out the explanatory telegrams from *Brus.* [Brusilov] and *Gurko* with the request to be allowed to continue the attack, which was then already in full swing, I gave my consent the next morning. Today *Br.* [Brusilov] asked permission to send General *Kaledin* to Lechitskii [General, commander of the Ninth Army] and to appoint *Gurko* commander over all these troops, including the Guards, which, from a military point of view,

is quite correct, and with which I thoroughly agree. Now I shall be calm in the assurance that *G.* [Gurko] will act energetically but with caution and intelligence. These details are for you alone—I beg you, my dear! Tell Him [Rasputin] only: Papa prikazal priniat' razumnye mery! [Papa has ordered that sensible measures be taken!]

[Stavka, November 5, 1916:]

Yesterday I received the famous General *Manikovskii,* the chief of the Ordnance Department. He told me much concerning the workers, the terrible propaganda among them, and the enormous amount of money distributed to them for strikes—and that on the other hand no opposition is offered, the police do nothing and nobody seems to care what may happen! The ministers are, as usual, weak—and here is the result!

[Stavka, November 10, 1916:]

I am sorry for *Prot.* [Protopopov]—he is a good, honest man, but he jumps from one idea to another and cannot make up his mind on anything. I noticed that from the beginning. They say that a few years ago he was not quite normal after a certain illness (when he sought the advice of *Badmaev*). It is risky to leave the Ministry of Internal Affairs in the hands of such a man in these times!

. . .

In any case, Trepov will try to do what he can. In all probability he will return on Sunday and will bring with him the list of persons whom we had discussed with him and *Sht.* [Shtiurmer].

Only, I beg you, do not drag our Friend into this. The responsibility is mine, and therefore I wish to be free in my choice.

[Stavka, February 23, 1917:]
My beloved Sunny,

. . .

I greatly miss my half-hour game of patience every evening. I shall take up dominoes again in my spare time. The stillness around here depresses me, of course, when I am not working. Old *Ivanov* [General N. Iu., commander of the Southwest Front] was amiable and charming at dinner. My other neighbor was Sir H. Williams [General Sir John Hanbury-Williams, the British attaché], who is delighted at having met so many of his compatriots here lately.

You write about my being firm—a master; that is quite right. Be assured that I do not forget; but it is not necessary to snap at people right and left every minute. A quiet, caustic remark or answer is often quite sufficient to show a person his place.

[Stavka, February 24, 1917:]

My brain is resting here—no ministers, no troublesome questions demanding careful consideration. I feel this is good for me, but only for my brain. My heart is suffering because of our separation. I hate this separation, especially at such a time! I shall not be away long—I shall direct things as best I can here, and then my duty will be fulfilled.

. . .

Ever your most loving little husband,
Nicky

XVIII:15. BUCHANAN ON RASPUTIN'S INFLUENCE, CA. 1910-1916

The following is an excerpt from the memoirs of Sir George Buchanan, who as British ambassador in Russia from 1910 to 1917 was well acquainted with the tsar and other high personages.

Reference: G. W. Buchanan, *My Mission to Russia and Other Diplomatic Memories*, 2 vols. (Boston: Little, Brown, 1923), 1:241-42.

By personal magnetism or by some form of hypnotic suggestion [Rasputin] did undoubtedly relieve the haemophilia from which the Tsarevitch—a charming boy, the idol of both his parents—had long suffered. Believing, as she did, that Rasputin could by his prayers preserve her son's life, the Empress centred all her hopes on him and regarded him with feelings akin to adoration. She absolutely declined to credit the stories of his debauched life, even when one of his drunken orgies had occasioned the intervention of the police.

For her he was always blameless—a Godfearing man, reviled and persecuted like the saints of old.

Rasputin had the natural cunning of the Russian peasant, but he was no ordinary impostor. He believed in himself—in his preternatural powers—in his gift of reading the decrees of fate. He warned the Empress that if his enemies succeeded in getting him sent away evil would befall the Tsarevitch, as his presence was indispensable to the latter's well-being.

XVIII:16. FATHER GEORGE SHAVEL'SKII ON THE EMPEROR AND RASPUTIN, CA. 1915-1916

One person who saw a good deal of the tsar in the last years of his reign was Father George Shavel'skii, who served from 1911 to 1917 as head chaplain (*protopresviter*) of the chaplains' corps in the Russian army and navy. In his two-volume memoirs Shavel'skii gives among other things his evaluation of the tsar and the influence of Rasputin, based in part on the impressions Shavel'skii gathered in 1915 and 1916 while serving at general headquarters.

Reference: G. Shavel'skii, *Vospominaniia poslednego protopresvitera russkoi armii i flota*, 2 vols. (New York: Chekhov, 1954), 1:58, 335; 2:260-62.

The tsar—kind, good-hearted, but weak willed— was completely overwhelmed by the authority, the obstinacy, and the iron will of his wife, whom he undoubtedly loved dearly, and to whom he was unwaveringly faithful. By nature he was neither a mystic nor a practical man; his upbringing and his life had made him a fatalist, and his domestic surroundings made him his wife's slave. He developed a kind of blind resignation to chance and to misfortune, in which he invariably saw the will of Providence. . . . Humbly submitting to all misfortunes, of which there was no shortage during his reign, he also submitted to the influence of his wife . . . grew accustomed to her, and even to a very considerable extent adopted her religious sentiments. If various *blazhennye* [deeply religious individuals who cut themselves off from worldly interests], God's fools, and other "clairvoyants" were essential to the empress, then he accepted them too. The empress could not live without them, and he quickly grew accustomed to them. Soon he even grew accustomed to Rasputin.

When [in 1911] I assumed the duties of head chaplain [protopresviter] . . . Rasputin at that time had already completely gained control of the minds of the tsar and tsaritsa. He had become a close friend of the imperial family. The attempts of some of the courtiers to paralyze the influence of the ignorant favorite ended in total failure.

. . .

The emperor himself represented a unique type. His character was woven from antitheses. Within him, each positive quality coexisted with its exactly opposite negative quality. Thus, he was gentle, kindly, and mild, but everyone knew that he never forgot an insult he had received. He quickly became attached to people, but just as quickly turned away from them. In some cases he was touchingly trustful and frank; in others, he was astonishingly secretive, suspicious, and cautious. He loved his homeland boundlessly and would have died for it if he thought it necessary, but at the same time he overvalued his tranquillity, his habits, and his health, and to preserve all these he sacrificed—perhaps unwittingly—the interests of the state.

The emperor was extremely susceptible to the influence of others, and was, in fact, always under one influence or another, to which he sometimes yielded almost unconsciously, under the impact of a first impression. Each minister after his appointment experienced a "honeymoon" of intimacy with the emperor and unlimited influence over him, and during this period was all-powerful. But after some time this minister's charm would wear off, and the influence over the emperor would pass into the hands of another lucky man, and again for a brief period.

. . .

. . .

On the one hand, Rasputin's reception room began to be filled with petitioners of every rank: from those who sought to be appointed as ministers, governors general, metropolitans, and so forth, down to those who were truly oppressed and burdened and hoped for his protection and aid. On the other hand, there was increasing indignation, especially among the upper circles, over the fact that the country was being ruled by a depraved, dirty, and venal peasant.

Whereas the tsar and tsaritsa showed Rasputin special attention because they believed in him and were inspired by a special respect for him, all these dignitaries fawned on Rasputin, hurried to fulfill his every demand, and sang his praises solely for base motives. In their hearts they all hated and despised the dirty peasant, while outwardly they did their best to flatter and please him, hoping through him to win the tsar's favor and all the ensuing benefits. The conduct of these flunkies of Rasputin is all the more reprehensible because it was dictated solely by selfish considerations. A number of other ministers, such as P. A. Stolypin, S. D. Sazonov, V. N. Kokovtsev, A. V. Krivoshein, A. A. Khvostov, and others shunned Rasputin and never fulfilled his requests.

. . .

Rasputin played a tremendous and fateful role in the destiny of Russia. His more than ten years of intimacy with the imperial family, his constant ignorant and shady interference in affairs of state, his patronage of every dolt and rascal antagonized and embittered all sections of the population not only against him, but also against the imperial family, weakened the spiritual bond that united the people with the tsar, and provided abundant nourishment for the enemies of the old regime who sought its downfall.

Tragic were the roles of the tsaritsa and the tsar in the Rasputin affair—a weak-willed, fatalist tsar and a neurotic empress. If there had not been such a tsaritsa, there would not have been a favorite like Rasputin.

XVIII:17. RODZIANKO'S MEMOIRS ON THE IMPACT OF THE WAR AND THE COLLAPSE OF THE TSARIST GOVERNMENT, 1914-1917

The following excerpts from the memoirs of Rodzianko (see above, Items XVIII:1 and 2) bear on the situation in Russia during the war and the factors leading to the downfall of the monarchy.

Reference: Rodzianko, "Gosudarstvennaia Duma i fevral'skaia 1917 g. revoliutsiia," in *Arkhiv russkoi revoliutsii,* 6:24, 36-37, 44, 45; and Rodzianko, "Krushenie Imperii," in *Arkhiv russkoi revoliutsii,* 17:154-55.

[From a section published in 1922:]

During the entire war the country's internal water routes were never adequately used for the cheap transportation of necessary food to railroad junctions, from which, in turn, grain could have been carried to given points, thus cutting down the demand for and use of the railroad's rolling stock. This same sort of thing was observed as regards other aspects of the distribution of the country's foodstuffs and other essential goods.

In some districts there was an abundance,

even a surplus, of such items, while elsewhere there was an acute shortage. All this was a result of the government's exceptional inability to organize and its unwillingness to heed the practical advice of public officials.

Another example of the government's absolute mismanagement is the quite unnecessary loss of livestock requisitioned for army rations. The requisitioning was conducted without any plan and without any correlation to the army's need for meat. The cattle, after being collected from the populace, were combined in huge herds which followed the armies about without plan or direction; therefore, they frequently came to localities not provided with feed and found there neither pasture, nor fodder, nor sufficient watering places. If one also takes into account the disruption in transport, then it is obvious that there would be no hope of properly supplying the army's herds of cattle. Livestock losses from hunger, sickness, and insufficient veterinary and hygienic care numbered in the thousands and inflicted incalculable misfortune on the population.

· · ·

The incredibly rapid and pointless changing and shuffling of ministers took on the characteristics of a system. State Duma member Purishkevich in a speech aptly and famously characterized it as "ministerial leapfrog." Clearly the rapid changing of department heads inflicted irreparable damage on the systematic conduct of affairs, introducing into the business of the departments a confusion that, of course, could only benefit our enemies. No one had any faith in the stability or longevity of the appointed ministers, not even the ministers themselves. As a result of such an atmosphere, people functioned lethargically. Not one of the appointees believed that he would succeed in putting into effect during his short tenure of office the measures or reforms that were planned. At the appointment of a new minister, betting pools were set up in the departments on how long a given individual would remain in office.

How did they pick, for example, the ministers who so quickly replaced one another? I will answer this question in their own words. When Ivan Logginovich Goremykin was appointed prime minister, I asked him: "Why did you, Ivan Logginovich, decide to accept such a responsible assignment at your advanced age?" Goremykin, a thoroughly honest man and government official, nevertheless literally replied with the following: "Oh, my friend, I don't know why; but this is the third time they have taken me out of mothballs." . . .

Because of a burning fear for the future of our fatherland, because of the ever growing chaos in transportation, because of the ever rising costs of staples, because of unnecessary levies of troops which tore workers away from necessary work within the country, and because the full weight of all this confusion fell chiefly on the lower strata of society, on the have-nots, there ripened a discontent which with sure strides was leading the people to revolutionary excesses. In view of the apparent disorder of the national economy and of the apparent and manifest inability of the government to create more or less normal conditions so that the burdens of war and its attendant sacrifices might possibly be borne at least tolerably, could the attitude of the people possibly be favorable to the government, and even to the supreme authority [i.e. the tsar], and could the State Duma . . . hold off the oncoming explosion? I assert with confidence, and take the responsibility for these words, that the Fourth State Duma did all that was required of it to remove the misunderstandings that cropped up. But neither the supreme authority nor the government ever sufficiently heeded its voice.

· · ·

The influence of Rasputin and that entire group around the empress Aleksandra Fedorovna, which affected through her the entire policy of the supreme authority and the government, grew to fantastic limits.

I assert without a moment's hesitation that this circle was undoubtedly under the influence of the enemy and served the interests of Germany. There is no other way to explain the groundless dismissal of those really useful government officials who, at the insistence of public opinion, were called to office in 1915 after the reverses in Galicia, and who undoubtedly could have led the country to victory through their well-known reasonable policies which agreed completely with the country's social forces. A talented, honest official had only to appear in a high government position and immediately Rasputin's clique would begin to persecute him, and he would be dismissed with breakneck speed and without explanation.

. . .

A second set of causes that contributed to the collapse of our government includes the clumsy and inconsistent distribution of authority which led to the complete dislocation of the economic life of the people who were left in the rear. Transportation was in the worst disorder, followed by finances. General mismanagement came to light. There was no adequate care for the prisoners and wounded after they left the infirmaries. No methods were established to combat the growing speculation, itself a negative phenomenon causing unprecedented price increases for the necessities of life.

To this set of causes must be added the unusually intense German propaganda carried on with German gold. . . .

In the third set of causes accounting for the ease with which the coup was accomplished, I place the beginnings of demoralization in the army. . . .

Finally, the fourth cause of the revolution was the extraordinary and complete duplicity of the government's internal policy. This two-faced system harassed Russian society to the point of desperation, since no one knew beforehand whether the government would behave the next day as it did today or completely the reverse. Therefore Russian society ceased to believe in the sincerity of government announcements, knowing that the government's course could change with startling ease.

[From a section published in 1926, after Rodzianko's death:]

We must completely and once and for all abandon the unkind idea of the "treason" of the empress Aleksandra Fedorovna. The committee of the Provisional Government under the chairmanship of Murav'ev with representatives from the Soviet of Workers' and Soldiers' Deputies participating, which studied this problem with special attention paid to documentary information, has completely repudiated this accusation. . . . Even less can one speak of the "betrayal" of the Russian cause by Emperor Nicholas II; he died a martyr's death specifically because of his fidelity to his given word.

But at the same time it is quite clear that our entire domestic policy, to which the imperial government strictly adhered from the beginning of the war, inevitably and methodically led to revolution, to sedition in the minds of the citizens, to the complete ruin of the country's economy.

One need only recall the ministerial leap-frog. From the autumn of 1915 to the autumn of 1916, there were five ministers of internal affairs: Prince Shcherbatov was replaced by A. N. Khvostov; he was replaced by Makarov; then followed Khvostov the elder [A. A. Khvostov, uncle of A. N.], and finally Protopopov. Each minister's share in the administration was two and one-half months. Under such conditions can one even speak of a serious domestic policy? During the same period there were three war ministers: Polivanov, Shuvaev, and Beliaev; four ministers of agriculture: Krivoshein, Naumov, Count A. Bobrinskii, and Rittikh. The regular functioning of the main sectors of the economy connected with the war was continually shaken by the changes. Obviously, nothing sensible could result from this. There was confusion, there were contradictory orders, there was a general perplexity, but no firm will, no pertinacity, no decisiveness, no single definite policy for victory. The people observed this; they saw and endured it. The popular conscience was confused, and in the minds of the ordinary people this logical train of thought was engendered: a war is going on; they do not spare our brother, the soldier; they are killing us by the thousands, while everywhere there is disorder because of the incompetence and negligence of the ministers and generals who rule us and who were appointed by the tsar.

Everything that went on during the war was not merely bureaucratic idiocy, petty tyranny, and unlimited authority; not merely an inability to cope with the enormous difficulties of the war. It was also a well-considered and persistently conducted system of disrupting our rear; and for those who worked deliberately in the rear, Rasputin was a very suitable tool.

XVIII:18. NAUMOV ON INTERNAL AFFAIRS IN 1915-1916

Aleksandr Nikolaevich Naumov (1868-1950), an estate owner, land captain, publisher, and zemstvo official in the Samara guberniia, was elected to the State Council (representing the

Samara guberniia zemstvo) in 1909, 1912, and 1915. From November 1915 to July 1916 he served as minister of agriculture. In these excerpts from his memoirs, which were published only long after the Revolution, Naumov provides some glimpses of the government and of Nicholas himself in 1915 and 1916.

Reference: A. N. Naumov, *Iz utselevshikh vospominanii 1868-1917*, 2 vols. (New York: A. K. Naumova and O. A. Kusevitskaia, 1955), 2:321, 427-28, 496-97, 514-15, 533-34.

The commission [i.e. the High Investigating Commission for a General Inquiry into the Circumstances That Caused Tardy and Insufficient Replenishment of Military Supplies, formed in the summer of 1915, to which Naumov had been appointed] was also greatly impressed by the extensive remarks of the chief of the Main Artillery Office, the intelligent and energetic general A. A. Manikovskii. He provided a great deal of interesting information about the state of our foreign orders and the organization of military supply in Germany.

The plan drafted before the war of 1914 by the war department in concert with the legislative chambers—the so-called Major Program of the War Ministry, which provided for a reorganization of the army and the establishment of adequate supply—could not have been completed before 1917. Breaking out in July 1914, the war caught the war department unprepared in many respects. The army had neither heavy artillery, nor a sufficient number of armored automobiles, nor an air force, nor even technical items such as binoculars, telephones, and telegraph instruments. It was short of both shells and cartridges.

From the very first months of the war the government, while taking measures to increase domestic production, was also compelled to resort to placing orders abroad. However, the higher military administration had no plans whatever for carrying out the needed urgent measures. Nor was it able to utilize the general enthusiasm that appeared in the early days of the war; thus it allowed this matter of exceptional importance to slip from its hands.

As a result, instead of planned and concerted action in the area of both military supplies manufactured in domestic factories and those ordered abroad, division of authority reigned at the top, critically hampering the work of supplying the army. Acting alongside the war department were entirely independent organizations, such as the All-

Russian Zemstvo and City Unions, the War-Industries Committee, the Red Cross, and others, competing with one another and bringing great confusion into the work of military supply.

. . .

[In January 1916, when Shtiurmer, or Stürmer, was appointed chairman of the Council of Ministers] fear and despair filled my whole being—fear for the throne, and despair because I faced the prospect of working with a person whose hand I was reluctant to shake when we met.

I must confess that this appointment aroused in me for the first time a truly chilling anxiety for the safety of the Russian throne and the tranquillity of the country. The emperor's choice was a challenge not only to antigovernment circles but to all the Russian public that had reasonable and loyal feelings toward the ruling strata. It was impossible to find any justification for the emperor's action. Rasputin's influence was coming out into the open in all its callous audacity. Everyone knew of the slavish adulation of this newly appointed head of a governing institution before the "Tobol'sk *starets*" [i.e. Rasputin]. Shtiurmer was a loyal and obedient tool in the hands of "Grigorii Efimovich"—that man so fatal for the destiny of Russia.

Shtiurmer's appointment lay heavily on the imperial crown and threw a shadow over all the large official family of the Russian state hierarchy. My first impulse was to resign at once from my ministerial post, to refuse to enter into any official association with a man for whom I felt only profound contempt. But when I spoke to the emperor about it, His Majesty refused to release me, pointing out that "one does not leave the trenches in the midst of war."

. . .

I must note here that my first ministerial report [to the tsar] left an indelible impression upon me. It took place in an atmosphere of remarkable simplicity, amicability, and sincere warmth. My acceptance of the ministerial post had, at the time, a most depressing effect upon my mood, but the cordial and gracious welcome I received from my monarch and his enchanting manner toward his ministers made me forget the difficulties of my new position and inspired me with a fervent desire to assist His Imperial Majesty to the best of my ability in his tremendous task of governing the state.

. . .

[In an audience at the imperial headquarters, May 20, 1916] I considered it my duty to acquaint His Majesty with the interesting impressions, of importance to the state, that I had gathered during my journey to the south of Russia. I attempted to report to His Majesty in detail about the state of the food supply, the harvests and the prospective yield, and the results of the organizing of agricultural work in the southern agricultural regions. The emperor repeatedly interrupted me with questions relating, not to the business aspects of my official journey, but rather to everyday trivia that interested him. . . . He asked . . . how the weather was, whether there were children, and flowers, and so forth, neglecting the serious part of my report.

I must confess that such an attitude on the part of the emperor toward matters of basic state importance was most discouraging to me at that time. As a matter of fact, during my visit of May 20, 1916, I became clearly aware of a certain characteristic of the emperor which I attribute to general nervous exhaustion brought about by all the adversities attending his reign and the extraordinary complications he had encountered in governing the country since the outbreak of the war in 1914. Like the neurotic who preserves his equanimity only until some vulnerable point is touched, the emperor, evidently exhausted under the pressure of the most complex state concerns and excessive responsibility, instinctively sought peace, preferring to think and speak about lighter and more pleasant things when we reported to him, rather than to hear and discuss urgent, difficult, and disturbing questions.

. . .

While he possessed unquestionable intelligence, a sharp memory, and a good measure of sensitivity and curiosity, Nikolai Aleksandrovich directed all these native endowments toward, as it were, trivial matters, and approached state problems of broad significance quite superficially. His thoughts, questions, and remarks, as I recall them, were in most instances rather narrow and not sufficiently serious in content. In our conversations on general political topics the emperor did not evince the depth and breadth of political thinking, the statesmanship that one would have wished to find in the supreme ruler of the vast Russian Empire. When I advised His Majesty of the importance of drawing up a plan for Russian national development for many decades in advance, his response was: "So long as it lasts through [my son] Aleksei's lifetime." . . . As a rule, the emperor raised no objections to anything during our reports to him. I do not recall a single instance when he did not grant his consent to my proposals. Because of this, the atmosphere of the official audiences was exceedingly pleasant for those submitting reports, facilitating a calm and unhampered presentation of the matters at hand. But this atmosphere also had its negative effect on the work of the reporting minister, who was not always able to rely firmly on the consent and promises of the well-meaning and mild-tempered tsar. Easily influenced, the emperor was capable of quickly and sharply altering his attitudes, and even of withdrawing his promises altogether.

On the whole, it must be admitted unquestionably that the excessively mild-tempered emperor usually manifested this distinguishing trait of his character, which was generally regarded as his shortcoming and was referred to as weakness of will. But I consider it my sacred duty to say, before the memory of the now departed martyr-tsar, that in some cases he showed in his actions and convictions a remarkable firmness and persistence. I can refer to a personal situation. When I fervently and persuasively pleaded with the emperor to release me from my appointment as minister, His Majesty listened to me at length but held his ground. I could do nothing but submit and undertake the work. This is an example of a personal nature. But all of us, and the entire thinking world, have incontrovertible testimony to the historic, valiant steadfastness of spirit of the martyred Russian emperor Nicholas II, who, despite everything, remained loyal to his allies to the very end.

XVIII:19. PLEKHANOV ON THE PEACE QUESTION IN 1916

In the years after 1905 Plekhanov (see Items XVI:28-30, 35), by then an elder statesman among Russian Marxists, preserved a mind of his own. His incisive criticism of what he regarded as ir-responsible policies, whether of the Bolshevik or right-wing socialist variety, is illustrated in his *Diary of a Social Democrat,* the first of a series of booklets published in Petrograd in 1916.

Reference: Georgii V. Plekhanov, *Dnevnik sotsial-demokrata,* vol. 1 (Petrograd: M. V. Popov, 1916), pp. 14-16, 20-21.

The peace described by N. S. Chkheidze be-fore the State Duma at the session of February 10 [1916] is nothing but utopian "verbiage." "Peace without annexations or reparations. . . . National self-determination. . . ."

Let us admit for the moment that these are fine things—though we shall presently see that, if anything, they are bad rather than good—and let us ask ourselves: How will such a peace as described by N. S. Chkheidze come about? To this natural and inescapable ques-tion our "leader" has given a reassuring an-swer: "We shall take the matter into our own hands"; and he has promised "to talk with the Germans." You can't believe what you read with your own eyes! Is that all?

"We are going to talk with the Germans!" We are very grateful for the effort you are prepared to make, but we would like to know, *at least approximately,* how long your negoti-ations might drag on. *And how ought we be-have while awaiting a favorable outcome?* Shall we fold our arms, submissively enduring the blows administered to us by the ruthless conqueror?

· · ·

If [Chkheidze] believes that while waiting for a favorable outcome from his talks with the Germans the populations of Belgium, France, Serbia, Montenegro, Poland, Lithu-ania, and western Russia, oppressed and rav-aged by these same Germans, can and must *defend with arms their right to live,* then this should be said plainly and openly, to avoid any misunderstanding in this regard.

N. S. Chkheidze has failed to speak out one way or the other. He has shown himself vacillating and irresolute. This is a great pity indeed.

Furthermore, who are the Germans with whom Chkheidze proposes to "talk"? The ones who proclaimed—and by their deeds continue to proclaim—that "the inhabitants of conquered countries should be left with only their eyes that they might weep over their misfortunes"? Of course not! There is so much goodness of heart in his *dreams* of a good peace! Well, what Germans? The Ger-man workers? But not all workers are alike. The worker who supports the policies of imperialism is in no way better than the other imperialists—the Junkers and the belligerent "captains of industry." Everybody knows, except Chkheidze, that the German trade unions openly support the aforesaid policy. What can we talk with them about?

· · ·

In describing his ideal peace [Chkheidze] says that no reparations should be imposed and at the same time declares that national self-determination must be established on a firm foundation. But whoever recognizes the Belgians' *right* to self-determination thereby postulates the Germans' *obligation* to in-demnify unhappy Belgium for its *innumerable and entirely undeserved* misfortunes. And whoever concedes this *right* to the French, the Serbs, the Montenegrins, the Poles, the Lithuanians, the West Russians, and so on, thereby recognizes the *obligation* of the Ger-mans and Austrians also to indemnify them. And what if the Germans and Austrians refuse to fulfill their obligations or even—what is ob-viously most likely—cynically refuse to dis-cuss the question? Obviously they will have to *be compelled to acknowledge and fulfill their obligations.* But in order to compel them you have to *fight* them. And if you have to fight, what will become of the *peace "without repa-rations"?*

But perhaps it is after all better to conclude a quick peace, stifling in one's heart all indigna-tion at the cynicism of the German imperialists and disclaiming any indemnification to those peoples who have suffered. If this is done, then why discuss the right of national self-determination? After all, *you sacrifice their right to your love of peace.* And in sacrificing it you render a service to that very imperialism against which you want to fight. . . .

He who wants a good peace must wage a good war until the mailed fist of the German conquerer has been reduced to impotence.

XVIII:20. PALÉOLOGUE ON VARIOUS DEVELOPMENTS OF 1916

The scope and spirit of the memoirs of the French ambassador (see Items XVIII:2, 4) is suggested by these short excerpts from his comments recorded under various dates during 1916 and published in 1921-23.

Reference: Paléologue, *Ambassador's Memoirs,* 4th ed. (1925), 2:166, 186-88, 316-17; 3d ed. (1924), 3:14-15, 112, 133.

[January 23 (February 5, N.S.), 1916:]

For the last three days I have been gathering information from all quarters about the new President of the [Ministers'] Council [Shtiurmer or Stürmer], and I have no reason to congratulate myself on what I have ascertained.

He is sixty-seven, and worse than a mediocrity—third-rate intellect, mean spirit, low character, doubtful honesty, no experience, and no idea of State business. The most that can be said is that he has a rather pretty talent for cunning and flattery.

His family origins are German. . . .

Neither his personal qualifications nor his administrative record and social position marked him out as fitted for the high office which has just been entrusted to him, to the astonishment of everyone. But his appointment becomes intelligible on the supposition that he has been selected solely as a tool; in other words, actually on account of his insignificance and servility. This choice has been inspired by the Empress's *camarilla,* and warmly recommended to the Emperor by Rasputin, with whom Sturmer is on the most intimate terms.

[February 9 (22, N.S.), 1916:]

The Imperial Duma resumed its work today.

. . .

[The Emperor] went to the Tauride Palace in person to open the session.

. . .

Since the establishment of representative government in Russia, it is the first time that the Emperor has visited the Duma. Previously it was the practice for the deputies to go to the Winter Palace to greet their Tsar.

. . .

As soon as the Emperor reached the altar the religious service began with those wonderful anthems, now broad and soaring, now pure and ethereal, which are the eternal interpretation of the infinite aspirations of orthodox mysticism and Slav emotion.

Everyone present was moved to the very depths. Among the reactionaries, the champions of absolute autocracy, glances of fury or consternation were exchanged, as if the Emperor, the Elect of God and the Lord's Anointed, was about to commit sacrilege. But on the faces of the parties of the Left was an expression of radiant and quivering ecstasy. I could see tears glistening in many eyes.

. . .

The Emperor listened to their service and singing with his usual composure. He was very pale, almost livid. . . .

But prayers were soon over; the clergy withdrew.

The Emperor then said a few words on patriotism and unity:

"I rejoice to be with you, among my people, whose representatives here you are, and I call down the blessing of God on your labours. I firmly believe that you will bring to your work, for which you are responsible to the Fatherland and myself, the whole of your experience, your knowledge of local conditions and love of country, and that your doings will be actuated solely by that love, which will serve you as a guiding star. With all my heart I wish the Imperial Duma fertile labours and complete success."

. . .

In his loud, deep bass the President of the Duma, Rodzianko, then replied to the imperial address in these terms:

"Your Majesty,

With the deepest emotion we have heard your pregnant words. We are filled with joy to see our Tsar among us. In this hour of trial you have once more emphasized that close union with your people which points the way to victory. . . . Hurrah for our Tsar! Hurrah!"

The public cheered this to the echo. Only the members of the Extreme Right were silent. For some minutes Potemkin's palace resounded with cheering.

[July 31 (August 13, N.S.), 1916:]

I have recently had opportunities of talking to French or Russian manufacturers and merchants . . . and I have asked them all if the conquest of Constantinople is still considered the indispensable war aim in circles in which they move.

Their replies have been almost identical; summarized, they are as follows:

Among the rural masses the dream of Constantinople, which has never taken definite shape, is becoming increasingly vague, remote and unreal. . . .

In working-class circles there is not the slightest interest in Constantinople. . . .

In the next higher stage, i.e., among the middle class, business men, industrial leaders, engineers, lawyers, doctors, etc., the importance of the problem with which the fate of Constantinople faces Russia is fully recognized; it is not forgotten that the outlet through the Bosphorus and the Dardanelles is necessary to the export of Russian grain, and everyone wishes to end a situation in which an order from Berlin can sever that outlet. But the historical and mystic doctrine of the Slavophiles is disregarded, and even reprobated, and the conclusion reached is that it would be enough to secure the neutralization of the Straits under the guarantee of an international organism.

The advocates of the idea of incorporating Constantinople in the Empire are now to be found only in the very small camp of the Nationalists and the group of doctrinaire Liberals.

[August 16 (29, N.S.), 1916:]

A former president of the Council [of Ministers], Kokovtsov, is passing through Petrograd and I called on him this afternoon.

I found him more pessimistic than ever.

The dismissal of Sazonov and General Beliaev has made him extremely uneasy.

"The Empress is now all-powerful," he said. "Sturmer is incapable and vain but astute and shrewd enough when his personal interests are at stake, and has known only too well how to make her serve his purposes. He reports regularly to her, tells her everything, consults her on all points, treats her as the regent and trains her in the notion that as the Emperor has received his power from God he has to account for it to God alone, so that it is sacrilege for anyone to take the liberty of opposing the imperial will. You can imagine how much an argument of that kind appeals to the brain of a mystic! Thus it has come about that Khvostov, Krivoshein, General Polivanov, Samarin, Sazonov, General Beliaev and myself are now regarded as revolutionairies, traitors and infidels!"

[November 21 (December 4, N.S.), 1916:]

The passage in the ministerial speech referring to Constantinople has fallen as flat among the public as it did in the Duma. There is the same phenomenon of indifference plus amazement, as if Trepov had exhumed an ancient Utopia, once fancied, but long since forgotten.

Several months ago I was already observing the progressive disappearance of the Byzantine dream. The charm has been broken.

[December 19, 1916 (January 1, 1917, N.S.):]

If I must judge solely by the constellations of the Russian sky, the new year is beginning under bad auspices. Everywhere I see anxiety and down-heartedness. No one takes any more interest in the war, no one believes in victory any longer; the public anticipates and is resigned to the most evil happenings.

XVIII:21. GUCHKOV'S LETTER TO ALEKSEEV, AUGUST 15, 1916

The Moscow industrialist and Octobrist leader Aleksandr Ivanovich Guchkov (1862-1936), serving as chairman of the Central War-Industries Committee, expressed himself as follows in concluding a letter dated August 15, 1916, to General Mikhail Vasil'evich Alekseev, who was the chief of staff of the supreme command under the tsar.

Reference: Vladimir P. Semennikov, ed., *Monarkhiia pered krusheniem, 1914-1917: Bumagi Nikolaia II i drugie dokumenty* (Moscow: Gosizdat, 1927), p. 282.

There is total disintegration in the rear; the government is rotting at its very roots. No matter how good the present situation at the front, the decaying rear threatens once more, as it did a year ago, to drag both your valiant front and your talented strategy, and indeed the whole country, into that deep mire from which we extricated ourselves once at the risk of our lives. . . . And when you realize that the whole government is headed by Mr. Shtiurmer—who has an established reputation (both in the army and among the people), if not as a traitor already, then as a man ready to betray—and that the course of diplomatic relations today and the outcome of the peace negotiations tomorrow, and thus our entire future, are in this man's hands, then you will understand, Mikhail Vasil'evich, what a mortal anxiety for the fate of our homeland has seized both public opinion and the feelings of the populace.

We in the rear are powerless, or almost powerless, to combat this evil. Our weapons for fighting are double-edged and, because of the excited mood of the masses, particularly the workers, may serve as the first spark of a conflagration, the extent of which no one can either foresee or localize. I will not even speak of what awaits us after the war. The deluge is imminent. But the pitiful, worthless, slimy government prepares to meet this cataclysm with those measures ordinarily used for protection against a good downpour: it puts on its rubbers and opens its umbrella.

Can you do anything? I do not know. But be assured that our abominable policy (including also our abominable diplomacy) threatens to cut across the line of your good strategy at present and completely to deform its fruits in the future. In history, and particularly in our own history, there are many dire examples of this.

Forgive me for this letter and do not deplore my ardor.

Perhaps never before have I been as convinced of the total validity of the public anxiety that has enveloped us as I am at this fateful hour.

God help us.

XVIII:22. SECRET POLICE REPORTS ON INTERNAL CONDITIONS, FEBRUARY-OCTOBER 1916

Rich material on internal conditions and the public mood in 1916, as well as in earlier years, was unearthed after the Revolution in the files of the security police. Here are samples from three reports that came up through these confidential channels in the year before the Revolution.

Reference: Tsentrarkhiv, ed., *Burzhuaziia nakanune fevral'skoi revoliutsii* (Moscow: Gosizdat, 1927), pp. 77-78 [Feb. 29], 136-37 [Oct. 30]; "Politicheskoe polozhenie Rossii nakanune fevral'-skoi revoliutsii v zhandarmskom osveshchenii," *Krasnyi arkhiv*, 17 (1926): 5-6, 11, 16.

[From a confidential report of February 29, 1916, from the Moscow department of the security police (*okhrannoe otdelenie*):]

In the present instance we must speak of even more than the decline in the prestige of the supreme power: the symptoms are present of an *antidynastic* movement which has already begun and is steadily developing, or, to be more exact, perhaps it is not so much a movement against the dynasty as a whole, not so much a movement with a definitely expressed republican character, as a movement of acute and profound resentment against the person of the currently reigning emperor. And all the recent happenings have intensified this mood to a terrifying degree. After mingling with diverse sections of society, we are pained to report that, should we respond to every instance of brazen and overt insults to His Majesty the emperor, the number of trials under article 103 [of the criminal code of 1903 concerning the punishments of those who insult the tsar or his family] would reach an unprecedented figure. And this is as much the mood of the middle and higher bourgeoisie led by Kadet circles as it is of the lower classes strongly attracted by the extreme Left.

The moment of acute crisis, of a turning in the direction of a complete rupture with the supreme authority, the moment of an extreme intensification of the [hostile] attitude toward the person of the emperor occurred when he refused to receive the deputation from the Unions of Zemstvos and of Towns. The congresses of these unions, which took place in August of this year [1915], sharply stressed that a *final attempt* was being made to open the eyes of the monarch, who was being pushed into an abyss by Goremykin's policies; and when the deputation was refused an audience, the leading opposition circles resolutely decided *no longer to take even the smallest steps toward contact with the monarch;* because events must now move *past* him, for he has placed himself in a position where "atonement" [*rasplata*] is the only way out.

. . .

Turning now to the factors that, insofar as Moscow is concerned, foster the steady decline in the prestige of the supreme authority, we must note the following.

Perhaps no one, not even the most unrestrained revolutionaries in their proclamations, has caused so much harm, has furthered to such a terrible degree the decline in the prestige of the supreme authority by blackening the person of the monarch, as has Samarin, the former chief procurator of the Holy Synod, by his recitation on practically every street and street corner of the reasons for his resignation. The details of the role played in public life at the present moment by the notorious "starets" [a monastic elder; here used ironically] Rasputin were heavy blows and insults, not only to His Majesty the emperor, but especially to Her Majesty the empress Aleksandra Fedorovna. The malicious or, perhaps, stupid tongue of this "most devoted monarchist" Samarin has been fully exploited by the leaders of the revolutionary movement, and . . . the filthy gossip about the tsar's family has now *become the property of the street.* . . .

We must also note together with this feeling of extreme disrespect for the person of Her Majesty the empress Aleksandra Fedorovna the widespread feeling of resentment against her as a "German." Her Majesty the empress is regarded, even in intellectual circles, as the inspirer and leader of the campaign for a separate peace with Germany.

[From a report of October 30, 1916, by the director of the Department of Police, Vasil'ev, summarizing the responses of the local police to a circular telegram from the deputy minister of internal affairs, inquiring about the mood of the people:]

All the reports agree without exception as to the principal causes of the present sentiments [of the public] and acknowledge these causes to be the current state of the food problem and, linked inseparably with this, the unparalleled, appalling rise in prices which is incomprehensible to the population. All the other grave features of our present life seem to be merely the consequences of these factors. . . .

The greatest degree of mass irritation and resentment resulting from the aforesaid causes is observed in the two capitals. A comparison of the attitudes of the population of Petrograd and Moscow toward the central government today and during the period 1905-06 establishes that today the mood of opposition has reached extraordinary dimensions which it never attained among the broad masses during the earlier period. The whole burden of blame for the misfortunes endured by our homeland is now being placed, not only on the government in the person of the Council of Ministers, but even on the supreme authority.

This extraordinarily excited mood of the population of the capitals provides grounds for the conclusion of the heads of security police departments that, unless the circumstances that provoke such tension both in Petrograd and in Moscow change, serious disorders of a purely spontaneous nature may break out. The strikes of purely spontaneous origin now taking place in Petrograd confirm, as it were, the correctness of this conclusion.

The mood in the interior [i.e. beyond the two capitals] is depicted as similarly tense, but, nevertheless, to a slightly lesser degree. It must be specified here, however, that this refers only to the cities, since the reports unanimously testify to the fact that in most of the villages—because economic conditions are quite favorable for the peasantry—not only is this excited mood not observed but even a satisfied population is noted with a peaceful or, rather, an indifferent attitude to virtually everything that so agitates the urban population.

However, the general dissatisfaction in the cities and even in the territory of the Don Cossacks has increased so greatly in depth and scope that, according to the unanimous opinion of the heads of investigative agencies, spontaneous disorders may break out everywhere in response to an immediate cause, or under the influence of rumors of such disorders beginning in the capitals. One may consider typical the conclusion of the head of the Kronstadt gendarmerie that mounting prices and the shortage of essential goods are creating a situation in which the outbreak of disorders among the workers is possible even in the fortress in a state of siege. And one cannot rely on their suppression by garrison troops, since the latter consist of recruits, militia, and reserves for whom the interests of the civilian population would be closer and more comprehensible than the fulfillment of military duty.

[From a report of the Petrograd security police to the Special Section of the Department of Police, in October 1916:]

The brilliant results of the offensive by General Brusilov's armies in the spring of this year, 1916, and the present state of the work of supplying the active front definitely indicate that the tasks undertaken in these directions by the government and by wide sections of the public have been more than successfully fulfilled. The problem of providing the army with military supplies may be considered solved and properly taken care of... But the gradually increasing disorganization of the rear—in other words, of the entire country—which has become chronic and is ever worsening, has at this moment achieved such an extreme and monstrous stage that it is even now beginning to threaten results achieved at the front and promises in the very near future to plunge the country into the destructive chaos of catastrophic and elemental anarchy.

The systematically growing disorganization of transport; the unrestrained orgy of pillaging and swindling of every kind by shady operators in the most diverse branches of the country's commercial, industrial, and sociopolitical life; the unsystematic and mutually contradictory orders of representatives of state and local administrations; the unconscientiousness of minor and lower agents of the government in the provinces; and, as a result of all the foregoing, the inequitable distribution of food products and essential goods, the incredible rise in prices, and the lack of sources and means of procuring food among the presently starving populations of the capitals and large population centers . . .

[here are inserted references to several preceding reports]—all this, taken together . . . shows categorically and definitely that a dire crisis is already upon us which must inevitably be resolved in one direction or another.

The above summary may be confirmed by the particularly troubled mood now observable among the masses of the people. By the beginning of September of this year an exceptional intensification of the feelings of opposition and animosity was distinctly noted among the most diverse sections of the residents of the capitals. Ever more frequent complaints against the administration and harsh and merciless condemnations of government policy have begun to be expressed.

By the end of September, according to well-informed sources, this spirit of opposition reached an exceptional scale, which it had not attained—in any case among the broad masses—even during the period 1905-06. Open and unconstrained complaints against "venality in the administration," against the enormous burdens of the war, and against the intolerable conditions of daily existence have begun to be heard. The outcries of radical and left-wing elements about the need "first to destroy the German here in our own country, and then to tackle the German abroad," have begun to elicit more and more sympathy.

. . .

Despite the great increase in wages, the economic condition of the masses is worse than terrible. While the wages of the masses have risen 50 percent, and only in certain categories 100 to 200 percent (metal workers, machinists, electricians), the prices on all products have increased 100 to 500 percent. According to the data collected by the sick benefit fund of the "Triangle" plant, a day's wages for a worker before the war were [as follows, in comparison with current wages]:

[Type of Worker]	[Prewar Wages]	[Present Wages]
Unskilled	1 rub. to 1 rub. 25 kop.	2 rub. 50 kop. to 3 rub.
Metalworker	2 rub. to 2 rub. 50 kop.	4 rub. to 5 rub.
Electrician	2 rub. to 3 rub.	5 rub. to 6 rub., etc.

At the same time, the cost of consumer goods needed by the worker has changed in the following incredible way:

[Item]	[Prewar Cost]	[Present Cost]
Rent for a corner	2 to 3 rub. monthly	8 to 12 rub.
Dinner (in a tearoom)	15 to 20 kop.	1 rub. to 1 rub. 20 kop. (at the same place)
Tea (in a tearoom)	7 kop.	35 kop.
Boots	5 to 6 rub.	20 to 30 rub.
Shirt	75 to 90 kop.	2 rub. 50 kop. to 3 rub., etc.

Even if we estimate the rise in earnings at 100 percent, the prices of products have risen, on the average, 300 percent. The impossibility of even buying many food products and necessities, the time wasted standing idle in queues to receive goods, the increasing incidence of disease due to malnutrition and unsanitary living conditions (cold and dampness because of lack of coal and wood), and so forth, have made the workers, as a whole, prepared for the wildest excesses of a "hunger riot."

. . .

If in the future grain continues to be hidden, the very fact of its disappearance will be sufficient to provoke in the capitals and in the other most populated centers of the empire the greatest disorders, attended by pogroms and endless street rioting. The mood of anxiety, growing daily more intense, is spreading to ever wider sections of the populace. Never have we observed such nervousness as there is now. Almost every day the newspapers report thousands of facts that reflect the extremely strained nerves of the people in public places, and a still greater number of such facts remains unrecorded. The slightest incident is enough to provoke the biggest brawl. This is especially noticeable in the vicinity of shops, stores, banks, and similar institutions, where "misunderstandings" occur almost daily.

XVIII:23. A LETTER FROM G. E. L'VOV TO RODZIANKO, OCTOBER 29, 1916

These assessments were contained in a letter to Duma chairman Rodzianko from the head of the All-Russian Union of Zemstvos, Prince Georgii Evgen'evich L'vov (1861-1925).

Reference: Tsentrarkhiv, *Burzhuaziia nakanune fevral'skoi revoliutsii*, pp. 144-45.

The chairmen of the guberniia zemstvo boards [*zemskie upravy*] who met in Moscow October 25 to discuss the food supply question considered it their duty to subject to discussion the general uneasy political situation in the country. Here is a summary of their unanimous opinion.

. . . The country is experiencing increasingly acute disorders in the fields of transport and the production of necessary goods and even of rations.

Disconnected, contradictory, devoid of any definite plan either in theory or in action, the decrees of the state authorities are steadily intensifying the general disorganization in all areas of public life. In the provinces all these decrees provoke feelings of perplexity, irritation, and sometimes absolute indignation and animosity. All the decrees of the higher authorities are directed, as it were, toward the specific goal of complicating still further the country's grave situation. This characteristic of the higher administration clearly manifests itself in the food question, which is becoming ever more acute and dangerous. Similar in character are the conditions under which mobilization has been organized for the past half year. The conduct of a series of measures related to the needs of the war automatically leads one to conclude that the government is allowing not only a pointless but even a thoroughly criminal waste of the human and material resources of the country. The constant change of ministers and high government officials which takes place under conditions involving continual changes in the policies pursued by these persons leads to a real paralysis of authority. . . . Influenced by all this, the whole country has come to feel that the government now in power is not capable of concluding the war or of preparing for its forthcoming settlement in accordance with the interests of Russia. The partial changes in personnel that are going on in the government do not alter the general policy of the government. They merely disorganize the regime radically and undermine the last remnants of its authority. But this is not enough. Agonizing, terrible suspicions, sinister rumors of treason and betrayal, of secret forces working in the interests of Germany and seeking, by destroying national unity and by sowing dissension, to prepare the ground for a shameful peace, have now turned into a lucid awareness that an enemy hand is secretly influencing the direction of the course of our state affairs. Naturally, because of this, rumors spring up that government circles acknowledge the pointlessness of further fighting, the timeliness of terminating the war, and the necessity of concluding a separate peace. Such were the profoundly anxious feelings that united all the chairmen of the guberniia zemstvo boards assembled in Moscow for discussion of the present situation in Russia.

XVIII:24. A LETTER FROM GRAND DUKE NIKOLAI MIKHAILOVICH TO THE TSAR, CA. NOVEMBER 1, 1916

Among the small group of persons who could speak with comparative frankness to the tsar, an important place was occupied by the tsar's elder cousin Grand Duke Nikolai Mikhailovich, son of Alexander II's brother. As a capable historian (author of a biography of Alexander I), Nikolai Mikhailovich made excellent use of the opportunities afforded by his social position for contacts with leading figures of his own and other countries. His letters to the tsar contain both straight reporting and avuncular counsel. This sample is from his letter of about November 1, 1916.

Reference: Golder, *Documents of Russian History*, pp. 244-45, citing *Rech'*, no. 58, Mar. 22, 1917; translation slightly revised.

You have said more than once that you wish to carry the war to a successful finish. Are you certain that, with the present conditions in the rear, this can be done? Are you acquainted with the internal situation, not only in the interior of the empire, but on the outskirts (Siberia, Turkestan, Caucasus)? Are you told all the truth, or is some of it concealed from you? Where is the root of the evil? Allow me to tell you briefly the essentials of the case.

So long as your method of selecting ministers [with the aid of Rasputin] was known to a limited circle only, affairs went on somehow, but from the moment that this method became generally known, it was impossible to govern Russia in that way. You have told me repeatedly that you could trust no one, that you were being deceived. If that is true, then the same must be true of your wife, who loves you dearly but is led astray by the evil circle that surrounds her. You trust Aleksandra Fedorovna, which is easy to understand, but that which comes out of her mouth is the result of clever fabrication and not the truth. If you are not strong enough to remove these influences from her, at least guard yourself against this steady and systematic interference by those who act through your beloved wife. If your persuasion is ineffective, and I am certain that you have more than once fought against this influence, try some other means, so as to end this system once and for all. Your first impulses and decisions are always remarkably right and to the point, but as soon as other influences come in, you begin to hesitate and end up by doing something other than what you originally intended. If you should succeed in repulsing this continuous invasion of the dark forces, the rebirth of Russia would take place at once, and the confidence of the great majority of your subjects would return to you. All other matters would soon settle themselves. You could find people who, under different conditions, would be willing to work under your personal leadership. At the proper time, and that is not far distant, you could, of your own free will, grant a ministry that would be responsible to you and to constitutional legislative institutions. This could be done very simply, without any pressure from outside, and not as was the case with the act of October 17, 1905. I have hesitated a long time before venturing to tell you this truth, and I have finally decided to do so after being urged by your mother and sisters. You are at the beginning of a new era of disturbances; I will go further and say at the beginning of an era of attempts at assassination. Believe me that in trying to loosen you from the chains that bind you, I do it from no motives of personal interest, and of this you and Her Majesty are convinced, but in the hope and in the expectation of saving you, your throne, and our dear country from the most serious and irreparable consequences.

XVIII:25. MILIUKOV'S SPEECH IN THE DUMA, NOVEMBER 1, 1916

On November 1, 1916, when in the preceding year or so such men as Shcherbatov, Samarin, Krivoshein, Kharitonov, Polivanov, and Sazonov had been forced out of the cabinet, Kadet leader Miliukov made a speech that ran in part as follows.

Reference: Gosudarstvennaia Duma, chetvertyi sozyv, *Stenograficheskie otchety, Sessiia 5,* 1st sitting (Nov. 1, 1916) (St. Petersburg: Gosudarstvennaia Tipografiia, 1917), cols. 36-37, 46-48; translation based largely on Golder, *Documents of Russian History,* pp. 155, 164-65. Another translation of this speech is given in Alfred E. Senn, ed., *Readings in Russian Political and Diplomatic History,* 2 vols. (Homewood, Ill.: Dorsey, 1966), 1:225-34.

As heretofore, we are striving for complete victory; as heretofore, we are prepared to make all the necessary sacrifices; and, as heretofore, we are anxious to preserve our national unity. But I say this candidly: there is a difference in the situation. We have lost faith in the ability of this government to achieve victory (*Voices:* "That's true"), because, as far as this government is concerned, neither the attempts at correction nor the attempts at improvement which we have made here have proved successful. All the Allied Powers have summoned to the ranks of their governments the very best men of all parties. They have gathered about the heads of their governments all the confidence and all those elements of organization present in their countries, which are better organized than our own. What has our own government accomplished? Our [Progressive Bloc] declaration has told that. When there was formed in the Fourth State Duma a majority [the Progressive Bloc] which the Duma had lacked theretofore, a majority ready to vote its confidence in a cabinet worthy of such confidence, then nearly all those men who might in some slight degree have been expected to receive such confidence were forced, systematically, one after another, every one of them, to leave the cabinet. And if we have formerly said that our government had neither the knowledge nor the talent necessary for the present moment, we say now, gentlemen, that this present government has

sunk beneath the level on which it stood during normal times in Russian life. (*Voices on the Left:* "True! Right!") And now the gulf between us and that government has grown wider and has become impassable.

. . .

Today we see and are aware that with this government we cannot legislate, any more than we can with this government lead Russia to victory. . . . We are telling this government, as the declaration of the Bloc stated: We shall fight you; we shall fight with all legitimate means until you go. . . . When the Duma with ever greater persistence insists that the rear must be organized for a successful struggle, while the government persists in claiming that organizing the country means organizing a revolution and deliberately prefers chaos and disorganization, then what is this: stupidity or treason? (*A voice on the Left:* "Treason!" *Adzhemov:* "Stupidity!" *Laughter.*) . . .

You must realize, also, why we, too, have no task left to us today other than that which I have already pointed out: to obtain the resignation of this government. . . . We have many, very many, separate reasons for being dissatisfied with the government. If we have time, we shall speak of them. But all these particular reasons boil down to this general one: the government, as presently composed, is incapable and ill intentioned. (*Voices on the Left:* "Correct!") This is the main evil, a victory over which will be tantamount to winning the whole campaign.

XVIII:26. N. E. MARKOV'S SPEECH IN THE DUMA, NOVEMBER 3, 1916

Miliukov's sharp attack on the government was followed on November 3, 1916, by, among others, the speech of Nikolai Evgen'evich Markov (Markov II), a rightist deputy from the Kursk guberniia and a member of the Union of the Russian People. Here is the gist of the plea he addressed to the majority in the Duma.

Reference: Gosudarstvennaia Duma, chetvertyi sozyv, *Stenograficheskie otchety, Sessiia 5,* 2d sitting (Nov. 3, 1916), cols. 97, 102.

If the people and the workers believe your words . . . then . . . be aware that the people and the workers are men of action, men with toil-hardened hands; they are not windbags, and, unfortunately, they do believe your words; and if you say "we shall fight against government authority during this terrible war," then realize that this means that the workers would strike, that they would raise the banner of revolt; and do not hide behind the pretense that you wish to confine yourself to words

alone. No, be aware that your words will lead to revolt, to rebellion, to an insurrection of the people, to a weakening of the state at a time when the state is trembling from the blows of a hateful, evil, despicable enemy.

. . .

Gentlemen, you apparently do not realize what you wish to accomplish, so I shall explain it to you: you wish to bring on a revolution in Russia so that a revolution would destroy the entire Russian state, well formed or not.

XVIII:27. SHUVAEV'S DECLARATION TO THE DUMA, NOVEMBER 4, 1916

In partial response to the criticisms voiced in the Duma, Minister of War Shuvaev on November 4, 1916, made a declaration, from which this is a brief excerpt.

Reference: Gosudarstvennaia Duma, chetvertyi sozyv, *Stenograficheskie otchety, Sessiia 5,* 4th sitting (Nov. 4, 1916), cols. 203, 204.

On the basis of my observations, gentlemen, I am deeply convinced, as an old soldier, that we are coming nearer to victory every day.

. . .

Everyone everywhere has applied himself to manufacturing what the army needs. . . . I shall cite the figures: taking January 1, 1915, as the basic unit, I shall tell you how much production was increased by January 1,

1916, and by today. Three-inch guns: . . . January 1, 1916—3.8 times [the January 1, 1915, level]; August 1916—8 times. . . . Rifles: [production] increased to 3 times by January 1916, and to 4 times by August 1916 as compared with January 1915. . . . Three-inch shells: [output] increased to 12.5 times [the January 1, 1915, level by] January 1916, and 19.7 times by August 1916.

XVIII:28. TREPOV'S DECLARATION TO THE DUMA, NOVEMBER 19, 1916

After Shtiurmer (or Stürmer) had been so sharply attacked in the Duma early in the November debates, the tsar—over the protests of his beloved Sunny—appointed as chairman of the Council of Ministers a man who would not be Rasputin's tool: Aleksandr Fedorovich Trepov (1862-1926). A. F. Trepov (not to be confused with any of his three brothers) had held several significant bureaucratic posts, had helped to draft the plan for a duma, and had served as a conservative member of the State Council (1914) and as minister of ways and communications (1915). One of his attempts to save the government during his less than six-week tenure was his declaration to the Duma on November 19, 1916. The excerpts from the stenographic record convey the burden of his argument. They are followed by the comment of a foreign eyewitness. (See also the comment of Paléologue, Item XVIII:20, above.)

Reference: Gosudarstvennaia Duma, chetvertyi sozyv, *Stenograficheskie otchety, Sessiia 5,* 6th sitting (Nov. 19, 1916), cols. 254, 257, 258; Buchanan, *My Mission to Russia,* 2:34.

CHAIRMAN OF THE COUNCIL OF MINISTERS TREPOV: On behalf of the government, I frankly and openly declare that it proceeds from the desire to devote its energies to positive, practicable work in conjunction with the legislative institutions.

. . .

We shall not stop halfway but must carry on the war until the German forces are smashed, until German militarism is smashed

and is no longer capable of speedy rebirth. We must destroy the constant threat of violence which for decades has hung over the entire civilized world, undermining peaceful, civilized labor and compelling all nations to arm feverishly against the hourly possibility of an attack from the enemy, for whom international agreements are but meaningless scraps of paper. The present war must end in victory not only over the external but also over the internal enemy. For many years Germanism has wormed its way into the flesh and blood of the Russian state and of the Russian people itself. The war has opened our eyes, and we have clearly realized for the first time the full burden that is stifling and ruining Russian life in all its manifestations. . . .

In discussing current problems underscored by the war, I cannot fail to touch upon a question close to the heart of every Russian. For over a thousand years Russia has striven to move southward, toward a free outlet of the open sea. The keys to the Bosporus and the Dardanelles, Oleg's shield on the gates of Tsar'grad—these are the age-old cherished dreams of the Russian people at all periods of its existence, and now this desire is near realization. At the beginning of the war . . . Turkey was given formal assurances and promises that in exchange for its neutrality it would be guaranteed its independence and the inviolability of its territory and would be granted various other advantages and privileges as well. But all efforts proved to be in vain and, blinded by the flattering promises of the Germans, Turkey, having treacherously attacked us, thereby signed its own condemnation. The vital interests of Russia are as clear to our faithful allies as they are to us, and, accordingly, the agreement concluded by us in 1915 with Great Britain and France, in which Italy also joined, establishes once and for all Russia's rights to the Straits and to Constantinople. (*Applause and cries of "Bravo" from the Right and from scattered sections of the Center and Left.*) The Russian people should know for what it is shedding its blood, and, in accordance with a mutual agreement just reached, our agreement with our allies is hereby proclaimed from this rostrum.

[From the report of Britain's Ambassador Buchanan:]

The opening sitting of the Duma was a very stormy one, and Trepoff, who was received with hoots and hisses, had to leave the tribune three times before he could obtain a hearing. I was much struck by his patience and forbearance, and felt that the Duma was making a great mistake and putting itself in the wrong. His declaration of policy was most satisfactory, and he was emphatic as to the necessity of fighting out the war to victory and of defeating the Germans at home as well as in the field. The chamber, however, continued hostile, and even the announcement, which the Allied Governments had authorized him to make with regard to the Constantinople Agreement, fell perfectly flat. The Duma and the public were so engrossed by the internal crisis that they could think of nothing else.

XVIII:29. PURISHKEVICH'S SPEECH IN THE DUMA, NOVEMBER 19, 1916

A dramatic moment in the latter portion of the Duma's debates of November 1916 was the long speech on November 19 by the ardent monarchist and extreme rightist Vladimir Mitrofanovich Purishkevich (1870-1920), founder of the Union of the Russian People.

Reference: Gosudarstvennaia Duma, chetvertyi sozyv, *Stenograficheskie otchety, Sessiia 5,* 6th sitting (Nov. 19, 1916), cols. 261, 265, 270, 286-87, 288; translation based largely, but with some changes, on Golder, *Documents of Russian History,* pp. 166-67, 168, 170, 174-75.

Gentlemen, I mount this tribune today with inexpressible emotional agitation, and not because I have left the ranks of my faction. I cannot abandon the ranks of the Right, for I am perhaps the Right-most of all those who are in the Right camp. But there are moments, gentlemen . . . when one cannot allow oneself to speak from the bell tower of an uezd or guberniia town but must ring the alarm from the bell tower of Ivan the Great [in the Kremlin in Moscow]. . . . Today, as formerly and in the future, there burns within me an infinite love for my native land and a selfless, boundless, and most devoted allegiance to my sovereign. I am living at this moment with but a single thought—that of a Russian victory. But today, as before, I have within me no slavish obsequiousness before the organs of the ruling power, and I could not enter my name as a member of the ministerial antechamber. (*Applause in the Center and on the Left. Voices in the Center:* "Bravo!") I clearly see, gentlemen, who and what it is that is harming Russia, impeding her, and postponing the hour of her certain victory over the external enemy.

. . .

The disorganization of our rear is undoubtedly being carried out by the enemy, and it is being done by a strong, relentless, and resolute hand. We have a single system, the system of devastation in the rear. This system was set up by Wilhelm himself and is being carried out by him with amazing consistency with the aid of the German party working in our rear.

. . .

What today, gentlemen, is the principal scourge of Russian public and official life? Here are four propositions: the first is the senseless censorship of that which ought not to be censored; the second is the hypocrisy and paralysis of the government; the third is the dangerous symptoms of the triumph of Germanophile tendencies among the organs of the government; and, in connection with this, the fourth is absolute uncertainty as to the morrow, with new government policies cooked up from day to day.

. . .

I take the liberty to say here, from the rostrum of the State Duma, that all this evil comes from those dark forces, from those influences which push this or that individual into position and which force up into high posts people who are not capable of filling them, from those influences headed by Grishka Rasputin. . . . It is necessary that the legislative body, being the voice of the entire country and now united in spirit on the question of victory, finally raise its voice about this, Russia's greatest evil, which is corrupting Russian public life. These past nights I couldn't sleep, I give you my word of honor. I lie with eyes open and imagine a series of telegrams, reports, notes which this illiterate peasant [*muzhik*] writes now to one minister, then to

another, and most frequently of all, it is said, to Aleksandr Dmitrievich Protopopov, and which he requests them to act upon. And we know there were instances when the failure to fulfill these demands entailed the fall of these strong and powerful men...

. . .

I shall take the liberty of addressing now the Council of Ministers, quite apart from the Duma, whose duty I have already indicated. If the ministers consider duty above career—and I believe that at this moment duty is above career—and if you really are a united cabinet, then go to the tsar and say that things cannot go on any longer in this way. This is not a boycott of authority, gentlemen, but your duty before the sovereign. If you are loyal to your sovereign, if the glory of Russia, her power, her future, intimately and inseparably bound up with the grandeur and splendor of the tsar's name, are dear to you, go to Imperial Headquarters, throw yourselves at the tsar's feet, and beg permission to open his eyes to the dreadful reality, beg him to deliver Russia from Rasputin and the Rasputinites both big and small...

. . .

Gentlemen, we must plead with the sovereign, and you (*turning to the ministers*), his loyal servants, chosen to carry out his will, you, primarily responsible for the course of the Russian ship of state, united with us, go to headquarters and plead with the sovereign that Grishka Rasputin not be the leader of Russian internal public life. (*Loud and prolonged applause from the Center, Left, and Right; voices:* "Bravo!")

XVIII:30. PURISHKEVICH ON THE PLOT TO KILL RASPUTIN, NOVEMBER 20-21, 1916

One step in the preparation of the plot to kill Rasputin is related as follows in the diary of one of the conspirators. Purishkevich records that on November 20, the day after he had spoken out in the Duma (see above), he received an uninterrupted succession of congratulatory telephone calls.

Reference: Golder, *Documents of Russian History*, pp. 176-77. The footnote cites V. Pourichkevitch, *Comment J'ai Tué Raspoutine*, trans. Lydie Krestovsky (Paris: Povolozky, 1924), pp. 37-46.

[November 20, 1916:]

Among those who telephoned was a Prince Iusupov, Count Sumarokov-Elston. He has aroused my curiosity. After expressing the usual compliments he inquired if he could see me to explain certain things about Rasputin's relation with the Court, things which he could

not tell over the telephone. I made an appointment for tomorrow morning at nine. I am anxious to know what he has to say and what he wants.

[November 21, 1916:]

He was on time . . . and at once made a very

good impression on me. . . . He looks as if he possessed a great deal of will power and much strength of character. . . .

"Your speech will not have the results you expect," said he. "The Emperor does not like to have one bring pressure on him. Rasputin's power will grow greater rather than less owing to his boundless influence over the Empress. It is she who really governs the State. The Emperor is at Headquarters much occupied with military operations."

"Well, what are we going to do about it?" I asked.

He gave a mysterious smile and looked me straight in the face.

"Get rid of Rasputin."

"That's easy to say. But who will do it? Russia has nobody with backbone enough

for such a deed. The Government could do it easily, but the Government clings to him and watches over him as if he were a treasure."

"Yes," said Iusupov, "one cannot count on the Government, but I dare say there are men in Russia who would do it."

"Do you think so?"

"I know it. One of them is right before you. . . ."

I smiled. "Prince," said I to him, "I am no longer astonished at anything that happens in Russia. I am not trying to get anything for myself; I have no personal ambitions. But if you wish . . . to deliver Russia from Rasputin, here is my hand. We are going to examine the means to bring it about, and we will undertake it if we can find some others to join us."

XVIII:31. A RESOLUTION ADOPTED BY THE CONGRESS OF THE UNION OF TOWNS, DECEMBER 9, 1916

After the November debates in the Duma, in which the regime had been sharply attacked, the Congress of the Union of Towns endorsed (December 9, 1916) a resolution addressed to the Duma and containing this appeal.

Reference: Tsentrarkhiv, *Burzhuaziia nakanune fevral'skoi revoliutsii*, p. 159.

It is entirely clear to all estates [*sosloviia*], all classes, all categories of honest people in Russia that the irresponsible criminals who are driven by superstitious fear, the fanatics who blasphemously mouth assertions of love for Russia, are preparing for her defeat, disgrace, and enslavement.

The eyes of Russia have finally been opened, and dire reality has come to light before them.

The life of the state has been shaken to its foundations by the government's measures;

the country has been brought to economic ruin; the food supply of the army and the population is in critical state; and the government's latest measures complete the disorganization and threaten [us] with social anarchy.

There is only one way out of the present situation which is leading Russia to certain catastrophe: the reorganization of the government and the establishment of a responsible ministry.

XVIII:32. THE TSAR'S SPECIAL ORDER OF THE DAY, DECEMBER 25, 1916

In December 1916 Germany, after her successes on the Rumanian front, proposed that peace talks be started. The Allies refused. In his special decree of December 25 to the army and navy, Nicholas explained that refusal. The full text, as given below, is contained in the significant memoirs of General A. S. Lukomskii, who had been assistant minister of war and who from November 1916 to April 1917 was "quartermaster general" to the chief of staff.

Reference: Aleksandr S. Lukomskii, *Vospominaniia Generala A. S. Lukomskogo*, 2 vols. (Berlin: Otto Kirchner, 1922), 1:114-16; translation based largely, but with some changes, on A. S. Loukomsky, *Memoirs of the Russian Revolution* (London: T. F. Unwin, 1922), pp. 47-48.

More than two years ago, in a time of profound peace, Germany, which had long been secretly preparing to enslave all the peoples of Europe, suddenly attacked Russia and her faithful ally, France, which obliged England to join us and take part in the struggle. The evident complete contempt of Germany for the fundamentals

of international law, which manifested itself in the infringement of Belgian neutrality and the merciless cruelty of the Germans toward the peaceful populations of the territories they seized, gradually united all the great powers of Europe against Germany and her ally, Austria-Hungary.

Under the pressure of the German armies, extremely strong because of their technical resources, Russia and France as well were obliged, in the first year of the war, to cede a part of their territory to the foe. This temporary reverse, however, crushed neither our faithful allies' spirit nor yours, my gallant troops. Meanwhile, by straining all the forces of the state, the difference between our technical resources and those of the Germans was gradually disappearing. But, even long before this, since the autumn of the past year, 1915, our enemy had been unable to occupy another inch of Russian territory; and in the spring and summer of this current year it has experienced a series of severe defeats and has gone from the offensive to the defensive along the whole of our front. Its forces are apparently wearing themselves out, while the might of Russia and her valorous allies continues to grow steadily. Germany feels that the hour of her final defeat, of retaliation for all her cruelties and violations of the law, is near. And so, just as Germany suddenly declared war at a time when she felt her military superiority over her neighbors, she now, feeling her weakness, proposes to the Allied Powers, united against her in an indissoluble bond, to enter into peace negotiations. She, naturally, wishes to begin these negotiations before the degree of her weakness becomes fully evident, before the total loss of her fighting capacity. Thus, she endeavors to use her temporary victory over Rumania, which has still not succeeded in acquiring military experience in contemporary warfare, to create a false impression of the strength of her armies. But if Germany had the opportunity of declaring war and attacking Russia and her ally France at the most unfavorable moment for them, then the allies, supported by noble Italy and powerful England, and fortified now by the struggle,

have the opportunity, in their turn, to enter into peace negotiations when they consider the time favorable for themselves. This time has not yet come: the enemy has not yet been expelled from the territories it has seized. Russia has not yet secured its aims fostered by the war: the possession of Tsar'grad [Constantinople] and the Straits as well as the establishment of a free Poland from its three existing, but as yet separate, parts. To conclude a peace at present would mean not to make use of the fruits of the heroic efforts of the Russian army and fleet.

These efforts, and even more the sacred memory of those gallant sons of Russia who have perished on the field of battle, forbid us even to think of peace before the final victory over the foe, who dared to think that, if he could begin the war, he can end it whenever he likes.

I do not doubt that every true son of Holy Russia—whether he, with weapon in hand, forms part of my glorious army, or works within the country to strengthen that army, or simply pursues his own peaceful toil—is imbued with the awareness that peace can be granted to the enemy only after he is driven from our boundaries, only when, entirely broken, he gives us and our faithful allies solid proofs of the impossibility of his repeating his treacherous attack and firm assurances that by the very force of circumstances he will be compelled to fulfill those obligations which he takes upon himself in the treaty of peace.

Let us then remain firm in our assurance of victory, and the Almighty will bless our banners; he will cover them once more with undying glory and will grant us a peace worthy of your heroic deeds, my glorious troops—a peace for which the generations to come will bless your memory, forever sacred to them.

Nikolai

XVIII:33. BUCHANAN'S AUDIENCE WITH THE TSAR, DECEMBER 30, 1916

For developments at the top in the final weeks of Nicholas's reign, the reports of the British ambassador once again have special value, as this excerpt will illustrate.

Reference: Buchanan, *My Mission to Russia*, 2:45-46, 48-49.

I went on to say that there was now a barrier between him and his people, and that if Russia was still united as a nation it was in opposing his present policy. The people, who had rallied so splendidly round their Sovereign on the outbreak of war, had seen how hundreds

of thousands of lives had been sacrificed on account of the lack of rifles and munitions; how, owing to the incompetence of the administration, there had been a severe food crisis, and—much to my surprise, the Emperor himself added, "a breakdown of the railways."

All that they wanted, I continued, was a Government that would carry on the war to a victorious finish. The Duma, I had reason to know, would be satisfied if His Majesty would but appoint as President of the Council a man in whom both he and the nation could have confidence, and would allow him to choose his own colleagues. The Emperor, while passing over this suggestion, referred by way of justification to certain changes which he had recently made in the Ministry. I therefore ventured to observe that His Majesty had of late changed his Ministers so often that Ambassadors never knew whether the Ministers of to-day with whom they were treating would still be Ministers on the morrow.

"Your Majesty, if I may be permitted to say so, has but one safe course open to you—namely, to break down the barrier that separates you from your people and to regain their confidence." Drawing himself up and looking hard at me, the Emperor asked: "Do you mean that *I* am to regain the confidence of my people or that they are to regain *my* confidence?" "Both, sir," I replied, "for without such mutual confidence Russia will never win this war."

. . .

"An Ambassador, I am well aware, has no right to hold the language which I have held to Your Majesty, and I had to take my courage in both hands before speaking as I have done. I can but plead as my excuse the fact that I have throughout been inspired by my feelings of devotion for Your Majesty and the Empress. If I were to see a friend walking through a wood on a dark night along a path which I knew ended in a precipice, would it not be my duty, sir, to warn him of his danger? And is it not equally my duty to warn Your Majesty of the abyss that lies ahead of you? You have, sir, come to the parting of the ways, and you have now to choose between two paths. The one will lead you to victory and a glorious peace—the other to revolution and disaster. Let me implore Your Majesty to choose the former. . . ."

The Emperor was visibly moved by the warmth which I had put into this appeal, and, pressing my hand as he bade me goodbye, said, "I thank you, Sir George."

XVIII:34. BURYSHKIN ON THE MOSCOW MERCHANT CLASS IN FEBRUARY 1917

Buryshkin (see Item XVII:50) in his memoirs makes these observations about the class solidarity of the Moscow bourgeoisie just before the February Revolution.
    Reference: Buryshkin, *Moskva kupecheskaia*, pp. 264-65, 280, 315.

By the beginning of the February Revolution there already existed a number of industrial groupings, and almost all the principal branches of industry and trade in the Moscow district were organized. In addition to . . . the Association of Cotton Manufacturers, which united all branches of this industrial sector, there were also an Association of Cloth Manufacturers headed by Kashtanov, and an organization of flax and linen producers with Tret'iakov as chairman. The silk manufacturers grouped themselves about the Shchenkovs; the leather manufacturers were under the chairmanship of Novoselov. . . . Recently there had also appeared the Association of Cement Makers and certain smaller commercial groupings, such as the Association of Shoe Merchants and others. There were also, of course, branches of nationwide syndicates—Prodamet [syndicate of metalworking firms], Produgol' [syndicate of coal producers], Krovlia [syndicate of Ural roofing-iron manufacturers], and so on.

. . .

Neither class nor even group consciousness emerged. No groups arose that could truly comprehend not so much their own rights as their responsibilities in connection with their role in the national economy. Therefore, when the "bourgeois" revolution occurred, the bourgeoisie, in essence, did not exist. In any case, there was no group that had its own ideology and was aware of both its rights and, above all, its obligations.

. . .

Commercial and industrial Moscow can by no means be considered a homogeneous group with a common political outlook. Among Moscow merchants, as among Russians of the commercial classes in general, there were men of diverse opinions, diverse shades of political thought. There were followers of the Right and of the Left. There were extremists on the right and there were, although not too often, also extremists on the left closely bound with the revolutionary movement.

XVIII:35. RODZIANKO'S REPORT ON THE ECONOMIC SITUATION IN FEBRUARY 1917

After the Revolution the Soviets came upon and published a report prepared for the tsar some-
time in February 1917 by Duma chairman M. V. Rodzianko. In this seventeen-page report, the
economic situation of the country is described with a wealth of data, including several tables.
These excerpts convey the tone of the report but unfortunately can barely dip into the supporting data.

Reference: Mikhail V. Rodzianko, "Ekonomicheskoe polozhenie Rossii pered revoliutsiei:
Zapiska M. V. Rodzianki," *Krasnyi arkhiv*, 10 (1925): 69-71, 73-74, 79, 81-82, 86.

Your Imperial Majesty:

In a moment of terrible danger the worst
policy is to shut one's eyes to the full serious-
ness of the actual situation. One must boldly
look it in the face since, in this case, there is
a possibility of finding some sort of favorable
solution. The situation in Russia today is
both catastrophic and profoundly tragic. Her
army is not defeated; it is better supplied
with arms than ever before. But behind the
army, in the rear, the breakdown is such that
it threatens to render useless all the sacrifices,
all the bloodshed, all the unparalleled heroism,
and, even more, to tip the military scales to
the advantage of our enemies. From every
corner of Russia come reports, each more
dismal and miserable than the other. The
mayor of Moscow reports in his memorandum
presented to the chairman of the Council of
Ministers that the situation in Moscow with
respect to the food supply is critical: instead
of 65 carloads of flour . . . in December the
daily flour supply in Moscow was not more
than 50 carloads, and in January it even fell
to 42 carloads, i.e. the supply met only a
little more than half the need. If the supply
of flour is not brought up to the norm, Moscow will soon have absolutely no reserves of
flour. The situation in Petrograd is no better.
The January supply of essential commodities
was 50 percent of the norm, as established by
the Special Conference; the supply of livestock, fowl, and butter was 25 percent of the
norm, and supply in the first half of January
was better than in the second half. Thus,
what was needed was 32 carloads of rye and
rye flour daily, but only 2, 1, 21, and 2 carloads were actually brought in; 40 carloads
of wheat flour were needed per day, but only
12, 10, 35, 8, and 2 were actually brought in.

The plight of the provinces, to which the
authorities naturally pay less attention, is even
worse. . . .

. . . The fuel situation is no better. Almost
all of Russia is suffering from an acute shortage of liquid and solid mineral fuels, and of

wood and peat. The same memorandum from
the mayor of Moscow cites facts whose significance is depressing. During the winter season
Moscow needs daily 475,000 poods of wood,
100,000 poods of coal, 100,000 poods of fuel
oil, and 15,000 poods of peat. But in January,
before the frosts set in, on the average only
430,000 poods of wood, 60,000 poods of
coal, and 75,000 poods of oil were brought in
to Moscow. . . . Because of the shortage of
fuel, many enterprises, including even those
working for defense, have already halted or
will soon halt operation. Buildings with central
heating systems have 50 percent of the fuel
they need, and the wood yards are empty.
. . . In people's apartments the temperature
seldom rises above 11-12° R [approximately
57-59° Fahrenheit], and in houses with central
heating it falls to 9 or 10° R [52-55° F]. In
educational institutions and in many establishments it is extremely difficult to work, since
the temperature in their buildings remains between 6 and 8° R [44-50° F]. . . . Because of
the fuel shortage . . . factories stand idle. . . .

. . . [In Petrograd] of the 73 plants standing
idle in December 1916, 39 were forced to suspend production because of a lack of fuel and
11 because of the suspension of electric power,
caused by the fuel shortage at the power stations.

· · ·

The country has everything it needs but
cannot make adequate use of it. There is not
the slightest doubt that agricultural production is able to satisfy the consumer needs of
the Russian population. . . . Russia has sufficient grain resources. . . . The yield in 1916
of only the four principal grain crops totaled
3,336,000,000 poods; their total consumption
was 2,643,000,000 poods. Nor is there anything to fear from the point of view of available resources in regard to providing the
country with fuel; our country possesses in-
exhaustible sources of fuel in all its various
forms: forests, coal beds, oil, peat, combusti-
ble shale, and so on. . . . And if all these very

rich resources are not exploited, it is only because proper organization of the rear is lacking.

We must, of course, cite first the poor organization of transportation, which does not permit us to move the requisite products in the necessary quantities from one place to another, and which therefore retards the proper pace of the national economy. Thus, the fuel crisis is caused only by the fact that the railroads do not manage to transport the required amount of fuel, although the latter is available.

. . .

The second major reason for the collapse of the rear is the confusion in the labor market. The huge depletions of the population caused by the mobilization, which took more than 50 percent of the able-bodied males between the ages of sixteen and fifty, have created an extremely complex and crucial situation in the rear. . . .

Skilled workers were mobilized and sent to the front, and all efforts to send them back from the army remained virtually fruitless until very recently. Under such conditions our enterprises had to resort to the labor of semiskilled or entirely unskilled workers, and

this had a number of harmful repercussions.

. . .

The third principal reason for the collapse of the rear is the improper utilization of the country's economic potential. . . . Public initiative is distrusted and is seen as a dangerous enemy; despite all the tremendous services they have rendered the country and the army, public organizations are persecuted. . . .

The fourth factor that must be mentioned here is the insane financial policy of the government.

. . .

It is essential . . . to enlist the services of all the vital forces of the country in the cause of putting the national economy in order; this necessarily presupposes the establishment not only of complete confidence but also of complete contact between the government and society. Only a government the country trusts and in which it has faith can compel the people to go forth to further sacrifices. Then, and only then, will the slogan "War to a victorious end" acquire a solid foundation.

. . . The twelfth hour is striking and the time is all too near when any appeal to the people's reason will be belated and useless.

XVIII:36. GENERAL KHABALOV'S REPORTS ON PETROGRAD, FEBRUARY 25 AND 26, 1917

These reports were contained in telegrams sent by the chief of the Petrograd military district to General Alekseev, chief of staff of the supreme command. The originals bear Alekseev's notes "reported to His Majesty the emperor" on February 26 and 27, respectively.

Reference: "Fevral'skaia revoliutsiia 1917 goda," *Krasnyi arkhiv*, 21 (1927): 4, 5.

[Sent February 25, 5:40 P.M.; received 6:08 P.M.:]

I report that, as a result of the bread shortage, a strike broke out in many factories on February 23 and 24. On February 24, around 200,000 workers were out on strike and forced others to quit their jobs. Streetcar service was halted by the workers. In the afternoons of February 23 and 24, some of the workers broke through to the Nevskii [Prospekt], whence they were dispersed. Violence led to broken windows in several shops and streetcars. Arms were not used by the troops. Four policemen received minor wounds.

[Sent February 26, 1:05 P.M.; received 1:40 P.M. (full text):]

To No. 486. I report that, during the after-

noon of February 25, crowds of workers who had assembled at Znamenskaia Square and near the Kazan' Cathedral were repeatedly dispersed by the police and the military. About 5 P.M. demonstrators near the Gostinyi Dvor began to sing revolutionary songs and hoisted red flags with the inscriptions "Down with War!" In response to the warning that arms would be used against them, there came from the crowd several revolver shots, one of which wounded a soldier of the Ninth Reserve Cavalry Regiment in the head. A troop of dragoons dismounted and opened fire on the crowd, killing three and wounding ten men. The crowd dispersed immediately. Around 6 P.M. a grenade was thrown at a detail of mounted gendarmes, wounding one gendarme and his horse. The evening passed relatively quietly. On February 25, 240,000 workers were out on strike. I issued a statement forbidding the people to gather in the streets and warning the populace that any manifestation of disorder would be suppressed by force of arms. Today, February 26, throughout the morning the city has been quiet. No. 3703. *Khabalov.*

XVIII:37. RODZIANKO'S TELEGRAMS TO THE TSAR, FEBRUARY 26 AND 27, 1917

On February 26 and the morning of February 27, 1917, Duma chairman M. V. Rodzianko sent these telegrams to the tsar. He received no reply.

Reference: Rodzianko, "Gosudarstvennaia Duma i fevral'skaia 1917 g. revoliutsiia," in *Arkhiv russkoi revoliutsii,* 6:59; translation based largely on Golder, *Documents of Russian History,* p. 278.

[Telegram of February 26, 1917:]

The situation is serious. The capital is in a state of anarchy. The government is paralyzed; the transportation system has broken down; the supply systems for food and fuel are completely disorganized. General discontent is on the increase. There is disorderly shooting in the streets; some of the troops are firing at each other. It is necessary that some person enjoying the confidence of the country be entrusted immediately with the formation of a new government. There can be no delay. Any procrastination is fatal. I pray to God that at this hour the responsibility not fall upon the sovereign.

[Telegram of February 27, 1917:]

The situation is growing worse. Measures must be taken, immediately, for tomorrow will already be too late. The final hour has struck, when the fate of the country and the dynasty is being decided.

XVIII:38. RODZIANKO'S TELEGRAM TO THE TSAR, EARLY AFTERNOON OF FEBRUARY 27, 1917

At 12:40 P.M. on February 27, Rodzianko sent this telegram to the tsar. It was marked received at 1:05 P.M. (complete text).

Reference: Rodzianko, "Fevral'skaia revoliutsiia 1917 goda," *Krasnyi arkhiv,* 21 (1927): 6-7.

By Your Majesty's decree, the work of the State Duma has been suspended until April. The last bulwark of order has been eliminated. The government is totally powerless to suppress disorders. Nothing can be expected from the garrison troops. The reserve battalions of the Guards regiments are seized with mutiny. Officers are being killed. Joining the crowd and the popular movement, they [the troops] make for the Ministry of Internal Affairs and the State Duma. Civil war has begun and is flaring up. Command the immediate summoning of a new government on the principles I reported to Your Majesty in yesterday's telegram. Revoke your imperial decree and command that the legislative chambers be convened again. Proclaim these measures at once by imperial manifesto. Your Majesty, do not delay. If the movement spreads to the army, the German will triumph, and the downfall of Russia, and, with it, the dynasty, is inevitable. In the name of all of Russia, I beg Your Majesty to take the above steps. The hour that will decide your destiny and that of our homeland has come. Tomorrow may be too late. Chairman of the State Duma *Rodzianko.*

XVIII:39. THE TELEGRAM FROM SOME STATE COUNCIL MEMBERS TO THE TSAR, FEBRUARY 28, 1917

On February 28, 1917, a telegram was sent to the tsar by twenty-two members of the State Council. It concluded with this appeal.

Reference: Golder, *Documents of Russian History,* p. 279, citing *Izvestiia* of the Committee of Petrograd Journalists, no. 2, Feb. 28 (Mar. 13 N.S.), 1917. Slight stylistic changes have been made. Full translations of this and many other documents pertaining to the fall of the tsarist government and the establishment of the Provisional Government are given in Robert Paul Browder and Alexander F. Kerensky, eds., *The Russian Provisional Government, 1917: Documents,* 3 vols. (Stanford: Stanford University Press, 1961).

Your Majesty, keeping the present government in power any longer means the complete breakdown of law and order and will bring with it inevitable defeat in war, ruin of the dynasty, and great miseries for Russia.

We think that the last and only remedy is for Your Imperial Majesty to make a complete change in domestic policy and, in agreement with the repeated requests of the popular representatives, classes, and public organizations, to call together at once the legislative chambers; dismiss the present Council of Ministers; and ask someone who has the confidence of the people to submit to you, for confirmation, a list of names for a new cabinet capable of governing the country in complete harmony with the representatives of the people. Every hour is precious. Further delay and hesitation may bring on uncountable miseries.

Your Imperial Majesty's faithful subjects, members of the State Council.

[Then follow twenty-two names.]

XVIII:40. SHUL'GIN ON THE FORMATION OF THE PROVISIONAL COMMITTEE OF THE DUMA, FEBRUARY 27, 1917

Vasilii Vital'evich Shul'gin (b. 1878), member of the Second, Third, and Fourth Dumas, was a "Progressive Nationalist" and member of the Progressive Bloc in 1915-17. In his memoirs concerning the February Revolution (*Dni*, published in 1925), Shul'gin paints a vivid picture. Here is a brief excerpt from his account of the events at the Taurida Palace on February 27.

Reference: V. V. Shul'gin, *Dni* (Belgrade: Novoe Vremia, 1925), pp. 161-63.

Someone proposed in a fiery speech that all members of the Duma—all, without party distinctions—should maintain complete unity in the trying times that had begun, in order that disintegration be prevented; and that a committee which would be invested with "dictatorial powers" should be elected to lead the members of the Duma... All members of the Duma were to be required to give unquestioning obedience to this committee...

In that agitated, frightened atmosphere, this proposal met with general support... Dictatorship is a function of danger: thus it has been, and thus it will be...

With great solidarity and by an overwhelming majority [the following members] were elected, from Left to Right:

Chkheidze	Social Democrat
Kerenskii	Trudovik
Efremov	Progressive
Rzhevskii	Progressive
Miliukov	Kadet
Nekrasov	Kadet
Shidlovskii, Sergei	Left Octobrist
Rodzianko	Zemstvo Octobrist
L'vov, Vladimir	Center
Shul'gin	Nationalist (Progressive)

In essence this was a committee of the Progressive Bloc with the addition of Kerenskii and Chkheidze. This was an extension of the bloc toward the Left, about which I had at one time spoken with Shingarev—but alas, under what conditions this extension took place!..

Fear of the street drove Shul'gin and Chkheidze into one "*kollegium*"...

But the street was advancing and suddenly broke upon them...

This crowd of thirty thousand which had been threatening since morning was no myth, no figment of our fears...

And it came exactly like a landslide, like a flood... They say (I did not see it myself) that Kerenskii tried to take the first bunch of soldiers who crept onto the porch of the Taurida Palace and make them into "the first revolutionary guard"...

"Citizen-soldiers, a great honor has fallen to your lot: to protect the State Duma... I declare you to be the first revolutionary guard"!..

But this "first revolutionary guard" did not even last the first minute... It was immediately overrun by the crowd...

I don't know how it happened... I can't recall... I do remember that instant when the black-grey mass pressing at the doors inundated the Duma in an unbroken, bursting torrent...

Soldiers, workers, students, intellectuals, just plain people... In a living, viscous, human stream they poured into the bewildered Taurida Palace and filled up hall after hall, room after room...

. . .

That which we had feared so much, which we had wished to avoid at any cost, was already a fact. The Revolution had begun.

From this moment the State Duma, properly speaking, ceased to exist.

XVIII:41. THE PROCLAMATION OF THE PROVISIONAL COMMITTEE OF THE DUMA, FEBRUARY 28, 1917

The twelve-man Provisional Committee of the State Duma, which had been formed on February 27, issued two proclamations at two o'clock the next morning. Here is one of them (complete text).

Reference: Rodzianko, "Gosudarstvennaia Duma i fevral'skaia 1917 g. revoliutsiia," *Arkhiv russkoi revoliutsii*, 6:59; translation based partly on Golder, *Documents of Russian History*, pp. 281-82.

Under the grave conditions of domestic collapse brought about by the measures of the old government, the Provisional Committee of members of the State Duma has considered itself obliged to take into its own hands the restoration of state and public order. Conscious of the full responsibility involved in the decision it has taken, the committee expresses its assurance that the populace and the army will help it in the difficult task of creating a new government which corresponds to the desires of the people and is able to enjoy its confidence.

XVIII:42. THE PROCLAMATION OF THE PROVISIONAL GOVERNMENT, MARCH 1, 1917

Here in its entirety is the proclamation of March 1, 1917, in which the Provisional Committee of members of the State Duma announced the formation of the Provisional Government and set forth its general aims.

Reference: *Zhurnal Ministerstva Iustitsii*, 1917, nos. 2-3 (February–March), pp. 6-7.

From the Provisional Government

Citizens!

The Provisional Committee of members of the State Duma, with the aid and sympathy of the troops and the population of the capital, has at present scored such a degree of success over the dark forces of the old regime that it can now proceed to a more durable organization of executive power.

To this end, the Provisional Committee of the State Duma appoints as ministers of the first public [*obshchestvennyi*] cabinet the following persons, the country's confidence in whom is guaranteed by their past public and political activities.

Chairman of the Council of Ministers and Minister of Internal Affairs: Prince G. E. L'vov

Minister of Foreign Affairs: P. N. Miliukov

Minister of War and the Navy: A. I. Guchkov

Minister of Means of Communications: N. V. Nekrasov

Minister of Trade and Industry: A. I. Konovalov

Minister of Public Education: A. A. Manuilov

Minister of Finance: M. I. Tereshchenko

Chief Procurator of the Holy Synod: V. N. L'vov

Minister of Agriculture: A. I. Shingarev

Minister of Justice: A. F. Kerenskii

State Comptroller: I. V. Godnev

Minister for Finnish Affairs: F. I. Rodichev

The Cabinet will be guided in its present activity by the following principles:

1. Full and immediate amnesty in all political and religious cases, including terrorist attempts, military uprisings and agrarian offenses, and so forth.

2. Freedom of speech, the press, unions, assembly, and strikes, with the extension of political freedoms to servicemen within limits permitted by military and technical conditions.

3. Abolition of all class, religious, and national restrictions.

4. Immediate preparations for the convocation—on the basis of universal, equal, direct, and secret suffrage—of a constituent assembly which will establish the form of government and the constitution of the country.

5. Replacement of the police by a people's militia with an elected command, subordinate to the organs of local self-government.

6. Elections to the organs of local self-government on the basis of universal, direct, equal, and secret ballot.

7. Non-disarmament and non-transfer from Petrograd of the military units that participated in the revolutionary movement.

8. Along with the preservation of strict military discipline in the ranks and during performance of military duty, the abolition of all restrictions upon the soldiers' enjoyment of those public rights that have been granted to all other citizens. The Provisional Government considers it its duty to add that it by no means intends to use the military situation to delay in any way the realization of the above reforms and measures.

Chairman of the State Duma M. V. Rodzianko

Chairman of the Council of Ministers Prince G. E. L'vov

Ministers: P. N. Miliukov, N. V. Nekrasov, A. I. Konovalov, A. A. Manuilov, M. I. Tereshchenko, Vl. N. L'vov, A. I. Shingarev, A. F. Kerenskii

XVIII:43. ORDER NO. 1, MARCH 1, 1917

Here is the text of the famous Order No. 1, issued March 1, 1917, by the Petrograd Soviet of Workers' and Soldiers' Deputies.

Reference: Golder, *Documents of Russian History*, pp. 386-87, citing *Izvestiia*, no. 3, Mar. 15, 1917. Minor changes have been made on the basis of the (evidently not quite complete) Russian version in *Arkhiv russkoi revoliutsii*, 6:73-74.

To the garrison of the Petrograd okrug, to all the soldiers of the guard, army, artillery, and navy, for immediate and strict execution, and to the workers of Petrograd for their information:

The Soviet of Workers' and Soldiers' Deputies has resolved:

1. In all companies, battalions, regiments, parks, batteries, squadrons, in the special services of the various military administrations, and on the vessels of the navy, committees of elected representatives from the lower ranks of the above-mentioned military units shall be chosen immediately.

2. In all those military units that have not yet chosen their representatives to the Soviet of Workers' Deputies, one representative from each company shall be selected, to report with written credentials at the building of the State Duma by ten o'clock in the morning of the third of this March.

3. In all its political activities the military branch is subordinated to the Soviet of Workers' and Soldiers' Deputies and to its own committees.

4. The orders of the military commission of the State Duma shall be executed only in such cases as they do not conflict with the orders and resolutions of the Soviet of Workers' and Soldiers' Deputies.

5. All kinds of arms, such as rifles, machine guns, armored automobiles and others, must be kept at the disposal and under the control of the company and battalion committees and must in no case be turned over to officers, even at their demand.

6. In the ranks and during their performance of the duties of the service, soldiers must observe the strictest military discipline, but outside the service and the ranks, in their political, general civic, and private lives, soldiers cannot in any way be deprived of those rights that all citizens enjoy. In particular, standing at attention and compulsory saluting, when not on duty, are abolished.

7. Also, the addressing of the officers with the titles "Your Excellency," "Your Honor," and the like, is abolished, and these titles are replaced by the address of "Mister General," "Mister Colonel," and so forth. Rudeness toward soldiers of any rank, and, especially, addressing them as "thou," is prohibited, and soldiers are required to bring to the attention of the company committees every infraction of this rule, as well as all misunderstandings occurring between officers and enlisted men.

The present order is to be read to all companies, battalions, regiments, ships' crews, batteries, and other combatant and noncombatant commands.

The Petrograd Soviet of Workers' and Soldiers' Deputies

XVIII:44. THE ABDICATION MANIFESTO OF NICHOLAS II, MARCH 2, 1917

The Provisional Committee of members of the State Duma, having decided on March 1 that Nicholas should be asked to abdicate, authorized two members, A. I. Guchkov and V. V. Shul'gin, to go to him secretly with the message. Shul'gin in his postrevolutionary account (*Dni*) describes the events of March 2—the trip to Pskov in a special train arriving about 10 P.M., the tsar's friendly reception of them, Guchkov's report of disorders in Petrograd, the tsar's calm and cooperative manner. Retiring for a little while with Guchkov's outline of suggested points, the tsar returned (it was now almost midnight) and handed Guchkov the text of his manifesto. It was typewritten on two or three quarter-sheets of the sort evidently used at the Stavka as telegraph forms. Shul'gin records that anguish gripped his heart as he read "these striking words which now are known to all."

Reference: Shul'gin, *Dni*, pp. 273-74; another Russian text in *Zhurnal Ministerstva Iustitsii*, 1917, nos. 2-3 (February-March), pp. 1-2; translation based largely on Pares, *Fall of the Russian Monarchy*, p. 467.

In these days of great struggle with a foreign enemy, who for nearly three years has striven to enslave our homeland, the Lord God has been pleased to send down on Russia a new, terrible ordeal. The internal popular disturbances that have begun threaten to have a disastrous effect on the further conduct of this persistent war. The destiny of Russia, the honor of our heroic army, the welfare of the people, the entire future of our dear fatherland demand that, whatever it may cost, the war be brought to a victorious end. The cruel enemy is straining his last forces, and already the hour is near when our gallant army, together with our glorious allies, will be able finally to crush the enemy. In these decisive days in the life of Russia, we have deemed it a duty of conscience to facilitate for our people a close union and consolidation of all national forces for the speediest attainment of victory; and, in agreement with the State Duma, we have thought it best to abdicate the throne of the Russian state and to lay down the supreme power. Not wishing to part with our beloved son, we hand down our inheritance to our brother, Grand Duke Mikhail Aleksandrovich, and give him our blessing on his accession to the throne of the Russian state. We enjoin our brother to direct state affairs in full and inviolable union with the representatives of the people in the legislative institutions, on those principles which they will establish. In the name of our dearly loved homeland we call on all faithful sons of the fatherland to fulfill their sacred duty to the tsar by obeying him at this grave moment of national tribulation, to help him, together with the representatives of the people, to bring the Russian state onto the road of victory, prosperity, and glory. May the Lord God help Russia!

                                                    Nikolai

[Shul'gin goes on to explain that at his suggestion the tsar added in pencil "taking an inviolable oath thereupon" after the word "establish" in the third from last sentence. Also at Shul'gin's suggestion, the document was antedated to three o'clock that afternoon, so that it would not appear to have been extorted.]

XVIII:45. KOKOVTSOV DESCRIBES THE TAURIDA PALACE, MARCH 3, 1917

Kokovtsov describes in these words the seat of the Duma on the day after the Provisional Government was announced. Kokovtsov had just been arrested and brought there.

Reference: Vladimir N. Kokovtsov, *The Memoirs of Count Kokovtsov: Out of My Past*, ed. Harold H. Fisher, trans. Laura Matveev (Palo Alto: Stanford University Press, 1935), p. 483, revised slightly on the basis of V. N. Kokovtsov, *Iz moego proshlogo, vospominaniia 1903-1919*, 2 vols. (Paris: Illiustrirovannaia Rossiia, 1933), 2:408.

Even the most vivid imagination could not picture what was taking place within the Taurida Palace. Soldiers, sailors, university students of both sexes, nondescript persons by the score, deputations to see someone, anyone, orators perched upon tables and chairs shrieking unintelligibly, arrested persons like me escorted by guards, "Frenchies" [those wearing a certain type of army tunic] dashing hither and yon, orderlies and unknown persons transmitting some sorts of orders to someone, a steady hum of voices! It was bedlam. And in the midst of it all wandered members of the Duma, recently so proud, who had been planning to show the world a miraculous revolution which would take place without the "shedding of a drop of blood."

XVIII:46. THE ABDICATION PROCLAMATION OF GRAND DUKE MIKHAIL ALEKSANDROVICH, MARCH 3, 1917

The day after Nicholas's abdication in favor of his brother Michael, Michael issued this proclamation. Shul'gin records that in the conversation he had with Michael during and after the preparation of the document, he was deeply impressed by him and thought to himself "what a good constitutional monarch he would have been."

Reference: *Zhurnal Ministerstva Iustitsii,* 1917, nos. 2-3 (February-March), p. 2; translation based to some extent (but with extensive changes) on Golder, *Documents of Russian History,* pp. 298-99.

A heavy burden has been entrusted to me by my brother in handing down to me the imperial all-Russian throne at a time of unprecedented war and popular disturbances. Animated by the thought that is in the minds of the whole people, that the good of our homeland comes before everything else, I have firmly decided to accept the supreme power only in the event that that be the will of our great people, who must by general balloting through their representatives to the Constituent Assembly establish the form of government and the new fundamental laws of the Russian state. Therefore, calling upon God for his blessing, I ask all citizens of the Russian state to subordinate themselves to the Provisional Government, which came into being and was invested with full authority on the initiative of the State Duma, until the Constituent Assembly, summoned at the earliest possible moment on the basis of universal, direct, equal, and secret suffrage, shall by its decision on the form of government express the will of the people.

XVIII:47. NICHOLAS'S LAST ADDRESS TO THE ARMY, MARCH 8, 1917

On March 8, 1917, when already under arrest and about to leave the general headquarters at Mogilev, Nicholas signed his last address to the army. Its significance lies in what it reveals about its author, for the Provisional Government did not allow the document to be disseminated.

Reference: Lukomskii, *Vospominiia Generala A. S. Lukomskogo,* 1:143-44; translation based largely on Pares, *Fall of the Russian Monarchy,* pp. 472-73.

For the last time I appeal to you, the troops whom I so fervently love. Since my abdication for myself and my son from the throne of Russia, the power has passed to the Provisional Government, which has arisen on the initiative of the State Duma.

May God help it to lead Russia along the road to glory and prosperity.

May God help you, my valiant troops, to defend our homeland against the cruel foe! For two and one-half years you have hourly borne the heavy burden of war. Much is the blood that has been shed; many are the efforts that have been made; and the hour is already near when Russia, bound to her gallant allies by a single common striving for victory, will crush the last efforts of the adversary.

This unprecedented war must be brought to full victory.

Whoever now dreams of peace, whoever wishes it—that one is a traitor to his fatherland, its betrayer. I know that every honest soldier thinks so. Carry out your duty then; protect our gallant homeland; subordinate yourselves to the Provisional Government; obey your commanders.

Remember that any weakening of the discipline of the service only plays into the hands of the enemy.

I firmly believe that unbounded love for our great homeland is not extinguished in your hearts. May the Lord God bless you and may Saint George the Holy Martyr and Conqueror lead you to victory.

Nikolai

BIBLIOGRAPHY

Note: This bibliography is limited to those works that were used in the preparation of the Source Book and does not include all of the collections mentioned in the reference notes as supplementary material. In general, the publisher is given only for works published since 1900.

Adrianova-Peretts, V. P., ed. *Vremennik Ivana Timofeeva.* Moscow: AN SSSR, 1951.

————, and D. S. Likhachev, eds. *Povest' vremennykh let.* Moscow: AN SSSR, 1950.

Aksakov, Ivan S. *Polnoe sobranie sochinenii I. S. Aksakova.* 7 vols. Moscow, 1886-87.

Aksakov, Konstantin S. *Polnoe sobranie sochinenii K. S. Aksakova.* Ed. I. S. Aksakov. 2 vols. Moscow, 1861-71.

————. *Zamechaniia na novoe administrativnoe ustroistvo krest'ian v Rossii.* Leipzig, 1861.

Akty sobrannye v bibliotekakh i arkhivakh Rossiiskoi Imperii arkheograficheskoiu ekspeditsieiu Imperatorskoi Akademii Nauk. 4 vols. St. Petersburg, 1836.

Akty sotsial'no-ekonomicheskoi istorii severovostochnoi Rusi. 3 vols. Ed. B. D. Grekov (vol. 1), L. V. Cherepnin (vols. 2 and 3). Moscow: AN SSSR, 1952-64.

Aleksandra Fedorovna: see *Letters of the Tsaritsa to the Tsar;* see also Tsentral'nyi Gosudarstvennyi Istoricheskii Arkhiv v Moskve, ed., *Perepiska . . .*

Annales Bertiniani. Ed. G. Waitz. Hanover, 1883.

Antonovich, Vladimir B. *Monografii po istorii zapadnoi i iugozapadnoi Rossii.* Vol. 1. Kiev, 1885.

Arkheograficheskaia Komissiia, ed. *Akty istoricheskie.* 5 vols. St. Petersburg, 1841-42.

————. *Akty otnosiashchiesia do iuridicheskogo byta drevnei Rossii.* Ed. Nikolai Kalachev. 3 vols. St. Petersburg, 1857, 1864, 1884.

————. *Akty otnosiashchiesia k istorii iuzhnoi i zapadnoi Rossii.* 15 vols. St. Petersburg, 1863-92.

————. *Akty otnosiashchiesia k istorii zapadnoi Rossii.* 5 vols. St. Petersburg, 1846-51.

————. *Dnevnik Liublinskogo seima 1569 g.* St. Petersburg, 1869.

————. *Dokumenty ob"iasniaiushchie istoriiu zapadno-russkogo kraia i ego otnosheniia k Rossii i Pol'she.* St. Petersburg, 1865.

————. *Dopolneniia k aktam istoricheskim.* 12 vols. St. Petersburg, 1846-72.

————. *Letopis' po Ipatskomu spisku.* St. Petersburg, 1871.

————. *Letopis' po Lavrent'evskomu spisku.* St. Petersburg, 1897.

————. *Novgorodskie letopisi (Novgorodskaia vtoraia i Novgorodskaia tret'ia letopisi).* St. Petersburg, 1879.

————. *Polnoe Sobranie Russkikh Letopisei.* 31 vols. St. Petersburg, 1841-1968.

————. *Russkaia istoricheskaia biblioteka.* 39 vols. St. Petersburg: Arkheograficheskaia Komissiia, 1872-1927.

————. *Sibirskie letopisi.* St. Petersburg: I. N. Skorokhodov, 1907.

Arkhiv iugo-zapadnoi Rossii. 35 vols. Kiev: Tip. G. T. Korchak-Novitskogo, 1859-1914.

Arkhiv russkoi revoliutsii. Ed. I. V. Gessen. 22 vols. Berlin: Slovo, 1921-27.

Avvakum, *The Life of Archpriest Avvakum, by Himself.* Trans. Jane Harrison and Hope Mirrlees. London: L. and V. Woolf at the Hogarth Press, 1924.

Bakunin, Mikhail A. *Izbrannye sochineniia.* 5 vols. Petrograd: Golos Truda, 1920-22. See also Maximoff.

Bartenev, Petr I., ed. *Deviatnadtsatyi vek.* 2 vols. Moscow, 1872. See also *Russkii arkhiv.*

Bazilevskii, B. [Vasilii Ia. Iakovlev], ed. *Literatura partii Narodnoi Voli.* Paris: Société nouvelle de librairie et d'édition, 1905.

————. *Revoliutsionnaia zhurnalistika semidesiatykh godov . . .* Paris [?], 1906.

Belinskii, Vissarion G. *Polnoe sobranie sochinenii.* 13 vols. Moscow: AN SSSR, 1953-59.

Belinsky, Vissarion G. *Selected Philosophical Works.* Moscow: Foreign Languages Publishing House, 1948.

Benedetto, L. F. *The Travels of Marco Polo*. Trans. Aldo Ricci. London: G. Routledge and Sons, 1931.

Berry, Lloyd E., and Robert O. Crummey, eds. *Rude and Barbarous Kingdom: Russia in the Accounts of Sixteenth-Century English Voyagers*. Madison: University of Wisconsin Press, 1968.

Bodemann, Eduard, ed. *Briefe der Kurfuerstin Sophie von Hannover an die Raugraefinnen und Raugrafen zu Pfalz*. Publicationen aus den K. Preussischen Staatsarchiven, vol. 37. Leipzig, 1888.

Bogoiavlenskii, S. K., and I. S. Riabinin, eds. *Akty vremeni mezhdutsarstviia (1610-1613)*, Moscow: Izd. Imperatorskogo Obshchestva Istorii i Drevnostei Rossiiskikh pri Moskovskom Universitete, 1915.

Bogucharskii: See Iakovlev, V. Ia.

Bolotov, Andrei T. "Nakaz dlia derevenskogo upravitelia." In Vol'noe Ekonomicheskoe Obshchestvo, *Trudy Vol'nogo Ekonomicheskogo Obshchestva*, Vol. 16, pp. 69-230. St. Petersburg, 1770.

Borozdin, Aleksandr K., ed. *Iz pisem i pokazanii dekabristov*. St. Petersburg: M. V. Pirozhkov, 1906.

Browder, Robert Paul, and Alexander F. Kerensky, eds. *The Russian Provisional Government, 1917: Documents*. 3 vols. Stanford: Stanford University Press, 1961.

Bruce, Peter H. *Memoirs of Peter Henry Bruce, Esq*. Dublin, 1783. Reprint. New York: Da Capo, 1968.

Bubnoff: see *The Russian Co-operator*.

Buchanan, George W. *My Mission to Russia and Other Diplomatic Memories*. 2 vols. Boston: Little, Brown, 1923.

Burtsev, Vladimir L., comp. and ed. *Za sto let, 1800-1896: Sbornik po istorii politicheskikh i obshchestvennykh dvizhenii v Rossii*. London, 1897. Reprint. The Hague: Europe Printing, 1965.

Buryshkin, Pavel A. *Moskva kupecheskaia*. New York: Chekhov, 1954.

Burzhuaziia nakanune fevral'skoi revoliutsii: see Tsentral'nyi Gosudarstvennyi Istoricheskii Arkhiv v Moskve.

Butashevich-Petrashevskii, Mikhail V. *Delo Petrashevtsev*. 3 vols. Moscow: AN SSSR, 1937-51.

Carpini, Giovanni de Plano. *The Mongol Mission*. Ed. and intro. Christopher Dawson. New York: Sheed and Ward, 1955.

Catherine II. *Memoirs of Catherine the Great*. Trans. Katherine Anthony. New York: Knopf, 1927. See also Reddaway; Chechulin.

———. *The Memoirs of Catherine the Great*. Ed. Dominique Maroger, intro. G. P. Gooch, trans. Moura Budberg. New York: Macmillan [1955].

———. *Pis'ma Imperatritsy Ekateriny II k Grimmu*. *Sbornik Imperatorskogo Russkogo Istoricheskogo Obshchestva*, vol. 23. St. Petersburg, 1878.

Chaadaev, Petr Ia. *The Major Works of Peter Chaadaev*. Trans. and commentary Raymond T. McNally. Notre Dame, Ind.: University of Notre Dame Press, 1969.

———. *Peter Yakovlevich Chaadayev: Philosophical Letters and Apology of a Madman*. Trans. and intro. Mary-Barbara Zeldin. Knoxville: University of Tennessee Press, 1969.

———. *Sochineniia i pis'ma P. Ia. Chaadaeva*. Ed. M. O. Gershenzon. 2 vols. Moscow: A. I. Mamontov, 1913-14. *See also* Moskoff.

Chancellor, Richard. "A Letter of Richard Chancellor . . . Touching His Discoverie of Moscovia." In *Hakluytus Posthumus or Purchas His Pilgrimes*, ed. Samuel Purchas. Vol. 11. Glasgow: J. MacLehose and Sons, 1906.

Chechulin, Nikolai D., ed. *Nakaz Imperatritsy Ekateriny II, dannyi Komissii o sochinenii proekta novogo Ulozheniia*. St. Petersburg: Tip. Imperatorskoi Akademii Nauk, 1907.

Cherepnin, Lev V., ed. *Akty feodal'nogo zemlevladeniia i khoziaistva XIV-XVI vekov*. Pt. 1. Moscow: AN SSSR, 1951.

———. *Pamiatniki prava pèrioda obrazovaniia russkogo tsentralizovannogo gosudarstva*. Pamiatniki russkogo prava, vol. 3. Moscow: Gosiurizdat, 1955.

Cherepnin, Lev V., and S. V. Bakhrushin, eds. *Dukhovnye i dogovornye gramoty velikikh i udel'nykh kniazei XIV-XVI vv*. Moscow: AN SSSR, 1950.

Cherniavsky, Michael, ed. *Prologue to Revolution: Notes of A. N. Iakhontov on the Secret Meetings of the Council of Ministers, 1915.* Englewood Cliffs, N.J.: Prentice-Hall, 1967.

Chernov, Viktor M. *Konstruktivnyi sotsializm.* Prague: Volia Rossii, 1925.

[Chernov, Viktor M.] *Ocherednoi vopros revoliutsionnogo dela.* London: Agrarian Socialist League, 1900.

Chernyshevskii, Nikolai G. *Polnoe sobranie sochinenii N. G. Chernyshevskogo.* 10 vols. St. Petersburg: I. Kraig, 1905-06.

———. *Selected Philosophical Essays.* Moscow: Foreign Languages Publishing House, 1953.

Chertkov, Vladimir G., ed. *Studencheskoe dvizhenie 1899 goda.* Purleigh, Eng.: Svobodnoe slovo, 1900.

Chronicle of Novgorod: see Michell.

Chteniia v Imperatorskom Obshchestve Istorii i Drevnostei Rossiiskikh pri Moskovskom Universitete: see Obshchestvo Istorii i Drevnostei Rossiiskikh.

Collins, Samuel. *The Present State of Russia.* London, 1671.

Constantine Porphyrogenitus. *De administrando imperio.* Greek text ed. Gy. Moravcsik, Eng. trans. R. J. H. Jenkins. Budapest: Institute of Greek Philology of Peter Pazmany University, 1949.

Coxe, William. *Travels into Poland, Russia, Sweden, and Denmark.* 3 vols. London: T. Cadell, 1784-90.

Cross, Samuel H., and Olgerd P. Sherbowitz-Wetzor, eds. and trans. *The Russian Primary Chronicle. Laurentian Text.* Cambridge, Mass.: Mediaeval Academy of America, 1953.

Custine, Astolphe, Marquis de. *Journey for Our Time: The Journals of the Marquis de Custine.* Ed. and trans. Phyllis P. Kohler. New York: Pellegrini and Cudahy, 1951.

Czartoryski, Adam J. *Memoirs of Prince Adam Czartoryski and His Correspondence with Alexander I.* Ed. Adam Gielgud. 2d ed. 2 vols. London, 1888.

Desiatiletie Ministerstva Narodnogo Prosveshcheniia, 1833-1843, St. Petersburg, 1864.

Desnitskii, V., ed. *Delo petrashevtsev. Pamiatniki obshchestvennoi mysli,* vol. 1. Moscow: AN SSSR, 1937.

Dewey, Horace W., comp., trans., and ed. *Muscovite Judicial Texts, 1488-1556.* Michigan Slavic Materials No. 7. Ann Arbor: Department of Slavic Languages and Literatures, University of Michigan, 1966.

———. *The Sudebnik of 1497.* Ann Arbor: University Microfilms, 1955.

———. "The White Lake Charter: A Mediaeval Russian Administrative Statute." *Speculum,* 32 (1957): 74-84.

D'iakonov, Mikhail A., ed. *Akty otnosiashchiesia k istorii tiaglogo naseleniia v Moskovskom gosudarstve.* 2 vols. St. Petersburg, 1895-97.

Dmitrieva, R. P. *Skazanie o kniaziakh vladimirskikh.* Moscow: AN SSSR, 1955.

Dmytryshyn, Basil, ed. *Imperial Russia: A Source Book, 1700-1917.* New York: Holt, Rinehart and Winston, 1967.

———, ed. *Medieval Russia: A Source Book, 900-1700.* New York: Holt, Rinehart and Winston, 1967.

Documents diplomatiques français, 1871-1914. Ser. 1 (1871-1900), 16 vols. Paris: Imprimerie Nationale, Alfred Costes, L'Europe Nouvelle, 1929-56.

Domostroi, intro. I. E. Zabelin. In *Chteniia v Imperatorskom Obshchestve Istorii i Drevnostei Rossiiskikh pri Moskovskom Universitete.* Moscow, 1881, bk. 2.

Domostroi po Konshinskomu spisku i podobnym. Ed. A. S. Orlov. 2 vols. Moscow: Sinodal'naia Tipografiia, 1908-10. Reprint. The Hague: Mouton, 1967.

Dostoevskii, Fedor M. *The Diary of a Writer: F. M. Dostoevsky.* Trans. Boris Brasol. 2 vols. New York: Charles Scribner's Sons, 1949.

———. *Polnoe sobranie sochinenii F. M. Dostoevskogo.* 12 vols. St. Petersburg: A. F. Marks, 1894-95.

Dovnar-Zapol'skii, Mitrofan V., ed. *Akty Litovsko-Russkogo Gosudarstva, vypusk I (1390-1529 gg.).* In *Chteniia v Imperatorskom Obshchestve Istorii i Drevnostei Rossiiskikh pri Moskovskom Universitete,* vol. 191, Moscow, 1899, bk. 4.

————. "Materialy dlia istorii votchinnogo upravleniia v Rossii," *Kievskie Universitetskie Izvestiia* (Kiev), 1903, no. 12; 1904, no. 6; 1909, no. 7; 1910, no. 11.

Druzhinin, Vasilii G., ed. *Pamiatniki pervykh let russkogo staroobriadchestva.* 3 vols. St. Petersburg: M. A. Aleksandrov, 1912-14.

Dubel't, M. L. "Iz epokhi osvobozhdeniia krest'ian, rasskaz gen.-leit. M. L. Dubel'ta, 1861." *Russkaia starina,* 69 (February 1891): 469-74.

Dubiecki, Marjan, comp. *Powstanie styczniowe w swietle zrodel.* Teksty zrodlowe do nauki historji w szkole sredniej, pt. 54. Krakow: Nakladem Krakowskiej Spolki Wydawniczej, 1924.

Dubrovin, Nikolai F., comp. *Sbornik istoricheskikh materialov izvlechennykh iz arkhiva Pervogo Otdeleniia Sobstvennoi Ego Imperatorskogo Velichestva Kantselarii.* 16 vols. St. Petersburg: Pervoe Otd. S. E. I. V. Kantseliarii, 1876-1917.

Dukhovnye i dogovornye gramoty velikikh i udel'nykh kniazei XIV-XVI vv. Moscow: AN SSSR, 1950.

Duma: see Gosudarstvennaia Duma.

Dumont, Jean. *Corps universel diplomatique du droit des gens.* 8 vols. bound in 16. Amsterdam, 1726-31.

Durnovo, P. N. "Zapiska." *Krasnaia nov',* no. 10 (November-December 1922). pp. 178-99.

Dzhivelegov, A. K., S. P. Mel'gunov, and V. I. Picheta, eds. *Velikaia reforma.* 6 vols. Moscow: Sytin, 1911.

Edie, James M., James P. Scanlan, and Mary-Barbara Zeldin, eds.; collab. George L. Kline. *Russian Philosophy.* 2 vols. Chicago: Quadrangle Books, 1965.

Entsiklopedicheskii Slovar'. 41 vols. St. Petersburg: Brokgauz and Efron, 1890-1904.

Fennell, John L. I., ed. and trans. *The Correspondence between Prince A. M. Kurbsky and Tsar Ivan IV of Russia, 1564-1579.* Cambridge: At the University Press, 1955.

Fennell, John L. I., and Dimitri Obolensky, eds. *A Historical Russian Reader: A Selection of Texts from the Eleventh to the Sixteenth Centuries.* Oxford: Clarendon Press, 1969.

"Fevral'skaia revolutsiia 1917 goda." *Krasnyi arkhiv,* 21 (1927 no. 2): 3-78; 22 (1927 no. 3): 3-70.

Filipowicz, Tytus, ed. *Confidential Correspondence of the British Government respecting the Insurrection in Poland: 1863.* Paris: Soudier, 1914.

Fischer, George. *Russian Liberalism.* Cambridge: Harvard University Press, 1958.

Fletcher, Giles. *Of the Rus Commonwealth.* Ed. Albert J. Schmidt. Ithaca, N.Y.: Cornell University Press, 1966. See also Berry.

————. *Of the Russe Commonwealth: Facsimile Edition with Variants.* Ed. John V. A. Fine, Jr., intro. Richard Pipes. Cambridge: Harvard University Press, 1966.

————. *Russia at the Close of the Sixteenth Century, Comprising the Treatise "Of the Russe Common Wealth" by Dr. Giles Fletcher and "The Travels of Jerome Horsey, Knt."* Ed. Edward A. Bond. London: Hakluyt Society, 1856.

Fonvizin, Mikhail A. "Obozrenie proiavlenii politicheskoi zhizni v Rossii." In *Obshchestvennye dvizheniia v Rossii v pervuiu polovinu XIX veka,* comp. V. I. Semevskii, V. Bogucharskii, and P. E. Shchegolev, vol. 1, pp. 97-202. St. Petersburg: Tipo-litografiia Gerol'd, 1905.

Garkavi, Avraam Ia. *Skazaniia musul'manskikh pisatelei o slavianakh i russkikh (VII-X vv.).* St. Petersburg, 1870. Reprint. The Hague: Mouton, 1969.

Ger'e, Vladimir [Guerrier, W.], ed. *Sbornik pisem i memorialov Leibnitsa otnosiashchikhsia k Rossii i Petru Velikomu.* St. Petersburg: Tip. Imperatorskoi Akademii Nauk, 1873. See also Guerrier.

Gertsen, Aleksandr I. *Byloe i dumy.* Moscow: OGIZ, 1946.

————. *Izbrannye filosofskie proizvedeniia.* 2 vols. Moscow: OGIZ, 1946.

————. *My Past and Thoughts: The Memoirs of Alexander Herzen.* Trans. Constance Garnett. 6 vols. London: Chatto and Windus, 1924-27. Rev. ed. by Humphrey Higgens. 4 vols.

(London: Chatto and Windus, 1968).

——. *Polnoe sobranie sochinenii i pisem.* Ed. M. K. Lemke. 22 vols. Petrograd-Leningrad-Moscow: Gosizdat and others, 1917-25.

——. *Sochineniia A. I. Gertsena.* 7 vols. bound in 3. St. Petersburg: F. Pavlenkov, 1905.

Giovanni de Plano Carpini: see Carpini.

Glinskii, Boris B. *Revoliutsionnyi period russkoi istorii (1861-1881).* 2 vols. St. Petersburg: A. S. Suvorin, 1913.

Gnevushev, A. M., comp. and ed. *Akty vremeni pravleniia tsaria Vasiliia Shuiskogo (19 maia 1606 g.-17 iiulia 1610 g.).* Moscow: Izd. Imperatorskogo Obshchestva Istorii i Drevnostei Rossiiskikh pri Moskovskom Universitete, 1914.

Goetz, Leopold K. *Deutsch-Russische Handelsvertraege des Mittelalters.* Hamburg: L. Friederichsen, 1916.

Golder, Frank A., ed. *Documents of Russian History 1914-1917.* Trans. Emanuel Aronsberg. New York: Century, 1927. Reprint. Gloucester, Mass.: Peter Smith, 1964.

Golovin, Nikolai N. *The Russian Army in the World War.* New Haven: Yale University Press, 1931.

Gorbachevskii, Ivan I. *Zapiski i pis'ma dekabrista.* Ed. B. E. Syroechkovskii. Moscow: Gosizdat, 1925.

Gosudarstvennaia Duma. *Stenograficheskie otchety Gosudarstvennoi Dumy I, II, III, i IV sozyvov.* 36 vols. St. Petersburg: Gosudarstvennaia Tipografiia, 1906-17.

Gosudarstvennyi Sovet: see *Otchet po . . .*

Got'e, Iu. V., ed. *Akty otnosiashchiesia k istorii zemskikh soborov. Pamiatniki russkoi istorii,* vol. 3. Moscow: N. N. Klochkov, 1909.

Granovskii, Timofei N. *Sochineniia T. N. Granovskogo.* 3d ed. 2 vols. Moscow, 1892.

——. *T. N. Granovskii i ego perepiska.* 2 vols. Moscow, 1897.

Grekov, Boris D., ed. *Pravda Russkaia.* 2 vols. Moscow: AN SSSR, 1940-47.

Grushevskii: see Hrushevsky.

Gudzii, Nikolai K., ed., and L. B. Lekhtblau, comp. *Russkie satiricheskie zhurnaly XVIII veka.* Moscow: Uchpedgiz, 1940.

Guerrier, W. *Leibniz in seinen Beziehungen zu Russland und Peter dem Grossen.* Leipzig, 1873. See also Ger'e.

Gurko, Vladimir I. *Features and Figures of the Past: Government and Opinion in the Reign of Nicholas II.* Palo Alto: Stanford University Press, 1939.

Hansard's Parliamentary Debates. 3d ser., vol. 132. London, 1854.

Hanway, Jonas. *An Historical Account of the British Trade over the Caspian Sea, with a Journal of Travels from London through Russia into Persia and Back.* 2 vols. London, 1753.

Harkavy: see Garkavi.

Haxthausen, Baron August von. *The Russian Empire, Its People, Institutions, and Resources.* Trans. Robert Farie. 2 vols. London, 1856.

——. *Studien ueber die innern Zustaende, das Volksleben und insbesondere die laendlichen Einrichtungen Russlands.* 3 vols. Hanover, 1847-52.

Hellie, Richard, trans. and ed. *Readings for Introduction to Russian Civilization: Muscovite Society.* Chicago: University of Chicago Syllabus Division, 1967.

Herberstein, Sigismund von. *Commentaries on Muscovite Affairs.* Ed. and trans. Oswald P. Backus III. Lawrence: University of Kansas Bookstore, 1956.

——. *Description of Moscow and Muscovy 1557.* Ed. Bertold Picard, trans. J. B. C. Grundy. London: J. M. Dent, 1969.

Herrmann, Ernst, ed. *Russland unter Peter dem Grossen: Nach den handschriftlichen Berichten Johann Gotthilf Vockerodt's und Otto Pleyer's.* Leipzig, 1872. See also *Rossiia pri Petre . . .*

Hertslet, Edward, ed. *The Map of Europe by Treaty since the General Peace of 1814.* 4 vols. London, 1875-91.

Herzen: See Gertsen.

Howes, Robert C., trans. and ed. *The Testaments of the Grand Princes of Moscow.* Ithaca, N.Y.: Cornell University Press, 1967.

Hrushevsky, Michael S. *Istoriia Ukraini-Rusi.* 10 vols. in 11 pts. New York: Knigospilka, 1954-58 (facsimile reprint of original edition of 1905-36).

Iablonskis, K. I., ed. *Statut velikogo kniazhestva litovskogo 1529 goda.* Minsk: AN BSSR, 1960.

Iakhontov, A. N. "Tiazhelye dni." *Arkhiv russkoi revoliutsii,* 18 (Berlin: Slovo, 1926): 5-136.

Iakovlev, A. I., ed. *Akty khoziaistva boiarina B. I. Morozova.* 2 pts. Moscow: AN SSSR, 1940-45.

———. *Pamiatniki istorii Smutnogo vremeni. Pamiatniki russkoi istorii,* vol. 4. Moscow: N. N. Klochkov, 1909.

Iakovlev, Vasilii Ia. [pseudonyms: B. Bazilevskii, V. Bogucharskii], ed. *Gosudarstvennye prestupleniia v Rossii v XIX veke, sbornik izvlechennykh iz ofitsial'nykh izdanii pravitel'stvennykh soobshchenii.* 3 vols. St. Petersburg: Russkaia Skoropechatnia, 1906. See also Bazilevskii.

Intelligentsiia v Rossii: Sbornik statei. St. Petersburg: Knigoizdat. "Zemlia," 1910.

Iosif Volotskii: see Sanin.

Iswolsky [Izvol'skii], Alexander P. *The Memoirs of Alexander Iswolsky.* Ed. and trans. C. I. Seeger. London: Hutchinson, 1920.

Iushkov, Serafim V., ed. *Pamiatniki prava feodal'no-razdroblennoi Rusi XII-XV vv. Pamiatniki russkogo prava,* vol. 2. Moscow: Gosiurizdat, 1953.

———. *Pamiatniki prava Kievskogo gosudarstva. Pamiatniki russkogo prava,* vol. 1. Moscow: Gosiurizdat, 1952.

Iuzefovich, T., ed. *Dogovory Rossii s vostokom: politicheskie i torgovye.* St. Petersburg, 1869.

Izveshchenie o III s"ezde Rossiiskoi Sotsial'-demokraticheskoi Rabochei Partii. Geneva: Izd. RSDRP, 1905.

Izveshchenie o vtorom ocherednom s"ezde Rossiiskoi Sotsial'-demokraticheskoi Rabochei Partii. Geneva: Izd. RSDRP, 1903.

Izvol'skii: see Iswolsky.

"Iz zapisnoi knizhki arkhivista: Dva dokumenta iz istorii Zubatovshchiny." *Krasnyi arkhiv,* 19 (1926, no. 6): 210-11.

Jakobson, Roman. "Saint Constantine's Prologue to the Gospels." *Saint Vladimir's Seminary Quarterly,* vol. 7, N.S., 1963.

Jordanes. *The Gothic History.* Trans. C. C. Mierow. Princeton: Princeton University Press, 1915. Photographically reprinted, Cambridge, Eng., and New York, 1960.

Kalachev, Nikolai V., ed. *Doklady i prigovory v . . . Senate v tsarstvovanie Petra Velikogo.* 6 vols. St. Petersburg: Tip. Imperatorskoi Akademii Nauk, 1880-1901.

Kalinychev, F. I., comp. *Gosudarstvennaia Duma v Rossii v dokumentakh i materialakh.* Moscow: Gosiurizdat, 1957.

Kapterev, Nikolai F. *Patriarkh Nikon i Tsar' Aleksei Mikhailovich.* 2 vols. Sergiev Posad: Tip. Sviato-Troitskoi Sergievoi Lavry, 1909-12.

Karamzin, Nikolai M. *Zapiska o drevnei i novoi Rossii.* Ed. Richard Pipes. Cambridge: Harvard University Press, 1959. See also Pipes.

Katkov, Mikhail N. *Sobranie peredovykh statei "Moskovskikh Vedomostei" s 1863 po 1887 god.* 24 vols. Moscow, 1897-98.

Kennan, George. *Siberia and the Exile System.* 2 vols. New York, 1891.

Khomiakov, Aleksei S. *Izbrannye sochineniia.* New York: Chekhov, 1955.

———. *Polnoe sobranie sochinenii A. S. Khomiakova.* 8 vols. Moscow: Tip. Imperatorskogo Moskovskogo Universiteta, 1900-07.

Khrestomatiia po istorii SSSR. Moscow: Gosudarstvennoe Uchebno-Pedagogicheskoe Izdatel'stvo Ministerstva Prosveshcheniia RSFSR. Vol. 1, *S drevneishikh vremen do kontsa XVII veka.* Comp. V. I. Lebedev, M. N. Tikhomirov, V. E. Syroechkovskii. 4th ed., 1951. Vol. 2, *1682-1856.* Comp. S. S. Dmitriev and M. V. Nechkina. 3d ed., 1953. Vol. 3, *1857-1894.* Comp. S. S.

Dmitriev. 2d ed., 1952.

Kireevskii, Ivan V. *Polnoe sobranie sochinenii I. V. Kireevskogo.* Ed. M. O. Gershenzon. 2 vols. Moscow: Tip. Imperatorskogo Moskovskogo Universiteta, 1911.

"K istorii Loris-Melikovskoi 'Konstitutsii.'" *Krasnyi arkhiv* 8 (1925, no. 1): 132-50.

Knox, Alfred. *With the Russian Army 1914-1917: Being Chiefly Extracts from the Diary of a Military Attaché.* 2 vols. New York: E. P. Dutton, 1921.

Kohn, Hans, ed. *The Mind of Modern Russia: Historical and Political Thought of Russia's Great Age.* New Brunswick, N.J.: Rutgers University Press, 1955.

Kokovtsov, Vladimir N. *Iz moego proshlogo: Vospominaniia, 1903-1919.* 2 vols. Paris: Illiustrirovannaia Rossiia, 1933.

———. *The Memoirs of Count Kokovtsov: Out of My Past.* Ed. Harold H. Fisher, trans. Laura Matveev. Palo Alto: Stanford University Press, 1935.

Korb, Johann G. *Diarium itineris in Moscoviam . . .* Vienna, 1700 or 1701.

———. *Diary of an Austrian Secretary of Legation at the Court of Peter the Great.* Trans. and ed. Count Macdonnell. 2 vols. London, 1863. Reprint. New York: Da Capo, 1968.

———. *Dnevnik puteshestviia v Moscoviiu (1698-1699 gg.).* Trans. and commentary, A. I. Malein. St. Petersburg: A. S. Suvorin, 1906.

Kormchaia Kniga. Republished from the edition of 1653 (under Patriarch Nikon). 2 pts. Moscow, 1787.

Korobkov, Nikolai M., ed. *Fel'dmarshal Kutuzov, sbornik dokumentov i materialov.* Moscow: OGIZ, 1947.

Korsakov, Dimitri A. *Votsarenie Imperatritsy Anny Ioannovny.* Kazan', 1880.

Kotoshikhin, Grigorii. *O Rossii v tsarstvovanie Aleksiia Mikhailovicha.* 3d ed. St. Petersburg: Arkheograficheskaia Komissiia, 1884. See also Uroff.

Krachkovskii, Ignatii Iu., ed. *Puteshestvie Ibn-Fadlana na Volgu.* Moscow: AN SSSR, 1939.

Krasnyi arkhiv. 106 vols. bound in 35. Moscow, 1922-41.

Kravchinskii [Stepniak], Sergei M. *The Russian Peasantry: Their Agrarian Condition, Social Life, and Religion.* New York: Harper and Brothers, 1905.

Krizhanich, Iurii. *Russkoe gosudarstvo v polovine XVII veka.* ed. P. Bezsonov. Moscow, 1859.

Kropotkin, Peter. *Memoirs of a Revolutionist.* Boston: Houghton Mifflin, 1930.

———. *Modern Science and Anarchism.* 2d ed. London: Freedom Press, 1923.

———. *Mutual Aid: A Factor of Evolution.* New York: MacLure Phillips, 1902.

Kurakin: see Semevskii.

Kurbskii, Prince Andrei M. *Sochineniia kniazia Kurbskogo. Russkaia istoricheskaia biblioteka,* vol. 31. St. Petersburg: Arkheograficheskaia Komissiia, 1914.

Kutrzeba, Stanislaw, and W. Semikowicz, eds. *Akta unji Polski z Litwa, 1385-1791.* Krakow: Nakladem Polskiej Akademji Umiejetnosci i Towarzystwa Naukowego Warszawskiego, 1932.

Kutuzov: see Korobkov.

Lamzdorf [Lamsdorff], Vladimir N. *Dnevnik 1891-1892.* Moscow: AN SSSR, 1934.

Langer, William L. *The Franco-Russian Alliance 1890-1894.* Cambridge: Harvard University Press, 1929.

Lannoy, Ghillebert de. *Oeuvres de Ghillebert de Lannoy, voyageur, diplomate, et moraliste.* Louvain, 1878.

Lantzeff, George V. *Siberia in the Seventeenth Century: A Study of the Colonial Administration.* Berkeley: University of California Press, 1943.

Lassota von Steblau, Erich. *Tagebuch des Erich Lassota von Steblau.* Ed. Reinhold Schottin. Halle, 1866.

Laue, T. H. von: See Von Laue.

Lavrov, Petr L. ["Mirtov"]. *Historical Letters.* Ed. and trans. James P. Scanlan. Berkeley: University of California Press, 1967.

———. *Istoricheskie pis'ma.* St. Petersburg, 1870.

Lazarevskii, N. I., ed. *Zakonodatel'nye akty perekhodnogo vremeni 1904-1908.* St. Petersburg: Izd. Pravo, 1909.

Lemke, Mikhail K., ed. *Politicheskie protsessy v Rossii 1860-kh gg.* 2d ed. Moscow: Gosizdat, 1923. Reprint. The Hague: Mouton, 1969. See also Gertsen.

Lenin, Vladimir I. *The Essential of Lenin in Two Volumes.* London: Lawrence and Wishart, 1947.

——. *Sochineniia.* 2d ed. 30 vols. Moscow: Gosizdat, 1926-30.

——. *What Is to Be Done?* Trans. Sergei V. and Patricia Utechin. New York: Oxford University Press, 1963.

Letters of the Tsar to the Tsaritsa: see Vulliamy.

Letters of the Tsaritsa to the Tsar, 1914-1916. Intro. Bernard Pares. London: Duckworth, 1923.

Levshin, A. I. "Dostopamiatnye minuty v moei zhizni, zapiska A. I. Levshina." *Russkii arkhiv,* 1885, no. 8, pp. 475-557.

Lewicki, Tadeusz, ed. *Zrodla arabskie do dziejow slowianszczyzny.* Vol. 1. Wroclaw and Krakow: Wyd. Polskiej Akademii Nauk, 1956.

Liubavskii, Matvei K. *Ocherk istorii litovsko-russkogo gosudarstva.* 2d ed. Moscow: Moskovskaia Khudozhestvennaia Pechatnia, 1915.

Loubat, J. F. *Narrative of the Mission to Russia, in 1866, of the Honorable Gustavus Vasa Fox, Assistant-Secretary of the Navy, from the Journal and Notes of J. F. Loubat.* New York, 1874.

Loukomsky [Lukomskii], Alexander S. *Memoirs of the Russian Revolution.* London: T. F. Unwin, 1922.

——. *Vospominaniia Generala A. S. Lukomskogo.* 2 vols. Berlin: Otto Kirchner, 1922.

Macartney, Carlile A. *The Magyars in the Ninth Century.* Cambridge: At the University Press, 1930.

Maklakov, Vasilii A. *The First Duma: Contemporary Reminiscences.* Trans. Mary Belkin. Bloomington: Indiana University Press, 1964.

——. *Iz vospominanii.* New York: Chekhov, 1954.

——. *Pervaia Gosudarstvennaia Duma: Vospominaniia sovremennika.* Paris: Dom Knigi, 1939.

——. *Vlast' i obshchestvennost' na zakate staroi Rossii: Vospominaniia sovremennika.* Paris: Illiustrirovannaia Rossiia, 1939.

——. *Vtoraia Gosudarstvennaia Duma: Vospominaniia sovremennika.* Paris [1946].

Malinin, Vasilii N. *Starets Eleazarova monastyria Filofei i ego poslaniia.* Kiev: Tip. Kievo-Pecherskoi Uspenskoi Lavry, 1901.

Manifest Rossiiskoi Sotsial'-demokraticheskoi Rabochei Partii, 1898 g. Geneva: T. A. Kuklin, 1903.

Manstein, Christopher Hermann von. *Mémoires historiques, politiques et militaires sur la Russie depuis l'Année 1727 jusqu'à 1744, par le Général de Manstein.* 2 vols. Paris, 1860.

——. *Memoirs of Russia from the Year 1727 to 1744.* Ed. David Hume. London, 1770.

——. "Zapiski Manshteina o Rossii, 1727-1744." *Russkaia starina,* 1875, no. 12, suppl.

Martens, Fedor F. *Recueil des traités et conventions conclus par la Russie avec les puissances étrangères.* 15 vols. bound in 8. St. Petersburg: A. Böhnke, 1874-1909.

Materialy po istorii SSSR. Vol. 2. Moscow: AN SSSR, 1955.

Matlaw, Ralph E., ed. and intro. *Belinsky, Chernyshevsky, and Dobrolyubov: Selected Criticism.* New York: E. P. Dutton, 1962.

Maximoff, G. P., comp. and ed. *The Political Philosophy of Bakunin: Scientific Anarchism.* Glencoe, Ill.: Free Press, 1953.

Mazour, Anatole G. *The First Russian Revolution, 1825: The Decembrist Movement.* Berkeley: University of California Press, 1937.

Memoirs of Catherine . . . .: see Catherine II, *Memoirs . . .*

Metternich, Prince Richard, ed. *Memoirs of Prince Metternich.* Arr. M. A. Klinkowström, trans. Mrs. Alexander Napier. 5 vols. New York, 1880-82.

Mezhdutsarstvie 1825 goda i vosstanie dekabristov v memuarakh i perepiske chlenov tsarskoi sem'i. Moscow: Gosizdat, 1926.

Michell, Robert, and Nevill Forbes, eds. and trans. *The Chronicle of Novgorod.* Intro. C. Raymond Beazley, commentary by A. A. Shakhmatov. London: Royal Historical Society, 1914 (Camden, 3d ser., vol. 25).

Mikhailovskii, Nikolai K. *Poslednie sochineniia N. K. Mikhailovskogo.* 2 vols. St. Petersburg: Russkoe Bogatstvo, 1905.

——. *Sochineniia N. K. Mikhailovskogo.* Vols. 1-3 (of 6), 4th ed. St. Petersburg: Russkoe Bogatstvo, 1906-09. Vols. 4-6, St. Petersburg: Russkoe Bogatstvo, 1897.

Miliukov, Pavel N. *God bor'by, 1905-06.* St. Petersburg: Obshchestvennaia Pol'za, 1907.

——. *Russia and Its Crisis.* London: T. F. Unwin, 1905.

——. *Vospominaniia 1859-1917.* 2 vols. New York: Chekhov, 1955.

Miliutin, Dmitrii A. *Dnevnik D. A. Miliutina, 1873-1882.* Ed. Petr A. Zaionchkovskii. 4 vols. Moscow [Bibl. Lenina], 1947-50.

Miliutina, Mariia A. "Iz zapisok Marii Aggeevny Miliutinoi." *Russkaia starina,* 98 (April 1899): 105-27.

Miller [Mueller], G. F. *Istoriia Sibiri.* 2 vols. Moscow: AN SSSR, 1937-41.

Mishulin, A. V. "Drevnie slaviane v otryvkakh greko-rimskikh i vizantiiskikh pisatelei po VII v. n. e." *Vestnik drevnei istorii,* 14 (1941, no. 1), suppl.

Monas, Sidney. *The Third Section: Police and Society in Russia under Nicholas I.* Cambridge: Harvard University Press, 1961.

Moskoff, Eugene A. *The Russian Philosopher Chaadayev: His Ideas and His Epoch.* New York: Colonial Printing and Publishing, 1937.

Mukhanov, Pavel A., ed. *Zapiski getmana Zholkevskogo o Moskovskoi voine.* 2d ed. St. Petersburg, 1871.

Naumov, Aleksandr N. *Iz utselevshikh vospominanii 1868-1917.* 2 vols. New York: A. K. Naumova and O. A. Kusevitskaia, 1954-55.

Nevskii, Vladimir I., comp. *1905: Sovetskaia pechat' i literatura o sovetakh: Materialy i dokumenty.* Vol. 3. Moscow: Gosizdat, 1925.

Nolde, Boris. *L'Alliance Franco-Russe.* Paris: Librarie Droz, 1936.

Nomad, Max. *Apostles of Revolution.* Boston: Little, Brown, 1939.

Novgorodskaia pervaia letopis'. Ed. A. N. Nasonov. Moscow: AN SSSR, 1950.

Novikov, Nikolai I., ed. *Drevniaia rossiiskaia vivliofika.* 2d ed. 12 vols. Moscow, 1788-91. Vol. 6, 1788.

——. *Satiricheskie zhurnaly N. I. Novikova.* Ed. P. N. Berkov. Moscow: AN SSSR, 1951.

Novosil'tsev, N. N. "N. N. Novosil'tsev's Project for a Constitutional Charter for the Russian Empire." Ed. David Urquhart. *The Portfolio,* 5 (1837): 512-22, 610-39; 6 (1837): 72-83.

Obshchestvo Istorii i Drevnostei Rossiiskikh. *Chteniia v Imperatorskom Obshchestve Istorii i Drevnostei Rossiiskikh pri Moskovskom Universitete.* 264 vols. Moscow: Universitetskaia Tipografiia, 1846-1918.

Obshchestvo Istorii i Drevnostei Rossiiskikh. *Vremennik Imperatorskogo Moskovskogo Obshchestva Istorii i Drevnostei Rossiiskikh.* 25 vols. Moscow, 1849-57.

Olearius, Adam. *Der Welt-beruehmten Adami Olearii Reise-Beschreibungen . . . nach Musskau und Persien.* 4th ed. Hamburg, 1696.

——. *The Travels of Olearius in Seventeenth-Century Russia.* Trans. and ed. Samuel H. Baron. Stanford: Stanford University Press, 1967.

Osvobozhdenie. Ed. and publ. P. B. Struve. Stuttgart, 1902-04; Paris, 1904-05.

Otchet po Gosudarstvennomu Sovetu za 1886 god. St. Petersburg, 1888.

Page, Stanley W., ed. *Russia in Revolution: Selected Readings in Russian Domestic History since 1855.* Princeton: Van Nostrand, 1965.

Paléologue, [Georges] Maurice. *An Ambassador's Memoirs.* Trans. F. A. Holt. 4th ed. 3 vols. New York: George H. Doran, 1924-25.

——. *La Russie des tsars pendant la grande guerre.* 6th ed. 3 vols. Paris: Plon-Nourrit, 1922.

Palitsyn, Avraamii. *Skazanie Avraamiia Palitsyna.* Commentary by O. A. Derzhavina and E. V. Kolosova, ed. L. V. Cherepnin. Moscow: AN SSSR, 1955.

Palmer, W. *The Patriarch and the Tsar.* 6 vols. London, 1871-76.

Pamiatniki russkogo prava. 8 vols. Moscow: Gosiurizdat, 1952-61. See also Cherepnin; Iushkov.

Pamiatniki russkoi istorii. Ed. members of the history faculty of Moscow University. 8 vols. Moscow: N. N. Klochkov, 1909-11. See also Got'e; Iakovlev; Pososhkov.

Pares, Bernard. *Day by Day with the Russian Army, 1914-15.* London: Constable, 1915.

——. *The Fall of the Russian Monarchy: A Study of the Evidence.* New York: Alfred A. Knopf, 1939.

Pawlowski, Bronislaw, comp. *Krolestwo kongresowe i powstanie listopadowe.* Teksty zrodlowe do nauki historji w szkole sredniej, pt. 49. Krakow: Nakladem Krakowskiej Spolki Wydawniczej, 1923.

Perepiska Nikolaia i Aleksandry Romanovykh 1914-1917: see Tsentral'nyi Gosudarstvennyi Istoricheskii Arkhiv v Moskve.

Peresvetov, Ivan. *Sochineniia I. Peresvetova.* Ed. A. A. Zimin and D. S. Likhachev. Moscow: AN SSSR, 1956.

——. *Sochineniia Ivana Peresvetova.* Ed. V. F. Rzhiga. In *Chteniia v Obshchestve Istorii i Drevnostei Rossiiskikh pri Moskovskom Universitete.* Moscow, 1908, no. I.

Perry, John. *The State of Russia under the Present Czar, By Captain John Perry.* London, 1716.

Pestel', Pavel I. *Russkaia Pravda.* Ed. and intro. P. Shchegolev. St. Petersburg: Izd. "Kul'tura," 1906.

"Petr Mikhailovich Bestuzhev-Riumin i ego pomest'e." *Russkii arkhiv.* vol. 42 (1904, no. 1), pp. 5-42.

Pipes, Richard. *Karamzin's Memoir on Ancient and Modern Russia: A Translation and Analysis.* Cambridge: Harvard University Press, 1959.

Pisarev, Dmitrii I. *Izbrannye sochineniia.* Vol. 1. Moscow: Gosudarstvennoe Izd. Khudozhestvennoi Literatury, 1935.

——. *Selected Philosophical, Social, and Political Essays.* Moscow: Foreign Languages Publishing House, 1958.

——. *Sochineniia.* 4 vols. Moscow: Gosudarstvennoe Izd. Khudozhestvennoi Literatury, 1955-56.

Pis'ma i bumagi Imperatora Petra Velikogo. 11 vols. Vols. 1-7, St. Petersburg: Gosudarstvennaia Tipografiia, 1887-1918. Vols. 8-11, Moscow: AN SSSR, 1948-64.

Plekhanov, Georgii V. *Dnevnik sotsial-demokrata.* Vol. 1. Petrograd: M. V. Popov, 1916.

——. *Nashi raznoglasiia.* St. Petersburg: Novyi Mir, 1906.

——. *Selected Philosophical Works.* 2 vols. Moscow: Foreign Languages Publishing House, 1959.

——. *Sochineniia.* 24 vols. Moscow: Gosizdat, 1923-27.

Pobedonostsev, Konstantin P. *Moskovskii sbornik.* Moscow, 1896.

——. *Pis'ma Pobedonostseva k Aleksandru III.* 2 vols. Moscow: Novaia Moskva, 1925-26.

——. *Reflexions of a Russian Statesman.* Trans. Robert C. Long. London, 1898.

Pokrovskii, Mikhail N., et al., eds. *Vosstanie dekabristov.* 11 vols. Moscow: Gosizdat, 1925-54.

"Politicheskoe polozhenie Rossii nakanune fevral'skoi revoliutsii v zhandarmskom osveshchenii." *Krasnyi arkhiv,* 17 (1926, no. 4): 3-35.

Polner, Tikhon J. *Russian Local Government during the War and the Union of Zemstvos.* Russian Series, "Economic and Social History of the World War," no. 9. New Haven: Yale University Press, 1930.

Polnoe Sobranie Zakonov Rossiiskoi Imperii . . . 1649-1913. 134 vols. St. Petersburg, 1830-1916 (1st ser., 46 vols., containing laws of 1649-1825; 2d ser., 55 vols., covering 1825-81; 3d ser., 33 vols., covering 1881-1913).

Polnyi sbornik platform vsekh russkikh politicheskikh partii. 4th ed. St. Petersburg, 1907.

Polovtsev, Aleksandr A. "Dnevnik A. A. Polovtseva, 1901-1908." *Krasnyi arkhiv,* 3 (1923): 75-172; 4 (1923): 63-128.

Ponomarev, A. I. *Pamiatniki drevnerusskoi tserkovno-uchitel'noi literatury.* Pt. 1. St. Petersburg: Izd. zhurnala "Strannik," 1894.

Pososhkov, Ivan T. "Donesenie boiarinu F. A. Golovinu o ratnom povedenii." In *Pamiatniki russkoi istorii,* vol. 8. Moscow: N. N. Klochkov, 1911.

——. *Kniga o skudosti i bogatstve.* Moscow: AN SSSR, 1937.

Po voprosam programmy i taktiki: Sbornik statei iz "Revoliutsionnoi Rossii." [Paris:] Tip. Sotsialistov-Revoliutsionerov, 1903.

Pravitel'stvennyi vestnik. St. Petersburg, 1869-1917.

Pravo (weekly legal journal). 1898-1917.

Priselkov, Mikhail D. *Khanskie iarlyki russkim mitropolitam.* St. Petersburg: Nauchnoe Delo, 1916.

Procopius. *History of the Wars.* Trans. H. B. Dewing. Loeb Classical Library, vol. 4. Cambridge: Harvard University Press, 1924.

Programma i organizatsionnyi ustav Partii Sotsialistov-Revoliutsionerov. Paris: Izd. TsK PS-R, 1906.

Programma i ustav Rossiiskoi Sotsial'-Demokraticheskoi Rabochei Partii, Paris: *Sotsial'demokrat,* 1909.

Protokoly ob"edinitel'nogo s"ezda Rossiiskoi Sotsial'-demokraticheskoi Rabochei Partii, sostoiavshegosia v Stokgol'me v 1906 g. Moscow: TsK RSDRP, 1907.

Protokoly pervoi obshchepartiinoi konferentsii P.S-R. 1908 g. Paris: Izd. TsK PS-R, 1908.

Protokoly zasedanii soveshchaniia . . . po peresmotru osnovnykh gosudarstvennykh zakonov. St. Petersburg: Gosudarstvennaia Tipografiia, 1906.

Pskovskie letopisi. Ed. A. N. Nasonov. Moscow: AN SSSR, 1941.

Pugachevshchina: see Tsentral'nyi Gosudarstvennyi Istoricheskii Arkhiv v Moskve.

Purchas, Samuel: see Chancellor.

Putnam, Peter, ed. *Seven Britons in Imperial Russia.* Princeton: Princeton University Press, 1952.

Radishchev, Aleksandr N. *A Journey from St. Petersburg to Moscow, by A. N. Radishchev.* Ed. Roderick Page Thaler, trans. Leo Wiener. Cambridge: Harvard University Press, 1958.

——. *Puteshestvie iz Peterburga v Moskvu.* Moscow: AN SSSR, 1935 (reprint of ed. of 1790).

Raeff, Marc. *The Decembrist Movement.* Englewood Cliffs, N.J.: Prentice-Hall, 1966.

——. *Plans for Political Reform in Imperial Russia, 1730-1905.* Englewood Cliffs, N.J.: Prentice-Hall, 1966.

——, ed. *Russian Intellectual History, an Anthology.* New York: Harcourt, Brace and World, 1966.

Reddaway, W. F., ed. *Documents of Catherine the Great: The Correspondence with Voltaire and the Instructions of 1767.* Cambridge: At the University Press, 1931.

Riasanovsky, Nicholas V. *Nicholas I and Official Nationality in Russia, 1825-1855.* Berkeley: University of California Press, 1959.

Riha, Thomas, ed. *Readings in Russian Civilization.* 3 vols. Chicago: University of Chicago Press, 1964. 2d ed. 1969.

Rittikh, Aleksandr A., ed. *Krest'ianskoe zemlepol'zovanie.* St. Petersburg: V. F. Kirsbaum, 1903.

Rockhill, William W., ed. *Journey of William of Rubruck to the Eastern Parts of the World, 1253-1255, as Narrated by Himself.* London: Hakluyt Society, 1900.

Rodzianko, Mikhail V. "Ekonomicheskoe polozhenie Rossii pered revoliutsiei: Zapiska M. V. Rodzianki." *Krasnyi arkhiv,* 10 (1925, no. 3): 69-86.

——. "Gosudarstvennaia Duma i fevral'skaia 1917 g. revoliutsiia." *Arkhiv russkoi revoliutsii,* 6 (1922): 5-80.

——. "Krushenie Imperii." *Arkhiv russkoi revoliutsii,* 17 (1926): 1-169.

Rossiia pri Petre Velikom, po rukopisnomu izvestiiu I. G. Vokerodta i O. Pleiera. Trans. A. N. Shemiakin. *Chteniia v Imperatorskom Obshchestve Istorii i Drevnostei Rossiiskikh pri Moskovskom Universitete,* vol. 89, pt. 4. Moscow, 1874, bk. 2.

Rousset de Missy, Jean. *Recueil historique d'actes . . . et traitez de paix depuis la Paix d'Utrect.* 21 vols. The Hague, 1728-55.

Rozen, Andrei E. *Zapiski dekabrista.* St. Petersburg: Obshchestvennaia Pol'za, 1907.

The Russian Co-operator: A Journal of Co-operative Unity. Ed. J. V. Bubnoff and A. N. Balakshin. London, 1916-21.

Russian Primary Chronicle: See Cross.

Russkaia istoricheskaia biblioteka: see Arkheograficheskaia Komissiia.

Russkaia starina. Ed. M. I. Semevskii. St. Petersburg, 1870-1918.

Russkii arkhiv. Ed. P. Bartenev. Moscow, 1863-1917.

Rychkov, Petr I. "Nakaz dlia derevenskogo upravitelia . . ." *Trudy Vol'nogo Ekonomicheskogo Obshchestva,* 16: 9-68. St. Petersburg, 1770.

Sanin [Volotskii], Iosif. *Prosvetitel' ili oblichenie eresi zhidovstvuiushchikh.* Kazan', 1855.

Sazonov, Sergei D. *Fateful Years 1909-1916: The Reminiscences of Serge Sazonov.* London: J. Cape, 1928.

Sbornik dogovorov i diplomaticheskikh dokumentov po delam Dal'nego Vostoka 1895-1905 gg.. St. Petersburg: Ministerstvo Inostrannykh Del, 1906.

Sbornik Imperatorskogo Russkogo Istoricheskogo Obshchestva. 148 vols. St. Petersburg: Tip. Imperatorskogo Russkogo Istoricheskogo Obshchestva, 1867-1916.

Segel, Harold B., ed. and trans. *The Literature of Eighteenth-Century Russia.* 2 vols. New York: E. P. Dutton, 1967.

Semennikov, Vladimir P., ed. *Monarkhiia pered krusheniem, 1914-1917: Bumagi Nikolaia II i drugie dokumenty.* Moscow: Gosizdat, 1927.

————. *Politika Romanovykh nakanune revoliutsii.* Moscow: Gosizdat, 1926.

Semenov, Nikolai P. *Osvobozhdenie krest'ian v tsarstvovanie Imperatora Aleksandra II: Khronika deiatel'nosti komissii po krest'ianskomu delu.* 3 vols. St. Petersburg, 1889-92.

Semevskii, M. I., ed. *Arkhiv kniazia F. A. Kurakina.* Vol. 1. St. Petersburg, 1890. (Contains "Zhizn' kniazia Borisa Ivanovicha Kurakina.")

Senn, Alfred E., ed. *Readings in Russian Political and Diplomatic History.* 2 vols. Homewood, Ill.: Dorsey Press, 1966.

Sergeev, A. A. "Pervaia Gosudarstvennaia Duma v Vyborge." *Krasnyi arkhiv,* 4 (1923, no. 2): 85-99.

Sergeevskii, Nikolai D., ed. *Konstitutsionnaia khartiia 1815 g. i nekotorye drugie akty byvshego Tsarstva Pol'skogo (1814-1881). Biblioteka Okrain Rossii,* vol. 5. St. Petersburg: Izd. Sergeevskogo, 1907.

Shavel'skii, Georgii. *Vospominaniia poslednego protopresvitera russkoi armii i flota.* 2 vols. New York: Chekhov, 1954.

Shcherbatov, Mikhail M. *On the Corruption of Morals in Russia.* Ed. and trans. A. Lentin. Cambridge: At the University Press, 1969.

————. *Sochineniia Kniazia M. M. Shcherbatova.* Ed. I. P. Khrushchov and A. G. Voronov. St. Petersburg, 1898.

Shchipanov, I. Ia., ed. *Izbrannye sotsial'no-politicheskie i filosofskie proizvedeniia dekabristov.* 3 vols. Moscow: Gosudarstvennoe izdatel'stvo politicheskoi literatury, 1951.

Shil'der, N. K. *Imperator Aleksandr Pervyi, ego zhizn' i tsarstvovanie.* 4 vols. St. Petersburg: A. S. Suvorin, 1897-98.

Shilovskii, Petr P. *Akty otnosiashchiesia k politicheskomu polozheniiu Finliandii.* St. Petersburg: M. M. Stasiulevich, 1903.

Shul'gin, Vasilii V. *Dni.* Belgrade: Novoe Vremia, 1925.

Skarga, Piotr. *Kazania sejmowe.* Ed. Stanislaw Kot. Krakow: Nakladem Krakowskiej Spolki Wydawniczej, 1925.

Smirnov, Ivan I. *Vosstanie Bolotnikova 1606-1607.* Moscow: AN SSSR, 1951.

Smith, Robert E. F. *The Enserfment of the Russian Peasantry.* Cambridge: At the University Press, 1968.

Solov'ev, Ia. A. "Zapiski Senatora Ia. A. Solov'eva." *Russkaia starina,* 27 (1880): 319-62; 30 (1881): 211-46, 721-56, 903-05.

Solov'ev, Sergei M. "Istoriia padeniia Pol'shi." *Sobranie sochinenii S. M. Solov'eva.* St. Petersburg: Obshchestvennaia Pol'za, 1900.

Solov'ev [Solovyof], Vladimir S. *The Justification of the Good.* Trans. Nathalie A. Duddington, note by Stephen Graham. London: Constable, 1918.

——. *Opravdanie dobra: Nravstvennaia filosofiia Vladimira Solov'eva.* 2d ed. Moscow, 1899.

——. *Sobranie sochinenii Vladimira Sergeevicha Solov'eva.* 9 vols. St. Petersburg: Obshchestvennaia Pol'za, [1901]-07.

Sovremennoe polozhenie i zadachi partii: Platforma, vyrabotannaia gruppoi Bol'shevikov. Paris: Izd. Gruppy "Vpered," 1910.

Spector, Ivar and Marion, eds. *Readings in Russian History and Culture.* Palo Alto: Pacific Books, 1968.

Speranskii, Mikhail M. *Plan gosudarstvennogo preobrazovaniia, vvedenie k "Ulozheniiu Gosudarstvennykh Zakonov" 1809 g.* Moscow: Izd. Russkoi Mysli, 1905.

Staden, Heinrich von. *Aufzeichnungen ueber den Moskauer Staat.* Ed. Fritz Epstein. Hamburg: Friederichsen, de Gruyter, 1930.

——. *The Land and Government of Muscovy: A Sixteenth-Century Account.* Trans. and ed. Thomas Esper. Stanford: Stanford University Press, 1967.

Staehlin-Storcksburg, Jacob von. *Original Anecdotes of Peter the Great.* London, 1788.

Statut velikogo kniazhestva litovskogo 1529 goda. Ed. K. I. Iablonskis. Minsk: An BSSR, 1960.

Steblau: see Lassota.

Stoglav: Tsarskie voprosy i sobornye otvety. Moscow, 1890.

Stroev, Pavel M. *Obstoiatel'noe opisanie staropechatnykh knig slavianskikh i rossiiskikh, khraniashchikhsia v biblioteke grafa F. A. Tolstova.* Moscow, 1829.

Struys, John. *The Voiages and Travels of John Struys.* Trans. John Morrison. London, 1684.

"Studencheskie volneniia v. 1901-1902 gg. Vvodnaia stat'ia A. Syromiatnikova." *Krasnyi arkhiv,* 89-90 (1938, nos. 4-5): 258-308.

"Studencheskoe dvizhenie v 1901 g., s predisloviem V. Orlova." *Krasnyi arkhiv,* 75 (1936, no. 2): 83-112.

"Sudebnik 1497 g." *Pamiatniki russkogo prava,* 3: 346-57. Moscow: Gosizdat, 1955.

"Sudebnik 1550 g." *Pamiatniki russkogo prava,* 4: 233-61. Moscow: Gosizdat, 1956.

Sudebniki XV-XVI vekov. Ed. B. D. Grekov. Moscow: AN SSSR, 1952.

Svod Zakonov Rossiiskoi Imperii. 3d ed. 16 vols. St. Petersburg: Gosudarstvennaia Tipografiia, 1857-1916.

Tatishchev, Sergei S. *Imperator Aleksandr II.* 2 vols. St. Petersburg: A. S. Suvorin, 1911.

Tolstoi, Iurii K., ed. *Pervye sorok let snoshenii mezhdu Rossiei i Angliei 1553-1593.* St. Petersburg, 1875. Reprinted by Burt Franklin. New York: 1963.

Tolstoi, Lev N. *Polnoe sobranie sochinenii.* 90 vols. Moscow: Gosudarstvennoe Izd. Khudozhestvennoi Literatury, 1928-58.

——. *Sochineniia grafa L. N. Tolstogo.* 12th ed. 20 vols. Moscow: T. and I. N. Kushnerev, 1911.

——. *The Works of Leo Tolstoy: Tolstoy Centenary Edition.* 21 vols. London: Oxford University Press, 1928-37.

Tooke, William. *The Life of Catharine II, Empress of Russia.* 2d ed. 3 vols. London, 1800.

——. *View of the Russian Empire during the Reign of Catherine the Second and to the Close of the Eighteenth Century.* 2d ed. 3 vols. London, 1800.

Traités et conventions entre L'Empire du Japon et les puissances étrangères. Tokyo: Z. P. Maruya, 1908.

Trudy Vol'nogo . . . : see Vol'noe Ekonomicheskoe Obshchestvo.

Tsentral'nyi Gosudarstvennyi Istoricheskii Arkhiv v Moskve, ed. *Burzhuaziia nakanune fevral'skoi revolutsii.* Moscow: Gosizdat, 1927.

——. *Perepiska Nikolaia i Aleksandry Romanovykh 1914-1917.* Vols. 3-5. Moscow: Gosizdat, 1923.

——. *Pugachevshchina.* 2 vols. Moscow: Gosizdat, 1926-29.

Tsentral'nyi Statisticheskii Komitet. *Ezhegodnik Rossii 1906 g.* St. Petersburg: Ministerstvo Vnutrennikh Del, 1907.

——. *Ezhegodnik Rossii 1910.* St. Petersburg: Ministerstvo Vnutrennikh Del, 1911.

——. *Statisticheskii Ezhegodnik Rossii 1914.* St. Petersburg: Ministerstvo Vnutrennikh Del, 1915.

Ulozhenie gosudaria tsaria i velikogo kniazia Alekseia Mikhailovicha. St. Petersburg: Gosudarstvennaia Tipografiia, 1913.

Uroff, Benjamin Phillip. "Grigorii Karpovich Kotoshikhin, *On Russia in the Reign of Alexis
Mikhailovich:* An Annotated Translation." 2 vols. Ph.D. dissertation, Columbia University,
1970.

Urusov [Urussov], Sergei D. *Memoirs of a Russian Governor, Prince S. D. Urussov.* Trans.
Hermann Rosenthal. New York: Harper and Brothers, 1908.

Ustrialov, Nikolai G. *Istoriia tsarstvovaniia Petra Velikogo.* 5 vols. (nos. 1-4, 6) St. Petersburg,
1858-63.

Valk, Sigizmunt N., ed. *Gramoty velikogo Novgoroda i Pskova.* Moscow: AN SSSR, 1949.

Vashkevich, Vladislav V., comp. *Sbornik uzakonenii kasaiushchikhsia evreev.* St. Petersburg,
1884.

Vasiliev, A. A. *The Russian Attack on Constantinople in 860.* Cambridge: Harvard University
Press, 1946.

"Vekhi," kak znamenie vremeni: Sbornik statei. Moscow: "Zveno," 1910.

Vekhi: Sbornik statei o russkoi intelligentsii. 4th ed. Moscow: T. and I. N. Kushnerev, 1909.
Reprint. Frankfurt-am-Main: Posev, 1967.

Vernadsky, George. *Bohdan, Hetman of Ukraine.* New Haven: Yale University Press, 1941.

———. *La Charte Constitutionelle de l'Empire russe de l'an 1820.* Paris: Librairie du Recueil
Sirey, 1933.

———. "Juwaini's Version of Chingis-Khan's Yasa." *Annales de l'Institut Kondakov,* 11 (1939):
39, 42-44.

———. *Medieval Russian Laws.* New York: Columbia University Press, 1947. Reprint. New York:
Octagon Books, 1955; New York: W. W. Norton, 1969.

———. *The Mongols and Russia.* George Vernadsky and Michael Karpovich, *A History of Russia,*
vol. 3. New Haven: Yale University Press, 1953.

———. *The Origins of Russia.* Oxford: Clarendon Press, 1959.

Vigel', Filipp F. *Vospominaniia F. F. Vigelia.* 7 vols. in 3. Moscow, 1864-65.

———. *Zapiski.* Ed. S. Ia. Shtraikh. 2 vols. Moscow: Artel' Pisatelei Krug, 1928.

Vitte: See Witte.

Vol'noe Ekonomicheskoe Obshchestvo. *Istoriia Imperatorskogo Vol'nogo Ekonomicheskogo
Obshchestva s 1765 do 1865.* Comp. A. I. Khodnev. St. Petersburg, 1865.

Vol'noe Ekonomicheskoe Obshchestvo. *Trudy Vol'nogo Ekonomicheskogo Obshchestva k
pooshchreniiu v Rossii zemledeliia i domostroitel'stva.* 280 vols. St. Petersburg, various publishers, 1765-1915. See also Bolotov, Rychkov.

Von Laue, Theodore H. "A Secret Memorandum of Sergei Witte on the Industrialization of
Imperial Russia." *Journal of Modern History,* 26 (March 1954): 60-74.

Voskresenskaia letopis'. Polnoe Sobranie Russkikh Letopisei, vols. 7-8. St. Petersburg, 1853.

Vossoedinenie Ukrainy s Rossiei: Dokumenty i materialy. 3 vols. Moscow: AN SSSR, 1954.

Vulliamy, C. E., ed. *The Letters of the Tsar to the Tsaritsa, 1914-1917.* Trans. A. L. Hynes.
London: J. Lane, 1929.

Wallace, Donald Mackenzie. *Russia.* Rev. and enlarged ed. London: Cassell, 1912.

Walsh, Warren B., ed. *Readings in Russian History.* 3 vols. 4th ed. Syracuse, N.Y.: Syracuse
University Press, 1963.

Weber, Friedrich Christian. *The Present State of Russia.* 2 vols. London, 1722-23.

Whitworth, Charles. *An Account of Russia As It Was in the Year 1710.* London, 1758.

Wiener, Leo, ed. *Anthology of Russian Literature from the Earliest Period to the Present Time.*
2 vols. New York: G. P. Putnam's Sons, 1902.

Wilhelm II. *The Kaiser's Letters to the Tsar.* Ed. N. F. Grant. London: Hodder and Stoughton,
1920.

Witte [Vitte], Sergei Iu. *Vospominaniia: Tsarstvovanie Nikolaia II.* 2 vols. Berlin: Slovo, 1922.
See also: Yarmolinsky; Von Laue.

Wolf, L., ed. *The Legal Sufferings of the Jews in Russia.* London: T. F. Unwin, 1912.

Wormeley, Katherine Prescott, ed. and trans. *Prince de Ligne: His Memoirs, Letters and Miscellaneous Papers.* 2 vols. Boston: Hardy, Pratt, 1899.

Yarmolinsky, Abraham, ed. and trans. *The Memoirs of Count Witte.* Garden City, N.Y.: Doubleday, Page, 1921.

Zablotskii-Desiatovskii, Andrei P. *Graf P. D. Kiselev i ego vremia.* 4 vols. St. Petersburg, 1882.

Zaionchkovskii, A. M., comp. "Iz zapisnoi knizhki arkhivista v gody reaktsii." *Krasnyi arkhiv,* 8 (1925, no. 1): 240-43.

Zapadnorusskie letopisi. Polnoe Sobranie Russkikh Letopisei, vol. 17. St. Petersburg: Arkheograficheskaia Kommissiia, 1907.

Zemskii s"ezd 6-go i sl. noiabria 1904 g. Paris: Izd. Red. "Osvobozhdenie," 1905.

Zenkovsky, Serge A., ed. and trans. *Medieval Russia's Epics, Chronicles, and Tales.* New York: E. P. Dutton, 1963.

Zhurnal Ministerstva Iustitsii, 1917, nos. 2-3 (February-March), pp. 1-7.

Zhurnal Ministerstva Narodnogo Prosveshcheniia. 362 vols. St. Petersburg, 1834-1905; n.s. 72 vols., 1906-17.

Zisserman, Arnold L. *Fel'dmarshal Kniaz A. I. Bariatinskii, 1815-1877.* 3 vols. Moscow, 1888-91.

Zolkiewski, Stanislas. *Expedition to Moscow: A Memoir by Hetman Stanislas Zolkiewski.* Trans. M. W. Stephan. Intro. and notes by Jedrzej Giertych. Preface by Robert Bruce Lockhart. Polonica Series no. 1. London: Polonica Publications, 1959. See also Mukhanov.

PERMISSIONS